THE OXFORD GUIDE TO BRITISH WOMEN WRITERS

THE OXFORD GUIDE TO

BRITISH WOMEN WRITERS

JOANNE SHATTOCK

Oxford New York

OXFORD UNIVERSITY PRESS

1993

Oxford University Press, Walton Street, Oxford OX2 6DP
Oxford New York Toronto
Delhi Bombay Calcutta Madras Karachi
Kuala Lumpur Singapore Hong Kong Tokyo
Nairobi Dar es Salaam Cape Town
Melbourne Auckland Madrid
and associated companies in
Berlin Ibadan

Oxford is a trade mark of Oxford University Press

Published in the United States
by Oxford University Press Inc., New York

British Library Cataloguing in Publication Data
Data available

Library of Congress Cataloging in Publication Data
Shattock, Joanne.
The Oxford guide to British women writers/Joanne Shattock.
Includes bibliographical references.
1. English literature—Women authors—Bio-bibliography.
2. Women and literature—Great Britain—Dictionaries.
3. English literature—Women authors—Dictionaries.
4. Women authors, English—Biography—Dictionaries. I. Title.
PR111.S48 1993
016.8208'09287—dc20 92–47232

ISBN 0–19–214176–7

1 3 5 7 9 10 8 6 4 2

Typeset by Barbers Ltd, Wrotham, Kent
Printed in Great Britain
on acid-free paper by
Butler and Tanner Ltd,
Frome and London

ACKNOWLEDGEMENTS

Many colleagues have assisted both directly and indirectly in the planning and preparation of this Guide. I am particularly grateful to Peter Woodhead, Peter Larkin, Richard Storey, Clare Hanson, Martin Stannard, Sharon Ouditt, Joanne Wilkes, John Sutherland, Andrew Gasson, and Lindeth Vasey. The staffs of the libraries of the University of Leicester and the University of Warwick have been both patient and generous with their time. The Research Committee of the Faculty of Arts at the University of Leicester offered timely support for some of the research on secondary sources. Kim Scott Walwyn, Frances Whistler, and Andrew Lockett of Oxford University Press have been unstinting in their encouragement and have also offered help on specific points. Finally I must thank my family, who have lived cheerfully with women writers and have each in individual ways made contributions.

INTRODUCTION

THIS book is designed as a guide to the enormous range of British women's writing from the medieval period to the present day. Its aim is twofold. The first is to make known and accessible over four hundred women writers whose work appears in a variety of genres, from the autobiographers, religious writers, and translators of the early periods to the novelists, poets, playwrights, children's writers, popular novelists, travel and film writers of the present day. The second is to indicate some of the important critical, theoretical, and scholarly work which has been produced on these writers, particularly the wealth of innovative and challenging research and criticism which has appeared in the last two decades.

Each entry offers a brief outline of the writer's life and career, her major publications, and the significant features of her work. There is also an attempt to place each writer in the context of her contemporaries, both male and female, and to highlight, where they existed, the networks of literary and personal connections which bound women writers together.

The field of coverage is British women writers, but in some instances national boundaries have been deliberately blurred. The term 'British' indicates birth within the United Kingdom and a writing life conducted mainly in Britain, although literary lives tend to resist such strict demarcation. Many women writers of the colonial period, such as Frances Brooke or Susanna Rowson, were born in Britain but spent part of their writing lives in North America. Anne Bradstreet was born in England but is better known as one of the earliest American women poets. Mina Loy, to use a later example, was born in London but spent her adult life alternating between the United States and Europe. Conversely Katherine Mansfield and her cousin Elizabeth von Arnim were both born in New Zealand, but their writing careers were largely British-based. Similarly South African-born Olive Schreiner and Doris Lessing, who grew up in British colonial Africa, can be regarded as part of the British literary scene. All of these writers are included in the Guide. Perhaps more controversially, Christina Stead, who was born in Australia and spent much of her career in the United States but a significant period in England, is included, as is Nadine Gordimer, who although incontrovertibly a South African writer, impinges significantly on modern British writing today. For the same reason, contemporary Irish writers like Molly Keane ('M. J. Farrell') and Edna O'Brien, who have for some time lived and worked in England, appear in the Guide, as does Sylvia Plath, an American, a crucial part of whose brief writing life was spent in England.

Any principles of selection are to an extent arbitrary. I have tried to emphasize, in my selection, the diversity of women's writing across genres and periods. As well as poets, dramatists, and novelists, there are diarists, autobiographers, letter writers, journalists, detective writers, children's writers, travel writers, and romantic novelists. I do not, however, claim to have been in any way inclusive, particularly with some of the latter categories, for whom specialist reference books offer wider coverage. Historians, biographers, translators, writers of conduct books, cookery writers, religious writers, and even a mathematician appear prior to 1900, when women moved easily across genres and before specialization began to take hold.

The twentieth century presents a particular problem as regards selection. Modern women's writing differs from the earlier periods in both its diversity and its professionalism. There are now many women historians, biographers, philosophers, anthropologists, and writers across the spectrum of academic disciplines, a range of writing so vast as to make selection and even token inclusion impossible. I have included these writers only when they combine academic or specialist writing with creative work, as is the case with Naomi Mitchison, Elspeth Huxley, and Freya Stark. Secondly, while I have not operated a specific cut-off point for contemporary writers, I have tended to choose women whose reputations were established by the early 1980s. I have attempted to highlight those writers who have been the subject of recent academic interest as well as others who are ripe for rediscovery and reassessment. The major writers of each period are of course included but they have not necessarily been given more extensive coverage than lesser-known figures.

The focus of the Guide is on writing lives. The majority of entries are therefore biographical, but there are also subject entries which provide information on subgenres of women's writing, literary organizations and periodicals relevant to women writers, and key publications and composite works involving women. The writers are listed alphabetically according to the names by which they are best known, whether pseudonym, married or maiden name. Where there is any doubt, or where several names are equally applicable, cross-references are included in the main alphabetical list.

Suggestions for further reading are given at the end of each entry, usually one or two significant books on a writer, a standard biography where it exists, and editions of letters, diaries, or notebooks. In the case of major writers this can only be a sample of the range of secondary work available, and I have tried in these instances to indicate important recent writing. Those requiring more extensive reading should consult the *Modern Language Association International Bibliography*, the *New Cambridge Bibliography of English Literature* (Cambridge, 1969–77), and specialized bibliographies, some of which are indicated in the entries.

I have not listed manuscript holdings of women writers. This information is given for a few women writers in the *Index of English Literary Manuscripts*, ed. Peter Beal, Barbara Rosenbaum, Pamela White, *et al.* (London, 1980–), in the *Location Register of Twentieth Century English Literary Manuscripts and Letters* (1988), and in *The Feminist Companion to Literature in English*, ed. Virginia Blain, Patricia Clements, and Isobel Grundy (London, 1990). It will appear in detail in the forthcoming third edition of the *Cambridge Bibliography* (Cambridge, 1995–).

The Guide concludes with a general bibliography of work on women's writing, divided into two sections, books written before and after 1920. The list of works prior to 1920 is important in several respects. Key publications like George Ballard's *Memoirs of Several Ladies of Great Britain who have been Celebrated for their Writing or Skill in the Learned Languages, Arts and Sciences* (1752), or George Colman and Bonnell Thornton's anthology of *Poems by Eminent Women* (1755), not only created a canon of women writers which influenced later generations, but registered a growing awareness of the impact of women's writing. Some, like Ballard, had the specific aim of pressing for recognition of these writers. Their successors in the nineteenth century, anthologies by Bethune, Rowton, and others, a range of biographical dictionaries which included a large proportion of women writers, and collections of essays on women writers, also served to establish a consensus about the significance of women's writing in the period. The increased numbers of such works in the later nineteenth century suggests not so much a need for polemic as a comfortable acceptance of the prominence and number of women writers.

The larger proportion of the post-1920 bibliography is in fact post-1970, reflecting the fruits of an exciting two decades of rediscovery and reassessment and the impact of contemporary feminist criticism. The books listed treat a range of writers or explore a particular subject or theme. Works devoted to single writers, or in some cases small groups of writers, have been cited in the entries for those writers and are not repeated in the general bibliography.

This is a beginners' handbook rather than a guide to research. It is aimed at the student or general reader who wants an overview of a particular writer, an indication of her major publications and the scope of her work, and information on collections of letters, biographies, and criticism. Its coverage of both primary and secondary material is selective rather than exhaustive. It is to be hoped, none the less, that the Guide will stimulate the ongoing process of rediscovery, rereading, and reassessment of women's writing in the next generation of readers.

A

Ackland, Valentine *see under* WARNER, Sylvia Townsend

Acton, Eliza, poet and writer on cookery (b. Battle, Sussex, 17 April 1799, d. Hampstead, London, February 1859).

The daughter of John Acton, an Ipswich brewer, Eliza Acton suffered from delicate health in her youth and was taken abroad for convalescence. After a broken engagement to a French army officer she returned to England and began her writing career with a volume of *Poems*, published by subscription in 1826. She contributed to various *annuals and periodicals and acquired a certain celebrity by presenting Queen Adelaide with some verses on the occasion of her visit to Tunbridge in 1837. She repeated the feat in 1842 with 'The Voice of the North', a welcome to Queen *Victoria on the occasion of her first visit to Scotland. Her reputation, however, was made and rests with *Modern Cookery* (1845), the most important general cookery book in English in the nineteenth century, which went through numerous editions in the 1840s. Dedicated to 'the young housekeepers of England', it addressed the needs of families on limited incomes and demonstrated an awareness of the new science of nutrition. Isabella *Beeton made use of several of Acton's recipes in her more famous *Household Management* (1861) and extended her manual to include all aspects of the running of a middle-class household, but Acton was reckoned to be the more innovative writer. She followed *Modern Cookery* with *The English Bread Book* (1857), to combat the distressing practices of commercial bakeries. After a long illness she died in Hampstead in her sixtieth year. *See* Elizabeth David's introd. to *The Best of Eliza Acton* (1974).

Adams, Sarah Fuller, née Flower, poet (b. Great Harlow, Essex, 22 February 1805, d. London, 14 August 1848).

Sarah Flower Adams, as she was known, was the younger daughter of Benjamin Flower, a radical journalist and active Unitarian, and his wife Eliza Gould, a teacher. After her father's death in 1829 she was sent to live with the eminent Unitarian divine William J. Fox, editor of the *Monthly Repository*, to which she became a regular contributor. She married William Bridges Adams, a railway engineer and inventor, in 1834; they had no children. She wrote several hymns which were set to music by her sister the composer Eliza Flower (1803–46) and used in services at Fox's South Place Chapel. Thirteen were published by Fox in *Hymns and Anthems* (1841) and the best known, 'Nearer my God to thee', was separately reprinted many times throughout the century. The words were changed on several occasions to obscure Adams's Unitarianism. 'He sendeth sun, he sendeth shower' was another of her popular hymns. Her longest work, *Vivia Perpetua* (1841), a five-act verse drama about an early Christian female convert, reflected her deeply felt Christian beliefs, and also her interest in the theatre. She was said to have had enough talent as an actress to consider the stage as a profession (Macready admired her 1837 Lady Macbeth), but her precarious health dictated a more sedentary career. She wrote *The Flock at the Fountain* (1845), a catechism and collection of hymns for children, and a series of poems for the Anti-Corn Law League, some of which were published in Fox's *Lectures Addressed Chiefly to the Working Classes* (1849). She died of tuberculosis at the age of 43. The 1893 edition of *Vivia Perpetua* contains a memoir by E. F. Bridell-Fox. *See* H. W. Stephenson, *The Author of Nearer my God to Thee* (1922); F. E. Mineka, *The Dissidence of Dissent: The Monthly Repository* 1806–1838 (1944).

Adcock, (Kareen) Fleur, poet (b. Papakura, near Auckland, New Zealand, 10 February 1934).

Fleur Adcock is the daughter of Cyril Adcock, a British-born professor of psychology who emigrated to New Zealand from Manchester as a child, and his Northern Irish wife Irene Robinson. The family spent the war in England, where she and her sister attended 'nine or ten schools and acquired a succession of English accents'. Her return to New Zealand, 'cosy, carefree, insular and deprived', was a disappointment. She went to Wellington Girls' College and then to Victoria University in Wellington, where she took an MA in classics with first-class honours. In 1952, at 18, she married Alistair Campbell, a poet; they had two sons. They later divorced and she taught classics at the University of Otago in Dunedin for a year, and then trained as a librarian. She began to publish her poems in *Landfall*, the *New Zealand Listener*, and other journals. In 1962 she made 'a brief and ill-considered second marriage', which ended the following year when she sailed to England with her younger son. She took a job in the library of the Foreign and Commonwealth Office and began to write. *The Eye of the Hurricane* (1964), her first collection of poems, was published in New Zealand after her departure. Many of the poems were reprinted in *Tigers* (1967), her first British collection, which also contained new poems written in England. *High Tide in the Garden* (1971) included much-discussed poems like 'Gas' and 'Country Station', and *The Scenic Route* (1974) drew on her travels in Nepal, Northern Ireland, and a return visit to New Zealand. *The Inner Harbour*, her fifth collection, was published in 1979, *Selected Poems* in 1983, *The Incident Book* in 1986, and *Time Zones* in 1991. She has edited *The Oxford Book of Contemporary New Zealand Poetry* (1982) and the *Faber Book of Twentieth Century Women's Poetry* (1987) and translated Latin poetry in *The Virgin and the Nightingales* (1983). *See* Jeni Couzyn (ed.), *The Bloodaxe Book of Contemporary Women Poets* (1985).

Aguilar, Grace, novelist (b. Hackney, London, June 1816, d. Frankfurt, 16 September 1847).

The daughter of Emanuel Aguilar, a Jewish merchant of Spanish descent, Grace Aguilar suffered from poor health for much of her life, and most seriously from deafness, the result of measles. She was educated at home and developed an interest in history, particularly Jewish history. She wrote her first work, 'Gustavus Vasa', a drama, before she was 12, and a collection of poems, begun when she was 14, was eventually published as *The Magic Wreath* in 1835. She began to write professionally in order to supplement her income after her father's early death from consumption. The *Spirit of Judaism*, her chief work on the Jewish religion, privately printed in England and published in America in 1842, advocated a return to the spiritual and moral aspects of Judaism as opposed to the formalism and traditionalism of the modern faith. A second work, *The Jewish Faith* (1846), reinforced these at times unpopular ideas. Shortly before her death she was presented with a testimonial and address by Jewish women in London as 'the first woman who had stood forth as the public advocate of the faith of Israel'. *Women of Israel* (1845) stressed the significance of women in the Jewish religion and culture. Her contributions to periodicals on religious subjects were posthumously published as *Sabbath Thoughts and Sacred Communings* (1851). Grace Aguilar was best known, however, as a novelist. Most of her fiction was published posthumously, edited by her mother. *Home Influence: A Tale for Mothers and Daughters* (1847) was the only work published in her lifetime, and went through thirty editions. The sequel, *A Mother's Recompense* (1850), and *Woman's Friendship* (1851), like *Home Influence*, were sentimental stories of domestic life, with emphasis on the mother and daughter relationship, a favourite subject. She also wrote two historical novels, *The Vale of Cedars* (1850), set in Spain during the Inquisition, and *The Days of Bruce* (1852), a costume melodrama with a Scottish setting, and a collection of short stories, *Home Scenes and Heart Studies* (1847). Aguilar died aged 31 while on a visit to Frankfurt in an attempt to secure treatment at a Continental spa.

Aiken, Joan (Delano), novelist and children's writer (b. Rye, Sussex, 4 September 1924).

Joan Aiken is the daughter of the American poet and novelist Conrad Aiken (1889–1973), who lived in England for extended periods in the 1920s and early 1930s, and was for a time London correspondent of the *New Yorker*, and his Canadian wife Jessie Macdonald. She was educated at home by her mother and then went to Wychwood School, Oxford. After working for the BBC and the UN Information Centre in London she married Ronald George Brown, by whom she has a daughter and a son, in 1945. After his death in 1955 she became features editor of *Argosy* magazine. In 1976 she married the painter Julius Goldstein. Aiken published stories and poems while in her teens (one of her stories was read on the BBC's *Children's Hour*) and turned in the 1950s to writing stories and full-length novels for children and later for adults. Her first books were two collections of stories, *All You've Ever Wanted* (1953) and *More than You Bargained For* (1955). She then began a sequence of original, deliberately unhistorical novels which assumed the extension of the Tudor–Stuart line into the nineteenth century with Kings James III and Richard IV and plots against them by the wily Hanoverians. *The Wolves of Willoughby Chase* (1962) was the first of these highly imaginative, action-packed, and humorous tales, followed by *Black Hearts in Battersea* (1964), *Nightbirds on Nantucket* (1966), *The Cuckoo Tree* (1971), and *The Stolen Lake* (1981). *The Whispering Mountain* (1968), about the rediscovery of a legendary harp in a Welsh monastery, won the Guardian Children's Fiction Award and was runner up for the Carnegie Medal. Another strand of Aiken's work for children includes modern fairy-tales, of which the collection *A Necklace of Raindrops* (1968) is the most inventive and the best known. Her adult fiction includes romantic thrillers like *The Butterfly Picnic* (1972, published in the USA as *A Cluster of Separate Sparks*) and *Last Movement* (1977) as well as several *Gothic fantasies. Aiken has published over eighty books and has written about her children's books in *The Way to Write for Children* (1982). *See* John Rowe Townsend, *A Sense of Story* (1971).

Aikin, Anna Laetitia *see* BARBAULD, Anna Laetitia

Aikin, Lucy, poet, historian, and children's writer (b. Warrington, Cheshire, 1781, d. Hampstead, London, 1864).

The daughter of Dr John Aikin, an author and physician who sacrificed his professional prospects to his religious principles, sister of Arthur Aikin, a chemist and scientific writer, and niece of Anna Laetitia *Barbauld, Lucy Aikin published her first work in magazines and reviews, including her brother's *Annual Review* (1803–8). Her first major work, *Epistles on Women* (1810), a poem, was followed in 1814 by *Lorimer: A Tale*, her only novel. She is best known for her historical works, *Memoirs of the Court of Queen Elizabeth* (1818), *Memoirs of the Court of James I* (1822), and *Memoirs of the Court of Charles I* (1833). Her *Life of Addison* (1843) contained many of his unpublished letters and formed the basis of Macaulay's essay on Addison in the *Edinburgh Review* in July 1843, in which he expressed modified admiration for Miss Aikin's ability as a historical writer ('the truth is that she is not well acquainted with her subject'). A selection of *Poetry for Children* (1803) went through many editions. She also published *An English Lesson Book* (1828) and a memoir of her father (1823). Aikin, like other members of her family, was a Unitarian. She corresponded for sixteen years with her fellow Unitarian the American William Ellery Channing. Her *Memoirs, Miscellanies and Letters* were edited by P. H. LeBreton in 1864.

Alexander, (Cecil) Frances, hymn writer (b. County Wicklow, 1818, d. Londonderry, 12 October 1895).

The second daughter of Major John Humphreys of the Royal Marines and his wife Elizabeth Reed, whose background was also military, Frances Alexander was educated at home, and began to write poetry at the age of 9. She was greatly influenced in her youth by the Oxford Movement and contributed a number of poems to a series of tracts written with her friend Lady Harriet Howard, collected as a volume in 1848. Her *Verses for Holy Seasons* (1846) was dedicated to John Keble, who contributed the preface to her *Hymns for Little Children* (1848). The collection included the well-known 'All things bright and beautiful', 'Jesus calls us o'er the tumult', 'Once in royal David's city', and 'There is a green hill far away'. In 1850 she married the Revd William Alexander, Bishop of Derry and Raphoe and later Archbishop of Armagh, by whom she had four children. She wrote secular verse as well, much of it suitable for musical settings, and some intended for children. Her admirers included the composer Gounod and Tennyson, who declared he would have been proud to have written her 'Legend of Stumpie's Brae'. Other volumes of poetry included *The Lord of the Forest and his Vassals: An Allegory* (1848), *Moral Songs* (1849), *Narrative Hymns for Village Schools* (1853), *Hymns Descriptive and Devotional for Village Schools* (1858), and *The*

Legend of the Golden Prayers (1859). She also edited *The Sunday Book of Poetry* (1864). Her collected *Poems*, which included Northern Irish dialect poems, were published posthumously in 1896 with a preface by her husband. *See* Ernest W. O. Lovell, *A Green Hill Far Away: The Life of Cecil Frances Alexander* (1970).

Allingham, Margery (Louise), detective story writer (b. Ealing, London, 20 May 1904, d. Colchester, Essex, 30 June 1966).

Margery Allingham was the eldest of the three children of Herbert John Allingham, editor of the *London Journal* and the *Christian Globe* and a prolific writer of serial fiction, and his wife Emily Jane Hughes. Her literary forebears included John Till Allingham, an early nineteenth-century writer of melodramas, and John Allingham, the author of 1890s boys' stories. Her grandfather was the proprietor of a religious newspaper. 'My father wrote, my mother wrote, all the weekend visitors wrote and . . . so did I,' she recalled later. When she was 7 her father gave her her own study and the plot for a fairy story, which she wrote and rewrote for nearly a year. She went to a private school in Colchester near the family home in Layer Breton, and then to the Perse School, Cambridge, where she wrote and acted in her own play 'Fairy Gold'. She left school at 15, determined to be an actress and a playwright, and enrolled in the Regent Street Polytechnic School of Speech and Drama. She wrote fiction for the magazines *Sexton Blake* and *Girls' Cinema* and in 1923 published her first book, the unsuccessful *Blackkerchief Dick. The Crime at Black Dudley*, published in 1929, introduced her detective hero Albert Campion, and her career as a crime writer was made. *Mystery Mile* the following year added Magersfontein Lugg, Campion's ex-burglar manservant, another Allingham perennial. Early mysteries included *Look to the Lady* (1931), *Sweet Danger* (1933), *Flowers for the Judge* (1936), and *The Fashion in Shrouds* (1938). During the war, in which she worked as an ARP warden and as a billeting officer for evacuees, she wrote *Dance of the Years* (1943), a mainstream novel based in part on family history, which was not a success, and *Traitor's Purse* (1941), one of the best of her adventure stories. Her detective fiction now entered a new and more mature phase in which she combined a talent for realist fiction with crime writing, a distinction which in any case she refused to acknowledge: 'I make no distinction between the novel and the thriller, between Dorothy *Sayers' *The Nine Tailors* . . . and Elizabeth *Bowen's *The Heat of the Day*.' Her best work was written in the post-war years, titles which included *More Work for the Undertaker* (1949), which introduced another Allingham character, Charles Luke of the CID, *Tiger in the Smoke* (1952), and her own favourite, *The Beckoning Lady* (1955). In 1927 she married the artist Philip Youngman Carter (d. 1969), who illustrated the dust-jackets of many of her books. They lived at Tolleshunt D'Arcy, in Essex, near the village where she grew up. Carter completed her last book, *Cargo of Eagles*, published in 1968, and wrote a memoir for the posthumous collection *Mr. Campion's Clowns* (1967). Allingham became an acknowledged leader of post-war detective fiction, noted, in the words of a colleague, for her 'colloquial raciness' of style and also for her many striking female characters. Her work formed the basis of a television series in 1989. She also wrote *The Oaken Heart* (1941), about England in wartime, and several plays. *See* Julia Thorogood, *Margery Allingham: A Biography* (1991).

'A.L.O.E.' (A Lady of England) *see* TUCKER, Charlotte Maria

Anderson, Wilhelmina Johnstone *see* MUIR, Willa

Andrews, Cicily Isabel *see* WEST, Dame Rebecca

'Anna Matilda' *see* COWLEY, Hannah

annuals.

Annuals were lavishly produced collections or albums of poetry, short stories, and essays, published annually, often at Christmas, illustrated by steel engravings and intended as gift books. The early Victorian equivalent of the coffee table book, the annuals flourished between the 1820s, with the founding of the *Forget-me-Not* (1823), until the 1850s, with the demise of the *Keepsake* (1857). Increasingly extravagant modes of production were used, as glazed figured boards and protective slipcases were replaced by silk and later morocco bindings. There were sometimes as many as twenty-five or thirty illustrations in each volume. In theory the illustrations complemented the text, but the reverse priority was not uncommon. Women writers featured prominently as editors and contributors. Lady *Blessington was the most successful of the annual editors. She took over the *Keepsake* in 1841 and continued until her death in 1850. Her contributors included Mrs Samuel Carter *Hall, Caroline *Norton, and Emmeline *Stuart-Wortley. Laetitia *Landon (L.E.L.), Mary *Howitt, Sarah *Ellis, and Caroline *Norton successively edited *Fisher's Drawing-Room Scrap Book* between 1832 and 1849. Blessington and Landon had both previously edited *Heath's Book of Beauty* (1833–47), another popular album, to which Adelaide *Procter contributed. Mary Russell *Mitford and Felicia *Hemans also wrote for the annuals. Wordsworth's quip that 'it would disgrace any name to appear in an annual' seems not to have deterred writers of either sex, who were offered substantial sums for what were usually sweepings from their worktables. *See* Andrew Boyle, *Index to the Annuals 1820–1850* (1967).

'Anodos' *see* COLERIDGE, Mary

Anspach, Elizabeth, Margravine of, née Craven, poet and dramatist (b. December 1750, d. 1828).

Elizabeth, Margravine of Anspach, was the youngest daughter of the fourth Earl of Berkeley. Her father died when she was 4, and her mother remarried three years later, leaving her to a lonely childhood. At the age of 16 she married William Craven, later sixth Earl of Craven, by whom she had four daughters. Elizabeth wrote and produced plays, beginning with an adaptation from the French of *The Sleep-Walker* (1778), published by Horace Walpole's private press at Strawberry Hill. She followed this by an experimental Christmas story, *Modern Anecdotes of the Ancient Family of Kinkvervankotsdarsprakengotchderns: A Tale for Christmas* (1779), and a comedy, *The Miniature Picture* (1780), which she had staged at Drury Lane, with herself in a prominent place in the audience. Her marriage was unhappy, however, and both partners unfaithful. They separated in 1783 and Elizabeth travelled extensively in Europe, publishing a series of letters, *A Journey through the Crimea to Constantinople* (1789). She took up residence with the Margrave of Anspach, ostensibly as his 'sister'. They were married in 1791, on the death of her first husband. The following year the couple settled in England, at Brandenberg House, Hammersmith, and at the estate of Benham in Berkshire, the seat of the Craven family. The Margrave was fond of horses and of drama. Elizabeth built a private theatre and organized the production of her own plays, which included *The Princess of Georgia* (1798), *Love Rewarded* (1799), and *The Soldier of Dierenstein* (1802), as well as several privately acted pieces which have not survived. She composed the music for several of the productions at Brandenberg House, and also frequently performed in them. Her *Letters* to the Margrave were published in 1785 and 1786, and *The Memoirs of the Margravine of Anspach, Written by Herself* in 1826, edited with an introduction by A. M. Broadley and L. Melville in 1914. *See* 'George Paston' [Emily Morse Symonds], *Little Memoirs of the Eighteenth Century* (1901).

Anstruther, Joyce *see* STRUTHER, Jan

'Anthony, C. L.' *see* SMITH, Dodie

Arnim, 'Elizabeth' von (Mary Annette Beauchamp, also 'Elizabeth', 'Anne Cholmondely'), novelist (b. New Zealand, 31 August 1866, d. Charleston, South Carolina, 9 February 1941).

Elizabeth von Arnim was the sixth and last child of English-born shipping magnate Henry Beauchamp and his Australian wife Elizabeth ('Louey')

Lassetter. Katherine *Mansfield was her cousin. The family moved to London via Switzerland when she was 3. She went to Miss Summerhayes's school in Ealing and then to the Royal College of Music, where she won a prize for organ playing. When she was 18 she was taken on a tour of Europe by her father, where she met the Prussian Count Henning August von Arnim-Schlagenthin, whom she married in 1891. His impoverished Pomeranian estate was the setting for her best-known book, *Elizabeth and her German Garden*, published anonymously in 1898, which presents a picture of her domestic life, her family of five children, and, humorously, her husband, 'the Man of Wrath'. The contrast between the freedom she experienced in nature and the restrictions of domestic life and the tyranny of marriage and motherhood was a theme which she developed in many of her twenty-odd novels. She wrote daily, shutting herself away after her domestic responsibilities were fulfilled. Most of her early books appeared as by 'Elizabeth', author of *Elizabeth and her German Garden*, apart from *Christine* (1917), which was published under the pseudonym Anne Cholmondely. *The Benefactress* (1901) was based on her husband's imprisonment on a false charge. *Fraulein Schmidt and Mr. Anstruther* (1907) and *The Caravanners* (1909) gently satirized aspects of German bourgeois life and German husbands. Count von Arnim died in 1910. Elizabeth looked after their children in a château in Switzerland until the outbreak of the First World War, when she returned to England. After an affair with H. G. Wells she married Francis, second Earl Russell and brother of the philosopher Bertrand Russell, in 1916. The marriage was disastrous and the couple separated in 1919. Her novels became more sombre after her widowhood and remarriage. *Vera* (1921), generally acknowledged to be her best work, presents a harsh picture of marital tyranny and is supposedly based on her marriage to Russell. *The Pastor's Wife* (1914) presents an equally bleak view of women's position within marriage. Her best seller *The Enchanted April* (1923), which was dramatized and also televised (1992), presents a more optimistic view of marital relationships. Her ambivalence towards men and marriage is reflected in her autobiography *All the Dogs of my Life* (1936) and in her last novel *Mr. Skeffington* (1940). Von Arnim moved to South Carolina on the outbreak of the Second World War and died there two years later. Barbara *Pym, Rebecca *West, and Alice *Meynell were among her admirers. Her daughter Leslie de Charms wrote a biography, *Elizabeth of the German Garden* (1940). *See* K. Usborne, *'Elizabeth': The Author of Elizabeth and her German Garden* (1986).

Arnold, Mary Augusta *see* WARD, Mrs Humphry

Ashford, Angela *see under* ASHFORD, Daisy

Ashford, 'Daisy' (Margaret Mary Julia), child writer, (b. Petersham, Surrey, 7 April 1881, d. Hellesdon, Norwich, 15 January 1972).

Probably the only woman writer to reach her peak at the age of 13, Daisy Ashford was the eldest of the three children of William Henry Roxburghe Ashford, a civil servant in the War Office, and his second wife Emma Georgina Walker, a soldier's widow who had five children by her previous marriage. The large amalgamated family was Roman Catholic and Daisy was educated by a governess, then by a private teacher, and for one year at a convent at Hayward's Heath. By the time she went to school at 17, her writing career was virtually over. She began precociously at 4 to tell stories to her middle-aged parents, who wrote them down. In 1885 she dictated 'The Life of Father McSwiney', which was eventually published in 1983 in *The Hangman's Daughter and Other Stories*. In 1889, after the family had moved to Lewes, in Sussex, she dictated two romances, 'A Short Story of Love and Marriage' and 'Mr Chapmer's Bride', which has not survived. The first book written in her own handwriting, complete with misspellings, was her best known, *The Young Visiters; or Mr. Salteena's Plan*, which presented a clever child's view of Victorian upper middle-class life. She then wrote a play, 'A Woman's Crime', now lost, and two further stories, 'The True History of Leslie Woodcock' (1892) and 'Where Love Lies Deepest' (1893). 'The Hangman's Daughter', which she wrote in 1894–5, like 'Where Love lies Deepest', was more sombre in tone than *The Young Visiters* and she regarded it as her 'greatest literary achievement'. Two chapters of 'A Romance of the Afghan War' were completed in 1896 but then abandoned. She spent five years at home after leaving school, moved with the family to Bexhill, and then joined her sister in London, where she worked as a secretary. Her early writings were rediscovered during the sorting out of her dead mother's papers in 1917. *The Young Visiters* was shown to Frank Swinnerton, a reader at Chatto & Windus, who published it under her name in 1919 with an introduction by J. M. Barrie. Its success was immediate. It was reprinted eighteen times in its first year, despite some reservations about its authenticity. A. A. Milne, Robert Graves, and Holbrook Jackson were among its enthusiastic reviewers. Barrie himself was widely believed to be the author, which markedly increased its American sales. The book was dramatized (1920) and made into a musical (1968) and into a film (1984). In the introduction to *Daisy Ashford: Her Book* (1920) Ashford claimed the stories were written by 'a Daisy Ashford of so long ago that she seems almost another person' and modestly attributed her success to Barrie's commendation. She worked at the British legation at Berne during the First World War, and in 1920 married James Devlin (d.

1956), by whom she had four children. They farmed near Norwich and later ran a hotel. Two collections of stories were reprinted before her death, *Love and Marriage* (1965) and *Where Love Lies Deepest* (1966). Her true identity was revealed at the end of her life in 1972. Her sister **Angela Ashford** wrote 'The Jealous Governes', which was included in several of the collections, at the age of 8. *See* R. M. Malcomson, *Daisy Ashford: Her Life* (1984).

Ashton, Dorothy Violet *see* WELLESLEY, Dorothy

Ashton, Winifred *see* DANE, Clemence

Askew, Anne, poet, autobiographer, and martyr (b. Lincolnshire, 1520, d. London, 16 July 1546).

Anne Askew or Ayscough was the second daughter of Sir William Askew, a Lincolnshire landowner and courtier to Henry VIII, and his wife Elizabeth Wrottesley. Her father believed in educating his daughters, but not in allowing them freedom in their marriage choice. Consequently she was highly educated, and married against her will to Thomas Kyme, the son of a large landowner, uneducated, and a staunch Roman Catholic, who had been intended for her elder sister. He was unsympathetic to his wife's developing Protestant sympathies and was encouraged by Lincolnshire priests to cast her out as a heretic. Askew, who had borne Kyme two children, in turn unsuccessfully sought a divorce. She left her husband's house and moved to London, associating with a group of Protestants who surrounded the Queen, Catherine Parr. She was twice tried for heresy, enduring interrogation and eventually racking, at the hands of the Lord Chancellor and senior members of the Church, partly with the intention of making her incriminate the Queen. She refused to confess, and was burnt at the stake at Smithfield at the age of 25. After her first trial, she set down her own account of her *First Examination*, one of the earliest instances of autobiographical writing by a woman. *The Latter Examination* was a record of her second imprisonment. The strength of her personality is equally evident in the often anthologized but possibly apocryphal 'Ballad which Anne Askewe Made and Sang when she was in Newgate'. The two *Examinations* were published separately in Wesel in 1546 and 1547 with an 'elucidation' by the Protestant polemicist John Bale, and in John Foxe's *Actes and Monuments* or *Book of Martyrs* (1563). Askew's reputation lived on in the seventeenth century and her story formed the basis of Anne *Manning's novel *The Lincolnshire Tragedy* (1866). *See* Elaine V. Beilin, *Redeeming Eve: Women Writers of the English Renaissance* (1987), and in *Contending Kingdoms: Historical, Psychological and Feminist Approaches to the Literature of Sixteenth-Century England and France*, ed. Marie-Rose Logan and Peter L. Rudnytsky (1991).

Astell, Mary, feminist and polemicist (b. Newcastle-upon-Tyne, 6 November 1666, d. Chelsea, London, 14 May 1731).

Mary Astell was the daughter of Peter Astell, a prominent Newcastle coal merchant, and Mary Errington, also from a prosperous Newcastle coal-mining family. She was educated in philosophy, logic, and mathematics by a clergyman uncle, and at the age of 22 went to London, proposing to live independently of her family. She settled in Chelsea, where she remained for the rest of her life, and began to engage in the intellectual and religious debates of her day. She first achieved celebrity in 1694 with the publication of *A Serious Proposal to the Ladies*, an appeal to wealthy women to use their dowries for the establishment of residential colleges for women who chose to remain single. The institutions would provide higher education for middle- and upper-class women and would, she pressed, become havens for 'hunted heiresses' and decayed gentlewomen. Others described them as 'protestant nunneries'. *A Serious Proposal to the Ladies Part II* (1697) elaborated rules of rational thought for women according to Cartesian principles. While attracting vociferous opposition, *A Serious Proposal* also aroused enthusiastic support and established her reputation as an intellectual and a combatant on behalf of women. Her extensive correspondence with John Norris (1657–1711), Cambridge Platonist and poet, was published in 1695 as *Letters Concerning the Love of God between the Author of the Proposal to the Ladies and Mr. John Norris*. Her next work, *Some Reflections on Marriage* (1700), presented that institution as potentially the most tyrannical of relationships and advised that women should not enter into it lightly. The preface added in 1706 asked, 'If all men are born free, how is it that women are born slaves?' Astell was a convinced and pugnacious churchwoman and her various writings in support of the Church of England, including *A Fair Way with Dissenters and their Patrons* (1704), a response to Defoe's *The Shortest Way with the Dissenters* (1702), won her supporters who might otherwise have been estranged by her feminism. Her own religious manifesto *The Christian Religion as Profess'd by a Daughter of the Church* (1705) set out the philosophical grounds for her belief in an attempt to refute materialist philosophers such as Locke. Her last work, *Bart'lemy Fair; or An Inquiry after Wit* (1709), was written in response to Lord Shaftesbury's *Letter Concerning Enthusiasm* and against the threat of latitudinarianism. *An Impartial Enquiry into the Causes of Rebellion* (1704) articulated her Tory and royalist principles. Mary Astell was one of the most formidable female intellectuals of her generation. Attacks on her in the *Tatler* and by Swift, Colley Cibber, and others, and outright borrowing of her work in Steele's *The Ladies Library* (1714), testified to the strength of her reputation as a polemicist. She was a friend of Lady Mary Wortley *Montagu, for whose *Letters* she wrote a preface, and had a powerful patron in Lady Elizabeth Hastings (1682–1739), a prominent philanthropist. She also befriended the impoverished scholar Elizabeth *Elstob. In her later years she opened a school for the children of pensioners at the Royal Hospital, Chelsea. She died in London after an operation for breast cancer. *See* Ruth Perry, *The Celebrated Mary Astell* (1986); Bridget Hill's introd. to *The First English Feminist* (1986).

Aubin, Penelope, novelist (b. London, *c.*1685, d. 1731).

Little is known of Penelope Aubin's personal life. She was born in London, probably the daughter of an *émigré* French officer. She published a volume of poems in 1708, and then nothing until her first novel, *The Strange Adventures of the Count de Vinevil and his Family*, in 1721. Her husband was known to have died before 1722, which suggests that writing may have been a necessity as a source of income. Several other novels followed in quick succession, *The Life of Madam de Beaumount, a French Lady* (1721), *The Noble Slaves* (1722), *The Life and Amorous Adventures of Lucinda* (1722), *The Life of Charlotta du Pont* (1723), *The Life and Adventures of the Lady Lucy* (1726), and *The Life and Adventures of the Young Count Albertus* (1728). The 'life and adventures' structure, in which the hero or heroine experienced shipwreck, imprisonment, persecution, followed by escape and reunion, was much influenced by the travel writing of the period and also served a moral purpose, that of testing and rewarding virtue. Female characters preserved their chastity and their Christian principles no matter what the trial. The narrator of *Charlotta du Pont* reinforced the author's point: 'Examples should convince us how possible it is for us to behave ourselves as we ought in our Conditions, since Ladies, whose Sex, and tender Manner of Breeding render them much less able than Men to support such Hardships, bravely endured Shipwrecks, Want, Cold, Slavery, and every Ill that Human Nature could be tried withal.' Aubin's model was Elizabeth *Rowe, to whom she dedicated *The Life of Charlotta du Pont* ('my much honoured Friend Mrs Rowe'), although the friendship may have been imagined. Rowe's influence was evoked to underline Aubin's determination to write moral tales in the teeth of the contemporary trend and the temptation to write 'more modishly . . . less like a Christian, and in a Style careless and loose'. She left that, she added, to 'other female Authors my Contemporaries, whose Lives and Writing have, I fear, too great a resemblance'. She was probably thinking of the popular Eliza *Haywood, to whose work her own was favourably compared by contemporaries. Samuel Richardson may have been the author of the preface to a 1739 collection of Aubin's novels which praised her for preserving 'Purity of Style and Manners' in her fiction. Aubin published several translations of plays from the French. Towards the end of her life she became a popular preacher, speaking from the York Buildings near Charing Cross. Shortly before her death she spoke the epilogue on the second night of her surprisingly ribald comedy *The Merry Masqueraders; or The Humorous Cuckold* (1730). *See* Jane Spencer, *The Rise of the Woman Novelist: From Aphra Behn to Jane Austen* (1986); April London, in *Fetter'd or Free? British Women Novelists 1670–1815*, ed. Mary Anne Schofield and Cecilia Macheski (1986).

Austen, Jane, novelist (b. Steventon, near Basingstoke, Hampshire, 16 December 1776, d. Winchester, 18 July 1817).

Jane Austen was the sixth of the seven children of the Revd George Austen, rector of Deane and Steventon, and his wife Cassandra Leigh, the daughter of a well-connected clergyman. The Leighs numbered a Master of Balliol and minor landed gentry among their relations. Two of Austen's brothers became admirals and another entered the Church. She and her elder sister Cassandra remained unmarried, although she was known to have had several suitors. She spent the first twenty-five years of her life at the rectory in Steventon, where she was taught the conventional French, Italian, music, and needlework. Encouraged by her father she also read widely, particularly the novels of Richardson, Fielding, Sterne, the work of many women novelists including Fanny *Burney and Maria *Edgeworth, the poetry of Cowper and Crabbe, and later the poetry and early novels of Scott. She also, it is claimed, took part in family theatricals. The family moved to Bath in 1801, and after her father's death in 1805 she and her mother and sister moved to Southampton, and then in 1809 to the village of Chawton, near Alton, in Hampshire, to a house owned by her brother. She spent the rest of her life at Chawton, apart from occasional visits to Bath and London. She began to write in her early teens, many of the stories satirizing the excesses of contemporary fiction. *Love and Freindship*, which she wrote at 14, was a burlesque of sensibility. *A History of England* satirized pomposity, *Lesley Castle* mocked the epistolary form. *Lady Susan*, her only genuine epistolary novel, is thought to have been written in 1793–4, but was not published until 1871. An early story entitled 'Eleanor and Marianne', written in 1795–6, was rewritten in 1797–8 as *Sense and Sensibility*, revised in 1809, and eventually published in 1811. *First Impressions*, written in 1797, was rejected by the publisher and revised and published as *Pride and Prejudice* in 1813. *Northanger Abbey* was written in 1798–9, prepared for the press in 1803, and sold to a publisher for £10. It was later bought back from him by one of her brothers and published posthumously in 1818. *The Watsons*, an unfinished novel, was written between 1804 and 1805, but abandoned, possibly due to her father's death. *Mansfield Park*, *Emma*, and *Persuasion* were all written in the family parlour at Chawton between 1811 and 1815. *Mansfield Park* was published in 1814, *Emma* in 1816. *Persuasion* was published posthumously along with *Northanger Abbey* in 1818. She was working on the unfinished *Sanditon* at the time of her death. The first four novels were published anonymously, and her authorship made public in a biographical note prefaced to the last two. Austen's work achieved only modest success during her lifetime. *Emma* was reviewed by Scott in the *Quarterly Review* in 1815 and he later contrasted his own 'big bow-wow strain' with her 'exquisite touch which renders ordinary common-place things and characters interesting'. After the publication of *Mansfield Park* the Prince Regent, later George IV, gave her permission to dedicate her next book to him, which she did, but declined the suggestion of his Librarian that she should write a romance about the House of Coburg. She died in Winchester of Addison's disease at the age of 40. Austen's reputation flourished after her death, Scott, Macaulay, and G. H. Lewes numbering among her most vociferous admirers. Women writers were less forthcoming in her praise. Charlotte *Brontë, in a famous letter to Lewes, declared her work to be 'a carefully fenced, highly cultivated garden, with neat borders and delicate flowers', but 'without poetry'. Mid-Victorian male critics, according to Elaine Showalter (*A Literature of their Own*, 1977), commended Austen as an example of female literary restraint to her more 'unruly' siblings, and polarized the female literary tradition into two distinct lines, those of Jane Austen and George Sand, the writer of intellect and cultivation versus the novelist of passion and rebellion. The publication in 1870 of J. E. Austen-Leigh's *Memoir* inaugurated a Jane Austen cult. Anne Thackeray *Ritchie wrote of her enthusiastically in *A Book of Sibyls* (1883). Her reputation in the twentieth century has remained high. Virginia *Woolf called her 'one of the most consistent satirists in the whole of literature' (*The Common Reader* (1925)). F. R. Leavis gave her a key position in his *Great Tradition* (1948). Recent feminist critics have debated the extent of her feminism. Her sister Cassandra edited all personal references out of her letters, the standard edition of which is by R. W. Chapman (1932, rev. 1952). The standard edition of the novels is by R. W. Chapman (6 vols., 1923–54). *See* Mary Lascelles, *Jane Austen: Her Mind and Art* (1939); *Jane Austen: The Critical Heritage*, ed. B. C. Southam (2 vols., 1968, 1987); Marilyn Butler, *Jane Austen and the War of Ideas* (1975 rev. 1984); Sandra Gilbert and Susan Gubar, *The Madwoman in the Attic* (1979); David Gilson, *Jane Austen: A Bibliography* (1982); Margaret Kirkham, *Jane Austen, Feminism and Fiction* (1983); Tony Tanner, *Jane Austen* (1986).

Austin, Sarah, translator and reviewer (b. Norwich, 1793, d. Weybridge, Surrey, 8 August 1867).

The daughter of John Taylor, a yarn manufacturer, and his wife Susanna Cook, Sarah Austin was educated by her mother and married the jurist John Austin (1790–1859) in 1820. They had one daughter, later Lady Lucie Duff *Gordon. She began to write in order to supplement her husband's income as a lawyer. In 1833 she published *Selections from the Old Testament* and the first of her translations, *Characteristics of Goethe*. In 1834 she translated Carove's *The Story without an End*, which was often reprinted, and Cousin's report on *The State of Public Instruction in Prussia*, to which she added a preface, arguing the case for a national system of education. Austin was a scrupulous and intelligent translator, and frequently added notes and explanatory material to her translations. She wrote for the *Edinburgh*, the *British and Foreign*, and the *Foreign Quarterly* reviews, one of only a handful of women contributors, and for the *Athenaeum*. Her best-known work during her lifetime, *Germany from 1760 to 1814* (1854), was the result of an extended residence in that country. That book and her translations from the German did much to make the work of German intellectuals and writers known in England, and her widely reviewed translation of Ranke's *History of the Popes* (1840) won her the praise of Macaulay and Henry Hart Milman. In addition to Goethe and Ranke, she translated Raumer's *England in* 1835 (1836), *Fragments from German Prose Writers* (1841), Niebuhr's *Stories of the Gods and Heroes of Greece* (1843), and Guizot's *Causes of the Success of the English Revolution* (1850). She prepared a posthumous edition of John Austin's *The Province of Jurisprudence Determined* in 1861, to which she prefaced a memoir, and in 1863 published an edition of his *Lectures on Jurisprudence*. She also edited Lucie Duff Gordon's *Letters from Egypt* (1865). Sarah Austin's reputation as an intellectual rested as much on her conversational powers and her wide acquaintance with intellectual circles as on her published work. John Stuart Mill was a particular admirer. She died of a heart attack in 1867. *See* Janet A. Ross, *Three Generations of Englishwomen* (1888); Lotte and Joseph Hamburger, *Troubled Lives: John and Sarah Austin* (1985) and *Contemplating Adultery* (1993).

'Aydy, Catherine' *see* TENNANT, Emma

b b b b b b b b b b b b b

B

Bacon, Ann, Lady, translator and letter writer (b. Gains Park, Essex, 1528, d. Gorhambury, Hertfordshire, August 1610).

Ann, Lady Bacon, was the second of five daughters among the nine children of Sir Anthony Cooke and his wife Ann Fitzwilliam. All of Cooke's daughters were liberally educated by their father, at one time tutor to Edward VI. According to some authorities Ann assisted him in the capacity of governess. She acquired a reputation for immense learning from an early age, and reportedly read Latin, Greek, Italian, and French, 'as her native tongue'. She was also a devout Puritan. She became the second wife of Sir Nicholas Bacon, Lord Keeper of the Seal to Elizabeth I, around 1557. Their sons Anthony and Francis were born in 1558 and 1561. Her translation of the sermons of the Italian Calvinist Bernardine Ochine, undertaken before her marriage, were published as 'by A.C.' (*c.*1550). In 1564 she published a translation from the Latin of the influential *Apologie of the Church of England* by John Jewel, Bishop of Salisbury, which contained a complimentary preface by Matthew Parker, Archbishop of Canterbury. The work was reissued in 1600 and again after her death, assuring her a place at the very centre of contemporary religious debate. Her attractive letters to her sons, upon whom she continued to be a formidable influence long after their childhood, were printed in James Spedding's *Life and Letters of Bacon* (1861–74). She became more ferociously Puritan in her old age, denouncing plays and masques, but urging fair treatment for Nonconformists. Her last years were marred by senility, one contemporary reporting that 'she was but little better than frantic in her age'. She died at 82. The daughters of Sir Anthony Cooke, like the daughters of

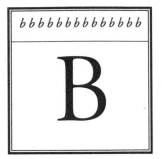

Sir Thomas More, were famed for their learning. Her elder sister **Mildred** (1526–89) became the second wife of William Cecil, Lord Burghley, and was a noted letter writer. One younger sister, **Elizabeth** (1529–1609), wife of Sir Thomas Hoby, and secondly of John, Lord Russell, was a translator and letter writer, and another, **Katherine** (1530?–83), wife of the diplomat Sir Henry Killigrew, was a Latin poet (*see DNB*). *See* Mary Ellen Lamb in *Silent but for the Word: Tudor Women as Patrons, Translators and Writers of Religious Works*, ed. Margaret P. Hannay (1985); Elaine V. Beilin, *Redeeming Eve: Women Writers of the English Renaissance* (1987).

Bagnold, Enid, novelist and playwright (b. Rochester, Kent, 27 October 1889, d. London, 31 March 1981).

Enid Bagnold was the eldest of the two children of Arthur Henry Bagnold, a military engineer, and his wife Ethel Alger, the daughter of a chemical and fertilizer manufacturer. She spent three years in Jamaica, where her father had been posted, and then went to a school in Godalming run by Julia Frances Huxley, the mother of Aldous and Julian and the granddaughter of Thomas Arnold. From there she was sent to a school in Switzerland, from which she ran away, and from there to Paris and Marburg. After school she studied drawing with Walter Sickert in London and moved in a world of artists and writers which included Gaudier-Brzeska, who sculpted her, Katherine *Mansfield, Vita *Sackville-West, and others. She wrote for *Hearth and Home*, edited by the notorious Frank Harris, with whom she had her first love affair. During the First World War she worked as a VAD (Voluntary Aid Detachment) nurse in a London hospital, recording her experiences frankly in *A Diary without Dates* (1918), which resulted in her dismissal from her post within a half-hour of the book's publication. H. G. Wells pronounced it one of the two most human books written about the war. Her later war experiences in France formed the basis of her first novel, *The Happy Foreigner* (1920). Strikingly beautiful, ebullient, and gregarious, she became a central figure in London society and, according to Nigel Nicolson's *DNB* entry, too fond of the great and grand to be taken seriously by the literary establishment. In 1920 she married Sir Roderick Jones, chairman of Reuters News Agency, by whom she had four children. *Serena Blandish; or The Difficulty of Getting Married*, her second novel, was published anonymously 'by a Lady of Quality' in 1924 and adapted as a play in 1929. *Alice and Thomas and Jane* (1930), a book for children, was illustrated by her daughter. In 1935 she published her best-known book, *National Velvet*, the story of a girl who wins a horse in a raffle and, disguised as a boy, then wins the Grand National. A famous film version in 1944 and a stage adaptation in 1946 secured its lasting success. She considered her next novel, *The Squire*

(1938), about pregnancy and childbirth, to be her best. *The Loved and Envied* (1951), based on her friend Lady Diana Cooper, was her last. She concentrated on play-writing for the latter part of her career, with mixed success. *Lottie Dundas* (1941), about a typist who becomes an actress, did well in both London and New York. She had several notable failures but one undoubted success. *The Chalk Garden* (1955) ran for two years in London and was extravagantly praised by the critic Kenneth Tynan as 'possibly the finest English comedy since those of Congreve'. *The Chinese Prime Minister* (1964) was another New York hit. Bagnold was actively involved in the productions of all her plays, and in 1975, at the age of 86, revised the unsuccessful *Call Me Jacky* (1968) into *A Matter of Gravity.* She published *Enid Bagnold's Autobiography* (1969), a selection of her *Poems* (1978), and in 1980 *Letters to Frank Harris and Other Friends.* Despite painful arthritis she remained active until her death at 91, describing herself as 'an old lady masking a sort of everlasting girl inside'. *See* Katherine Mansfield, *Novels and Novelists* (1930); Kenneth Tynan, *Curtains* (1961); Anne Sebba, *Enid Bagnold: The Authorized Biography* (1987).

Baillie, Lady Grizel or Grisell, poet (b. Redbraes Castle, Berwickshire, 25 December 1665, d. Mellerstein, Berwickshire, 6 December 1746).

The daughter of Sir Patrick Hume, later Earl of Marchmont, a Scots Protestant patriot, and his wife Grizel Ker, Grizel Baillie is as famous for her heroism as for her writing. When she was 12 'little Grizel' gave evidence of her courage and tenacity when she conveyed secret messages to her father's devoted friend, the famous Robert Baillie of Jerviswood. In the course of this exploit she met his son George, whom she later married. She demonstrated equal courage and resourcefulness during her own father's hiding, when she kept him alive in a burial vault for a month on smuggled food. After Baillie of Jerviswood had been hanged, the Hume family moved into exile in Holland, where, as her mother was an invalid, Grizel ran the household and later declared it to be the happiest time of her life. Her heroic exploits were recorded and publicized by her descendant Joanna *Baillie in her *Metrical Legends of Exalted Characters* (1821). At the accession of William and Mary in 1688 Grizel was offered the post of Maid of Honour to the Princess of Orange but declined it in order to marry her childhood sweetheart in 1692, by whom she had a son and two daughters. Baillie was an MP between 1708 and 1734, and the couple moved to London. She began to write from an early age and left fragments of poems in a notebook, 'many of them interrupted, half writ, some broken off in the middle of a sentence', as her daughter later described them. Some of her songs were published in Allan Ramsay's *Tea-Table*

Miscellany (1723–40) and in other collections of Scottish songs. The best known was 'And werena my heart light I wad dee', of which a later anthologist wrote: 'Its sudden inspiration has fused and cast into one perfect line, the protest of thousands of stricken hearts in every generation.' She also left numerous account books and 'Day Books' for the period 1692–1733, important for the study of domestic history. A selection was published as *The Household Book of Lady Griselle Baillie 1692–1733*, ed. R. Scott-Moncrieff, in 1911. Her daughter Grizel Murray wrote about both parents in *Memoirs of the Lives and Characters of the Right Honourable George Baillie of Jerviswood, and of Lady Grisell Baillie* (1922).

Baillie, Joanna, poet and dramatist, (b. Bothwell, Lanarkshire, 11 September 1762, d. Hampstead, 23 February 1851).

Joanna Baillie was the daughter of the Revd James Baillie, Church of Scotland minister of Bothwell, and later professor of divinity at Glasgow University, and of Dorothea Hunter. William and John Hunter, the famous surgeons, were her uncles. The Baillies claimed descent from William Wallace. Joanna was educated at a boarding school in Glasgow where she early demonstrated a talent for writing and performing plays, and also for music. Her father died in 1778, and in 1783 her uncle Dr William Hunter left the use of his house in London to her brother Matthew, who later became a physician. Joanna, her elder sister Agnes, and her mother moved to London, where, despite her shyness, she gradually obtained an entry into literary circles. Her first volume of poems, published in 1790, went virtually unnoticed and some were later reprinted in her *Fugitive Verses* (1840). She then resolved to write a group of plays demonstrating each of the passions, a comedy and a tragedy for each passion. *A Series of Plays in which it is Attempted to Delineate the Stronger Passions of the Mind*, usually known as the *Plays on the Passions*, was published in three volumes between 1798 and 1812. The first volume secured her the friendship and admiration of Sir Walter Scott, and *De Monfort*, a tragedy on hatred, was produced at Drury Lane with John Kemble and Mrs Siddons in the leading roles. The second volume (1802) contained a comedy on hatred which was produced at the English Opera House, but the others were considered not sufficiently dramatic for performance. A volume of *Miscellaneous Plays* (1804) included two tragedies, *Rayner* and *Constantine Paleologus*, the second of which she hoped Kemble would also produce. He declined, but it was eventually performed at the Surrey Theatre and then in Liverpool, Dublin, and Edinburgh. Another tragedy, *Family Legend* (1810), about a Highland feud, was also performed in Edinburgh, under Scott's patronage and with an epilogue by Henry Mackenzie, but in general Baillie's dramas were regarded as too 'literary'. She published a volume of *Metrical Legends* (1821) mainly on Scottish subjects, including one on her ancestress Lady Grizel *Baillie, and edited a collection, *Poetic Miscellanies* (1823), which included contributions by Scott, Wordsworth, and Southey. Another play, *The Martyr*, was published in 1826, and in 1836 she produced a three-volume collection of *Miscellaneous Plays*, some of them extensions to *Plays on the Passions* and several of which were performed to a lukewarm reception. Joanna Baillie had a wide circle of literary friends, including Anna *Barbauld, Lucy *Aikin, Maria *Edgeworth, and Francis Jeffrey, the last of whom had begun by attacking her in the *Edinburgh Review*. Byron proclaimed her the only exception to his assertion that women could not write tragedy. She died unmarried and still holding court to her friends at her home in Hampstead at the age of 88. *See* M. S. Cathcart, *The Life and Work of Joanna Baillie* (1923).

Bainbridge, Beryl (Margaret), novelist, (b. Liverpool, 21 November 1934).

Beryl Bainbridge's father Richard, a failed businessman turned salesman and a socialist, died when she was 17. 'All my childhood was spent with people who were disappointed,' she once wrote. 'They'd married the wrong person, failed in business, been manipulated by others.' As a child she wrote constantly, encouraged by her mother Winifred Baines, who bought her exercise books and sharpened her pencils. Her father read Dickens to her and told her stories. But home life was marred by her father's violent rages and general domestic disharmony. She went to Merchant Taylors' School in Liverpool and later studied ballet at a school in Tring. She began a career as an actress while in her teens, performing in provincial repertory companies and also on the radio. In 1954 she married Austin Davies, a painter, and had three children before divorcing him in 1959. She wrote her first novel after the birth of her first child. It was returned by one publisher because its characters were 'repulsive beyond belief' and one scene 'too indecent and unpleasant even for these lax days'. A second publisher mislaid it. It was eventually published as *Harriet Says*, her third novel, in 1972. Her first two, *A Weekend with Claud* (1967) and *Another Part of the Wood* (1968), received muted critical approval and were later revised, but the enthusiastic reception of *Harriet Says* inaugurated a productive period in which she published virtually a novel a year: *The Dressmaker* (1973, published in New York as *The Secret Glass*, 1974), *The Bottle Factory Outing* (1974), derived from her experiences in a London wine-bottling plant, which won the Guardian Fiction Award, *Sweet William* (1975), for which she wrote the screenplay in 1980, *A Quiet Life* (1976), *Injury Time* (1977), which won the Whitbread Award, *Young Adolf* (1978), loosely based on a visit of Hitler to his half-brother in Liverpool in 1912, *The Winter*

Garden (1980), and *Watson's Apology* (1984), which drew on a Victorian murder case. She has also written several television plays, a collection of short stories, *Mum and Mr. Armitage* (1985), and *English Journey; or the Road to Milton Keynes* (1984), a revisiting of the itinerary of J. B. Priestley's *English Journey* (1932). *An Awfully Big Adventure* (1989) was shortlisted for the Booker Prize. *The Birthday Boys*, a reworking of Scott's Antarctic expedition, was published in 1991. Bainbridge's novels combine banal domesticity with menace, ordinariness with the absurd. Black comedy features prominently. The books are distinguished by their economy of style and by the build-up of an atmosphere of violence, either generalized and in the background, or as an abrupt, often bizarre element in the plot. 'I am not very good at fiction,' she once commented. 'It is always me and the experiences I have had.'

Balfour, Mary *see* BRUNTON, Mary

Ballard, George, *Memoirs of Several Ladies of Great Britain* (1752).

Ballard (1706–55) was a self-educated antiquary and Anglo-Saxon scholar and a mantua maker by trade who in 1750 was made one of the eight clerks at Magdalen College, Oxford. In 1752 he published his two-volume *Memoirs of Several Ladies of Great Britain* 'who have been celebrated for their writings or skill in the learned languages, arts and sciences'. He selected sixty-four women from the sixteenth to the eighteenth centuries, scholars, historians, and some poets, most of them proficient in classical languages or some form of learning. Novelists and playwrights were not included. All were amateurs in the world of learning, and as such were much like Ballard himself, whose life of scholarship had been conducted outside the academic establishment until his recent appointment. The inspiration for the venture came from Elizabeth *Elstob, whom Ballard met some twenty years after she had ceased to be an active Anglo-Saxon scholar and whose miserable existence spurred him to record the lives of similar learned women whose achievements might otherwise have gone unrecognized. Elstob herself had begun a project to record women of achievement in 1709, but like her major scholarly work it had been abandoned on her brother's death in 1715. Ballard's preface stated that the purpose of the work was to remove 'that vulgar prejudice of the supposed incapacity of the female sex'. The epigraph reiterated that 'surely those who deny that the other sex is suited to scholarship have already been refuted by all philosophers'. He used his associates in the antiquarian world to help him compile a biographical sketch of each subject, complete with sources. The first volume was dedicated to a Mrs Talbot, a Warwickshire gentlewoman, and the second, to her slight irritation, to Mary *Delany, 'the truest judge and brightest pattern of all the accomplishments which adorn her sex'. The subscribers included Samuel Richardson, Edward Gibbon, William Blackstone, Bonnell Thornton, Mrs Delany, and Elizabeth Elstob (under the name Frances Smith). Critical reception was muted and many of Ballard's male associates questioned the point of the project. But a second edition was published in 1775, some twenty years after his death. Most subsequent biographical works which included women drew on his list and his sources. Like George Colman and Bonnell Thornton's anthology **Poems by Eminent Ladies* (1755) and John Duncombe's **Feminiad* (1754), it helped to establish a *de facto* canon of women writers for future generations. *See* Ruth Perry's introd. to her edn., *Memoirs of Several Ladies of Great Britain* (1985).

Banks, Isabella (Mrs Linnaeus Banks) (b. Manchester, 25 March 1821, d. Dalston, Cumbria, 5 May 1897).

Isabella Banks was the daughter of James Varley, a Manchester chemist and amateur artist, and his wife Amelia Daniels. She had her eyesight damaged by a smoking chimney as a child but did not let this deter her literary activities, publishing her poem 'A Dying Girl to her Mother' in the *Manchester Guardian* at the age of 16. Her father lost a substantial amount of money in a lawsuit over a bleaching process he had invented and Isabella in consequence ran a school at Cheetham, near Manchester, from the age of 18 until her marriage in 1846 to George Linnaeus Banks (1821–81), a journalist, poet, and lecturer. She contributed to various local newspapers edited by Banks, and, as the family finances became precarious due to his apparent mental instability and later drunkenness, she began to write intensively to support their eight children, five of whom died. Her first novel, *God's Providence House*, was published in 1865, and her best-known book *The Manchester Man* appeared in 1876, when she was 55. The rags to riches story of a foundling who rises to become a partner in a Manchester firm and marries his former master's daughter, it contained an accurate and detailed picture of Manchester in the early decades of the nineteenth century, including a description of the Peterloo riots of 1819. It went through four editions by 1881. *Forbidden to Marry* (1883), *Bond Slaves* (1893), and the earlier *Stung to the Quick: A North Country Story* (1867) earned her the title of 'The Lancashire Novelist'. Despite the breakdown of her health and her husband's rapidly deteriorating condition, Isabella Banks worked energetically to produce further novels, mainly romances, until her death in 1897, winning a loyal following. She published two volumes of poetry, *Ivy Leaves* (1844) and *Daisies in the Grass*, written jointly with her husband in 1865, some of which reveal her views of women's difficult role within marriage. She was also highly skilled in embroidery design, producing an original pattern every month for forty-five years. A uniform collected edition of her works begun in 1881 was never completed. She was granted a civil-list pension in 1891. *See* Edward L. Burney, *Mrs. G. Linnaeus Banks* (1969).

Barbauld, Anna Laetitia, poet and essayist (b. Kibworth Harcourt, Leicestershire, 20 June 1743, d. Stoke Newington, London, 1825).

Anna Barbauld was the only daughter and eldest child of Dr John Aikin, a Dissenting preacher who became a schoolmaster, and his wife Jane Jennings. When she was 15 her father became a tutor at the newly established Warrington Academy for Dissenters, where Anna's precocious talents were encouraged by her father's colleagues in a liberal and highly intellectual community. She could read before she was 3, became fluent in French and Italian, and later added a knowledge of Latin and Greek. She nevertheless lacked confidence in her own abilities, and it was only with the encouragement of her brother John that she published her first volume of *Poems* (1773), which included the well-known 'Corsica'. The same year they published *Miscellaneous Pieces in Prose* by J. and A. L. Aikin, which included her essays on 'Inconsistency in our Expectations' and 'On Romances'. In 1774 she married the Revd Rochemont Barbauld, a clergyman of French Protestant descent, who had himself been educated at Warrington, and who unfortunately suffered from an increasingly severe mental disorder. The couple opened a boys' school at Palgrave, in Suffolk, where Anna Barbauld bore the brunt of the organization and was responsible for the school's success. The Barbaulds had no children, but adopted a nephew, Charles Aikin, who was the inspiration for her *Lessons for Children* (1778). She also wrote her popular *Hymns in Prose for Children* (1781) at Palgrave. In 1785 they sold the school, spent some time travelling on the Continent, and then settled first in Hampstead, and eventually near her brother at Stoke Newington, where the Revd Barbauld had charge of a small congregation. Her literary work increased. She wrote a series of pamphlets on political subjects, *An Address to the Opposers of the Repeal of the Corporation and Test Acts* (1790), *Civic Sermons to the People* (1792), and *Sins of the Government, Sins of the Nation* (1793), against the war with France. Encouraged to return to poetry by her brother, she wrote an *Epistle to William Wilberforce* (1791), attacking the slave-trade. She subsequently contributed poetry to the *Monthly Magazine* of which he was the literary editor, collaborated in his *Evenings at Home* (1792–5), and edited the poetry of Akenside (1794) and William Collins (1797) in a series which he published. She also edited Richardson's *Letters* (1804). Her husband's condition worsened, and after several acts of violence against her he was eventually placed in an institution, where he was found drowned in 1808. Although deeply affected by the tragedy, she turned her entire energies to her work. In 1810 she undertook a fifty-volume edition of *The British Novelists* with biographical introductions to each of the writers, which included many women, and a prefatory essay on the 'Origin and Progress of Novel Writing'. In 1811 she published *The Female Speaker*, a selection of prose and poetry for young ladies. In the same year she produced a controversial anti-war poem, 'Eighteen Hundred and Eleven', which prophesied that at some time in the future a traveller standing on a crumbling Blackfriars Bridge would survey the ruins of St Paul's. The poem was severely criticized, particularly in the *Quarterly Review* in 1812, and proved to be her last publication. Despite her prominence in literary circles and her wide acquaintance with women writers, Mrs Barbauld had no sense of a common cause, or of a female literary tradition. When pressed by Elizabeth *Montagu to become the principal of an academy for women she responded that she saw no point in producing learned women rather than 'good wives or agreeable companions'. She died at Stoke Newington in 1825. In the same year her niece Lucy *Aikin produced an edition of her *Works* with a memoir. *See* Anne Thackeray *Ritchie, *A Book of Sibyls* (1883); B. Rodgers, *Georgian Chronicle: Mrs. Barbauld and her Family* (1958); Catherine E. Moore, in *Fetter'd or Free? British Women Novelists 1670–1815*, ed. Mary Anne Schofield and Cecilia Macheski (1986).

Barber, Margaret Fairless *see* FAIRLESS, Michael

Barber, Mary, poet (b. Ireland, 1690?, d. 1757).

Mary Barber was the wife of Jonathan Barber, a Dublin woollen draper and tailor. Of their several children, Constantine became president of the Dublin College of Physicians and Rupert a miniature painter and engraver. Mrs Barber began writing poetry for use in her children's lessons while at the same time helping her husband in his shop. She came to prominence in 1725 when she sent a poem, 'The Widow's Address', through the poet Thomas Ticknell to Lord Carteret, the Lord Lieutenant, to plead the case of an officer's widow who had fallen on hard times. As a result she was introduced to Swift, who became her patron, referring to her as 'Sapphira', generously correcting her poetry, and introducing her to influential literary figures in Ireland and England, including Arbuthnot, Gay, Pope, and Sir Robert Walpole, who eventually became subscribers to her first volume of poetry. She settled for a while in England, accompanied by her husband, who capitalized on these acquaintances in his business. A letter forged under Swift's signature praising her as 'the best female poet of this or perhaps of any age' was probably not written by her, and Swift did not allow the incident to prevent the publication of her *Poems on Several Occasions* (1734), prefaced by a commendatory letter from him to Lord Orrery and some verses by Constantia *Grierson. The volume was printed by Samuel Richardson. The critical response was muted, but a second and third printing followed. Mrs Barber made several attempts to settle in England, most notably in Bath. Swift offered assistance, particularly after she was arrested in 1734 for smuggling the manuscripts of some of his poems into the country. She was plagued by gout, and once the money from the subscription had run out asked for the rights to the London edition of his *Complete Collection of Genteel and Ingenious Conversation* (1738), which he granted. A selection of her poems was included in **Poems by Eminent Ladies* (1755), edited by George Colman and Bonnell Thornton, an indication of her contemporary standing. She died in 1757, her husband having predeceased her probably in 1733.

Barker, Jane ('Galesia'), poet and novelist (b. Northamptonshire, 1652, d. *c.*1727).

Jane Barker was the daughter of Thomas Barker, formerly a Royalist soldier and the agent for a Northamptonshire landowner, and his wife Anne Connock, a member of a Cornish Royalist family. When she was 10 the family moved to Wilsthorpe, near Stamford in Lincolnshire, where her father acquired a lease on some land. She was taught Latin and medicine by her brother, a student at Cambridge, whose early death was a considerable blow. An arch-Royalist and strong supporter of the Stuarts, Barker converted to Roman Catholicism. Her mother and father as well as her brother predeceased her, and after the Revolution of 1688 she followed the Stuarts to France, where she lived at the court of Saint-Germain. She returned to England sometime after the turn of the century. Her first publication, *Poetical Recreations* (1688), a two-volume collection, includes poems on 'a Virgin's life', medicine, religion, her brother's death, and an ode to the Muses. Her writing was strongly autobiographical from the outset. She wrote under two personae, Fidelia and Galesia (sometimes 'Galecia' or 'Galaecia'), both aspects of herself, the former employed mainly in her poetry to declare her fidelity to Jacobitism and Catholicism, and the latter used particularly in her fiction to examine her vocation as a woman writer. She appears to have gone blind by 1700, but continued to write, dictating her work to an amanuensis. She revised her poetry, much of it political, and on her return to Wilsthorpe as a spinster on a diminished income began to write fiction. In *Love's Intrigues; or The History of the Amours of Bosvil and Galesia* (1713), 'Galesia' is both narrator and heroine, and the story records an unhappy love affair with the heroine ending up single and a poet. *A Patch-Work Screen for the Ladies* (1723) and *The Lining for the Patch-Work Screen* (1726), both collections of interpolated tales, extend the self-portrait to Galesia's old age as a chaste spinster and writer. Barker's anxiety about her acceptability as a woman writer is evident throughout, as is her plea for a better understanding of the single woman. Katherine *Philips was her model woman writer, and the adoption of the persona Galesia a possible imitation of Philips's Orinda. Barker's other fiction included *Exilius; or The Banished Roman* (1715), based on a French heroic romance. *The Entertaining Novels of Mrs. Jane Barker* (1719) collected both *Exilius* and *Bosvil and Galesia*, along with other tales, and a second edition was published posthumously in 1736. Barker was one of the first women novelists to examine writing as a vocation for women. Her work never attained the popularity of her contemporaries Aphra *Behn or Delarivier *Manley, but emphasis on her spinsterhood and her chastity ensured that her reputation remained 'respectable' to eighteenth-century readers when theirs did not. *See* Jane Spencer, *The Rise of the Woman Novelist: From Aphra Behn to Jane Austen* (1986); Jean B. Kern, in *Fetter'd or Free? British Women Novelists 1670–1815*, ed. Mary Anne Schofield and Cecilia Macheski (1986).

Barnard, Lady Anne, poet and travel writer (b. Balcarres, Fifeshire, 8 December 1750, d. London, 6 May 1825).

Lady Anne Barnard was the eldest daughter of James Lindsay, fifth Earl of Balcarres, and Anne Dalrymple. She grew up in Fife, but spent winters in Edinburgh, where she gained entry to intellectual circles which included David Hume, Henry Mackenzie, Lord Monboddo, and others, and was introduced to Dr Johnson when he visited Edinburgh in 1773. She later moved to London to live with her sister. Her best-known work was a ballad, 'Auld Robin Gray', which she wrote at Balcarres in 1771 at the age of 21. The name Robin Gray was taken from an old shepherd on the estate. According to her account, she remembered a ballad with 'improper words' sung to her in childhood by a servant and had determined to write new ones. *The History of Old Robin Gray* was published anonymously in 1783, and it was only when Scott published *The Pirate* in 1821 that her authorship was revealed. She then wrote to Scott, explaining the circumstances of its composition and her desire for secrecy, confessing her 'dread of being suspected of writing anything, perceiving the shyness it created in those who could write nothing'. He later published a new edition which included her narrative of its composition and two inferior continuations, in 1825. In 1793, when she was 42, to the amazement and amusement of her friends, she married Andrew Barnard, son of Thomas Barnard, Bishop of Limerick, whom she had met in London. He was twelve years her junior and newly appointed Colonial Secretary to the Governor of the Cape of Good Hope. She accompanied him there in 1797, and her *Journal of a Residence at the Cape of Good Hope* (1840) provides one of the best accounts of life in the colony. The couple returned to England in 1806, and lived in Wimbledon. Barnard returned to Africa the following year and died of fever. Lady Anne Barnard remained a prominent figure in London society for another decade, living again with her sister and creating a fashionable salon which attracted Burke, Sheridan, and even the Prince of Wales as regular visitors. Her journals from the Cape of Good Hope remained unpublished until 1840, when extracts formed part of *The Lives of the Lindsays*, by A. C. W. Lindsay. It was first published separately in 1924 as *Lady Anne Barnard and the Cape of Good Hope 1797–1801*, ed. D. Fairbridge. Another edition in 1825 included a memoir, and *South Africa a Century Ago: Letters Written from the Cape of Good Hope 1797–1891*, ed. W. H. Wilkins (1901), contained her letters.

Barrett, Elizabeth *see* BROWNING, Elizabeth Barrett

Bawden, Nina, novelist and children's writer (b. London, 19 January 1925).

Nina Bawden is the daughter of Charles Mabey, an engineer, and his wife Ellalaine Ursula Cushing. She was educated at Ilford County High School and briefly in Wales as a wartime evacuee, an experience on which she drew for one of her best children's books, *Carrie's War* (1973). She won a scholarship to Somerville College, Oxford, taking her BA in 1946, and in the same year married Henry Walton Bawden, by whom she had two sons. In 1954 she married Austin Steven Kark, later head of the BBC World Service, by whom she had a daughter. She worked briefly for the Town and Country Planning Association and in 1953 published her first novel, *Who Calls the Tune.* Of the demands of writing for adults as well as children, she once commented, 'The things I write about for adults, I write about for children, too; emotions, motives, the difficulties of being honest with oneself, the gulf between what people say and what they really mean.' Her more than thirty books are middle-class based, and focus on broken marriages and disrupted families, children's misconceptions about adult behaviour, and adult disregard for children. Her children's books began with adventure stories: *Devil by the Sea* (1957), *The Secret Passage* (1963), *On the Run* (1964), *The White Horse Gang* (1966), *The Witch's Daughter* (1966), *A Handful of Thieves* (1967), and *The Runaway Summer* (1969). *Squib* (1971) marked a transition to more serious themes, and *Carrie's War* was followed in 1975 by *The Peppermint Pig*, about an Edwardian family who face an abrupt change in their financial circumstances, which won the Guardian Children's Fiction Award. Later titles for children include *Rebel on a Rock* (1978), a sequel to *Carrie's War*, *The Robbers* (1979), and *Kept in the Dark* (1982), a psychological thriller.

Bawden admits to making a distinction between writing for children and writing for adults, adding, 'I consider my books for children as important as my adult work, and in some ways more challenging.' Some of the most significant of her 'adult' fiction titles include *A Little Love, a Little Learning* (1965), *A Woman of My Age* (1967), *The Grain of Truth* (1968), *The Birds on the Trees* (1971), *George beneath a Paper Moon* (1974), *Afternoon of a Good Woman* (1976), *Familiar Passions* (1979), *Walking Naked* (1981), and *The Ice-House* (1983).

Bayly, Ada Ellen *see* LYALL, Edna.

Beauchamp, Kathleen Mansfield *see* MANSFIELD, Katherine

'Beaumont, Averil' *See under* HUNT, Violet

Beauvoir, Simone de, French philosopher, novelist, and feminist (b. Paris, 9 January 1908, d. Paris, 14 April 1986).

Simone de Beauvoir was the daughter of middle-class Parisian parents, the fervently Catholic Françoise Brasseur and George Bertrand de Beauvoir, a lawyer. She was educated at private girls' schools and studied mathematics at the Institut Catholique in Paris. She took a degree at the Sorbonne in 1928 and in 1929 came second in the national examinations for the Agrégation (a teaching qualification). The first place went to the philosopher and writer Jean-Paul Sartre, with whom she had an intimate, unorthodox relationship until his death in 1980. (They agreed not to marry and to be free to have love affairs without recrimination.) She taught at *lycées* in Marseilles and Rouen and eventually in Paris between 1938 and 1943. She remained in Paris during the German occupation, distributing information for the French Resistance, and in 1943 gave up teaching in order to devote herself to writing and to political activism. *L'Invitée*, her first novel, was published in 1943 (translated as *She Came to Stay*, 1954), followed by *Le Sang des autres* (1944; *The Blood of Others*, 1948), about France during the occupation. De Beauvoir and Sartre became the centre of French existentialism after the war. Together they founded *Les Temps modernes*, which became the organ of the movement, and de Beauvoir published several philosophical works, among them *Pour une morale de l'ambiguité* (*The Ethics of Ambiguity*, 1947). She toured America in 1947 and began a four-year relationship with the American writer Nelson Algren. She also published *L'Amérique au jour le jour* (*America Day by Day*, 1952), based on diary extracts, which revealed her sharply anti-American attitudes. But it was her provocative study *Le Deuxième Sexe* (1949; *The Second Sex*, 1953) which established her reputation. Probably the most influential theoretical book about the position of women and the construction of femininity in the twentieth century, *The Second Sex* attracted fierce opposition as well as admiration. In it de Beauvoir criticized the patriarchal ideology which had created the myths of womanhood, an ideology which embraced areas as diverse as literature written by men, psychoanalysis, and Marxism (which had marginalized women). The American anthropologist Margaret Mead pronounced it 'rare, exasperating . . . torrential, brilliant, wonderfully angry', but argued that its 'partisan selectivity' worked against any claim to dispassionate scholarship. Others were disturbed by de Beauvoir's ambiguous attitude to the female body. (She was later to campaign vigorously to free women from unwanted pregnancy through the group Choisir, and by signing, along with other eminent women, the famous Manifesto 343, acknowledging that she herself had had an abortion.) De Beauvoir and Sartre became sympathetic to the Communist Party in the 1950s, although they never joined. They travelled to Russia several times, and to China, about which de Beauvoir wrote *La Longue Marche* (*The Long March*, 1957). *Les Mandarins* (1954; *The Mandarins*, 1960), a novel about the dilemmas facing politically committed intellectuals after the Liberation, won the prestigious Prix Goncourt. Between 1952 and 1958 she had an affair with a young Communist journalist, Claude Lanzmann. In 1958 she published the first part of her four-volume autobiography, *Mémoires d'une jeune fille rangée* (1958; *Memoirs of a Dutiful Daughter*, 1959). This was followed by *La Force de l'âge* (1960; *The Prime of Life*, 1962), *La Force des choses* (1963; *Force of Circumstance*, 1964), and *Tout Compte fait* (1972; *All Said and Done*, 1974). *Une mort très douce* (1964; *A Very Easy Death*, 1966) was a moving account of her response to the death of her mother. Her political activism increased during th 1960s. With Giselle Halimi she wrote *Djamila Boupacha* (1962), a powerful attack on the war in Algeria. She and Sartre attended the international Russell Tribunal on Vietnam in 1967 and the following year she joined student demonstrations in Paris. She began the feminist section of *Les Temps modernes* in 1973, and as president of the League for the Rights of Women 1974–85 she campaigned for aid to victims of rape and wife battering, and advocated a new style of radical revolutionary feminism. In 1979, with Monique Wittig and Christine Delphy she began the journal *Questions féministes*. Other works included *Brigitte Bardot and the Lolita Syndrome* (1962) and an essay on the Marquis de Sade (1962), reprinted from *Les Temps modernes*. *La Vieillesse* (*The Coming of Age*, 1970) was a study of old age, signalling her own advancing years. In 1981, the year after Sartre's death, she published *La Cérémonie des adieux* (*Adieux: A Farewell to Sartre*), a frank and some said uncharitable account of his last years. In 1983 she published his letters to her, written between 1926 and 1963. The revelations in her *Lettres à Sartre 1930–1963* created a furore when they were published in 1990. The first volume of her diaries, *Journal de guerre, septembre 1939–janvier 1941*, was also published in 1990. *See* Mary Evans, *Simone de Beauvoir: A Feminist Mandarin* (1985); Judith Okely, *Simone de Beauvoir* (1986); Joy Bennett and Gabriella Hochmann, *Simone de Beauvoir: An Annotated Bibliography* (1988); Elizabeth Fallaize, *The Novels of Simone de Beauvoir* (1988); Jane Heath, *Simone de Beauvoir* (1989); Deirdre Bair, *Simone de Beauvoir: A Biography* (1990); Toril Moi, *Feminist Theory and Simone de Beauvoir* (1990); Margaret Crosland, *Simone de Beauvoir: The Woman and her Work* (1992).

Bedford, Sybille, novelist (b. Charlottenburg, Berlin, 16 March 1911).

Sybille Bedford is the daughter of Maximilian von Schoenebeck, an impoverished German aristocrat, and his English wife Elizabeth Bernard. After the First World War, which she spent in Berlin, her mother sent her to a village school in Baden and then to schools in Italy, France, and England. She considered studying law but abandoned the idea, and instead wrote essays and a novel while in her teens, and in 1935 married Walter Bedford. As a journalist she covered the Auschwitz trial at Frankfurt at the end of the war, followed by a series of celebrated trials, of the murderer John Bodkin Adams, of Jack Ruby (the Kennedy assassination) in Dallas, of Stephen Ward (the Profumo affair) in London, and the *Lady Chatterley* trial. Two works of non-fiction, *The Best we Can Do* (1958, published in New York as *The Trial of Dr. Adams*, 1959) and *The Faces of Justice: A Traveller's Report* (1961), reflect her concern with justice and judicial procedures. Her travel book *The Sudden View: A Mexican Journey* (1953), republished as *A Visit to Don Otavio*, won critical attention, as did her first novel, *A Legacy* (1956), a satirical story of two wealthy German families, one Catholic and one Jewish, prior to 1914, based in part on her own family. Her second novel, *A Favourite of the Gods* (1963), presented three generations of women, beginning with an American heiress married to a philandering Italian prince, their liberated Italian daughter, and, in turn, her English daughter. The last is the middle-aged writer heroine of Bedford's third novel, *A Compass Error* (1969), who is seduced by the wife of her mother's lover. Interconnections between personal relationships and wider political contexts, complex female relationships, and innocent Americans set amongst scheming Europeans are constant elements in Bedford's fiction, the last at times inviting comparisons with Henry James. Her friendship with Aldous Huxley led to an invitation to write the official biography (2 vols., 1973–4), which was much acclaimed. She published her 'biographical novel' *Jigsaw: An Unsentimental Education* in 1989. Bedford became a fellow of the Royal Society of Literature in 1964, and she was vice-president of PEN in 1979. *See* Robert O. Evans, in *British Novelists since 1900*, ed. Jack I. Biles (1987).

Beer, Patricia, poet and critic (b. Exmouth, Devon, 4 November 1924).

Patricia Beer is the daughter of Andrew William Beer, a railway clerk, and his wife Harriet Jeffrey, a teacher and a member of the Plymouth Brethren. Her autobiography *Mrs. Beer's House* (1968) gives a vivid description of her Devon childhood and her family background. She was taught at home by her mother and then went to Exmouth Grammar School, followed by Exeter University, where she took a first in English. She did postgraduate work at St Hugh's College, Oxford, lectured briefly at the University of Padua and the British Institute in Rome, and returned to London as a lecturer at Goldsmith's College 1962–8. She married architect Damian Parsons in 1964. She began to write at the age of 10. Her first book of poetry, *The Loss of the Magyar* (1959), is a sequence of eight sections dealing with her sea captain great-grandfather's death by shipwreck. The next, *The Survivors* (1963), also deals with family history. Others include *Just like the Resurrection* (1967), *The Estuary* (1971), *Spanish Balcony* (1973), *Driving West* (1975), *Selected Poems* (1979), and *The Lie of the Land* (1983). Her *Collected Poems* were published in 1989. Beer's later work moves away from traditional metres and experiments with free verse and syllabics. Her subjects are solid, recognizable, everyday matters, with occasional hints at darker possibilities and sometimes an element of surprise. She often draws on family and childhood experiences, although deeply personal or confessional poetry, she insists, is 'not for me'. Yeats, Robert Lowell, and Ted Hughes are poets she admires. She has also published a study of the metaphysical poets (1972) and a book on major nineteenth-century women novelists, *Reader I Married Him* (1974). Her novel *Moon's Ottery* (1978) is set in Elizabethan Devon. She has also edited several modern anthologies.

Beeton, Isabella Mary, journalist and cookery writer (b. London, 1836, d. Greenhithe, Kent, 1865).

Isabella Beeton was the eldest of four daughters of Benjamin Mayson, a linen draper who died when she was 4, and his wife Elizabeth Jerram. In 1843 her mother married Henry Dorling, a widower with four children, and together they produced thirteen more. Isabella and her sister Bessie looked after their numerous siblings in a house near the Epsom Downs race course of which her stepfather was clerk. Their parents lived separately on nearby Epsom High St. and visited frequently. She went to Islington School for a short period, and later to a school in Heidelberg. In 1856 she married Samuel

Orchart Beeton, a publisher and the proprietor of numerous periodicals. She published her first article in the *Englishwoman's Domestic Magazine* in 1857 and became the magazine's fashion correspondent and in 1860 its editor. She also contributed to the *Queen*, inaugurated in 1861, and helped with the *Young Englishwoman*, all of which were owned and managed by her husband. But her most celebrated publication was *The Book of Household Management*, published in monthly parts from September 1859. It sold over 60,000 copies in its first year, was published in book form in 1861, and became a standard work of reference for middle-class Victorian women. It was intended as an all-purpose manual for the management of the Victorian home, and covered everything from the duties of servants and the dressing of children to the menus for family meals and for wedding breakfasts. Beeton's aim, she claimed, was to avert 'family discontent' and to reduce the temptation of men to dine at their clubs by making their wives competent at cookery and conversant with all the domestic arts. There were later spin-offs from the original, including *The Englishwoman's Cooking-Book* (1862), a *Dictionary of Every-Day Cookery* (1865), *How to Manage House-Servants and Children* (1871), and various specialized cookery books. The Beetons' first son died in infancy and a second at the age of 3. Two more were born in 1863 and 1865. Mrs Beeton died of puerperal fever after the birth of the last, at the age of 28. *See* Nancy Spain, *Mrs Beeton and her Husband* (1948); *The Beeton Story* (1956); H. M. Hyde, *Mr and Mrs Beeton* (1951); S. Freeman, *Isabella and Sam: The Story of Mrs Beeton* (1977).

Behn, Aphra, playwright, novelist, and poet (b. Wye, Kent, 10 July 1640, d. London, 16 April 1689).

Aphra Behn was born in Kent, the daughter of Bartholomew Johnson, an innkeeper, and his wife Elizabeth. During her youth she spent some time in Surinam, where a member of her family had an official post. On her return in 1664 she married a Mr Behn, thought to be a London merchant of Dutch descent. The marriage lasted two years, during which time Aphra moved in court circles, where it was said Charles II admired her wit. When war broke out with Holland the king sent her as an official spy. She obtained accurate intelligence of a planned Dutch invasion but the information was then disregarded. Now husbandless (Behn may have died from the plague) and virtually penniless, she turned to writing as her only recourse, becoming the first Englishwoman to live by her pen. She began with a series of plays, eighteen for certain, possibly more, four of which were performed at court, making her one of the most prolific Restoration dramatists of either sex. Politically she was Royalist, and also, secretly, Roman Catholic. She published anonymously, sometimes deliberately disguising her sex behind the required bawdy and sexual innuendo of the period. Her plays were witty, densely plotted, and she openly borrowed and adapted from the work of her predecessors. *The Forc'd Marriage*, a tragicomedy performed at Lincoln's Inn Fields (1670), included the young Thomas Otway in the cast on the first night. Two comedies, *The Amorous Prince* (1671) and *The Dutch Lover* (1673), were followed by *Abdelazer*, a tragedy, and *The Town Fop*, another comedy, both performed in 1676. Her most celebrated play, *The Rover*, a comedy produced at Dorset Garden in 1677, was a perennial in theatre repertoire until the end of the eighteenth century, but the second part (1681) did not quite equal its success. *Sir Patient Fancy* (1678) contained an introduction protesting against the double standards for male and female playwrights regarding bawdy and an epilogue defending a woman's right to authorship. *The Lucky Chance* (1686) similarly defended her right to write as freely as men. Other plays included *The Feigned Courtesans* (1679), a comedy dedicated to Nell Gwyn, *The Roundheads* (1681), about the last days of the Civil War, and *The City Heiress* (1682), which lampooned Shaftesbury and the Whigs. One of the most successful of all her plays, *The Emperor of the Moon* (1687), a farced based on the Italian *commedia dell'arte*, helped to make the Harlequinade popular. She published fifteen prose works, of which the best known were *The Fair Jilt* (1688) and *Oroonoko; or The Royal Slave* (1688), which drew on her experiences in Surinam, and which is regarded as the first anti-slavery fiction. *Love Letters to a Gentleman*, published with the 1696 collection of her novels, is thought to have been based on her letters to her long-time lover John Hoyle, a lawyer with an unsavoury reputation for low life who was continuously unfaithful to her. She wrote poems commemorating the death of Charles II and celebrating the accession of James II and Queen Mary. She also published translations from French, Latin, and Greek. Her last years were spent combating illness. She died in 1689 and was buried in Westminster Abbey. Undoubtedly the most highly profiled of seventeenth-century women writers, her reputation until the twentieth century was tinged with scandal relating to her personal life and an exaggerated sense of the 'indecency' of her work. But the significance of her achievement was undeniable. As Virginia *Woolf pointed out in *A Room of One's Own* (1929): 'Now that Aphra Behn had done it, girls could say . . . I can make money by my pen.' A complete edition of her *Works* is in progress, edited by Janet Todd (1992–). *See* V. *Sackville-West, *Aphra Behn: The Incomparable Astrea* (1927); Maureen *Duffy, *The Passionate Shepherdess* (1977); Mary Ann O'Donn *Aphra Behn: An Annotated Bibliography of Primary and Secondary Sources* (1986); Janet Todd, *The Sign of Angellica: Women, Writing and Fiction, 1660–1800* (1989); Mary Anne Schofield and Cecilia Macheski (eds.),

Curtain Calls: British and American Women and the Theater 1660–1820 (1991); Ros Ballaster, *Seductive Forms: Women's Amatory Fiction 1684–1740* (1992).

Bell, Acton, Currer, and Ellis *see* BRONTË, Anne; BRONTË, Charlotte; BRONTË, Emily

Bell, Gertrude (Margaret Lowthian), travel writer and archaeologist (b. Washington Hall, County Durham, 14 July 1868, d. Baghdad, 11–12 July 1926).

Gertrude Bell was the elder child and only daughter of Thomas Hugh Bell, an iron master, later the second baronet, and his first wife Mary Shield, who died when Gertrude was 3. She was educated at Queen's College, Harley St., and at Lady Margaret Hall, Oxford, where in 1888 she became the first woman to take a first in modern history. Her father's second marriage in 1876, to **Florence Olliffe** (1851–1930), novelist and playwright, whose family were high-ranking diplomats, opened doors for foreign travel and she spent periods in Bucharest, Tehran, and Berlin as well as travelling round the world. In 1892, despite family opposition, she became engaged to Henry Cadogan, a young diplomat who died of pneumonia a year later. After a period in Tehran she learnt Persian and in 1894 published a series of sketches, *Persian Pictures* (*Safar Nameh*), and a translation of the fourteenth-century Persian poet Hafiz, *Poems from the Divan of Hafiz* (1897). She spent the winter of 1899 in Jerusalem in order to learn Arabic and gained an enthusiasm for desert travel and Syrian archaeology. She was also a formidable mountaineer and made some important first ascents in the Alps between 1901 and 1904. She made her first journey from Jerusalem through Syria to Asia Minor in 1905, writing *The Desert and the Sown* about her journey in 1907. She became a self-taught and highly competent field archaeologist, publishing *The Thousand and One Churches* (1909, with W. M. Ramsay), about work undertaken in Asia Minor, and *The Palace and Mosque at Ukhaidir* (1914), about excavations in what is now central Iraq. A journey through Mesopotamia to Asia Minor was recalled in *Amurath to Amurath* (1911). Her knowledge of Arabic and her familiarity with the area made her an obvious choice to join the Arab intelligence bureau based in Cairo in 1915. A love affair with Lieutenant-Colonel Charles Doughty-Wylie, a married man, ended when he was killed at Gallipoli. She undertook a mission to Delhi in 1916 and in the same year became oriental secretary in the secretariat attached to the Mesopotamian Expeditionary Force. Her knowledge of Arab politics and her pre-war Arab friendships led her to retain the post at the end of the war, attached to the British High Commissioner in Baghdad. A liberal, and fiercely pro Arab independence, she was closely involved in the setting up of the new state of Iraq. Her *Review of the Civil Administration of Mesopotamia* was published as a White Paper in 1921. She also played a crucial role in the establishment of the national museum at Baghdad, where she died suddenly in 1926 at the age of 58. Paradoxically, despite her pioneering activities in so many fields, Gertrude Bell was not a feminist. She was a founder member of the Women's Anti-Suffrage League in 1908 and in many respects was surprisingly conventional. Apart from her travel books, the selected *Letters of Gertrude Bell*, edited by her stepmother (1927), and *The Earlier Letters of Gertrude Bell*, edited by Elsa Richmond (1937), give an evocative picture of desert life and landscape. Her diaries were extensively quoted in *Gertrude Bell: From her Personal Papers*, ed. Elizabeth Burgoyne (2 vols., 1958). *See* J. Kamm, *Gertrude Bell: Daughter of the Desert* (1956); H. V. F. Winstone, *Gertrude Bell* (1978); Susan Goodman, *Gertrude Bell* (1985).

Bell, Priscilla *see* WAKEFIELD, Priscilla

Belloc-Lowndes, Marie Adelaide, novelist (b. Saint-Cloud, near Paris, 1868, d. Eversly Cross, Hampshire, 14 November 1947).

Marie Belloc-Lowndes was the daughter of Louis Belloc, son of a French painter and his Irish wife, and of Bessie Rayner *Parkes, a prominent English feminist and writer. Another French grandfather was a painter of the Delacroix school and her French grandmother translated Harriet Beecher Stowe's *Uncle Tom's Cabin* into French. The writer Hilaire Belloc (1870–1953) was her brother. Both children were raised as Catholics, Bessie Parkes having converted to Catholicism before her marriage to Belloc. After Louis Belloc died in 1872 his widow brought the children to London. A rash stock market investment reduced her to near poverty and she retired to Slindon in Sussex. The family spent half the year in Sussex and half with Belloc's family at Saint-Cloud, near Paris, which Marie later claimed gave her an intimate knowledge of the literature of both countries. 'My heart is all French,' she once wrote. While relations assisted in sending her brother to the Oratory School at Edgbaston, Marie had virtually no formal education. She married *Times* journalist Frederick Sawray Lowndes in 1896, and they had two sons and a daughter. She wrote from the age of 16 onwards, and began her career by working for W. T. Stead of the *Pall Mall Gazette*. Her early publications included royal biographies and historical novels, but *The Lodger* (1913), based on the Jack the Ripper case, established her as a writer of crime fiction, a designation which she did not altogether relish. She wrote over sixty books, including forty novels, together with several plays and volumes of short stories. She is probably best known for a series of autobiographical works *and Friendship Dwelt* (1943), *The Merry Wives of Westminster* (1946), and *A Passing World*, published posthumously in 1948. The first provides a portrait of her mother, and also the early years of her brother Hilaire, to whom she and her husband were particularly generous. She secured a small sum from Stead to enable him to travel in France and then submit some of his impressions for publication. Later their assistance enabled him to contemplate going to Oxford. Her *The Young Hilaire Belloc* was published in 1956. *See Diaries and Letters of Marie Belloc-Lowndes 1911–1947*, ed. E. Iddesleigh and S. Lowndes-Marques (1971).

Bennett, Anna Maria, novelist (b. Merthyr Tydfil, Glamorgan, *c.*1750, d. Brighton, Sussex, 12 February 1808).

Anna (sometimes misnamed Agnes) Maria Bennett's origins are obscure. Her father David Evans has been variously described as a grocer and a customs officer, her brother as a City attorney, and her husband as a tanner. She left the last after moving with him from Wales to London, worked in a chandler's shop, and then became 'housekeeper' to the recently court-martialled Admiral Sir Thomas Pye, who was the father of two of her children. One of them, Harriet Pye Esten, became an actress and Bennett vigorously managed her theatrical career as well as her own literary one. Pye died in 1785, the year her first novel, *Anna; or Memoirs of a Welch Heiress*, was published. The entire print run sold out on the first day of publication, readers apparently hoping for personal revelations. *Juvenile Indiscretions* (1786), which followed, was attributed to Fanny *Burney. She published two others, the epistolary *Agnes De-Courci* (1789), which was modelled on Richardson's *Clarissa*, and *Ellen; or The Countess of Castle Howel* (1794), before her most popular book, *The Beggar Girl and her Benefactors* (1797), a satire on female *Gothic novelists, which made her a *Minerva Press best seller. *Vicissitudes Abroad; or The Ghost of my Father*, her last completed work, reportedly sold 2,000 copies on the first day of publication in 1806. Bennett's novels were characterized by low-born heroines whose virtues contrasted with those in higher stations, plots which contained financial reversals, and sexual comedy, which later proved her undoing. Scott and Coleridge both expressed enthusiasm for her work at the height of her fame, and several of her books were translated into French. *See* J. F. Fuller, 'A Curious Genealogical Medley', in *Miscellanea Genealogica et Heraldica* (1913); J. M. S. Tompkins, *The Popular Novel in England, 1770–1800* (1932); D. Blakey, *The Minerva Press, 1790–1820* (1939).

Benson, Stella, novelist (b. Lutwyche Hall, Much Wenlock, Shropshire, 6 January 1892, d. Hongay, Tongking, North Indochina, 6 December 1933).

Stella Benson was the third child of Ralph Beaumont Benson, a Shropshire landowner, and Caroline Essex Cholmondeley, daughter of the Revd Richard Hugh Cholmondeley, rector of Hodnet, and sister of the novelist Mary *Cholmondeley. Her health was delicate, and she was educated at home. When she was 20 she undertook a journey to the West Indies, which furnished the material for her first novel, *I Pose* (1915). On her return she took up social work in Hoxton, a deprived area of London, and then opened her own business making paper bags, and employing a local woman as partner. At the same time she became interested in women's suffrage. Her second novel, *This is the End* (1917), was published during this period. She took a job as a landworker until her poor health dictated a warmer climate, and spent some time in California, working as a maid, a bill collector, a book agent, and then, more suitably, as a tutor at the University of California and a reader for the University Press. She published a volume of poems, *Twenty* (1918), and completed her third novel, *Living Alone* (1919). Loneliness and alienation were to be the themes of much of her work, derived in part from her own experience. *The Poor Man* (1922) was a satire on American life, which she found uncongenial. She then travelled to the Far East, where more new occupations ensued, including teaching in a mission school in Hong Kong and working in the X-ray department of an American hospital in Peking. In 1921 she married John O'Gorman Anderson, an Irishman employed in the Chinese customs service. Their honeymoon journey across America in a Ford car was described in *The Little World* (1925). To her disappointment there were no children of the marriage. Apart from occasional travels, the couple spent the remainder of their lives in China, part of it against the dangerous background of civil war. Benson helped to organize a successful campaign against prostitution in Hong Kong, but most of her energies were devoted to writing novels and short stories. *Goodbye Stranger* (1926), a retelling of familiar myths and stories, was followed by *The Man who Missed the 'Bus* (1928), a fantasy. Her most important novel was *Tobit Transplanted* (1931, first published in New York in 1930 as *The Run-Away Bride*), which won the Femina Vie Heureuse Prize and the A. C. Benson Silver Medal of the Royal Society of Literature. It was based on the life of the White Russian community of Manchuria. Benson's novels combine fantasy and realism, and a variety of contrasting narrative techniques and perspectives. She died of pneumonia in China just before her 45th birthday. *Some Letters of Stella Benson*, ed. C. Clarabut, were published in 1938. *See* R. E. Roberts, *Portrait* *of Stella Benson* (1939); R. Meredith Bedell, *Stella Benson* (1983); Joy Grant, *Stella Benson: A Biography* (1988).

Bentley, Phyllis (Eleanor), novelist and critic (b. Halifax, Yorkshire, 19 November 1894, d. Halifax, 27 June 1977).

Phyllis Bentley was born in Halifax, in the midst of Yorkshire manufacturing and provincial life, which was to provide the setting and subject-matter of most of her fiction. She was the fourth child and only daughter of Joseph Edwin Bentley, a master dyer and finisher, and Eleanor Kettlewell of Huddersfield, whose family was also engaged in textile manufacture. She was educated at Princess Mary High School for Girls, Halifax, and at Cheltenham Ladies' College, from where she obtained an external London University pass degree. Her war work included school-teaching and a job in the Ministry of Munitions, followed by a period spent cataloguing local libraries. Her first novel, *Environment* (1922), was semi-autobiographical and was followed by a sequel, *Cat-in-the-Manger*, in 1923. Ten years and seven novels later she achieved her first major success with *Inheritance* (1932), a family saga set in Yorkshire, which established her in the genre which she made her own, the regional novel. She published twenty-eight novels in all, many of them with Yorkshire settings, of which *Carr* (1929), which contained portraits of her parents, *A Modern Tragedy* (1934), and the sequels to *Inheritance*, *The Rise of Henry Morcar* (1946), *A Man of his Time* (1966), and *Ring in the New* (1968), are among the best known. *The English Regional Novel* (1941), and several studies of the *Brontës, in particular *The Brontës* (1947) and *The Brontës and their World* (1969), established her reputation as a critic. She wrote several historical books for children, three volumes of short stories, an autobiography, *O Dreams, O Destinations* (1962), and edited various works of the Brontës (1949, 1954). She was a prolific journalist, writing detective stories for American magazines and contributing a fortnightly review of fiction to the *Yorkshire Post* up until her death aged 83. She was unmarried.

Berners, Juliana, or Julians Barnes, prose writer (b. *c*.1388).

Juliana Berners is believed to have been either the daughter of Sir James Berners, a favourite of Richard II who was beheaded as an enemy to the public shortly after her birth in 1388, or the wife of the holder of the manor of Julians Barnes near St Albans, hence the title Dame Julians Barnes. Legend has it that she was a woman of great beauty and also great learning, that like many noblewomen of the day she participated in field sports, and that she wrote a treatise on hunting, a portion of a treatise on hawking, and a short list of beasts of the chase and another of beasts and fowls, which formed part of a composite early book known as *The Book of St. Albans*, the last work printed in 1486 on the press established at St Albans around 1479. The *Book* had multiple authors. The legend that Juliana Barnes or Berners was prioress of Sopwell Abbey near St Albans is now believed false. Doubtful too is the extent of her contribution to the *Book.* She may have contributed only some miscellaneous items to the sections on hawking and hunting. Whatever the exact circumstances, the contributions represent some of the earliest published writings in English by a woman. Berners or Barnes consequently appeared in many early anthologies of women's writing, notably those by *Ballard, Bethune, and Rowton (see Bibliography), as one of the first British women writers. *See New Cambridge Bibliography of English Literature*, i (1974); Rachel Hands, *Review of English Studies* (1967).

Besant, Annie, writer on social and religious topics (b. London, 1 October 1847, d. Adyar, near Madras, India, 20 September 1933).

Annie Besant was the daughter of William Persse Wood, a London businessman who had studied medicine but never practised it, and Emily Morris of Clapham. Both parents were of Irish extraction. Her father died when she was 5. Her mother channelled all the family's finances into sending her brother to Harrow and Cambridge, leaving Annie to be educated by a sister of Frederick Marryat, the novelist. As a child she experienced a strong sense of neglect, and her sense of grievance was later increased by an unhappy marriage. In 1867 she married Frank Besant, then a master at Cheltenham, and later the vicar of Sibsey in Lincolnshire. He was also the brother of Walter Besant, the novelist and man of letters. They had a son and a daughter. Besant was a narrow-minded clergyman who was unsympathetic to his wife's growing religious scepticism. A pamphlet entitled *The Deity of Jesus of Nazareth by the Wife of a Beneficed Clergyman* led to their separation in 1873. She was given the custody of their daughter but lost both children when in 1874 she joined the National Secular Society and formed a close friendship with Charles Bradlaugh, a leading free-thinker. She became co-editor with him of the *National Reformer*, the organ of the free-thinkers, and a co-speaker on public platforms. She was tried and convicted of circulating a pamphlet on birth control, a celebrated case which ultimately prevented her from obtaining a divorce from her husband, who died in 1917. Annie Besant's life was taken up with a series of causes which she embraced consecutively and with equal fervour. She broke with Bradlaugh in 1885, resigned from the *National Reformer*, and joined the Fabian Society, and later the Social Democratic Federation. She established the Law and Liberty League, and with the crusading journalist W. T. Stead edited the League's periodical the *Link.* She helped to organize and win a famous strike of girls in the Bryant & May match factory in 1888. She served on the London School Board and the London County Council and did a great deal to help homeless girls and deprived children. She matriculated at London University and passed the preliminary scientific examination with honours. From socialism she moved to theosophy, where through Stead she came under the influence of Helena Blavatsky. She became president of the Theosophical Society in 1907 and remained in that office until her death. She found theosophy compatible with Hindu religion and philosophy and through that link became intensely interested in Indian nationalism. She founded the Central Hindu College at Benares and later a girls' school which in 1916 became the nucleus of a university. She fell foul of the British authorities several times in her enthusiasm to promote Indian independence and on one occasion was interned. Her influence waned in later years, but she remained committed to the Indian cause until her death in India in 1933. Annie Besant wrote over a hundred books, pamphlets, and lectures, including *On the Deity of Jesus of Nazareth* (1873), *On the Nature and Existence of God* (1875), *The Gospel of Atheism* (1877), *Reincarnation* (1892), *The Self and its Sheaths* (1895), *Esoteric Christianity* (1901), *Theosophy and the New Psychology* (1904), *Thought Power* (1911), *Lectures on Political Science* (1919), and *Shall India Live or Die?* (1925). She published her *Autobiography* in 1893. Her interests and influence were far wider than those reflected in her journalism and occasional writing. Her lasting reputation is that of a tireless campaigner and propagandist, rather than a writer. *See* Arthur H. Nethercot, *The First Five Lives of Annie Besant* (1961), and *The Last Four Lives of Annie Besant* (1963). Anne Taylor, *Annie Besant: A Biography* (1992).

Betham, Mary Matilda, poet and woman of letters (b. Stonham Aspel, Suffolk, 1776, d. London, 30 September 1852).

Mary Matilda Betham was the eldest daughter of the fifteen children of the Revd William Betham of Stonham Aspel, Suffolk, and rector of Stoke Lacy, Herefordshire, a well-known antiquary and the compiler of a five-volume *Baronetage of England* (1801–5). Her mother was Mary Damant, daughter of William Damant of Eye, in Suffolk. Her brother William became Ulster King-of-Arms. She was educated at home, like her niece Matilda *Betham-Edwards, mainly by being given free access to her father's library, combined with some teaching from him. She was sent to school, according to the *DNB*, 'only to learn sewing and prevent a too strict application to books'. She taught herself miniature painting, and developed a love of literature and history. In 1804 she published a *Biographical Dictionary of the Celebrated Women of Every Age and Country*, the result of her own researches. Around the same time she went to London, where she gave readings from Shakespeare and exhibited her portraits at the Royal Academy. She became friendly with Coleridge,

Southey, Mrs *Barbauld, and Charles and Mary *Lamb. She published two volumes of poetry, *Elegies* (1797) and *Poems* (1808), and in 1816 her *Lay of Marie*, based on the work of a thirteenth-century Anglo-Norman woman poet. A decline in health and in family circumstances forced her return to the country, where she spent the remainder of her life in retirement until her very last years, when she returned to London and resumed her place in literary circles. *See* Matilda Betham-Edwards, *Six Life Studies of Famous Women* (1880).

Betham-Edwards, Matilda Barbara, novelist and writer on French life (b. Westerfield, Suffolk, 4 March 1836, d. Hastings, Sussex, 4 January 1919).

Matilda Betham-Edwards was the daughter of Edward Edwards, an East Anglian farmer, and Barbara Betham, the daughter of the Revd William Betham, a Suffolk clergyman. The family had a tradition of literary and historical scholarship. Her aunt was Mary Matilda *Betham, a poet and woman of letters, her grandfather was a genealogist, and her great-uncle Sir William Betham was Ulster King-of-Arms. She was often confused with her cousin Amelia Blandford *Edwards, the Egyptologist and novelist, much to her annoyance. Matilda Betham-Edwards was largely self-educated, with the help of her father's library, but attended a day school at Ipswich and for a while a boarding school at Peckham, which she hated. She had an aptitude for languages, and visited Germany and France in order to improve them. She managed her father's farm for a year after his death with the help of a sister, but when the latter died in 1865 Matilda moved to London, where she met Barbara *Bodichon, George *Eliot and George Henry Lewes, and other literary figures. She continued to travel in France, and became throughly familiar with French society, about which she wrote for the benefit of English readers. She was honoured by the French government for these services in 1891. Her publications included an edition of the Suffolk-born Arthur Young's *Travels in France* (1889) and his *Autobiography and Correspondence* (1898). Her strengths as a writer were in her prose writings, particularly those about France, but she also wrote a large number of novels, beginning with *The White House by the Sea* (1857), which like much of her fiction had a Suffolk setting. *The Lord of the Harvest* (1899), set before the repeal of the Corn Laws, is thought to be her best Suffolk novel. *Dr. Jacob* (1864), *Kitty* (1869), and *A Suffolk Courtship* (1900) are also well known. Betham-Edwards was an energetic and extremely well-organized writer. In 1917, celebrating what she regarded as the 'diamond jubilee' of her literary career, she reckoned that there had been only eight out of the sixty years in which she had not produced a new book or a new edition. She included her aunt Mary Matilda

Betham in her *Six Life Studies of Famous Women* (1880) and published her autobiographical *Reminiscences* (1898) and *Mid-Victorian Memories* (1919).

Bird, Isabella Lucy, later Bishop, travel writer (b. Boroughbridge Hall, Yorkshire, 15 October 1831, d. Edinburgh, 7 October 1904).

Isabella Bird was the daughter of the Revd Edward Bird and his second wife Dora Lawson. Both families were fervently evangelical, the Birds numbering William Wilberforce and John [Bird] Sumner among their kinsmen. Her childhood was spent successively in Cheshire, Birmingham, and Huntingdonshire as her father moved benefices. She taught Sunday school from an early age and made her literary début with a privately printed essay on the seemingly unpromising subject of fiscal protection in 1847. She suffered from a spinal complaint and deliberately lived out of doors, learned to ride and also to row. After an operation on her spine she was recommended a sea voyage for her health, and in 1854, at the age of 23, spent seven months in the United States and Canada. *The Englishwoman in America* (1856) was the result, her first travel book, and the beginning of a life spent in travel, missionary work, and writing. She settled for a while with her mother and sister in Edinburgh and became active in schemes to encourage emigration to Canada from the Scottish Highlands. Driven by her poor health, loneliness (a succession of her immediate family died), by missionary zeal, and by a genuine enthusiasm for travel, she set out in 1871 for Australia and New Zealand, the Sandwich Islands, and eventually the Rocky Mountains. Two notable books, *The Hawaiian Archipelago: Six Months among the Palm Groves, Coral Reefs and Volcanoes of the Sandwich Islands* (1875) and *A Lady's Life in the Rocky Mountains* (1879), first published in the *Leisure Hour*, brought her to the attention of the scientific community and to a wider reading public. She shared her interest in the work of medical missionaries with her sister's medical adviser Dr John Bishop, some ten years her junior. They married in 1881, the year after her sister's death, when she was nearly 50. Bishop died five years later. Meanwhile seven months in Japan, and five weeks in the Malay Peninsula and a return via Egypt, produced *Unbeaten Tracks in Japan* (1880) and *The Golden Chersonese and the Way Thither* (1883). After her husband's death she devoted herself to medical missions, founding in all five hospitals in memory of her husband, sister, and parents. She travelled to Tibet (*Among the Tibetans* (1894)), to India, Persia, Kurdistan, (*Journeys in Persia and Kurdistan* (1891)), Korea (*Korea and her Neighbours* (1898)), and China (*The Yangtze Valley and Beyond* (1899)). She addressed the British Association in 1891, 1892, and 1898, and became the first female fellow of the Royal Geographical Society in 1892. At the age of 69 she made a six-month journey to Morocco, riding over a thousand miles, but was prevented by illness from writing more than an article. She died in Edinburgh just before her 73rd birthday, still hoping to return to China. Of her nine travel books, which made her reputation as one of the outstanding travel writers of her day, those on Asia, particularly *Among the Tibetans* and *The Yangtze Valley and Beyond*, were among the most highly regarded. *See* Anna M. Stoddart, *The Life of Isabella Bird* (1906); Dorothy Middleton, *Victorian Lady Travellers* (1965); Pat Barr, *A Curious Life for a Lady* (1970).

Birley, Julia *see under* KENNEDY, Margaret Moore

Bishop, Isabella Bird *see* BIRD, Isabella

Blachford, Mary *see* TIGHE, Mary

Black, Clementina *see under* GARNETT, Constance

Blamire, Susanna, poet (b. The Oaks, Dalston, near Carlisle, 1747, d. Carlisle, 5 April 1794).

Susanna Blamire was the youngest of the four children of William Blamire, a yeoman farmer, and his wife Isabella Simpson. Her mother died when she was 7, and on her father's remarriage she was sent to live with her aunt on a farm at nearby Thackwood. She went to the village school at Raughton Head, near Stockdalewath, read enthusiastically, and began to write poems in imitation of her favourite writers, despite the disapproval of her aunt and her elder brother. Her earliest poem, 'Written in a Churchyard, on Seeing a Number of Cattle Grazing in it' (1766), for example, was reminiscent of Gray's 'Elegy'. Another, 'Stoklewath; or The Cumbrian Village', recalled Goldsmith's 'Deserted Village' and also the work of William Collins. She spent some time in the Scottish Highlands, visiting her sister, who had married a Lieutenant-Colonel Graham of Gartmore, in Perthshire, and was introduced to a family with strong literary interests. She also accompanied her sister and brother-in-law on visits to London and Ireland. It was common for wealthy Cumbrian families to spend the winter in Carlisle, and there she met Catharine Gilpin of Scaleby Castle, who was also a poet, and with whom she shared lodgings and jointly wrote several poems. Most of her work was published anonymously in single sheets and then reprinted in magazines and collections such as *Calliope; or The Musical Miscellany* (1788) and Johnson's *Scots Musical Museum* (1790). She wrote in both the Scots and Cumbrian dialects and some of her songs were included in Robert Anderson's *Ballads in the Cumbrian Dialect* (1808). Some of her best known included 'The Nabob' or 'The Traveller's Return', 'The Waefu' Heart', 'The Siller Crown', and 'Auld Robin Forbes'. She suffered from rheumatism from an early age and other ailments accelerated the decline in her health in her forties. She died in Carlisle at the age of 46. Susanna Blamire's reputation was almost entirely posthumous. Her works were collected by Dr Henry Lonsdale, an Edinburgh medical student who was a native of Carlisle, and by Patrick Maxwell, who contacted her friends and family in search of manuscript poems, many of which were written on the backs of recipes and old letters. In 1842 they published *The Poetical Work of Miss Susanna Blamire, the 'Muse of Cumberland'*, with a preface, memoir, and notes by Maxwell. Lonsdale added more information about her in his *Worthies of Cumberland* (vol. iv, 1873) and further unpublished poems were included in *The Songs and Ballads of Cumberland*, edited by Sidney Gilpin in 1866.

Bland, Edith *see* NESBIT, E

Blessington, Marguerite, Countess of, novelist and editor (b. Knockbrit, near Clonmel, County Tipperary, 1 September 1789, d. Paris, 4 June 1849).

The fourth of the seven children of Edmund Power, a dissolute Irish landowner and a brutal magistrate, and his wife Ellen Sheehey, both from County Tipperary, Marguerite Power was forced into marriage with an Irish army officer, Captain Maurice St Leger Farmer, at the age of 14. Farmer was rumoured to suffer bouts of insanity. After three months Marguerite fled to her parents' home but was not officially freed until Farmer fell from a window to his death in a drunken brawl in 1817. She then married, as his second wife, the enormously wealthy first Earl of Blessington. Their London home became a popular salon and in 1823, on a Continental tour, they became friendly with Byron, with whom they spent two months. Also of the party was Alfred, Count d'Orsay, a popular young dandy with whom the Countess became intimate, and who later married her stepdaughter. The Earl died of apoplexy in Paris in 1829, leaving his finances in a precarious state. The Countess returned to London, re-established her salon at Gore House, Kensington, with d'Orsay, now estranged from his wife, and began to write to supplement her diminished income. She had earlier published *The Magic Lantern* (1822) and two other travel books but she now concentrated on fiction, mainly of the 'silver-fork' (novels of fashionable life) variety and some with an Irish setting. *Grace Cassidy; or The Repealers* (1833) was followed by, among others, *The Confessions of an Elderly Gentleman* (1836), *The Victims of Society* (1837), *The Governess* (1839), *The Lottery of Life* (1842), and *Strathern* (1845), which included a character based on Bulwer-Lytton. In her lifetime Blessington's most famous publication was her *Conversations with Lord Byron* (1834), reprinted from the *New Monthly Magazine* and a prudent use of her earlier association which brought substantial financial reward. In the same year she began her editorship of *The Book of Beauty*, an *annual owned by the engraver Charles Heath, to which she was also a prolific contributor, and in 1841 became editor of Heath's most famous publication, the *Keepsake*. The Irish famine of 1845 dealt the final blow to the Blessington fortunes, and in 1849 the Countess went bankrupt. She died a few months later of apoplexy, in Paris, where she had fled with d'Orsay after the bankruptcy. *See* R. R. Madden, *The Literary Life and Correspondence of the Countess of Blessington* (1855); M. Sadleir, *Blessington-Dorsay* (1933, repr. 1947); Ernest J. Lovell, introd. to *Lady Blessington's Conversations of Lord Byron* (1968).

Blind, Mathilde ('Claude Lake'), poet, critic, and translator (b. Mannheim, Germany, 21 March 1841, d. London, 26 November 1896).

Mathilde Blind was the daughter of a German banker named Cohen. She adopted the name Blind after her mother's second marriage to Karl Blind, a political activist and later a well-known German political writer who was exiled from Germany following the suppression of the 1848 revolutionary movement. She was educated in 'more or less bad' private schools in Brussels and London, and later in Zurich. Rosa *Carey was a fellow pupil at her London school. The family settled permanently in London, where she met many of the European refugees who frequented her stepfather's house. She was particularly influenced by Mazzini, about whom she later published some reminiscences in the *Fortnightly Review* (1891). Her first known work was an ode in German on the occasion of the Schiller centenary, which she recited in 1859. She then wrote a tragedy about Robespierre, which was praised by Louis Blanc but never published. Her first book was a volume of *Poems* published in 1867 under the pseudonym Claude Lake. Two long poems, written after a visit to Scotland, *The Prophecy of St. Oran* (1881) and *The Heather on Fire* (1886), about the Highland clearances, came next, and a prose romance, *Tarantella* (1885). Her most ambitious work was another long poem, *The Ascent of Man* (1889), written in response to Darwin's theories and reissued in 1899 with an introduction by Alfred Russell Wallace. She translated two influential European works, D. F. Strauss's *The Old Faith and the New* (1873) and *The Journal of Marie Bashkirtseff* (1890), to which she contributed a sharply feminist introduction. She also wrote two volumes for the 'Eminent Women' series, on George *Eliot (1883) and on Madame Roland (1886). She edited a selection of Shelley's poems (1872) and published a lecture and also an article on him in the *Westminster Review*, both in 1870. She also edited the *Poems* and *Letters and Journals* of Byron (1886). She lived for a while in Manchester to be near the painter Ford Madox Brown and his wife. Later she travelled extensively in Italy and Egypt, experiences which were reflected in three volumes of poetry: *Dramas in Miniature* (1891), *Songs and Sonnets* (1893), and *Birds of Passage* (1895). *Shakespeare's Sonnets* (1902), her last collection, was written at Stratford. Blind was an ardent advocate of women's rights and in particular supported the cause of women's education. She left the greater part of her estate to Newnham College, Cambridge, when she died in 1896. *The Poetical Works of Mathilde Blind* (1900), ed. Arthur Symons, included a memoir by Richard Garnett. *See* E. S. Robertson, *English Poetesses* (1883).

Bluestocking Circle.

This was the name given to a group of women in the late eighteenth century who were known for their literary and scholarly interests. They included Elizabeth *Montagu, Elizabeth *Carter, Catherine *Talbot, Elizabeth *Vesey, Hester *Chapone, and Mary *Delany. The name originated in 1756 from a joke at the expense of Benjamin Stillingfleet, an eccentric scholar who was in the habit of attending parties given by Elizabeth Montagu and others wearing the blue cotton stockings traditionally only worn by working-class men. The term became a private joke, a codeword used to refer to the various members of the circle, which included men as well as women. Dr Johnson, Edmund Burke, David Garrick, Sir Joshua Reynolds, Horace Walpole, Lord Lyttleton, and the Earl of Bath were frequent visitors at Mrs Montagu's salons. She in turn was dubbed 'Queen of the Blues', although there were other hostesses, including Frances Boscawen, Mrs Vesey, Mrs Fulke Greville, and the Duchess of Portland. Latterly 'bluestocking' became a pejorative term and referred exclusively to learned women. A younger generation of women writers, including Hannah *More and Fanny *Burney, joined the circle, which More celebrated in her poem *The Bas bleu* (1786). *See* Sylvia H. Myers, *The Bluestocking Circle* (1990).

Blyton, Enid (Mary), children's writer (b. East Dulwich, London, 11 August 1897, d. Hampstead, London, 28 November 1968).

Enid Blyton was the eldest of the three children of Thomas Carey Blyton, a modestly successful businessman, and his wife Theresa Mary Harrison. Her father's ambition that she should be a concert pianist was thwarted when he walked out on the family for another woman when she was 13. She instantly abandoned her music and wrote poetry as a means of escape, publishing her first poem in a children's magazine when she was 14. After St Christopher's School for Girls in Beckenham, where she was head girl, she trained as a teacher in Ipswich and taught at Bickley Park School in Kent. The next year she became a governess in Surbiton. *Child Whispers*, a collection of poems, was published in 1922. By 1921–2 her short stories and poems were appearing regularly in magazines, and by 1925 she was earning over £1,200 from her writing, enough to enable her to give up teaching. In 1924 she married Major Hugh Alexander Pollock, an editor in the publishing house of Newnes. They had two daughters. Through Pollock she became editor of a new Newnes weekly, *Sunny Stories for Little Folks*, with which she was associated for over twenty-five years, 1926–52. She produced collections of fairy-tales and children's stories, edited *The Teacher's Treasury* (1926) and other serials for teachers, and had her own 'Enid Blyton's Children's Page' in *Teacher's World*. She wrote her first full-length children's book, *The Adventures of the Wishing Chair*, in 1937. By 1940 she was producing thirteen titles a year and in 1942 wrote the first of her 'Famous Five' titles, *Five on a Treasure Island*. The 'Adventure' series and also the 'Secret Seven' series followed, the latter initiated by a book of that title, in 1949. She launched various school stories which also became series, beginning with *The Naughtiest Girl in the School* (1940), *The Twins at St. Clare's* (1941), and *First Term at Malory Towers* (1946). But it was with her character Little Noddy, inspired by a line drawing by the Dutch artist Harmsen van der Beek, that she became a major public figure. Little Noddy, Big Ears, and the other inhabitants of Toyland Village became an unprecedented commercial success, reproduced in everything from dolls to cereal packets as well as in Blyton's books and a television series. By the 1950s she had over forty separate publishers, with whom she negotiated herself, employing a literary agent only during the last fifteen years of her career. At her peak she stipulated a minimum printing of 25,000 copies. She wrote at the rate of 10,000 words a day, and could complete a full-length children's book between Monday and Friday of the same week. By the end of her career in 1965 she had published over 400 titles, translated into twenty languages or dialects (from Afrikaans to Swahili, she liked to claim). In 1977, nearly ten years after her death, her English-language sales alone were in excess of 200 million and increasing at the rate of five million copies a year. Her success brought a negative response from reviewers and also public libraries, some of which refused to stock her books. Her critics accused her of using a limited and unchallenging vocabulary, of sexual stereotyping, of racism, and of a middle-class bias. It had little effect on her popularity or her sales. She was the first best-selling children's writer of the twentieth century and the first major children's writer to appear in paperback. Her marriage to Pollock ended in 1942 and six months later she married Kenneth Darrell Waters, a London surgeon, who died a year before she did, in 1967. She published her *Story of my Own Life* in 1952. *See* Barbara Stoney, *Enid Blyton* (1974); Sheila G. Ray, *The Blyton Phenomenon* (1982); Imogen Smallwood, *A Childhood at Greenhedges* (1989).

Bodichon, Barbara Leigh Smith, feminist and journalist (b. Wathington, Sussex, 8 April 1827, d. Scalands Gate, Sussex, 11 June 1891).

Barbara Leigh Smith, later Bodichon, was the eldest of the five children of Benjamin Leigh Smith, a Radical MP and a Unitarian, and his common-law wife Anne Longden, a milliner's apprentice who died when Barbara was 7. Political discussion and debate were a feature of family life and the family tradition of producing activist reformers and iconoclasts was a long one. Her grandfather had been one of Wilberforce's supporters in the campaign to abolish the slave-trade. Her great-grandfather had supported the American colonists in their campaign against the British government. She was educated at home by a tutor who encouraged her to read the *Arabian Nights* and she later followed a course in painting and drawing at the Ladies' College, Bedford Square. Her talents were by no means dilettante. She continued to draw and to paint throughout her life and to exhibit and sell her work. Her father's settlement of an annual income of £300 when she came of age was crucial to the development of her ideas about women's independence and the right to own property. She used some of the money to establish Portman Hall, a co-educational, non-denominational school in which she also taught. In 1854 she wrote 'A Brief Summary in Plain Language of the Most Important Laws Concerning Women', and campaigned vigorously for a Married Women's Property Act, legislation which did not in fact take place for nearly twenty years. Her essay *Women and Work* (1857) argued that paid work for women was both desirable and a necessity and that dependence was degrading. In 1858 she and her friend Bessie Rayner *Parkes established the **English Woman's Journal* to promote their ideas about women's rights and their campaigns for legal reform. The money for the *Journal* was provided by Barbara Leigh Smith and Bessie Parkes became the editor. In 1857 Leigh Smith had met and married Dr Eugène Bodichon, an Algerian of French extraction sixteen years her senior. He was a medical doctor who shared many of her radical ideas and who was prepared to enter into a marriage in which both partners retained a degree of independence. As a result they spent part of each year in Algeria and part in England. Barbara Bodichon next became involved in the movement for the higher education of women. With her friend Emily Davies she helped to establish Girton College, Cambridge. She also left a large sum, realized from the sale of her paintings, to the college in her will. She was largely responsible for the foundation, in 1866, of the Women's Suffrage Committee, the origin of the more sustained campaign for women's suffrage. Her two pamphlets on suffrage, *Reasons for the Enfranchisement of Women* (1866) and *Objections to the Enfranchisement of Women*

Considered (1866), outlined her views. Her only other publication was a diary written during an extended visit to the southern states of America which she undertook shortly after her marriage, published as *An American Diary (1857–8)*, ed. Joseph W. Reed (1972). Barbara Bodichon is better known as an active reformer than a writer, and as such she was a central and powerful figure in the women's movement in the 1850s and 1860s. As well as Bessie Rayner Parkes and Emily Davies, her close friends included George *Eliot and Elizabeth Garrett Anderson, the first woman to qualify in medicine. Bodichon was thought to have been a model for Eliot's *Romola.* In 1877 she suffered a stroke from which she only partially recovered. Her husband also became ill and unable to spend winters in England. As a result her separation from him increased. He died in 1885 and she lived on as an invalid until 1891, dying in a house in Sussex which she had built for herself. *See* Hester Burton, *Barbara Bodichon 1827–91* (1949); Sheila R. Herstein, *A Mid-Victorian Feminist: Barbara Leigh Smith Bodichon* (1985).

Bonhote, Elizabeth, novelist (b. Bungay, Suffolk, 1744, d. Bungay, July 1818).

Elizabeth Bonhote was the daughter of James Mapes, a baker, of Bungay, in Suffolk. She married Daniel Bonhote, a local solicitor and captain of the 2nd Bungay Volunteers, by whom she had several children. Her first work, *Rambles of Mr. Frankly,* published anonymously 'by his sister' in four volumes (1772–6), was a series of sketches contrasting city and country life, modelled on Sterne's *Sentimental Journey. The Fashionable Friend* (1773), an epistolary novel, and *Hortensia* (1777) followed. Several of her novels were published by William Lane's *Minerva Press: *Olivia; or The Deserted Bride* (1787), *Darnley Vale; or Emma Fitzroy* (1789), and *Ellen Woodley* (1790). *Bungay Castle* (1796), a *Gothic story set during the Wars of the Roses, and also a Minerva Press book, took its title from Bonhote's home, which she purchased and renovated and later sold to the Duke of Norfolk, the book's dedicatee. In 1788 she published by subscription *The Parental Monitor,* a two-volume conduct book, one volume for girls and the other for boys. Intended as a guide to her children in the event of her death it advocated acceptance of one's lot and dependence on adults. It was reprinted in 1790 and 1796. She also published *Feeling; or Sketches from Life,* 'a desultory poem with other poems by a lady', in 1810. She died in 1818, aged 74. Her husband predeceased her in 1804. *See* Dorothy Blakey, *The Minerva Press, 1790–1820* (1939), which lists her works.

Boston, Lucy M(aria), children's writer (b. Southport, Lancashire, 10 December 1892, d. Hemingford Grey, Huntingdonshire, 25 May 1990).

Lucy Boston was the fifth of the six children of James Wood, an engineer, and his wife Mary Garrett. The family were strict Methodists and wealthy. She later described the household as 'rigidly, rabidly puritanical' and claimed it set her on a course of 'outrageous and defiant unconventionality whenever opportunity offered'. She also attributed her love of parties, dancing, and good food and wine in her adult life to early restrictions. She went to Downs School, in Seaford, Sussex, then to a Quaker school in Surrey, followed by finishing school in Paris. In 1914 she went up to read classics at Somerville College, Oxford, but left after two terms in order to train as a VAD (Voluntary Aid Detachment) nurse. She worked at a French military hospital near Le Havre and in 1917 married her cousin Harold Boston, an army officer. They lived on the Continent for some time and had one son, Peter, who later became the illustrator of her books. The marriage was dissolved in 1935 and after an itinerant life in Italy and Austria she returned to England and purchased Hemingford Grey, a twelfth-century manor house in Huntingdonshire. The house became the 'Green Knowe' of the series of children's books for which she is best known and which she began to write when she was over 60. The novels revolve around Mrs Oldknow, the owner of Green Knowe, who tells stories of the children who have lived in the house over the centuries to her great-grandson Tolly. The historical children variously reappear without seeming to be ghosts and the house becomes a focus for the conjunction of past and present, a symbol of timelessness and an antidote to a modern world which has culminated in two World Wars. The series began with *The Children of Green Knowe* (1954), followed by *The Chimneys of Green Knowe* (1958), *The River at Green Knowe* (1959), *A Stranger at Green Knowe* (1961), which won the Library Association's Carnegie Medal, and *The Enemy at Green Knowe* (1964). *The Stones of Green Knowe* (1976) is the story of the building of the house as seen through the eyes of a child of the time. Boston's other children's stories, *The Sea Egg* (1967), *Nothing Said* (1971), and *The Fossil Snake* (1975), similarly turn on an unlikely or impossible event (a sea egg, a dryad, a fossil which comes alive) which children through their imaginations none the less perceive as true. Her work has been praised for its evocation of the natural world and its haunting sense of the past but criticized at times for its lack of credibility and the absence of memorable characters. She wrote two 'adult' novels, *Yew Hall* (1954) and *Persephone* (1969, published in the USA as *Strongholds*), in which Hemingford Grey features, but they received little attention. *Time is Undone* (1977) is a collection of poems written over a period of fifty years and includes the sonnet sequence 'Poems in Old Age' which was praised by I. A. Richards. Boston wrote *Memory in a House* (1973), about the restoration of Hemingford Grey, at 81, and her autobiography *Perverse and Foolish: A Memoir of Childhood and Youth* (1979) in her 85th year. She died at Hemingford Grey at 97. *See* John Rowe Townsend, *A Sense of Story* (1971).

Bottome, Phyllis, novelist (b. Rochester, Kent, 31 May 1884, d. Hampstead, London, 22 August 1963).

Phyllis Bottome was the third of the four children of the Revd William Macdonald Bottome, an American clergyman, and his Yorkshire-born wife Margaret Leatham. The family moved to New York when Phyllis was 9 but returned to England four years later. According to her autobiography she began to write at an early age ('I may truthfully say I became a novelist at age four or five'), but her prime ambition was a theatrical career. The onset of tuberculosis prevented this and she turned to writing. Her first book, *Life the Interpreter* (1902), was published when she was 18. Other novels followed at intervals, none attracting much critical attention. After her father's death in 1913 she lived in London and looked after her mother, met Ezra Pound and other literary figures, and continued to write. Her novel the topical *Secretly Armed* (1916, published in New York as *The Dark Tower*) became an overnight sensation. In 1917 she married Captain Alban Ernan Forbes-Dennis, whom she had first met in Switzerland, where she had gone for a tuberculosis cure. He was posted to Vienna after the war and she threw herself into the turbulent life of the city, organizing a food distribution centre with the Austrian psychologist Alfred Adler and his wife. *Old Wine* (1926) drew on her experiences during these years and was the first of her books to gain critical recognition. Bottome became an enthusiastic publicist of Adlerian psychology, the alienated heroes of many of her novels attesting to the impact of his theories. *Private Worlds* (1934) was one of the best novels to emerge from her interest in Adler. She and her husband moved between Austria, Switzerland, and Germany in the 1930s, where she witnessed Hitler's rise to power at first hand. The anti-war novel *The Mortal Storm* (1937), and the fiercely anti-Nazi *Within the Cup* (1943, published in the USA as *Survival*), the story of an Austrian psychologist forced to flee his country, were both highly popular. Her biography of Adler, published in 1939, was written at his request. She and her husband settled in Austria at the end of the war but eventually returned to England. Her autobiographies *Search for a Soul* (1947), *The Challenge* (1952), and *The Goal* (1962) give a detailed picture of her life. She wrote a brief pamphlet on Stella *Benson (1934). Daphne *du Maurier collected her short stories (1963). Bottome published a total of forty-seven novels, continuing to write until within a year of her death at 79.

Bowen, Elizabeth (Dorothea Cole), novelist and short story writer (b. Dublin, 7 June 1899, d. London, 22 February 1973).

Elizabeth Bowen was the only child of Henry Charles Cole Bowen, a barrister, and his wife Florence Isabella Pomeroy Colley. Both sides of her family were long-standing members of the Anglo-Irish ascendancy. Her Dublin childhood was described in *Seven Winters* (1942). When she was 7 her father suffered a severe nervous breakdown and the family moved to England. A lifelong stammer dated from this early upheaval. She was educated at Harpenden Hall School, Hertfordshire, and Down House, Kent. Her mother's death from cancer when she was 13 was another serious blow and was reflected in her fiction in the sense of displacement experienced by many of her child characters. She was brought up by what she called 'a community of aunts' and spent her summers at Bowen's Court, the family's eighteenth-century home at Kildorrery, County Cork, to which her father returned after his recovery and subsequent remarriage. She inherited the house at his death in 1930 and chronicled the family history in *Bowen Court* (1942). The house also featured as Danielstown in *The Last September* (1929). In 1923 she married Alan Charles Cameron, a local education officer who later worked with the BBC schools service. They lived near Oxford and then in Regent's Park, London, where her circle of friends extended to include Oxford dons as well as London literary figures. *Encounters*, a collection of short stories, was published in the first year of her marriage. *The Hotel*, her first full-length novel, appeared in 1927. Other early works included *Friends and Relations* (1931), *To the North* (1932), and *The House in Paris* (1935). Her two best-known novels were written in London immediately prior to and at the end of the Second World War, *The Death of the Heart* (1938) and *The Heat of the Day* (1949). The latter's evocative London setting was characteristic of many of her works. Some of her best short stories were set in the blitz, particularly 'Mysterious Kor' in *Penguin New Writing* (1944). Others demonstrated an interest in and skilful deployment of the supernatural, as in the title story of *The Cat Jumps* (1934). At the end of the war she and her husband moved to Bowen's Court, where Alan Cameron died in 1952. She found the upkeep of the house difficult in spite of her earnings from lecture tours of America and elsewhere, periods as writer-in-residence at various American universities, and a prodigious amount of journalism. In 1959 she sold the house, which was promptly demolished by its new owner. She returned to England, living first in Oxford and then at Hythe in Kent. Up until the 1950s her novels had focused on the world of the middle and upper middle classes, particularly in Ireland, a world whose structure and codes of behaviour had undergone serious disintegration by the end of the war. She concentrated on what she called 'the cracks in the surface of life', strong feelings, disruptions, shocks, which took place beneath a conventional exterior. *A World of Love* (1955) was the last of her Anglo-Irish novels. Her two final books, *The Little Girls* (1964) and *Eva Trout* (1969), which won the James Tait Black Memorial Prize, had begun to move in new directions, which she did not live long enough to consolidate. She was appointed CBE in 1948 and C.Lit. in 1965, was a member of the Irish Academy of Letters, and received honorary doctorates from Trinity College, Dublin, and Oxford. *Collected Impressions* (1950) included her introduction to *The Faber Book of Modern Stories* (1937) as well as reviews and prefaces written for various editions of the works of other writers. As well as the autobiographical title piece, *Pictures and Conversations* (1975) contained her 'Notes on Writing a Novel' (1945) and fragments of a last novel, 'The Move-In'. *The Collected Stories of Elizabeth Bowen*, ed. Angus Wilson, was published in 1980. *See* Harriet Blodgett, *Patterns of Reality: Elizabeth Bowen's Novels* (1975); Victoria Glendinning, *Elizabeth Bowen: Portrait of a Writer* (1977); Hermione Lee, *Elizabeth Bowen: An Estimation* (1981); Harold Bloom (ed.), *Elizabeth Bowen: Modern Critical Views* (1987); Phyllis Lassner, *Elizabeth Bowen* (1990).

'**Bowen,** Marjorie' (Gabrielle Margaret Vere Campbell, also 'George R. Preedy', 'Joseph Shearing'), historical novelist (b. Hayling Island, Hampshire, 29 October 1886, d. London, 23 December 1952).

Marjorie Bowen was the second daughter of Vere Douglas Campbell and his wife Josephine Elizabeth Ellis, the daughter of a Moravian clergyman. She resented the impecunious and eccentric lives of her parents and grew up introspective, reserved, and deeply distrustful of anything bohemian. She was educated, in her own words, 'by life' and 'by herself', studied art at the Slade School in London, and spent a year in Paris. She worked for a time as a research assistant in the British Library and taught herself Italian and French. In 1912 she married a Sicilian, Zefferino Emilio Costanza, by whom she had two children, one of whom died in infancy. She nursed her husband through a long illness in Italy during the First World War. He died in 1916 and the following year she married Arthur Long, an Englishman, by whom she had two sons. Bowen resolved at an early age to earn her living by writing, partly to pay for the extravagances of her mother, now separated from her father. Her pseudonym derived from her maternal great-grandfather. *The Viper of Milan*, a historical novel, rejected by eleven publishers and then published in 1906 when she was 20, was an instant and phenomenal best seller. She capitalized on a talent for story-telling with a prodigious output which at her death totalled more than 150 books. Throughout the 1920s and 1930s she published at least a novel a year, usually more. Her books recreated either a historical period, The Netherlands in the seventeenth century, the reign of Richard III, revolutionary France, or a historical character, Mary Stuart, Lady Hamilton, William Hogarth, John Wesley. A trilogy on the Renaissance begun in the late 1920s, *The Golden Roof* (1928), *The Triumphant Beast* (1934), and *Trumpets at Rome* (1936), was followed by another set in England in the seventeenth century, *God and the Wedding Dress* (1938), *Mr. Tyler's Saints* (1939), and *The Circle in the Water* (1939). In 1920 she adopted a second pseudonym, George R. Preedy, who became the masculine author of more historical novels including the successful *General Crack* (1928), which was made into a film. Her third pseudonym, Joseph Shearing, was first used in 1932 for the author of a series of historical novels based on actual criminal cases. His identity was not revealed until 1942. She once claimed that the adoption of a new pen-name helped her to assume a new personality when writing in a different vein. She had upwards of ten by the end of her career, including John Winch and Robert Paye, who were the authors of children's books. Bowen published her autobiography *The Debate Continues* under her maiden name Margaret Campbell in 1939. *See* Margaret Crosland, *Beyond the Lighthouse: English Women Novelists in the 20th Century* (1981).

Bowles, Caroline Anne, later Southey, poet (b. Lymington, Hampshire, 7 October 1786, d. Lymington, 20 July 1854).

The second wife of the poet Robert Southey, Caroline Anne Bowles was the daughter of Captain Charles Bowles of the East India Company and his wife Anne Burrard. Her father retired shortly after her birth and the family, which included her grandmother and her great-grandmother, settled in Lymington, in Hampshire. After the deaths of both parents she lost most of her property through the dishonesty of a guardian. She decided to support herself by writing and sent the manuscript of a narrative poem to Robert Southey. Southey recommended it to John Murray, who declined it, but it was eventually published by Longman as *Ellen Fitzarthur* in 1820. *The Widow's Tale and Other Poems* followed in 1822. Southey and Caroline Bowles met in 1820. He persuaded her to assist him in a projected poem about Robin Hood, a project which came to grief when she proved unable to master the stanza form of *Thalaba. Robin Hood: A Fragment* 'by the late Robert Southey and Caroline Southey' was published in 1847. She visited him in Keswick, when he deputed Wordsworth to show her around the countryside. She published *Solitary Hours* (1826), a collection of prose and verse, and in 1829 a series of stories, *Chapters on Churchyards*, first published in *Blackwood's Magazine.*

Her *Tales of the Factories* (1833) in verse anticipated Caroline *Norton's *A Voice from the Factories* (1836) and Elizabeth Barrett *Browning's 'Cry of the Children' (1843). Her long poem *The Birth-Day* (1836) prompted Henry Nelson Coleridge to pronounce her 'the Cowper of our modern poetesses' in the *Quarterly Review* (September 1840). In 1839 Southey, whose second wife had died after a lengthy mental illness, and who was now in failing health himself, proposed marriage, which she accepted. Despite their compatibility it proved disastrous. Within three months Southey's own mental health rapidly deteriorated. Her stepchildren, apart from Southey's eldest daughter Edith, detested her and Southey's death in 1843 came as a release. 'The last three years have done upon me the work of twenty,' she wrote to a friend. She is scarcely mentioned in Cuthbert Southey's edition of his father's correspondence (1849–50), a work which she refused even to look at. She returned to her cottage at Lymington and wrote nothing more. Southey left her £2,000, which was modest when compared to his legacies to his children and did not compensate for an annuity which she had had to forfeit on her marriage. She was granted a crown pension of £200 in 1854 and died two years later. Her letters were published as *The Correspondence of Robert Southey with Caroline Bowles* (1881). Caroline Bowles was no relation of the poet William Lisle Bowles.

Brackley, Lady Elizabeth *see under* NEWCASTLE, Margaret Cavendish, Duchess of

Bradby, Anne Barbara *see* RIDLER, Anne

Braddon, Mary Elizabeth, novelist and editor (b. London, 4 October 1835, d. Richmond, Surrey, 4 February 1915).

Mary Elizabeth Braddon, probably the most successful Victorian woman novelist in terms of sales, was the youngest daughter of Henry Braddon, a solicitor and writer on sporting subjects, and his Irish wife Fanny White. Her mother left her feckless husband when Mary was 4, taking her children first into the country and then returning to London. Mary was educated at home, mainly by her mother, wrote for the magazines in order to add to the family income, and also had a brief period on the stage under the name Mary Seyton. In 1856 she was offered £10 by a printer in Beverley for a serial which should combine 'the humour of Dickens with the dramatic quality of G. W. M. Reynolds'. The story was later rewritten and published as *The Trail of the Serpent; or Three Times Dead* (1861). Her first acknowledged publications were an epic poem on Garibaldi and *Lady Lisle*, a short novel, both published in 1861. She wrote her most famous novel, *Lady Audley's Secret*, in 1862 for *Robin Goodfellow*, a serial owned by the Irish publisher John Maxwell. It was transferred to the *Sixpenny Magazine* and published in three volumes in the same year by William Tinsley. It established Braddon's reputation and made Tinsley's fortune (he built a villa at Barnes, which he called Audley Lodge, on the proceeds). The novel, which involved a bigamous heroine, arson, several murder attempts, and probable insanity, was one of the first of the so-called *sensation novels of the 1860s. John Maxwell, the novel's original publisher, became the central figure in Braddon's life. She lived with him, and bore their first child in 1862. Maxwell was unable to marry her because his wife was alive in a lunatic asylum. They eventually married in 1874 amidst scandal and innuendo, and had six more children. Braddon's energy was phenomenal and her output prodigious. Her books earned as much as £2,000 each in the 1860s. She followed *Lady Audley's Secret* with *Aurora Floyd* (1863), which again involved bigamy and was admired by Henry James, *Eleanor's Victory* (1863), which centred on a murder, and *John Marchmont's Legacy* (1863), the intricate plot of which included a secret marriage, a train crash, a wife presumed dead, and a suicide. Other titles appeared remorselessly, among them *Henry Dunbar* (1864), *The Doctor's Wife* (1864), *Birds of Prey* (1867), and *Charlotte's Inheritance* (1868), in a similar vein and at similar speed, all popular with the circulating library public and the emerging railway reader. By 1899 fifty-seven of her titles were available in the cheap, so-called yellowback editions. Braddon published in a number of periodicals, including *Reynolds' Miscellany*, the *London Journal*, *Temple Bar*, and *All the Year Round*. She also edited *Belgravia* (1866–76) and the *Belgravia Annual* (1867–76), which were owned by Maxwell, as well as the Christmas *annual *Mistletoe Bough* (1878–92). Her later fiction, which she went on producing into her seventies, was less sensational and more psychological in its concerns. Her eightieth book, *The Green Curtain*, was published in 1911, when she was 74, and *Mary*, her last novel, appeared posthumously in 1916. Braddon was the best known of the sensation novelists of the 1860s. Despite the lurid appeal of bigamy and murder in her books, wrongdoing was always punished and virtue rewarded. Two of her sons, William Babington and Gerald Maxwell, wrote novels. *See* William B. Maxwell, *Time Gathered* (1937); Robert Lee Wolff, *Sensational Victorian: The Life and Fiction of Mary Elizabeth Braddon* (1979); Winifred Hughes, *The Maniac in the Cellar: Sensation Novels of the 1860s* (1980).

Bradley, Katherine Harris *see* FIELD, Michael

Bradstreet, Anne, poet (b. Northampton (prob.), 1612, d. Andover, Massachusetts, 16 September 1672).

Regarded as one of the earliest American poets, Anne Bradstreet was born in

England, the second of the six children of Thomas Dudley, a steward to the Earl of Lincoln, and his wife Dorothy Yorke. The family were prominent Puritans. She was educated at home by tutors with the use of her father's and the Earl's libraries. Most members of her family wrote poetry (her father, her sister **Mercy Woodbridge,** and later her son), as she did from her teens onward. In 1628, when she was 16, she contracted smallpox. In the same year she married Simon Bradstreet, the son of a Lincolnshire Nonconformist minister, who had served under her father in the Earl of Lincoln's household and was then in the service of the Puritan Countess of Warwick. In 1630 the Dudleys, the Bradstreets, and others sailed for Salem, Massachusetts. They settled in Ipswich and later in Andover. Thomas Dudley became Governor of the colony. Anne Bradstreet continued to write poetry, despite precarious health and the birth of eight children. Some of her poems were personal, others were on historical and heroic themes. They were distributed in manuscript, and she was praised by the Puritan writer and divine Cotton Mather as 'a crown to her father'. A later anthologist less equivocally pronounced her 'the most celebrated poet of her time in America'. Unknown to her, a collection of her poems was taken back to England by her sister's husband John Woodbridge and published in 1650 as *The Tenth Muse Lately Sprung up in America* 'by a Gentlewoman in Those Parts'. Despite failing health she continued to write in her later years, mainly the personal and contemplative poetry for which she is best known. In 1661, after another long illness, she wrote her *Poetical Epistles* to her husband and in 1665 and 1669 poems on the deaths of her grandchildren. She died of consumption in 1672 at the age of 60. A second edition of her *Poems* was printed in Boston in 1678, the title-page announcing that the works had been 'corrected by the Author'. Extracts from a manuscript notebook of meditations written for her children were published for the first time in 1844. The meditations were published in full in her complete *Works* (1867). Her husband later became Governor of Massachusetts. Oliver Wendell Holmes and William Ellery Channing were among her descendants. Her reputation waned until modern American poets Conrad Aiken and John Berryman praised her, the latter in his *Homage to Mistress Bradstreet* (1956). *The Complete Works of Anne Bradstreet* (1981) have been edited by Joseph R. McElrath and Allan P. Robb. *See* Elizabeth Wade White, *Anne Bradstreet: The Tenth Muse* (1972); Pattie Cowell and Ann Stanford, *Critical Essays on Anne Bradstreet* (1983).

Brand, Barbarina *see* DACRE, Lady

Bray, Anna Eliza, née Kempe, novelist (b. Newington, Surrey, 25 December 1790, d. London, 21 January 1883).

Anna Eliza Kempe was the daughter of John Kempe, a bullion porter in the Royal Mint, and his wife Ann Arrow. At one time she intended to follow a theatrical career, but illness prevented her début in 1815 and she did not pursue the ambition further. In 1818 she married the artist and illustrator Charles Alfred Stothard. Her first book, *Letters Written during a Tour in Normandy, Britanny and Other Parts of France in 1818* (1820), was illustrated by him. He died in 1821 after falling from a ladder in a church while sketching stained glass for a book on church monuments. Their only child, born after his death, died in infancy and Anna Kempe married for the second time, the Revd Edward Atkyns Bray, vicar of Tavistock, in Devon. She wrote a memoir of her first husband and completed his *The Monumental Effigies of Great Britain* (1832) with the help of her brother. She then turned to novel writing. Between 1826 and 1874 she wrote at least twelve novels, mainly historical romances and family sagas set in Devon and Cornwall, like *Fitz of Fitz-Ford* (1830), *Trelawney of Trelawne* (1837), and *Courtenay of Walreddon* (1844). Probably her best-known book was based on a series of letters about West Country traditions and superstitions which she wrote to Robert Southey between 1832 and 1835, published as *A Description of the Part of Devonshire Bordering on the Tamar and the Tavy* (1836), later retitled *The Borders of the Tamar and the Tavy* (1879). *A Peep at the Pixies; or Legends of the West* (1854) capitalized on its success and was aimed at children. Bray's second husband died in 1857. She moved to London, where she edited his poetry and sermons and wrote a life of Handel, several volumes of popular history, and three more novels. Her later years were clouded by a report that she had stolen a piece of the Bayeux tapestry while on a tour of France in 1816. The rumours were eventually quashed by leaders in *The Times*. She died in London at the age of 93. Longman issued a collected edition of her novels in 1845–6, which was reprinted by Chapman & Hall in 1884. Her *Autobiography*, covering her life up to 1843, was edited by her nephew J. A. Kempe in 1884.

Brazil, Angela, writer of girls' stories (b. Preston, Lancashire, 30 November 1868, d. Coventry, 13 March 1947).

Angela Brazil (she changed the pronunciation to rhyme with 'dazzle') was the fourth and youngest child of Clarence Brazil, manager of a cotton mill, and his wife Angelica McKinnell. She went to Miss Knowles's Select Ladies' School in Preston, then to the junior department of Manchester High School, and eventually as a boarder to Ellerslie College in Manchester, where she was head girl. The school was considered 'advanced' in educational methods and had no organized games or prefects, two predominant features of the schools which were to figure in her own stories. She studied at Heatherley's Art College, in London, where Baroness *Orczy was a fellow student, and then worked as a governess. After her father's death in 1899 she travelled in Europe and the Middle East with her mother and sister and began to write professionally at the age of 36. Her first works were *The Mischievous Brownie* (1899), four plays for children, and *A Terrible Tom Boy* (1904). *The Fortunes of Philippa* (1906), her first girls' school story, was followed by nearly fifty titles, in the course of which she established a sub-genre of children's writing and made her name. At her peak she produced several books a year, and by the end of her career she was writing to a formula. Her best books on the whole were the earliest: *The Third Class at Miss Kaye's* (1908), *The Nicest Girl in the School* (1910), her most popular work, *A Fourth Form Friendship* (1912), *The Jolliest Term on Record* (1915), *The Madcap of the School* (1917), *Monitress Merle* (1922), and *Captain Peggie* (1924). Brazil's heroines were characterized by their intense emotional attachments to those of the same sex, their notorious slang, which led to the books being banned in some schools, their respect for authority, and their devotion to games, especially hockey. Brazil recalled her own 'white-hot' friendships with other girls and in middle age declared herself 'still an absolute school girl'. Her books appealed primarily to upper- and middle-class female readers and their sales made her a rich woman. She also wrote for periodicals like *Little Folks* and *Our School Magazine.* She never married, and lived with her unmarried older brother and sister in Coventry, to which she had banished many of her fictional schoolgirls. Her last novel, *The School on the Loch,* was published in 1946, the year before her death. She published her autobiography *My Own Schooldays* in 1925. *See* Gillian Freeman, *The Schoolgirl Ethic: The Life and Work of Angela Brazil* (1976); Patricia Craig and Mary Cadogan, *You're a Brick, Angela* (1986).

Bridges, Elizabeth *see* DARYUSH, Elizabeth

Brittain, Vera (Mary), autobiographer, novelist, and journalist (b. Newcastle under Lyme, Staffordshire, 29 December 1893, d. London, 29 March 1970).

Vera Brittain was the only daughter of Thomas Arthur Brittain, a paper manufacturer, and his wife Edith Mary Bervon. Her brother Edward, a close companion and formative influence in her youth, was killed in action in France in 1918. She grew up in Macclesfield and Buxton, whose provinciality she resented. St Monica's School in Surrey provided intellectual stimulus and despite parental opposition she won an open exhibition to Somerville College, Oxford, in 1914. The outbreak of war made university intolerable to her, and she left in 1915 to become a VAD (Voluntary Aid Detachment) nurse, first in Malta and then in France. The death of her fiancé Roland Leighton as well as her brother and most of the young men of her generation and the horrors of the war turned her, in her words, 'from an ordinary patriotic young woman into a convinced pacifist'. After the war she returned to Oxford, where she got a second in history and formed a close friendship with a fellow student, Winifred *Holtby, with whom she moved to London, both having the intention of embarking on a literary career. Her novels *The Dark Tide* (1923) and *Not without Honour* (1924) had a muted reception, but the first brought her to the attention of George Catlin, a former Oxford student and then an assistant professor of politics at Cornell University. They married in 1925. Vera Brittain found American campus life uncongenial and by mutual agreement their 'semi-detached' marriage enabled her to remain in England with their son John and daughter Shirley (later Williams, politician and cabinet minister), while her husband spent the academic year in the United States. In 1933 she published *Testament of Youth*, 'to write history in terms of personal life' and 'to show what the whole War and the post-war period . . . has meant to the men and women of my generation'. The book went through five editions in the same year, and made her reputation overnight. It was the first war memoir to chronicle the impact of the war on non-combatants. It was also a poignant autobiography. It drew on her early years, her fight for education, her love affairs, and her nursing experience, and made an intense impression on a post-war generation. She made three lecture tours of the United States up to 1940 and threw herself into both pacifist and feminist campaigns. She lectured for the League of Nations Union, joined the Peace Pledge Union, and wrote for *Peace News*. She provoked considerable hostility by speaking publicly and repeatedly against the saturation bombing of Germany throughout the Second World War. She joined the Six Point Group, a women's rights organization, and wrote for **Time and Tide*, the feminist review. The death of Winifred Holtby in 1935 was a severe personal blow, and she wrote her tribute to their sixteen-year friendship in *Testament of Friendship* (1940). She also assisted with the posthumous publication of Holtby's novel *South Riding* in 1938, the impact of which undoubtedly assisted the popularity of *Testament of Friendship*. The second part of her autobiography, *Testament of Experience*, was published in 1957, and covered her life between 1925 and 1950. Brittain's literary output was formidable. She was an energetic journalist, writing for the *Manchester Guardian* and the *Yorkshire Post* as well as for pacifist and feminist periodicals. She wrote a number of works of non-fiction, including *England's Hour* (1941), the controversial *Seeds of Chaos: What Mass Bombing really Means* (1944), *Women's Work in Modern Britain* (1928), *Lady into*

Woman (1953), a history of modern women, *The Woman at Oxford* (1960), and *Radclyffe Hall: A Case of Obscenity?* (1968). Her first response to her war experiences was *Verses of a V.A.D.* (1918), which was expanded in 1934 into *Poems of the War and After*. Her five novels, which included *Honourable Estate* (1936), *Account Rendered* (1945), and *Born 1925* (1948), contained autobiographical elements, and some of the preoccupations of her non-fiction, but are undistinguished. It is as the writer of the two autobiographical 'Testaments' that she is best known. She died in London in 1970. Posthumous collected writings include *Chronicle of Youth: War Diary 1913–1917*, ed. A. Bishop (1981), *Testament of a Generation: The Journalism of Vera Brittain and Winifred Holtby*, ed. Paul Berry and Alan Bishop (1985), and *Chronicle of Friendship: Diary of the Thirties 1932–1939*, ed. A. Bishop (1986). *See Selected Letters of Winifred Holtby and Vera Brittain*, ed. V. Brittain and G. Handley-Taylor (1960); Hilary Bailey, *Vera Brittain* (1987); Jean Kennard, *Vera Brittain and Winifred Holtby: A Working Partnership* (1989); Paul Berry, *Vera Brittain: A Life* (1990).

Brontë, Anne ('Acton Bell'), novelist (b. Thornton, Yorkshire, 25 March 1820, d. Scarborough, Yorkshire, 28 May 1849).

The youngest of the six children of the Revd Patrick Brontë (1777–1861), perpetual curate of Haworth, in Yorkshire, and his Cornish wife Maria Branwell, who died the year after Anne was born, Anne Brontë was brought up with her siblings in the parsonage at Haworth by her father and her mother's elder sister 'Aunt Branwell'. Parsonage life was an enclosed world, which few visitors interrupted. Around 1826 Anne and her sister *Emily began secretly to write a series of stories and poems, set in the imaginary kingdom of Gondal, which they continued possibly as late as 1845. At the same time their sister *Charlotte and brother Branwell were writing long romantic serials set in Angria, another imaginary world which, like Gondal, drew on the children's early and voracious reading of Romantic poetry and *Gothic fiction. Anne accompanied Charlotte to Miss Wooler's school at Roe Head in 1836–7, until the symptoms of consumption became so acute she was forced to leave. She became a governess to the Ingham family at Blake Hall in 1839, and to the Robinson family at Thorp Green Hall, near York, between 1841 and 1845. Branwell was employed as a tutor by the Robinsons until his embarrassing involvement with Mrs Robinson resulted in a well-publicized dismissal which caused his family great pain. Her experiences with the children of both households were reflected in her first novel, *Agnes Grey*, published under the pseudonym Acton Bell in 1847. Over twenty of her poems, along with a selection of those of Emily and Charlotte, had been published as 'by Currer, Ellis and Acton Bell' in 1846. Anne's second novel,

The Tenant of Wildfell Hall (1848), contained a portrait of Branwell in the drunken and debauched Arthur Huntingdon. Charlotte's 1850 'Biographical Notice' prefaced to the novel commented that her sister's 'choice of subject was an entire mistake'. Newby the publisher was nevertheless sufficiently encouraged to offer the early sheets to an American publisher in the belief that the novel was by the author of *Jane Eyre.* Charlotte and Anne went to London in July 1848 to make their distinctive identities known to George Smith and W. S. Williams, of Smith Elder. Branwell Brontë died in September 1848, Emily in December. Anne's consumption became acute; she went to Scarborough, on the Yorkshire coast, and died in May 1849. Most of her poems were published posthumously, and were collected in *The Complete Poems of Anne Brontë*, ed. C. K. Shorter and C. W. Hatfield (1923). There is a more recent edition of her poems by Edward Chitham (1979). The best edition of Brontë letters is *The Brontës: Their Lives, Friendships and Correspondence* (1932). *See* Winifred Gerin, *Anne Brontë* (1959); Inga-Stina Ewbank, *Their Proper Sphere: A Study of the Brontë Sisters as Early Victorian Female Novelists* (1966); Elizabeth Langland, *Anne Brontë: the Other One* (1989); Edward Chitham, *A Life of Anne Brontë* (1991).

Brontë, Charlotte ('Currer Bell'), novelist and poet (b. Thornton, Yorkshire, 21 April 1816, d. Haworth, Yorkshire, 31 March 1855).

Charlotte Brontë was the third of the six children of the Revd Patrick Brontë, perpetual curate of Thornton, and later of Haworth, both in Yorkshire, and his wife Maria Branwell, of Penzance. Mrs Brontë died of cancer in 1821, and the children were brought up by her elder sister, the reserved and unloved Aunt Branwell. They were initially educated at home but in 1824 Maria, Elizabeth, Charlotte, and *Emily Jane were sent to a recently established school for daughters of the clergy at Cowan Bridge, a harsh, ill-equipped institution which was the original of the notorious Lowood in *Jane Eyre.* The two elder girls died of consumption the following year, possibly as a result of a fever epidemic which broke out at the school. Charlotte and Emily were removed from the school and taught by their father, with the help of books from the parsonage library and the local Mechanics Institute. Around 1826 Charlotte and her talented but wayward brother Branwell (1817–48) began to write in secret, creating the imaginary world of Angria in a series of long romantic serials which filled dozens of closely written manuscript notebooks. Emily and her youngest sister *Anne similarly co-operated in creating the so-called Gondal sagas. In 1831 Charlotte was sent to a school kept by a Miss Wooler at Roe Head, between Leeds and Huddersfield, where she met her lifelong friend Ellen Nussey, and also Mary and Martha Taylor, the originals of Rose and Jessie Yorke in *Shirley.* She taught at Miss Wooler's between 1835 and 1838, accompanied first by Emily and then by Anne as pupils, until her health declined and she returned to Haworth. She went as a governess to several private families, declined two proposals of marriage from clergymen, and then, with her sisters, hit upon the idea of starting a school at the parsonage. To acquire experience of foreign languages Charlotte and Emily went to a school in Brussels kept by M. and Mme Heger in 1842. Charlotte fell hopelessly in love with Constantin Heger, whom she later portrayed as Paul Emmanuel in *Villette.* She found the experience intellectually stimulating but culturally isolating, and the country's Catholicism particularly repugnant. The sisters returned to Haworth and only Charlotte went back to Belgium for a second period in 1843. Plans for the school did not materialize, and the tensions in the parsonage increased as Branwell's drinking and probably an opium addiction prevented him from staying in any form of employment for long. A dismissal from a tutor's post for a supposed liaison with his employer's wife was the subject of painful local gossip. In 1846 Charlotte organized the publication of a collection of poems by the three sisters under the pseudonyms 'Currer, Ellis and Acton Bell'. They met with little response, but the following year the publisher Thomas Newby accepted Emily's *Wuthering Heights* and Anne's *Agnes Grey.* Charlotte's *The Professor* was rejected by Smith Elder, but the autobiographical *Jane Eyre* was enthusiastically accepted and created a minor sensation when it was published in October 1847. Newby published Anne's *Tenant of Wildfell Hall* the following year on the strength of *Jane Eyre's* success and Charlotte and Anne went to London to prove that Currer and Acton Bell were two separate individuals. Branwell died in September 1848. Emily's health declined rapidly and she died in December. Anne succumbed to consumption the following May. Charlotte was left in the parsonage with her father, exhausted and depressed. *Shirley* was published in October 1849, a tale of Yorkshire life set during the Luddite Riots of 1811–12, a story 'as unromantic as Monday morning', its narrator announced. Charlotte made several visits to London, meeting her publisher George Smith, Thackeray, to whom she had dedicated the second edition of *Jane Eyre,* and other members of the London literary establishment, several of whom, including G. H. Lewes and Harriet *Martineau, were to review her novels. Her meeting in 1850 with Elizabeth *Gaskell led to a celebrated literary friendship and in 1857 to Mrs Gaskell's controversial *Life of Charlotte Brontë. Villette,* Charlotte's last novel, which like *The Professor* drew on her Brussels experiences, but substituted a female first person narrator for the awkward male voice of the earlier work, was completed at the end of 1852 and published the following year. At the end of 1852 she received a proposal of marriage from the Revd Arthur Nicholls, her father's curate, which, under her father's instruction, she refused. In the spring of 1854 she reversed her decision, and they were married in June. She died the following March, of complications arising from pregnancy. Her father survived her for six years, living with Mr Nicholls, who died in 1906. Brontë's work, both individually and collectively with that of Anne and Emily, has always attracted attention, beginning with the furore surrounding the publication of *Jane Eyre* and also Gaskell's *Life*. Virginia *Woolf used *Jane Eyre* as an illustration of the latent anger she detected in nineteenth-century women's writing in *A Room of One's Own* (1929). Feminist critics Sandra Gilbert and Susan Gubar explored this further in *The Madwoman in the Attic* (1979), the title of which alludes to the plot of *Jane Eyre*. Charlotte Brontë's adaptation of *Gothic elements has also interested feminist critics. Christine Alexander has edited *The Early Writings of Charlotte Brontë 1826–35* (3 vols., 1987–93). Charlotte's poems have been edited by Tom Winnifrith (1984). The best available edition of Brontë letters is T. J. Wise and J. A. Symington, *The Brontës: Their Lives, Friendships and Correspondence* (4 vols., 1932). *See* Virginia Woolf, *The Common Reader* (1925); Robert B. Martin, *The Accents of Persuasion* (1966); Winifred Gerin, *Charlotte Brontë: The Evolution of a Genius* (1967); Terry Eagleton, *Myths of Power: A Marxist Study of the Brontës* (1975); Sandra Gilbert and Susan Gubar, *The Madwoman in the Attic: The Woman Writer and the Nineteenth-Century Literary Imagination* (1979); Christine Alexander, *The Early Writings of Charlotte Brontë* (1983); Helene Moglen, *Charlotte Brontë: The Self Conceived* (1984); Pauline Nestor, *Female Friendships and Communities: Charlotte Brontë, George Eliot, Elizabeth Gaskell* (1985) and *Charlotte Brontë* (1987); Rebecca Fraser, *Charlotte Brontë* (1988); Penny Boumelha, *Charlotte Brontë* (1990).

Brontë, Emily Jane ('Ellis Bell'), novelist and poet (b. Thornton, Yorkshire, 20 August 1818, d. Haworth, Yorkshire, 19 December 1848).

Emily Brontë was the fifth of the sixth children of the Revd Patrick Brontë and his wife Maria Branwell. Shortly before the birth of her sister *Anne the family moved from Thornton to Haworth, where Mr Brontë had accepted the perpetual curacy. Mrs Brontë died in November 1821 and the children were looked after by their aunt Elizabeth Branwell, in the isolated surroundings of Haworth parsonage. Emily went with her sisters to Cowan Bridge school for daughters of the clergy in September 1824 but was removed the following year because of poor health. The elder daughters Maria and Elizabeth having died from the effects of fever in 1825, the surviving children were taught at home by their aunt and supervised by their sister *Charlotte. Around 1826, Emily and Anne began their collaborative writing of the 'Gondal' sagas, a series of stories and poems, set in the imaginary kingdom of Gondal, which they continued possibly as late as 1845. At the same time Charlotte and her brother Branwell were writing long romantic serials set in Angria. Both series reflected the children's early and intensive reading, of Aesop's *Fables*, the *Arabian Nights*, as well as Romantic poetry and *Gothic novels. In 1835 Emily went as a pupil to Miss Wooler's school at Roe Head, where Charlotte was a teacher, but left after three months because of homesickness. The following year she tried teaching for six months at a school in Halifax but again found absence from Haworth unbearable. A plan by the sisters to establish a school at the parsonage led Emily and Charlotte to attend a school in Brussels run by Professor and Madame Heger in 1842 in order to improve their French. The death of Aunt Branwell brought them home prematurely, and only Charlotte returned to Brussels the following year. In 1845 Charlotte accidentally found some poems written by Emily and as a consequence planned the publication of *Poems* by 'Currer, Ellis and Acton Bell' in 1846. The book went unremarked apart from a notice in the *Athenaeum* (July 1846), but on the strength of this modest success the three planned publication of their novels. *Wuthering Heights*, written between October 1845 and June 1846, was published by T. C. Newby in December 1847 along with *Agnes Grey*. The work met with incomprehension at one extreme and disapproval of its 'coarseness' at the other. Branwell Brontë died in September 1848. Emily caught a cold at his funeral which aggravated a tubercular condition. She declined rapidly and died in December 1848, aged 30. Her literary reputation was almost entirely posthumous. Charlotte's 'Biographical Notice' prefixed to the 1850 edition of *Wuthering Heights* constructed the persona which was further developed by the myths and legends surrounding the Brontë family. Her poetry, only a fraction of which was published during her lifetime, has come to be recognized as some of the most original of the nineteenth century. Much of it is closely related to the Gondal material. Two of her notebooks into which she copied some of her poems are extant and throw further light on her methods of composition. *Wuthering Heights* was gradually reassessed, beginning with Mrs Humphry *Ward's preface to the 1899 Haworth edition, and accorded the unique status it has continued to hold in the twentieth century. The *Complete Poems* were first edited by C. W. Hatfield (1941) and more recently by Barbara Lloyd-Evans (1992) and by Janet Gezari (1992). Fannie E. Ratchford, in *The Brontës' Web of Childhood* (1941), was the first to connect the Gondal and Angrian material with the mature work of the sisters. She also edited *Gondal's Queen: A Novel in Verse* (1955), and *Five Essays Written in French by Emily Jane Brontë* (1948), Brontë's 'devoirs' or school exercises. *See* Virginia *Woolf, *The Common Reader* (1925); Winifred Gerin, *Emily Brontë: A Biography* (1971); Terry Eagleton, *Myths of Power: A Marxist Study of the Brontës* (1975); Anne Smith (ed.), *The Art of Emily Brontë* (1976); Margaret Homans, *Women Writers and Poetic Identity* (1980); Edward Chitham, *A Life of Emily Brontë* (1987); James Kavanagh, *Emily Brontë* (1985); Stevie Davies, *Emily Brontë* (1988); Lyn Pykett, *Emily Brontë* (1989).

Brooke, Frances ('Mary Singleton'), novelist and playwright (b. Claypole, Lincolnshire, 1724, d. Sleaford, Lincolnshire, January 1789).

Frances Brooke was the daughter of the Revd William Moore, who died when she was 3, and his wife Mary Knowles. After her mother's death she and her younger sister were brought up by relations in Lincolnshire. Another sister died in childhood. She moved to London, where in 1755–6 she edited a weekly periodical called the *Old Maid*, under the pseudonym 'Mary Singleton, Spinster'. She also wrote a verse tragedy, *Virginia* (1756), which was refused by Garrick, to her great irritation. In 1756 she married Dr John Brooke, rector of Colney, in Norfolk. Their only son was born in 1757, and in the same year Dr Brooke left for North America as a military chaplain. Frances translated Marie-Jeanne Riccoboni's *Letters from Juliet, Lady Catesby* (1760) a popular French novel, and in 1763 wrote her own highly successful sentimental and epistolary novel *The History of Lady Julia Mandeville*, which went through ten editions by 1792. In 1763 she sailed for Quebec, where her husband was garrison chaplain. The epistolary *History of Emily Montague* (1769) drew on her experience in the colony between 1763 and 1768, and came to be regarded as the first Canadian novel. A translation of Milot's *History of England* (1771) and various other translations were followed by *The Excursion* (1777), yet another epistolary novel, with education as a theme. It also contained an attack on Garrick, thereby settling an old score. Other novels have been ascribed to her, including *Charles Mandeville* (1790), a sequel to *Lady Julia*. Brooke renewed her theatrical contacts on her return to London. She jointly managed the Haymarket opera house with her friend the actress Mary Ann Yates. In 1781 her tragedy *Sinope* ran for ten nights at Covent Garden, with Yates playing the lead. Her most successful theatrical venture was *Rosina* (1783), a musical which went through numerous editions up until the middle of the nineteenth century. Another musical, *Marian* (1788), again with William Shields's music, remained popular until the turn of the century. Anna Laetitia *Barbauld commended Frances Brooke in her *British Novelists* as 'about the first who wrote in a polished style'. *See* John Moss (ed.), *Beginnings: A Critical Anthology* (1980); Jane Spencer, *The Rise of the Woman Novelist: From Aphra Behn to Jane Austen* (1986); Janet Todd, *The Sign of Angellica: Women, Writing and Fiction, 1660–1800* (1989).

Brooke-Rose, Christine, novelist, short story writer, and critic. (b. Geneva, 1926).

Christine Brooke-Rose's mother Evelyn Blanche Brooke, was half-Swiss, half-American. Her father Alfred Northbrook Rose was English. They separated early in her childhood and she was brought up in Brussels by her grandparents. She was completely bilingual but French was her first language, a situation to which she later attributed her slow development as a writer. ('I felt neither in one language nor in another'). She was sent to school in England after her father's death, and worked as an intelligence officer with the British Women's Auxiliary Air Force during the war. She read English and philology at Somerville College, Oxford, and did a Ph.D. in English at London University, out of which came her first critical work, *A Grammar of Metaphor* (1958), an analysis of the metaphorical language of fifteen poets from Chaucer to Dylan Thomas. While at Oxford she met her future husband Jerzy Peterkiewicz, a Polish writer and academic, whom she married in 1948. They divorced in 1975. His serious illness in 1956 caused her to write her first novel as a means of distraction. *The Languages of Love* (1957), a satire about philologists, was followed by three more traditional novels, *The Sycamore Tree* (1958), *The Dear Deceit* (1960), and *The Middlemen* (1961). Her own serious illness in 1962 while in France led her to read the experimental fiction of French novelists Nathalie Sarraute and Alain Robbe-Grillet as well as Samuel Beckett. Her first metafictional narrative, *Out*, appeared in 1964, followed by *Such* (1966), *Between* (1968), and *Thru* (1975), all demonstrating the influence of the *nouveau roman*. 'I had at last found what I wanted to do, even if it took me four novels to learn,' she recalled. *Such*, the story of the awakening to consciousness for three minutes, the time-span of the narrative, of a dead physicist-psychiatrist, was a joint winner of the James Tait Black Memorial Prize. *Thru* was experimentally modelled on Joyce's *Finnegans Wake*. The central subject of *Between*, whose main character is an interpreter, is language. *Thru* and *Amalgamemnon* (1984) are both set in the modern academic world, while *Xorander* (1988) concerns the science fiction world of modern computing. All three involve Brooke-Rose's characteristic exploration of language and word-play. Later novels include *Verbivore* (1990) and *Textermination* (1991). She has written two books on Ezra Pound (1971 and 1976), and a collection of studies on narrative and structure, *A Rhetoric of the Unreal* (1981). Her translation of Robbe-Grillet's novel *Dans le labyrinthe* won the Arts Council Translation Prize in 1969. Brooke-Rose's prolific free-lance journalism in the 1950s and 1960s (she reviewed for the *TLS*, *The Times*, the *Sunday Times*, the *Observer*, the *Listener*, the *Spectator*, and the *London Magazine*) helped to introduce the *nouveau roman* and

French literary theory (structuralism and post-structuralism) to the English reading public. From 1975 to 1988 she was professor of English language and literature at the University of Paris VIII, Vincennes. Four of her novels have been collected in *The Christine Brooke-Rose Omnibus* (1986). *See* Richard Martin, in *Breaking the Sequence: Women's Experimental Fiction*, ed. Ellen G. Friedman and Miriam Fuchs (1989); Robert L. Caserio, in *Why the Novel Matters: A Postmodern Perplex*, ed. Mark Spilka and Caroline McCracken-Flesher (1990).

Brookner, Anita, novelist and art historian (b. London, 16 July 1928).

The only child of Polish-Jewish parents, Newsom Bruckner, a businessman, and Maude Schiska, a singer, who changed the spelling of their name because of anti-German feeling, Anita Brookner went to James Allen's Girls' School in Dulwich and then to King's College, London. She took her Ph.D. at the Courtauld Institute of Art, lectured at Reading University, and then became a lecturer and later a reader in history of art at the Courtauld. She was also Slade Professor of Art at Cambridge in 1967–8. Her first books established her international reputation as an authority on late eighteenth- and early nineteenth-century French painting. These included studies of Watteau (1968), Greuze (1972), and David (1980), and *The Genius of the Future* (1971), on French art criticism. Most of her novels, which she began to write annually from 1980, are stories of intelligent women's lives, women in search of relationships or on the verge of extricating themselves from them, women who feel not in control of their lives. Her heroines are often single, financially independent, middle-aged. Several are novelists. The heroine of *A Start in Life* (1981), a university lecturer, looks back and 'at forty, knew that her life had been ruined by literature'. The heroines of *Providence* (1982), and *Look at Me* (1983), her next two novels, are young women who fail to find the romantic love they crave, love denied them by their families. *Lewis Percy* (1989), a later work, transposes this predicament to a male protagonist who in contrast finds happiness after a loveless marriage. The novelist heroine of *Hotel du Lac* (1984), which won the Booker Prize, and the heroine of *A Friend from England* (1987) are older women in the process of ending relationships. *A Misalliance* (1986) and *Brief Lives* (1990) examine the lives of two older women by exploring their past. *Family and Friends* (1985) and *Latecomers* (1988) are family chronicles, the first projected from a series of wedding photographs and the second a retrospect of the families of two Jewish refugees. The spinster heroine of *Fraud* (1992) faces life after the death of her widowed mother and decides not to continue to live up to the 'fraudulent' exterior she has presented to the world. Betrayal, disillusion, disappointment, the attrition of time, the contradictions in marriage and romantic love are the themes of Brookner's short, sombre, elegantly written, and richly allusive novels. Rosamond *Lehmann and Elizabeth *Taylor are the English women novelists she most admires. *Hotel du Lac* was filmed for television in 1986. *See* John Haffenden (ed.), *Novelists in Interview* (1985); Olga Kenyon, *Women Novelists Today* (1988); Robert Burchfield, in *The State of the Language*, ed. Christopher Ricks and Leonard Michaels (1990); John Skinner, *The Fiction of Anita Brookner: Illusions of Romance* (1992).

Brophy, Brigid (Antonia), novelist and critic (b. London, 12 June 1929).

Although born in London, Brigid Brophy claims to be 'mainly Irish', to have begun writing 'two or three years after I was born', and to have been an experienced playwright and producer at 8. She learned the elements of writing prose from her father, the novelist John Brophy (1899–1965), and the principles of syntax from her mother Charis Grundy, a teacher. An 'idyllic' childhood was disrupted by the war, during which she was moved from school to school, eventually settling at St Paul's Girls' School, London. She won a scholarship to read classics at St Hugh's College, Oxford, but was sent down in her second year. She worked as a shorthand typist and in 1953 published two books, *The Crown Princess and Other Stories* and *Hackenfeller's Ape*, which won the Cheltenham Festival Prize for a first novel. Like most of her fiction it reflects her various philosophical and ethical concerns, in this instance an opposition to vivisection, against which she later became a vigorous campaigner. In 1954 she married Michael Levey, an art historian and later Director of the National Gallery. Her fiction is experimental, often erudite, and frequently controversial. It explores among other themes the nature of the erotic and connections between sex and death, an interest highlighted in her psychoanalytical essay on the death instinct, *Black Ship to Hell* (1962). *Flesh* (1962) is about a sexual awakening, and *The Snowball* (1964) about a love of death. *The Finishing Touch* (1963) and the Kafkaesque *Place without Chains* (1978) have lesbian principal characters. *In Transit* (1969) is a transsexual fantasy. She has published studies of Mozart (1964), Aubrey Beardsley (1968 and 1976), and the novelist Ronald Firbank (1973). The flippant *Fifty Works of Literature we could do without* (1967) was written with Michael Levey and Charles Osborne. Her journalism has been collected in *Don't Never Forget* (1966) and *Baroque-'n'-Roll* (1987). She has written several plays, notably *The Burglar* (1967, published 1968), and with Maureen *Duffy organized a Pop Art Exhibition in 1969. She was active in the campaign for the Public Lending Right, 1972–81, to which she has written a

Guide (1983), and was a member of the Copyright Council from 1976 to 1980. She has suffered from multiple sclerosis since 1984.

Broughton, Rhoda, novelist (b. Denbigh, North Wales, 29 November 1840, d. Oxford, 5 June 1920).

Rhoda Broughton was the youngest of the family, consisting of three daughters and a son, of the Revd Delves Broughton, a younger son of a Staffordshire landowner, and Jane Bennett, the daughter of a Dublin lawyer. Her father was given the living of Broughton in Staffordshire, one of the family seats, and Rhoda Broughton grew up in an Elizabethan manor house with a good library and was encouraged in her reading, particularly of poetry, by her father. She never married, but after the death of her parents lived with her sisters at Surbiton, then with a married sister in Wales and in Richmond, and eventually with a cousin near Oxford. She began to write in imitation of Anne Thackeray *Ritchie's *The Story of Elizabeth* (1863), and published her first novel, *Not Wisely but Too Well*, in the *Dublin University Magazine* in 1867 when she was 27. The novel which followed, *Cometh up as a Flower* (1867), was an immediate success, and earned her top rates of payment for fiction. Broughton wrote extremely quickly. Her plots turned on the dilemma of love versus duty, and she had a good eye and ear for the manners and dialogue of country house and upper-class town life. Further titles included *Red as a Rose is She* (1870), *Goodbye Sweetheart* (1872), *Nancy* (1873), *Belinda* (1883), and *Doctor Cupid* (1886), all published in the three-volume format of the day. With the decline of the 'three-decker' Broughton found her style suited the new, shorter one-volume format. Later novels worth noting include *A Beginner* (1894), *Dear Faustina* (1897), *Foes in Law* (1900), and *Lavinia* (1902), which had an anti-Boer War hero. Broughton had a reputation for creating 'fast' heroines and sexually audacious situations, a reputation which she outlived as the climate for fiction changed. She was said to have reflected that she had begun her career as a Zola and ended it as a Charlotte *Yonge. She was one of the most successful novelists, in terms of sales, of the late Victorian period. *See* an appreciation by Marie *Belloc-Lowndes in Broughton's *A Fool in her Folly* (1920).

Browning, Elizabeth Barrett, poet (b. Coxhoe Hall, Kelloe, County Durham, 6 March 1806, d. Florence, 30 June 1861).

The eldest of the eleven children of Edward Moulton Barrett and Mary Graham Clarke, Elizabeth Barrett grew up on her father's estate of Hope End, near Ledbury, Herefordshire. She was a precocious reader, and was much encouraged in her reading of the classics by her father, who allowed her to share her brother's classical tutor, and later arranged for tuition from a local scholar. A series of illnesses from her teenage years onward left her unable to leave home, and increased the amount of time devoted to reading. Her mother's death in 1828 was followed by the reversal of her father's financial fortunes, and necessitated the selling of Hope End and removal to London, eventually to Wimpole Street. In 1838 Elizabeth was sent to Torquay to recover from a lung haemorrhage. Against her father's wishes her brother Edward remained with her to help her recuperation. His death in a sailing accident off Torbay left her bereaved and burdened with guilt. She began to write poetry at the age of 13. *The Battle of Marathon* was published at her father's expense in 1820. Her *Essay on Mind* followed in 1826 and her translation of *Prometheus Bound* in 1833. *The Seraphim and Other Poems* was published in 1838 and she helped R. H. Horne with a series of biographical essays published as *A New Spirit of the Age* (1844). Her first important volume was her *Poems* (1844), which won her the admiration of the poet Robert Browning and led to a clandestine courtship, partly by correspondence, and eventually their elopement and marriage in September 1846, against her father's wishes. They settled in Florence, at Casa Guidi, which remained her home until her death. Their son 'Pen' was born in 1849. From the time of her marriage onward Elizabeth Barrett Browning's work went from strength to strength. Her famous sonnnet sequence 'Sonnets from the Portuguese', love poems addressed to her husband, and written secretly during their courtship, was published as part of *Poems* (1850). A spurious 'edition' of 1847 was in fact a forgery by T. J. Wise. *Casa Guidi Windows* (1851) reflected her passionate interest in contemporary Italian politics, as did a later volume, *Poems before Congress* (1860). The volume she regarded as her most mature work was *Aurora Leigh* (1857, ed. Margaret Reynolds, 1992), a narrative poem in nine books which set out her views on the position of women in contemporary society and the difficulties which beset a woman poet. Her posthumously published *Last Poems* (1862) is widely regarded as containing some of her best poetry. During her lifetime Barrett Browning's reputation easily eclipsed that of her husband. On Wordsworth's death in 1850 hers was one of the names suggested as his successor as Poet Laureate. Despite her relatively secluded life she had many literary friends, including Anna *Jameson and Mary Russell *Mitford. *The Letters of Elizabeth Barrett Browning* were originally edited by F. G. Kenyon (2 vols., 1897). A modern edition of *The Brownings' Correspondence* is in progress, ed. Philip Kelley and Ronald Hudson *et al.* (1984–). Daniel Karlin has edited *Robert Browning and Elizabeth Barrett: The Courtship Correspondence* (1987). *See* Virginia *Woolf, *The Common Reader: 2nd Series* (1932) and *Flush: A Biography* (1933); Cora Kaplan's introd. to *Aurora Leigh* (1978); Angela Leighton, *Elizabeth Barrett Browning* (1986); Deirdre David, *Intellectual Women and Victorian Patriarchy*

(1987); Dorothy Mermin, *Elizabeth Barrett Browning: The Origins of a New Poetry* (1989); Glenis Stephenson, *Elizabeth Barrett Browning and the Poetry of Love* (1989); Marjorie Stone, *Elizabeth Barrett Browning* (1992).

Brunton, Mary, novelist (b. Barra, Orkney, 1 November 1778, d. Edinburgh, 19 December 1818).

Mary Brunton was the daughter of Colonel Thomas Balfour of Elwick, Orkney, and Frances Ligonier, the daughter of an army officer and niece of the first Earl of Ligonier. She was educated at home and taught French, Italian, and some German by her mother, who died when she was 16. She took charge of her father's household for four years, and when she was 20 declined an invitation to live fashionably in London with her titled relations, choosing instead to marry the Revd Alexander Brunton, a scholarly Church of Scotland clergyman who had acquired the living of Bolton, near Haddington, East Lothian. They read philosophy, theology, and history together, and in 1803 moved to Edinburgh, where Dr Brunton became professor of oriental languages at Edinburgh University, and one of the preachers at the Tron Church. Mary was introduced into Edinburgh literary circles, and began secretly to write a novel. She showed the first volume of *Self Control* to her husband, who made suggestions, some of which she adopted. The remaining two volumes were completed in daily instalments which she read aloud to him in the evenings. It was published in 1811, dedicated to Joanna *Baillie, and went through three editions in the first year. *Discipline*, her second novel, published in 1814, continued the themes of duty, self-reliance, and prudence in marriage choice. It contained scenes set in the Highlands, which she had intended to expand upon, following the example of Maria *Edgeworth's Irish stories. The success of Scott's *Waverley* in 1814 dissuaded her from continuing with the plan, although she retained some Highland scenes in the novel. A third novel, *Emmeline*, a cautionary story of a woman who divorces her husband in order to marry another man, remained unfinished when she died of a fever following the birth of a stillborn son in 1819. It was published posthumously in 1819 by Alexander Brunton, prefixed with a memoir. *See* Sarah W. R. Smith and Katrin R. Burlin, in *Fetter'd or Free? British Women Novelists 1670–1815*, ed. Mary Anne Schofield and Cecilia Macheski (1986).

'Bryher' (Annie Winnifred Ellerman), novelist, autobiographer, and patron of the arts (b. Margate, Kent, 2 September 1894, d. Vaud, Switzerland, 28 January 1983).

Annie Winnifred Ellerman, better known by her pen-name Bryher, which she took from one of the Scilly Isles, was born fifteen years before the marriage of her parents John Reeves Ellerman (later Sir John), a self-made shipping magnate and newspaper owner, and his wife Hannah Glover. Winnifred educated herself by voracious reading, particularly history and the adventure stories of G. A. Henty, and was taken by her parents on extensive travels in Europe, Africa, and the Near East. Her parents eventually married in 1908 in time for the birth of her brother, which precipitated her departure for Queenswood, a girls' boarding school in Eastbourne, which she hated for its constraints and gender stereotyping: 'To possess the intellect, the hopes, the ambitions of a man, unsoftened by any feminine attribute, to have these sheathed in convention, impossible to break without hurt to those she had no wish to hurt, to feel so thoroughly unlike a girl, this was the tragedy.' The frustrations of the heroine of her first novel, *Development* (1920), were in fact her own. Her father arranged for the publication of a book of poems, *Region of Lutany* (1914), and she worked as a journalist during the First World War, reviewing for the *Sphere* and the *Saturday Review*. In 1917 she encountered the work of the Imagists, in particular Amy Lowell. She sent her pamphlet *Amy Lowell: A Critical Appreciation* (1911) to the American poet H(ilda) D(oolittle), then living in London. Their resulting intensely emotional relationship, sexual as well as intellectual, lasted until H.D.'s death in 1961. Through her Bryher was introduced to literary circles in London and Paris and in 1921 she married the American writer Robert McAlmon, a marriage of convenience, deliberately undertaken to provide her with the freedom reserved only for married women. Using Bryher's money, McAlmon founded the Contact Publishing Company, which numbered Gertrude Stein, Hemingway, H.D., Djuna Barnes, Mina *Loy, Mary *Butts, Joyce, Pound and William Carlos Williams among its authors. Later it published May *Sinclair and Dorothy *Richardson and the sequel to Bryher's *Development,* the autobiographical Two Selves (1923). Bryher also supported Sylvia Beach's famous English bookshop in Paris, Shakespeare & Co., as well as Harriet Weaver's Egoist Press in London. She published a travel book, *West* (1925), and *Civilians* (1927), about women's work during the First World War (she tried to sign up as a land-worker). In 1927 she divorced McAlmon and married Kenneth Macpherson, a lover of H.D.'s. The marriage enabled her to regain her British citizenship. She and Macpherson lived amicably in a triangular relationship with H.D. until the end of the Second World War. They eventually adopted H.D.'s daughter. Through Macpherson Bryher became interested in the contemporary cinema and together they started *Close-up,* the first periodical in English devoted to the art of the film, to which Dorothy Richardson, H.D., Gertrude Stein, and Bryher contributed regularly. They also founded a film company, Pool Productions, which made the films *Foothills* and *Borderline,* starring H.D. and Paul Robeson. Bryher and H.D. next became interested in psychoanalysis. Both were analysed (H.D.

by Freud) and Bryher gave financial support for the establishment of the *Psychoanalytic Review.* In 1935 she used her considerable business skills to run the literary journal *Life and Letters Today.* Bryher and Macpherson were divorced in 1947 and she embarked on a series of successful historical novels, including *The Fourteenth of October* (1954), *Roman Wall* (1955), *The Player's Boy* (1957), *Gate to the Sea* (1959), *Visa for Avalon* (1965), and *This January Tale* (1966). At H.D.'s death in 1961 Alice B. Toklas commented that it was impossible to believe in Bryher without H.D. She in fact lived on for more than twenty years, writing more fiction and the two volumes of autobiography which are possibly her best works, *The Heart to Artemis* (1962) and *The Days of Mars: A Memoir 1940–46* (1972). *See* Barbara Guest, *Herself Defined. The Poet H.D. and her World* (1984); Robert McAlmon, *Being Geniuses Together* (1984); Shari Benstock, *Women of the Left Bank: Paris 1900–1940* (1987); Gillian Hanscombe and Virginia L. Smyers, *Writing for their Lives; The Modernist Women 1910–1940* (1987).

Bulwer-Lytton, Rosina, Lady Bulwer-Lytton, novelist (b. Ballywhire, County Limerick, 2 November 1802, d. Upper Sydenham, London, 12 March 1882).

Rosina Bulwer-Lytton was the youngest daughter of Francis Wheeler and his wife Anna Doyle, the daughter of an archdeacon. When her parents separated, Rosina lived for a while with her mother in Guernsey and Caen, and was then sent to London to live with her uncle General Sir John Doyle, the retired Governor of Guernsey. She was clever, accomplished, impetuous, and beautiful, and entered the literary circle which surrounded Lady Caroline *Lamb. In 1826 she met Edward George Lytton Bulwer, later the novelist Bulwer-Lytton, then on the brink of a literary career. Bulwer's strongly possessive mother, on whom he was dependent for an allowance, disapproved of the match. He felt honour bound to marry Rosina, as they had become lovers, and the marriage took place in August 1827. The couple settled at Woodcot House, near Pangbourne, Berkshire, and then in Hertford Street, Mayfair, where they lived on Bulwer's literary earnings plus Rosina's income of £80. The birth of a daughter in June appears to have been traumatic for Rosina in that she could not nurse the baby and became indifferent to motherhood, but it led to a partial reconciliation with Lady Lytton. She restored Bulwer's allowance but refused to see Rosina. Bulwer in turn refused to take her money. A son was born in 1831, but the family disapproval and Bulwer's volatile temperament meant that the marriage was unstable from the beginning. There is a suggestion of physical violence on his part. Even Leslie Stephen, in his otherwise sympathetic *DNB* entry, maintained that Bulwer 'must be counted among the eminent authors who have not made and not deserved success in married life'. The couple travelled to Italy in 1833, where their quarrels increased. They returned in 1834, and after living apart a legal separation was effected in 1836. The two children were first given to Rosina, and then, in 1838, taken from her. She saw her daughter again only once before the latter's death at the age of 20 in 1848. Bulwer made her an allowance of £400 a year in 1836, much of which she used to fight a series of legal battles against him. In 1839 she published her first novel, *Cheveley; or The Man of Honour*, whose hero, a brutish, philandering aristocrat, was intended as a thinly disguised version of her husband. Its *succès de scandale* gave her an exaggerated sense of what she could earn from fiction. Subsequent novels, which included *The Budget of the Bubble Family* (1840), *The Prince-Duke and the Page* (1841), *Bianca Capello: An Historical Romance* (1842), *Behind the Scenes* (1854), *Very Successful* (1856), and *The World and his Wife* (1858), earned less money and there was some evidence that Bulwer had put pressure on publishers to reject her work. Several of her novels were written as 'histories', including *Memoirs of a Muscovite* (1844) and *School for Husbands* (1852), which contains a fictional account of Molière. Rosina lived for some years on the Continent in straitened financial circumstances, and returned to England in 1847, eventually settling in Taunton in 1857. In 1858, on the day of Bulwer's election as MP for Hereford, she appeared at a public meeting and denounced him. He promptly had her declared insane and placed in a mental institution. She was released after three weeks, but her son publicly defended the action. Her debts were paid and she was given an increased allowance, but she continued to attack Bulwer until his death in 1873, accusing him of personal violence, infidelity, and other forms of cruelty. She lived until 1882, moving from Taunton to Dulwich and from there to Upper Sydenham, where she lived as a recluse. After her death some letters to her from her husband were published in 1884 and then suppressed by Lord Lytton's successor in 1885. Louisa Devey, the editor of the letters, published a *Life of Rosina, Lady Lytton* in 1887. *See* Michael Sadleir, *Bulwer, a Panorama: Edward and Rosina 1803–36* (1931).

Burnett, Frances Hodgson, novelist and children's writer
(b. Manchester, 24 November 1849, d. Long Island, New York,
29 October 1924).

Frances Hodgson Burnett was the eldest daughter of Edwin Hodgson, a hardware merchant who died in 1853, and his wife Eliza Boone. The depression in Lancashire caused by the impact of the American Civil War on the textile industry and the difficulties of managing the business after Hodgson's death encouraged the family's emigration to Tennessee in 1865 to live with an uncle. Frances supported herself by writing stories for American magazines, although her use of English settings and Lancashire dialect was viewed with suspicion by editors. Her mother died in 1870 and in 1873 she married Dr Swan M. Burnett, of Knoxville, an eye and ear specialist. Her first son was born in 1874, and she continued to supplement the family income by her writing while her husband pursued his medical studies. *That Lass o' Lowrie's* (1877), her first novel, set in a Lancashire coal-mining town, was an unexpected success, selling 30,000 copies in England and more in America. Charles Reade paid her the dubious compliment of dramatizing it, piratically, as *Joan* in 1878. *Haworth's* (1879), also set in the English north, followed, and then two books with American settings, *Louisiana* (1880), and *A Fair Barbarian* (1881). *Through One Administration* (1883) was an ambitious attempt to deal with American politics. Her greatest success came with her first children's book, *Little Lord Fauntleroy* (1886), whose hero was based on her second son Vivian, much to his later embarrassment. It set a fashion for a particular kind of suit for boys, was made into a play, and earned its author a substantial income for the rest of her career. It was also criticized for its sentimentality and for the unrealistic perfection of its hero. Other children's books followed, of which the best known were *Sara Crewe* (1888), *A Little Princess* (1905), based on an earlier story, and *The Secret Garden* (1911), which was originally not intended as a children's novel. It had the distinction of presenting two thoroughly unattractive children who become self-reliant, unlike the stereotypes of nineteenth-century children's fiction. She published in all more than forty novels and several plays, of which *A Lady of Quality* (1896) was regarded as the best. Burnett's personal life was fraught. Her elder son Lionel died in 1890. She and her husband divorced in 1898 (he died in 1906), and in 1900 she impulsively married Stephen Townsend, an English doctor ten years her junior, whom she divorced the following year. She became a naturalized American in 1905, but travelled often between England and America. Her vigorous stance against the unauthorized English dramatizations of *Little Lord Fauntleroy* helped to bring about international copyright legislation in 1891. Her autobiography *The One I Knew Best of All* (1893) gives a vivid account of her youth. Her son Vivian quoted from her letters in his biography *The Romantick Lady* (1927). *See* Marghanita Laski, *Mrs. Ewing, Mrs. Molesworth and Mrs. Hodgson Burnett* (1950); Ann Thwaite, *Waiting for the Party: The Life of Frances Hodgson Burnett* (1974).

Burney, Charlotte, Sarah Harriet, and Susanna *see under* BURNEY, Fanny

Burney, Fanny (Frances, later d'Arblay), novelist (b. King's Lynn, Norfolk, 13 June 1752, d. 6 January 1840).

Fanny Burney, as she was known, was the third of the six children of Dr Charles Burney, organist and music historian, by his first wife Esther Sleepe, the granddaughter of a French refugee. After their mother's death in 1762 her two elder sisters were sent to school in Paris while Frances was kept at home. Her father's remarriage in 1766 and his increased social and professional activity in London left no time for teaching her. As a result she had no formal education. She was reported to be backward, and did not know her letters at 8. But she read voraciously and from the age of 10 began to write compulsively, in a variety of literary forms. On her 15th birthday she impulsively burnt all her manuscripts, a great heap of 'Elegies, Odes, Plays, Songs, Stories, Farces,—nay Tragedies and Epic Poems', as she later recorded, possibly under the influence of her stepmother, who persuaded her that she had wasted her time with frivolous pursuits. Within a few months she had begun her now famous journals, written 'for my Genuine & most private amusement', and continued one of the stories, 'Carolyn Evelyn', which became *Evelina*, published anonymously in three volumes in 1778. Her father's friends, who included Dr Johnson, Sir Joshua Reynolds, Edmund Burke, David Garrick, Mrs Thrale (later *Piozzi), and other members of the *Bluestocking Circle, enthusiastically welcomed the novel, as did the public at large. It went through four editions in rapid succession, and her reputation was established. *Cecilia* followed in 1782, its first edition of 2,000 selling out in three months. Elizabeth *Montagu joined her circle of admirers, and introduced her to Mary *Delany, who had recently been granted a house at Windsor by the King. Through these connections Frances was offered the position of Second Keeper of the Robes to the Queen in 1786. She accepted the post in the hope that it would improve her father's chances of preferment, but found court life trivial and irksome. In 1791 she asked for and was granted leave to resign. Her *Diary* of her later years 1778–1840 (published in 1842–6) gives a lively and detailed account of court life, just as the volumes which cover her earlier years 1768–78 (published in 1889) present an invaluable account of the Johnson circle. At the home of one of her sisters, near Mickleham, in Surrey, she was introduced to General Alexandre d'Arblay, a French refugee officer who had been an adjutant to General Lafayette. They were married in 1793, with her father's reluctant consent, and the following year, at the age of 42, she had a son. Her pension of £100 a year was scarcely adequate, and Madame d'Arblay, as she then became known, attempted a tragedy, *Edwy and Elgiva*, which was performed at Drury Lane in March 1795. Despite Sarah Siddons and John Philip Kemble in the title roles it failed after one night and was withdrawn. It was the only one of the eight plays which she wrote (four comedies and four tragedies) which was ever performed. An early satire on the Bluestockings, *The Witlings*, was suppressed on parental instructions. She published her third novel, *Camilla*, by subscription in 1796, Jane *Austen being among the subscribers. The novel was less highly regarded than her first two, but the proceeds provided enough money to build a cottage near Mickleham. The d'Arblays moved to France in 1802, where they settled until 1812. Frances then returned to England in order to prevent her son's conscription and nursed her father until his death in 1814. In the same year she published her last novel, *The Wanderer*, generally thought inferior to her other books, but a financial success. General d'Arblay's military rank was restored with the fall of Napoleon. The family returned permanently to England, where he died in 1818. Her last literary task was the preparation of *The Memoirs of Dr. Burney* for publication in 1832. These consisted largely of her own narrative with excerpts from her father's copious journals. (She subsequently burned twelve manuscript volumes to prevent further publication.) Her son predeceased her in 1837 and she died after an illness in 1840, aged 87. Her three best books, *Evelina*, *Cecilia*, and *Camilla*, chart the development of their young, inexperienced but intelligent heroines as they enter society and record the various levels of that society with a sharply satirical eye and an ear for dialogue. The first edition of her earlier journals, begun secretly before her 16th birthday, and covering the period 1768 to 1791, contained extracts from the journals of her sisters **Susanna,** later **Phillips** (1755–1800), and **Charlotte,** later **Francis** (1761–1838). Their half-sister **Sarah Harriet Burney** (1772–1844), the only child of Dr Burney's second marriage, published several successful novels, including *Clarentine* (1796), *Geraldine Fauconberg* (1808), and *Traits of Nature* (1812), plus collections of shorter stories. Charlotte's daughter Charlotte Francis Barrett (1786–1870) edited the first edition of her aunt's later journals (1842–6). A modern edition of *The Early Journals and Letters of Fanny Burney*, covering the period 1768–91, is in progress, ed. Lars E. Troide (1988–). *The Journals and Letters of Fanny Burney* 1791–1840 have been edited by Joyce Hemlow (12 vols., 1972–84). Joseph A. Grau has edited *Fanny Burney: An Annotated Bibliography* (1981). *The Complete Plays of Fanny Burney* are being edited by Peter Sabor *et al.* (1994–). *See* J. Hemlow, *The History of Fanny Burney* (1958); Winified Gerin, *The Young Fanny Burney: A Biography* (1961); Roger H. Lonsdale, *Dr. Charles Burney: A Literary Biography* (1965); Judy Simons, *Fanny Burney* (1987); Margaret Anne Doody, *Frances Burney: The Life in the Works* (1988); Katherine M. Rogers, *Frances Burney: The World of 'Female Difficulties'* (1991).

Burton, Isabel, Lady, travel writer (b. London, 20 March 1831, d. London, 22 March 1896).

Isabel Burton was the daughter of Henry Raymond Arundell, a member of an old Catholic family and a descendant of the sixth Baron Arundell of Wardour. (The first baron had been created a hereditary count of the Holy Roman Empire.) She was educated at a convent near Chelmsford, and later at Boulogne, where in 1851 she met the explorer and Arabic scholar Richard Burton. They met again in 1856 and became unofficially engaged, knowing that her parents would object to her marrying a non-Catholic. They married in 1861, without her parents' consent, but having obtained a dispensation for a mixed marriage from Cardinal Wiseman. Isabel Burton subsequently became her husband's companion, confidant, secretary, and amanuensis, and, as the *DNB* entry suggests, shared his life in travel and literature 'so far as a woman could'. She rode, and swam and fenced with him, and took a full part in his writing and publishing. She saw many of his books through the press and devised the method of issuing his translation of the *Arabian Nights* to private subscribers which ensured its financial success. She also arranged for an edition in six volumes without notes for household reading, an enterprise which resulted in a financial loss in 1887–8. Queen *Victoria, however, accepted the first copy printed. Burton encouraged her to write independently, and as a result she published two travel books, *The Inner Life of Syria* (1875) and *Arabia, Egypt, India* (1879). Other works were ascribed to her, including *How to Deal with the Slave Scandal in Egypt* (1881) and a translation of *Iracema the Honey-Lips: A Legend of Brazil* (1885). She devoted most of her energies to furthering her husband's career and, after his death, to preserving his memory. Her success in this respect was a matter of some controversy. Her two-volume *Life of Sir Richard Burton* (1893), though derived in part from autobiographical reminiscences dictated by Burton and from his private journals, was not approved of by the rest of his family. Her own autobiography *The Romance of Isabel, Lady Burton, Told in Part by Herself* (1897) was also thought to be a glamourized version of the truth. Burton left her his translation of the erotic Persian text *The Perfumed Garden*, on which he had been working for fourteen years, intending that it should provide an income for her. She was offered £6,000 by a publisher, but thought it unfit for publication and, in an article in the *Morning Post*, confessed to having burnt it in her garden. She was widely believed to have burnt other manuscripts and letters of Burton's as well. She was granted a civil-list pension in 1891. She died in 1896 and in her will requested that her body should be embalmed so that it could be kept by the side of her husband in the mausoleum tent in the Mortlake cemetery. *See The Romance of Isabel Lady Burton*, ed. W. H. Wilkins (1897).

Bury, Lady Charlotte (Susan Maria), novelist, poet, and diarist (b. London, 28 January 1775, d. London, 31 March 1861).

Lady Charlotte Bury was the youngest child of the fifth Duke of Argyll and Elizabeth Gunning, the daughter of an Irish landowner and widow of the sixth Duke of Hamilton. In her youth she was a society beauty with literary inclinations, and in 1796 married her impecunious cousin Colonel John Campbell, one-time MP for Ayr. Campbell died in 1809, leaving her with nine children. She obtained the post of Lady-in-Waiting to the Princess of Wales, later Queen Caroline, where she remained until 1815, and augmented her income by writing. In 1818, against her family's wishes, she married the Revd Edward John Bury, rector of Lichfield, by whom she had two daughters. She again began to supplement the family income by writing, producing a series of novels about high society, the so-called 'silver-fork novels'. The titles are self-explanatory: *Self-Indulgence* (1812), *Conduct is Fate* (1822), *Flirtation* (1827), *The Exclusives* (1830), *The Disinherited and the Ensnared* (1834), *The Devoted* (1836), *The Divorced* (1837), *The History of a Flirt* (1840). She was said to have received as much as £200 per novel at the peak of her career. Bury died in 1832, and, possibly for financial reasons, Lady Charlotte published anonymously the diary she had kept while Lady-in-Waiting to Queen Caroline, with the title *Diary Illustrative of the Times of George the Fourth* (1838). Despite the anonymity, the diary was attributed to her and the attribution was not denied. It was sympathetic to the Queen but also indiscreet, and charges of disloyalty and vulgarity were levelled at her. Perhaps because of this, the diary retained its popularity and was reissued in 1896 and again in 1908. She also edited two diaries by contemporaries, Catherine *Gore's *Memoirs of a Peeress* (1837) and Caroline Lucy Scott's *A Marriage in High Life* (1828). She continued to write fiction, including *The Manœuvring Mother* (1842), *The Lady of Fashion* (1856), and the posthumously published *The Two Baronets* (1864). She was known exclusively for her fiction and for the diary. Her *Poems on Several Occasions* (1797) went virtually unnoticed, as did her *Suspirium Sanctorum* (1826), a book of prayers, and *The Three Great Sanctuaries of Tuscany* (1833), a volume of verses in memory of her husband, with his illustrations. Despite her one-time financial success, she died impoverished at the age of 86. *See* W. M. Rosa, *The Silver-Fork School: Novels of Fashion Preceding Vanity Fair* (1936).

Butler, Lady Eleanor *see* LLANGOLLEN, Ladies of

Butler, Frances Anne *see* KEMBLE, Fanny

Butts, Mary Francis, novelist (b. near Poole, Dorset, 1890, d. Cornwall, 5 March 1937).

Mary Butts was the only daughter of Frederick John Butts, a naval captain, and his second wife Mary Jane Briggs. She grew up on the family estate Salterns, near Poole, a period recorded in her autobiography *The Crystal Cabinet* (1937). The sale of the estate after her father's death was a deeply felt loss which was frequently represented in her fiction. As a child she was closely attached to her brother Tony, although they were later estranged. His friend the novelist William Plomer caricatured her cruelly as Lydia Delap in *Museum Pieces* (1952). She went to St Leonard's School for Girls in St Andrews and then to Westfield College, London, which she left before taking a degree, possibly because of an involvement with a lecturer. She worked for a time in an East End Settlement and during the First World War moved in a circle which included Ezra Pound, H(ilda) D(oolittle), Richard Aldington, May *Sinclair, and Ford Madox Ford. In 1918 she married the poet and publisher John Rodker. They had a daughter the following year and she left them both shortly after to live with Cecil Maitland, a Scottish painter and writer with aristocratic connections and severe personal problems. She also began to write, publishing excerpts of her first novel, *Ashe of Rings*, about ritual, witchcraft, and the disruption of war, in the *Little Review* in 1919. Maitland and Butts moved to Paris, where they became friendly with *Bryher and the group surrounding the expatriate Americans Sylvia Beach and Djuna Barnes. Butts experimented with drugs, dabbled in black magic, drank to excess, and continued to write. Her stories and poems were published in the *Little Review*, the *Transatlantic Review*, and other magazines. Her first collection of stories, *Speed the Plough*, each of which dealt with manifestations of the unconscious, was published in 1923. Robert McAlmon's Contact Press published *Ashe of Rings* in 1925 and included some of her work in the *Contact Collection of Contemporary Writers* in the same year. *Imaginary Letters*, an epistolary novel about a young woman's love for a 'psychically sick' homosexual was published in 1928, illustrated by Jean Cocteau. The heroine's predicament was largely autobiographical, and a series of hopeless relationships with men who needed her but did not love her further complicated Butts's life after her separation from Cecil Maitland and his eventual death. In 1930 she returned to England and married the painter and cartoonist Gabriel W. Aiken. They separated in 1934. She published *The Death of Felicity Taverner* (1932) and two historical novels, *The Macedonian* (1933) and *Scenes from the Life of Cleopatra* (1935). A third, *Julian the Apostate*, remained unpublished. She wrote for Bryher's magazine *Life and Letters Today* and published another collection of stories, *Several Occasions* (1932). *Last Stories* were selected by Bryher and published posthumously. She died of a misdiagnosed ruptured appendix at 47. *See* Gillian Hanscombe and Virginia L. Smyers, *Writing for their Lives: The Modernist Women 1910–1940* (1987).

Byatt, A(ntonia) S(usan), novelist (b. Sheffield, 24 August 1936).

Antonia Byatt is the eldest of the four children of John Frederick Drabble, a circuit judge, and his wife Kathleen Marie Bloor. Like her sister the novelist Margaret *Drabble she was educated at the Mount School, York, where her mother had taught, and at Newnham College, Cambridge, where she took a first in English. She did postgraduate work at Bryn Mawr College in Pennsylvania, and research on Renaissance allegory at Somerville College, Oxford, before lecturing at the Central School of Art and Design, London, 1965–9, and then at University College London 1972–83. She married Ian Charles Rayner Byatt, an economist, in 1959 and had a daughter and a son (now deceased). They divorced in 1969 and she married Peter John Duffy, by whom she has two daughters. Her first novel, *Shadow of a Sun* (1964), about a teenager's relationship with a novelist father, was followed by *The Game* (1967), a story of sibling rivalry between two sisters, an Oxford don and a popular novelist. *The Virgin in the Garden*, published in 1978, was the first volume of a projected quartet chronicling the new Elizabethan age. A study of provincial life in the 1950s and a realist fiction, the novel is also rich in literary allusion and Renaissance iconography and has a double time scheme in which the main characters perform a neo-Elizabethan play in the grounds of a country house in Coronation year, 1953, while the prologue looks back from the perspective of 1968. Its sequel *Still Life* (1985) takes the same characters forward to 1980, the year of the Post-Impressionist exhibition in London. Byatt's most widely acclaimed work is the Booker Prize winning *Possession: A Romance* (1990), the interwoven narratives of the relationships of two Victorian poets and two twentieth-century academics engaged in researching them. *Angels and Insects* (1992), a pair of linked novellas, further displays her grasp of Victorian literature and culture. Byatt has also written a study of Iris *Murdoch (1965), with whom she has often been compared, and a book on Wordsworth and Coleridge (1970, repr. 1989). She has edited George *Eliot's *The Mill on the Floss* (1979) and her essays (1990) and has written introductions to the novels of Willa Cather. *Sugar and Other Stories* was published in 1987. She was a member of the Kingman Committee on the English Language (1987–8), and is an active member of the Society of Authors and of PEN. She was appointed CBE in 1990. In an interview in 1982 Byatt claimed to 'derive my sense of an order behind things from T. S. Eliot and Pound. I write the way I do from James via T. S. Eliot rather than from a line of women writers. . . . Literature has always been my way out, my escape from the limits of being female.' *See* Janet Todd (ed.), *Women Writers Talking* (1983).

Byrne, Charlotte *see* DACRE, Charlotte

c c c c c c c c c c c c c c c c

C

Caffyn, Kathleen *see under* NEW WOMAN

Caird, (Alice) Mona (Henryson) ('G. Noel Hatton'), novelist (b. Isle of Wight, 1858, d. 4 February 1932).

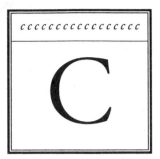

Mona Caird was the only daughter of John Alison, an inventor, and his wife Matilda Hector. She spent part of her childhood in Australia, an experience reflected in her first novel, *Lady Hetty* (1875), published anonymously when she was 17. In 1877 she married J. Alexander Henryson-Caird (d. 1921). They had one son. Under her masculine pseudonym G. Noel Hatton she published *Whom Nature Leadeth* (1883), a melodramatic novel, followed by *One that Wins* (1887), neither of which was particularly successful. *The Wings of Azrael* (1889) attracted more attention with its sensational plot in which the heroine stabbed her sadistic husband to death and then threw herself off a cliff. Caird's fervent anti-marriage position was made clear in the widely read *The Daughters of Danaeus* (1894), whose title derived from the women in classical mythology who were doomed to an eternity of drawing water in sieves in punishment for killing their husbands. Caird's contemporary heroine rebelled against the constraints of a modern English marriage but was ultimately defeated. Her treatise *The Morality of Marriage* (1897) expanded her views on the subject, some of which had earlier generated a heated correspondence in the *Daily Telegraph*. Other novels offered oblique criticism of marriage and the harm it could do women, as in *A Romance of the Moors* (1891) and *The Stones of Sacrifice* (1915). Caird also held strong anti-vivisectionist views, publicized in *A Sentimental View of Vivisection* (1895), *Beyond*

the Pale (1897), and *The Inquisition of Science* (1903). She travelled widely. The novel *The Pathway of the Gods* (1898), a fantasy, was set in Rome and she published a travel book, *Romantic Cities of Provence* (1906). Her last novel, *The Great Wave* (1931), gave scope to her penchant for mysticism, which was latent in most of her works. *See* Margaret M. Gullette's afterword to *The Daughters of Danaeus* (1989).

Caldwell, Anne *see* MARSH, Anne

Callander, Caroline Henrietta *see under* NORTON, Caroline

Cameron, Lucy Littleton *see under* SHERWOOD, Mary Martha

Campbell, Lady Charlotte Susan Maria *see* BURY, Lady Charlotte

Campbell, Gabrielle Margaret Vere *see* BOWEN, Marjorie

Carey, Rosa Nouchette ('Le Voleur'), novelist (b. Stratford-le-Bow, London, 1840, d. Putney, 19 July 1909).

Rosa Nouchette Carey was the eighth child and fourth daughter of William Henry Carey, a London ship broker, and his wife Maria Jane Wooddill (or Woodhill). She grew up in Hackney and was educated at home and then at the Ladies' Institute, St John's Wood, where Mathilde *Blind was also a pupil. They were close friends until a divergence in religious views (Carey embraced High Church principles) separated them. As a child Carey wrote plays and poetry, started a magazine, and entertained her siblings by telling them stories. The latter formed the basis of her first immensely successful novel, *Nellie's Memories* (1868), composed in her teens and written down much later. It sold more than 50,000 copies, and was regularly reprinted well into the twentieth century. Carey published forty-one novels between 1868 and her death in 1909, mainly wholesome stories with a moral, directed at young girls, their large sales attesting to their popularity. Among the most popular were *Wee Wifie* (1869), *Wooed and Married* (1875), and her best-received novel *Not like Other Girls* (1884), in which three daughters and their widowed mother turn to dressmaking after the death of their father, a situation with some autobiographical connections. Others included *Only the Governess* (1888), *Rue with a Difference* (1900), and her last, *The Sunny Side of the Hill* (1908). *Heriot's Choice* (1879) was originally published in Charlotte *Yonge's *Monthly Packet*. Her fiction as a whole shows the clear influence of Yonge, whose religious views she shared. Carey also wrote short stories, many of which were published by the Religious Tract Society, as well as serials for the *Girl's Own Paper* and a volume of biographies, *Twelve Notable Good Women of the Nineteenth Century* (1899). Under her pseudonym Le Voleur she produced a number of slightly racier titles: *By Order of the Brotherhood* (1895), *For Love of a Bedouin Maid* (1897), *In the Tsar's Dominions* (1899), and *The Champington Mystery* (1900). Rosa Carey remained unmarried, devoting herself to the care first of her widowed mother, then of various of her siblings and their children. She lived for thirty-nine years in Hampstead, and then in Putney, sharing her house for some of that time with Helen Marion Burnside, a children's writer. Mrs Henry *Wood was also a friend. *See* Helen C. Black, *Notable Women Authors of the Day* (1893); Jane Crisp (ed.), *Rosa Nouchette Carey (1840–1909): A Bibliography*, Victorian Fiction Research Guides 16 (1989).

Carlyle, Jane Welsh, poet and letter writer (b. Haddington, East Lothian, 14 July 1801, d. London, 21 April 1866.

Jane Baillie Welsh, as she was born, was the only child of Dr John Welsh, a country doctor, and his wife Jane Welsh (no relation), whose mother's family claimed descent from William Wallace. Her father's family in turn numbered John Knox among their ancestors. As a child she was both strong-willed and clever, insisted on learning Latin, and went to Haddington school, where Edward Irving, later the famous and controversial preacher, was a master. On her 10th birthday she burnt her doll on a funeral pyre in imitation of Dido, and at 14 she wrote a tragedy. She continued to write poetry for many years. Her father's death from typhus in 1819 was a severe blow which affected her health. Known as the 'flower of Haddington', she was not short of suitors, but retained her early affection for Irving, an affection apparently reciprocated, but from which a previous engagement forced him to extricate himself. He introduced her to Thomas Carlyle in 1821. Their mutual attraction was based on intellectual compatibility as well as affection, and their courtship, like their later marriage, was stormy. Despite the opposition of her mother, who regarded Carlyle as an ill-tempered atheist as well as a social inferior, they were married in 1826 and settled in Edinburgh. Carlyle's difficulty in finding publishers made their finances precarious and they withdrew to Jane's family farm at Craigenputtock in 1828, where their solitary life and the strains imposed by poverty took a toll on her already delicate health. Carlyle's irritability, caused in part by dyspepsia and by worry over his work, and Jane's penchant for uttering unpleasant truths exacerbated the tensions between them. In 1834 they moved to London, to a house in Cheyne Row, Chelsea, which was to remain their home until both their deaths. Jane Carlyle earned a considerable reputation as a hostess, known for her forthright opinions and acerbic wit. She entertained most of the eminent literary figures of the day, Tennyson, Browning, Dickens, Forster, Macready, Thackeray, and political *émigrés* like Mazzini and Cavaignac. She created a circle of friends of her own, apart from those of Carlyle, among them Geraldine *Jewsbury, who became her closest companion. She was a special favourite of Francis Jeffrey, to whom, as with her other intimates, she confided the misery created by Carlyle's bad temper and the periods of enforced isolation occasioned by his work. He kept her closely involved with his writing but was apparently insensitive to the solitariness of long periods of her life. She in turn grew jealous of his growing attachment to Lady Harriet Baring, Lady Ashburton, the wife of one of his friends, her resentment and hostility ceasing only at the latter's death in 1857. Her health oscillated in the easier decades of Carlyle's literary success in the 1850s and early 1860s. Some of her complaints were clearly psychosomatic, but in 1863 she was knocked down by a horse-drawn London cab. She died suddenly in April 1866 after rescuing a dog from an oncoming carriage. Reading the large collection of her intimate and revealing letters, many of them to friends as well as to himself, spurred Carlyle to write his *Reminiscences* in the summer of 1866 and through 1867, and to prepare the letters for publication. He then entrusted the letters and his memoir of her to his friend, the historian James Anthony Froude, leaving his ultimate intention unclear at his death in 1881. Froude's publication of the *Reminiscences* in 1881 and the *Letters and Memorials of Jane Welsh Carlyle* in 1883 created a furore, revealing as they did the tensions and jealousies between husband and wife. The suggestion that the marriage may have been unconsummated because of Carlyle's impotence was addressed directly in Froude's posthumous *My Relations with Carlyle* (1903), having become a popular talking point after the publication of the letters. Froude defended his right to publish the *Reminiscences* and letters against the charge that Carlyle had forbidden it 'without fit editing'. Irrespective of the disturbing revelations, Jane Carlyle remains one of the outstanding letter writers of the nineteenth century, her talents for observation and narrative and her wit leading frequently to the suggestion that she might have written novels. The letters offer a unique insight not only into her personality, and into an extraordinary relationship, but into the mid-Victorian world of letters. Rodger L. Tarr has edited *The Collected Poems of Thomas and Jane Carlyle* (1986). *See New Letters and Memorials of Jane Welsh Carlyle*, ed. A. Carlyle (1903); *The Collected Letters of Thomas and Jane Welsh Carlyle*, the Duke-Edinburgh edn., ed. C. R. Sanders, K. J. Fielding, C. de L. Ryals, *et al.* (1970–). As the edition is still incomplete it can be supplemented by collections by Leonard Huxley, *Jane Welsh Carlyle: Letters to her Family 1839–63* (1924); T. Scudder, *Letters of Jane Welsh Carlyle to Joseph Newbert 1848–62* (1931); T. Bliss, *Jane Welsh Carlyle: A New Collection of her Letters* (1950); A. and M. M. Simpson, *I Too am Here: Selected Letters of Jane Welsh Carlyle* (1977). For her poetry, see I. W. Dyer, *A Bibliography of Carlyle's Writings* (1928). *See also* Virginia * Woolf,

'Geraldine and Jane', *The Common Reader: Second Series* (1932); E. Hardwick, *Seduction and Betrayal* (1974); Norma Clarke, *Ambitious Heights: Writing, Friendship, Love: The Jewsbury Sisters, Felicia Hemans and Jane Welsh Carlyle* (1990).

Carr, Philippa *see* HIBBERT, Eleanor

'Carrington' (Dora de Houghton Carrington), artist, diarist, and letter writer (b. Hereford, 29 March 1893, d. Ham Spray, Hampshire, 11 March 1932).

Carrington, as she called herself from her student days onward, was the daughter of Samuel Carrington, a retired railway builder, and his much younger wife Charlotte, who had been governess to one of his nieces. She went to school in Bedford and then between 1910 and 1913 to the Slade School of Art, London, with painters Mark Gertler, Stanley Spencer, Roger Fry, and others, where she developed a crippling sense of her own inferiority. 'It's rather maddening to have the ambition of Tintoretto and to paint like a mouse,' she once commented. Through Virginia and Leonard *Woolf she met and fell in love with Lytton Strachey, with whom she lived from 1917. He in turn encouraged her marriage to Ralph Partridge, whom he also loved and with whom they set up a *ménage à trois* in 1921, first at Tidmarsh Mill, near Pangbourne, and then at Ham Spray, which Strachey bought from the royalties from *Queen *Victoria*, published in 1921. Carrington became entangled in various love affairs, including one with Gerald Brenan, while at the same time slavishly devoting herself to Strachey, decorating, entertaining, and acting as housekeeper. When he was dying of cancer she unsuccessfully attempted suicide and then shot herself six weeks after his death. She did illustrations for the Woolfs' publications, but otherwise published nothing during her lifetime. She left a collection of poetry, short fiction, and drama at her death, together with the letters and diaries for which she has become best known. She was an idiosyncratic and engaging letter writer. Virginia Woolf read her letters enthusiastically and parodied her punctuation. The letters and diaries are important for their self-revelations as well as for their insight into the Bloomsbury world in which Carrington moved. They reflect a woman's attitude to her work, to creativity, and to the conflicts these created within her. An exhibition of her work was held in 1970. David Garnett edited her *Letters and Extracts from her Diaries* (1970), which contains a memoir by her brother Noel Carrington, who edited her *Paintings, Drawings and Decorations* (1978). *See* Gretchen Gerzina, *Carrington* (1989); Mary Ann Caws, *Women of Bloomsbury: Virginia, Vanessa, Carrington* (1990).

Carroll, Susanna *see* CENTLIVRE, Susanna

Carswell, Catherine Roxburgh, novelist and biographer (b. Glasgow, 27 March 1871, d. London, 18 February 1946).

Catherine Carswell was the second of the four children of George MacFarlane, a textile exporter, and his wife Mary Anne Lewis. Both her grandfathers were Scottish ministers who supported the formation of the United Free Church of Scotland, and she was brought up in an atmosphere of rigorous Calvinism with an emphasis on good works. She attended schools in Glasgow and studied music at the Frankfurt Conservatorium for two years. In 1904, after a short courtship, she married Herbert Jackson, an artist whose increasing mental instability led to the breakdown of the marriage. In 1908 she made legal history by securing an annulment on the grounds of insanity. She had been attending lectures in English literature at Glasgow University (women were not then admitted to degrees) and in 1907 became a reviewer and drama critic for the *Glasgow Herald*. The most important event in her early life occurred in 1914, when she met D. H. Lawrence, of whom she became a close friend and colleague. She was dismissed from the *Herald* for a favourable and extremely perceptive review of *The Rainbow* in the same week in 1915 that the novel itself was withdrawn from sale. In the same year she married Donald Carswell, a writer and civil servant, by whom she had a son. A daughter by her first husband died of pneumonia in 1913. She and Lawrence planned to write a novel together, which did not materialize, but they exchanged manuscripts of her first novel, *Open the Door!*, and *Women in Love*. The frank acknowledgement of women's sexuality in the former was a demonstration of Lawrence's influence. *Open the Door!*, published in 1920, was a *Bildungsroman* whose heroine sought to free herself from a stifling family environment. It won the Melrose Prize for a first novel and was followed by *The Camomile* (1922), about a woman struggling to become a writer. Carswell made her name with her first biography, *The Life of Robert Burns* (1930), and followed it by the book for which she was best known, *The Savage Pilgrimage* (1932), a life of Lawrence which professed to challenge what she termed the 'destructive hagiography' of John Middleton Murry's *Son of Woman* (1931). The first edition of the book was withdrawn from circulation after a writ for libel was served by Murry, who then countered with *Reminiscences of D. H. Lawrence* (1933), which contained a reply to Carswell's book. *The Tranquil Heart* (1937), a life of Boccaccio, was the last book she completed. Her husband was killed in a black-out accident in 1940, and she spent the remainder of the war working on her autobiography *Lying Awake*, which was published posthumously by her son in 1950, and which contained some of her poems and a selection of letters. She died in London in 1946.

John Carswell explored the literary world of his parents in *Lives and Letters* (1978). *See* John Carswell's memoir in the reprint of *The Savage Pilgrimage* (1982), and his introd. to the reprint of *Open the Door!* (1986).

Carter, Angela, novelist and essayist (b. Eastbourne, Sussex, 17 May 1940, d. London, 16 February 1992).

Angela Carter was the daughter of Hugh Alexander Stalker, a journalist, and his wife Olive Farthing. She grew up in a south Yorkshire mining village, her mother's birthplace, where the family had moved to escape wartime bombing. They later returned to south London, where she went to a girls' grammar school at Streatham and then worked as a journalist on the *Croyden Advertiser.* In 1960 she married Paul Carter, an industrial chemist, and moved to Bristol. She read English at Bristol University from 1962 to 1965, specializing in medieval literature, from which she developed an interest in myth and folklore. She also read anthropology, sociology, and psychology on the side. She wrote her first novel, *Shadow Dance* (1966), in the summer vacation of her second year. Her next book, *The Magic Toyshop* (1967), won the John Llewellyn Rhys Memorial Prize and established her as a leading practitioner of the 'magic realism' school, combining as it did realism with extravagant fantasy, nightmarish dislocation, and *Gothic horror. Her third novel, *Several Perceptions* (1968), won the Somerset Maugham Award. *Heroes and Villains* (1969), with its post-atomic holocaust setting, *Love* (1971), *The Infernal Desire Machine of Doctor Hoffman* (1972), and *The Passion of the New Eve* (1977) variously offered strongly feminist perspectives on Western patriarchy and capitalism, while at the same time combining pastiche, black humour, eroticism, and the macabre. Carter spent two years in Japan in the 1970s, an experience of cultural isolation which she described in a series of essays in *New Society*, later collected in *Nothing Sacred* (1982). She also held creative writing fellowships at Sheffield and Brown universities. She was divorced in 1972 and later settled in London with Mark Pearce, by whom she had a son in 1982. Her collection of stories *The Bloody Chamber* (1979), with its original and erotic rewriting of fairy-tales, won the Cheltenham Festival of Literature Award. Her trenchant 'exercise in cultural history' *The Sadeian Woman* (1979), a reconsideration of women's response to sexual violence and repression, brought critical acclaim and generated controversy. *Nights at the Circus* (1984), a joint winner of the James Tait Black Memorial Prize, presented a fantastic late nineteenth-century *New Woman with the ability to fly. Her story 'The Company of Wolves', a reworking of the tale of Little Red Riding Hood, was made into a film (1984) for which she co-authored the screenplay, as she did for the film version of *The Magic Toyshop* (1986). Her last work, *Wise Children*, about indecorous old age, was published in 1992. Carter also wrote radio plays, several books for children, and collections of short stories, including *Fireworks: Nine Profane Pieces* (1974) and *Black Venus* (1985). She died of lung cancer. *Expletives Deleted: Selective Writings* was published posthumously (1992). *See* Ellen Cronan Rose, in *The Voyage In: Fictions of Female Development*, ed. Elizabeth Abel, Marianne Hirsch, and Elizabeth Langland (1983); Paulina Palmer, in *Women Reading Women's Writing*, ed. Sue Roe (1987); Avis Lewallen, in *Perspectives on Pornography: Sexuality in Film and Literature*, ed. Gary Day and Clive Bloom (1988); Elaine Jordan, in *Plotting Change: Contemporary Women's Fiction* (1990); Lorna Sage, *Women in the House of Fiction: Post-War Women Novelists* (1992).

Carter, Elizabeth, poet, translator, and letter writer (b. Deal, Kent, 16 December 1717, d. London, 19 February 1806).

Elizabeth Carter was the eldest daughter of the Revd Dr Nicholas Carter, perpetual curate of Deal and a preacher at Canterbury Cathedral, and of Margaret Swayne, of Bere Regis, Dorsetshire. Her mother lost her fortune in the South Sea Bubble fiasco and died of a consequent decline when Elizabeth was 10. She was educated in ancient and modern languages by her father and had difficulty in keeping up with the vigorous pace and intensity of the tuition. She took snuff and green tea in order to read late at night and the severe headaches which resulted plagued her for the rest of her life. She spoke French fluently and taught herself Italian, Spanish, and German, and later Portuguese and Arabic. She was also interested in astronomy, ancient and modern history, and ancient geography. Her father was a friend of Edward Cave, the proprietor of the *Gentleman's Magazine*, where she published her first work in 1734 at the age of 16, under the pseudonym Eliza. Cave published her *Poems upon Particular Occasions* in 1738 and her translations from the French of Crousaz's *Examination of Mr. Pope's Essay on Man* (1738) and of Algarotti's Italian handbook *Sir Isaac Newton's Philosophy Explain'd for the Use of the Ladies* (1739). Through the *Gentleman's Magazine* she became friendly with Samuel Johnson and contributed two essays to the *Rambler* (nos. 44 and 100). Four of her poems were included in the publisher Robert Dodsley's *Collection of Poems* (1758). Her 'Ode to Wisdom' was published without acknowledgement by Richardson in *Clarissa*, an oversight for which he later apologized. Her major work, however, was a translation of *Epictetus*, from the Greek, begun in 1749 and published by subscription in 1758. She had been encouraged in this by her friend Catherine *Talbot and given practical assistance by the latter's mentor Thomas Secker, Bishop of Oxford. The subscription raised nearly £1,000. Her friends persuaded her to publish *Poems on Several Occasions* in 1762, her last publication. She was a central figure in literary circles, her friends including Elizabeth *Montagu, Elizabeth *Vesey, William Pulteney, Earl of Bath, Lord Lyttleton, and later Hannah *More and Joanna *Baillie. She was supportive of fellow women writers, helping with the posthumous publication of Catherine Talbot's *Works* (1772) and reading the work of younger women who aspired to a literary career. Her views about women were essentially conservative, however, and she disapproved of the radical ideas of Mary *Wollstonecraft and Charlotte *Smith. She never married, although her name was linked with several eminent figures, but chose rather to act as her father's housekeeper in their house at Deal until his death in 1774. Despite the *bluestocking image, she enjoyed domesticity, hence Dr Johnson's compliment that she 'could make a pudding as well as translate Epictetus'. Mrs Montagu gave her a small annuity after her husband's death, as did the family of the Earl of Bath, and she lived in modest comfort in apartments in Clarges Street until her death in 1806. Her nephew edited her *Memoirs* (1807) and published two collections of her letters (1809 and 1817). *See* Patricia Meyer Spacks, in *The Private Self: Theory and Practice of Women's Autobiographical Writings*, ed. Shari Benstock (1988); Sylvia H. Myers, *The Bluestocking Circle* (1990).

Cartland, (Mary) Barbara (Hamilton) (also 'Barbara McCorquodale'), romantic novelist (b. Edgbaston, Birmingham, 9 July 1901).

Barbara Cartland is the daughter of Major Bertram Cartland of the Worcestershire Regiment and his wife Mary Scobell, both of whom came from wealthy backgrounds. Her father's family's loss of money in 1903 followed by his death in the First World War led to a reduction in the family's living standards. She nevertheless went to Malvern Girls' College and then Abbey House in Hampshire, 'came out' as a débutante in 1919, and was presented at court in 1925. In 1927 she married Alexander McCorquodale, the son of a printing magnate. They had a daughter, but divorced in 1933. In 1936 she married his cousin Hugh McCorquodale, by whom she had two sons. She began her writing career as a gossip columnist for the *Daily Express* in 1923. Her first novel, *Jig-Saw* (1925), was supposedly written while bored on a family holiday in the country. Her novels depict the London social life she herself relished, with vulnerable, virginal heroines attracted to older, wealthy, and more experienced men. Many are set in the nineteenth century. She appears in the *Guinness Book of Records* as the most prolific living author, with over 300 titles and sales of 390 million. She writes by dictating to a secretary and claimed an average of twenty-three books a year at her peak. Some have been written as Barbara McCorquodale. She has also written biographies on, among others, Elizabeth, Empress of Austria, Diane de

Poitiers, Josephine, Empress of France, advice books on marriage and sex, and books on food and health. She was active in the St John's Ambulance Brigade and the ATS during the Second World War, and has campaigned on behalf of gypsies. There are five volumes of autobiography: *The Isthmus Years* (1943), *The Years of Opportunity* (1947), *I Search for Rainbows* (1967), *We Danced All Night: 1919–1929* (1971), and *I Seek the Miraculous* (1978). She was appointed DBE in 1991. *See* H. Cloud, *Barbara Cartland: Crusader in Pink* (1979); Rosalind Brunt, in *Popular Fiction and Social Change*, ed. Christopher Pawling (1984); G. Robyns, *Barbara Cartland* (1985).

Cary, Lady Elizabeth, Viscountess Falkland, playwright and translator (b. Burford, Oxfordshire, *c.*1585, d. London, October 1639).

Elizabeth Cary was the only child and heiress of a wealthy Oxford lawyer, Lawrence Tanfield, later Lord Chief Baron of the Exchequer, and his wife Elizabeth Symondes. As a child she was precocious, teaching herself French, Spanish, Italian, Latin, Hebrew, and Transylvanian. Despite parental restrictions she read through the night, borrowing from servants to buy forbidden candles. She completed French and Latin translations, including Ortellius' *The Mirror of the World*, and took issue with Calvin's *Institutes of Religion.* At the age of 15 or 16 she married Henry Cary, then a professional soldier, who left her with his parents while he completed his military service abroad. She wrote plays secretly, after her mother-in-law disapproved of her constant reading. *Mariam, the Fair Queen of Jewry*, a Senecan tragedy based on Josephus' *Jewish Antiquities*, the first of many plays about Herod and his wife Mariamne, was completed by 1602 but not published until 1613, making Cary the first woman playwright in England to publish a full-length, original play. (Mary Herbert, Countess of *Pembroke, had published *Antonie*, an adaptation of Robert Garnier's *Marc-Antoine*, in 1592.) On Henry Cary's return, Elizabeth became a dutiful wife and mother, bearing eleven children and mortgaging the estate settled on her at her marriage to further her husband's career, whereupon her father disinherited her. She satisfied her craving for an intellectual life by reading theology, and as a result secretly converted to Roman Catholicism in 1626. Henry Cary, now Viscount Falkland, a member of the Privy Council, and Lord Chief Deputy of Ireland, separated from her, taking custody of the children, and stripping her of virtually all personal possessions. She lived in poverty until the Privy Council ordered her husband to support her. She sought solace in writing, producing *The History of Edward II* (1627), religious poems, and lives of the saints. She translated Catholic polemical works, including Cardinal Perron's *The Reply to the King of Great Britain* (1630), which was publicly burned. Two of her daughters remained loyal to her, and she defied her husband to kidnap two of her sons in order to take them to the Continent as Catholics. They eventually took orders, and several of her daughters became nuns. She and her husband were reconciled on his return to England but continued to live separately. She died of a lung disease in 1639. Her son Lucius Cary, second Viscount Falkland (1610–43), became an influential Royalist and the centre of a circle of liberal thinkers based at Great Tew, in Oxfordshire. Elizabeth Cary's reputation rests on *Mariam*, written when she was little more than 17, and reflecting ambivalent attitudes to wifely duty, marital fidelity, and an independent intellectual life for women. John Marston and Michael Drayton both dedicated works to her. A manuscript biography, by one of her daughters, either Anne (1615–71) or Mary (1622–93), was edited by Richard Simpson as *The Lady Falkland: Her Life* (1861), and formed the basis of two later biographies, Georgiana *Fullerton's *Life of Elizabeth, Lady Falkland* (1883) and Kenneth B. Murdock, *The Sun at Noon* (1939). *See* Sandra K. Fischer, in *Silent but for the Word: Tudor Women as Patrons, Translators and Writers of Religious Works* ed. Margaret P. Hannay (1985); Elaine V. Beilin, *Redeeming Eve: Women Writers of the English Renaissance* (1987); Betty S. Travitsky, in *Ambiguous Realities: Women in the Middle Ages and Renaissance*, ed. Carole Levin and Jeanie Watson (1987); Tina Krontiris, in *The Renaissance Englishwoman in Print: Counterbalancing the Canon*, ed. Anne M. Haselkorn and Betty S. Travitsky (1990); Margaret Ferguson, in *Tradition and the Talents of Women*, ed. Florence Howe (1991).

Cavendish, Lady Jane *see under* NEWCASTLE, Margaret Cavendish, Duchess of

Cavendish, Margaret *see* NEWCASTLE, Margaret Cavendish, Duchess of

Centlivre, Susanna, née Freeman ('Susanna Carroll'), playwright (b. Whaplode, near Holbeach, Lincolnshire, *c.* 1669, d. London, 1 December 1723).

According to most accounts, Susanna Centlivre's parents both died before she was 12. Her father William Freeman was a dissenter and a Parliamentarian who endured persecution after the Restoration in 1660 and fled to Ireland. Her mother Ann Marham was a gentleman's daughter from Norfolk. Susanna was self-taught and clever and stories of her youthful exploits proliferate, including that of running away to become an actress when she was 16 and entering Cambridge disguised as a boy. She was twice married at an early age, first to a nephew of Sir Stephen Fox, and the second time to an army officer named Carroll. Her first play, *The Perjur'd Husband*, a tragi-comedy, was produced at Drury Lane in 1700, when she was 31. She went on to write a total of sixteen plays and three farces, as well as some poetry and a series of letters, earning considerable literary celebrity and becoming one of the most successful dramatists of her day. She was friendly with dramatists like Nicholas Rowe, George Farquhar, Colley Cibber, and Steele, and her known Whiggish views earned her a mention in *The Dunciad.* Her correspondence with the Huguenot historian and journalist Abel Boyer was published in his *Letters of Wit, Politicks, and Morality* (1701). Her early plays were signed 'S. Carroll', but others were published anonymously because her publishers feared prejudice against women writers. She joined a theatrical company, touring provincial towns and performing occasionally in her own plays. It was supposedly at Windsor that she attracted the attention of Joseph Centlivre, chief cook to Queen Anne, whom she married in 1707. Her best plays were comedies, notably *The Gamester* (1705), *The Busie Body* (1709), the name of one of whose characters, Marplot, became synonymous with an interfering busybody, *The Wonder: A Woman Keeps a Secret* (1714), which provided Garrick with one of his best parts, and *A Bold Stroke for a Wife* (1718), in which the Quaker character Simon Pure gave rise to the phrase 'the real Simon Pure'. Several of her plays were translated into French and German and there was even a Danish translation of *The Busie Body.* Throughout her career she contributed poetry and prose pieces to various periodicals and collections, including (probably) a poem on the death of Dryden included in *The *Nine Muses* (1700), a preface to the *Poems* of Sarah Fyge *Egerton (1703), a pastoral on the death of Nicholas Rowe (1719), a series of anti-Jacobite letters in the *Weekly Journal* (1720), and a separately published poem on the accession of George I (1715). She died in Buckingham Court, Spring Gardens, London, which had been her home since 1712. *See* 'Life', prefaced to *The Works of the Celebrated Mrs. Centlivre* (3 vols., 1760–1); J. W. Bowyer, *The Celebrated Mrs. Centlivre* (1952); F. P. Lock, *Susanna Centlivre* (1979); Douglas R. Butler, in *Curtain Calls: British and American Women and the Theater 1660–1820*, ed. Mary Anne Schofield and Cecilia Macheski (1991).

Challans, Eileen Mary *see* RENAULT, Mary

Chapone, Hester, née Mulso, poet and prose writer (b. Twywell, Northamptonshire, 27 October 1727, d. Hadley, Middlesex, 25 December 1801).

Hester Chapone was the only daughter of Thomas Mulso, a wealthy gentleman farmer, and his wife Hester Thomas. Her three brothers, to whom she was closely attached, became clergymen, and her mother's brother was successively Bishop of Peterborough, Salisbury, and Winchester. Hester's literary precocity was resented and discouraged by her mother. After the latter's death and while acting as her father's housekeeper, she taught herself French, Latin, and Italian as well as music and drawing. She contributed to Johnson's *Rambler* and made the acquaintance of Elizabeth *Carter, to whose translation of Epictetus she contributed a prefatory ode (1758). Through other acquaintances she joined the circle of admirers surrounding Samuel Richardson, who called her 'a little spitfire', a compliment to her powers of conversation. Through Richardson she met a lawyer, John Chapone, whom she married in 1760, despite her father's opposition. Chapone died nine months later, and although it was alleged that the marriage had been unhappy, her friends testified to her sincere and prolonged grief. She remained a widow for the next forty years, engaging in a modestly successful writing career. Her best-known work, *Letters on the Improvement of the Mind* (1773), was written for a niece, and dedicated to Elizabeth *Montagu. It proposed a course of self-education for women, in history, science, geography, and philosophy, as well as advocating the traditional virtues of politeness, economy, and religion. It went through twenty-five editions by 1844 in Britain, France, and America. John Hawkesworth had published her 'Story of Fidelia' in *The Adventurer* (1753) and Johnson used a stanza of her then unpublished 'To Stella' to illustrate a quatrain in his dictionary. Some of these earlier pieces were collected in *Miscellanies in Prose and Verse*, published in 1775. A two volume collection of her *Works* was published in 1786 and another, containing many of her letters and a memoir, was published posthumously by her family in 1807. *See* J. Cole, *Memoirs of Mrs. Chapone, from Various Authentic Sources* (1839).

Charke, Charlotte, playwright, novelist, and autobiographer (b. 1713, d. London, 6 April 1760).

Charlotte Charke was the youngest of the twelve children of Colley Cibber (1671–1757), the playwright and later Poet Laureate, and his wife Katherine Shore. She was sent to a school run by a Mrs Draper in Westminster, where she learnt Latin and Italian plus music and dancing. She already knew French. As a child she enjoyed the masculine activities of hunting, shooting, and riding, frequently dressed as a boy, and eschewed feminine accomplishments. When about 16 she married Richard Charke, an actor and theatre musician, by whom she had a daughter. They separated after a year, and to support herself she joined the Drury Lane company and later Fielding's company at the Haymarket, where she acted in a variety of roles, including male leads. She also acted in her own comedy *The Carnival; or Harlequin Blunderer* in 1735. She responded to her dismissal from Drury Lane in the same year for supposed immorality with a splenetic play, *The Art of Management; or Tragedy Expelled*, most copies of which were confiscated by the theatre manager. Relations were restored through her father's intervention, but by this time her family had washed its hands of her. Charke's death around 1738 had freed her to marry for a second time, one John Sacheverell, but this marriage too was short-lived. She undertook a variety of jobs, including valet, waiter, managing a puppet show, selling sausages, and running a public house. *Tit for Tat; or Comedy and Tragedy at War* (1743), written for puppet theatre, was probably by her. She regularly wore masculine dress and as 'Mr Brown', accompanied by her daughter and a 'Mrs Brown', toured provincial theatres as a strolling player for over nine years. In 1755 she published, in parts, her *Narrative of the Life of Mrs. Charlotte Charke, Youngest Daughter of Colley Cibber*, which contained a detailed account not only of her personal life, but of the provincial theatre of the time. Contemporary accounts of her later life underline its squalor and further descent into poverty. She died in London in 1760, shortly after her last stage appearance. She wrote a novel, *The History of Henry Dumont and Mrs. Charlotte Evelyn* (1756), and three short novellas, *The Mercer; or Fatal Extravagance* (1755), *The Lover's Treat; or Unnatural Hatred* (*c.*1758), and *The History of Charles and Patty* (n.d.). Her *Narrative* was published in full in 1775. Maureen *Duffy paraphrased parts of it in her novel *The Microcosm* (1966). *See* N. Cotton, *Women Playwrights in England* c.*1363–1750* (1980); Pat Rogers, in *Sexuality in Eighteenth-Century Britain*, ed. Paul-Gabriel Bouce (1982); Lynne Friedl, in *Sexual Underworlds of the Enlightenment*, ed. G. S. Rousseau and Roy Porter (1988).

Charles, Elizabeth, née Rundle, novelist (b. Tavistock, Devon, 2 January 1821, d. London, 28 March 1889).

Elizabeth Charles was the only child of John Rundle, MP for Tavistock, where she grew up. She was educated at home by governesses and tutors and wrote poetry from an early age, some of which was read by Tennyson and the historian J. A. Froude. Her first published story, 'Monopoly', was inspired by Harriet *Martineau's *Illustrations of Political Economy*. The Oxford Movement was another formative influence on her early life. Her first book, the didactic *Tales and Sketches of Christian Life in Different Lands and Ages*, was published in 1850. The following year she married Andrew Paton Charles, a barrister and the owner of a soap and candle factory at Wapping. They moved to London, where they were joined by her parents, who had lost their fortune. She was offered £400 by the editor of a Scottish magazine to write her best-known book, *The Chronicles of the Schonberg-Cotta Family* (1863). This life of Martin Luther as told by the children of a local printer who eventually prints Luther's texts was one of the most popular religious novels of the nineteenth century. Its unexpected success taught her never again to sell a copyright. *The Diary of Mrs. Kitty Trevylyan* (1864), which followed it, was based on the lives of the Methodists Whitfield and Wesley. *Against the Stream* (1873), about an evangelical revival, contained a tribute to William Wilberforce. Other successful titles included *The Bertram Family* (1876), which showed the influence of Charlotte *Yonge, and *Joan the Maid* (1879), based on the story of Joan of Arc. The deaths of her father in 1864 and of her husband (from consumption) in 1868 left her with no financial resources, but she was able to live comfortably on her royalties. She was active in several London charities and founded a 'home for the dying' or hospice in Hampstead in 1885. Sixteen of her books were published by the Society for the Promotion of Christian Knowledge. She also wrote several hymns. *Our Seven Homes: Autobiographical Reminiscences* (ed. M. Davidson) was published in 1896, the year of her death.

Charlesworth, Maria Louisa, children's writer (b. Blakenham Parva, near Ipswich, 1 October 1819, d. Nutfield, Surrey, 16 October 1880).

The only daughter of a hard-working clergyman, the Revd John Charlesworth, rector of Flowton, in Suffolk, and later of a London parish, Maria Charlesworth helped her father in his work with the poor from the age of 6. After his death in 1864 she lived for a while with her clergyman brother in Limehouse and then set up a ragged school and a mission in Bermondsey. She drew on her youthful experiences in her first book, *The Female Visitor to the Poor* (1846), which went through various editions and translations. A fictionalized version, *Ministering Children* (1854), directed at the juvenile market, sold over 170,000 copies during her lifetime and became one of the best known of the 'reward books' offered as Sunday school prizes and on similar occasions. It was translated into French, German, and Swedish, and various parts were published separately. She wrote a sequel in 1867. Other improving fiction included *Oliver of the Mill* (1876) and *The Old Looking-Glass; or Mrs. Dorothy Cope's Recollections of Service* (1877), but it was for *Ministering Children* that she was best known. A semi-invalid towards the end of her life, Charlesworth died at 61 at Nutfield, in Surrey, where she made her permanent home after her father's death. *See* Gillian Avery, *Nineteenth-Century Children* (1965) and *Childhood's Pattern* (1975); M. C. Cutt, *Ministering Angels* (1978).

'Charlotte Elizabeth' *see* TONNA, Charlotte Elizabeth

Cholmondeley, Mary, novelist (b. Hodnet, Shropshire, 8 June, 1859, d. London, 15 July 1925).

Mary Cholmondeley was the eldest daughter and third child of the Revd

Richard Hugh Cholmondeley, rector of Hodnet, and of Emily Beaumont. Her grandmother Mary Heber was the sister of Bishop Reginald Heber, the hymn writer. Mary Cholmondeley suffered from ill health for most of her life. She never married, endured an unhappy love affair, and spent most of her life in the company of her parents, helping her father in his parochial duties until his retirement in 1896, after which the family moved to London. She was later to regard her childhood and youth as a period of unmitigated repression. She wrote her first novel when she was 17, but her first published work was *The Danvers Jewels*, a sensational detective novel which owed its inspiration to Wilkie Collins, and which appeared in the magazine *Temple Bar* in 1887. She was introduced to Richard Bentley, the publisher of *Temple Bar*, by her friend Rhoda *Broughton. A sequel, *Sir Charles Danvers*, was published in 1889, and her third novel, *Diana Tempest*, dedicated to her sister Hester, who wrote poetry and who died aged 22, in 1893. But the novel for which she was best known was *Red Pottage* (1899), which was sharply critical of middle-class hypocrisies, particularly contemporary religious practice, and also contained some forceful comments on the exploitation of women. The novel was denounced from a London pulpit, which no doubt enhanced its popular success both in England and America. Mary Cholmondeley wrote several other novels, including *The Devotee: An Episode in the Life of a Butterfly* (1897), described by R. L. Wolff in *Nineteenth-Century Fiction: A Bibliographical Catalogue* (1981–6) as a 'Freudian case-history . . . observed with clinical detachment', *Moth and Rust* (1902), and *Prisoners* (*Fast Bound in Misery and Iron*) (1906), on which she worked for three years and which was regarded as libellous by those who were portrayed in it. She also published a series of reminiscences, *Under One Roof: A Family Record* (1918). The novelist Stella *Benson was her niece, the daughter of her younger sister Caroline. *See* Percy Lubbock, *Mary Cholmondeley: A Sketch* (1928); Jane Crisp, *Mary Cholmondeley 1859–1925: A Bibliography*, Victorian Fiction Research Guides 6 (1981).

'Cholmondely, Anne' *see* ARNIM, Elizabeth von

Christie, Dame Agatha (Mary Clarissa), later Mallowan ('Mary Westmacott'), crime novelist, playwright, and short story writer (b. Torquay, Devon, 15 September 1890, d. Wallingford, Oxfordshire, 12 January 1976).

Agatha Christie was the youngest child and second daughter of Frederick Alvah Miller, an American of independent means who died during her early childhood, and his wife Clarissa Margaret Boehmer. She had no formal schooling, not even a governess, but was taught instead by her mother, who believed that no child should read until the age of 8. Despite the maternal injunction, she read voraciously, composed stories in her head, and published a poem in the local newspaper when she was 11. She studied piano and singing in Paris but her temperamemt was unsuited to public performance and her voice not strong enough. She returned to Torquay, where in 1914 she rejected an intended suitor and at two days' notice married Archibald Christie, who was about to join the Royal Flying Corps. They had one daughter. She worked as a VAD (Voluntary Aid Detachment) nurse during the war and, observing Belgian refugees in Torquay, invented Hercule Poirot, her retired Belgian policeman hero who first appeared in *The Mysterious Affair at Styles* (1920). The success of that book encouraged a steady output until *The Murder of Roger Ackroyd* (1926), with its surprise ending, caused a minor sensation and was acknowledged as a classic of modern detective fiction. Christie was recognized as a major contributor to the genre. Her husband's infidelity at this time and her mother's death led her to stage a much-publicized disappearance in 1928, followed by a divorce. In 1930 she married Max Mallowan, an archaeologist, with whose professional career and interests she became closely associated for the rest of her life. Several of her novels, including *Death Comes as the End* (1945), reflect the archaeological life, and *Come and Tell me how you Live* (1946) was a personal account of expeditions undertaken with her husband. Christie was now in her most productive period, bringing out one or more books every year. Her best work is considered to be the twenty-five novels produced up to the end of the Second World War. Two titles written during this period, *Curtain: Hercule Poirot's Last Case* and *Sleeping Murder*, were deliberately saved, to be published at the end of her career in 1975 and 1976. The latter contained the last appearance of the intuitive spinster Miss Marple, Christie's other main detective, who was first introduced in short stories and then in the well-known *Murder at the Vicarage* (1930). Her strengths as a detective writer were her narrative skill and her ingenuity. She was a mistress of variations on the 'least likely person' theme, the trailing of red herrings, and the planting of clues. Characterization was slight, she relied mainly on dialogue, and physical description was minimal. She rarely strayed from what she knew best, comfortable upper middle-class English life. Christie had considerable success as a playwright, most notably with *Witness for the Prosecution* (1953), adapted from a story of the same title, and *The Mousetrap* (1952), adapted from her story 'Three Blind Mice', whose West End run has exceeded that of any other play. Other stage adaptations include *Ten Little Niggers* (1943), retitled *Ten Little Indians* (New York, 1944), and *Murder on the Nile* (1943), from *Death on the Nile* (1937). Between 1930 and 1956 she wrote six romantic novels under the pseudonym Mary Westmacott, another as Agatha Christie Mallowan, and a book of children's stories, *Star over Bethlehem* (1965). The sales of her more than sixty novels and thirty collections of short stories were so phenomenal that her publishers and literary agent claimed to be unable to reach a total. Her works were translated into 103 languages, and film and television rights were sold for record sums. She was appointed DBE in 1971 and died at her home in Oxfordshire in her 86th year. *An Autobiography* was published posthumously in 1977. *See* Patricia D. Maida and Nicholas Spornick, *Murder she Wrote: A Study of Agatha Christie's Detective Fiction* (1982); Janet Morgan, *Agatha Christie* (1984); D. Sanders and L. Lovallo (ed.), *The Agatha Christie Companion* (1985); Marion Shaw and Sabine Vanacker, *Reflecting on Miss Marple* (1991); Alison Light, *Forever England: Femininity, Literature and Conservatism between the Wars* (1991).

Chudleigh, Mary, Lady, poet (b. Winslade, Devon, 1656, d. Ashton, Devon, 1710).

Mary, Lady Chudleigh, was the daughter of Richard Lee of Winslade, Devon. At the age of 17 she was married to the son of Sir George Chudleigh of Ashton, also in Devon. He succeeded to his father's title in 1691. They had two sons and a daughter who died early, but the marriage was not happy. Life at Ashton was lonely and without intellectual stimulus, although she corresponded with Mary *Astell, with the Cambridge Platonist John Norris of Bemerton, and with the poet Elizabeth *Thomas. She greatly admired and was influenced by Astell's work and in 1701 published *The Ladies' Defence* in response to a wedding sermon preached by the Nonconformist John Sprint, which advocated total subordination of women to their husbands. The *Defence* is in the form of a verse debate in which 'Melissa' argues with three male speakers, Sir John Brute, Sir William Loveall, and a parson, about women's education and wifely duties. The prefatory address to the work was signed 'M——y C——'. Writing and reading filled her life and provided a creative solace. In 1703 she published *Poems on Several Occasions. The Ladies' Defence* was added to the second edition (1709) without her permission. The volume went through two posthumous editions in 1713 and 1720. *Essays upon Several Subjects in Prose and Verse* (1710) was a miscellany of religious and moral writing. Her correspondence as Melissa to Elizabeth Thomas's Corinna was published with the *Poetical Works* of Philip, Duke of Wharton (vol. ii, 1731), and in R. Gwinnett, *Pylades and Corinna* (vol. ii, 1732). She died in 1710, having suffered for some time with rheumatism. Manuscripts of unpublished plays and translations, and of her poems, are in the Houghton Library, Harvard, and the Huntington Library. Some of her poems were included in **Poems by Eminent Ladies* (1755).

Churchill, Caryl, playwright (b. London, 3 September 1938).

Caryl Churchill is the only child of Robert Churchill, a political cartoonist. Her mother was an actress. She lived in Montreal between the ages of 10 and 17 because of her father's work and went to Trafalgar School. In 1955 the family returned to England. She read English at Lady Margaret Hall, Oxford, where her first three plays were produced, *Downstairs* (1958), *Having a Wonderful Time* (1960), and *Easy Death* (1962). In 1961 she married David Harter, a barrister, by whom she had three sons. While at home with her children in the 1960s she wrote radio plays 'about the bourgeois middle-class life and the destruction of it'. The plays were Brechtian in form and often used songs as well as documentary and historical material, a technique which she developed in her work for the theatre and television. *The Ants* (1962) established a predominant theme, the oppression of the individual by a capitalist and sexist society. In 1972 she was commissioned to write a play for the Royal Court. The result was *Owners* (1972), a savage play about property ownership, power, and exploitation, in which the property owner and exploiter is a woman. As resident dramatist at the Royal Court in 1974–5 she wrote *Objections to Sex and Violence*, which contrasts two sisters, one a putative feminist, the other a suburbanite. In the mid-1970s Churchill began to involve herself in workshop productions with two repertory companies. *Light Shining in Buckinghamshire* (1976), about seventeenth-century millennialists, was written for the Joint Stock Company. *Vinegar Tom*, written in the same year and based on seventeeth-century witch-hunts, was produced with the feminist touring company Monstrous Regiment. Both were overtly political plays, the former employing dramatized documentaries on the merits of freedom and democracy, the latter combining contemporary songs with historical material about the persecution of women. *Cloud Nine* (1979) was also written for Joint Stock. It explores sexual politics by juxtaposing Victorian colonial Africa in the 1880s with a London park in the 1970s. Cross-sex casting and the fact that characters age by twenty-five years while the play moves forward by a hundred serve to underline the farcical nature of gender roles, the changes in sexual morality, and the links between colonial, sexual, and class repression. *Top Girls* (1982), probably her best-known play, brings together successful women in history with a 1980s newly promoted business woman and then counterpoints her with her working-class sister and her abandoned, slightly retarded daughter. *Softcops* (1984), with an all-male cast in contrast to the all-female cast of *Top Girls*, was written in 1978 after reading Foucault's *Discipline and Punish* (1977), and later revised. It is set in nineteenth-century France and explores contemporary ideas about state control. *Fen* (1983), set in rural East Anglia, was written with

Joint Stock and based on an actual murder case. *Serious Money* (1987) is a play about greed, adventurously written in couplets, which incorporates a scene from Thomas Shadwell's *The Volunteers; or The Stock-Jobbers* (1692) to comment on 1980s speculators and the ethics of high finance. Other plays include *A Mouthful of Birds*, written with David Lan, about women, possession, and violence, which takes Euripides' *The Bacchae* as its starting-point, and *Ice Cream* (1989), about the interrelated lives of an American husband and wife and an English brother and sister. Churchill once described herself as combining 'a fairly strong political commitment and an antipathy to capitalism with a fairly wobbly theoretical grasp'. Her later work has concentrated more on issues of gender and class power. She has written an introduction to her collected *Plays One* (1985). *Plays Two* was published in 1990. *See* Phyllis R. Randall (ed.), *Caryl Churchill: Casebook* (1988); Geraldine Cousin, *Churchill the Playwright* (1989); Enoch Brater (ed.), *Feminine Focus: The New Women Playwrights* (1989); Amelia Howe Kritzer, *The Plays of Caryl Churchill: Theatre of Empowerment* (1991).

Clarke, Frances Elizabeth *see* GRAND, Sarah

Clarke, Mary (Victoria) Cowden, Shakespearian scholar, critic, and novelist (b. London, 22 June 1809, d. Genoa, 12 January 1898).

Mary Cowden Clarke was the eldest daughter of the eleven children of musician and composer Victor Novello and his wife Mary Hehl. Eminent artists and writers, including Charles and Mary *Lamb, Keats, and Leigh Hunt, frequented the family home and Mary and her siblings grew up in a thriving cultural environment. Mary Lamb gave her lessons in Latin and in reading poetry. Afterwards she was sent to a school in Boulogne. She became a governess for a short while but abandoned it due to ill health. In 1828 she married the scholar and critic Charles Cowden Clarke (1787–1877), a friend of her father's and thirty-two years her senior. Mary had begun to contribute to periodicals, including Hone's *Table Book*, before her marriage. In 1829 she began her major work, the *Concordance to Shakespeare*, which was eventually published in eighteen monthly parts in 1844–5. It superseded existing concordances and remained the standard work until the end of the century. She pressed ahead with her interest in popularizing Shakespeare, publishing a collection of *Shakespeare Proverbs* in 1848 and a three-volume series of tales, *The Girlhood of Shakespeare's Heroines*, in 1851–2. The latter were designed to emphasize desirable character traits in young women, using the heroines as examples. She also wrote several works of fiction, including *Kit Bam's Adventures* (1849), moralizing tales for children illustrated by George Cruikshank, and two adult novels, *The Iron Cousin* (1854) and *A Rambling Story*

(1874). She edited the *Musical Times*, to which she was also a contributor, between 1853 and 1856, and was an active participant in the amateur theatricals organized by Dickens and others to raise money for what later became the Shakespeare Birthplace Trust. In 1856 the Cowden Clarkes moved permanently to Italy, living first at Nice, and then at Genoa. Mary published *World-Noted Women; or Types of Womanly Attributes* (1858), an edition of Shakespeare (1860), and a biography of her father (1864). She and her husband together prepared an annotated cheap edition of Shakespeare published by Cassell in weekly numbers and completed in 1868. *The Shakespeare Key: Unlocking the Treasures of his Style* (1879) was devised as a companion to the *Concordance*. They also wrote *Recollections of Writers* (1878), which contained letters and memoirs of their extensive literary friendships with Keats, Leigh Hunt, Douglas Jerrold, the Lambs, and Dickens. Charles Cowden Clarke died in Italy in 1877. Mary survived him by twenty-one years, wrote a biographical sketch which was privately printed in 1887, and published her own autobiography *My Long Life* in 1896, the year before she died. See Richard D. Altick, *The Cowden Clarkes* (1948); Robert Gittings's edn. of *Recollections of Writers* (1969).

'Cleeve, Lucas' *see under* NEW WOMAN

Clifford, Lady Anne, diarist and biographer (b. Skipton Castle, Yorkshire, 30 January 1590, d. Brougham Castle, Westmorland, 22 March 1676.

Anne Clifford was the only surviving child of George Clifford, the third Earl of Cumberland, a naval commander and buccaneer, and his wife Lady Margaret Russell, daughter of the second Earl of Bedford. She was tutored by the poet Samuel Daniel, who addressed verses to her, and was twice married, in both cases with social advantage and personal unhappiness. By her first husband Richard Sackville, later Earl of Dorset, she had three sons who died in infancy and two daughters. In 1630, six years after his death, and after a severe attack of smallpox, she married Philip Herbert, fourth Earl of Pembroke and Montgomery. There were no children of this marriage, and Herbert died in 1650. Her father's death in 1605 initiated an extensive legal battle undertaken by her mother and later by Anne herself to regain his estates, which had been left to his brother. Both her husbands opposed her in this ambition, which was eventually realized in 1643. She relished her inheritance, and, as the *DNB* records, 'her passion for bricks and mortar was immense'. She restored six castles and seven churches, endowed schools and hospitals, and engaged in numerous charitable activities. From 1643, as if released by the success of her legal battle, she began to write her 'Great Books of the Records of Skipton Castle', an extensive manuscript which was an amalgam of family history, autobiography, and the biographies of her parents. The portion dealing with her own life and that of her parents was published in 1916, edited by J. P. Gilson. Part of her extensive diary, to which she contributed until she died, was edited with an introduction by V. *Sackville-West, a descendant, in 1923. Anne Clifford had a reputation for learning and formidable intellect. In a fulsome funeral sermon, published in 1677, Edward Rainbow, Bishop of Carlisle, claimed that 'her penetrating wit soared up to pry into the highest mysteries' and quoted John Donne's remark that 'she knew well how to discourse of all things, from predestination to slea-silk'. *See* George Williamson, *Lady Anne Clifford, Countess of Dorset, Pembroke and Montgomery* (1922, 2nd edn, 1967); Martin Holmes, *Proud Northern Lady: Lady Anne Clifford 1590–1676* (1975).

Clifford, Ethel *see under* CLIFFORD, Lucy

Clifford, (Sophia) Lucy, novelist (1853–21 April 1929).

Lucy Clifford was born in the West Indies, the daughter of John Lane, a well-known Barbadian. In 1875 she married William Kingdon Clifford, a brilliant and youthful Cambridge mathematician and philosopher who was then professor of applied mathematics at University College London. They had two daughters. Clifford's intellectual interests were broadly based. He was a prominent member of the Metaphysical Society, and their home became a meeting-place for a varied circle of friends, including eminent members of the scientific community, as well as George *Eliot, Leslie Stephen, and Henry and William James. Clifford died suddenly of tuberculosis in 1879, leaving his wife with the sole care of their young family. Various of her literary acquaintances, including George Eliot and Mary Elizabeth *Braddon, encouraged her to write. *Anyhow Stories* (1882), a book for children, was followed in 1885 by the controversial and successful *Mrs. Keith's Crime*, the story of a widowed and dying mother who kills her only surviving child to prevent her being left alone. The solitary and struggling woman was a familiar figure in Clifford's fiction. Other novels included *Love Letters of a Worldly Woman* (1891), *Aunt Anne* (1892), the story of a woman of 68 who falls in love with and marries a young man of 27 which Arnold Bennett pronounced her most precious novel, *A Wild Proxy* (1893), *A Flash of Summer* (1895), *The Getting Well of Dorothy* (1904), *Sir George's Objection* (1910), and *The House in Marylebone* (1917). She also wrote several plays, including *The Likeness of the Night* (1900), produced at the St James's Theatre 1901, *A Long Duel* (1901), *The Searchlight*, produced in Manchester in 1910 by Annie Horniman, the theatre patron and manager, *Hamilton's Second Marriage*

(1907), and *A Woman Alone* (1914), devised from a novel originally published in 1901. Her daughter **Ethel Clifford** also wrote novels. *See* Leon Edel, *Henry James: The Master* (1971); Robert Lee Wolff, *Sensational Victorian: The Life and Fiction of Mary Elizabeth Braddon* (1979).

Clive, Caroline, née Meysey-Wigley (Mrs Archer Clive, 'V'), novelist (b. Brompton Green, London, 24 June 1801, d. Whitfield, Herefordshire, 13 July 1873).

Caroline Clive was the second daughter and co-heiress of Edmund Meysey-Wigley, a wealthy Worcestershire landowner, and of Anna Maria Watkins Meysey. An illness left her lame at the age of 3, and she was therefore excluded from the normal activities of childhood and adolescence. At the relatively late age of 39 she married the Revd Archer Clive, rector of Solihull in Warwickshire, a handsome and cultivated clergyman, and the son of the MP for Hereford. They had two children. Mrs Clive's first work, a volume of poetry published in 1840 as *IX Poems by V,* was favourably reviewed by H. N. Coleridge in the *Quarterly Review,* among others. A series of volumes, also by V, followed, *I watched the Heavens* (1842), *The Queen's Ball* (1847), *The Valley of the Rea* (1851), and *The Morlas* (1853). But Caroline Clive is best remembered for one remarkable novel, *Paul Clifford* (1855), the sympathetic portrait of a man who murders his wife in order to marry his first love. In the course of the complicated plot, sometimes regarded as a precursor of the *sensation novels of the 1860s, Clifford not only escapes punishment, but succeeds in emigrating, in the care of his daughter by his second wife, and her husband. Clive followed *Paul Clifford* with a less polished and more moralistic sequel, *Why Paul Clifford Killed his Wife* (1860), and then wrote *John Greswold* (1864), a fictionalized autobiography generally regarded as a failure. Clive suffered a stroke while travelling on the Continent in 1865, and died in 1873 as a result of a macabre accident in which her dress was set on fire while she was writing in her boudoir. Eric Partridge edited *IX Poems by V* (1928), with a biographical introduction, and Mary Clive compiled extracts from her diary in 1949. *See* A. Sergeant (ed.) *Women Novelists of Queen Victoria's Reign* (1897); Eric Partridge, 'Mrs. Archer Clive', *Literary Sessions* (1932, repr. 1970).

Clive, 'Kitty' (Catherine), playwright (b. 1711, d. Twickenham, Middlesex, 1785).

Catherine, or 'Kitty', Clive, as she was popularly known, was the daughter of William Raftor, a well-connected Irish lawyer from Kilkenny who lost his property as the result of his support for James II. He settled in London and married a Miss Daniels, from a prosperous metropolitan family. The family was large, and Kitty's education scanty as a result. A good voice and innate theatrical presence brought her to the attention of Colley Cibber, then manager of Drury Lane. He cast her in a series of comic roles, particularly those of chambermaids, and she quickly rose to a position of eminence on the London stage in a theatrical career which lasted for over forty years. About 1733 she married George Clive, a barrister. The marriage resulted in an amicable separation soon after, although Kitty's name was never linked with anyone else. Generous and impulsive, she used her earnings liberally in the support of her family, particularly her brother James. She also engaged in several celebrated theatrical quarrels, with Theophilus Cibber, who wanted to cast his wife Susannah in a role which she wanted, with David Garrick, on many occasions, although they remained friends, and with the management of Drury Lane and Covent Garden whom she accused of operating a cartel, in *The Case of Mrs. Clive submitted to the Publick* (1744). Her brief career as a playwright began at the end of her stage career when she wrote an afterpiece, *The Rehearsal; or Bays in Petticoats*, for a benefit in 1750. The play was a spoof on female playwrights, in which the main character, the playwright Mrs Hazard, played by Kitty Clive, wants to write a play for the famous actress Mrs Clive. Published in 1753, it remained a popular afterpiece, and was produced as late as 1762. Many of the points made in jest, exploiting some of the clichés about women playwrights, were those made in savage earnest in *The *Female Wits*, the anonymous satire of 1696 against Delarivier *Manley, Mary *Pix, and Catharine *Trotter. Clive went on to write several other afterpieces for her own benefits, *Every Woman in her Humour* (1760), *The Island of Slaves* (1761), which is now thought likely to be hers, and *The Sketch of a Fine Lady's Return from a Rout* (1763), expanded into *The Faithful Irishwoman* (1765). After her retirement from the stage, Horace Walpole gave her a small house near Strawberry Hill at Twickenham, where she lived until her death. *See* Percy Fitzgerald, *The Life of Mrs. Catherine Clive* (1888).

Cobbe, Frances Power, journalist and feminist (b. Dublin, 4 December 1822, d. Hengwrt, North Wales, 5 April 1904).

Frances Power Cobbe was the fifth child and only daughter of Charles Cobbe, an Irish landowner, and his wife Frances Conway. The family were strongly attached to the Evangelical wing of the Church of England and counted five archbishops and a bishop among their connections. Frances was educated at home, and then at an expensive but ineffective school at Bristol. She learned some Greek and mathematics from a local clergyman and read widely in history, astronomy, and architecture. She disliked the social life of a county family and began to question the tenets of conventional religion. After her mother's death in 1847 she ceased regular attendance at church and family prayers and in 1855 published her *Essay on Intuitive Morals*, which set out her own position on religion and morals. It also caused a serious rift with her father. After his death in 1857 she left the family home, which had passed to her eldest brother, and set out on a series of travels in Europe and the East. Travel became one of her passionate interests, and *Italics* (1864) was the result of six visits to Italy. In 1858 she became associated with Mary Carpenter and her work with the Ragged Schools movement in Bristol. Further philanthropic work with sick and unemployed girls crystallized her interest in women's rights. In 1862 she read a paper to the Social Science Congress advocating the admission of women to university, published as *Female Education and how it would be Affected by University Examinations*. She joined the women's suffrage committee and worked on the married women's property committee. She wrote a series of influential pamphlets on violence to women, including *Wife Torture* (1878), which proposed that assault should be grounds for legal separation. This influenced the Matrimonial Causes Act of the same year. *Criminals, Idiots, Women and Minors* (1868) argued that women's economic dependence made it possible for men to go on abusing their wives. Yet her lectures *The Duties of Women* (1881) were highly conservative, advocating that the roles of wife and mother should make all other interests subordinate. Cobbe's other main interest was anti-vivisection, which occupied her attentions from the 1870s onward, and possibly deflected her energies from women's rights. She helped to found the Anti-Vivisection Society in 1875 and then in 1898 the British Union for the Abolition of Vivisection. *Darwinism in Morals and Other Essays* (1872), reprinted from her journalism, was an influential publication. A woman of limited means, she financed many of her activities through her earnings from writing, contributing regularly to the *Echo* between 1868 and 1875 and to the *Standard* and editing the *Zoophilist*. Cobbe lived with her friend Mary Lloyd from 1860 onwards and the two retired to Wales in 1884 on the strength of a legacy. She published an autobiography in 1894. *See The Life of Frances Power Cobbe by Herself* (1894); Jo Manton, *Mary Carpenter* (1976); Barbara Caine, *Victorian Feminists* (1992).

Cockburn, Catharine *see* TROTTER, Catharine

Colegate, Isabel (Diana), novelist (b. 10 September 1931).

Isabel Colegate is the daughter of Sir Arthur Colegate, a one-time MP, and his wife Lady Winifred Mary Worsley. She went to a boarding school in Shropshire and then to Runton Hill School, Norfolk, which she left at 16 in order to write. She worked as a literary agent for the publisher Anthony Blond and in 1953 married Michael Briggs. They have three children. Blond published her first novel, *The Blackmailer*, in 1958. Colegate's fiction anatomizes English society, its obsession with class and with the aristocracy, and the social upheavals caused by two world wars. *The Blackmailer*, *A Man of Power* (1960), and *The Great Occasion* (1962), which were reissued as *Three Novels* (1983), are set during the Second World War and its aftermath and depict aristocratic alliances with new sources of wealth. *Statues in a Garden* (1964) and *The Shooting Party* (1980) reflect the disintegration of the Edwardian social fabric on the eve of the First World War. *The Shooting Party* won the W. H. Smith Literary Award and was filmed in 1985. The 'Orlando Trilogy' (*Orlando King* (1968), *Orlando at the Brazen Threshhold* (1971), *Agatha* (1973)) loosely adapts the Oedipus myth and moves through the 1930s and the inter-war period to the 1950s and the Suez Crisis. Other books include *A Glimpse of Sion's Glory* (1985), a collection of short stories, and *The Summer of the Royal Visit* (1991). She became a fellow of the Royal Society of Literature in 1981.

Coleridge, Mary ('Anodos'), poet and novelist (b. London, 23 September 1861, d. Harrogate, Yorkshire, 25 August 1907).

Mary Coleridge was the daughter of Arthur Duke Coleridge, Clerk of the Assize on the midland circuit, and his wife Mary Anne Jameson. The great-great-niece of Samuel Taylor Coleridge, she was educated at home, where there were frequent literary visitors, and began to write verses and stories at an early age, encouraged by her father's friend the poet William Johnson Cory (1823–92), who became her tutor. She contributed to the *Monthly Packet* and other magazines and in 1893 published her first novel, *The Seven Sleepers of Ephesus*, which was praised by Robert Louis Stevenson, but went virtually unnoticed by the critics. *Fancy's Following* (1896), a book of poems published by Oxford University Press at the instigation of Robert Bridges, had more success, and *Fancy's Guerdon*, a selection with some additions, was published the following year. Both appeared under a pseudonym. *The King with Two Faces* (1897), a historical romance based on the assassination of Gustavus III of Sweden, established her reputation and went through ten editions by 1908. Other novels, mostly historical, included *The Fiery Dawn* (1901), based on the Duchesse de Berri, *The Shadow on the Wall* (1904), and *The Lady on the Drawing-Room Floor* (1906). She wrote for the *Monthly Review*, the *Guardian*, the *Cornhill Magazine*, and, from 1902, the *Times Literary Supplement*. She also devoted much of her time to teaching working women both in her own home and at the Working Women's College. Mary Coleridge never married. She died suddenly of appendicitis in 1907, a month before her 46th birthday, and just after finishing a short *Life of Holman Hunt* (1908). Over 200 of her *Poems New and Old* were published in 1907. Further poems were added in a new edition in 1954. It is as a poet that she is now remembered. Two of her sonnets, 'True to myself am I' and 'Go in the deepest, darkest dead of night', have been frequently anthologized. Many of her lyrics have been seen to anticipate twentieth-century poetry in their preoccupation with dreams, psychic states, and the problems of identity. Her poem 'The Other Side of the Mirror', which deals with self-alienation, is the focus of an extended discussion in Sandra Gilbert and Susan Gubar's *The Madwoman in the Attic* (1979). *Non Sequitur*, a collection of prose sketches, was published in 1900 and *Gathered Leaves*, a posthumous collection of stories and essays, which also included letters and fragments from her diaries, in 1910. *See* her *Collected Poems*, ed. T. Whistler (1954); Robert Bridges, *Collected Essays*, v (1931); Sandra Gilbert and Susan Gubar, *The Madwoman in the Attic: The Woman Writer and the Nineteenth-Century Literary Imagination* (1979).

Coleridge, Sara, poet, editor, and translator (b. Greta Hall, near Keswick, Cumberland, 22 December 1802, d. London, 3 May 1852).

The daughter of Samuel Taylor Coleridge and his wife Sara Fricker, Sara Coleridge grew up in a literary environment, with her father's friends and colleagues, particularly Southey and Wordsworth, close at hand. She married her cousin Henry Nelson Coleridge in 1829. She was fluent in Latin and French as well as other languages, and in 1821 translated from Latin Martin Dobrizhöffer's *Account of the Abipones*, which her father pronounced 'unsurpassable'. She translated the memoirs of the Chevalier Bayard from the French in 1825. Her *Pretty Lessons in Verse for Good Children* (1834) went through several editions, but her most important original work was *Phantasmion* (1837), a fairy-tale with lyrics. She and her husband jointly undertook the task of editing S. T. Coleridge's unpublished work, which she continued after H. N. Coleridge's death in 1843. Her edition of the *Poems* was published in 1844, the *Notes on Shakespeare* in 1849, and *Essays on his Own Times* in 1850. Their joint edition of *Biographia Literaria* appeared in 1847 and she published a new edition of the *Poems* in 1852 with her brother Derwent Coleridge. Sara Coleridge was a woman of formidable intellect, with a firm grasp of contemporary issues in psychology, philosophy, and theology. Like her father she suffered the affliction of an addiction to opium in her later years. She was a friend of Macaulay and the Carlyles and appears with Dora Wordsworth and Edith Southey in Wordsworth's poem 'The Trias' (1828). Her *Memoirs and Letters* were edited by her daughter in 1873. *See* E. L. Griggs, *Coleridge Fille: A Biography of Sara Coleridge* (1940); Virginia *Woolf, *The Death of the Moth and Other Essays* (1942); Bradford Keyes Mudge, *Sara Coleridge: A Victorian Daughter: Her Life and Essays* (1989).

Collier, Jane *see under* FIELDING, Sarah

Collier, Mary, poet (b. near Midhurst, Sussex, 1690?, d. *c.* 1762).

The title-page of Mary Collier's first published work described her as 'a WASHER-WOMAN, at Petersfield in Hampshire'. She was the daughter of 'poor but honest parents' who taught her to read, but she was not sent to school, probably because of the early death of her mother. After her father died in 1720 she moved to Petersfield, where, she recorded, 'my chief employment was Washing, Brewing and such labour, still devoting what leisure time I had to Books'. A later comment that 'I had learn'd to write to assist my memory' suggests that her first poems were memorized rather than transcribed. The publication in 1736 of Stephen Duck's *Poems on Several Occasions*, and in particular his well-known 'The Thresher's Labour' prompted her to reply to his unflattering portrait of rural working women. As a result she was encouraged to publish her poems. *The Woman's Labour: An Epistle to Mr. Stephen Duck*, was published in 1739, and gave a vivid picture of the rigours of women's work both in the fields and in the home. The prefatory advertisement expressed the hope that 'the Novelty of a Washer-Woman's turning poetess, will procure her some readers'. The third edition in 1740 was accompanied by a statement signed by nine Petersfield residents vouching for the authenticity of the poems, which suggests that working-class women poets were usually received with suspicion. Collier continued to work as a washerwoman until the age of 63, then ran a farmhouse until she was 70, when she retired 'to a Garret' in Alton, as 'an Old Maid'. Her *Poems on Several Occasions* (1762) secured local subscribers and added some new work, including an 'Elegy upon Stephen Duck', written in response to his suicide in 1756, and 'An Epistle to an Exciseman, who Doubted her being the Author of the Washerwoman's Labour'. It also contained prefatory 'Remarks of the Author's Life, drawn by herself'. A later edition of *The Poems of Mary Collier* (n.d. [1765?]) was published at Petersfield. *See* Donna Landry, *The Muses of Resistance: Laboring-Class Women's Poetry in Britain, 1739–1796* (1990).

Collins, An, religious poet, (fl. 1653).

The only source of biographical information about this seventeenth-century poet comes from autobiographical hints in 'To the Reader', the 'Preface', and 'The Discourse' of her *Divine Songs and Meditacions* published in London in 1653, only one original copy of which survives. It was reprinted by the Augustan Reprint Society in 1961. From this it is hinted that An Collins was a celibate, middle-aged woman who had been ill since childhood and who had from an early age read and then written her way, if not to health, then to some form of serenity. She turned, she reveals, first to 'profane histories' like Spenser's *Shepheardes Calendar*, then to the writing of religious poetry and to the exposition of 'divine truth', finding in religion and in a life of seclusion a serenity which she could not have reached in a world torn by civil war. Despite her withdrawal, the political and religious ferment of her age is not excluded from her writing. Seemingly Royalist and anti-Calvinist in her sympathies, she argues for the re-establishment of order and authority in both Church and State and calls on God to provide the only source of unity in families divided by the war. Her *Divine Songs*, many of which are imitations of the Psalms, used a variety of stanza forms and metres and drew on biblical and conventional religious imagery. Some may have been intended to be set to music. Her poems, the 'offspring of my mind', are, she says, 'a fruit most rare | That is not common with every woman | That fruitful are'. *See* Elaine Hobby, *Virtue of Necessity: English Women's Writing 1649–1688* (1988).

Collyer, Mary, novelist and translator (1716/17–1762/3).

Mary Mitchell, as she was born, married Joseph Collyer the elder (d. 1776), a compiler and translator and the son of a London bookseller. Their son, also Joseph (1748–1827), became a well-known engraver. Her translation of Marivaux's *La Vie de Marianne* as *The Virtuous Orphan; or The Life of Marianne* (1742) showed the strong influence of Samuel Richardson, and was reissued several times and also pirated. She published another translation, *Memoirs of the Countess de Bressol* (original unknown), in 1743 and in 1744 her best-known work, *Felicia to Charlotte: Being Letters from a Young Lady in the Country to her Friend in Town*, a sentimental novel about a young Londoner who discovers the delights of love in the country. A second edition in 1749 added another volume in which the heroine has a child, and the novel in part parodied the conventions of romantic fiction. It also bore the hallmarks of Rousseau's ideas on nature and theories of education and brought Collyer to the attention of *bluestockings Elizabeth *Montagu, Elizabeth *Carter, and Catherine *Talbot, who approved of the fact that she wrote to support her family. Collyer later published a popular translation of Salomon Gessner's *The Death of Abel* (1761) which went through twenty-seven editions by 1786 and another nineteen by 1845. Her translation of Klopstock's *Messiah*, incomplete at her death, was finished by her husband (1763–72). *See* Jane Spencer, *The Rise of the Woman Novelist: From Aphra Behn to Jane Austen* (1986).

Colville, Elizabeth *see* MELVILLE, Elizabeth

Compton-Burnett, Ivy, novelist (b. Pinner, Middlesex, 5 June 1884, d. London, 27 August 1969).

Ivy Compton-Burnett was the eldest of the seven children of James Compton

Burnett, a homeopathic doctor, and his second wife Katharine Rees. The surviving children of Dr Compton Burnett's first wife, who died in 1892, did not get on with their stepmother, nor she with them. Mrs Compton-Burnett (who added the hyphen) became a difficult and demanding head of the family after her husband's death in 1901. The large, often divided families of Compton-Burnett's novels, with their emotional tensions, tyranny, and power struggles, were clearly based on her own family. She was educated at Addiscombe College ('for the daughters of gentlemen') at Hove, in Sussex, where the family moved in 1892, and briefly at Howard College, Bedford. She then read classics at Royal Holloway College (now part of the University of London), where she took a second. After she left Royal Holloway her mother insisted that she act as governess to her four younger sisters. Following her mother's death in 1911, she herself became a tyrannical and insensitive head of the family, causing such resentment that her sisters refused to allow her to share a new London home they set up in 1915. Various other psychological blows left their mark in her twenties. Her brother Guy, to whom she was strongly attached, died of pneumonia in 1905. Noel, who replaced him in her affections, was killed on the Western Front in 1916. Her two youngest sisters died of overdoses of sedatives in 1917 and she herself nearly died as a result of a flu epidemic in 1918. In 1919 she established herself in a flat in London with Margaret Jourdain, an art historian and an expert on antique furniture, with whom she lived until the latter's death in 1951. She had begun to write in Hove, during the dreary period of governessing. *Dolores* (1911), her first novel, was untypical, and she later claimed that much of it had been written by Noel. Her happiest and most successful period began in London. *Pastors and Masters* (1925), followed by *Brothers and Sisters* (1929) established a pattern and a steady rhythm of writing in which she produced a new novel nearly every two years up to a total of twenty. The titles had a deliberate similarity and included *Men and Wives* (1931), *More Women than Men* (1933), *A House and its Head* (1935), *Daughters and Sons* (1937), *A Family and a Fortune* (1939), probably her best-known book, *Parents and Children* (1941), *Elders and Betters* (1944), *Manservant and Maidservant* (1947), *Two Worlds and their Ways* (1949), *Darkness and Day* (1951), *The Present and the Past* (1953), *Mother and Son* (1955), which won the James Tait Black Memorial Prize, *A Father and his Fate* (1957), ending with *A God and his Gifts* (1963). *The Last and the First* was published posthumously in 1971. Compton-Burnett's often-quoted remark 'I do not feel that I have any real or organic knowledge of life later than about 1910' is reflected in her novels' concern with upper middle-class Edwardian family life. Their most distinctive feature is their concentration on dialogue. Elizabeth *Bowen commented that 'costume and accessories play so little part that her characters sometimes give the effect of being physically as well as psychologically in the nude'. There is virtually no description in her books and little action. 'As regards plots', she once wrote, 'I find real life no help at all. Real life seems to have no plots.' Servants and children in her books speak in the same formal style as their masters and parents. Compton-Burnett resisted the often evoked comparison with Jane *Austen, insisting that their books did not have any real likeness but that 'I think there is possibly some likeness between our minds'. She was appointed DBE in 1967 and was made a Companion of Literature by the Royal Society of Literature in 1968. She died in London after an attack of bronchitis in 1969. *See* Elizabeth Bowen, *Collected Impressions* (1950); Pamela Hansford *Johnson, *Ivy Compton-Burnett* (1951); Robert Liddell, *The Novels of Ivy Compton-Burnett* (1955); Hilary Spurling, *Ivy when Young* (1974) and *Secrets of a Woman's Heart: The Later Life of Ivy Compton-Burnett 1920–1969* (1984); Robert Liddell, *Elizabeth* [*Taylor] *and Ivy* (1986); Kathy Justice Gentile, *Ivy Compton-Burnett* (1991); Alison Light, *Forever England: Femininity, Literature and Conservatism between the Wars* (1991).

Cook, Eliza, poet and journalist (b. Southwark, London, 24 December 1818, d. Wimbledon, Surrey, 23 September 1889).

Eliza Cook was the youngest of the eleven children of Joseph Cook, a London brazier. When she was 9 her father retired and the family moved to a small farm near Horsham, in Sussex. She was almost entirely self-taught, encouraged by her mother. She wrote many of her most popular poems before she was 15, including 'I'm Afloat', 'Lines to my Pony', 'Charlie O'Ross', and 'Star of Glengarry', and published her first collection, *Lays of a Wild Harp*, in 1835, when she was 17. She also sent poems anonymously to the *Metropolitan Magazine*, Colburn's *New Monthly Magazine*, and the *Weekly Dispatch*, including the most popular of all her poems, 'The Old Arm Chair', about the death of her mother. The title poem of her second collection, *Melaia and Other Poems* (1838) revealed a talent for satire. Cook established her own weekly magazine, *Eliza Cook's Journal*, priced at 1½*d.* to attract a popular readership. She wrote much of the material herself and was responsible for its strongly feminist slant, publishing articles on women's employment, the problems of single women, the need for a married women's property act, the reform of female dress, and improvements in women's education. Its fiction, too, had a message, as in 'The Solitary Child' (1851), which urged a more compassionate attitude to illegitimacy and unmarried mothers. Cook's feminism was qualified, however, and the journal stopped short of support for female suffrage. Its circulation was said to have exceeded that of Dickens's *Household Words*, but Cook's health broke down and it was discontinued in 1854. Some of the contents were reprinted in *Jottings from my Journal* (1860).

In her heyday, Cook's strikingly masculine appearance, with short hair, a tailored jacket with open lapels, and a shirt, attracted comment. At one point she had a 'romantic friendship' with the American actress Charlotte Cushman. She received a civil-list pension in 1863 and apart from a few poems in the *Weekly Dispatch* published little else. *New Echoes and Other Poems* (1864) was less successful than her previous collections. She became more or less an invalid in later years, but royalties from her earlier publications continued until her death at 71. Her middle-brow, sentimental, and domestic poetry had a wide appeal. She was sometimes compared with Thomas Hood, and her poem 'Poor Hood', according to the *DNB*, helped to erect a monument to his memory in Kensal Green cemetery. Several collected editions of her poems were published during her lifetime, including two American editions (1859, 1882) and a selection in German in 1865. *Poems: Second Series* (1845) contains a biographical preface. *See* Sally Mitchell, *The Fallen Angel: Chastity, Class and Women's Reading 1835–1880* (1981).

Cooke, Elizabeth, Katherine, and Mildred *see under* BACON, Ann, Lady

Cookson, Catherine ('Catherine Marchant'), popular novelist (b. Tyne Dock, South Shields, 20 June 1906).

The illegitimate daughter of Catherine Fawcett, a domestic servant, whom she believed to be her sister for most of her childhood, and an unnamed 'gentleman', Catherine Cookson was brought up a Catholic, went to school until she was 14, and then went into service. She worked as a checker in a workhouse laundry and in 1929 moved south to Hastings, in Sussex, where she managed a laundry. In 1940 she married Thomas Henry Cookson, a teacher. In the 1940s she joined the Hastings Writers' Circle and began to write. Despite nervous breakdowns and problems of physical health she has published over fifty popular novels, some as Catherine Marchant, many with Northumberland settings. *The Round Tower* (1968) won the Winifred Holtby Prize for a regional novel. Her heroines tend to be strong, determined to win respectability, usually by hard work. Her plots are often predictable, with the same spirited heroines eventually captivating attractive, aloof or initially patronizing men. The 'Mary Ann' series (1954–67) chronicle a strong-minded heroine who saves her father from alcoholism. The four historical 'Mallen' novels (1973–4), tales of the landed gentry, were adapted for television in 1979–80, as well as for film, stage, and radio. Cookson has written children's books and two autobiographies, *Our Kate: An Autobiography* (1969) and *Catherine Cookson Country* (1986). *Let me Make myself*

Plain (1988) is a collection of poems and meditations. She lives in Northumberland.

Cooper, Edith Emma *see* FIELD, Michael

Cooper, Lettice (Ulpha), novelist (b. Eccles, Lancashire, 3 September 1897).

Lettice Cooper is the daughter of Leonard Cooper, the proprietor of an engineering firm, and his wife Agnes Helena Fraser. She grew up in Eccles, in Lancashire, went to St Cuthbert's School, Southbourne, and then read classics at Lady Margaret Hall, Oxford. Rejecting teaching as a career, she worked for a while in her father's firm in Leeds and developed an interest in social work among the unemployed which took her into the Labour Party. She began her first novel at 7 in the family laundry book. Her first novels to be published were historical: *The Lighted Room* (1925), *The Old Fox* (1927), *Good Venture* (1928), *Likewise the Lyon* (1928). *The Ship of Truth* (1930), set in the present, won a prize for religious fiction. The settings of later novels have varied from the contemporary to the topical. *We Have Come to the Country* (1935) takes place in a centre for the unemployed in the 1930s. *The New House* (1936) describes the tensions of an upper middle-class mother and daughter's move from the family home. *National Provincial* (1938), her best-known novel, depicts socialist battles amongst the northern lower middle classes. *Late in the Afternoon* (1971) is set against the unrest of 1968, and *Snow and Roses* (1976) involves a miners' strike. *Desirable Residence* (1980) describes modern-day squatters and *Unusual Behaviour* (1986) an IRA bombing. *Fenny* (1953), sometimes considered her best novel, is set in Florence, which she visited often. Cooper worked briefly as an associate editor of the weekly **Time and Tide* and in the Ministry of Food during the Second World War. She has also been president of international PEN (1979–81). As well as her more than twenty novels she has written books for children and a series of biographies, of Florence *Nightingale (1960), Queen *Victoria (1961), Robert Louis Stevenson (1969), Dickens (1971), and a short study of George *Eliot (1951).

'Corelli, Marie' (Mary Mills, later Mackay), novelist (b. Bayswater, London, 1855, d. Stratford-upon-Avon, 21 April 1924).

Marie Corelli was the only child of the Scottish poet Charles Mackay by Mary Ellen Mills, a servant who became his second wife in 1859. The household moved to Fern Dell, near Box Hill in Surrey, where they were neighbours of George Meredith, who encouraged the young Mary in her musical accomplishments, which were prodigious. 'Marie Corelli' was a name adopted in anticipation of a musical career, but within months of her first successful concert, Corelli decided to abandon performing and to write instead. Her first novel, *The Romance of Two Worlds*, was published by Richard Bentley in 1886. She later described this about-turn in her career as due to a 'psychic experience', the first of many self-dramatizing episodes which were to characterize her later career and her life. Her next novel *Vendetta* (1886), like the first, made little stir, but it was with her third, *Thelma: A Society Novel* (1887), that she became a celebrity overnight. *Ardath: The Story of a Dead Self* (1889), which followed, was admired by Gladstone, and Corelli considered it her best work. By this time she was widely read by an admiring public, while sceptical critics poured scorn on her achievements. It was with *Barabbas: A Dream of the World's Tragedy* (1893), a melodrama based on the story of the crucifixion, that she achieved her biggest success to date. It was written, she claimed, to counter the 'agnosticism' of Mrs Humphry *Ward's *Robert Elsmere*, Mary Ward being a hated rival. *Barabbas* was published by the new firm of Methuen after Bentley had unwisely rejected it. Its successor, *The Sorrows of Satan* (1895), was, if possible, an even bigger hit, helped by the fact that it was one of the first to be published in a six-shilling one-volume format. It combined a religious theme with a salacious attack on the vices of the rich. Corelli was now a best-selling novelist who reportedly earned £10,000 per novel. She also took her art, and the various social messages it propounded, seriously. *The Mighty Atom* (1896) was an attack on secular education. *Ziska* (1897), set in Egypt, was on the theme of reincarnation. *The Master Christian* (1900) was a plea for peace. *Temporal Power* (1902) attacked socialism. In 1901 Corelli purchased Mason's Croft in Stratford-upon-Avon, a house believed to have belonged to Shakespeare's daughter, and set herself up consciously as a public figure and benefactress. Irritated neighbours had her prosecuted for food hoarding during the war, an ungenerous and unfounded accusation, especially in view of her sincere public spiritedness and concern for the preservation of Stratford. She lived all her adult life with her childhood friend and companion Bertha Vyver, who later wrote her memoirs. She died of heart disease in 1924, having just completed her twenty-eighth novel. Her extravagantly romantic fiction had long passed from public adulation but at her peak, in the dozen years after *The Sorrows of Satan*, she was, in terms of sales, the most popular novelist in Britain. *See* B. Vyver, *Memoirs of Marie Corelli* (1930); Michael Sadleir, 'The Camel's Back', in *Essays presented to Sir Humphrey Milford* (1930); E. Bigland, *Marie Corelli* (1953); W. S. Scott, *Marie Corelli* (1955); Brian Masters, *Now Barabbas was a Rotter: The Extraordinary Life of Marie Corelli* (1978).

'Corinna' *see* THOMAS, Elizabeth

Corinne (1807).

Corinne was a novel by Germaine de Staël-Holstein (Madame de Staël), translated into English by D. Lawler in 1807 and by Isabel Hill in 1833. De Staël's tale of two contrasting heroines, a dark and a blond, of whom the former, Corinne, a writer, artist, musician, and 'improvisatrice', sacrifices love and marriage for her career, and then dies, caught the imagination of many nineteenth-century women writers. Its oblique comment on the restricted lives offered to women in English society, on the suspicion of 'genius' in women, and on the insupportable sacrifices necessary for women to sustain an artistic career led to its being variously adapted, by Maria Jane *Jewsbury in *The History of an Enthusiast* (1830), Geraldine *Jewsbury in *The Half Sisters* (1848), Elizabeth Barrett *Browning in *Aurora Leigh* (1857) and George *Eliot in *The Mill on the Floss* (1860). Anna *Jameson and Felicia *Hemans were also influenced by *Corinne*, and Laetitia *Landon provided the translation of Corinne's improvisations for Hill's 1833 version, which was the most widely read edition. Other nineteenth-century novels which contrast 'dark' and 'light' heroines include Charlotte *Brontë's *Jane Eyre* (1847), Mrs. Henry *Wood's *East Lynne* (1861), and Eliot's *Adam Bede* (1859), *Middlemarch* (1871–2), and *Daniel Deronda* (1876). *See* Ellen Moers, *Literary Women* (1977); Avriel H. Goldberger's introd. to *Corinne; or Italy* (1987), a new translation; M. Gutwirth, A. Goldberger, and K. Szmurlo (eds.), *Germaine de Staël: Crossing the Borders* (1991).

Cornford, Frances Crofts, née Darwin, poet and translator (b. Cambridge, 30 March 1886, d. Cambridge, 19 August 1960).

Frances Cornford was the only child of Francis Darwin, later Sir Francis, a Cambridge botanist and the son of Charles Darwin, and Ellen Wordsworth Crofts, his second wife, niece of the poet and a lecturer at Newnham College. She was educated at home in Cambridge, where she spent most of her life. In 1908, while helping with a production of Milton's *Comus*, part of the tercentenary celebrations, she met Francis Cornford, a young classical scholar and fellow of Trinity, later professor of ancient philosophy, whom she married the following year. They had five children, of whom the eldest, the poet John Cornford (1915–36), was killed in the Spanish Civil War. Their son Christopher became an artist. Their house off the Madingley Road in Cambridge, was a meeting-place for a circle of artists, writers, and intellectuals, among whom were William Rothenstein, Eric Gill, Lowes Dickinson, Bertrand Russell, and sometimes exotic visitors like Rabindranath Tagore. Constantly labelled as the mother of John Cornford and the granddaughter of Charles Darwin, she none the less carved a place for herself. She began to write poetry at 16. Her first collection, *Poems* (1910), was followed by a morality play, *Death and the Princess* (1912). Between 1910 and 1960 she published eight volumes of poetry, establishing herself among the poets of the Georgian period and after. Rupert Brooke was a friend until his death in 1915. Her other volumes included *Spring Morning* (1915), *Autumn Midnight* (1923), *Different Days* (1928), published by Leonard and Virginia *Woolf, and *Mountains and Molehills* (1934). *Spring Morning* and *Mountains and Molehills* were illustrated with woodcuts by her cousin the artist Gwen Raverat. *On a Calm Shore* (1960), her last volume, was illustrated by her son. Cornford's poems were short, unpretentious, some almost epigrams, some elegiac, others humorous. Her triolet 'To a Fat Lady Seen from the Train' is frequently quoted. She was unrepentantly immune to modernist influence. Her *Collected Poems* (1954) was the official choice of the Poetry Book Society and in 1959 she won the Queen's Medal for Poetry. She also published several translations, including *Poems from the Russian* (1943), with Esther Polianowsky Salaman, and Paul Éluard's *Le Dur Désir de durer*, with Stephen Spender (1950). Some of her translations were published posthumously in 1976. Gwen Raverat's *Period Piece* (1950) gives a picture of their late Victorian extended family. Some of her letters were included in *Understand the Weapon/Understand the Wound: Selected Writings of John Cornford*, ed. John Galassi (1976). *See* Alan Anderson, *A Bibliography of the Writings of Frances Cornford* (1975); P. Delaney, *The Neo-Pagans* (1987).

Cory, Vivian *see under* NEW WOMAN

Cowan, Charlotte Elizabeth Lawson *see* RIDDELL, Mrs J. H.

Cowley, Hannah ('Anna Matilda'), dramatist and poet
(b. Tiverton, Devon, 1743, d. Tiverton, 11 March 1809).

Hannah Cowley was the daughter of Philip Parkhouse, a bookseller who had been educated for the Church and whose mother was a cousin of John Gay. In 1772 (probably) she married Thomas Cowley, a clerk in the Stamp Office. The couple moved to London where, after seeing a performance of an indifferent play, she reportedly claimed to be able to write a better one herself. The result was *The Runaway*, written in a fortnight, and produced by Garrick at Drury Lane in 1776. She was said to have received £800 for the work and launched herself on a literary career. Twelve more plays were produced by 1795, including *Who's the Dupe* (1779), a farce, *Albina* (1779), a tragedy, and *The Belle's Stratagem* (1780), *Which is the Man* (1782), *A Bold Stroke for a Husband* (1783), and *A School for Greybeards* (1786), all comedies, at which she excelled. She was probably the most productive woman dramatist of her day. Her poetry was less distinguished and less successful. She published *The Maid of Aragon: A Tale* (1780) and *The Scottish Village; or Pitcairn Green*

(1786) and then responded, under the pseudonym Anna Matilda, to the poetry of Robert Merry, published in the *World* in June 1787 under the signature 'Della Crusca'. This poetical correspondence led to the founding of the so-called Della Cruscan school of poets, whose sentimental and florid verse appeared in collections variously titled *The Poetry of Anna Matilda* (1788), *The Poetry of the World* (1788), and *The British Album* (1790). The group, whose members included Hester *Piozzi and Mary *Robinson, were later satirized by William Gifford in *The Baviad* (1791) and *The Maeviad* (1795). Cowley's last play, *The Town before you*, was produced at Covent Garden in 1794, and her last published work, *The Siege of Acre: An Epic Poem*, appeared in 1801. Her prickly personality was referred to by several contemporaries. She accused Hannah *More of plagiarizing the plot of *Albina* in what became a public confrontation. Despite the success of her plays she shunned literary society, preferring to retire to Devon in 1801. Her husband joined the East India Company as a soldier and in 1783 left for India, where he died in 1797. The eldest of their three children, a daughter, predeceased him in 1790. Her collected *Works* (3 vols.) were published posthumously in 1813. *See* Ellen Donkin, in *Curtain Calls: British and American Women and the Theater 1660–1820*, ed. Mary Anne Schofield and Cecilia Macheski (1991).

Craigie, Pearl Mary Teresa *see* HOBBES, John Oliver

Craik, Dinah Maria, née Mulock, novelist (b. Stoke-on-Trent, Staffordshire, 20 April 1826, d. Bromley, Kent, 12 October 1887).

Dinah Mulock was the daughter of Thomas Mulock, a Nonconformist minister, and his wife Dinah Mellard. Her father's instability led to the loss of his chapel and the family moved to Newcastle under Lyme. Dinah, who was both clever and precocious, helped her mother to teach school at the age of 13. The family eventually moved to London, where Mrs Mulock and the children separated from her husband. Her mother's death left Dinah with responsibility for her siblings which she resolved to undertake by writing. Friendship with Alexander Macmillan of the publishing house, and Charles Edward Mudie, proprietor of the famous circulating library, helped in the establishment of a literary career. Her first publication, *Cola Monti* (1849), was a children's book. *The Ogilvies* (1850), her first novel, turned on the problems of the marriage choice, a favourite subject. *Olive* (1850), about a deformed heroine, and *The Head of the Family* (1852), a family saga, were well received. Her reputation, however, was made and sustained by one best seller, *John Halifax, Gentleman* (1856), the story of a tanner's apprentice who rose to become master of his own concern. The novel predated Samuel Smiles's *Self-Help* (1859) but embodied its principles. The story, set in the pre-Reform

Bill era, involved actual historical figures. *A Life for a Life* (1859) did not equal the success of *John Halifax*, but was one of the few novels of the period to have a Crimean War setting. It also had two narrators, male and female, whose diaries are interwoven. In 1865 Dinah Mulock married George Lillie Craik, nephew of the literary critic and Shakespearian scholar of the same name. He was eleven years her junior, and shortly after became a partner in Macmillan's. The couple adopted a daughter. Mrs Craik continued to write fiction and non-fiction, including *A Noble Life* (1866), about a crippled hero, and two novels with a purpose, *A Brave Lady* (1870), an argument for married women's property rights, and *Hannah* (1871), for the right of in-laws to marry after the death of a spouse. *King Arthur: Not a Love Story* (1886) states her views on adoption. Her best-known book for children was *The Little Lame Prince* (1875). Her *A Woman's Thoughts about Women* (1858) was a conservative plea for more meaningful lives for women, not in new areas of activity, but in the traditional spheres of teaching, art, music, and writing. Two of her poems, 'Philip my King' and 'Douglas, Douglas, tender and true', were well known during her lifetime. She published a collection, *Thirty Years: Poems Old and New*, in 1881. She died suddenly of a heart attack at her home in Kent during preparations for her daughter's wedding. *See* A. Sergeant (ed.), *Women Novelists of Queen Victoria's Reign* (1897); Louisa Parr, *The Author of John Halifax, Gentleman: A Memoir* (1898); Sally Mitchell, *Dinah Mulock Craik* (1983).

Craven, Elizabeth *see* ANSPACH, Elizabeth, Margravine of

'Crompton, Richmal' (Richmal Crompton Lamburn), children's writer (b. Bury, Lancashire, 15 November 1890, d. Farnborough, Kent, 11 January 1969).

Richmal Crompton was the second of the three children of the Revd Edward John Sewell Lamburn, a master at Bury Grammar School and a curate, and his wife Clara Crompton. She attended St Elphin's Clergy Daughters' School, first in Warrington and then in Darley Dale, Derbyshire, won a scholarship to Royal Holloway College, University of London, and took a second in classics in 1914. She became a classics mistress at her old school between 1915 and 1917, and then taught at Bromley High School for Girls until 1924. One of her first short stories, about a tough, anarchic schoolboy called William, was published in the *Home Magazine* in February 1919, based in part on her brother John and a nephew. Feeling the need for anonymity, especially as a teacher, she used her Christian names, Richmal being a family name of long standing. More stories appeared in the same magazine and then transferred to the *Happy Mag.* In 1922 George Newnes published two volumes of selected stories, *Just William* and *More William.* Their enormous popularity and an attack of polio in 1923 which left her lame encouraged her to leave teaching and to put her energies into writing. She produced thirty-eight titles in all between 1922 and 1969. They had sold an estimated nine million copies by the mid-1970s, several years after her death, and were translated into thirteen languages. They were adapted in four 'William' films, and one radio and two television series. The books were at their best in the 1920s and 1930s, but their popularity endured to the end of her life, the last title, *William the Lawless*, appearing posthumously in 1970. Despite the enormous social changes between the 1920s and the 1960s, the contrast between the resilient schoolboy, at once irreverent, selfish, shrewd, and yet still innocent, and the smug middle-class assumptions of his parents and their world retained the attention and affection of a large reading and later a watching public. The almost mythic 'Just William' figure conjured up a popular image even to those who had not read the books. Of her polio attack, Richmal Crompton later declared philosophically that she had had 'a much more interesting life because of it'. As well as the William books she published over fifty other titles, many of them family chronicles and collections of short stories. She was a staunch Conservative, although the William books frequently criticize Conservative values, and a member of the Church of England. Towards the end of her life she became interested in mystical interpretations of Christianity. She died at the age of 79. *See* W. O. G. Lofts and D. Adley, *William: A Bibliography* (1980); Mary Cadogan, *Richmal Crompton* (1986); Kay Williams, *Just Richmal: The Life and Work of Richmal Crompton Lamburn* (1986).

'Crosse, Victoria' *see under* NEW WOMAN

Crowe, Catherine, novelist and short story writer (b. Borough Green, Kent, 1790, d. Folkestone, Kent, 1876).

Born in Kent, the daughter of John Stevens, Catherine Crowe lived for most of her life in Edinburgh after her marriage in 1822 to Lieutenant-Colonel John Crowe. They had one son. She became a disciple of the phrenologist George Combe, and thus acquired a reputation as an intellectual in Edinburgh scientific and medical circles. When Robert Chambers's anonymous *Vestiges of Creation*, published in 1844, was rumoured to have been the work of a woman, Catherine Crowe derived considerable pleasure from the fact that her name was one of those mentioned as a possible author. She had strong views on the need for education for women as well as for their economic independence. In her novel *Lilly Dawson* (1847) she commented that, if men's education had its deficiencies, 'six hours a day at Latin and

Greek are better than six hours a day at worsted work and embroidery; and time is better spent in acquiring a smattering of mathematics than in strumming Hook's lessons on a bad pianoforte'. She also showed a sympathetic attitude to the pressures of working-class women's lives, particularly sexual pressures. Several of her novels are about heroines who cross class lines. *Susan Hopley; or Circumstantial Evidence* (1841) is a romance about a servant who discovers her brother's murderer and also finds out that she is a colonel's daughter. In *Lilly Dawson* the pattern is slightly changed, as a middle-class heroine is shipwrecked, forced to become a servant, restored to her original life, but then chooses to marry her working-class lover. Two of Crowe's novels, *Men and Women; or Manorial Rights* (1844), a melodrama centring on a murder, and *Lilly Dawson*, were adapted for the stage. She also wrote *Aristodemus* (1838), a tragedy, and *The Cruel Kindness: A Romantic Play* (1853), which was performed at the Haymarket. She was fascinated by psychical phenomena and the paranormal. Her most famous work was *The Night Side of Nature*, a collection of stories about haunted houses, apparitions, and supernatural events, which were all declared to be authentic by the author. A treatise on *Spiritualism and the Age we Live in* (1859) precipitated a severe mental breakdown, after which she wrote very little. Other works of fiction, written before her illness, include *The Adventures of a Beauty* (1852), a conventional novel about fashionable life, *Light and Darkness*, a collection of short stories, and *Linny Lockwood* (1854), about a deserted wife who forms an alliance with her husband's mistress and refuses to pardon him. Despite their mixture of sensational events, conventional morality, and sentimental plots, Crowe's novels are distinguished by tough-minded heroines, aware of female oppression, who overcome disadvantages and circumstance by force of will. She also wrote books for children and published an abridged version of Harriet Beecher Stowe's *Uncle Tom's Cabin* (1853). John Crowe died in 1860. Catherine Crowe lived an invalid's life in Folkestone until her death at the age of 86. (The *DNB* gives her date of birth as 1800, which would mean she died at 76.) *See* A. Sergeant (ed.), *Women Novelists of Queen Victoria's Reign* (1897); Sally Mitchell, *The Fallen Angel: Chastity, Class and Women's Reading 1835–1880* (1981).

Currie, Mary Montgomerie Lamb *see* FANE, Violet

d d d d d d d d d d d d d

D

Dacre, Lady (Barbarina Brand), poet, playwright, and translator (b. 1768, d. London, 17 May 1854).

Barbarina Brand, Lady Dacre, was the youngest of three daughters of Admiral Sir Chaloner Ogle and his wife Hester Thomas, a bishop's daughter. She was educated at home and taught French and Italian in particular. In 1789 she married Valentine Henry Wilmot, a Guards officer, by whom she had a daughter and from whom she later separated. In 1819 she married Thomas Brand, Baron Dacre, a Whig peer. There were no children of the second marriage. In 1821 she published (privately) her *Dramas, Translations and Occasional Poems.* These included four verse dramas: *Ina* (1815), set in Anglo-Saxon England and produced unsuccessfully at Drury Lane for one night (22 April 1815), *Gonzalvo of Cordova* (1810), *Pedarias* (1811), and *Xarifa.* She was best known, however, for her translations of Petrarch's sonnets, some of which had been privately printed in 1818 and 1819 and which Ugo Foscolo (1778–1827), the Italian poet and critic, reprinted in his *Essays on Petrarch* (1823). They were also included in her *Translations from the Italian* (1836). Lady Dacre was well known in the literary, political, and social circles of her day, not only for her writing, but also for her skills in wax modelling. She edited her daughter **Arabella Sullivan's** (1796(?)–1839) two novels *Recollections of a Chaperon* (1831) and *Tales of the Peerage and Peasantry* (1835), both published anonymously. Her daughter's death in 1839 was a severe blow as was her own deafness in later years. She died at the age of 86. *See* Barbarina, Lady Grey, *A Family Chronicle,* ed. G. Lyster (1908).

Dacre, Charlotte, later Byrne ('Rosa Matilda'), novelist and poet (*c.*1782–*c.*1841).

Charlotte Dacre was the daughter of John King or Jacob Rey, a notorious London Jewish money-lender, radical writer, and blackmailer, by his first wife Deborah Lara, whom he divorced by Jewish law in 1785 in order to marry a countess. King was arrested for bankruptcy in 1788. Charlotte and her sister **Sophia**, who also became a writer, dedicated their juvenile poems, *Trifles from Helicon*, to their father in the same year to show 'the education you have afforded us has not been totally lost'. As Rosa Matilda Charlotte published *The Confessions of the Nun of St. Omer* (1805), dedicated to the well-known *Gothic novelist Matthew Gregory Lewis. Her best-known novel *Zofloya; or The Moor*, subtitled 'a romance of the fifteenth century' (1806), owes much to Lewis's *The Monk* (1796). Male aggression and female sexual neuroses are brought to the surface of the novel, which is intended as a warning against illicit love and unbridled passion. The climax of the story has the heroine proclaiming her devotion to the Moor, who reveals himself to be Satan and throws her over an Alpine ravine. Immensely popular in its day, it was abridged and reprinted as one of the 'bluebooks' or chapbooks of the period, under the title *The Daemon of Venice* (1810). It also influenced Shelley's *Zastrozzi* (1810). *The Libertine* (1807) appeared in three editions and a French translation by 1816. *The Passions* (1811) is an epistolary novel. *Hours of Solitude* (1805), a collection of poems, was published under her own name and contains poems by her sister. Little is known of her later life, except that she became Mrs Byrne in 1806. *See* Montague Summers, *The Gothic Quest* (1938, repr. 1965).

Dacre, Sophia *see under* DACRE, Charlotte

Dalton, Regina Maria *see* ROCHE, Regina Maria

'Dane, Clemence' (Winifred Ashton), novelist and playwright (b. Greenwich, London, 21 February 1888, d. London, 28 March 1965).

Clemence Dane derived her pseudonym from the Church of St Clement Danes in the Strand, in an area of London in which she lived for the greater part of her life. She was the daughter of Arthur Charles Ashton, a commission merchant, and his wife Florence Bentley. She was educated in England, Germany, and Switzerland, studied art in Dresden and at the Slade School in London, and had a brief career as an actress. When her health broke down during the First World War she abandoned the theatre to teach briefly at a girls' school in Ireland and also began to write. Her first novel, *Regiment of Women* (1917), was a devastating critique of life at a girls' school. *Legend*

(1919), her third book, was a study of a woman writer. These, together with *Broome Stages* (1931), the story of the Plantagenets, but based on a contemporary English theatrical family, constituted her most successful fiction. Her career as a playwright was a disappointment. It began well with *A Bill of Divorcement* (1921), based on the theme of inherited insanity, which ran for over 400 performances in London and was equally successful in New York. *Will Shakespeare*, produced in the same year and based on the poet's life, was a much publicized flop, due, it was suggested subsequently, to the fact that Dane could write good parts for women but not for men. None of her later plays equalled her initial success. She wrote two others based on literary lives, *Wild Decembers* (1932), about the *Brontës, and *Come of Age* (1933), based on the life of Thomas Chatterton. Her friends Sybil Thorndike and Lewis Casson staged *Granite* (1926) and *Mariners* (1927) but both were failures. *Adam's Opera* (1928) was slightly more successful. She adapted Rostand's *L'Aiglon* for the stage in 1934, Max Beerbohm's *The Happy Hypocrite* in 1936, and Friedrich Hebbel's *Herodes und Mariamne* in 1938. In 1951 a play based on an earlier radio play about Elizabeth I and Essex folded after the death of Sir Charles Cochran, who had taken one of the leading roles. Her last play, *Eighty in the Shade* (1959), was written for Sybil Thorndike. Dane wrote three detective novels jointly with the Australian-born novelist **Helen Simpson** (1897–1940), including *Sir John* (1930) and *Enter Sir John* (1932), with an actor-manager as the central character. She published *The Woman's Side*, a collection of feminist essays, in 1926, and a biography of Mary *Kingsley, *A Woman among Wild Men*, in 1938. *Tradition and Hugh Walpole* (1929) gave her views on the English novel. *London has a Garden* (1964), a history of the Covent Garden district, contains some reminiscences. She also wrote seven film scripts, including that for *Anna Karenina* (1935). She was appointed CBE in 1953.

D'Arblay, Frances *see* BURNEY, Fanny

D'Arcy, Ella, short story writer and novelist (b. London, 1851, d. Kent, 1937(?)).

Ella D'Arcy was born in London, the daughter of aristocratic Irish parents, and educated in France and Germany. She lived in the Channel Islands for a period and attended the Slade School of Art until deficient eyesight made a career as an artist impossible. Little is known of her life apart from her involvement as assistant editor of the *Yellow Book*, the famous 'illustrated quarterly' of the 1890s, published by John Lane, whose contributors included John Davidson, Henry James, George Gissing, H. G. Wells, and Richard LeGallienne. Aubrey Beardsley was for a time its art editor. D'Arcy published several stories in the *Yellow Book* and others in *Blackwood's Magazine, All the Year Round*, and *Temple Bar*. They were collected as *Monochromes* (1895) and formed a volume in Lane's Keynote series, named after the original book by George *Egerton. Like Egerton's work they reflected a strongly feminist perspective and the advanced views of the *New Woman. A further collection of her stories was published as *Modern Instances* (1898). Her novel *The Bishop's Dilemma* was published in the same year. D'Arcy never married, but reportedly had affairs with John Lane and the novelist Henry Harland ('Sidney Luska'). Charlotte *Mew was said to have fallen in love with her. She lived for part of her life in Paris and published a translation of André Maurois's *Ariel*, a fictionalized biography of Shelley (1924). *See* Katharine Mix, *A Study in Yellow* (1960); Penelope Fitzgerald, *Charlotte Mew and her Friends* (1984).

Darwin, Frances Crofts *see* CORNFORD, Frances Crofts

Daryush, Elizabeth, née Bridges, poet (b. London, 5 December 1887, d. Boar's Hill, Oxford, 7 April 1977).

Elizabeth Daryush, who also published as Elizabeth Bridges, was the daughter of the poet Robert Bridges (1844–1930), later Poet Laureate, and his wife Mary Monica Waterhouse, daughter of the nineteenth-century architect Alfred Waterhouse. She grew up first in Yattendon in Berkshire, and then in the family home at Boar's Hill, near Oxford. Through family connections she knew the poets John Masefield, Robert Graves, and Thomas Hardy, and according to a family story was observed in her cradle by Gerard Manley Hopkins. Her first book of poems, *Charitessi*, was published in 1911, when she was 23, and was praised by Yeats. Her second, entitled simply *Verses* (1916), inaugurated a series published in the 1930s, consecutively titled *Second Book Verses* (1932), *Third Book Verses* (1933), *Fourth Book Verses* (1934), *The Last Man and Other Verses* (1936), and *Sixth Book Verses* (1938). In 1923 she met Ali Akbar Daryush, a Persian government official then at Oxford, whom she married in the same year and with whom she went to Persia. She studied Persian poetry and published a translation, *Sonnets from Hafez and Other Verses* (1921). They returned to England in 1927 because of her husband's ill health and settled in a house in Boar's Hill, where she lived for the rest of her life. For most of her writing career Elizabeth Daryush's reputation was overshadowed by that of her father. The runs of her books were small and her work was better known in the United States, where she was enthusiastically championed by the critic Yvor Winters. The poet Roy Fuller joined the ranks of her admirers in the early 1970s and contributed a preface to *Verses: Seventh Book*, published by Carcanet Press in 1971. The result was a late flowering of her reputation. She was sought out by poets of a younger generation and her *Collected Poems* were published in 1976 with an introduction by Donald Davie. Daryush's work was associated with metrical experiment, particularly syllabic metres. Her poetry was unashamedly traditional. Modernist poetry she described as 'the weedy garden of instant verse'. *The Times* described her death as 'the breaking of the last thin strand which bound [English verse] in flesh and spirit to the poetry of the Victorian era'. *See* Yvor Winters, *Uncollected Essays and Reviews* (1973); Roy Fuller's preface to *Verses: Seventh Book* (1971); Donald Davie's introduction to her *Collected Poems* (1976).

'**Daviot,** Gordon' *see* MACKINTOSH, Elizabeth

Davys, Mary, novelist and playwright (b. Dublin, 1674, d. Cambridge, 1732).

Mary Davys was born in Dublin, where she later married the Revd Peter Davys, the headmaster of the Free School of St Patrick's and a friend of Swift. After he died in 1698 she left Ireland for York, where she settled and began to write. She published *The Amours of Alcippus and Leucippe* (1704), for which she received three guineas (it became *The Lady's Tale* in 1725), and the loosely autobiographical *The Fugitive* (1705), rewritten as *The Merry Wanderer* in 1725. These modest successes did not alleviate her financial difficulties, however. Swift sent her money on several occasions and in 1716 her comedy *The Northern Heiress* was successfully staged at the New Theatre in Lincoln's Inn Fields. She moved to Cambridge and set up a coffee house on the proceeds. Her later works found no difficulty in obtaining subscribers, usually from Cambridge, but those for her well-known *The Reform'd Coquet* (1724) included Pope, Gay, and Pope's friend Martha Blount. Two volumes of her collected *Works* were published in 1725 and included an unacted play, *The Self Rival*, in the prologue to which she complained of the prejudice against women writers. *Familiar Letters betwixt a Gentleman and a Lady* (n.d.), a pre-Richardsonian epistolary novel, was published in facsimile in 1955. Her last novel, *The Accomplish'd Rake* (1727), satirical, humorous, and realistic, is highly regarded by some modern readers, but her reputation in her own lifetime was not high. She was attacked for bawdy in the *Grub-Street Journal* and vigorously defended herself. She is alleged also to have published a reply in verse to Susanna *Centlivre's *Epistle to the King of Sweden* (1717). Davys's preface to her *Works* defended the right of a clergyman's widow to write plays, defied her readers to find 'any thing there offensive either to God or Man, any thing either to shock their morals or their Modesty'. Of the plays she wrote, 'I never was so vain as to think they deserv'd a Place in the first Rank, or so humble, as to resign them to the last.' She died in 1732 leaving her estate to a Cambridge grocer, whose descendant, Dr W. H. Ewan, later claimed that thirty-six letters from Swift to Mary Davys and her husband were in his possession. *See* Nancy Cotton, *Women Playwrights in England c.1363–1750* (1980).

'Delafield, E. M.' (Edmée Elizabeth Monica de la Pasture), novelist (b. Steyning, Sussex, 9 June 1890, d. Cullompton, Devon, 2 December 1943).

E. M. Delafield was the daughter of Count Henry Philip Ducarel de la Pasture, a member of an aristocratic French Catholic family who had settled in England after the Revolution, and his wife Elizabeth Bonham, who as **Mrs Henry de la Pasture** (1866–1945) wrote novels. The last years of Edwardian country society in which her youth was spent were reflected in her fiction, as was the genteel, upper middle-class provincial life which succeeded it. She joined the VAD (Voluntary Aid Detachment) in Exeter at the outbreak of war, worked for the Ministry of National Services in Bristol, and in 1919 married Major Arthur Paul Dashwood of the Royal Engineers, the second son of a baronet, by whom she had a son and a daughter. After two years in Malaysia they settled in Devon, where Elizabeth joined the Women's Institute and became a magistrate. She had published her first novel, *Zella Sees Herself,* in 1917, and this initiated a steady stream of over forty works in the next two decades, mainly fiction. Her strength was a gentle satire of mundane middle-class life, which was most successfully realized in a serial, *The Provincial Lady,* begun for the feminist weekly **Time and Tide* in 1930. Sequels included *The Provincial Lady goes Further* (1932), *The Provincial Lady in America* (1934), and *The Provincial Lady in War-Time* (1940). *Thank Heaven Fasting* (1932) is generally agreed to be her best novel. Some of her fiction addressed social issues as in *Nothing is Safe* (1937), which dealt with the impact of divorce on children. Another, *Messalina of the Suburbs* (1924), was based on the infamous Thompson–Bywaters murder case (as a decade later was F. Tennyson *Jesse's *A Pin to See the Peep Show* (1934)). She wrote three plays, *To See Ourselves* (1930), *The Glass Wall* (1933), and *The Mulberry Bush* (1935), and a successful series for *Punch,* 'As Others Hear us' (repr. 1937). *The Bazalgettes* (1935) was a convincing pastiche of Rhoda *Broughton. She also published a study of the *Brontës (1938). *See* Violet Powell, *The Life of a Provincial Lady* (1988).

Delaney, Shelagh, playwright and short story writer (b. Salford, Lancashire, 25 November 1939).

Shelagh Delaney is the daughter of Joseph Delaney, a bus-inspector, and his wife Elsie. After failing the eleven-plus exam she went to a secondary modern school and later transferred to a grammar school. She left at 16 intending to write, and to earn enough money to live on worked as a salesgirl, a cinema usherette, and as an assistant in a photographic laboratory. Her best-known work was written when she was 18, the award-winning play *A Taste of Honey* (1958), which was first produced by Joan Littlewood's Theatre Workshop Company in Stratford East. It transferred to the West End, winning the Charles Henry Foyle New Play Award, and an Arts Council bursary, and then to Broadway, where it won the New York Drama Critics Circle Award. Her 1961 screenplay won the British Film Academy Award. Centring on a working-class single parent, her teenage daughter, and the men in their lives, the play was linked with the work of post-war playwrights Arnold Wesker and John Osborne, whose domestic realism and focus on working-class life was seen as a reaction to the drawing-room comedies of dramatists like Terrence Rattigan and Noel Coward and the highbrow verse drama of T. S. Eliot and Christopher Fry. Delaney's next play, *The Lion in Love* (1960), was produced at the Royal Court. Since the publication of *Sweetly Sings the Donkey* (1963), a collection of autobiographical short stories, she has written primarily for film and television. She wrote the screenplay for *The White Bus* (1966), directed by Lindsay Anderson, and won the Writers' Guild Award for the screenplay for *Charley Bubbles* (1968), directed by Albert Finney. *Dance with a Stranger* (1985), a screenplay based on the case of Ruth Ellis, the last woman to be executed in England, won the Prix Film Jeunesse-Étranger at Cannes. Her plays for television include *St. Martin's Summer* (1974), *Find me First* (1979), and the series *The House that Jack Built* (1977). She has also written radio plays. *A Taste of Honey* was revived on Broadway in 1981. Shelagh Delaney has a daughter and lives in London.

Delany, Mary, née Granville, formerly Pendarves, bluestocking and letter writer (b. Coulston, Wiltshire, 14 May 1700, d. London, 15 April 1788).

Mary Delany was the daughter of Bernard Granville, the younger son of a West Country Tory family, and Mary Westcombe. Her father's brother George became Lord Lansdowne, a Tory politician and grandee, and his sister was a member of the Royal Household. Mary was sent to live with her aunt in the hope of a place in Queen Anne's Household, but the Granville fortunes fell with the Tories at the Queen's death in 1714. She lived for a while at Lord Lansdowne's house Longleat, in Wiltshire, where at the age of 17 she met his friend the wealthy Alexander Pendarves, querulous, drunken, and over forty years her senior. She was forced into marriage by her family, despite the existence of another relationship. The marriage was wretched and Pendarves died in 1725, leaving his wife without an income but free. She spent some time in Ireland, where she met Swift, and also Patrick Delany, an Irish churchman and a friend of Swift's, then on the point of marrying a wealthy widow. After his wife's death in 1741 Delany proposed marriage, which she accepted, despite her family's opposition to his humble origins. Through her connections he was appointed Dean of Down and they lived in Ireland and occasionally in England until his death in 1768. Mary Delany's interest in literature and her taste for literary society, begun through her acquaintance with Swift and his circle, was furthered through her friendship with Lady Margaret Cavendish Harley, daughter of the Duke of Oxford and later Duchess of Portland. It led to introductions to Elizabeth *Montagu and other members of the so-called *Bluestocking Circle, of which she became a central member after Patrick Delany's death. It also led to introductions to members of the royal family, who were generous in their patronage, eventually granting her an annuity of £300 and a house in Windsor. Through Hester *Chapone she met Fanny *Burney, who became a close friend for the rest of her life. Although not primarily a writer herself, she knew most of the eminent literary and artistic men and women of her day. She wrote some occasional verse, but her talents and personality were best expressed through her autobiography and her letters, published in six volumes in 1861–2. An earlier collection of her letters, to Mrs Frances Hamilton was published in 1820. She was also known during her lifetime for her exquisite paper mosaics of flowers, a collection of which is housed in the British Museum. *See* 'George Paston', *Mrs. Delany: A Memoir* (1900); Ruth Hayden, *Mrs. Delany: Her Life and Flowers* (1980); Patricia Meyer Spacks, in *The Private Self: Theory and Practice of Women's Autobiographical Writings*, ed. Shari Benstock (1988).

de la Pasture, Edmée Elizabeth Monica *see* DELAFIELD, E. M.

de la Pasture, Mrs Henry *see under* DELAFIELD, E. M.

de la Ramée, Marie Louise *see* OUIDA

Dell, Ethel M(ary), popular novelist (b. Streatham, London, 2 August 1881, d. Hereford, 17 September 1939).

Ethel M. Dell was the younger of two daughters of John Vincent Dell, who worked for an insurance company, and his wife Irene Parrott. She and her sister were taught at home by their mother. She then went to Streatham College for Girls, where she wrote stories for her classmates. Her father had some privately printed and others she placed in the *Red Magazine*, the *Universal and Ludgate Magazine*, and similar popular papers. Her first novel, *The Way of an Eagle*, was rejected thirteen times, and after many redraftings was published in 1912. It became an instant best seller. Dell published thirty-five novels as well as collections of short stories and a book of poems. She was generous in the distribution of her profits, particularly to members of her family. Her novels invariably had happy endings, designed to comfort rather than challenge. The marriage bond was supreme, class lines strictly adhered to, her heroes chivalrous, and love idealized. Sexual attraction was presented in coded form. Her heroines 'quivered', 'thrilled', or were 'scorched' by passion but rarely succumbed to sex before marriage. They did occasionally say 'damn' and 'hell'. At the height of her fame in the 1920s and 1930s Dell had a nation-wide following. *By Request* (1927) was written 'at the request of some of my readers' and carried on the story of two characters in a previous novel. Her books continued to be reprinted into the 1950s. Barbara *Cartland condensed many of them in the 1970s and 1980s. In 1922, at the age of 41, she married Lieutenant-Colonel Gerald Tahourdin Savage and retired with him to the country. She published her last novel in 1939, the year of her death. *See* Penelope Dell, *Nettie and Sissie: The Biography of Ethel M. Dell and her Sister Ella* (1977).

Desai, Anita, novelist and short story writer (b. Mussourie, North India, 24 June 1937).

Born in India of a Bengali father, D. N. Mazumbar, and a German mother, Toni Nime, Anita Desai went to Queen Mary's School, Delhi, and to Miranda House (a women's college), University of Delhi, where she took a degree in English literature in 1957. In 1958 she married Ashvin Desai, by whom she had two daughters and two sons. By her own account she has been writing in English since the age of 7, 'as instinctively as I breathe'. Her first story was published in 1946, when she was 9. She has been a free-lance novelist and book reviewer since 1963, when her first novel, *Cry, the Peacock*, was published, but has also held academic appointments at Girton College, Cambridge, and at Smith and Mount Holyoke colleges in Massachusetts. Her subsequent novels variously depict the Indian bourgeoisie since Independence. She focuses on unsatisfied lives, unfulfilled ambition, self-deception, illusions. Many of her novels centre on women from Westernized, upper middle-class families, wives, widows, and single women who have gained freedom and yet are trapped by circumstance. *Fire on the Mountain* (1977) is about an older woman suddenly made responsible for her great-granddaughter but who ironically causes her death. It won the Winifred Holtby Award of the Royal Society of Literature. *Voices in the City* (1965) and *Bye-Bye Blackbird* (1971) both focus on the emotional life of women, in the latter, an immigrant to England. *Clear Light of Day* (1980) is about the disillusionment of contemporary women. *In Custody* (1985) is a comedy about the problems of preserving Indian culture in a post-colonial era. Desai has published several books for children, among them *The Village by the Sea* (1983), which won the Guardian Children's Fiction Award. She is a fellow of the Royal Society of Literature. *See* her essay 'Indian Women Writers', in *The Eye of the Beholder*, ed. Maggie Butcher (1983).

Diver, (Katherine Helen) Maud, novelist and writer on India (b. Murree, Northern Punjab, India, 1867, d. Hindhead, Surrey, 14 October 1945).

Born at a hill station in the Himalayas, Katherine Maud Diver was the eldest daughter of Colonel C. H. T. Marshall of the Indian army and his wife (née Pollock). She and her sister were sent to England for their education, but she returned willingly to India and in 1890 married a subaltern in the Royal Warwickshire Regiment, later Lieutenant-Colonel T. Diver (d. 1941). They settled permanently in England in 1896 and she began at once to write short stories and articles for the *Pall Mall Gazette*, *Longman's*, *Temple Bar*, the *Cornhill*, and other magazines. She published her first novel, *Captain Desmond V.C.*, in 1907 at the age of 40. Its instant success established her as a novelist of British life in India, the subject of later books like *The Great Amulet* (1908), *Candles in the Wind* (1909), and *Lilamani: A Study in Possibilities* (1911). These, as well as the non-fictional *The Englishwoman in India* (1909), underlined the tensions between East and West which were central to Anglo-Indian life. Two volumes of historical biography, *The Hero of Herat* (1912), and *The Judgment of the Sword* (1913), about the soldier-diplomat Eldred Pottinger, preceded a further group of novels, *Desmond's Daughter* (1916), *The Unconquered* (1917), *Strange Roads* (1918), and its sequel *The Strong Hours* (1919), the last two about the First World War. Two historical works, *Kabul to Kandahar* (1935), about the second Afghan war, and a biography in 1936 of her great-aunt Honoria Lawrence, the intrepid and influential wife of Sir Henry Lawrence, hero of the Indian Mutiny, brought her an increased reading public. *A Wild Bird* (1929) and *Ships of Youth* (1931), both about India, won her a hitherto elusive American public. *Sylvia Lyndon* (1940) was her last novel and *Royal India* (1942) and *The Unsung: A Record of British Service in India* (1945) her last books about India. She was working on a study of Warren Hastings at the time of her death. Her books about India were aimed at a popular audience and carefully avoided contemporary politics.

Dixie, Lady Florence (Caroline), novelist, poet, and travel writer (b. London, 24 May 1857, d. Glen Stuart, Annan, Dumfriesshire, 7 November 1905).

Lady Florence Dixie was the youngest of the six children of Archibald

William Douglas, seventh Marquis of Queensberry, and Caroline Margaret Clayton, the daughter of a baronet who was also a general. As a child she was precocious, talented, and adventurous. She published poetry when she was 10, was a first-rate horsewoman, a good shot, and a swimmer. While still a girl she took up big game hunting and became one of the first women to pursue the sport, visiting Africa, Arabia, and the Rocky Mountains. In 1875 she married Sir Alexander Beaumont Churchill Dixie, by whom she had two sons. She refused to let marriage and motherhood restrict her activities. In 1878, the year in which her second child was born, she made an exploratory journey to Patagonia with her husband and others, and published her best-known travel book, *Across Patagonia* (1880). During the Zulu War in South Africa she became war correspondent for the *Morning Post* and a vociferous advocate of Zulu independence, publishing her views in *A Defence of Zululand and its King* (1882) and *In the Land of Misfortune* (1882). She became a supporter of Home Rule in Ireland and an early and original campaigner for sex equality, advocating changes in women's dress, in the line of succession to the throne, in the marriage service, and in the divorce laws. Despite or perhaps because of her early game hunting experience, she later denounced these activities in *Horrors of Sport* (1891) and *Mercilessness of Sport* (1901). Her fiction embodied many of her strong views as well as her personal experiences. *Redeemed in Blood* (1889), a melodramatic first novel, was set in Patagonia. *Gloriana; or The Revolution of 1900* (1890) was a futurist novel in which the female protagonist assumed a male persona, entered Parliament, and brought about an ideal state. In 1902 she published a verse drama, *Isola; or The Disinherited*, about the oppression of women. *The Story of Ijain* (1903) was an autobiographical account of her childhood. *Izra; or A Child of Solitude* (1906) which was being serialized at the time of her death, explored the restraints of women's lives and advocated a more liberal attitude to sexuality. Dixie published two children's stories, *The Young Castaways* (1889) and *Aniwee; or The Warrior Queen* (1890), both of which resisted gender stereotyping in their heroines. *Abel Avenged* (1877) was an early verse tragedy and *Songs of a Child* (1901–2) a volume of juvenilia published under the pseudonym Darling. An elder sister, **Lady Gertrude Georgina Douglas**, was also a novelist, publishing under the pseudonym **George Douglas**. *See* B. Roberts, *Ladies in the Veld* (1965); C. B. Stevenson, *Women Travel Writers in Africa* (1982); Nan Bowman Albinski, in *Feminism, Utopia, and Narrative*, ed. L. F. Jones and S. W. Goodwin (1990).

'Dods, Margaret' *see* JOHNSTONE, Christian Isabel

Dorset, Catherine Ann *see under* SMITH, Charlotte

'Douglas, George' (Lady Gertrude Georgina Douglas) *see under* DIXIE, Lady Florence

Dowriche, Anne, poet (*fl.* 1589–96; b. Mount Edgecumbe, Honiton, Devon).

Anne Dowriche was the daughter of Peter Edgecumbe, a Devonshire landowner, and his wife Margaret Luttrell. She married the Revd Hugh Dowriche, later rector of Honiton, in 1580 and had four children. She is known for one work, *The French Historie: A Lamentable Discourse of Three of the Chief and most Famous Bloodie Broiles that have Happened in France for the Gospell of Jesus Christ* (1589), a long poem in defence of the Protestant cause. Dedicated to her brother Pearse Edgecumbe, the *Historie* was based on an English translation of a commentary on the French civil wars and written in iambic hexameter and heptameter couplets. Dowriche effaced her gender by inventing two male personae in the poem and in her dedication begged that if her brother was not pleased with it he should 'remember I pray, that it is a womans doing'. Her purpose in writing, she emphasized, was 'to edifie, comfort and stirre up the godlie mindes unto care, Watchfulnesse, Zeale and firventnesse in the cause of Gods truth'. She wrote her history in verse, 'to restore againe some credit if I can unto Poetrie, having been defaced of late so many waies by wanton vanities'. In the course of the poem Satan appears in league with the Catholics, and Catherine de Medici is seen villainously urging the massacre of the Huguenots. *See* Elaine V. Beilin, *Redeeming Eve: Women Writers of the English Renaissance* (1987).

Drabble, Margaret, novelist and critic (b. Sheffield, 5 June 1939).

The second of the four children of the Honourable John Frederick Drabble, QC, a circuit judge, and his wife Kathleen Marie Bloor, and the sister of novelist Antonia *Byatt, Margaret Drabble went to the Mount School, York, where her mother had taught, and then to Newnham College, Cambridge, where she took a first in English. In 1960 she married Clive Swift, an actor and fellow student by whom she had two sons and a daughter. They divorced in 1975 and in 1982 she married the biographer Michael Holroyd. Her first novels, written in the early years of marriage and motherhood, were, by her own admission, circumscribed by her experiences. They all have middle-class, intelligent, and educated heroines who try to relate what they experience to what they have read, sometimes by defining themselves as characters in nineteenth-century novels. *A Summer Birdcage* (1962), *The Garrick Year* (1964), *The Millstone* (1965), *Jerusalem the Golden* (1967), and *The Waterfall* (1969) variously address marriage, motherhood, pregnancy, adultery, and careers for women in England in the 1960s and 1970s. Drabble professes herself interested in problems of fate and free will, accident and determinism, like her nineteenth-century predecessors, and also questions of equality and social justice. Later novels have enlarged their scope to consider the public as well as the private life while also becoming technically more sophisticated. These include *The Needle's Eye* (1972), *The Realms of Gold* (1975), *The Ice Age* (1977), *The Middle Ground* (1980), *The Radiant Way* (1987), and its sequel *A Natural Curiosity* (1989). *The Gates of Ivory* (1992) contrasts the world of north London's intellectual middle classes with that of the inhabitants of present-day Cambodia, in a plot structure that owes much to Conrad. Drabble has published books on Wordsworth (1966) and Arnold Bennett (1974), the latter sharing a Potteries background with her maternal grandparents. She has also edited a collection on Hardy (1976), and the *Oxford Companion to English Literature* (1985). *A Writer's Britain* (1979) emphasizes the relationship between landscape and writing. She has won the John Llewellyn Rhys Memorial Prize (1966), the James Tait Black Memorial Prize (1968), and the E. M. Forster Award of the American Academy of Arts and Letters (1973), and has been chairman of the National Book League. She was appointed CBE in 1980. *See* Valerie Grosvenor Myer, *Margaret Drabble: Puritanism and Permissiveness* (1974); Ellen Cronan Rose, *The Novels of Margaret Drabble: Equivocal Figures* (1980) and E. C. Rose (ed.), *Critical Essays on Margaret Drabble* (1985); Dorey Schmidt and Jan Seale (eds.), *Margaret Drabble: Golden Realms* (1982); Mary Hurley Morin, *Margaret Drabble: Existing within Structures* (1983); Joanne V. Creighton, *Margaret Drabble* (1985); Joan Garret Packer, *Margaret Drabble: An Annotated Bibliography* (1988); Lorna Sage, *Women in the House of Fiction: Post-War Women Novelists* (1992).

Duffy, Maureen (Patricia), novelist, poet, and playwright (b. Worthing, Sussex, 21 October 1933).

The daughter of Cahia Patrick Duffy and Grace Rose Wright, Maureen Duffy went to Trowbridge High School for Girls in Wiltshire and then to Sarah Bonnell High School for Girls and King's College, London, where she took a degree in English in 1956. She wrote plays and poetry at university followed by novels. *That's How it Was* (1962), her first novel to be published, was a semi-autobiographical story of the intense relationship of a working-class mother and her illegitimate daughter. Duffy's novels focus on working-class culture, sexual identity, and the politics of gender, and combine realism and fantasy. *The Microcosm* (1966), her best-known novel, describes underground lesbian society in London and draws on the writing of Charlotte *Charke. *The Paradox Players* (1967) describes the restorative effect of a hard Thames winter on a suffering novelist. *I Want to Go to Moscow* (1973) is about radical anti-vivisectionists. *Gor Saga* (1982) reflects her concern for animal rights and was televised in 1988. *The Change* (1987) records the effects of the Second World War on a variety of characters. *Illuminations* (1991) juxtaposes a contemporary English lecturer against her *alter ego*, an eighth-century nun whose letters she translates. A trilogy of plays, *Rites* (1969), *Solo*, and *Old Tyme* (both 1970), draws on Greek myth. Another play, *A Nightingale in Bloomsbury Square* (1974), centres on the reflections of the dying Virginia *Woolf. Her *Collected Poems 1949–84* were published in 1985. Duffy has made a major contribution to the revival of interest in Aphra *Behn with her biography *The Passionate Shepherdess* (1977), an edition of *Oronooko* (1986), an introduction to *Love/Letters between a Nobleman and his Sister* (1987), and a collection of Behn's plays (1990). *The Erotic World of Faery* (1972) is a Freudian study of literature. She has played a prominent role in various professional bodies, including the Writers' Action Group, the Writers' Guild of Great Britain, the Authors' Lending and Copyright Society, and the British Copyright Council. *See* Jane Rule, *Lesbian Images* (1975); Christine Wick Sizemore, *A Female Vision of the City: London in the Novels of Five British Women* (1989).

du Maurier, Daphne, novelist and short story writer (b. London, 13 May 1907, d. Par, Cornwall, 19 April 1989).

Daphne du Maurier was a member of the third generation of a distinguished Anglo-French family whose talents were directed towards literature and popular entertainment. Her grandfather George du Maurier (1834–96) was a well-known *Punch* artist and the author of *Peter Ibbetson* and *Trilby*. She was the daughter of actor-manager Sir Gerald du Maurier and his wife Muriel Beaumont. She and her two sisters were educated at home, apart from six months spent in Paris when she was 18. Her biography of her father, *Gerald: A Portrait* (1934), made no attempt to disguise her dislike of the stereotypically glamorous, party-going life of the theatrically successful which she witnessed at first hand while growing up. Her attachment to her father, on the other hand, was intense. She read widely in English and French and began to write poems and short stories while a teenager. Katherine *Mansfield, Mary *Webb, and Guy de Maupassant were acknowledged early influences on her writing, while in mid-career she eschewed contemporary fiction and read only Jane *Austen, Trollope, and R. L. Stevenson, the last an important influence on her major work. In 1932 she married Lieutenant-Colonel, later Lieutenant-General, Sir Frederick Arthur Montague Browning (d. 1965) of the Grenadier Guards, a war hero, Olympic athlete, and later a member of the Royal Household. They had two daughters and a son. Her first three novels, all romances, *The Loving Spirit* (1931), *I'll Never be Young Again*

(1932), and *The Progress of Julius* (1933), made little impact. But the two which followed, *Jamaica Inn* (1936) and *Rebecca* (1938), won her an enormous reading public which she never lost. According to *The Times* (20 April 1989), her books 'embodied in currently acceptable terms some of the abiding fantasies of half the human race'. Her major novels divided readily into two categories. The first were historical tales of smuggling and piracy, violence and romantic love, set in seventeenth- and eighteenth-century Cornwall, which included *Jamaica Inn*, *Frenchman's Creek* (1941), *Hungry Hill* (1943), and *The King's General* (1946). The second were modern *Gothic stories, featuring mystery and suspense, and included *Rebecca*, *My Cousin Rachel* (1951), *The Scapegoat* (1957), and *The Flight of the Falcon* (1965). *Rebecca*, her best-known novel, the story of a second wife who is haunted by the memory of her predecessor, who turns out to have been hated, was the subject of two unsuccessful plagiarism cases in 1941 and 1948. Many have noted similarities with Charlotte *Brontë's *Jane Eyre*. *Mary Anne* (1954) was based on the life of her great-great-grandmother, the mistress of the Duke of York, son of George III, and *The Glass-Blowers* (1963) on her du Maurier ancestors. As well as the biography of her father, she wrote a family history, *The du Mauriers* (1937), and edited a selection of George du Maurier's letters (1951). *Vanishing Cornwall* (1967), which contained photographs by her son, was an elegy for the county which had been her home for many years, and which provided the setting of many of her novels. She also published a study of Branwell Brontë (1960) and over fourteen collections of short stories, notably *Come Wind, Come Weather* (1940), *Nothing Hurts for Long* (1943), *Breaking Point* (1959), *Not after Midnight* (1971), and *The Rendezvous and Other Stories* (1980). Her short story 'The Birds' was adapted by Alfred Hitchcock for a film of the same name, as was *Rebecca*, which she also adapted for the stage (1940). *Jamaica Inn*, *Frenchman's Creek*, and *Hungry Hill*, for which she co-wrote the screenplay, were also successful films. Du Maurier also wrote two plays, *The Years between* (1944) and *September Tide* (1948). *Growing Pains*, her autobiography, was published in 1977 and *The Rebecca Notebook and Other Memories* in 1980. She was made a fellow of the Royal Society of Literature in 1952 and created DBE in 1969. Margaret *Forster is writing the authorized biography, and the novelist Susan Hill has been commissioned to write a sequel to *Rebecca*. *See* Jane S. Bakerman (ed.), *And then there Were Nine* (1985); Judith Cook, *Daphne: A Portrait* (1991); Alison Light, *Forever England: Femininity, Literature and Conservatism between the Wars* (1991).

Dunn, Nell (Mary), novelist and playwright (b. London, 1936).

The daughter of middle-class London parents, Nell Dunn left her convent school at 14. In 1956 she married the writer Jeremy Sandford (they later separated), by whom she had three sons. While living in Battersea, south London, she began to observe and to assemble material on the haphazard and downwardly spiralling lives of working-class women, trapped without the security of money and education. She published documentary-style stories in the *New Statesman* and in 1963 *Up the Junction*, a collection of sketches about working-class life in Clapham, which won the John Llewellyn Rhys Memorial Prize for fiction. It was adapted for television in 1965. The heroine of *Poor Cow* (1967), her first and best-selling novel, is a woman of 22, a single parent and one-time prostitute whose self-produced epitaph gives the book its title: 'To think when I was a kid I planned to conquer the world and if anybody saw me now they'd say, "She's had a rough night, poor cow."' Dunn later wrote the screenplay with Ken Loach (1967). Other fiction includes *The Incurable* (1971), about a middle-class woman whose husband develops multiple sclerosis, and *I Want* (1972), the story of a sixty-year love affair between a convent-educated girl and a Liverpool scholarship boy, written with the poet Adrian Henri and adapted for the stage in 1983. *Tear his Head off his Shoulders* (1974) is about middle-class women and sexual conflict, and *The Only Child* (1978) about maternal possessiveness. Dunn's early reputation was revived in 1981 by her play *Steaming*, set in a decaying London Turkish bath where six women of mixed ages and class gradually develop a sense of sisterhood and band together to prevent the closure of the bath. An ear for dialogue, particularly the rhythm of working-class speech, and an unabashed acknowledgement of female sexuality prevail in this as in most of Dunn's work. The play won the Susan Smith Blackburn Prize and the Evening Standard and Society of West End Theatre awards. She has also published a series of interviews, *Talking to Women* (1965), and edited another collection about alternative families, *Living like I Do* (1977, published in the USA as *Different Drummers*). Her latest work includes a play, *The Little Heroine*, and a play for television, *Every Breath you Take* (both 1988). Margaret *Drabble has written the introduction to a reprint of *Poor Cow* (1988). *See* Hélène Keyssar, *Feminist Theatre: An Introduction to Plays of Contemporary British and American Women* (1984).

Dunne, Mary Chavelita *see* EGERTON, George

eeeeeeeeeeeeeeee

E

Eastlake, Elizabeth, Lady, née Rigby, reviewer, translator, and writer on art (b. Norwich, 17 November 1809, d. London, 2 October 1893).

The fourth daughter and one of twelve children of Dr Edward Rigby, a physician, and his second wife Anne Palgrave, Elizabeth Rigby wrote her first review, a highly critical article on Goethe, for the *Foreign Quarterly Review* in 1836. An introduction to John Murray and later to John Gibson Lockhart secured her regular reviewing in the *Quarterly Review*, mainly on literary subjects. Her most celebrated coup was her pugnacious attack on *Vanity Fair* and *Jane Eyre* in 1848, in which she accused the supposedly male author of the latter of writing in an anti-Christian and revolutionary spirit. Her *First Residence on the Shores of the Baltic* (1841) was the result of a visit to Russia in 1838, and she published two works of fiction, *The Jewess* (1843) and *Livonian Tales* (1846), which also drew on her Russian experiences. Her marriage to the painter Sir Charles Eastlake, later Keeper of the National Gallery, in April 1849 extended her already large number of acquaintances in literary and political circles and also her opportunities for European travel. She translated G. F. Waagen's *Treasures of Art in Great Britain* (1845–7) and completed Mrs *Jameson's *History of our Lord as Exemplified in Works of Art* (1864). Following the death of her husband in 1865, she published *Fellowship: Letters Addressed to my Sister Mourners* (1868), which won the admiration of Queen *Victoria and provided an entrée to court circles. She edited her husband's *Contributions to the Literature of the Fine Arts* (1870), to which she added a memoir, and in 1874 revised his edition of Kugler's *Schools of Painting in Italy*. She wrote a biographical sketch of her close friend Harriet *Grote (1880) and in the same year edited her father's *Letters from France*. Her horrified response to the Rossetti exhibition of 1883 resulted in the re-publication of essays on *Five Great Painters* (1883). In 1887 she translated A. Brandl's *Samuel Taylor Coleridge and the English Romantic School*. Lady Eastlake was one of the most productive and influential female reviewers in the nineteenth century and her energetic work for the *Quarterly* on English and European literature and art continued into the 1880s. Her *Journals and Correspondence* were published in 1895, edited by her nephew Charles Eastlake Smith, and the introduction to the 1887 edition of Kugler's *Schools of Painting* contains an account of her. *See* Marion Lochhead, *Elizabeth Rigby, Lady Eastlake* (1961).

Eden, the Honourable Emily, novelist and traveller (b. Westminster 3 March 1797, d. Richmond, Surrey, 5 August 1869).

Emily Eden was the seventh daughter and one of fourteen children of George Eden, first Baron Auckland, a prominent Whig politician and diplomat, and his wife Eleanor Elliot. She and her sister Frances accompanied their brother George, the second Lord Auckland, to India, where he was Governor-General from 1835 to 1842. She acted as his hostess and on her return to England in 1844 published *Portraits of the People and Princes of India*, and much later, in 1866, a series of travel notes, *Up the Country: Letters Written to her Sister from the Upper Provinces of India* 'by the Hon. Emily Eden'. She also produced two novels, *The Semi-Detached House*, published anonymously, 'edited by Lady Theresa Lewis' (1859), and *The Semi-Attached Couple* (1860), first written in 1829, which became a minor classic. Eden's strengths were a shrewd eye for social contrasts, a mastery of dialogue, and a talent for satire. Jane *Austen was her favourite writer. She never married and in the last years of her life entertained the higher echelons of society at morning receptions at her house Eden Lodge, Kensington. Her *Letters from India* were published posthumously in 1872, and her *Letters* were edited by Violet Dickinson in 1919. *See* J. Dunbar, *Golden Interlude: The Edens in India* (1955).

Edgeworth, Maria, novelist and children's writer (b. Black Bourton, Oxfordshire, 1 January 1767, d. Edgeworthstown, County Longford, 22 May 1849).

Maria Edgeworth was one of the twenty-two children of Richard Lovell Edgeworth (1744–1817), an Anglo-Irish landowner, educationalist, and author, by his first wife Anna Maria Elers, who died in 1773. She was born at her mother's family home in Oxfordshire, moved to Ireland with her father after his second marriage, and was then sent to school in England when her stepmother became ill. She was clever at school, good at French and Italian, and amused her schoolfellows by telling them stories. She returned to Edgeworthstown, the family's Irish home, in 1782, after her father's third marriage, and helped him to run the estate. When left in charge of her siblings, she told them stories, which she copied out on a slate when they approved of them. Under her father's encouragement she completed a translation of Madame de Genlis's *Adelaide and Theodore*, one volume of which was printed in 1783. Her first major publication was *Letters for Literary Ladies* (1795), a defence of female education. *The Parent's Assistant* (1795), stories for children, which followed, went through numerous editions, English, Irish, and American, until well into the mid-nineteenth century. It was also translated into French. Her next work, *Practical Education* (1798), a treatise which showed the influence of Rousseau's theories of education, was written with her father, who was a formative intellectual presence throughout her career as well as a collaborator. Her reputation was established by her first novel, *Castle Rackrent* (1800), which with its Irish setting and historical background, 'taken from facts, and from the manners of the Irish squires, before the year 1782', as the title-page announced, began a tradition of historical and regional novels which had a far-reaching influence on fiction of the period. Scott, for one, claimed in the preface to the Waverley edition of his novels in 1829 that he would never have thought of a Scottish novel had he not read Maria Edgeworth's 'exquisite pieces of Irish character'. Her second Irish novel, *The Absentee*, published as part of *Tales of Fashionable Life* (1812), was another chronicle of an adventuresome Irish landed family. The humorous *Ennui* (1809) and *Ormond* (1817) were her other important Irish tales. Other novels depicted contemporary English society, including *Belinda* (1801), *Leonora* (1806), *Patronage* (1814), and *Helen* (1834). The writing of adult fiction was interspersed with collections of didactic stories for children such as *Early Lessons* (1801), begun by her father, which had various sequels, *Moral Tales for Young People* (1801), *The Mental Thermometer* (1801), and *Popular Tales* (1804). As with *The Parent's Assistant* the collections went through numerous editions, usually by reprinting one or two of the original stories and adding others. Maria lived at Edgeworthstown all her adult life, surrounded by her large family, having rejected a proposal of marriage from a Swedish count in 1803. She was distraught by her father's death in 1817, but prepared his *Memoirs* for publication in 1820. Despite her relative seclusion she had numerous admirers in English literary circles. She was fêted on trips to London and Paris, and corresponded with many writers, including Anna Laetitia *Barbauld, Elizabeth *Inchbald, Elizabeth *Hamilton, and Jane Marcet. She visited Scott at Abbotsford in 1823 and he returned the visit in

1825. Jane *Austen sent her a copy of *Emma.* She continued to run the estate until near her death, her American admirers sending barrels of flour 'to Miss Edgeworth for her poor' during the famine of 1846. She died there at the age of 82 after a writing career of over fifty years. *See* A. T. Ritchie, *A Book of Sibyls* (1883); Virginia *Woolf, *The Common Reader* (1925); A. J. C. Hare, *The Life and Letters of Maria Edgeworth* (1894); Marilyn S. Butler, *Maria Edgeworth* (1972) and *Jane Austen and the War of Ideas* (1975, 1987); Mary Anne Schofield and Cecilia Macheski (eds.), *Fetter'd or Free? British Women Novelists 1670–1815* (1986); Elizabeth Kowaleski-Wallace, *Their Fathers' Daughters: Hannah More, Maria Edgeworth, and Patriarchal Complicity* (1991).

Edwards, Amelia (Ann Blandford), novelist, journalist, and Egyptologist (b. London, 7 June 1831, d. Weston-super-Mare, Somerset, 15 April 1892).

Amelia Edwards was the daughter of a retired army officer turned London banker. She was educated at home by her mother, the daughter of an Irish barrister, and showed early promise in drawing, writing, and music. A poem written at the age of 7 and a story written when she was 12 were both published in magazines. A downturn in the family fortunes turned her to writing for a living. She published stories in *Chambers' Journal* and in Dickens's periodicals *Household Words and All the Year Round,* and later wrote for the *Saturday Review* and the *Morning Post.* She also began to write fiction, eight novels in total, each of which she claimed took her two years to complete, so meticulous was her research for their background and setting. The first, *My Brother's Wife,* was published in 1855, but it was with *Barbara's History* (1864), which was influenced by *David Copperfield* and involved the plot device of bigamy fashionable in the 1860s, that her reputation was made. It was republished by Harper in America and by Tauchnitz in Germany and was translated into German, Italian, and French. Other novels included *Debenham's Vow* (1870), set during the American Civil War, *The Days of my Youth* (1873), about a French upbringing, and *Lord Brackenbury* (1880), a novel of English country life, which was originally published in the *Graphic* with illustrations by Luke Fildes. In the 1870s she embarked on some extensive travels, particularly to Egypt and the Middle East. Her first travel book, *Untrodden Peaks and Unfrequented Valleys* (1872), an account of her journey through the Dolomites, was followed by *A Thousand Miles up the Nile* (1877), which took her two years to write, and recorded her discovery of various Egyptian monuments and treasures. More than a travel book, it was a scholarly introduction to the civilization of ancient Egypt and went through three editions. Her experience of the irresponsible destruction of antiquities in Egypt prompted her resolve to further the scientific excavation and preservation of such monuments and artefacts. She was instrumental in the establishment of the Egyptian Exploration Fund in 1882 and remained involved with its activities until her death. In her will she left a bequest to found the first chair of Egyptology at University College London. A second book on Egyptian culture, *Pharaohs, Fellahs and Explorers*, the substance of a series of lectures in America (she did not choose the title), was published in 1891. In her later years she became involved in various public activities. She was a member of the Bible Archaeological Society and of the Society for the Promotion of Hellenic Literature. She was also a member of a society for promoting women's suffrage. Just before her death she received a civil-list pension for her services to literature and to archaeology. A broken arm which she suffered during the American lecture tour of 1889–90 was the beginning of a marked decline in health. She did not long survive the death in 1892 of a friend with whom she had lived for many years. *See* A. Sergeant (ed.), *Women Novelists of Queen Victoria's Reign* (1897).

'**Egerton,** George' (Mary Chavelita Dunne), short story writer and playwright (b. Melbourne, Australia, 14 December 1859, d. Crawley, Sussex, 12 August 1945).

George Egerton was the daughter of a vagabond Irish army officer, John J. Dunne, and his Welsh wife Isabel George Bynon. The facts of her life are complicated by the various 'official' versions she put out during her lifetime. As a child she witnessed some of the incidents in the New Zealand wars against the Maoris and also spent some time in Chile. She had hoped to study art, but family finances did not permit it, and she studied nursing instead. She worked for a time in New York, Dublin, and London and in 1888 eloped with Henry Higginson, a married man and a friend of her father's (he is listed as H. H. W. Melville in her *Who's Who* entry). They lived in Norway, where she was introduced to the work of Ibsen, who later became a prominent influence on her own writing. She also met the novelist Knut Hamsen, whose novel *Hunger* she translated (1899) and to whom she dedicated her first book, *Keynotes*. She left Higginson after a year, moved to England, and in 1891 married George Egerton Clairmonte, a minor Canadian writer. They lived in Ireland, had one child, and were divorced in 1901. (Her 'official' account has both husbands die.) In the same year she married Reginald Golding Bright, a theatrical agent. *Keynotes* (1893), a collection of short stories, was one of the most influential of the *New Woman fictions of the late nineteenth century. Published by John Lane, with whom Egerton probably had an affair, and with a frontispiece by Aubrey Beardsley, its success led to several more collections, all with musical titles, *Discords* (1894), *Symphonies* (1897), and *Fantasies* (1898). The stories or sketches in each collection present women at psychologically significant moments, often at points of crisis, on the brink of suicide, suffering from alcoholism, or beset by sexual problems. Egerton's work was crucial to the establishment of a feminist literary voice in the 1890s. On the strength of her first book Lane established a 'Keynotes' series which included works by Grant Allen, Ella *D'Arcy, 'Fiona Macleod' (William Sharp), and others. Egerton published *The Wheel of God* (1898), a semi-autobiographical fiction, *Rosa Amorosa* (1901), which also drew on her own experiences, and *Flies in Amber* (1905), a collection of short stories. She wrote several plays, including *His Wife's Family* (1908), *The Backsliders* (1910), and *Camilla States her Case* (1925), and adapted the work of various European playwrights, among them Pierre Loti, Judith Gautier, and Henry Bernstein. Her plays attracted the interest of prominent actresses but failed to win either commercial success or critical approval. Very much an 1890s figure, she lived until 1945, listing languages, dialects, needlework, and genealogy as her recreations in her *Who's Who* entry. She was a founder member of the Irish Genealogical Research Society. *See A Leaf from the Yellow Book: The Correspondence of George Egerton*, ed. Terence de Vere White (1958); Gail Cunningham, *The New Woman and the Victorian Novel* (1978); Patricia Stubbs, *Women and Fiction: Feminism and the Novel 1880–1920* (1979).

Egerton, Sarah, née Fyge, poet and polemicist (b. London, 1670, d. 13 February 1723).

Sarah Fyge Egerton was one of six daughters of Thomas Fyge, a physician and city councillor descended from a landowning family in Winslow, Buckinghamshire, and Mary Beecham of Seaton, in Rutlandshire. When she was 14 she wrote an answer to Robert Gould's misogynist satire *Love Given O're; or, A Satyr against the Pride, Lust and Inconstancy etc. of Woman* (1682), which was published anonymously as *The Female Advocate*, with a preface signed 'S.F.', in 1686. A second and expanded edition was published the following year, the success of which prompted her father to send her to live with relations in the country, at Shenley in Buckinghamshire. She was married against her will to a lawyer, Edward Field, who died in the mid-1690s, leaving her well off and childless. Her infatuation with his friend Henry Pierce, the 'Alexis' of her poems, continued throughout her second marriage to her cousin the Revd Thomas Egerton, rector of Adstock, in Buckinghamshire, and many years her senior. Her *Poems on Several Occasions* was published in 1703 and reissued in 1706. Also in 1703 the couple became embroiled in an acrimonious, highly public, and apparently unsuccessful divorce suit. The marriage was extravagantly satirized by Fyge's one-time friend Delarivier *Manley, in *The New Atlantis* (1709), and ridiculed in a popular broadside in 1711, but the couple remained married until Egerton's death in 1720. Sarah Fyge published an ode on Dryden's death in *Luctus Britannici; or The Tears of the British Muses* (1700) and contributed three poems to *The *Nine Muses; or Poems on the Death of the Late Famous John Dryden* (1700), edited by Manley. Her last known poem was the unpublished 'The Essay, Address'd to the Illustrious Prince and Duke of Marlbrow after the Long Campaigne', written in 1708. She died in 1723, leaving some plate to the church in Winslow where she was buried, and a bequest of £1 a year to the poor of the parish, which was not carried out due to the corruption of her executor. Her monument depicted her as a victim of fate, an image she would probably have approved of.

Elgee, Jane Francesca *see* WILDE, Lady

'Eliot, George' (Mary Ann Evans), novelist (b. Arbury, Chilvers Coten, Warwickshire, 22 November 1819, d. London, 22 December 1880).

George Eliot was the third child of Robert Evans, the agent for the Newdigate estates in Derbyshire and Warwickshire, and his second wife Christiana Pearson. Known for his integrity and devotion to his work, Robert Evans was the model for Caleb Garth in *Middlemarch*, and in part for the hero of *Adam Bede*. Mary Ann's childhood was rural and happy, and much of it, particularly her close relationship with her older brother Isaac, is reflected in the first two books of *The Mill on the Floss*. She went to various local schools including Miss Wallington's at Nuneaton, where one of her teachers, Maria Lewis, a strong Evangelical, was an important influence, and then to a boarding school run by the Misses Franklin in Coventry. After her mother's death in 1836 she returned home to become her father's housekeeper, while also putting herself through a formidable programme of reading. Philosophy, theology, the works of Scott, and the Romantic poets, particularly Wordsworth, were combined with extensive reading in German literature. She also took lessons in Italian and German from a local teacher and read Greek and Latin with the headmaster of a nearby grammar school. Her brother Isaac took over the management of the Arbury estate in 1841 and Mary Ann and her father moved to a house in Foleshill, Coventry, where she became friends with Charles Bray, a philanthropic ribbon manufacturer and progressive intellectual, and his wife Caroline. Her strong Evangelical sympathies gradually waned under the influence of the Brays and of Caroline Bray's brother Charles Hennell, another free-thinker, until she eventually lost her faith, much to her father's distress. In 1844 Hennell persuaded her to translate D. F. Strauss's controversial *Das Leben Jesu* into English. It was published in 1846. Her father's death in 1849 left her with a small annuity and the freedom to work in London, eventually as the assistant editor of John Chapman's radical *Westminster Review*. She wrote a number of lengthy reviews for the quarterly herself, including 'Silly Novels by Lady Novelists' and 'The Natural History of German Life' (both in 1856), which contained important personal statements on the nature of fiction. In 1854 she published a translation of Ludwig Feuerbach's *Essence of Christianity*, a work which was to have a profound influence on her own thought. An emotional involvement with Chapman, and then an unreciprocated attraction to the philosopher Herbert Spencer, preceded her relationship with George Henry Lewes (1817–78), a journalist, philosopher, and scientist and also a married man. Lewes had condoned his wife's adultery with his friend Thornton Hunt, which, according to law, prevented his subsequently obtaining a divorce. Marian, as she was now known, and Lewes entered into a common-law 'marriage' in 1854, one result of which was her complete ostracism by her family and, most painfully, by her brother Isaac. Lewes became a crucial figure in her literary career, encouraging her to write fiction, protecting her against insensitive criticism, and organizing the business side of her life. *Scenes of Clerical Life* (1858), a collection of three stories initially published in *Blackwood's Magazine*, was the first work to appear under her pseudonym George Eliot. *Adam Bede* (1859), which followed, reinforced an already meteoric reputation, and addressed, among other things, the problem of seduction and the sexual double standard already tackled by Elizabeth *Gaskell in *Ruth* (1853) and by Elizabeth Barrett *Browning in *Aurora Leigh* (1857). The autobiographical *The Mill on the Floss* (1860), with its controversial ending, established her as a major novelist. It was followed by *Silas Marner* (1861), a pastoral tale of a child's redemptive love. *Romola* (1863) marked a change of subject and a change of publisher, a historical novel set in fifteenth-century Florence, serialized first in the *Cornhill Magazine* and published by Smith Elder. *Felix Holt the Radical* (1866), her only political novel, reflected the debate surrounding the impending second Reform Bill and revealed an innate conservatism. It also marked her return to the house of Blackwood. Shorter works like 'The Lifted Veil' (1859), a story of clairvoyance, 'Brother Jacob' (1864), 'The Spanish Gypsy' (1868), a long poem, and 'Armgart' (1871), a verse drama about a woman artist, were interspersed with the writing of her major fiction. *Middlemarch: A Story of Provincial Life*, her best-known, and probably her best, work, was published in eight parts (1871–2). *Daniel Deronda* (1876), her last novel, was also her most radical, and encompassed contemporary English upper middle-class society and a search for a new Jewish state. Lewes died suddenly in 1878, followed by John Blackwood in 1879. Eliot edited the remaining volumes of Lewes's *Problems* *of Life and Mind*, which was in the process of publication, and in 1880 married John Walter Cross (1840–1924), twenty years her junior, who had been a friend of both Lewes and herself. Her family, including Isaac Evans, restored relations with her almost immediately, after a gap of twenty-five years. She died of a kidney disorder seven months later. The publication of Cross's *The Life of George Eliot* in 1885 initiated a general re-evaluation of her work and a reconsideration of her especially by women writers, a process which continued into the twentieth century, with the responses of Virginia *Woolf (1919) and Vita *Sackville-West (1932). The psychological seriousness of her characters, her exploration of the complex forces determining an individual's relationship with his society, and the philosophical underpinning of her fiction made her one of the major Victorian novelists, an assessment which modern criticism from the 1950s onward has endorsed. A recent generation of feminist critics has focused on her female characters and her presentation of the constricted lives of nineteenth-century women. *The George Eliot Letters* have been edited by Gordon S. Haight (9 vols., 1954–79), the *Essays of George Eliot* by Thomas Pinney (1963). William Baker has edited her notebooks from the Pforzheimer Library (4 vols., 1976–85), J. C. Pratt and V. A. Neufeldt the *Middlemarch* notebooks (1979), and Joseph Wiesenfarth *A Writer's Notebook 1854–79 and Uncollected Writings* (1981). A. S. *Byatt and Nicholas Warren have edited *Selected Essays, Poems and Other Writings* (1990). *See* Virginia Woolf, *The Common Reader* (1925); V. Sackville-West, in *Great Victorians*, ed. H. J. Massingham (1932); Gordon S. Haight, *George Eliot: A Biography* (1968); Barbara Hardy, *The Novels of George Eliot* (1959) and *Particularities: Readings on George Eliot* (1982); David Carroll (ed.) *George Eliot: The Critical Heritage* (1977); Sandra Gilbert and Susan Gubar, *The Madwoman in the Attic* (1979); Gillian Beer, *Darwin's Plots* (1983) and *George Eliot* (1986); Sally Shuttleworth, *George Eliot and Nineteenth Century Science* (1984); Margaret Homans, *Bearing the Word* (1986); George Levine with Patricia O'Hara, *An Annotated Critical Bibliography of George Eliot* (1988); David Carroll, *George Eliot and the Conflict of Interpretations* (1992).

'Elizabeth' *see* ARNIM, Elizabeth von

Elizabeth I, Queen of England, poet, translator, and letter writer (b. Greenwich, 7 September 1533, d. Richmond, Surrey, 24 March 1603).

Elizabeth I was the daughter of Henry VIII and Anne Boleyn. Her early education was undertaken by the eminent scholars Roger Ascham and his pupil William Grindal. She had a perfect command of French, Italian, Latin, and Greek, both written and spoken, as well as some German, Spanish, and

Flemish. When she was 11 she translated Marguerite of Navarre's *Le Miroir de l'âme pécheresse* as *The Glasse of the Sinful Soul* (printed in 1548 as *The Godly Medytacyon*, ed. P. Ames, 1897, and R. Salminen, 1979). Her other translations, from Petrarch and Boethius' *De consolatione philosophiae* to Horace's *Ars poetica*, attempted when she was 65, are competent but not exceptional (ed. C. Pemberton, 1899). She wrote *A Book of Devotions*, her private prayers, in four languages in the 1570s (trans. A. Fox and introd. J. Hodges, 1970). Six original poems are known to be hers, three of which are short epigrams. Of the remaining three, 'The doubt of future foes' on the plotters for Mary Queen of Scots, was carefully selected by George Puttenham in his *The Art of English Poesy* (1589) to illustrate the rhetorical figure of the Gorgeous. Not surprisingly other contemporary references to her poetic talents erred towards hyperbole. Her letters deserve more notice than they have received, and at least twelve of her speeches remain, including the famous address to her troops at Tilbury before the arrival of the Armada, and her last oration to Parliament. *See The Poems of Elizabeth I*, ed. Leicester Bradner (1964); *The Letters of Elizabeth I*, ed. G. B. Harrison (1935) and E. I. Kouri (1982); *The Public Speaking of Queen Elizabeth I: Selections*, ed. G. Rice (1951). Biographies include J. Neale, *Queen Elizabeth* (1934); Edith *Sitwell, *Fanfare for Elizabeth* (1946; repr. 1988); Susan Bassnett, *Elizabeth I: A Feminist Perspective* (1988).

Ellerman, Annie Winnifred *see* BRYHER

'**Ellis,** Alice Thomas' (Anna Margaret Haycraft), novelist (b. Liverpool, 9 September 1932).

Alice Thomas Ellis is the daughter of John and Alexandra Lindholm. She grew up in Penmaenmawr, North Wales, and went to Bangor County Grammar School ('in a way it was rather like heaven') and then to the Liverpool School of Art. A convert to Roman Catholicism, she spent a period as a postulant in a Liverpool convent and then married publisher Colin Haycraft in 1956. They had seven children, of whom five survive. She published two cookery books as Alice Haycraft, in 1977 and 1980. Food, like Roman Catholicism, plays a prominent part in her fiction. She published her first novel, *The Sin Eater*, in 1977, under the pseudonym Alice Thomas Ellis. It won the Welsh Arts Council Award. Her novels are comedies of upper-class manners, set alternately in London and in the country, usually Wales, both familiar territory. The women in her fiction are confronted by moral choices, often precipitated by love, marital crises, bereavement, jealousy, or bizarre sexual attraction. Eccentric characters and events are juxtaposed with the conventional and the prosaic, good is tested against the tangible presence of evil, and the comedy often verges on the macabre, as in *The Twenty-Seventh Kingdom* (1982), *The Other Side of the Fire* (1983), and *Unexplained Laughter* (1985), which won the Yorkshire Post fiction award. Her acute ear for dialogue underpins each book. *The Clothes in the Wardrobe* (1987), *The Skeleton in the Cupboard* (1988), and *The Fly in the Ointment* (1989) form a trilogy. Ellis's columns in the *Spectator*, on chaotic north London domestic life, have been collected as the *Home Life* series (1986), *More Home Life* (1987), *Home Life 3* (1988), *Home Life 4* (1989). Her autobiography *A Welsh Childhood* was published in 1990. She is fiction editor of her husband's publishing firm of Duckworth, who also publish Beryl *Bainbridge.

Ellis, Sarah, née Stickney, novelist and writer of conduct books (b. Hull, 1812, d. Hoddesdon, Hertfordshire, 16 June 1872).

Sarah Ellis was born into the Quaker family of William Stickney, a farmer, but rejected the Society of Friends and joined the Congregationalists in her youth. In 1837 she became the second wife of William Ellis, chief foreign secretary of the London Missionary Society, who had achieved considerable fame for his work in the South Sea Islands and later in Madagascar. The Ellises, who had no children, were united in their devotion to the temperance cause and to the work of Christian missions. Sarah Ellis was also interested in education of working-class women and founded a school, Rawdon House, which she ran herself. She had published *The Poetry of Life* (1835) before her marriage, and followed this with a series of 'conduct books' which advised women on their role in society, in the home, and within marriage. *The Women of England, their Social Duties and Domestic Habits* (1839), *The Daughters of England* (1842), *The Mothers of England* (1843), and *The Wives of England* (1843) advocated submission to male authority, insisted on the superior role of men in society, and advised women to restrict their activities to those of motherhood and the home. Ellis's books were probably the best known of the many such conduct books which appeared during the Victorian period. *The Women of England* alone went through more than twenty editions. She regarded fiction as another means of disseminating her views, from her first novel *Pictures of Private Life* (1833) and *Home; or The Iron Rule* (1836) to *Pique* (1850), which demonstrated the duties of marriage, and the submission of woman in that institution. She wrote other 'improving' works, the titles of which are self-evident: *Family Secrets; or Hints to those who would Make Home Happy* (1841), *Mrs. Ellis' Housekeeping Made Easy* (1843), *Temper and Temperament* (1844), *The Young Ladies' Reader* (1845), *The Mothers of Great Men* (1859), *Share and Share Alike; or The Grand Principle* (1865), *Rainy Days and how to Meet them* (1867), *Education of the Heart: Woman's Best Work* (1872). Ellis published over thirty books, many of which infuriated her more liberated sisters. Some twentieth-century readers have seen her works as survival guides to a system which could not be changed, rather than an admission of female inferiority, and have pointed out her emphasis on female solidarity. An ironic note is added by the *DNB*, which does not grant her a separate entry, but incorporates her within her husband's. She also edited *Fisher's Drawing-Room Scrap Book* (1844–5) and *Fisher's Juvenile Scrap Book* (1840–8), both *annuals. She died within days of her husband, having caught the cold which led to his death. *See The Home Life and Letters of Mrs. Ellis*, compiled by her nieces (1893).

Elstob, Elizabeth, Anglo-Saxon scholar (b. Newcastle upon Tyne 29 September 1683, d. 3 June 1758).

Elizabeth Elstob was the daughter of Ralph Elstob, a Newcastle merchant whose family claimed descent from Welsh kings, and of Jane Hall. Her father died when she was 5 and her mother, 'a great admirer of learning, especially in her own sex', as she recalled, died three years later. Her uncle and guardian discouraged her education, arguing that 'one tongue is enough for a woman', but she learnt French, and eventually eight languages, including Latin. Her brother William was sent to Eton, followed by Oxford. He became a fellow of University College and later held two London livings. A noted Anglo-Saxon scholar, it was probably through his encouragement and the influence of their patron George Hickes (1642–1715), the acknowledged leader of the first generation of Anglo-Saxon scholars, that Elizabeth's interest in the subject, a hitherto unknown pursuit for a woman, developed. She lived with William in Oxford for a while and then in London. Her first publication was a translation of Madame de Scudéry's *Essay on Glory* (1708). She also published *An English-Saxon Homily on the Birthday of St. Gregory* (1709), dedicated to Queen Anne, which attracted subscribers among a number of women of rank. In her preface she apologized for using a language 'few Men and none of the other Sex have ventured to converse with' and vigorously defended women's right to learning against the argument that it encouraged neglect of household duties. She also anticipated the charge that the work might not be all her own but her brother's. She dedicated her next work, an Anglo-Saxon grammar, *Rudiments of Grammar for the English-Saxon Tongue First Given in English with an Apology for the Study of Northern Antiquities* (1715), to Princess Caroline and received help from Mary *Astell in finding subscribers. Her preface referred to 'the Pleasure I my self had reaped from the Knowledge I have gained from this Original of our Mother Tongue' and her hope that 'others of my own Sex might be capable of the same Satisfaction'. She planned an edition of *The English Saxon Homilies of Aelfric*, of which some testimonies in its favour and proposals appeared but only two gatherings of the work were published in 1715, possibly because financial support was not forthcoming. Both her brother and her patron died in 1715, leaving her more or less penniless. She moved to Evesham where she became mistress of a charity school under the patronage of Lady Elizabeth Hastings, doubting her ability to teach the housewifely accomplishments of spinning and knitting. During this period she met the antiquary George *Ballard, who was so moved by her plight that he was inspired to compile his *Memoirs of Several Ladies of Great Britain* (1752). Elstob had herself planned to compile a record of women of achievement, the early stages of which were contained in a notebook, but like her other scholarly projects it came to an end with her brother's death. After twenty years of isolation and privation at the school she obtained a pension from Queen Caroline, through the influence of Mary *Delany and of Sarah Chapone, mother-in-law of Hester *Chapone. After the Queen's death Mrs Delany introduced her to the Duchess of Portland, who employed her as governess to her children from 1738 until her death in 1756. Her health gradually declined, and she died at the age of 73. After her early burst of productivity during the years spent with her brother, she wrote virtually nothing for the last forty years of her life. She left a brief manuscript autobiography, dated *c.*1738. *See* Myra Reynolds, *The Learned Lady in England, 1650–1760* (1920); Mary Elizabeth Green, in *Female Scholars: A Tradition of Learned Women before 1800*, ed. J. R. Brink (1980); Ruth Perry, introd. to G. Ballard, *Memoirs of Several Ladies of Great Britain* (1985).

Emecheta, Buchi, novelist, children's writer, and publisher (b. Yaba, Nigeria, 21 July 1944).

Buchi Emecheta is the daughter of Ibo parents, Alice Ogbanje and Jeremy Nwabudike Emecheta, both of whom died when she was young. She won a scholarship to the Methodist Girls' High School in Lagos and at 17 married Sylvester Onwordi, whom she accompanied to England in 1962. They had five children and then separated. She worked as a librarian for nine years while bringing up her children and wrote in the mornings before work. She took a degree in sociology from the University of London (1970–4) and became a youth worker and then a community worker in Camden. Her novels *In the Ditch* (1972) and *Second-Class Citizen* (1974) are in part autobiographical and deal with her early life in Britain. They were published together as *Adah's Story* (1983). Her autobiography *Head above Water* (1986) further explores the problems of adjustment for an immigrant family, racism, and family relationships. *The Bride Price* (1976), an early manuscript of which was burned by her husband, and *The Slave Girl* (1977) draw on the African experiences of her mother and grandmother. The latter won the Jock Campbell Award for Britain's most promising writer. Another novel, *The*

Joys of Motherhood (1979), examines social injustices against women and girls in African society, and their complicity in the system. *Destination Biafra* (1982), a fictional account of the civil war, draws on first-hand accounts of friends and family. *Double Yoke* (1982) is based on her experiences as a visiting professor of English at Calaba University in Nigeria and *The Rape of Shavi* (1983) is a futuristic satire. *Gwendolen* (1989) is about a sexually abused Jamaican girl who moves to London in the 1970s. Emecheta's children's books include *Titch the Cat* (1979), *Nowhere to Play* (1980), and *The Moonlight Bride* and *The Wrestling Match* (both 1981). She writes for the *New Statesman*, the *TLS*, and the *Guardian* and has written plays for the BBC. Her work has been crucial in drawing attention to black women's writing in Britain. She has been a member of the Arts Council and of the Home Secretary's advisory council on race. She established a publishing house, Ogwugwu Afor, which publishes her own books. *See* Lauretta Ngcobo (ed.), *Let it be Told: Essays by Black Women in Britain* (1987).

English Woman's Journal (1858–64).

The periodical which gave the women's movement in Britain a voice in the 1860s. The monthly *Journal* was founded in March 1858 by Bessie Rayner *Parkes and Barbara *Bodichon, to provide a vehicle through which to publicize and debate current issues related to women. Bodichon provided the money for the venture, and Parkes became joint editor with Mary Hays. Contributors included Bodichon, Jessie Boucherett, Emily Davies, Isa Craig, Adelaide *Procter, Emily *Faithfull, and others. It began as a literary magazine with a feminist bias, but before the year was out had become a feminist magazine with some literary contributions in the form of fiction, poetry, and book reviews. The journal campaigned for improvements in women's employment, for the reform of women's education, and for the extension of legal rights. Its columns contained profiles of famous and successful women and an 'Open Council' column for readers' views. The journal's office at Langham Place provided a meeting-place for a number of women active in feminist causes, and the 'Langham Place Circle' became a nucleus from which other organizations sprang, notably the Society for the Promotion of the Employment of Women (SPEW). Women's suffrage was first mentioned in the last issue of the magazine in August 1864. Its circulation was never more than 500 but its readership is likely to have been much greater. *See* Jane Rendall, *Equal or Different? Women's Politics, 1800–1914* (1987).

'Ephelia', poet and playwright (*b. c.* 1650 d. after 1681).

Ephelia was the favourite pen-name of an unidentified Royalist woman writer with court connections, and the author of a handsomely produced volume, *Female Poems on Several Occasions: Written by Ephelia*, published in 1679 and again in 1682. The collection of sixty-five poems, written in a variety of forms, includes a group which explores a love affair between the writer and 'Strephon', or 'J. G.', a merchant-adventurer in the Tangier trade and more than twice her age. The poems move through the full cycle of the relationship from early rapture to bitter betrayal in which J. G. eventually leaves Ephelia for a wealthy Tangier beauty. The writer transforms the themes and conventions of the courtly love tradition to register their implications for women, particularly the plight of a sexually 'free' woman who is abandoned. *Female Poems* also contained the prologue, epilogue, and songs of a lost play, *The Pair Royal of Coxcombs* (*c*.1678), a satiric comedy directed at Charles II and his brother James, and a political broadside on the Popish Plot, 'A Poem to his Sacred Majesty, on the Plot, Written by a Gentlewoman', first published in 1678. 'Advice to his Grace' (1681), addressed to the Duke of Monmouth and urging him to remove himself from plots against his father, is also known to have been written by Ephelia, as is an elegy lamenting the death of the Archbishop of Canterbury in 1677. Speculations by Henry Wheatley in the nineteenth century that Ephelia was a Mrs Joan Philips have been proved groundless, as has Edmund Gosse's follow-on suggestion that she was the daughter of Katherine *Philips. She may have died around 1681, occasioning the second edition of *Female Poems*, which contained verses by Rochester, Etheredge, John Crowne, Aphra *Behn, and others of her circle, possibly a coterie similar to that which surrounded Philips. *See* Myra Reynolds, *The Learned Lady in England, 1650–1760* (1920); Elaine Hobby, *Virtue of Necessity: English Women's Writing 1649–1688* (1988).

'Evans, Margiad' (Peggy Eileen Arabella Williams), novelist and poet (b. Uxbridge, London, 1909, d. Tunbridge Wells, Kent, (18 March 1958).

Margiad Evans appropriated her pen-name from her paternal grandmother to emphasize her literary allegiance to Wales and to the Welsh–English border near Ross-on-Wye which had been her childhood home. She was born Peggy Whistler, the daughter of Geoffrey Whistler, an insurance clerk, and his wife Katharine Wood. She went to Ross-on-Wye High School, which she left at 16, and then to Hereford School of Art. She worked as a teacher and a book illustrator and published her first novel, *Country Dance*, which she illustrated under her own name, in 1932. *The Wooden Doctor*, published the following year, was about an unrequited passion, as was *Turf or Stone* (1934). *Creed* (1936), considered her best book, was the story of a religious fanatic. Her four novels, published within the space of four years, were all set in the remote Herefordshire countryside to which she was passionately attached. All were, in the words of D. S. Savage, 'bitter, passionate cries of protest against the frustrations of personal life'. In 1940 she married Michael Mendus Williams and after the war moved with him to Hartfield, in Sussex. They had one daughter. She published two volumes of poems, *Poems from Obscurity* (1947), and *A Candle Ahead* (1956), which won the Welsh Arts Council Poetry Award. Her unconventional *Autobiography* (1943) was followed by the autobiographical *A Ray of Darkness* (1952). She published a book of short stories, *The Old and the Young* (1948), but a planned book on the *Brontës, whom she greatly admired, remained unfinished. During her last years she suffered from epileptic fits, the result of a brain tumour which eventually left her paralysed. She died at the age of 49. *See* D. S. Savage, *The Withered Branch* (1950); Moira Dearnley, *Margiad Evans* (1982).

Evans, Mary Ann *see* ELIOT, George

Ewing, Juliana Horatia, née Gatty, children's writer (b. Ecclesfield, Yorkshire, 3 August 1841, d. Bath, 13 May 1885).

Juliana Ewing was the second of eight surviving children of Dr Alfred Gatty, vicar of Ecclesfield, and of Margaret Scott *Gatty, founder editor of *Aunt Judy's Magazine* and a noted children's writer. Juliana entertained her seven siblings with stories (Aunt Judy was her family nickname), and the family kept a manuscript magazine in circulation. Juliana's first published story was 'A Bit of Green', published in Charlotte *Yonge's *Monthly Packet* in July 1861. Her first volume of stories, *Melchior's Dream*, followed the next year. In May 1866 Margaret Gatty launched *Aunt Judy's Magazine*, which became Juliana's main vehicle of publication for the rest of her career. She and her sister Horatia Katharine edited it together for two years after their mother's death in 1873, and Horatia continued as editor until 1885. *Mrs. Overtheways Remembrances* (1869), *The Brownies and Other Tales* (1870) (which gave Robert Baden-Powell the idea for the name of his organization for younger girls), *A Flat Iron for a Farthing* (1872), *Lob-lie-by-the-Fire* (1874), *Jackanapes* (1884), and *The Story of a Short Life* (1885) were some of her best-known works, all of which first appeared in the *Magazine*. Her stories represented a shift away from the solidly moralizing and didactic nature of earlier children's fiction. In 1867 she married Major Alexander Ewing of the Army Pay Department and travelled with him to New Brunswick. They settled eventually at Aldershot, and Mrs Ewing used her knowledge of army life and overseas settings as background to some of her stories. She became too ill to accompany her husband in later years, and for the last part of her life lived at Taunton. She died of cancer in 1885. *See* Horatia K. F. Gatty, *Juliana Horatia Ewing and her Books* (1885); A. Sergeant (ed.), *Women Novelists of*

Queen Victoria's Reign (1897); Marghanita Laski, *Mrs. Ewing, Mrs. Molesworth and Mrs. Hodgson Burnett* (1950); G. Avery, *Mrs. Ewing* (1961); Christabel Maxwell, *Mrs. Gatty and Mrs. Ewing* (1949).

ffffffffffff

F

'Fairless, Michael' (Margaret Fairless Barber), religious writer (b. Yorkshire, 7 May 1869, d. Castle Hill, Yorkshire, 24 August 1901).

Michael Fairless was the youngest of the three daughters of Fairless Barber, a lawyer with antiquarian interests, and his wife Maria Musgrave. She was educated at home, then at schools in Torquay and London, and read voraciously as a child. Travels in Germany when she was young had a profound influence on her. She trained as a nurse and worked in the East End of London, where she was known as 'the Fighting Sister', until a serious spinal injury forced her retirement. After the death of both of her parents she lived in the country with only the company of a mentally retarded girl and began to write. A novella, *The Gathering of Brother Hilarius*, the story of a medieval monk who eventually becomes a prior, which contained a powerful Black Death scene, was published in 1901. Her best-known work was the posthumously published *The Roadmender* (1902), a work of popular philosophy first published in the *Pilot*, the magazine of the British sailors' society. In the story the roadmender, Fairless herself, watches life tranquilly by the side of the pathway to heaven. It sold 250,000 copies by 1922. An edition by her friend M. E. Dawson in 1926 contained additional material. Her health deteriorated to such an extent that at times she wrote lying down, using her left hand, and eventually she dictated her work. Three more books were published after her death: *The Child King*, Christmas stories published in 1902, *The Grey Brethren and Other Fragments in Prose and Verse* (1905), and

Stories Told to Children (1914). *See* M. E. Dowson [W. S. Palmer] and A. M. Haggard, *Michael Fairless: Her Life and Writings* (1913).

Faithfull, Emily, editor and publisher (b. Headley, Surrey, 1835, d. Manchester, 1895).

Emily Faithfull was the youngest daughter of Ferdinand Faithfull, vicar of Headley, near Epsom, in Surrey. She went to a boarding school in Kensington, was presented at court, and had a social life typical of an upper middle-class girl. When she was in her early twenties she met some of the Langham Place Group of feminists and became involved in the Society for Promoting the Employment of Women. She was convinced that typesetting was a suitable job for women, taught herself to typeset, and in 1860 founded the Victoria Press, in which the compositors, although not all the employees, were women. The Press won the approval of Queen *Victoria, and Emily Faithfull received the honorary title of 'Printer and Publisher in Ordinary to her Majesty.' In 1863 she founded and edited the * *Victoria Magazine*, which published fiction and also pressed the claims of women to properly paid employment. In 1864 her reputation was severely damaged by her involvement in a highly publicized divorce case between Henry (later Admiral) and Helen Codrington. She withdrew from the Victoria Press, but joined the Women's Trade Union League, became involved in the Women's Printing Society, and in 1877 founded the *West London Express*, again staffed by women compositors. She was also on the staff of the *Ladies' Pictorial*. During this period she wrote a novel, *Change upon Change: A Love Story* (1868). Several visits to the United States, including a lecture tour, were described in *Three Visits to America* (1884) and her novel was republished there in 1873 as *A Reed Shaken with the Wind*. She published many articles and pamphlets on the subject of women's employment, which became the main preoccupation of her later years. She also founded the International Musical, Dramatic and Literary Association, in order to promote improvement in the matter of copyright. In the early 1860s she was involved with the Women's Suffrage Society, but it is likely that the scandal surrounding the Codrington divorce made her less acceptable as a colleague in women's suffrage circles. She died in 1895 at the age of 60.

'Falconer, Lanoe' (Mary Elizabeth Hawker), novelist (b. Inverary, Aberdeenshire, 29 January 1848, d. Broxwood Court, Herefordshire, 16 June 1908).

Lanoe Falconer was the daughter of Peter William Lanoe Hawker, an officer in the 74th Highlanders, and his wife Elizabeth Fraser. Her paternal grandfather was the author of a well-known sportsman's manual. Her education was perfunctory, but she read assiduously, and after her father's death in 1857 her mother's remarriage took the family to France and Germany and she became fluent in both languages. She wrote stories and essays, publishing sporadically in periodicals, but her first success came in 1890, when her short novel *Mademoiselle Ixe* inaugurated Fisher Unwin's Pseudonym Library. The series, to which *Ouida contributed and for which John Oliver *Hobbes invented her pen-name, was intended to rival John Lane's Keynotes series. The novels were pocket-sized, and shaped to fit in a reticule. 'Lanoe' was a family name, and 'Falconer' a synonym of 'hawker'. *Mademoiselle Ixe* concerned a governess who became involved in a Russian nihilist plot, and was pronounced by the *Saturday Review* to be 'one of the finest short stories in England'. Gladstone praised it, Russia forbade its circulation, and it was translated into French, German, Dutch, and Italian. It also enjoyed large English and American sales. She followed it with *Cecilia de Noel* (1891), a ghost story, and *The Hotel d'Angleterre* (1891), a collection of stories. She also published *Old Hampshire Vignettes* (1907) and two short tales, *Shoulder to Shoulder* (1891) and *The Wrong Prescription* (1893). Her mother's death in 1901 was a blow from which she did not recover. She died of rapid consumption in 1908. *See* E. M. Phillipps, *Lanoe Falconer (Author of Mademoiselle Ixe)* (1915).

Falkland, Lady *see* CARY, Elizabeth, Lady

'Fane, Violet' (Mary Montgomerie Lamb, later Singleton, later Lady Currie), poet and novelist (b. Beauport, near Littlehampton, Sussex, 24 February 1843, d. Harrogate, Yorkshire, 13 October 1905).

Violet Fane was the eldest daughter of Charles James Saville Montgomerie Lamb and Anna Charlotte Grey. Both sides of the family were literary by inclination as well as socially distinguished, but did not, it seems, approve of women writing. Despite parental discouragement she wrote both stories and poetry as a child and etched illustrations for a reprint of Tennyson's 'Mariana' (1863). In 1864 she married Henry Sydenham Singleton, an Irish landowner, by whom she had two sons and two daughters. The legacy of family disapproval prompted the adoption of a pseudonym, 'Violet Fane', after a character in Disraeli's *Vivian Grey*, for her first volume of poetry, *From Dawn to Noon* (1872). *Denzil Place* (1875), a novel in verse, contained an adulterous relationship which critics found distasteful. *The Queen of the Fairies and Other Poems* (1876) and a play, *Anthony Bebington* (1877), were followed by her *Collected Verses* (1880). According to a reviewer for the *Academy* Violet Fane bore 'somewhat the same relation to the true poets of today as L.E.L. [Laetitia *Landon] did to those forty years ago'. Mary Singleton was a well-known figure in London society. W. H. Mallock dedicated his *New Republic* (1877) to her and she featured in it as Mrs Sinclair, 'who has published a volume of poems, and is a sort of fashionable London Sappho'. She published three novels, *Sophy; or The Adventures of a Savage* (1881), *Thro' Love and War* (1886), and *The Story of Helen Davenant* (1889), all of them lengthy, three-volume love stories which appealed to popular taste. She also wrote essays and sketches for periodicals, republished as *Edwin and Angelina Papers* (Essays by 'V' reprinted from the *World*, 1878) and *Two Moods of a Man* (1901). Her first husband died in 1893, and the following year she married Sir Philip Henry Wodehouse Currie, later Baron Currie, ambassador to Constantinople and then Rome. *Under Cross and Crescent* (1896) and *Betwixt Two Seas* (1900), both volumes of poetry, were produced during her time in Constantinople. She also translated the *Memoirs of Marguerite de Valois* (1892). She died of heart failure at the Grand Hotel, Harrogate.

Fanshawe, Lady Anne, memoirist (b. London, 25 March 1625, d. Ware Park, Hertfordshire, 30 January 1680).

Anne Fanshawe was the elder daughter and fourth child of Sir John Harrison, of Balls, Hertfordshire, a prominent Royalist and friend of Charles I, and of Margaret Fanshawe. She received an education appropriate to her social position, which included French, music, needlework, and dancing. She was described as 'a hoyting girl', with a love of physical activity and adventure which was to stand her in good stead in later life. When her father was imprisoned in 1642 and deprived of his property the family moved into lodgings in Oxford. There Anne met Sir Richard Fanshawe, a poet and translator, twelve years her senior and an eminent Royalist. He was also her mother's first cousin. They married in 1644 and in a remarkably happy and intimate marriage she loyally followed and supported him in what was to become a frenetic diplomatic career, in the service first of Charles I, and then of the Duke of York, later James II, in Jersey, France, Ireland, Portugal, and Spain. She and her family of six sons and eight daughters, of whom only five survived to adulthood, endured Fanshawe's imprisonment, the sequestration of their property, mounting debts, shipwreck, and even an attack by pirates, during which she stood on deck by her husband's side. After the Restoration life became less precarious, as Fanshawe was appointed an ambassador, first to Portugal and then to Spain. His sudden death in 1666, however, left her with large debts, which she successfully recovered from the King. Her *Memoirs*, completed in 1676 and only published in 1829, combine autobiography with a vigorous if partial narrative of her adventures during the Commonwealth. They also present a devoted portrait of her husband. Horace Walpole though they dwelt too much on 'private domestic distresses' while Delarivier *Manley in *The New Atlantis* described Anne Fanshawe as a woman with 'affected learning, eternal tattle, insipid gaiety and a false sense of wit', which the *DNB* primly pronounced to be 'the scorn of a woman of doubtful reputation for one of unblemished character'. The *Spectator's* reviewer in 1829 linked the *Memoirs* with those of Lucy *Hutchinson. Virginia *Woolf reviewed the 1907 edition, based on the manuscript in the British Library which is not in Anne Fanshawe's hand, but is signed by her. The memoirs have been subsequently reprinted, together with those of another seventeenth-century memoirist, Anne, Lady *Halkett, as *The Memoirs of Anne, Lady Halkett and Ann, Lady Fanshawe*, ed. John Loftis (1979). Richard Fanshawe's best-known work was a translation of Camoens's *The Lusiad* (1655). *See The Essays of Virginia Woolf* I (1986); Mary Beth Rose (ed.), *Women in the Middle Ages and the Renaissance: Literary and Historical Perspectives* (1986); Dale Spender, *Mothers of the Novel* (1986).

Fanshawe, Catherine Maria, poet (b. Chipstead, Surrey, 6 July 1765, d. Putney Heath, London, 17 April 1834).

Catherine Fanshawe was the second daughter and one of five children of John Fanshawe of Shabden, who was first clerk of the board of green cloth in the household of George III, and his wife Penelope Dredge. On the death of her parents and two brothers, she moved with her two sisters to a house in Berkeley Square and later to Midhurst House, Richmond, where, apart from some European travels, she spent most of her life. She was an accomplished artist as well as a poet and also a lively letter writer. Despite her secluded life she made the acquaintance of many literary figures of her day. She responded to a loan of a poem by Cowper by adding 'Stanzas Addressed to Lady Hesketh', to which Cowper in turn replied. Several of her poems were published in Joanna *Baillie's *Poetic Miscellanies* (1823). Her best-known poem was a riddle on the letter H, ''Twas in heaven pronounced, and 'twas muttered in hell', which was once attributed to Byron. Her 'Speech of the Member for Odium', a squib on Cobbett, was privately printed. Testimonies to her talents were given by Scott and by her friend Mary Russell *Mitford. John Gibson Lockhart, Scott's biographer, pronounced her 'a woman of rare wit and genius'. Most of her poems remained in manuscript until after her death. *Memorials of Miss C. M. Fanshawe*, compiled by her nephew William Harness and privately printed, contains most of her poems, and some etchings. Her *Literary Remains* were published in 1876.

Farjeon, Eleanor, children's writer (b. London, 13 February 1881, d. Hampstead, London, 5 June 1965).

Eleanor Farjeon was the third of the five children of Benjamin Farjeon

(1838–1903), a prolific novelist (he wrote over fifty-one books) and the son of an orthodox Jew from North Africa, and Margaret Jefferson, the daughter of Joseph Jefferson, an American actor. Although her father did not convert to Christianity he did not impose Judaism on his children. Their Hampstead home was a meeting-place for writers, actors, and musicians, and the theatre featured centrally in family life. She had no formal education, but had the run of her father's 8,000–volume library. She was a reclusive child, wrapped up in her own fantasy world, as she later recorded: 'I was a dreamy, timid, sickly, lachrymose, painfully shy, sensitive, greedy, ill-regulated little girl.' Only after her father's death in 1903 was she forced to face the real world, at the age of 22. He had left no money and she turned to writing for a living, helped by her friendship with the poet Edward Thomas (1878–1917). His death in France in 1917 was another crucial blow which hastened her maturing as a writer. She recorded this period in her life much later in *Edward Thomas: The Last Four Years* (1958). She spent two years living alone in a cottage in Sussex after Thomas's death. *Martin Pippin in the Apple-Orchard* (1921) was the result, a romantic fantasy combining prose, verse, and folklore, which established her reputation as a writer. One of its enthusiastic reviewers was Rebecca *West. It was not intended as a children's book but its appeal to younger readers over the years ensured its reissue in 1952 as a children's story. She returned to Hampstead in 1920, where she began a stream of children's stories, poetry, rhyming games, and retold folk-tales. Her first volume of poems, *Pan-Worship* (1908), was followed by *Nursery Rhymes of London Town* (1916), one of her best-known titles. As Tom Fool she wrote topical daily verse for thirteen years for the *Daily Herald*, and as Chimaera a weekly poem for the feminist **Time and Tide* in the 1920s. Her fantasy *The Soul of Kol Nikon* (1923) was serialized in the *Irish Review*. She collaborated with her brother Herbert on a Victorian operetta, *The Two Bouquets* (1936, published 1948), a children's play, *The Glass Slipper* (1944, published 1955), and *The Silver Curlew* (1949, published 1953). Her adult books included *Ladybrook* (1931), *Humming Bird* (1936), *Miss Granby's Secret* (1940), and *Ariadne and the Bull* (1945). The best of her children's books appeared in the last fifteen years of her life, often reissues of previously published work: *Silver-Sand and Snow* (1951), *The Children's Bells* (1957), both volumes of poetry, and *The Little Bookroom* (1955), a collection of stories which won the Carnegie and the Hans Andersen medals for children's literature. She was also awarded the American Regina Medal. Her best-known poem is probably the hymn 'Morning has broken', which she wrote in the 1920s. *A Nursery in the Nineties* (1935), the story of her life up to her father's death, presents a compelling picture of bohemian family life. Farjeon had a liaison with George Earle, a scholar who was already married, for over thirty years. She became a Roman Catholic in 1951, and died at her cottage in Hampstead at the age of 84. The Eleanor Farjeon annual award for children's writing was established in her honour in 1965. *See* E. H. Colwell, *Eleanor Farjeon* (1961); Denys Blakelock, *Eleanor: Portrait of a Farjeon* (1966); Annabel Farjeon, *Morning has Broken: A Biography of Eleanor Farjeon* (1986).

'Farrell, M. J.' *see* KEANE, Molly

Feinstein, Elaine, poet and novelist (b. Bootle, Lancashire, 24 October 1930).

Elaine Feinstein is the daughter of Isador Cooklin, a shopkeeper, and his wife Fay Compton. She went to Wyggeston Grammar School, Leicester, and then read English at Newnham College, Cambridge. She took her degree in 1952 and read for the bar but never practised law. In 1956 she married Arnold Feinstein, an immunologist, by whom she had three sons. She worked as an editor at Cambridge University Press 1960–2, and then became a lecturer, first at Bishop Stortford College of Education and then at the University of Essex. She began to write poetry from the early 1960s, influenced particularly by the American poets Wallace Stevens, William Carlos Williams, and Emily Dickinson. Her first poems were 'reactions to personal experience', particularly daily life, as in her early volumes *In a Green Eye* (1966) and *The Magic Apple Tree* (1971). It was the process of translating the work of the Russian poet Marina Tsvetayeva (*Selected Poems* 1971 and 1981) which opened a new door in her own poetic development. Admiring Tsvetayeva's 'wholeness of self-exposure' she began to write longer poems, to use longer lines and new rhythms, and to extend the range of her material. *The Celebrants* (1973) was a sequence of poems tracing the human obsession with knowledge, often forbidden or arcane knowledge, and death through the ages. *Some Unease and Angels: Selected Poems* was published in 1977. *The Feast of Euridice* (1980) demonstrated new experiments with myth and legend, and *Badlands* (1986) was a series of landscapes of exile, suffering, and loss, ranging from classical mythology to the present day. Feinstein's fiction, like her poetry, shows a progressive widening of focus. It has provided, in her own words, 'a channel for the exploration of my humanist concerns'. Tsvetayeva's influence again encouraged her 'to say not what I knew was expected' in her fiction. *The Circle* (1970), her first novel, is a study of a marriage. *The Amberstone Exit* (1972) is about a young girl's hunger for sexual experience and freedom. Her Jewishness became a reality when she was old enough to register the horrors of the Second World War. Several of her novels treat the themes of the holocaust and Jewishness directly or indirectly: *Children of the Rose* (1982), *The Survivors* (1982), *The Border* (1984), *Mother's Girl* (1988). Feinstein has published several collections of short stories, and television and radio plays. She has written a biography of Tsvetayeva (1987), and has translated the work of other Russian women poets (1979 and 1988).

***Female Eunuch**, The* see GREER, Germaine

female Gothic *see* GOTHIC NOVEL

***Female Wits**, The.*

The Female Wits; or The Triumvirate of Poets at Rehearsal was an anonymous play by 'W.M.' performed at Drury Lane in 1696, published in 1704, satirizing three prominent women playwrights, Mary *Pix, Delarivier *Manley, and Catharine *Trotter.

***Feminiad**, The.*

The Feminiad was a poem by John Duncombe (1729–86), written in 1751, published in 1754, as a celebration of modern female genius, to encourage the 'thousands yet unborn' who might want to emulate them. The 370–line poem takes the form of an exemplary list or 'gallery' of women writers, intended as a source of national pride as well as inspiration. 'Genius' is interpreted mainly as poetic genius. Poets, scholars, essayists, and autobiographers are listed but no writers of fiction. Playwrights, on the whole, are disapproved of. The selection is democratic. There are peeresses as well as working-class women writers, reinforcing the belief that 'native genius' is not the preserve of a particular social class. Among those named in the poem are Aphra *Behn, Frances *Brooke, Elizabeth *Carter, Susanna *Centlivre, Catharine *Trotter, Judith Cowper Madan, Hester Mulso *Chapone, Frances Thynne, Countess of Hertford, Mary *Leapor, Delarivier *Manley, Katherine *Philips, Laetitia *Pilkington, Elizabeth *Rowe, and Anne *Finch, Countess of Winchilsea. The pen is no threat to domestic order, the poem insists, and no husband need fear a female genius in his house. But although women writers pose no threat, it is made clear that a woman writer must be virtuous as well as talented. Manley, Centlivre, and Behn are singled out as causing the Muse to throw a veil of pity over each 'bold, unblushing mien' and grieve 'to see One nobly born disgrace | Her modest sex, and her illustrious race'. *The Feminiad* was often reprinted. A new edition was published (as *The Feminead*) in 1757 and Dodsley included it in the fourth volume of his *Miscellany* in 1755. It was also frequently anthologized. A Miss Scott was inspired to write *The Female Advocate: A Poem: Occasioned by Reading Mr. Duncombe's Feminead* (1774) in response to it. As part of a general acknowledgement by male writers of women's 'right to literature' in the mid-eighteenth century, it was preceded by Thomas Seward's (father of

Anna *Seward) 'The Female Right to Literature', printed in Dodsley's 1748 collection, and by George *Ballard's *Memoirs of Several Ladies of Great Britain* (1752). George Colman and Bonnell Thornton's anthology of **Poems by Eminent Ladies*, which followed in 1755, along with *The Feminiad* helped to establish a canon of women writers to which later writers could refer. *See* Jocelyn Harris's introd. to *The Feminiad*, Augustan Reprint Society Publication no. 207 (1981).

Fenn, Lady Eleanor, née Frere ('Mrs Teachwell', 'Mrs Lovechild', 'Solomon Lovechild'), children's writer (1743–1 November 1813).

Lady Eleanor Fenn, born Frere, was the childless wife of the antiquary Sir John Fenn (1739–94) of East Dereham, in Norfolk, the first editor of the *Paston Letters*, whom she married in 1766. She was an energetic philanthropist, running Sunday schools and superintending the revival of the cottage spinning industry in her area. She also wrote books for her nieces and nephews, undertaking their entire production herself, including the binding. The publisher John Marshall, whose authors included Sarah *Trimmer and Mary Jane and Dorothy Kilner, later published her books, most of which appeared between 1780 and 1790, under various pseudonyms and sometimes anonymously. They were intended to amuse as well as instruct. Her *Juvenile Tatler* (1789) and *Fairy Spectator* (1789), both by Mrs Teachwell, were humorous, despite being written to a pattern. *Cobwebs to Catch Flies; or Dialogues in Short Sentences* (*c.*1783), her best-known and the most frequently pirated work, was a manual designed to increase vocabulary, the first volume containing words of six letters, the second increasing to words of four syllables. The work resembled Mrs *Barbauld's *Lessons for Children.* Other well-known works included *Fables by Mrs. Teachwell* (1783) and *Rational Sports* (1783). She also wrote several grammars, invented a *Game of Grammar*, and produced several works on natural history. She died in her 70th year. *See* F. J. Harvey Darton, *Children's Books in England* (3rd edn. 1982).

Ferrier, Susan Edmonstone, novelist (b. Edinburgh, 7 September 1782, d. Edinburgh, 5 November 1854).

Susan Ferrier was the youngest of the six sons and four daughters of James Ferrier, an Edinburgh lawyer, and his wife Helen Coutts, the daughter of a farmer. Her mother died when she was 15, and after her three sisters married she acted as her father's housekeeper until his death in 1829. As a Writer to the Signet and principal Clerk of Session her father was a colleague of Sir Walter Scott. Through this connection Susan was placed in the midst of the Edinburgh literary scene at one of its most glittering periods. James Ferrier also managed the estates of the fifth Duke of Argyll, which provided an introduction to fashionable Scottish life, as well as two important friendships, with Lady Charlotte *Bury, the Duke's daughter, and his niece Charlotte Clavering, who was largely responsible for encouraging Susan Ferrier to write her first novel, *Marriage* (1818). They had intended it as a joint production, although in the end Charlotte Clavering wrote only a short section, 'The History of Mrs. Douglas'. The publisher John Blackwood paid her £150 for it and it was a mark of its success that he offered £1,000 for her next work, *The Inheritance*, published in 1824. Through Scott, Robert Cadell was encouraged to bid for her final work, *Destiny*, published in 1831 and dedicated to Scott. She received £1,700 for the work. All three novels engaged in veiled didacticism on the theme of prudence in marriage, but with it Ferrier demonstrated a sure hand at comedy and a sharp eye for satire. Literary figures of all persuasions were among her admirers, including John Wilson and John Gibson Lockhart of *Blackwood's Magazine* and the *Quarterly Review*, Sydney Smith, Henry Brougham, Sir James Mackintosh, and T. B. Macaulay of the *Edinburgh*, as well as Joanna *Baillie and Scott, who was her most enthusiastic champion. Failing eyesight in her later years forced her into a life of semi-retirement, but the enduring nature of her popularity was demonstrated by the constant reprinting of her works in Bentley's Standard Novels in 1831, in the Parlour Library in 1847, in a posthumous edition by Bentley in 1856, which she had corrected, and further posthumous editions in 1873–4 and 1882. She died in Edinburgh in 1854. *See* J. A. Doyle, *Memoir and Correspondence of Susan Ferrier 1782–1854* (1898); Mary Cullinan, *Susan Ferrier* (1984).

'**Field,** Michael', poet and dramatist, joint pseudonym of Katherine Harris Bradley (b. Birmingham, 27 October 1846, d. 26 September 1914) and Edith Emma Cooper (b. Kenilworth, Warwickshire, 12 January 1862, d. 13 December 1913).

Michael Field was the pseudonym adopted by Katherine Harris Bradley, the daughter of Charles Bradley, a Birmingham tobacco manufacturer, and his wife Emma Harris, and her niece Edith Emma Cooper, the daughter of Katherine's eldest sister Emma and James Robert Cooper, a merchant. Katherine Bradley joined the Cooper household when her sister became ill after the birth of a second child, and she and Edith lived together as devoted companions for the rest of their lives. Katherine had been privately tutored and in turn taught her niece. She attended Newnham College, Cambridge, for a short period and also the Collège de France, in Paris, where she fell in love with a Frenchman, many years her senior, who died shortly afterward. When the family moved to Bristol in 1878 both women attended classes in classics and philosophy at University College, Bristol. Financially independent, they moved first to Reigate and later to Richmond, in Surrey, where they lived a near reclusive life, devoted to their writing, which was undertaken in partnership. Their first publications were Katherine Bradley's *The New Minnesinger and Other Poems*, published as by Arran Leigh (1875), and the joint *Bellerophon and Other Poems* by Arran and Isla Leigh (1881). The first Michael Field work was a play, *Callirrhoe* (1884), which was widely acclaimed. They produced altogether twenty-seven tragedies, mostly verse plays on historical and classical subjects, only one of which was ever performed, and that disastrously. There were also eight volumes of lyrics, many closely reflecting the aestheticism of the 1890s, notably *Long Ago* (1889), a rewriting of Sappho, *Sight and Song* (1892), *Under the Bough* (1893), *Poems of Adoration* (1912), mainly by Edith Cooper, and *Mystic Trees* (1913), by Katherine Bradley. To their friends Katherine Bradley was known as 'Michael', and Edith Cooper as 'Field', or more intimately 'Henry'. Sir William Rothenstein, the artist, described Michael as 'stout, emphatic, splendid and adventurous in talk, rich in wit'; Field, as 'wan and wistful, gentler in manner than Michael but equally eminent in the quick give and take of ideas'. The early Michael Field works were widely praised by reviewers. Once their identity was known, however, critics were less enthusiastic. Despite their secluded lives, they were friends with Browning, George Meredith, Herbert Spencer, Oscar Wilde, and George Moore. Katherine Bradley had also corresponded with Ruskin between 1875 and 1880. In 1907 they both became Roman Catholics, and both died of cancer within months of one another in 1913–14. A journal kept between 1888 and 1914 was left to the poet T. Sturge Moore, their literary executor, with instructions to open it at the end of 1929 and to publish what he thought fit. A selection, together with some of their letters, was published as *Works and Days*, ed. T. and D. C. Sturge Moore (1933). *The Wattlefold*, a collection of their unpublished poems, was issued posthumously by Edith C. Fortey in 1930. *See* Mary Sturgeon, *Michael Field* (1922); Lillian Faderman, *Surpassing the Love of Men* (1981); Angela Leighton, *Victorian Women Poets: Writing against the Heart* (1992).

Fielding, Sarah, novelist (b. East Stour, Dorset, 8 November 1710, d. Bath, April 1768).

Sarah Fielding was the third daughter and one of six children of Edmund Fielding, an army officer from a genteel but impoverished family, and his first wife Sarah Gould, a judge's daughter. The novelist Henry Fielding (1707–54) was her brother. Their mother died in 1718 and the children were put in the care of their maternal grandmother and a great-aunt. A domestic crisis developed when their father married a Roman Catholic whom the children disliked. As a result the family was dispersed and Sarah was sent to a boarding school in Salisbury. Her extensive knowledge of Latin and Greek and also her wide reading in English literature, however, were acquired through private study. She moved to London in the 1740s, living sometimes with Henry and his family and at times with her sisters. Her financial circumstances were precarious and the preface to her first novel, the picaresque *The Adventures of David Simple* (1744), explained that she wrote because of financial difficulties. *Familiar Letters between the Characters in David Simple* (1747) and a sequel, *Volume the Last* (1753), profited from the success of the first work, the second edition of which was revised by Henry, who also supplied a preface disclaiming any responsibility for its composition. She joined the circle of friends and admirers who surrounded Samuel Richardson and wrote a celebrated defence of *Clarissa* in an anonymous pamphlet in 1749. Richardson printed three of her novels. Also in 1749 she published *The Governess; or Little Female Academy*, a didactic tale which has been regarded as the first full-length children's novel in English. With her friend the writer **Jane Collier** (1710–55) she wrote *The Cry* (1754), an allegory about truth and falsehood, which is relevant to contemporary discussions about the nature of fiction. *The Countess of Dellwyn* (1759) and *Ophelia* (1760), like *David Simple*, have innocent main characters who struggle against a hostile world, and in *Cleopatra and Octavia* (1757) the original historical figures tell their life stories. Her last work, *Memoirs of Socrates* (1762), was a translation from the Greek of Xenophon. Despite the popularity of *David Simple* and the full subscription lists of subsequent works, Sarah Fielding lived in comparative poverty, receiving some financial assistance from her brother and some, too, from Elizabeth *Montagu. Henry predeceased her in 1754, and she died near Bath in 1768, after a period of illness. *The Correspondence of Henry and Sarah Fielding* has been edited by Martin C. Battestin and Clive T. Probyn (1993). *See* Mary Anne Schofield and Cecilia Macheski (eds.), *Fetter'd or Free? British Women Novelists 1670–1815* (1986); Jane Spencer, *The Rise of the Woman Novelist: From Aphra Beha to Jane Austen* (1986); Janet Todd, *The Sign of Angellica: Women, Writing and Fiction, 1660–1800* (1989).

Fiennes, Celia, travel writer (b. Newton Toney, near Salisbury, 1662, d. London, 1741).

Celia Fiennes was the daughter of Nathaniel Fiennes and his wife Frances Whitehead, both members of prominent Puritan families. Her grandfather, the first Viscount Saye and Sele, had been one of the most powerful opponents of Charles I and her father was a member of the Council of State and the Keeper of the Great Seal under Cromwell. Adventurous, tough, and unconventional, she undertook a series of journeys through England, sometime between the years 1685 and 1703, supposedly for the sake of her health, covering every county and providing, fortuitously, the first comprehensive survey of the country since those of Harrison and Camden in the sixteenth century. She travelled usually on horseback, accompanied by one or two servants, staying sometimes with relations, but often in local inns. Her earliest journey was in the south. The northern journey and tour of Kent was made in 1697 and her 'Great Journey' to Newcastle and to Cornwall the following year. There are almost no dates in her accounts of her travels, but it is thought that she wrote the main account in 1702, while recording her impressions of London. Her now famous travel book *Through England on a Side Saddle in the Time of William and Mary* first came to notice when Southey included two anonymous extracts in a miscellany in 1812, acknowledged as 'from the manuscript journal of a lady'. It was first published in 1888 by the Honourable Mrs Griffiths, a descendant who had acquired the manuscript. The first modern edition was published as *The Journeys of Celia Fiennes*, ed. Christopher Morris (1947). The journals have come to be regarded as valuable source books for economic and social history, similar to Defoe's better-known *Tour through the Whole Island of Great Britain* (1724–6) and, much later, Cobbett's *Rural Rides* (1830). Fiennes noted in engaging detail the workings of various trades and emerging industries, mining and agricultural processes, the architecture of towns, as well as the food she ate and what she paid for it, religious practices she encountered, and the interiors of cathedrals and country houses. The journals are rarely personal. Her prose is artless, her vocabulary at times limited, but the freshness of her response and her enthusiasm outweigh her deficiencies. There are two modern editions, *The Illustrated Journeys of Celia Fiennes 1685–c1712*, ed. Christopher Morris (1982), and *The Journeys of Celia Fiennes*, ed. John Hillaby (1983). *See* Margaret Willy, *Three Women Diarists* (1964).

Finch, Anne, Countess of Winchilsea, poet (b. Sydmonton, near Newbury, Berkshire, 1661, d. Eastwell Park, Kent, 5 August 1720).

Anne Finch was the daughter of Sir William Kingsmill and his wife Anne Hazlewood. Her parents died when she was young and she and her sister were brought up by an uncle. The Kingsmills were an old Hampshire family who had suffered during the Civil War. The Restoration brought a change in their fortunes and when she was about 20 Anne became Maid of Honour to Mary, wife of the Duke of York, later James II. At court she met Captain Heneage Finch, second son of the Earl of Winchilsea and Gentleman of the Bedchamber to the Duke of York, whom she married in 1684. He succeeded his nephew as the fourth Earl in 1712. The Finch fortunes declined with the flight of James II. Heneage Finch was arrested for a time, and after his release the couple settled at Eastwell Park in Kent, where they lived a retired but cultivated life, spending the winters in London and periods in Tunbridge Wells. They had no children. Heneage became interested in antiquarian pursuits and Anne continued to write poetry, as she had already been doing for some time. Her first publication was a group of four poems, including 'The Spleen', her best-known work, which were included in Charles Gildon's *New Collection of Poems on Several Occasions* (1701). Her literary circle was wide and her admirers included Nicholas Rowe, Swift, and even Pope, who exchanged verses with her. Her husband was connected with the Thynne family at Longleat, and she thus became friends with the Countess of Hertford and with Elizabeth *Rowe. Her poetry was increasingly included in miscellanies, and possibly as a response to this she published, in 1713, *Miscellany Poems on Several Occasions*, which included a tragedy, 'Aristomenes'. The first edition was anonymous, but subsequent issues bore her name. A serious illness in 1715 turned her towards religious verse. She contributed prefatory poems to Pope's collected *Works* in 1717 and he included some of her unpublished poems in his *Poems on Several Occasions*, also in 1717. She left many unpublished poems at her death, some of which were published in Thomas Birch's *General Dictionary* (1741). She was also included in **Poems by Eminent Ladies* (1755). Anne Finch was one of the outstanding women poets of her generation. Her poetry contained satire, burlesque, metaphysical wit, and religious feeling, and her imaginative response to nature won the admiration of Wordsworth, among others. He mentioned her 'Nocturnal Reverie' in the supplementary essay to the 1815 edition of his *Poetical Works* and included a number of her poems in an anthology, *Poems and Extracts*, prepared for Lady Mary Lowther in 1819 (published 1905). Finch's introduction to some of her unpublished work expresses strong feminist sentiments and an awareness of the predicament of the woman writer. Myra Reynolds edited her *Poems* (1903), Katherine M. Rogers her *Selected Poems* (1979), and Jean M. Ellis D'Alessandro the *Wellesley* [College] *Manuscript Poems* (1988). Finch is in need of a full contemporary edition. *See* Katherine M. Rogers, in *Shakespeare's Sisters: Feminist Essays on Women Poets*, ed. Sandra Gilbert and Susan Gubar (1979); Jean Mallinson, in *Gender at Work: Four Women Writers of the Eighteenth Century*, ed. Ann Messenger (1990); Jean M. Ellis D'Alessandro, *When in the Shade . . . Imaginal Equivalents in Anne the Countess of Winchilsea's Poetry* (1989); Barbara McGovern, *Anne Finch and her Poetry: A Critical Biography* (1992).

Flower, Sarah Fuller *see* ADAMS, Sarah Fuller

Forster, Margaret, novelist, biographer, and critic (b. Carlisle, 25 May 1938).

Margaret Forster is the second of the three children of Arthur Gordon Forster, a fitter, and his wife Lilian Hind ('better educated, but though intelligent and artistic, no more a reader than he was'). She went to Carlisle and County High School for Girls, won an open scholarship to Somerville College, Oxford, and took a BA in modern history, 1960. After Oxford she married the writer Hunter Davies (also from Carlisle) and had three children. She taught at Barnsbury Girls' School in Islington for three years, and in 1964 published the first of her novels, *Dames' Delight. Georgy Girl* (1965), her first major success, was made into a film. Her books treat, often ironically, of love, relationships, growing up, growing old, of fraying marriages (*Marital Rites*, 1981), of parents and children (*The Travels of Maudie Tipstaff* (1967), *Private Papers* (1986), *Have the Men had Enough* (1989)), of the impact of the old on the young and vice versa (*Mr. Bone's Retreat* (1971), *The Seduction of Mrs. Pendlebury* (1974), *Mother can you Hear me?* (1979)). *Lady's Maid* (1990) is the story, told partly in her letters, of Elizabeth Barrett *Browning's maid Elizabeth Wilson. Forster has written several biographies: of Prince Charles Stuart (1973), of Thackeray (1978), of Barrett Browning (1988). *Significant Sisters: The Grassroots of Active Feminism 1839–1939* (1984) includes studies of Caroline *Norton and Florence *Nightingale. She has edited Thackeray's journalism (1984) and a selection of Barrett Browning's poetry (1988). She has also been a member of a BBC advisory panel on the social effects of television, 1975–7, a member of the Arts Council literary panel, 1978–81, and a reviewer for the *Evening Standard*, 1977–80. She lives in London.

Fothergill, Caroline *see under* FOTHERGILL, Jessie

Fothergill, Jessie, novelist (b. Cheetham Hill, Manchester, June 1851, d. Berne, Switzerland, 28 July 1891).

Jessie Fothergill was the eldest child of Thomas Fothergill, a cotton merchant who died when she was 15, and his wife Anne Coultate, the daughter of a Burnley doctor. The family were Quakers, but her father's marriage to a non-Quaker forced him to leave the Friends. She was educated at a private school at Bowden, in Cheshire, and then at a boarding school in Harrogate. Her father's death left the family in reduced financial circumstances and led to their removal to the small town of Littleborough, near Rochdale, where Jessie Fothergill, who remained a spinster, spent most of her life. It provided the opportunity for a close study of the lives of workers in the cotton mills, which was to form the background to her best fiction. A visit to Germany in 1874 gave her a chance to study German and to indulge her love of music, which also figured prominently in her novels. She published her first novel, *Healey*, set in Lancashire, after her return from Germany in 1875. It was followed by *Aldyth* (1876), and then by her most successful book, *The First Violin* (1877), begun while in Germany and first published in *Temple Bar*. Despite its popularity (it was dramatized as late as 1899) its preposterous romantic plot, in which the heroine escapes marriage by going to Germany and becomes involved with a leading violinist, made it one of the least typical and least satisfactory of her novels. It was the only one to be published anonymously, probably because her family objected to the *Ouidaesque plot. Other titles among her twelve full-length novels included *Probation* (1879), set against the background of the 1862 cotton famine, *Kith and Kin* (1881), *Borderland* (1886), and *Lasses of Leverhouse* (1888), another Lancashire story which was partly autobiographical. Reviewers praised Fothergill's accurate rendering of north-country dialect. Her strong-minded heroines, often masculine in their aspirations, reflected her admiration for the 'burning radicalism', in her words, of *Jane Eyre* and her acknowledged enthusiasm for the works of the *Brontës, George *Eliot, and George Sand. She suffered from a lung complaint, which encouraged her to travel abroad. She spent some time in America in 1884 and, after teaching herself Italian, visited Italy. Her last novel, *Oriole's Daughter*, published posthumously in 1893, was set in Rome, where she spent the winter of 1890–1. She died in Switzerland the following summer. Her sister **Caroline Fothergill** published a total of eight novels between 1883 and 1898, many of them with regional settings. *See* Helen C. Black, *Notable Women Authors of the Day* (1893); Jane Crisp, *Jessie Fothergill 1851–1891: A Bibliography*, Victorian Fiction Research Guides 2 (1980).

Frere, Eleanor *see* FENN, Lady Eleanor

Fullerton, Lady Georgina Charlotte, novelist (b. Tixall Hall, Staffordshire, 23 September 1812, d. Bournemouth, 19 January 1885).

The daughter of Lord Granville Leveson Gower, afterwards first Earl Granville, and Lady Harriet Elizabeth Cavendish, second daughter of the fifth Duke of Devonshire, Georgina Fullerton was born into the uppermost of aristocratic circles. Her father became ambassador to Paris, and most of her formative years were spent at the British Embassy, where she met and in 1833 married Alexander George Fullerton, a young Irish Guards officer and embassy attaché. They continued to live in Paris until her father's retirement in 1841. Her husband's conversion to Roman Catholicism profoundly affected her. She followed suit in 1846, after a period of intense interest in the Oxford Movement. Her first and most famous novel, *Ellen Middleton* (1844), espoused the need for confession and was praised by Gladstone and Lord

Brougham among others. *Grantley Manor*, which followed in 1847, was the story of a secret Catholic–Protestant marriage, set, like most of Fullerton's novels, in aristocratic circles. A later novel, *Mrs. Gerald's Niece* (1869), described marital discord resulting from the Oxford Movement. The death of her only son in 1854 at the age of 21 made her resolve to devote the rest of her life to philanthropic pursuits. She and her husband wore mourning for the rest of their lives. She founded a religious community and was instrumental in bringing a Catholic sisterhood to England. Her remaining novels, the proceeds of which she sent to charities, were historical rather than religious in subject-matter. Of these the best known were *Lady Bird* (1852) and *Too Strange not to be True* (1864). Two were written in French. She was involved in 1864 in the founding of the Catholic periodical the *Month*, which serialized her story *Constance Sherwood* (1865). It was her two early novels, however, so vividly reflecting the background to the Oxford Movement and subsequent popular conversion to Roman Catholicism, which made her name, and on which her reputation rests. *See* P. Craven, *The Life of Lady Georgiana Fullerton*, trans. H. J. Coleridge (1888); Charlotte *Yonge, 'Lady Georgina Fullerton', in A. Sergeant (ed.), *Women Novelists of Queen Victoria's Reign* (1897); Margaret Maison, *Search your Soul, Eustace* (1961); Robert Wolff, *Gains and Losses* (1977).

Fyge, Sarah *see* EGERTON, Sarah

G

'Gabrielli', *see* MEEKE, Mary

'Galesia' *see* BARKER, Jane

Garnett, Constance, translator (b. Brighton, 19 December 1861, d. Edenbridge, Kent, 17 December 1946).

Constance Garnett was one of the eight children of David Black, a coroner, and his wife Clara Patten. Her paternal grandfather, a Scottish sea captain, had served as naval architect to Tsar Nicholas I of Russia. Her maternal grandfather George Patten was a portrait painter and her sister **Clementina Black** (1855–1923) was an active trade unionist and novelist. Delicate until the age of 6, she eventually went to Brighton High School, from where she won a scholarship to Newnham College, Cambridge. She took a first in the classical tripos in 1883, although women were not then admitted to degrees. She joined the Fabian Society, worked as a librarian in the People's Palace in the East End of London, and in 1889 married Edward Garnett (1868–1937), a writer and critic. Their only child was the novelist David Garnett (1892–1981). Through her husband she met a number of Russian exiles living in London, including the anarchist Peter Kropotkin and Felix Volkhovsky, who encouraged her interest in the Russian language and literature. She began to learn Russian in earnest while awaiting the birth of her son. On a trip to Russia the following year she took money for famine relief and messages for various socialist colleagues of her Russian friends. She also met Tolstoy. On her return she began what was to become her life's work, the translation from

Russian into English of all the major Russian prose writers. Between 1894 and 1928 she translated over seventy books, including all of Turgenev, most of Dostoevsky and Chekhov, Tolstoy, Gogol, Ostrovsky, Gorky, and Herzen. Garnett was a Fabian in her youth and sympathized with many of the Russian revolutionaries whom she met, but in her old age she became a strong Conservative. Her eyesight deteriorated in her later years and she dictated her translations after hearing the Russian read aloud. Many of her translations have been superseded, some were criticized as banal or prudish, but she did more than any other single translator to make Russian literature available to English readers in the early decades of the twentieth century. Katherine *Mansfield wrote to her in 1921: 'These books have changed our lives, no less.' *See* David Garnett, *The Golden Echo* (1953); Carolyn Heilbrun, *The Garnett Family* (1961); Richard Garnett, *Constance Garnett: A Heroic Life* (1991).

Gaskell, Mrs Elizabeth Cleghorn, novelist (b. Chelsea, London, 29 September 1810, d. Holybourne, near Alton, Hampshire, 12 November 1865).

Mrs Gaskell, as she was always known, was the only surviving daughter of William Stevenson, a one-time Unitarian minister, also a farmer, who became Keeper of the Records to the Treasury, and his first wife Elizabeth Holland of Sandle Bridge in Cheshire. Her mother died shortly after she was born and she was sent to live with her Aunt Lumb in Knutsford, Cheshire, the original of Cranford, and of several other small country towns in the midst of farming communities which featured in her fiction. She was brought up as a Unitarian, and sent to local schools and then to a boarding school at Stratford-upon-Avon, where she was taught Latin, French, and Italian. In 1828 her only brother John, a lieutenant in the merchant navy, disappeared at sea, an emotional loss which was reflected in the various missing brothers who return in her fiction (Peter Jenkyns in *Cranford*, Frederick Hale in *North and South*). Her father's remarriage to a woman Elizabeth did not like had a later fictional equivalent in Mrs Gibson in *Wives and Daughters*. She nevertheless remained with him until his death in 1829. In 1832 she married the Revd William Gaskell, assistant minister at the Unitarian Cross St Chapel, Manchester, a happy marriage which was also a working partnership, each taking a keen interest in the other's professional life. They had four daughters, and a son who died of scarlet fever in 1845. Gaskell's first publication was a descriptive poem in the style of Crabbe, 'Sketches among the Poor', published in *Blackwood's Magazine* in 1837. But it was her son's death which prompted her to write her first novel as a means of consolation. *Mary Barton*, subtitled 'a tale of Manchester life', eventually found a publisher in 1848. The story of fraught industrial relations, which included a strike, an assassination, and a feminine plea for better understanding, found admirers in Carlyle and Dickens, as well as eloquent critics among the Manchester manufacturers, notably W. R. Greg. Dickens pressed her to contribute to his new weekly *Household Words*, an association which was to prove fruitful to her in the 1850s. She published *Libbie Marsh's Three Eras* and two other stories in *Howitt's Journal*, run by her friends William and Mary *Howitt, in 1847–8. But *Household Words* had a wider audience. She wrote 'Lizzie Leigh' for the first number, 'The Old Nurse's Story' in 1852, and in 1851–3 *Cranford*, a series of sketches of a small town with exclusively female inhabitants. Her second full-length novel, *Ruth* (1853), dealt with a fallen woman, the sexual double standard, and the problem of illegitimacy, and proved as controversial as its predecessor. Charlotte *Brontë lamented its sentimental ending, Elizabeth Barrett *Browning rewrote the story in the subplot of *Aurora Leigh*, and George *Eliot responded with the tale of Hetty Sorrel in *Adam Bede*. Her next novel, *North and South*, set in Manchester, and designed to argue a case for the vitality of the industrial north as opposed to the deadening traditionalism of the agricultural south, followed Dickens's *Hard Times* in *Household Words* in 1854–5. Mrs Gaskell's friendship with Charlotte Brontë began in 1850, and despite the wide differences in their background and writing, or perhaps because of them, it developed and deepened until Brontë's death in 1855. As a result Mrs Gaskell was commissioned by Brontë's husband and father to write her biography. *The Life of Charlotte Brontë* (1857) is one of the most celebrated literary biographies of the period, widely praised, but also the subject of threatened litigation by various individuals referred to in the work. Mrs Gaskell's reputation as a major writer was by this time secure. She travelled in Italy and France, and developed a wide circle of literary friends, including the American Charles Eliot Norton. *My Lady Ludlow*, a shorter fiction, was serialized in *Household Words* (1858) and formed the central part of a collection of stories, *Round the Sofa* (1859). She did extensive research for her next novel, *Sylvia's Lovers*, set in Whitby, in Yorkshire, during the Napoleonic Wars, and followed it with the pastoral *Cousin Phillis* (1864), which many consider her best work. *A Dark Night's Work*, serialized in *All the Year Round*, the successor to *Household Words*, in 1863, was one of several of her stories which involved the supernatural. Her last novel, *Wives and Daughters*, a story of changing country society, was being serialized in the *Cornhill Magazine* at the time of her sudden death in 1865, and remains incomplete. *See Letters*, ed. J. V. Chapple, and A. Pollard (1966); Coral Lawsbury, *Elizabeth Gaskell: The Novel of Social Crisis* (1975); Angus Easson, *Elizabeth Gaskell* (1979); Pauline Nestor, *Female Friendships and Communities: Charlotte Brontë, George Eliot, Elizabeth Gaskell* (1985); Catherine Gallagher, *The Industrial Reformation of English Fiction 1832–1867* (1986); Patsy Stoneman, *Elizabeth Gaskell* (1987); Angus Easson (ed.), *Elizabeth Gaskell: The Critical Heritage* (1991); Jane Spencer, *Elizabeth Gaskell* (1992); Jenny Uglow, *Elizabeth Gaskell: a Habit of Stories* (1993).

Gatty, Horatia Katharine Frances *see under* GATTY, Margaret

Gatty, Juliana *see* EWING, Juliana Horatia

Gatty, Margaret, née Scott, children's writer and editor (b. Burnham, Essex, 3 June 1809, d. Ecclesfield, Yorkshire, 4 October 1873).

Margaret Gatty was the youngest daughter and co-heiress of the Revd Dr Alexander John Scott, who had been Nelson's chaplain on the *Victory*, and of Mary Frances Ryder, who died when Margaret was 2. She was brought up by her father and grandfather and educated at home. Her father encouraged her love of literature and she showed a precocious talent in drawing and calligraphy. In 1839 she married the Revd Alfred Gatty, vicar of Ecclesfield, in Yorkshire, where she spent the rest of her life. Of their ten children, eight survived into adulthood, and formed a lively and united family, in which story-telling and writing was a central activity. Juliana *Ewing, her second daughter, entertained her siblings with stories, and it was her family nickname of 'Aunt Judy' which Margaret Gatty gave to her own successful volume of children's fiction, *Aunt Judy's Tales* (1859), and to the children's magazine she founded in 1866. Her writing career began in 1842, with a biography of her father, but it was not until 1852, when she was 42, that she published her first work of fiction, *The Fairy Godmothers and Other Tales*. This was followed in 1855 by the first series of *Parables from Nature*, which she illustrated herself, and which continued until 1871. The *Parables* were frequently reprinted and widely translated. Later editions were illustrated by Holman Hunt and John Tenniel, among others. Mrs Gatty was an accomplished botanist as well as a writer of fiction. Her *History of British Seaweeds* (1863), which she illustrated, remained authoritative long after her death, and both a seaweed and a sea serpent were named after her. Gatty edited and contributed to *Aunt Judy's Magazine* from 1866 until 1873, when ill health forced her to hand it over to her two daughters **Juliana** and **Horatia**, the latter of whom carried on the editorship until 1885. Other works included *Aunt Judy's Letters* (1862), a less successful sequel to the *Tales*, a book on emblems (1872), and another on sundials (1872). A debilitating disease which brought increasing paralysis confined her to the vicarage at Ecclesfield, where she died. *See* Christabel Maxwell, *Mrs. Gatty and Mrs. Ewing* (1949).

Gibbons, Stella (Dorothea), novelist and poet (b. London, 5 January 1902, d. December 1989).

Stella Gibbons, best known and possibly only known as the author of *Cold Comfort Farm* (1932), was born in London, the eldest of the three children of Telford Charles Gibbons, a north London doctor, and his wife Maud Williams. Home life was unhappy and she told stories to her younger brothers and read books with exotic settings (Disraeli's *Alroy* and Thomas Moore's *Lalla Rookh*) as a means of escape. Her father would not send his children to school but had them educated at home by governesses. At 13 she went to North London Collegiate School, where she was equally unhappy but wrote school stories for the other girls to read. At 19 she took a journalism course at University College London and worked first as a decoder of cables for the British United Press, where, she claimed, she first learned to write. She spent ten years in Fleet St. in various jobs, doing special reporting, literary and drama criticism, fashion writing, and at the same time producing poetry and short stories. Reviewing novels for the *Lady*, she was later to claim, stimulated her gift for satire. In 1933 she married Allan Bourne Webb, an actor and opera singer, by whom she had a daughter. She published her first book, *The Mountain Beast and Other Poems*, in 1930. But it was in 1932 that she received immediate celebrity with *Cold Comfort Farm*, a satire on the contemporary rural novel, which won the Femina Vie Heureuse Prize the following year. Through the Starkadder family and her believable heroine Flora Poste, she parodied the hackneyed conventions and what she saw as the pretensions and absurdities of contemporary regional novelists like Mary *Webb, T. F. Powys, Sheila *Kaye-Smith, as well as Hardy and Lawrence. It was a measure of the book's success that it outlived most of the novels that occasioned it. A musical version in 1965 derived its title from the most quoted line in the book, *Something Nasty in the Woodshed*, and it was adapted for television in 1968. The success was at a price, however, as none of the works which followed was regarded as its equal and they suffered from the comparison, 'like a mother with one unusually precocious offspring who continually overshadows the quiet, worthy members of her brood', as one reviewer put it. She wrote twenty-five novels over the next forty years, together with four volumes of poetry, and three collections of short stories. *Christmas at Cold Comfort Farm* (1940) and *Conference at Cold Comfort Farm* (1949), both collections of stories, attempted to capitalize on earlier success. *The Priestess and Other Poems* (1924) and *The Lowland Venus and Other Poems* (1938) preceded her *Collected Poems* in 1950. Gibbons claimed to see herself as a poet rather than a novelist, but she had some successes in the latter role, including *Bassett* (1934), *Nightingale Wood* (1938), and *The Bachelor* (1944).

Many of her novels were set in literary north London, which she knew well, and showed her sharp eye for social contrasts. Among her last were *The Charmers* (1965), *Starlight* (1967), *The Snow Woman* (1969), and *The Woods in Winter* (1970). She was elected a fellow of the Royal Society of Literature in 1950 and died, still writing, at the age of 87.

'Girl of the Period' *see under* LINTON, Eliza Lynn

Glyn, Elinor (Sutherland), novelist (b. Jersey, 17 October 1864, d. London, 23 September 1943).

Elinor Glyn was the younger daughter of Douglas Sutherland, a Scottish civil engineer, and his wife Elinor Saunders. Her mother's family combined English, Irish, and French aristocratic ancestry and had settled in Ontario. When her father died three months after her birth, having failed to prove himself heir to the seventh Lord Duffus, her mother returned to Canada, where Elinor was partly brought up by her French grandmother. Her mother's remarriage to an elderly Scot whom his stepchildren detested occasioned the family's removal to Jersey. Elinor was taught by a series of governesses, was bilingual in French and English, read voraciously, and lived in a fantasy world. Red-haired and green-eyed, she made a dramatic entrance into society in both Paris and London, where various eligible suitors pursued her. Her marriage to wealthy landowner Clayton Glyn in 1892 was not happy, partly because they had no shared interests, and partly because she bore him two daughters and no son, but it provided a secure world of country house society interspersed with foreign travel. Her first novel, *The Visits of Elizabeth* (1900), was written during a period of convalescence, and presented a revealing picture of that society. Its success occasioned other novels of high society, including a sequel, *Elizabeth Visits America* (1909). She then turned to romantic novels, of which the most publicized was *Three Weeks* (1907), the sexually explicit story of an affair between an Englishman and a Balkan queen. Two of Glyn's most celebrated admirers, Lord Curzon, former Viceroy of India, and the statesman Lord Milner, presented her with a tiger skin, which featured controversially in the story. In 1908 Clayton Glyn's imminent bankruptcy forced her to write in earnest. A winter spent at St Petersburg provided the background for *His Hour* (1910), one of her best romances. *Halcyone* (1912) contained recognizable portraits of both Curzon and another admirer, the philosopher F. H. Bradley. The best known of all her romances was probably *It* (1927), which was later made into a film. As a result of the novel's popularity 'it' became synonymous with sex appeal. She worked as a Hollywood scriptwriter in the 1920s, when several of her books were turned into films but her financial affairs remained precarious. She continued to write until she was well into her seventies, a glamorous and exotic figure until the end of her life. She wrote from London at the height of the blitz: 'I am enjoying it all.' Her autobiography *Romantic Adventure* was published in 1936. *See* 'Anthony Glyn' [G. L. S. Dawson], *Elinor Glyn* (1955; rev. 1968); Jeremy Pilcher, *The 'It' Girls* (1955).

Godden, Jon *see under* GODDEN, Rumer

Godden, (Margaret) Rumer, novelist and children's writer (b. Eastbourne, Sussex, 10 December 1907).

Rumer Godden is the second of four daughters of Arthur Leigh Godden, who worked for a steamer company in India, and his wife Katherine Norah Hingley. She grew up in East Bengal, where she and her sisters were educated, mainly by their parents, and where they collectively wrote long books which were illustrated by **Jon Godden** (b. 1908), who also became a novelist. *Two under the Indian Sun* (1966), written by Rumer and Jon, described their Anglo-Indian childhood. The sisters were sent to various schools in England (five in six years), where they found difficulty in settling. Rumer eventually went to Moira House in Eastbourne. She trained as a dancing teacher and returned to Calcutta, where she started a dancing school. In 1934 she married Lawrence Sinclair Foster, a stockbroker, by whom she had two daughters, and a son who died shortly after birth. Her first novel, *Chinese Puzzle* (1936), was accepted the day her first daughter was born (two others had been rejected). *Black Narcissus*, her first successful book, also one of her best known, about a community of nuns in the Himalayas, was published in 1939 and subsequently translated into several languages. She continued to write, and also to run a small day school in Calcutta, until 1941, when her husband left her after going bankrupt. She took the children to stay on a tea estate in Darjeeling, publishing the diary of their experiences as *Rungli-Rungliot* (1943). *Bengal Journey* (1945) was an account of women's war work in Bengal. Several of her novels deal sensitively with adolescence, particularly *The River* (1946), made into a film by Jean Renoir, *Greengage Summer* (1958), for which she co-wrote the film script, and *Loss of Innocence* (1961). *An Episode of Sparrows* (1955), about London street urchins, was also made into a film. She has written successful children's fiction, beginning with *The Dolls' House* (1947), in which dolls depict adult conflicts and predicaments. Others include *Impunity Jane* (1954), another doll story, and *The Mousewife* (1951), the story of a friendship between a mouse and a caged bird, based on an entry in Dorothy *Wordsworth's *Journal*. In 1949 she married James Lesley Haynes Dixon, and returned to England, where they lived for several years in Lamb House, at Rye, in Sussex, once the home of Henry James. She lives in

Dumfriesshire, where she continues to write. Her novels number over twenty, with as many children's books. The latest include *Thursday's Children* (1984), *Fu-dog* (1989), and *Coromandel Sea Change* (1991). She has written two further books about India, both with Jon Godden, *Shiva's Pigeons* (1972) and *Indian Dust* (1989), and books on Hans Christian Andersen (1955) and on Beatrix *Potter (1971). She published the first part of her autobiography *A Time to Dance, No Time to Weep* in 1987. *See* Hassell A. Simpson, *Rumer Godden* (1973).

Godwin, Mary *see* SHELLEY, Mary

Godwin, Mary Wollstonecraft *see* WOLLSTONECRAFT, Mary

Gordimer, Nadine, novelist and short story writer (b. Springs, Transvaal, South Africa, 20 November 1923).

Nadine Gordimer is the daughter of Isidore Gordimer, a Jewish watchmaker who emigrated to South Africa from a town on the Baltic, and his English-born wife Nan Myers. She was brought up in a mining town in the Transvaal where she had 'a scrappy and uninspiring minimal education' at a convent school and a 'deadly dull colonial social background'. The act of writing, which she began at the age of 9, in her words, 'brought me to life'. A heart complaint kept her away from school between the ages of 10 and 15 or 16. 'My particular solitude as an intellectual by inclination was so complete I did not even know I was one,' she recalled. She went to Witwatersrand University, which introduced her to the broader cultural life of Johannesburg and gave her a sense of personal and political commitment to a multiracial South Africa. She was married first to G. Gavron in 1949, and had a daughter, and secondly in 1954 to Reinhold Cassirer, a company director, by whom she has a son. Her early stories were published in the *New Yorker*, *Harper's*, and other American magazines and later collected in *Face to Face* (1949) and *The Soft Voice of the Serpent* (1952). Her acknowledged literary mentors are Lawrence, Henry James, and Hemingway. Her first novel, *The Lying Days* (1953), has a semi-autobiographical heroine. The second, *A World of Strangers* (1958), has as a protagonist a young Englishman on a visit to South Africa who finds that a solely private life is impossible. *Occasion for Loving* (1963) shows the inadequacy of white liberal attitudes through an affair between a married white woman and a black South African. The death of old liberal ways is underlined again in *The Late Bourgeois World* (1966), which contrasts a senile white woman and her progressive granddaughter. In *A Guest of Honour* (1971), which won the James Tait Black Memorial Prize, a former colonial officer returns to a newly independent African state from which he had previously been expelled for supporting black activists. The ambiguity of the

European's role in Africa is underlined as the political situation slips out of control. *The Conservationist* (1974), joint winner of the Booker Prize, is a subtle picture of the white community under apartheid, centring on a conservative Afrikaans farmer. Gordimer's work has been criticized for political shrillness. Her writing, according to one critic (*TLS*, 11 October 1991), survives 'on a knife-edge between the demands of private truths and the imperatives of commitment', but occasionally falls off the edge. *Burger's Daughter* (1979), which was banned in South Africa, and *A Sport of Nature* (1987), with its futuristic vision of an African utopia, have both been criticized for lack of detachment, whereas *July's People* (1981) and *My Son's Story* (1990) have been acclaimed for their treatment of individual predicaments within the context of political horrors. Gordimer's short stories, of which *Jump* (1991) is the most recent collection, convey the pain of the South African context sometimes more acutely than her novels. She has published a study of black South African writers, *The Black Interpreters* (1973), and directed a film on the black activist Allan Boesak. Her essays have been collected in *The Essential Gesture: Writing, Politics and Places*, ed. Stephen Clingman (1988). Gordimer was awarded the Nobel Prize for Literature in 1991. *See* Stephen Clingman, *The Novels of Nadine Gordimer: History from the Inside* (1986); Judie Newman, *Nadine Gordimer* (1988); Rowland Smith (ed.), *Critical Essays on Nadine Gordimer* (1990); Bruce King (ed.), *The Later Fiction of Nadine Gordimer* (1992).

Gordon, Lady Lucie Duff, travel writer and translator (b. Westminster, London, 24 June 1821, d. Cairo, 14 July 1869).

Lucie or Lucy Duff Gordon was the only child of John Austin, an eminent lawyer, and his wife Sarah Taylor *Austin, a well-known translator and woman of letters. Her childhood playmates included the young John Stuart Mill and Henry Reeve, later the editor of the *Edinburgh Review*. A period in Germany with her parents when she was 5 made her fluent in German. Her mother taught her Latin, but she had little formal education apart from a short period at a mixed school in Hampstead where she learned Greek, and later at Miss Shepherd's school in Bromley while her parents were abroad. Although both parents were Unitarian she was confirmed as a member of the Church of England at 16. In 1840 she married Sir Alexander Cornewall Duff Gordon, a treasury civil servant and later Commissioner for Inland Revenue. Their London home at Queen Anne's Gate became a meeting-place for eminent men and women of letters as well as politicians and distinguished foreign visitors. Tennyson, Dickens, Thackeray, Landseer, Macaulay, Meredith, and Caroline *Norton were among the regular visitors, as well as the German historian Leopold von Ranke. Duff Gordon began her literary career with translations from German of Niebuhr, Meinhold, von Moltke, P. J. A. von Feuerbach, and, with her husband, von Ranke's *Memoirs of the House of Brandenburg* (1849). Tuberculosis forced her to travel for her health and she spent some time at the Cape of Good Hope in 1860. Her *Letters from the Cape* were published in 1864 as part of Francis Galton's *Vacation Tourist in 1862–3*. In 1862 she left England and settled in Egypt, which became her home for the rest of her life. Her many letters to her family formed the basis of *Letters from Egypt* (1865), edited by Sarah Austin. Her enthusiasm and understanding of Middle Eastern life and culture, her intolerance of blinkered European attitudes to other races, as well as her critical view of Turkish rule in Egypt made her an engaging and discerning travel writer. *Later Letters from Egypt* was published posthumously in 1875 and included her *Letters from the Cape* and a memoir by her daughter Janet Ross. She died of consumption in 1869 and was buried in the English cemetery in Cairo. *See* Janet Ross, *Three Generations of Englishwomen* (1888); O. H. G. Waterfield, *Lucie Duff Gordon in England, South Africa and Egypt* (1937).

Gore, Catherine Grace Frances, née Moody, novelist and dramatist (b. East Retford, Nottinghamshire, 1799, d. Linwood, Hampshire, 29 January 1861).

Catherine Gore was the daughter of C. Moody, a Nottinghamshire wine merchant. She wrote poetry from an early age, earning her nickname 'the Poetess' from her friends and praise from Joanna *Baillie, although none of it was published. She married Captain Charles Arthur Gore of the Life Guards in 1823, and from the time of her marriage began a writing career which was to produce over seventy novels and made her the unchallenged queen of the so-called 'silver-fork' school of novelists of fashionable life. Her first printed work was a narrative poem 'The Two Broken Hearts', which was followed in 1824 by her first novel, *Theresa Marchmont; or The Maid of Honour*. Her first major success for her publisher Henry Colburn was *Women as They Are; or The Manners of the Day* (1830), which George IV observed was 'the best bred and most amusing novel published in my remembrance'. Gore's novels of the 1830s present a revealing picture of social mobility and the pressures of life among the upper middle classes, of which the best are probably *The Hamiltons* (1834), *Mrs. Armytage; or Female Domination* (1836), *Cecil; or The Adventures of a Coxcomb* (1841), and *The Banker's Wife* (1843). She dealt interestingly with the theme of money and social class in novels like *Stokeshill Place; or The Man of Business* (1837), *Men of Capital* (1846), and *Mammon; or The Hardships of an Heiress* (1855). Thackeray parodied her work with humour rather than animus as *Lords and Liveries* 'by the author of *Dukes* *and Déjeuners, Hearts And Diamonds, Marchionesses And Milliners* etc.' in his *Punch's Prize Novelists* (1847). Henry Colburn puffed Gore's fiction in his various periodicals, and she in turn learned to manipulate the fiction market to her advantage. She published two novels during the same week in 1841 in deliberate rivalry with one another. She intimated in her preface to *Cecil* that it was a first novel in order to secure the public's interest in a new writer. Anonymity was a key to her success, so much so that the total number of her novels is still not entirely certain. Her career as a dramatist was less successful. Her comedy *The School for Coquettes* ran for five weeks at the Haymarket in 1831, but its successor *Lords and Commoners* was withdrawn after a few nights at Drury Lane. In 1832 Mrs Gore moved to France and supported her ailing husband and their ten children by her writing. An inheritance in 1850 should have meant the end of financial insecurity, but she was defrauded of £20,000 by her guardian Sir John Dean Paul. Her novel *The Banker's Wife*, about a corrupt banker, was thought to have been about Paul. Mrs Gore promptly had it reissued when Paul was imprisoned after the scandal in 1855. She lost her sight towards the end of her life, but carried on writing until her death aged 61. Only two of her ten children survived her. *See* R. H. Horne, *A New Spirit of the Age* (1844); W. M. Rosa, *The Silver-Fork School: Novels of Fashion Preceding Vanity Fair* (1936); Alison Adburgham, *Silver Fork Society* (1983).

Gothic novel.

This was the most popular fiction in England between 1790 and 1820 and a sub-genre which women writers in particular found attractive. Gothic novelists experimented with a new kind of fiction which dealt primarily with emotional and imaginative awareness and the non-rational, darker side of experience. Coral Ann Howells sees the Gothic world as 'a fraught fantasy world of neurosis and morbidity', 'obsessionally self-enclosed', and 'full of curiosity, doubt and anxiety'. In this respect Gothic fiction represented the extreme development of the eighteenth-century cult of sensibility. Sublimated sexual fantasy and masochism were often close to the surface in repetitive and clichéd plots involving persecuted heroines, lascivious villains, and perverted priests as well as ghosts and nightmares. Other Gothic conventions included the use of the supernatural, the macabre, and the fantastic. Haunted castles, abbeys, and graveyards, set against picturesque landscapes suggestive of emotional states, were standard features. Women novelists saw the Gothic as a vehicle for expressing hitherto inexpressible emotions and experience. Eminent practitioners among the first generation of female Gothic writers included Ann *Radcliffe, Mary Ann *Radcliffe, Isabella *Kelly, Sophia *Lee, Mary *Meeke, and Regina *Roche, many of them published by William Lane's *Minerva Press. Later women writers who variously adapted Gothic conventions include Mary *Shelley, Charlotte and Emily *Brontë, and Christina *Rossetti in the nineteenth century, and Daphne *du Maurier, Emma *Tennant, and Angela *Carter in the twentieth. Jane *Austen famously mocked Gothic novels but also acknowledged their potential in *Northanger Abbey* (1818). The mid-Victorian *sensation novel is often seen as a descendant of Gothic fiction. *See* Rosemary Jackson, *Fantasy: The Literature of Subversion* (1975); Ellen Moers, *Literary Women* (1977); Coral Ann Howells, *Love, Mystery and Misery: Feeling in Gothic Fiction* (1978); David Punter, *The Literature of Terror* (1980); Tania Modleski, *Loving with a Vengeance: Mass Produced Fantasies for Women* (1982); Juliann E. Fleenor (ed.), *The Female Gothic* (1983); Eugenia C. Delamotte, *Perils of the Night: A Feminist Study of Nineteenth Century Gothic* (1990).

Goudge, Elizabeth, novelist and children's writer (b. Wells, Somerset, 24 April 1900, d. Peppard Common, near Henley-on-Thames, Oxfordshire, 1 April 1984).

Elizabeth Goudge was the only child of the Revd Dr Henry Leighton Goudge, vice-principal of a theological college, and his wife Ida de Beauchamp Collenette, a member of an old Guernsey Norman-French family. Her childhood was solitary, apart from the company of neighbouring children with whom she wrote a magazine, and of her invalid mother who told her stories. The family moved to Ely and then in 1923 to Oxford, where her father became Regius Professor of Divinity. She was pleasantly but imperfectly taught by governesses and then sent remedially to a boarding school in Southbourne in Hampshire when she was 14. She studied art for two years at Reading College and then taught art and design. The stimulus of Oxford helped her early inclination to write. She began with plays, of which only one, *The *Brontës of Haworth*, had a single performance in 1932. Another, based on Fanny *Burney, went unnoticed. A publisher suggested she try novels instead. Her first, *Island Magic* (1934), was inspired by a family holiday on Guernsey. Another, *A City of Bells* (1936), was set in Wells, and a third, *Towers in the Mist* (1938), in sixteenth-century Oxford. A nervous breakdown in the 1930s resulted in a hiatus in her writing. After her father's death in 1939 she moved with her mother to Devon. Her best-selling work *Green Dolphin Country* (1944), a historical romance set in the Channel Islands and nineteenth-century New Zealand, won a Literary Guild Award and was made into a film (1947). *Gentian Hill* (1949) and *The Child from the Sea* (1970), the story of Lucy Waters, the secret wife of Charles II, were, along with *Green Dolphin Country*, her best-known historical novels. After her mother's death she moved to Peppard Common, near Henley-on-Thames, where she lived for more than twenty years with her friend Jessie Monroe.

The Heart of the Family (1953) completed a family trilogy, begun with *The Bird in the Tree* (1940) and *The Herb of Grace* (1948) and known collectively as 'The Eliots of Damerosehay'. Goudge's fiction for children is possibly better known than her other work. *The Little White Horse* (1946), combining realism and fantasy and set in the nineteenth century, won the Carnegie Medal in 1947. Others included *Smoky-House* (1940), the story of smuggling in the post-Napoleonic era, *The Valley of Song* (1951), a fable about eighteenth-century shipbuilders, and *Linnets and Valerians* (1964), about two families. Goudge published over forty titles in all, short stories, novels, children's books, and non-fiction on religious themes. A sense of place and a sense of history and often both figured prominently in both her adult and children's fiction. Her later fiction, such as *The Scent of Water* (1963), and her autobiography *The Joy of the Snow*, published in 1974, reveal her strongly felt Christianity. *See Patterns of People: An Elizabeth Goudge Anthology*, ed. Muriel Grainger (1978).

Graham, Catherine *see* MACAULAY, Catherine

'**Graham,** Ennis' *see* MOLESWORTH, Mary Louisa

'**Grand,** Sarah' (Frances Elizabeth McFall), novelist
(b. Donaghadee, County Down, 1854, d. Calne, Wiltshire, 12 May 1943).

Sarah Grand was the fourth of the five children of Edward John Bellenden Clarke, a lieutenant in the Royal Navy, and his wife Margaret Bell Sherwood. Her parents were English, but she was brought up in Northern Ireland in an atmosphere redolent of violence, sexuality, and squalor which is vividly described in the early chapters of her autobiographical novel *The Beth Book* (1897). The family returned to England in 1861, where she was sent to two indifferent boarding schools, emerging less well educated than her two brothers, much to her later chagrin. In 1870, at the age of 16, she married Lieutenant-Colonel David McFall, an army surgeon twenty-three years her senior and a widower with two children. The marriage was unhappy but it provided an opportunity for five years of travel in China, Japan, and the Far East. They had one son, but eventually separated. Frances began to write her first novel in 1880. Her pseudonym Sarah Grand was chosen carefully to suggest feminist pride and aspirations and with it came a new persona. She used the profits of *Ideala* (1888), her first novel, to separate permanently from her husband, taking her son with her to London. Her reputation was made and rests on two feminist novels, *The Heavenly Twins* (1893) and *The Beth Book*. The former caused a scandal when it was published, addressing as it did sex-role conditioning, venereal disease, the double standard, and women's right to independence. It sold 20,000 copies immediately and was reprinted six times in the first year. *The Beth Book* was a thinly veiled autobiography which explored the creative psychology of the woman artist and drew closely on Grand's childhood and adult life. It also contained an unflattering portrait of her husband. Two other novels dealt with controversial issues. The heroine of *Ideala* lives defiantly in sin and *A Domestic Experiment* (1891) is also the story of an adultery. *The Heavenly Twins* and *The Beth Book* have continued to interest feminists up to the present day. The latter was the high-water mark of Grand's career. She became active in the suffrage campaign as a member of the *Women Writers' Suffrage League and became president of her local branch of the National Union of Women's Suffrage societies. She also undertook an arduous lecture tour of the United States. But the end of the suffrage campaign meant the end of her own era as a celebrity. She published several other books including *Adnam's Orchard* (1912), *The Winged Victory* (1916), and *Variety* (1922), a collection of stories, but these made little impact. After her husband's death in 1898 she lived in Tunbridge Wells but in 1920 moved to Bath, where she was elected mayoress on six separate occasions. The role of provincial dignitary was a faintly ridiculous contrast to her earlier literary and feminist aspirations. She died in Bath in 1843, over twenty years after her last book was published. *See* Gail Cunningham, *The New Woman and the Victorian Novel* (1978); Joan Huddleston, *Sarah Grand 1854–1943: A Bibliography*, Victorian Fiction Research Guides no. 1 (1979); Gillian Kersley, *Darling Madame: Sarah Grand and Devoted Friend* (1983).

Grant, Anne, known as Mrs Grant of Laggan, poet and prose writer (b. Glasgow, 21 February 1755, d. Edinburgh, 8 November 1838).

The daughter of Duncan Macvicar, a Highlander who in 1757 obtained a commission in a British regiment stationed in New York during the Seven Years War, Anne Grant spent formative years among the Dutch and British colonists prior to the Revolutionary War. The family returned to Scotland in 1768, living in Fort Augustus, where Anne's father became barrack master. In 1779 she married the Revd James Grant, chaplain of Fort Augustus, who had been given the living of the village of Laggan in Inverness-shire. Immediately after their marriage the couple moved to Laggan, where Anne Grant ran the farm attached to the manse virtually single-handedly and integrated herself into the life of the Highland community. She also learned Gaelic and became an authority on folklore. Of their twelve children eight reached adulthood, but only one survived her. The sudden death of her husband in 1801 left her without an income, and she was obliged to give up the farm, which went with the living. She was persuaded by friends to publish a volume of *Poems* (1803) by subscription in order to relieve her financial difficulties. In 1807, for the same reason, she published her *Letters from the Mountains*, which won instant acclaim for its colourful pictures of Highland life and capitalized on the vogue for literature about Scottish rural life and traditions created by, among others, James 'Ossian' Macpherson (1736–96), one of her neighbours. It also brought her recognition in Scottish literary circles, including the friendship of Scott and of Francis Jeffrey, who reviewed her work in the *Edinburgh Review*. Her *Memoirs of an American Lady: With Sketches of Manners and Scenery in America* published the following year recalled her childhood experiences in New York. It went through several editions both in England and America and made her a minor celebrity. She published *Essays on the Superstitions of the Highlanders of Scotland* (1811) and a poem, *Eighteen Hundred and Thirteen* (1814), neither of which were as successful as her *Letters* or the *Memoirs*. After her husband's death she moved first to Stirling and then to Edinburgh, where a fall in 1820 caused her to spend the remainder of her life on crutches. Scott and others secured her a civil-list pension in 1826. She died of flu in 1838. Her son J. P. Grant edited her *Memoirs and Correspondence* (1844), which supplements the autobiographical elements in her earlier works. *See* 'George Paston' [Emily Morse Symonds], 'Mrs. Grant of Laggan', in *Little Memoirs of the Eighteenth Century* (1901).

Granville, Mary *see* DELANY, Mary

Greenaway, 'Kate' (Catherine), children's writer and illustrator (b. Hoxton, London, 17 March 1846, d. Hampstead, London, 6 November 1901).

Kate Greenaway was the second of four children of John Greenaway, a wood engraver, and his wife Elizabeth Jones. The household was firmly London based, but shortly after she was born her father sent the family to live in the country for two years so that he could work undisturbed. The experience of life in the village of Rolleston, in Nottinghamshire, was crucial to the formation of Kate Greenaway's vision of childhood in a rural setting which was to become her hallmark. She was educated at home and at a series of indifferent dame schools. The close relationship which she developed with her father, based on their shared interest in art, was also an important aspect of her education. She studied at Heatherley's Art School and later at the Slade and had her first public exhibition at the age of 22. She began commercial work by designing Christmas cards and valentines and also book illustrations. Her quaintly dressed children, their costumes partly invented, partly influenced by late eighteenth-century fashion, set against tidy rural backgrounds, sunlit and filled with flowers, were distinctive from the beginning. They later established a popular 'Kate Greenaway' style in children's clothes. Her first successful publication was undertaken in collaboration with the printer Edmund Evans. *Under the Window: Pictures and Rhymes for Children* (1878), a collection of her own verses with illustrations, sold a phenomenal 70,000 copies with 30,000 more in French and German translations. It paved the way for a series of collaborations, with Greenaway providing the illustrations for collections of nursery rhymes, fairy-tales, almanacs, and picture-books. She illustrated Charlotte *Yonge's *Heir of Redclyffe* and *Heartsease* (1879), a collection of the work of Ann and Jane *Taylor (1883), Browning's *Pied Piper of Hamelin* (1888), and Elizabeth von *Arnim's *April Baby's Book of Tunes* (1900). *Marigold Garden: Pictures and Rhymes*, the only other work for which she provided the text as well as the illustrations, was published in 1885. Greenaway's verses are of little significance when separated from her illustrations. The latter, by contrast, had the effect of transforming the text they illustrated. The most important influence on her work was that of Ruskin, whose *Fors Clavigera* (1883) and *Dame Wiggins of Lee* (1885), a collection of nursery rhymes, she illustrated. He gave her drawing lessons and tried to teach her perspective, publicly praised her work, and wrote her flirtatious letters. She visited him for a month at his home in the Lake District and grew to depend on his advice and affection, causing him later to distance himself. She never married, but lived with her parents, whom she supported, in Hampstead. One of the penalties of her success in the 1880s was the ease with which she was imitated, a factor which cut into her sales in the 1890s. Reviewers latterly complained that her work was repetitive. She took up oil painting in order to profit from the higher prices such work fetched, but died at 55 before she could perfect the technique. *See* M. H. Spielmann and G. S. Layard, *Kate Greenaway* (1905); Rodney Engen, *Kate Greenaway: A Biography* (1981).

Greenwell, Dora, poet (b. Greenwell Ford, County Durham, 6 December 1821, d. Clifton, near Bristol, 29 March 1882).

Dora Greenwell was one of three children and the only daughter of William Thomas Greenwell, a country gentleman, magistrate, and at one time Deputy Lieutenant of County Durham, and his wife Dorothy Smales. She was educated at home by governesses, knew Latin and modern languages, and taught herself philosophy and political economy. She began to write poetry when young, modelling her work on Tennyson and Elizabeth Barrett *Browning. She also developed a strong social conscience. Her father's bankruptcy in 1847 forced the family to move in with each of her clergymen brothers in turn, first in Northumberland and then in Lancashire. After her father's death in 1854 she and her mother returned to County Durham. Her first volume of *Poems* was published in 1848 and a second book, *Stories that Might be True with Other Poems*, in 1850. She wrote on social problems for various journals, most notably 'On the Education of the Imbecile' (1868), based on her experience of the Durham workhouse and prison, and 'Our Single Women' (1862), both for the *North British Review*. In the latter she pleaded for more work opportunities for women. Her 1861 volume of *Poems* contained new work and was reprinted in 1867 with some additions, including a poem about the Lancashire cotton famine and others about the American Civil War. While living in Northumberland she met the feminist Josephine Butler, who became a close friend, as did Christina *Rossetti, whom she met in the home of the critic William Bell Scott. Rossetti's poem 'Autumn Violets' is addressed to Greenwell, who in turn wrote 'To Christina Rossetti'. She wrote two prose works on Christian subjects, *The Patience of Hope* (1860), which she dedicated to Butler, and *Two Friends* (1862). She also wrote biographies of the Dominican monk Lacordaire (1867) and the Quaker John Woolman (1871). Later volumes of poetry included *Carmina Crucis* (1869), *Songs of Salvation* (1873), some of which are better known as hymns, *The Soul's Legend* (1873), and *Camera Obscura* (1876). After her mother's death in 1872 she lived for a while in London and then moved to her brother's home at Clifton, near Bristol. In later years she became an outspoken anti-vivisectionist and a campaigner for women's suffrage, although her declining health precluded an active role in either. Towards the end of her life she became addicted to opium and in 1881 she suffered a nearly fatal accident. She died at the age of 61. *See* W. Dorling, *Memoirs of Dora Greenwell* (1885); H. Bett, *Dora Greenwell* (1950).

Greer, Germaine, feminist, critic, journalist (b. Melbourne, Australia, 29 January 1939).

Germaine Greer is the daughter of Eric Reginald Greer, a newspaper advertising manager, and Margaret May Lafrank. She chronicled her search for her father's hidden identity in the prize-winning *Daddy We Hardly Knew You* (1989). She was convent-educated in Melbourne and won scholarships to the University of Melbourne, where she took a degree in English and French, followed by an MA in English at Sydney University in 1962. She won a Commonwealth Scholarship to Newnham College, Cambridge, and wrote a Ph.D. thesis on 'The Ethics of Love and Marriage in Shakespeare's Early Comedies' (1967). Greer lectured at the University of Warwick from 1967 to 1973 and for a short period in 1968 was married to the journalist and building worker Paul de Feu. Her first book, *The Female Eunuch* (1970, published in the USA in 1971), a vigorous and outspoken critique of female conditioning and stereotyping, became a classic text of the women's movement in the 1970s and beyond. In the wake of its publication she became an international celebrity, a television personality, and a highly profiled journalist. A much-publicized debate on the women's liberation movement with the American writer Norman Mailer in New York in 1971 was one of a number of occasions which enhanced her reputation for plain speaking and controversy. Her next book, *The Obstacle Race* (1979), analysed the factors which have inhibited women's achievement in the world of art. Her attacks on the West's enforcement of family planning on the underdeveloped world and her emphasis on the importance of motherhood to women in *Sex and Destiny: The Politics of Human Fertility* (1984) were widely interpreted as a recantation of her position in *The Female Eunuch. The Madwoman's Underclothes* (1986) collected essays and journalism written between 1968 and 1985 for the *Spectator, Oz, Playboy*, the *Sunday Times, Spare Rib, Esquire, Harper's Magazine*, and other publications and included a highly regarded essay 'Women and Power in Cuba', first published in *Women: A World Report* (1985). From 1980 to 1983 she was Professor of Modern Letters at the University of Tulsa and Founding Director of the Tulsa Centre for the Study of Women's Literature. Her interest in establishing the texts of early women writers resulted in *Kissing the Rod* (1988), an anthology of seventeenth-century women's poetry which she co-edited, and an edition of the uncollected verse of Aphra *Behn (1989). She has also written an introduction to Christina *Rossetti's *Goblin Market* (1975) and a book on Shakespeare (1986). *The Change* (1991) is a combative approach to the menopause. She currently lives in England. *See* Janet Todd (ed.), *Women Writers Talking* (1983).

Gregory, (Isabella) Augusta, Lady, playwright and folklorist (b. Roxborough, County Galway, 15 March 1852, d. Coole Park, County Galway, 22 May 1932).

Augusta Gregory was the twelfth child and youngest daughter of Dudley Persse, a wealthy Irish landowner, and his wife Frances Barry. She was educated at home, and developed an interest in Irish folklore and legends from her Irish-speaking nurse. In 1880 she became the second wife of Sir William Henry Gregory, an Irish MP and former Governor of Ceylon thirty-five years her senior. She travelled widely with her husband and shared his fervent nationalism. Their only son Robert, an artist killed in action as an airman in Italy in 1918, was commemorated in two poems by Yeats, 'An Irish Airman Foresees his Death' and 'In Memory of Major Robert Gregory'. After her husband's death in 1892 she prepared his autobiography for publication (1894) and edited his grandfather's letters as *Mr. Gregory's Letter*

Box 1813–30 (1898). She then turned her energies to collecting and publishing Galway tales and legends, inspired by the publication of Yeats's *Celtic Twilight* and Douglas Hyde's *Love Songs of Connacht* in 1893. She learned Gaelic and translated collections of ancient epics and Irish folklore into English as in *Cuchulain of Muirthemine* (1902), *Poets and Dreamers* (1903), *Gods and Fighting Men* (1904), *A Book of Saints and Wonders* (1906), and *Visions and Beliefs in the West of Ireland* (1920). In 1898 she met Yeats for the first time, and became involved in the Irish Literary Theatre, along with Edward Martyn, with the aim of encouraging Irish drama. The circle widened to include J. M. Synge, George Moore, Padraic Colum, and others, and in 1904 they moved into the Abbey Theatre, Dublin, with Lady Gregory as co-director with Yeats and Synge. Her administrative and organizational skills were crucial to the development and flowering of the Abbey. She became known as its 'godmother' or alternatively, according to Shaw, its 'charwoman'. She published a personal account of the period in *Our Irish Theatre: A Chapter of Autobiography* (1913). Her association with active playwrights encouraged her own latent dramatic talents and she had her first play produced in her fiftieth year. She wrote a total of twenty-seven plays, mainly one-act comedies, adapted four by Molière, translated a play by Goldoni, and collaborated with both Yeats and Douglas Hyde. She developed a representation of Irish country speech or dialect which she called 'Kiltartan', which formed the basis of peasant dialogue in her own plays and in those of Yeats and Synge. The best of her one-act comedies were published in *Seven Short Plays* (1909) and included *Spreading the News*, *Hyacinth Halvey*, *The Rising of the Moon*, *The Jackdaw*, *The Workhouse Ward*, and *The Gaolgate*. The best of her later plays, which combined realism and fantasy, were *The Golden Apple* (1916), *The Dragon* (1920), and *Aristotle's Bellows* (1923). She also wrote a passion play, *The Story Brought by Brigit* (1924). Her plays were written with the purpose of the Abbey in mind, to reach as wide an audience as possible, and to enhance national identity and an awareness of Irish culture. Coole Park, her estate in Galway, became the unofficial headquarters of the so-called Irish Revival or literary renaissance. Yeats immortalized it in his poems 'Coole Park' and 'Coole Park and Ballylee'. Yeats, Shaw, Synge, G. W. Russell ('AE'), Douglas Hyde, and J. B. Yeats spent much time there and Lady Gregory died there in 1932, aged 80. Her *Journals 1916–1930* were edited by L. Robinson (1946) and her works collected in *The Coole Edition of Lady Gregory's Writings*, ed. Colin Smythe (1970). *Seventy Years*, her autobiography, was edited by Colin Smythe (1974). *See* Elizabeth Coxhead, *Lady Gregory: A Literary Portrait* (1961); Ann Saddlemyer, *In Defense of Lady Gregory, Playwright* (1966); Ann Saddlemyer and Colin Smythe (eds.), *Lady Gregory: Fifty Years After* (1987).

Grierson, Constantia, poet and classical scholar (b. Graiguenamanagh, County Kilkenny, *c.*1705, d. Dublin, 2 December 1732).

Constantia Grierson, née Crawley, was the daughter of poor parents who none the less encouraged her reading, as did the local clergyman. She studied midwifery in Dublin with Dr van Lewen, father of Laetitia *Pilkington, and according to the latter knew Hebrew, Greek, Latin, French, and mathematics. Another friend, Mary *Barber, noted her accomplishments in history, divinity, and philosophy as well. In 1726 she married George Grierson, a Dublin printer born in Scotland, and corrected the press for his editions of Terence (1727) and Tacitus (1730), writing Latin dedications of the former to the son of Lord Carteret, Lord Lieutenant, and of the latter to Carteret himself. These contributed directly, it was said, to Grierson's appointment as King's Printer in Dublin in 1733. She became a member of the circle surrounding Swift, who praised her classical learning to Pope, among others. She also wrote poetry, about which she was extremely modest. Mary Barber included several of her poems in her *Poems on Several Occasions* (1734), published after Grierson's death, and Laetitia Pilkington published others in her *Memoirs*, vol. i (1748). Her work was included in the collection **Poems by Eminent Ladies* ed. G. Colman and B. Thornton (1755). Another poem, 'The Art of Printing', was distributed as a single broadside and later published in 1764. Further manuscript poems have recently been discovered. Grierson had four children, two sons and two daughters, three of whom died in infancy. Her remaining son, who succeeded his father as King's Printer, was 'a gentleman of uncommon learning, great wit and vivacity', according to the *DNB*, and admired by Dr Johnson. Constantia Grierson died of tuberculosis.

Griffith, Elizabeth, playwright and novelist (b. Glamorganshire, *c.*1720, d. Millicent, Nass, County Kildare, 5 January 1793).

Elizabeth Griffith was the daughter of Thomas Griffith, a well-known Dublin actor-manager, and his wife Jane Foxcroft, daughter of a Yorkshire clergyman. She was born in Wales, where Thomas Griffith's immediate family lived, but brought up in Ireland, where her father educated her probably with the theatre in mind. She read both French and English, particularly new novels and plays, and learnt to recite verse. Her father's death in 1744 hastened her theatrical début, and by 1749 she was acting with Thomas Sheridan's Dublin company. Around 1752 she was secretly married to Richard Griffith (?1714–88), then a feckless gentleman farmer with aristocratic origins, with whom she had carried on an extensive correspondence for several years. They had two children. In 1753 Elizabeth moved to London, where she played minor roles at Covent Garden. When Griffith's linen factory failed in the mid-1750s, the couple decided to publish their courtship letters by subscription. The first two volumes of *A Series of Genuine Letters between Henry and Frances* was published in 1757, and enlarged to six volumes by 1770. Its immediate success encouraged her to write for a living. She produced *Amana*, a dramatic poem, in 1764 and in 1765 her first comedy, *The Platonic Wife*, adapted from a play by Marmontel, which played for six nights at Drury Lane in January of that year. She moved permanently to London, buying a house on the proceeds of her next play, *The Double Mistake* (1766), and entered into a series of protracted negotiations for employment with Garrick. He suggested a version of Beaumarchais's *Eugénie*, which was produced as *The School for Rakes* at Drury Lane in February 1769. Her next play, *A Wife in the Right*, produced at Covent Garden in March 1772, was a failure, mainly due to the drunkenness of the leading actor. Her last main play, *The Times*, based on an adaptation of Goldoni's *Bourru bienfaisant*, was performed at Drury Lane in December 1779, after Garrick's retirement. Elizabeth Griffith also wrote three successful epistolary novels, all of them concerned with the sentimental idealization of womanhood and critical of the fashionable and mercenary marriage market. *The Delicate Distress* (1769) was published together with *The Gordian Knot* by Richard Griffith as *Two Novels in Letters* 'by the authors of Henry and Frances'. The others were *The History of Lady Barton* (1771) and *The Story of Juliana Harley* (1776). She also edited *A Collection of Novels* (1777) which included work by Penelope *Aubin, Aphra *Behn, and Eliza *Haywood. *Essays to Young Married Women* (1782) advised domesticity. She stopped writing when her son returned home rich from India. *See* J. M. S. Tompkins, *Polite Marriage* (1938); D. Eshelman, *Elizabeth Griffith: A Biographical and Critical Study* (1949); Jane Spencer, *The Rise of the Woman Novelist: From Aphra Behn to Jane Austen* (1986).

Grote, Harriet, biographer (b. The Ridgeway, near Southampton, 1 July 1792, d. Shere, Surrey, 29 December 1878).

The brilliant daughter of Thomas Lewin, an Indian civil servant, and a Miss Chaloner, Harriet Lewin fell in love with the son of a neighbour near Bexley in Kent, George Grote, under whose careful tuition she prepared to share in his historical and political interests and whom she married in 1820. They had one son who died soon after his birth in 1821. Harriet Grote devoted her considerable intellectual and practical talents to furthering her husband's political career as a Radical Member of Parliament and later became closely involved in the preparation of his celebrated *History of Greece* (1845–56). Her vivacity and attested conversational skills made their home a natural centre for the parliamentary Radicals and for George Grote's later literary and administrative activities. Harriet Grote forged particular links with French public men and according to the *DNB* became one of the chief intermediaries of her time between France and England. She was an accomplished musician and the friend of many composers and performers, including Mendelssohn and Jenny Lind, taking charge of the latter during some of her early visits to England. Her friend and biographer Elizabeth *Eastlake once pronounced her 'the cleverest woman in London'. Her first work was a brief biography of the painter Ary Scheffer (1860). In 1862 she published her *Collected Papers in Prose and Verse*, mainly essays on literary, political, and economic subjects, many of them in accordance with the old Radical views. She was a compulsive diarist and a lively letter writer and with the materials at her disposal began to write a biography of her husband before his death in 1871. *The Personal Life of George Grote* was published in 1873. Several of her pamphlets were printed for private circulation, including a sketch in 1866, 'The Philosophical Radicals of 1832: Comprising the Life of Sir William Molesworth', and 'A Brief Retrospect of the Political Events of 1831–2' (1878), both attesting to the centrality of her role in Radical politics of the Reform era. *See* Lady Eastlake, *Mrs. Grote: A Sketch* (1880).

Grymeston, Elizabeth, essayist (before 1563–1603).

Elizabeth Grymeston was the fifth child of Martin Bernye of Gunton in Norfolk and his wife Margaret Flint. A Catholic, she had by 1584 married Christopher Grymeston, a student and then bursar at Caius College, Cambridge, who later entered Gray's Inn and was called to the bar. They had nine children, of whom only one, Bernye, survived. This, together with a childhood scarred by her mother's uncontrolled anger and fear that she was dying, 'a dead woman among the living' as she described herself, led her to compile a miscellany and handbook of advice for her surviving son. *Miscellanea, Meditations, Memoratives*, published after her death in 1604, went through four editions by 1618 and parts of it were reprinted in the nineteenth century. This 'portable veni mecum' as she described it, offered 'the true portrature of thy mothers minde' and was derived from her extensive reading in Latin, Greek, Italian, the Church Fathers, and contemporary poetry. The book is divided into fourteen so-called chapters, mainly brief essays on religious topics, together with scattered verses. The 'Memoratives' were a collection of moral maxims. Her method was a combination of paraphrase and direct quotation. 'Neither could I ever brooke to set downe that haltingly in my broken stile which I found better expressed by a graver authour,' she admitted candidly. The book reflects a remarkable degree of learning for a woman of the sixteenth century. *See* Elaine V. Beilin, *Redeeming Eve: Women Writers of the English Renaissance* (1987).

Gunning, Elizabeth *see under* GUNNING, Susannah

Gunning, Susannah, née Minifie, novelist (b. 1740, d. London, 28 August 1800)

Susannah Gunning was the daughter of the Revd Dr James Minifie, of Fairwater in Somerset. Little is known of her early life before the publication of the *Histories of Lady Frances S . . . and Lady Caroline S . . .* (1763), which she wrote with her sister **Margaret Minifie** and published by subscription. Three other novels followed, *Family Pictures* (1764), *The Picture* (1766), also written jointly, and *The Hermit* (1770), characterized by conventional plots which turned on love and marriage in aristocratic circles. Her writing career came to an abrupt halt in 1768 with her marriage to Captain, soon to be Lieutenant-General, John Gunning, of the 65th Regiment of Foot, a dissolute soldier who had distinguished himself in the Battle of Bunker's Hill. His sisters, both beauties, had married advantageously into the aristocracy, and his advancement may have had something to do with his brother-in-law the Duke of Argyll. The marital prospects of the Gunnings' only daughter Elizabeth caused a public family row in 1791, an affair accompanied by squibs, satires, and cartoons which Horace Walpole dubbed the 'Gunninghiad'. Each parent supported an aristocratic suitor, and when Elizabeth chose her mother's candidate she and Susannah were turned out of the family home. Susannah Gunning responded with a public 'Letter' to the Duke of Argyll declaring her innocence of any connivance or deception. (The intrigue had involved a forged letter.) The family separated after the scandal. Shortly afterwards General Gunning was sued for damages over an affair with his tailor's wife. He removed to Naples with his mistress and died in 1797, changing his will the day before he died in order to leave money to his wife and daughter and his Irish estate to his wife. Susannah Gunning now resumed her writing career, plundering the affair, although she denied it, for her novel *Anecdotes of the Delborough Family* (1792), her poem *Virginius and Virginia* (1792), and her novel *Memoirs of Mary* (1793), in which the heroine suffers as a result of a forged letter. *Delves* (1796) was a picaresque novel with a Welsh setting. *Love at First Sight* (1797) and *Fashionable Involvements* (1800), her last works, were both stylized novels of manners. Her well known tendency to hyperbole in dramatic scenes prompted a contemporary to coin the term 'minific'. She died in London three years after her husband, at the age of 60. **Elizabeth Gunning,** later **Plunkett** (1769–1823), published nine novels, two collections of didactic stories for children, and several French translations. Her best-known works were probably *The Packet* (1794), *The Orphans of Snowden* (1797), and *The Gipsy Countess* (1799). Margaret Minifie is now considered to have been the author of *Barford Abbey* (1768), *The*

Cottage (1769), and *Combe Wood* (1783), once thought to have been written by Susannah Gunning. *See* Janet Todd, *The Sign of Angellica: Women, Writing and Fiction, 1660-1800* (1989).

H

Halkett, Anne, Lady, religious writer and autobiographer (b. London, 4 January 1622, d. 22 April 1699).

Anne Halkett was the younger daughter of Thomas Murray and his wife Jane Drummond, both members of Scottish noble families, who held posts as tutor and governess to the children of James I. Her father subsequently became Provost of Eton. He died when she was 3 and she was educated by her mother, who taught her French, dancing, music, and needlework as well as physic and surgery in order to help her work with the poor. She was also given an extensive religious education, with daily prayers and Bible readings and regular church attendance. Her mother forbade her marriage to her first suitor, Thomas Howard, because of his small fortune. The ensuing quarrel with her mother ended only after her threat to enter a Protestant nunnery. She then became involved with the Royalist Joseph Bampfield and assisted in the elaborately planned escape of the future James II. Bampfield proposed marriage, posing as a widower. Their relationship lasted for some years, until the existence of his wife was proved incontrovertibly. She nursed Royalist soldiers after the Battle of Dunbar in the summer of 1650 and remained in Scotland for two years practising medicine. In 1656 she married Sir James Halkett, a genuine widower with two daughters. Before the birth of their first child (three others died in infancy) she wrote 'The Mother's Will to her Unborn Child', the manuscript of which is now lost. After her husband's death in 1676 she taught children of the nobility in her house at Dunfermline. James II gave her a pension in reward for her services after his accession in

1685. She left numerous manuscript volumes at her death, mainly on religious subjects, written between 1644 and 1699, and an autobiography, written in 1677–8 and first published in 1875 by the Camden Society. Remarkably candid, the autobiography combines a record of political events with a narrative of her own experiences and feelings. It reveals a strong religious faith and a belief in providence which extended to the Royalist cause. *The Life of Lady Halkett*, published in 1701, contained two of her religious meditations, together with 'Instructions for Youth', and a 'Life', derived from the autobiography. *See* J. Loftis (ed.), *The Memoirs of Anne, Lady Halkett and Ann, Lady *Fanshawe* (1979); Mary Beth Rose (ed.), *Women in the Middle Ages and the Renaissance: Literary and Historical Perspectives* (1986).

Hall, Anna Maria (Mrs Samuel Carter Hall), novelist, journalist, and editor (b. Dublin, 6 January 1800, d. East Moulsey, Surrey, 30 January 1881).

Anna Hall's father died while she was a child. She was brought up by her mother, first in Dublin, and after 1815 in London. In 1824 she married the journalist and editor Samuel Carter Hall (1800–89). Her first short story was not published until she was 29, but this was followed by a collection of stories, *Sketches of Irish Character* (1829), which went into a second series in 1831. They caught the vogue for stories of Irish life, but although Hall's name was often linked with Maria *Edgeworth's, her work more closely resembled that of Mary Russell *Mitford. The stories were never popular in Ireland, partly because they were geared to an English audience. Hall was critical of Irish life, and took pains to emphasize the English extraction of her characters. She dramatized one of her stories, 'The Groves of Blarney', for the actor Tyrone Power, and also wrote several plays which had considerable success. She wrote a total of nine novels, beginning with *The Buccaneer* (1832), set during the period of Cromwell's Protectorate. Others included *Marian; or A Young Maid's Fortunes* (1840), and probably her best, *Can Wrong be Right?* (1862), whose heroine struggles to protect her virtue from the advances of a local lord. As well as contributing to Henry Colburn's *New Monthly Magazine* and the *Art Union Journal*, both of which were edited by her husband, she edited *Sharpe's London Magazine* for a year, and also the short-lived *St. James's Magazine*, founded as a rival to the *Cornhill* in 1862–3. Hall was an energetic philanthropist, helping to found the Hospital for Consumption at Brompton, the Governesses' Institution, the Home for Decayed Gentlewomen, and the Nightingale Fund. She also worked for temperance causes, for women's rights (although she opposed female suffrage), and helped street musicians. She was granted a civil-list pension in 1868 and died at the age of 81. *See* Samuel Carter Hall, *Book of Memories* (1876) and *Retrospect of a Long*

Life (1883); *Mary *Howitt: An Autobiography*, ed. Margaret Howitt (1889); Margaret *Oliphant, *The Autobiography and Letters of Mrs. Oliphant*, ed. A. L. Coghill (1899).

Hall, Marguerite Radclyffe, novelist and poet (b. Bournemouth, 1880, d. Lynton, Devon, 7 October 1943).

Marguerite Radclyffe Hall was the younger daughter of dilettante Radclyffe ('Rat') Radclyffe Hall and his American-born wife Mary Jane ('Marie') Diehl. Her father left shortly after her birth, and her mother's stormy second marriage to a teacher at the Royal College of Music left Marguerite isolated and did little to recommend conventional married life. She was taught by governesses, went to London day schools, and then left home to live with her grandmother. She inherited the family fortune, made from a sanatorium in Torquay, after her father's death in 1898. As a child she had written verses which she set to music. After a year at King's College, London, and a period spent travelling in the United States she began to write seriously. Five volumes of poetry were published in quick succession by 'Marguerite Radclyffe-Hall': *Twixt Earth and Stars* (1906), *A Sheaf of Verses* (1908), *Poems of the Past and Present* (1910), *Songs of Three Counties* (1913), and *The Forgotten Island* (1915). Many were subsequently set to music by various composers. In 1907 she fell in love with Mabel Veronica Batten, known as 'Ladye', a married socialite and *Lieder* singer many years her senior. They lived together for seven years, after which Ladye was superseded in Hall's affections by Una Vincent Troubridge, the wife of an admiral, and later the translator of Colette. Ladye's death the following year left a legacy of guilt which was never quite erased. Hall had converted to Roman Catholicism and now became interested in spiritualism and psychical research. In 1924 she published *The Unlit Lamp*, the first of her books to deal with relationships between women. It had been rejected ten times. *The Forge* (1924), written later, was published before *The Unlit Lamp* in the same year. *A Saturday Life* followed in 1925 and in 1926 *Adam's Breed* won both the James Tait Black Memorial Prize and the Femina Vie Heureuse Prize. By this time she was publishing as Radclyffe Hall, abandoning the hyphen and also her Christian name. In 1928, at the height of her career, she published the largely autobiographical *The Well of Loneliness*, an explicit study of a lesbian writer. There was a celebrated attack on the book in the *Sunday Express*. The book was declared an obscene libel and Hall and Jonathan Cape the publisher became the subjects of an obscenity trial. The book was withdrawn from sale in August 1928 but published in Paris, using the original stereotypes. Writers including Virginia *Woolf, Violet *Hunt, and others rallied to her support, but with no effect. Although much shaken by the trial she published three further books, *The*

Master of the House (1932), *Miss Ogilvy Finds Herself* (1934), a collection of stories, and *The Sixth Beatitude* (1936), none of which was controversial. In 1933 she fell in love with Evguenia Souline, a half-Russian and much younger nurse with whom she lived in a sometimes anguished *ménage à trois* with Una Troubridge until 1942. Hall died of cancer in 1943. Una Troubridge's *The Life and Death of Radclyffe Hall*, written after her death in 1945, was not published until 1961. The *Well of Loneliness* was eventually reissued in England in 1949. See Vera *Brittain, *Radclyffe Hall: A Case of Obscenity?* (1968); Claudia Stillman Franks, *Beyond 'The Well of Loneliness': The Fiction of Radclyffe Hall* (1982); R. Ormrod, *Una Troubridge: The Friend of Radclyffe Hall* (1985); Michael Baker, *Our Three Selves: The Life of Radclyffe Hall* (1985); Rebecca O'Rourke, *Reflecting on The Well of Loneliness* (1989); Jane Marcus, in *Lesbian Texts and Contexts: Radical Revisions*, ed. Karla Jay and Joanne Glasgow (1990).

Hamilton, Cicely, playwright, journalist, novelist, and actress (b. Kensington, London, 15 June 1872, d. London, 5 December 1952).

Cicely Hamilton was the daughter of Captain Denzil Hammill, the commander of a Highland regiment, and his Irish wife Maude Piers. She was educated at private schools in Malvern and later at the Bad Homberg in Germany. A decline in the family fortunes necessitated a stint as a pupil-teacher in the Midlands and she then took up various kinds of hack journalism, mainly novelettes and detective serials, in order to earn her living. She began a career as a playwright with a series of one-act plays for the Pioneer Players, an all-women company. Her first major success was *Diana of Dobson's* (1908), about a shopgirl who eventually captures a wealthy husband. The play's serious point, about inequality of wealth and the exploitation of working women, was somewhat marred by a sentimental ending, which was probably the reason for the play's phenomenal success and a run of 141 performances. She adopted the name Hamilton when she went on the stage with various provincial touring companies, her most notable performances being in Shaw's *Fanny's First Play* (1911) and J. M. Barrie's *The Twelve-Pound Look* (1913). She was an ardent feminist and suffragist as well as a pacifist, principles which informed each element of a varied career. She was the co-founder with Bessie Hatton, in 1908, of the *Women Writers' Suffrage League, an auxiliary of the National Union of Suffrage Societies. Two of her plays, *How the Vote was Won* (1909), a comedy about a women's general strike, and *A Pageant of Great Women* (1909), which celebrated women's achievements and starred Ellen Terry, were popular successes at the height of the suffrage agitation. Of her remaining plays, only *The Child in Flanders*

(1917), a modern nativity play, and *The Old Adam* (1925), about the durability of the war spirit in men, which Asquith, the Prime Minister, reportedly saw three times, received any critical attention. Hamilton's anti-war novel *William: An Englishman* (1919), won the Femina Vie Heureuse Prize. *Theodore Savage* (1922), an apocalyptic story of civilization destroyed by total scientific warfare, reinforced her point. Hamilton's major contribution to the 'woman question' was a witty polemic, *Marriage as a Trade* (1909), in which she argued against the 'largely compulsory character of that institution as far as one-half of humanity is concerned'. She never married. She wrote a history of the Old Vic (1926) with her friend Lilian Baylis, and in 1931 a perceptive travel book about Germany. This was followed by a series of travel books on the major countries of Europe, the last published in 1950. Her autobiography *Life Errant* appeared in 1935. Hamilton was awarded a civil-list pension in 1938 and died in 1952 at 80. *See* Dale Spender, *Women of Ideas and what Men have Done to them* (1982).

Hamilton, Elizabeth, novelist and writer on education (b. Belfast, 21 July 1758, d. Harrogate, Yorkshire, 23 July 1816).

Elizabeth Hamilton was a member of an old Scottish family of declining fortunes, the Hamiltons of Woodhall. Her father Charles Hamilton had joined a mercantile house in London, settled in Dublin, and married Katherine Mackay of that city. Elizabeth was the youngest of their three children. At her father's death in 1759 she was sent to live with her aunt and uncle near Stirling, where she was educated at a day school run by a master. For nearly twenty years she lived a solitary rural life, devoting herself to her aunt and uncle until the latter's death in 1790, lamenting in her memoirs that 'women cannot escape out of the rubbish in which they may happen to be buried', yet in a poem proclaiming herself 'a cheerful, pleased old maid'. Although there were few visitors, evenings were routinely set aside for reading aloud history, books of travel, and the occasional novel. This seclusion was interrupted in 1786 by a visit from her brother Charles, an oriental scholar and historian, who was in the military service of the East India Company and who had returned to England to continue his research. He took her on visits to London, where she was introduced into literary circles and encouraged to continue the writing she had begun to relieve her solitude. Her first publication was a contribution to Henry Mackenzie's periodical the *Lounger* (no. 46, 1785). A novel based on the life of Lady Arbella Stuart (1576–1615), one-time claimant to the throne, and with Shakespeare as a character, remained unpublished. Her correspondence with Charles, who died suddenly in 1792, formed the basis of her first literary success, the *Translation of the Letters of a Hindoo Rajah* (1796), a satire on contemporary society as seen through the eyes of a visiting oriental. *Memoirs of Modern Philosophers* (1800), a novel published anonymously, satirized contemporary radical philosophers, particularly the Godwin circle including Mary *Hays, although Mary *Wollstonecraft got off lightly. Her interest in education grew out of observation and also experience. *Letters on the Elementary Principles of Education* (1801), which went through several editions, advocated equality for boys and girls and an emphasis on both the moral and intellectual life. *Letters to the Daughter of a Nobleman* (1806), which was written during a period spent as a companion to motherless children, was directed to the upper classes. Her *Exercises in Religious Knowledge* (1809) was addressed to working-class girls after her involvement with a Female House of Industry. *Hints Addressed to the Patrons and Directors of Public Schools* (1815) recommended the methods of Pestalozzi. Her most popular works were the sentimental poem 'My ain Fireside' and *The Cottagers of Glenburnie* (1808), a story unashamedly aimed at reforming the living habits of the Scottish peasantry. Francis Jeffrey suggested in his review in the *Edinburgh* (1808) that the latter should be widely circulated, and that it would do much more good than Hannah *More's *Cheap Repository Tracts*. After her brother's death, Mrs Hamilton, as she liked to be called, although she never married, lived with her sister in England. They travelled extensively, and then settled in Edinburgh, where she became a celebrity, opening her home on Mondays to literary society. Dugald Stewart, Joanna *Baillie, and Mrs *Grant of Laggan were among her admirers, and George III granted her a pension in 1804. She had suffered for many years from gout and latterly from weak eyesight, and a return to England was thought essential for her health. She died suddenly in Harrogate in 1816, aged 58. Her journal, kept between 1788 and 1815, was posthumously published. *See* E. O. Benger, *Memoirs of Mrs. Elizabeth Hamilton with Selections from her Correspondence and Unpublished Writings* (1818); Marilyn Butler, *Jane Austen and the War of Ideas* (1975, 1987).

Harraden, Beatrice, novelist and suffragist (b. Hampstead, London, 24 January 1864, d. Barton-on-Sea, Hampshire, 5 May 1936).

Beatrice Harraden was the daughter of Samuel Harraden, a musical instrument importer, and his wife Rosalie Lindstedt. She was educated in Dresden, and went to Cheltenham Ladies' College and later to Queen's and Bedford Colleges in London, obtaining a London University BA. She devoted much of her time to the cause of women's suffrage, eventually becoming a prominent member of the Women's Social and Political Union, travelling and lecturing in England and also on the Continent and in America in support of the suffragettes. She was introduced to London literary society through

Eliza Lynn *Linton, her guardian, who patronizingly described her as 'my little BA.'. Her first stories were published in *Blackwood's Magazine* and she then wrote *Things will Take a Turn* (1891), a children's story. Her first novel, *Ships that Pass in the Night* (1893), a weepy love story about two convalescing consumptives, one of whom is killed in an accident, was an unprecedented best seller. *In Varying Moods* (1894), a collection of stories, *Hilda Strafford* (1897), *Untold Tales of the Past* (1897), children's stories, and *The Fowler* (1899), about a sexual predator, are among her best later books. Michael Sadleir's *DNB* entry notes Harraden's preoccupation with fleeting love affairs between strangers, in which one partner 'Excelsior-fashion "passes on"', and attributes it to her passion for a man who embezzled his client's money and whose body was later found in a crevasse in a Swiss glacier. Harraden received a civil-list pension in 1930 for services to literature and died at the age of 72.

Harrison, Mary St Leger Kingsley *see* MALET, Lucas

'**Hatton,** G. Noel' *see* CAIRD, Mona

Havergal, Frances Ridley, poet and hymn writer (b. Astley, Worcestershire, 14 December 1836, d. Caswell Bay, Swansea, 3 June 1879).

Frances Ridley Havergal was the youngest of the six children of the Revd William Henry Havergal, rector of Astley, Worcestershire, and a composer of religious music, and his first wife Jane Head. She was delicate as a child and rigorous study was discouraged, so she was taught by her mother and then by her elder sister Jane. She nevertheless knew French, German, Greek, and Hebrew and spent a year at a school in Düsseldorf when accompanying her father and stepmother to Germany in 1852–3. She wrote poetry from the age of 7 and published in *Good Words* and various religious periodicals. Her poems were admired in evangelical circles, as were her hymns, of which the best known were 'Take my life and let it be', 'O Saviour, precious Saviour', and 'Tell it out among the heathen'. They were widely used in contemporary collections and set to music by well-known composers including Gounod. Her first collection of poems, *The Ministry of Song* (1869), launched a prolific decade of publication. There were collections of poems and hymns, *Under the Surface* (1874), *Loyal Responses; or Daily Melodies for the King's Minstrels* (1878), and volumes of scriptural texts with accompanying poems, *Little Pillows; or Good-Night Thoughts for the Little Ones* (1875), *Morning Bells; or Waking Thoughts for the Little Ones* (1875). She prepared a new edition of her father's *Old Church Psalmody* for the press after his death in 1870. Her charitable activities, church-going, and Christian piety (she turned down proposals of marriage in order to devote herself to a spiritual life) were highlighted in her autobiography, written in 1859 and published as part of the posthumous *Memorials* edited by her sister **Maria Vernon Graham Havergal** in 1880. She lived for a while with Jane in order to teach her children, then with her father and stepmother in Leamington until the latter's death in 1878, and then moved to South Wales to be with Maria. She died in 1879 at the age of 42. Maria immediately published *Frances R. Havergal: The Last Week* (1879), an account of her death, followed by the *Memorials*, the *Poetical Works* (1884), and the *Letters* (1885). These sparked off a virtual Havergal industry which extended into the twentieth century and which was largely presided over by Maria. Several volumes of selections like *Ivy Leaves* (1884) and *Gems from Havergal* (1912) were edited by her friend Frances Shaw, and there was a spate of admiring biographies, but most of the posthumous publications were edited or compiled by her sister. The British Library catalogue lists nearly sixty separate volumes, collections like *Life's Chords* (1880) and *Life's Echoes* (1883) and popular compilations such as *Messages for Life's Journey* (1883), *Mottoes for the Month* (1893), and *Forget Me Nots of Promise* (1895). **Jane Havergal**, later **Crane**, in turn edited Maria's autobiography (1887), which included letters and journals, and published a brief biography of their father (1882). *See* T. H. Darlow, *Havergal: A Saint of God* (1927).

Havergal, Jane *see under* HAVERGAL, Frances Ridley

Havergal, Maria Vernon Graham *see under* HAVERGAL, Frances Ridley

Hawker, Mary Elizabeth *see* FALCONER, Lanoe

Haycraft, Anna Margaret *see* ELLIS, Alice Thomas

Hays, Mary, novelist and feminist (b. Southwark, London, 1760, d. London, 1843).

Mary Hays grew up in Southwark with her widowed mother and two sisters, members of a Dissenting family. A love affair with John Eccles, also from Southwark, was opposed by his father and her mother, and was conducted largely by letter. It ended with his death in 1780. She attended lectures at the Dissenting Academy in Hackney, and in 1792 she published her *Cursory Remarks*, under the pseudonym Eusebia, in defence of public worship against the attack of Gilbert Wakefield, one of the teachers at the Academy. This brought her to the attention of eminent radicals, including Joseph Johnson the printer, Joseph Priestley, the poet George Dyer, William Godwin, and Mary *Wollstonecraft, who became a forceful influence on her thought. Wollstonecraft encouraged her in the publication of *Letters and Essays, Moral* *and Miscellaneous* (1793), which bore witness to her influence in its arguments against despotism in religion, in society, and in the relations between men and women. William Godwin became a confidant, especially on the subject of her unrequited passion for the Unitarian William Frend, a situation directly reflected in her first novel, *Memoirs of Emma Courtney* (1796), in which the heroine declares her love for her beloved, against the advice of a philosopher/confidant. The heroine's offer to live with her lover outside marriage brought the novel and Hays unexpected notoriety. She was caricatured in Elizabeth *Hamilton's *Memoirs of Modern Philosophers* (1800) and attacked by the *Anti-Jacobin Review*, by Coleridge, and by the poet Charles Lloyd, among others. Her second novel, *The Victim of Prejudice* (1799), the story of an illegitimate heroine whose seduced mother is eventually hanged, argued for sexual equality and was similar in its concerns to Wollstonecraft's *The Wrongs of Women*, published in 1798. Hays became a close friend of Wollstonecraft and helped to nurse her in her last months. She wrote a warm tribute in the *Monthly Magazine* after her death and another less fulsome one in the *Annual Necrology for 1797–8*, published in 1800. The anonymous *An Appeal to the Men of Great Britain in Behalf of Women* (1798) has been ascribed to Hays. She also wrote a six-volume *Female Biography* (1803), on historical women of achievement, and several collections of 'improving' tales, *The Brothers; or Consequences* (1815), and *Family Annals; or The Sisters* (1817). Latterly she knew Southey and Crabb Robinson, Charles and Mary *Lamb, and also Hannah *More. She taught school for a while in Oundle, Northamptonshire, and in 1824 settled in London, where she died aged 83. *See* Annie F. Wedd, *The Love Letters of Mary Hays* (1925); Marilyn Butler, *Jane Austen and the War of Ideas* (1975, 1987); Ellen Moers, *Literary Women* (1977); Jane Spencer, *The Rise of the Woman Novelist: from Aphra Beha to Jane Austen* (1986); Janet Todd, *The Sign of Angellica: Women, Writing and Fiction, 1660–1800* (1989).

Haywood, Eliza, novelist, playwright, and journalist (b. London, *c.*1693, d. London, 25 February 1756).

Eliza Haywood was the daughter of a London shopkeeper named Fowler, and at an early age married the Revd Valentine Haywood, a clergyman some fifteen years her senior. They had one son, born in 1711. Public scandal including newspaper reports linked her name with one Andrew Yeatman in 1715. Separation from her husband followed and she appeared as an actress in Dublin in the same year, playing there until 1717, when she appeared at Lincoln's Inn Fields. She acted occasionally until 1720, but in 1719 began a new career with the publication of a successful romance, *Love in Excess*, which went through at least nine editions by 1750. Her official separation from her husband was announced by a statement in the press in which he absolved himself from any financial responsibility for her. She then launched herself on a highly successful, if controversial, literary career over a period of thirty years. Her publications, more than fifty volumes in total, included plays, poems, popular novels, *romans à clef*, and several periodicals. She also tried her hand as a publisher for a brief period in 1744–6. Her career as a playwright began with a tragedy, *The Fair Captive* (1721), a revision of an early play by Captain Hurst. *A Wife to be Lett*, a more successful comedy, followed in 1723, in which she acted the female lead. Her best-known theatrical work was an adaptation of Fielding's *Tragedy of Tragedies* into a popular opera, *The Opera of Operas; or Tom Thumb the Great* (1733), set to music by Thomas Arne. An attempt to secure royal favour in 1729 with a historical tragedy, *Frederick, Duke of Brunswick-Lunenburgh*, dedicated to the Prince of Wales, failed, perhaps because in her *Secret History of the Present Intrigues of the Court of Caramania* (1727) she had, among other things, publicized a liaison of George II's. Her fiction was popular, notorious, and prolific. Scandal-novels in which thinly veiled portraits of contemporary notables were identified by an accompanying key were a speciality, as in *Memoirs of a Certain Island Adjacent to Utopia* (1725). That work and the *Court of Caramania* prompted a savage attack by Pope in *The Dunciad* (1728), in which he called her a 'shameless scribbler' and alleged she had had two 'love-children'. Haywood put in a mild retaliation by contributing to *The Female Dunciad* (1729), a collection of attacks on Pope organized by Edmund Curll. Swift in turn lampooned her in his portrait of 'Corinna' (1727–8), intended for her and not for Delarivier *Manley, as was once thought. *The Adventures of Eovaai, Princess of Ijaveo* (1736) pretended to be a translation, but was actually a satire attacking Robert Walpole. Apart from scandalous pot-boilers, her early fiction perfected a formula for amorous misadventure, as in *The British Recluse* (1722), modelled on the fiction of Penelope *Aubin, *Idalia; or The Unfortunate Mistress* (1723), and *The Fatal Secret* (1724), all of which ran through multiple editions. Several later domestic novels are generally regarded as her best, including *The History of Miss Betty Thoughtless* (1751), which went through at least eight editions up until 1800, and *The History of Jenny and Jemmy Jessamy* (1753), which was commended by Scott for its pathos. She established several short-lived periodicals, including the *Tea Table* (1724), the *Parrot* (1728, 1746), and in 1744–6 the *Female Spectator.* She died in London after a short illness, in 1756. *See* G. F. Whicher, *The Life and Romances of Mrs. Eliza Haywood* (1915); Mary Anne Schofield and Cecilia Macheski (eds.), *Fetter'd or Free? British Women Novelists 1670–1815* (1986); Janet Todd, *The Sign of Angellica: Women, Writing and Fiction, 1660–1800*

(1989); Ros Ballaster, *Seductive Forms: Women's Amatory Fiction 1684–1740* (1992).

Hedgeland, Isabella *see* KELLY, Isabella

Hemans, Felicia Dorothea, née Browne, poet (b. Liverpool, 25 September 1793, d. Dublin, 16 May 1835).

Felicia Hemans was the fifth of the seven children born to George Browne, a Liverpool merchant, and his wife Felicity Wagner, who claimed a mixture of German, Italian, and Lancashire descent. Two of her brothers had distinguished careers in the Peninsula War and a third in government service in Upper Canada. She was taught at home by her mother and considered to be something of a prodigy. In 1808 her parents arranged for the publication of a volume of *Poems*, which was severely reviewed. She survived this set-back and in the same year published *England and Spain; or Valour and Patriotism.* Shelley read her first volume and having heard of her beauty wrote to suggest they enter into correspondence, a proposal which was firmly quashed by her mother. Her second volume, *The Domestic Affections and Other Poems*, was published in 1812, the same year as her marriage to Captain Alfred Hemans, an Irishman whom she had known for three years and who had served in the Peninsula War like her brothers. The couple had five sons in six years, after which Captain Hemans left for Italy and did not return. The reason for the break-up of the marriage was never given, although it was said that Mrs Hemans offered to join him in Italy after her mother's death in 1827, an offer which was refused. She wrote prolifically after her marriage in order to support her family and to educate her children. *Modern Greece* (1817), a narrative poem about the Greek revolution, won Byron's disapproval, but was followed by *Translations from Camoens and Other Poets* (1818), *Tales and Historic Scenes* (1819), and a prize-winning poem, *Wallace's Invocation to Bruce* (1819). There were other prize-winning poems, and also three plays, of which only one, *The Vespers of Palermo* (1823), was ever performed. *The Sceptic* (1820) was her first religious poem, and on the strength of it she was encouraged by Reginald Heber, the hymn writer and later Bishop of Calcutta, to produce another poem in defence of religion, *Superstition and Error* (1822). Mrs Hemans knew French, Italian, Spanish, and Portuguese as well as some Latin. *Lays of Many Lands* (1825) drew on her study of German, which she began when she was in her thirties. The second edition of *The Forest Sanctuary*, her favourite work, first published in 1825, contained 'Casabianca' ('The boy stood on the burning deck'), the best known of her poems, and for many twentieth-century readers the only familiar one. *Records of Women with Other Poems* (1828) was dedicated to Joanna *Baillie and based on stories of noble women. Other popular volumes were *Songs of the Affections* (1830), two volumes of hymns, *Hymns on the Works of Nature* (1833) and *Hymns for Childhood* (1834, first published in the USA in 1827), and *National Lyrics and Songs for Music* and *Scenes and Hymns of Life*, both published in 1834. Mrs Hemans was one of the most popular poets of her day. She was almost as well known in America, where an edition of her poems was published in 1825 and she was invited to become editor of a Boston periodical, an invitation which she refused. In the early 1830s she travelled to Scotland and met Scott and also Francis Jeffrey, both of whom were admirers of her work. She also visited Wordsworth, another admirer, at Rydal. Her friend Maria Jane *Jewsbury wrote of her as Egeria in her *Three Histories* (1830) and the Countess of *Blessington, John Wilson, and even Byron later professed their admiration for her work. Her health declined after her mother's death, and she eventually moved to Dublin to be close to one of her brothers and died there at the age of 41. Her sister Harriet M. B. Hughes prefaced a memoir to the collected *Works of Mrs. Hemans* (1839). *See* H. F. Chorley, *Memorials of Mrs. Hemans* (1836); Norma Clarke, *Ambitious Heights: Writing, Friendship, Love: The Jewsbury Sisters, Felicia Hemans and Jane Welsh Carlyle* (1990); Angela Leighton, *Victorian Women Poets: Writing against the Heart* (1992).

Hepburn, Edith Alice Mary Harper *see* WICKHAM, Anna

Herbert, Mary *see* PEMBROKE, Mary Herbert, Countess of

'Herring, Geilles' *see* SOMERVILLE, Edith

Heyer, Georgette ('Stella Martin'), historical novelist and detective writer (b. Wimbledon, Surrey 16 August 1902, d. London, 4 July 1974).

Georgette Heyer was the eldest of the three children and only daughter of George Heyer, a teacher at King's College School, Wimbledon, and his wife Sylvia Watkins, the daughter of a Thames tugboat owner. She was educated at 'numerous high class seminaries' in Paris and London and attended history lectures at Westminster College. At the age of 17 she told the story of what was to become her first novel, *The Black Moth* (1921), to amuse a younger brother who was recovering from an illness. She published it with her father's encouragement and followed it with *The Great Roxhythe* (1922), *Powder and Patch* (1923), and *These Old Shades* (1926), the latter two, like *The Black Moth*, set in the Georgian period. In 1925 she married George Ronald Rougier, a mining engineer. She wrote her next Georgian novel *The Masqueraders* (1928) while accompanying her husband on a prospecting expedition to Tanganyika and Macedonia. They settled in England in 1930, where Rougier, under her encouragement, studied to become a barrister and eventually a QC. Their only son, born in 1932, followed suit. Between the 1930s and the early 1950s she wrote a number of detective novels based on plots and legal problems suggested by her husband. Of these *Death in the Stocks* (1935) proved the most popular. Her reputation rests, however, on her historical novels, of which the most distinguished were those set in the Regency period. She was meticulous in her research into manners, social customs, dialogue, and the minutiae of daily life. The work of Jane *Austen, including her letters, was a favourite source, and Austen was her choice of an author to take to a desert island. She was capable of a wider scope. *An Infamous Army* (1937) and *The Spanish Bride* (1940) presented accomplished accounts of the Battle of Waterloo and the Peninsular War and demonstrated a knowledge of military history. Other period settings included the Restoration (*The Great Roxhythe*), the Elizabethan age (*Beauvallet* (1929)), and the Norman Conquest (*The Conqueror* (1931)). In her later years she devoted much time to research for a trilogy on the life of John, Duke of Bedford, the brother of Henry V. The first volume *My Lord John* was nearly complete at her death and prepared for publication by her husband in 1975. She published an early novel, *The Transformation of Philip Jettan* (1923), under the pseudonym Stella Martin but otherwise wrote her more than sixty novels under her own name. *See* Jane Aiken Hodge, *The Private World of Georgette Heyer* (1984); Harmony Raine, *The Georgette Heyer Compendium* (1984).

Hibbert, Eleanor (Alice), née Burford ('Jean Plaidy', 'Victoria Holt', 'Philippa Carr'), romantic and historical novelist (b. Kennington, London, 1 September 1906, d. 18 January 1993).

Eleanor Hibbert, who wrote under a variety of pseudonyms, was the daughter of Joseph Burford, an unsuccessful but bookish businessman, and his wife Alice Tate. She learned to read at 4, and read Dickens at 7, and Hugo and Tolstoy at 11. She went to a church primary school and won a scholarship to a London secondary school but left at 17 to work first in a restaurant and then for a Hatton Garden jeweller. She also began to write 'long, verbose imitations' of Victorian classics, eight of which were rejected by publishers. (She reworked the material later.) Marriage in her early twenties to G. H. Hibbert, a leather merchant twenty years her senior, gave her the financial freedom to write. She published stories in the *Daily Mail* and the *Evening News* and was encouraged by the literary editor of the *Mail* to write romantic novels. She read twenty and then wrote one, published under her maiden name Eleanor Burford. More than thirty others followed. From these she turned to historical fiction, writing under the pseudonym Jean Plaidy. These were usually based on an historical, frequently female, figure, narrated by a female observer, often royal, and designed to instruct as well as entertain. The first of these, *Together they Ride* (1945), was followed by nearly ninety more, at the rate of two a year. They appeared annually in the list of the top 100 library titles (borrowed at least 300,000 times). An American agent suggested she revive the *Gothic novel, which she did with *Mistress of Mellyn* (1961), under the pseudonym Victoria Holt. This became her first best seller, serialized in the *Ladies' Home Journal* followed by selection by the Readers' Digest Book Club and the sale of the film rights. It was followed by *Kirkland Revels* (1962), *The Bride of Pendorric* (1963), and *The Legend of the Seventh Virgin* (1965), all historical adventures influenced by her early reading of the *Brontës, Wilkie Collins, and other Victorians. The 'Victoria Holt' titles, numbering over thirty, were Hibbert's most successful works latterly, included in the annual top ten library titles. She distinguished her Jean Plaidy novels from her Victoria Holts by claiming that the former were written for 'a very special, very loyal public, who want to learn something', while the latter were for 'the housewife in the mid-west of America, who has never heard of Louis XV and doesn't want to'. Her third and most recent pseudonym was Philippa Carr, the author of nearly twenty romantic sagas, beginning with *The Miracle at St. Bruno's* (1972), which combine the historical interest of the Plaidy novels and the Holt plots and melodrama. After her success with Jean Plaidy Hibbert experimented with other pseudonyms, Elbur Ford, Ellalice Tate, and Kathleen Kellow, none of which caught on. Her titles total over 200 in twenty different languages, her sales estimated at seventy-five million. In her mid-eighties she continued to produce three books a year, writing as she had done since the early days of her marriage, for five to six hours, seven days a week, beginning at 7.30 in the morning. *See* Juliann E. Fleenor (ed.), *The Female Gothic* (1983).

Hinkson, Katharine and Pamela *see under* TYNAN, Katharine

'**Hobbes,** John Oliver' (Pearl Mary Teresa Craigie), novelist and dramatist (b. Chelsea, near Boston, Massachusetts, 3 November 1867, d. London, 13 August 1906).

Pearl Craigie was the daughter of John Morgan Richards, a successful Massachusetts businessman who had made money from patent medicines, and his wife Laura Hortense Arnold, also of Massachusetts. The family moved to London when their daughter was only a few months old. Pearl was educated at a boarding school at Newbury, Berkshire, and at London day schools. The family were Congregationalists. Pearl began to write at an early age, and had stories accepted from the age of 9 for a Congregationalist newspaper, the *Fountain.* At the age of 19 she married Reginald Walpole

Craigie, a banker with a reputation for drunkenness and infidelity. The marriage was extremely unhappy, and a few months after the birth of their son in August 1890 Craigie left her husband and sued for divorce. The emotional upheaval of her unhappy marriage helped to lead her in the direction of the Roman Catholic Church, which she joined in July 1892, taking the additional names Mary Teresa. During the early years of her marriage she wrote dramatic and art criticism for periodicals and resolved to continue her education. She had herself tutored in mathematics, and after her separation enrolled at University College London for courses in Greek, Latin, and English. She published her highly successful first novel *Some Emotions and a Moral* in 1891 in Fisher Unwin's Pseudonym Library, which occasioned the invention of John Oliver Hobbes, John after her father and son, Oliver in memory of Cromwell, and Hobbes after the English philosopher she much admired. *The Sinner's Comedy*, her second novel, followed in 1892, and in 1895 the again successful *The Gods, Some Mortals and Lord Wickenham*. Apart from their arresting titles, her novels were characterized by their portrayals of unhappy marriages as well as a sophisticated cynicism which caught the mood of the times. *The School for Saints* (1897) and its sequel *Robert Orange* (1900) were based in part on the career of Disraeli, who also appeared separately as a character. The two novels dealt with Catholicism and the conflicts it produced. Other notable novels included *The Herb Moon* (1896), *The Vineyard* (1904), and *The Dream and the Business* (1906), the last of which was also about Catholicism. Craigie wrote a series of plays which met with variable success. Her first was *Journeys End in Lovers Meeting*, produced in 1895 with Ellen Terry and Forbes Robertson in the leading roles. Her best-known play was *The Ambassador* (1898). Craigie had a tempestuous relationship with the novelist George Moore, and was represented unflatteringly in a number of his novels. The late nineteenth-century novelist she most resembled, in terms of style, was George Meredith. She continued to write for newspapers and periodicals, republishing a series of articles on India as *Imperial India* (1903). *Her Letters from a Silent Study* (1904) were reprinted from the *Academy*, which her father bought in 1896. She wrote the article on George *Eliot for the tenth edition of the *Encyclopedia Britannica*. She was president of the Society of Women Journalists 1895–6 and, like her fellow novelist Mrs Humphry *Ward, a member of the Anti-Suffrage League. She died of heart failure in 1906. *See* J. M. Richards, *The Life of John Oliver Hobbes, Told in her Correspondence* (1911); W. L. Courtney, *The Feminine Note in Fiction* (1904; repr. 1973); M. Maison, *John Oliver Hobbes* (1976).

'**Hockaby,** Stephen' *see* MITCHELL, Gladys

Hoey, Frances Sarah (Mrs Cashel Hoey), novelist (b. Bushy Park, County Dublin, 14 February 1830, d. Beccles, Suffolk, 9 July 1908).

Mrs Cashel Hoey, as she was popularly known, was one of eight children of Charles Bolton Johnston, secretary and registrar of Mount Jerome Cemetery, Dublin, and his wife Charlotte Jane Shaw. She was educated at home, largely by teaching herself, and at the age of 16 married Adam Murray Stewart, by whom she had two daughters. In 1853 she began to contribute reviews and articles on art to the *Freeman's Journal*, the *Nation*, and other Dublin papers, the beginning of a career in journalism which was to continue until her death. Stewart died in 1855 and, armed with an introduction to Thackeray, she moved to London, where she began to write for both the *Morning Post* and the *Spectator*. In 1858 she married John Cashel Hoey (1828–93), a well-known Irish journalist and a member of the Young Ireland Party. At the same time she converted to Roman Catholicism. In 1865 she began a thirty-year connection with *Chambers's Journal*, then under the editorship of James Payn. Two of her novels, *A Golden Sorrow* (1892) and *The Blossoming of an Aloe* (1894), were first serialized in *Chambers's*. She wrote a total of eleven novels, mostly stories of high life in exotic settings, some using the devices of *sensation fiction, of which the best known were *The House of Cards* (1868), *Falsely True* (1870), *The Question of Cain* (1882), which was partly set in India, and *A Stern Chase* (1886), set in Cuba, which she admitted in the preface she had never visited. According to the publisher William Tinsley, she was 'largely responsible' for five novels usually attributed to the journalist Edmund Yates (1831–94), *Land at Last* (1866), *The Black Sheep* (1867), *The Forlorn Hope* (1867), *The Rock Ahead* (1868), and *A Righted Wrong* (1870), the last, according to the *DNB*, entirely her own work. She had helped Yates to found his periodical the *World* in 1874. Hoey was also a prolific translator of French and Italian works and a publisher's reader. For more than twenty years she contributed a fortnightly 'Ladies Letter' to an Australian newspaper, and she was the first English journalist to report news of the Paris Commune in 1870. She was awarded a civil-list pension in 1892. *See* P. D. Edwards's bibliography, Victorian Fiction Research Guides 8 (1982).

Hofland, Barbara, later Hoole, novelist and children's writer (b. Sheffield, 1770, d. 9 November 1844).

Barbara Hofland was the daughter of Robert Wreaks, a Sheffield manufacturer, who died when she was an infant. She was brought up by an aunt and in 1796 married T. Bradshawe Hoole, a merchant, by whom she had a son. Hoole's death from consumption two years later left her wealthy but the money was subsequently lost through a bad investment, and she turned to writing. A volume of *Poems* (1805) attracted 2,000 subscribers, mainly out of sympathy. She opened a boarding school at Harrogate on the proceeds, and when this failed she began to write fiction. *The History of a Clergyman's Widow* (1812) sold 17,000 copies in various editions. In 1808 she married the landscape painter Thomas Christopher Hofland (1777–1843). The precariousness of an artist's life together with Hofland's natural improvidence and subsequent illness meant that she had to work even harder at her fiction. By 1824 she had produced upwards of twenty titles, the most successful of which, and probably her best, was *The Son of a Genius*, which drew on her experience of the artistic temperament and also on the emotional legacy of her son's death from consumption. She followed it with *The Daughter of a Genius* (1823). She was a popular as well as a prolific writer although her fiction, which extended to nearly seventy works, was remorselessly didactic in tone. Towards the end of her career she turned out conventional Victorian three-deckers, including *The Czarina* (1842), *The King's Son* (1843), *The Unloved One* (1844), and *Daniel Dennison* (1846). She was also an energetic journalist, having begun as early as 1795 with 'Characteristics of Some Leading Inhabitants of Sheffield', which she published in the *Sheffield Courant.* She expanded this vein later by contributing gossipy letters about London literary life to provincial newspapers. Her children's books include both history and travel and, despite their moralizing, are attractive and readable. Hofland was a friend of Mary Russell *Mitford. Some of her letters are preserved in A. G. K. L'Estrange's *Friendships of Mary Russell Mitford* (1882). *See* Thomas Ramsay, *The Life and Literary Remains of Barbara Hofland* (1849).

Holme, Constance, novelist (b. Milnthorpe, Westmorland, 1880, d. Carnforth, Westmorland, 17 June 1955).

Constance Holme was one of fourteen children of John Holme, a Westmorland land agent, and his wife Elizabeth Cartmel, who claimed part-Spanish descent. The family had been land agents for generations and most of her life was spent in or near her birthplace at Milnthorpe, in Westmorland. She told stories at school and published an early novel, *Hugh of Hughsdale*, in the *Kendal Mercury and Times* (1909). Another, written in 1912, remained unpublished. Her first major work was *Crump Folk Going Home*, set, like all her books, in Westmorland, most of the scenes being composite pictures of places she knew. *The Lonely Plough* (1914), her best-known novel, and *The Old Road from Spain* (1916) completed the trio of early works which dealt with the rural county society in whose midst she lived. In 1916 she married Frederick Burt Punchard (d. 1946), land agent to Lord Henry Bentinck of Underley Hall, Kirby Lonsdale, and a brother of Lady Ottoline *Morrell, who became an admirer of her work. Her next quartet of novels was regarded as her central achievement and marked a change of emphasis as well as growing technical sophistication. *Beautiful End* (1918), *The Splendid Fairing* (1919), which won the Femina Vie Heureuse Prize, *The Trumpet in the Dust* (1921), and *The Things which Belong* (1925) were each set in a single day, using flashbacks, anticipating the work of Virginia *Woolf. Unlike Woolf, Holme did not develop the stream of consciousness technique, but used instead the device of free association. The novels also explored rural society more broadly, moving away from the farmers and gentry of the early family chronicles to explore the lives of elderly working people. Her last novel, *He-Who-Came?*, a pastoral fantasy, was published in 1930. Holme also published a collection of one-act plays (1932) and a book of short stories, *The Wisdom of the Simple* (1937). Her novels have been described as regional, in the best sense of the term, in the tradition of Wordsworth and Coleridge in their presentation of and response to landscape, and at times resembling the work of Elizabeth *Gaskell in the sensitivity of her perceptions. *See* Glen Cavaliero, *The Rural Tradition in the English Novel 1900–1939* (1977); Margaret Crosland, *Beyond the Lighthouse: English Women Novelists in the 20th Century* (1981).

'**Holt**, Victoria' *See* HIBBERT, Eleanor

Holtby, Winifred, novelist (b. Rudstone, Yorkshire, 23 June 1898, d. London, 25 September 1935).

Winifred Holtby was the daughter of David Holtby, a farmer, and his wife Alice Winn, a Yorkshire County Councillor. She was a brilliant pupil at Queen Margaret's School, Scarborough, and went from there to Somerville College, Oxford. Like her friend Vera *Brittain, whom she met at Oxford, she interrupted her degree to take on war duties with the Women's Auxiliary Army Corps. After Oxford she and Brittain shared a flat in London, where they launched themselves on literary careers. Their friendship was the most important relationship in Winifred Holtby's life. She lived with Brittain and her children, during the latter's 'semi-detached' marriage, and was a central figure in the household. Holtby's first book was produced, unknown to her, at the age of 13 when her mother arranged for the publication of *My Garden and Other Poems* (1911). Like Brittain she campaigned vigorously for feminist and pacifist causes, lectured for the League of Nations Union and the Six Points Group (for women's rights), and was a director of **Time and Tide*, the feminist review. More than Brittain, she felt a tension between her literary ambitions and her reformist ideals. Much of her energy was directed towards the improvement of working conditions of black workers in South Africa, which she visited in 1926. Her first novel, *Anderby Wold* (1923), was based on the farming community of her childhood. Most of her fiction was set in the provincial world of her youth, including *The Crowded Street* (1924), *The Land of Green Ginger* (1927), and *Poor Caroline* (1931). *Mandoa! Mandoa!* (1933) was a satire set in a primitive African community. Her masterpiece, and the work for which she has remained famous, was *South Riding*, a novel about local government which she completed four weeks before her death. It was published posthumously with an introduction by Vera Brittain in 1936 and won the James Tait Black Memorial Prize the following year. Holtby's non-fiction included an important critical study of Virginia *Woolf (1932), *Women and a Changing Civilization* (1934), and a play, *Take Back your Freedom*, which was published in 1939. She had suffered from heart disease and latterly from kidney failure, and died in 1935 aged 37. Vera Brittain's tribute to their friendship was *Testament of Friendship: The Story of W. Holtby* (1940). *See* G. Handley Taylor, *Winifred Holtby: A Concise and Selected Bibliography Together with Some Letters* (1955); *Selected Letters of Winifred Holtby and Vera Brittain* ed. V. Brittain and G. Handley-Taylor (1960); Jean E. Kennard, *Vera Brittain and Winifred Holtby: A Working Partnership* (1989).

'Home, Cecil' *see* WEBSTER, Augusta

Hoole, Barbara *see* HOFLAND, Barbara

Horovitz, Frances, poet (b. London, 1938, d. 2 October 1983).

The daughter of F. E. Hooker, about whom she wrote her powerful 'Elegy' in *Water over Stone* (1980), Frances Horovitz grew up in Walthamstow and then read English and drama at Bristol University. She went to the Royal Academy of Dramatic Art and worked as an actress in repertory, films, and television. She married the poet Michael Horovitz in 1964 and had a son (b. 1971). Her first poems were published in the magazine *New Departures*, edited by Horovitz. *Poems*, a pamphlet, appeared in 1967, followed by *The High Tower* (1970), *Water over Stone* (1980), her first major collection, and *Snow Light, Water Light* (1983). Frances Horovitz, according to the preface to her *Collected Poems* (1985), was 'a severe judge of her own work' and wrote 'sparely and sparingly'. Her subjects are the natural world, relationships, love, landscape, and history. The poems in *Water over Stone*, written during ten years spent in Gloucestershire, celebrate relationships, particularly those of parent and child, the birth of her son, the death of her father. They also recall historical landscapes and places. The poems in *Snow Light, Water Light* reflect the landscape, both historical and contemporary, of Hadrian's Wall, near which she lived between 1980 and 1982. Together with the poet Roger Garfitt and other poets and artists she produced *Wall* (1981), an exploration in verse and picture of Hadrian's Wall, and contributed to a landscape anthology, *Presences of Nature* (1982). The poems of a projected last volume to be called 'Voices Returning' were incorporated in her *Collected Poems*, together with unpublished poems and fragments. She moved to Herefordshire in 1982, the setting for six *Rowlstone Haiku* (1982), which she wrote with Garfitt, whom she married in 1983. Horovitz was a celebrated poetry reader, both in public and on the radio. In partnership with the biographer Robert Gittings she read Keats and Hardy at various festivals and at the National Theatre. She recorded poetry readings for the Open University and made three programmes for the BBC reading the work of Russian women poets. She died of cancer at the age of 45. *See* Roger Garfitt's introd. to *Collected Poems* (1985); Brocard Sewell (ed.), *Frances Horowitz, Poet: A Symposium* (1987).

Howitt, Mary, novelist, editor, translator, and children's writer (b. Coleford, Gloucestershire, 12 March 1799, d. Rome, 30 January 1888).

Mary Howitt was the daughter of Samuel Botham, a prosperous Quaker businessman, and Anne Wood, a descendant of Andrew Wood, the patentee attacked by Swift in the *Drapier Letters*. She was educated at home and at various Quaker schools and began to write poetry from an early age. In 1821 she married William Howitt (1792–1879), a fellow Quaker and writer. They had five children, and lived for some of their married life in Nottingham, later in Surrey, and for a period in Heidelberg. Most of her professional career as a writer was bound up with that of her husband. Their friends referred to them as 'William and Mary' and joked that they had been crowned together like their royal namesakes. Much of the Howitts' writing was done for periodicals and annuals. A selection of their work was published as *The Forest Minstrel and Other Poems* (1823) and *The Desolation of Eyam* (1827). They were friends and popularizers of many of the major literary figures of their day, including Wordsworth, Keats, and Byron, and later the Pre-Raphaelites. Mary Howitt translated the novels of the Swedish writer Fredrika Bremer and introduced them to English readers. She also translated some of the work of Hans Christian Andersen into English. She and her husband founded the short-lived *Howitt's Journal*, which published some of the early work of Elizabeth *Gaskell, who became a close friend. The early failure of that publication led to William Howitt's bankruptcy. Mary Howitt also edited the *annual *Fisher's Drawing-Room Scrap-Book* for three years. She supported many of the activities of the women's movement in the mid-nineteenth century, including the efforts which led to the passing of the Married Woman's Property Act of 1857. She was a friend of Bessie Rayner *Parkes,

Barbara *Bodichon, and Octavia Hill. She also supported movements for political reform, the reform of working conditions in factories, and the extension of education. Her novels include *Wood Leighton* (1836), *The Heir of Wast-Waylan* (1847), and *The Cost of Caergwyn* (1864). She wrote many books for children, including *The Children's Year* (1847) and its companion *Our Cousins in Ohio* (1849). She wrote the lion's share of *The Literature and Romance of Northern Europe* (1852), published with her husband, and a *Popular History of the United States* (1859). Her *Collected Tales of English Life* was published in 1881. Her autobiographical 'Reminiscences of my later Life' was published in *Good Words* in 1886. According to the *DNB*, she wrote, edited, or translated at least 110 works. Both William and Mary Howitt became interested in the cults of spiritualism and mesmerism and in her later years Mary became a Roman Catholic. They moved to Italy in 1870, and William Howitt died in 1879. Mary lived with their daughter Margaret, herself a novelist, in the Tyrol, and died of bronchitis while on a visit to Rome in 1888. Margaret Howitt edited *Mary Howitt: An Autobiography* (1889). *See* R. H. Horne, *A New Spirit of the Age* (1844); 'George Paston' [Emily Morse Symonds], *Little Memoirs of the Nineteenth Century* (1902); C. R. Woodring, *Victorian Samplers: William and Mary Howitt* (1952); A. Lee, *Laurels and Rosemary: The Life of William and Mary Howitt* (1955).

Hunt, Margaret Raine *see under* HUNT, Violet

Hunt, (Isobel) Violet, novelist (b. 1866, d. London, 16 January 1942).

Violet Hunt was the daughter of Alfred William Hunt (1830–96), a landscape painter and water-colourist, and his wife **Margaret Raine Hunt** (1831–1912), a novelist who sometimes wrote under the pseudonym **Averil Beaumont**. The Hunt household was a centre for the Pre-Raphaelite circle of artists and writers; Violet's contemporaries at Notting Hill High School included the daughters of William Morris and Edward Burne-Jones, and her first poems were given to Christina *Rossetti for appraisal. Two of her early novels, *The Celebrity at Home* (1904) and *The Celebrity's Daughter* (1913), however, present an ambivalent and at times harshly satirical picture of fashionable artistic households and the predicament of having famous parents. Political radicalism was also part of the family atmosphere and Violet inherited her mother's commitment to women's suffrage. Later she founded and supported the *Women Writers' Suffrage League, and also supported Marguerite Radclyffe *Hall in her fight against the suppression of *The Well of Loneliness*. Her father intended that she should become a painter rather than a writer. Consequently she was encouraged to paint from an early age, and did not abandon it until the age of 28. She also studied at the Kensington Art School. In 1908 she met Ford Madox Hueffer (later Ford), then the founding editor of the *English Review*, whose contributors included James, Hardy, Conrad, Galsworthy, and Wells, and later Yeats, Lawrence, Pound, and Wyndham Lewis. Ford published one of her short stories and she immersed herself in the affairs of the review, acting as a literary hostess and contributing money, finding herself at the centre of the foremost literary circle of the day. Her relationship with Hueffer developed into a passionate involvement which lasted for over ten years. Hueffer's wife refused to divorce him and won a lawsuit against a weekly paper which had referred to Violet Hunt as Mrs Hueffer. Hunt none the less entered 'married 1911' into her *Who's Who* entry. The scandal divided her friends and family. Wells, Pound, Rebecca *West, and Wyndham Lewis remained loyal to Hunt, while others shunned her. Relations between Hunt and Hueffer cooled and by 1918 they were permanently estranged. Violet Hunt's background, appearance, and behaviour suggested an almost stereotypical *New Woman. She was intelligent, independent, and 'advanced' in her attitudes, both politically and sexually. Her novels tended to reinforce the image, with their emphasis on sexual relationships, their neurotic heroines, and their frankness regarding adultery, promiscuity, and prostitution, as in *A Hard Woman* (1895), *The Way of Marriage* (1896), and *Unkissed, Unkind* (1897). Several drew on autobiographical situations, including *The Celebrity at Home* (1904), *Sooner or Later* (1904), and *White Rose of Weary Leaf* (1908). Henry James among others preferred her short stories to her novels. *Tales of the Uneasy* (1911), *The Tiger Skin* (1924, first included in *Tales of the Uneasy*), and *More Tales of the Uneasy* (1925) demonstrated psychological complexity, sexual explicitness, and narrative control. She and Hueffer together wrote *The Desirable Alien* (1913), an account of their travels in Germany. As well as for the *English Review* Hunt wrote for the *Pall Mall Gazette* and *Black and White*. Her autobiography *The Flurried Years* (1926), intended as her version of the relationship with Hueffer, only served to reawaken the scandal and exacerbated the rift between them. It was followed by more controversy with *The Wife of Rossetti* (1932), a biography of Elizabeth Siddall, which drew in part on remembered anecdotes and the gossip of her childhood, and implied that Rossetti may have hastened her death by neglect. The debate raged in **Time and Tide*, the *TLS*, and elsewhere, until Hunt's position, in the end, appeared untenable. At her peak Violet Hunt lived at the centre of literary London, her work admired by James, Lawrence, Rebecca West, and May *Sinclair, among others. She died in virtual isolation, in 1942, at South Lodge, her London house, with its famous Gaudier-Brzeska bust of Ezra Pound in the front garden, surrounded by her Persian cats. *See* Douglas Goldring, *South Lodge: Reminiscences of Violet Hunt, Ford Madox*

Ford and the English Review Circle (1943; repr. 1977); Marie and Robert Secor, *Ford Madox Ford and Violet Hunt's 1917 Diary* (1983).

Hutchinson, Lucy, biographer (b. London, 1620, d. *c.*1675).

Lucy Hutchinson was the daughter of Sir Allen Apsley, Lieutenant of the Tower of London, by his third wife Lucy St John. By her own account she could read at 4 and by the time she was 7 she had eight tutors in language, music, dancing, writing, and needlework, 'but my genius was quite averse from all but my book'. She was taught French by her nurse and Latin by her father's chaplain. She also knew Greek and Hebrew. In 1638 she married John Hutchinson, a Parliamentarian who became Governor of Nottingham Castle during the Civil War and later a member of the Long Parliament for Nottinghamshire. They had four sons and four daughters, the last born in 1662, when she was 42. In the early years of her marriage she translated six books of Lucretius' *De rerum natura*, working in the schoolroom with her children while they were being given lessons. ('I remembered the syllables of my translation by the thread of the canvas I wrought in.') The first English translation of Lucretius was not published until 1682. Hers remained unpublished, but she later came to regard it as frivolous in the light of her increasing Puritanism. John Hutchinson had a prominent role in the events of 1649, acting as one of the King's judges and signing the death sentence. He played little part in public affairs after the end of the Long Parliament in 1653, retiring to his country seat at Owthorpe, thus escaping the treatment meted out to other regicides after the Restoration. In 1663, however, he was imprisoned, first in the Tower of London and then in 1664 in Sandown Castle in Kent, where he died of fever four months later. Lucy Hutchinson interceded on her husband's behalf during his imprisonment, despite his disapproval, and between 1664 and 1671 wrote her *Memoirs of the Life of Colonel Hutchinson*, 'to moderate my woe, and if it were possible to augment my love'. She overrated her husband's importance and was both prejudiced and partial in her account of his enemies, but her moving description of her courtship and marriage, her portrait of the life of a Puritan family, and her account of the Civil War in Nottinghamshire make it one of the most important seventeenth-century memoirs. It was not published until 1806. It stands with the Duchess of *Newcastle's life of her husband as one of two seventeenth-century biographies which transcended the status of dutiful and pious eulogies. Like the Duchess, Lucy Hutchinson remained best known as her husband's biographer, but in her case, deservedly so. She also wrote a treatise *On the Principles of the Christian Religion*, addressed to one of her daughters, and another *On Theology*, both published in 1817. A fragment of autobiography, 'The Life of Mrs. Hutchinson Written by Herself', was printed in the first edition of the *Life* and the 1885 edition contained some of Hutchinson's letters. It was translated into French in 1823. One of the poems she was known to have written was included in the 1806 edition of the *Life*, but a translation of part of the *Aeneid* remained unpublished. The manuscript of the *Life*, according to the *DNB*, has not survived. *See* Sara Heller Mendelson, *The Mental World of Stuart Women: Three Studies* (1987);

Huxley, Elspeth (Josceline), novelist, biographer, travel writer, and writer on Africa (b. London, 23 July 1907).

Elspeth Huxley is the daughter of Major Josceline Grant, a Kenyan coffee planter, and his wife Eleanour Lillian Grosvenor. The family moved to Kenya when she was 5 and the experience of being a European in Africa is variously reflected in all of her writing from her fiction through to her work on African history and society. Her African childhood is evocatively recalled in the first two volumes of her best-selling autobiography, *The Flame Trees of Thika* (1959) and *The Mottled Lizard* (1962, published in the USA as *On the Edge of the Rift*). *The Flame Trees of Thika* was a Book Society choice in the USA and was filmed in 1981. She went to school in England during the First World War and then to a school for European children in Nairobi. Her student days at Reading University and then at Cornell in the 1920s, where she studied agriculture, are revisited in the third volume of the autobiography, *Love among the Daughters* (1968). She worked as an assistant press officer to the Empire Marketing Board between 1929 and 1932 and in 1931 married Gervas Huxley (d. 1971), a writer and the first cousin of Julian and Aldous Huxley. They had one son. Her husband's involvement in the tea trade led to extensive travel in the 1930s, mainly by sea. She took up writing detective stories to pass the time and to avoid playing bridge. *Murder at Government House* (1937), *Murder on Safari* (1938), and *Death of an Aryan* (1939, published in the USA as *The African Poison Murders*) all have African settings. *Red Strangers* (1939), her first non-detective fiction, focuses on the effect of colonization on a native Kikuyu family. Huxley's other African novels deal sensitively with the contrasts between European and African social groups as in *The Walled City* (1948), also a Book Society choice, *A Thing to Love* (1954), and *Red Rock Wilderness* (1959). She has published several important non-fictional works on Africa, beginning with *White Man's Country: Lord Delamere and the Making of Kenya* (1935), a study of one of the pioneers of modern Kenya, *Race and Politics in Kenya*, with Margery Perham (1944), *Livingstone and his African Journeys* (1974), and *Out of the Midday Sun: My Kenya* (1985). *Back Streets, New Worlds* (1964) investigates immigrant society in Britain. She has also written several biographies, of the Kingsleys (1973), Florence *Nightingale (1975), and Scott of the Antarctic (1977), and several books of travel, *The Sorcerer's Apprentice* (1948) and *Four Guineas* (1954), on East and West Africa, *Their Shining Eldorado* (1967), about Australia, and *The Challenge of Africa* (1971). Huxley served on the Monkton Advisory Commission on Central Africa in 1959, which provided the background for a detective story, *The Merry Hippo* (1963), and on the General Advisory Council of the BBC, 1952–59. She was appointed CBE in 1962 and now lives in Wiltshire.

I

Inchbald, Elizabeth, actress, dramatist, and novelist
(b. Stanningfield, near Bury St Edmunds, Suffolk, 15 October 1753,
d. Kensington, London, 1 August 1821).

Elizabeth Inchbald was the second youngest child of John Simpson, a Roman Catholic farmer, and his wife Mary Rushbrook. Her father died when she was 7, and she had no formal education, although she and her sisters taught themselves to spell. When she was 18 she ran away to London, hoping to find work in the theatre. A speech impediment, which she never quite lost, made this initially difficult, and her striking beauty made her the prey of actors and managers alike. Partly to escape one unwelcome advance in 1772 she impulsively married Joseph Inchbald, an actor and portrait painter and a fellow Catholic more than twice her age, whom she had previously refused. The couple eked out a precarious existence in the provincial theatre, often playing opposite one another, until Inchbald's sudden death in 1779. Elizabeth was given a benefit and an engagement at Covent Garden the following year. She retired from the London stage eventually in 1789. She had begun to write farces while acting, and also a novel. She had a small part in her own first performed play, *A Mogul Tale; or The Descent of the Balloon*, at the Haymarket Theatre in 1784. It was followed by more than twenty others, comedies, farces, and adaptations of French and German plays. The best known of the last group is probably her adaptation of Kotzebue's *Lovers Vows* (1798), which the Bertram family and friends perform in Jane *Austen's *Mansfield Park*. Her novel *A Simple Story*, begun in 1777 and eventually published in 1791, with its interesting variation on the familiar plot of older lover as mentor and reformer of the undisciplined heroine, was an instant success. *Nature and Art*, which followed in 1796, in which a seduced and criminal heroine is sentenced to death unwittingly by her original seducer, did not equal its success, despite its feminist point. She wrote biographical and critical introductions for a twenty-five-volume collection of plays, *The British Theatre* (1808), and assembled a seven-volume *Collection of Farces* (1809) and another collection, *The Modern Theatre* (1811). She declined the editorship of the fashionable magazine *La Belle Assemblée* and also John Murray's invitation to write for the *Quarterly Review* but became one of the first women contributors to the *Edinburgh Review*. Her beauty, even in her later years, attracted many followers, but she never remarried. William Godwin and Thomas Holcroft were among her admirers as was John Philip Kemble, but the last did not, as she had hoped, ask her to marry him after her husband's death. She invested her earnings from her writings prudently, fearing the return of the poverty of her youth and married life, and used some of her savings to help various members of her family, all of whom predeceased her. She lived frugally, spending most of her later years in a series of inexpensive lodgings in London, and died in a home for Roman Catholic women in Kensington. She had compiled four volumes of memoirs but was persuaded to burn them before her death. Her friends (and admirers) included Anna Laetitia *Barbauld and Maria *Edgeworth. *See* James Boaden, *Memoirs of Mrs. Inchbald* (1833); W. McKee, *Elizabeth Inchbald: Novelist* (1935); Marilyn Butler, *Jane Austen and the War of Ideas* (1975, 1987); Katherine Sobba Green, *The Courtship Novel 1740–1820: A Feminised Genre* (1991); Jane Spencer, *The Rise of the Woman Novelist: From Aphra Behn to Jane Austen* (1986); Mary Anne Schofield and Cecilia Macheski (eds.), *Curtain Calls: British and American Women and the Theater 1660–1820* (1991).

Ingelow, Jean, poet and novelist (b. Boston, Lincolnshire, 17 March 1820, d. Kensington, London, 20 July 1897).

Jean Ingelow was the eldest of the large family of William Ingelow, a banker, and his wife Jean Kilgour of Aberdeenshire. Her maternal great-grandfather had been Bishop of Aberdeen. She grew up among a lively and supportive family, and was educated at home, first in Lincolnshire, then Ipswich, and eventually in London. She and her brothers and sisters produced their own periodical, which was typeset by a friend, and to which she contributed poems. She also wrote in secret, sometimes burning her manuscripts, sometimes hiding them, and occasionally using the folded shutters of her bedroom as a substitute for paper. She sent some short stories to the evangelical *Youth's Magazine* under the pseudonym of Orris, a name she continued to use. Her first published volume, *A Rhyming Chronicle of Incidents and Feelings* (1850), was admired by Tennyson, but her reputation was established with her collected *Poems* (1863), which went through twenty-three editions by 1880. The volume contained several of the poems on which her subsequent reputation rested, including 'Divided', 'Song of Seven', 'Supper at the Mill', and 'High Tide on the Coast of Lincolnshire, 1571', a ballad based on an actual disaster. A second series of *Poems* was published in 1880 and a third in 1885. *The Story of Doom and Other Poems* (1867), another popular volume, went through six editions by 1880. Ingelow had a wide American as well as a British reading public. Many American editions were issued, for some of which she received royalties, although she also suffered from piracy before the establishment of international copyright in 1891. She wrote novels and short stories, many of the latter intended for children. *Tales of Orris* (1860) was republished as *Stories Told to a Child* (1865) and, like *Studies for Stories* (1864), was illustrated by J. E. Millais. Her most famous and probably her best children's book was *Mopsa the Fairy* (1869). *Off the Skelligs* (1872) was her best-known novel, a love and adventure story set on islands off the south-west coast of Ireland. It was followed by a sequel, *Fated to be Free* (1875). Another novel, *Sarah de Berenger* (1879), was a melodrama of the *sensation school, with a plot reminiscent of Mrs Henry *Wood's *East Lynne* (1861). Ingelow became a well-known figure in literary and artistic circles. Later volumes of her stories and poems were illustrated by eminent artists, and she became a friend of Tennyson, Browning, Ruskin, and Christina *Rossetti. She never married, and lived with her brother in Kensington after her parents' death. *See* H. C. Black, *Notable Women Authors of the Day* (1893); Maureen Peters, *Jean Ingelow: Victorian Poetess* (1972); Kathleen Hickok, *Representations of Women: Nineteenth-Century British Women's Poetry* (1984); Angela Leighton, *Victorian Women Poets: Writing against the Heart* (1992).

'Iota' *See under* NEW WOMAN

'Iron, Ralph' *see* SCHREINER, Olive

jjjjjjjjjjjjjjjjjj

J

James, Dame P(hyllis) D(orothy), mystery and crime novelist (b. Oxford, 3 August 1920).

P. D. James is the second of the three children of Sidney Victor James, an Inland Revenue officer, and his wife Dorothy May Hone. She spent her childhood in Shropshire and then in Cambridge, where she attended Cambridge Girls' High School 1931–7. After school she worked variously in a tax office, as an assistant stage manager with the Cambridge Festival Theatre, and as a Red Cross nurse during the Second World War. In 1941 she married Ernest Connor Bantry White, a doctor with the Royal Army Medical Corps. Her husband's severe mental illness and prolonged periods of hospitalization after the war left her with sole responsibility for their two daughters. She became a clerk in the National Health Service, working for a diploma in hospital administration and medical record keeping at night. She then became principal administrative assistant wih the Northwest Metropolitan Regional Medical Board and after her husband's death in 1964 became an administrative grade civil servant. She began her first novel, *Cover your Face,* a country house mystery in the Dorothy L. *Sayers/Margery *Allingham tradition, in 1959, and published it in 1962. Her next three books, *A Mind to Murder* (1963), *Unnatural Causes* (1967), and *Shroud for a Nightingale* (1971), established her reputation as well as that of her Scotland Yard detective hero Adam Dalgliesh, who resembled his amateur predecessors Lord Peter Wimsey and Hercule Poirot. *An Unsuitable Job for a Woman* (1972) introduced Cordelia Gray, her female detective heroine. *Innocent Blood* (1980), a tale of an adopted daughter who discovers her parents have been guilty of child abuse and murder, is regarded more as a 'serious' crime novel than as a detective story. *The Skull beneath the Skin* (1982) marked a return to the detective story, with an Agatha *Christie-type house party on an island. *A Taste for Death* (1986) is her most sombre book to date, and introduced a second female detective, the ambitious Kate Miskin. Later titles include *Devices and Desires* (1989). She has also written *The Maul and the Pear Tree* (1971), with Thomas Critchley, based on a series of crimes which took place in the East End in 1811. James sees herself as 'more or less in the English classical tradition' of detective writers, one of a line beginning with Sayers and Christie and extending through Allingham to the present. Her work in the health service and later in the police and criminal policy departments of the Home Office has provided the background as well as the expert knowledge for most of her fiction. *A Mind for Murder* is set in a psychiatric hospital, *Shroud for a Nightingale* in a training college for nurses, *The Black Tower* in a home for incurables, and *Death of an Expert Witness* (1977) in a forensic science laboratory. *The Children of Men* (1992) is a futuristic story set in Oxford in 2021. James has emphasized the connections between crime writers and traditional novelists. The former, she once remarked, 'are as much concerned as are other novelists with psychological truth and the moral ambiguities of human actions'. She was appointed OBE in 1983 and DBE in 1991. *See* Norma Siebenheller, *P. D. James* (1981); Nancy Carol Joyner, in *10 Women of Mystery*, ed. Earl F. Bargainnier (1981); Bruce Harkness, in *Art in Crime Writing: Essays on Detective Fiction*, ed. Bernard Benstock (1983); Carolyn G. Heilbrun, in *Reading and Writing Women's Lives: A Study of the Novel of Manners*, ed. Bege K. Bowers and Barbara Brothers (1990).

Jameson, Anna Brownell, writer on art (b. Dublin, 17 May 1794, d. Ealing, London, 17 March 1860).

The eldest of the five daughters of Dennis Brownell Murphy, an Irish miniature painter, and his English wife, Anna Murphy became a governess at the age of 16 and worked for fifteen years helping to support her family, as she was to do off and on for most of her life. A broken engagement to her future husband Robert Jameson, a young and taciturn barrister, sent her on a tour of France and Italy, again as a governess. Her fictionalized travel journal *A Lady's Diary* (1826) was sold to a publisher on the understanding that she received a guitar from the profits. It was later published with considerable success by the more astute Henry Colburn as *The Diary of an Ennuyée*. In 1825 she married Jameson, but the marriage was not happy, and four years later they separated. Mrs Jameson published successively *Loves of the Poets* (1829), *Memoirs of Celebrated Female Sovereigns* (1831), and in 1832 her well-known *Characteristics of Women*, essays on Shakespeare's heroines, which went through several editions and was translated into German. It was in this work that her concern for improvements in the position of women was first presented. Her extended travel and residence in Germany was reflected in *Visits and Sketches at Home and Abroad* (1834). A brief reconciliation with her husband, who had taken up the position of Attorney-General of Upper Canada, was followed by a final separation in 1837, and she threw herself of necessity into a professional literary career. *Winter Studies and Summer Rambles in Canada* (1838), ostensibly a travel book, contained an impassioned discussion of the condition of women, and the need for improvements in their education to fit them for useful work. In 1842 the first of her publications on art, the *Handbook to the Public Galleries of Art in or near London*, appeared, followed by a *Companion to the Most Celebrated Private Galleries* in 1844. In 1845 she edited a collection of her articles from the *Penny Magazine*, *Memoirs of the Early Italian Painters*. The following year she published a collection of *Memoirs and Essays*, which included two of her best short works, 'The House of Titian' and 'Xanthian Marbles'. Elizabeth Barrett (*Browning) made two translations from the *Odyssey* for the latter. The remainder of her life was devoted to the publication for which she is best remembered, her *Sacred and Legendary Art*, published in four parts beginning in 1848 with *Legends of the Saints*, followed by *Legends of the Monastic Orders* (1850) and *Legends of the Madonna* (1852). The final part, *The History of our Lord as Exemplified in Works of Art*, was completed by her friend Lady *Eastlake in 1864. Mrs Jameson had a wide circle of female friends, of whom the most celebrated was Lady Byron, from whom she became estranged, a quarrel which clouded her last years. Other friends included the Brownings, Mrs *Gaskell, and Fanny *Kemble. She published *A Commonplace Book of Thoughts, Memories and Fancies* (1854), and two influential public lectures, *Sisters of Charity* (1855) and *The Communion of Labour* (1856), which set out the principles of her feminism. She placed particular emphasis on the need for women to lead useful lives, and to have the opportunity for earning their livings. The lectures also condemned the double standard of contemporary morality. Anna Jameson gradually became involved with the women's movement of the 1850s, giving her patronage to leading feminists like Adelaide *Procter, Bessie Rayner *Parkes, and Barbara *Bodichon when her declining health prevented more active participation. She died in 1860 from the results of a cold caught while returning from a day's work on the last section of *Sacred and Legendary Art* at the British Museum. Her niece and companion Geraldine ('Geddie') Bate, later Macpherson, wrote her *Memoirs* (1878). *See* R. H. Horne, *A New Spirit of the Age* (1844); Harriet *Martineau, *Biographical Sketches* (1869); Fanny *Kemble, *Records of a Girlhood* (1878); Mrs Steuart Erskine (ed.), *Anna Jameson: Letters and Friendships 1812–60* (1915); Clara

Thomas, *Love and Work Enough: The Life of Anna Jameson* (1967); Pauline Nestor, *Female Friendships and Communities: Charlotte Brontë, George Eliot, Elizabeth Gaskell* (1985).

Jameson, (Margaret) Storm, novelist (b. Whitby, Yorkshire, 8 January 1891, d. Cambridge, 30 September 1986).

Storm Jameson was the daughter of William S. Jameson, a sea captain and member of a Yorkshire shipbuilding family, and his wife Hannah Margaret Gallilee. Her mother, a strict Congregationalist, berated her for reading before breakfast but then encouraged her to compete for a scholarship at Scarborough Municipal School. She read English at Leeds University, where she was the first woman to take a first class degree, in 1912, and then won a scholarship to King's College, London. In 1913 she married Charles Douglas Clarke ('K'), by whom she had a son. They divorced in 1925 and in 1926 she married Guy Patterson Chapman, a historian. She published her MA thesis on *Modern Drama in Europe* in 1920, worked as a copy-writer and a drama critic, and edited a weekly magazine, the *New Commonwealth*, 1919–22. The publication of *The Pot Boils* (1919) signalled the start of a prolific output of fiction which included two trilogies. The first, titled the *Triumph of Time* (1932), chronicled a family of Yorkshire shipbuilders resembling her own in *The Lovely Ship* (1927), *The Voyage Home* (1930), and *A Richer Dust* (1931). The second, the *Mirror in Darkness* trilogy, (1939) comprising *Company Parade* (1934), *Love in Winter* (1935), and *None Turn Back* (1936), carried on the story of her earlier heroine Mary Hervey Russell, now a *New Woman much like herself. Jameson was president of the English branch of PEN from 1938 to 1945, when she worked on behalf of refugee writers and European intellectuals, and she continued this while on the governing body of international PEN. Three of her best novels reflect European political life between the wars, and drew on her European journeys on behalf of PEN, *Cousin Honoré* (1940), *Europe to Let* (1940), and *Cloudless May* (1943). Her novels of the 1930s and 1940s attracted attention from critics and readers alike, whereas those written in the 1950s and 1960s experienced a decline in interest. Among those which she herself regarded as her best and which received critical approval were *That was Yesterday* (1932), *A Day Off* (1933), *Farewell Night, Welcome Day* (1939), *The Journal of Mary Russell Hervey* (1945), *The Green Man* (1952), *A Cup of Tea for Mr. Thorgill* (1957), *The Road from the Monument* (1962), and *The White Crow* (1968). Her two-volume autobiography *Journey from the North* was published in 1969–70, when she was 78. Her last but one work, *Parthian Words* (1970), an attack on modern fiction, she insisted, 'contains my declaration of faith as a writer'. Her last book, *Speaking of Stendhal* (1979), published when she was 82, conveyed her continuing interest in and enthusiasm for French culture. She once said of herself, 'If I could begin my life again . . . I would not live by writing. I am not what you call a born writer; and I should have been much happier as an engineer'. Jameson published three novels in 1937–8 under the pseudonyms James Hill and William Lamb, and edited her husband's autobiography *A Kind of Survivor* (1975). *See* Elaine *Feinstein's introduction to *Company Parade* (1985, 1st pub. 1934).

Jennings, Elizabeth (Joan), poet (b. Boston, Lincolnshire, 18 July 1926).

Elizabeth Jennings is the younger daughter of Henry Cecil, a medical doctor. The family, who were converts to Roman Catholicism, moved to Oxford when she was 6. She went to Oxford Girls' High School and then read English at St. Anne's College, Oxford, 1946–9. Between 1950 and 1958 she worked as an assistant at Oxford City Library. The urge to write poetry came at 13 after reading part of G. K. Chesterton's *Lepanto.* Her school was not encouraging, but an uncle was. She was influenced briefly by W. H. Auden and T. S. Eliot and admired Edwin Muir, Wallace Stevens, and, above all, Yeats. Her poems were published in the *Spectator* and in *Poetry Review* and she was included in the 1949 edition of *Oxford Poetry. Poems* (1953), her first collection, won an Arts Council prize and the next, *A Way of Looking* (1955), the Somerset Maugham Award. In 1956 Robert Conquest included her in his *New Lines* anthology along with Philip Larkin, Kingsley Amis, Donald Davie, Thom Gunn, and others considered to be members of the so-called 'Movement'. Elizabeth Jennings was the only woman and the only Catholic included, and combined with the group, it was said by one wag, like 'a school-mistress in a . . . train with a bunch of drunken marines'. Her later poetry in fact retained many of the characteristics of the Movement. *A Sense of the World* (1958), *Song for a Birth or a Death* (1961), and *Recoveries* (1964) helped to establish her as one of the most accomplished poets of her generation. Around 1960 she suffered a severe mental breakdown followed by a suicide attempt. She recovered gradually, after analysis. Many of the poems included in *The Mind has Mountains* (1966) reflect her experiences and those of her fellow patients in hospital. It won the Richard Hillary Prize. Her *Collected Poems* were published in 1967 and were followed by *The Animals' Arrival* (1969) and *Lucidities* (1970). Jennings worked as a publisher's reader between 1958 and 1960 and has since worked as an editor, reviewer, and translator. *Let's Have some Poetry* (1960) is an introduction to poetry for children and *Every Changing Shape* (1961) a study of the relationship between mystical experience and the writing of poetry. She has written a study of Robert Frost (1964) and edited a number of collections, including *The*

Batsford Book of Children's Verse (1958), *An Anthology of Modern Verse* (1961), and a selection of Christina *Rossetti's poetry (1970). She has also translated the sonnets of Michelangelo (1961). Later volumes of poetry include *Growing Points* (1975), *Moments of Grace* (1979), *Selected Poems* (1979), *Celebrations and Elegies* (1982), *Tributes* (1989), and *Times and Seasons* (1992). A second *Collected Poems* was published in 1986. She won the W. H. Smith Literary Award in 1987 and was appointed CBE in 1992. *See* Blake Morrison, *The Movement* (1980; repr. 1986); Michael Wheeler, in *Hopkins among the Poets: Studies in Modern Responses to Gerard Manley Hopkins* (1985).

Jesse, F(ryniwyd Marsh) Tennyson, novelist and playwright (b. Chislehurst, Kent, 1888, d. London, 6 August 1958).

Fryn Tennyson Jesse's maternal grandmother was Emily Tennyson, sister of the poet and fiancée of the drowned Arthur Hallam. She was the second of three daughters of the Revd Eustace Tennyson d'Eyncourt Jesse and Edith Louisa James. As a child she travelled extensively in Europe and South Africa with her parents. When she was 10 her father became chaplain to the wine growers at Marsala in Sicily. Later she went to school in Paris and then studied art at the Newlyn School, run by Stanhope Forbes in Cornwall. She tried her hand at painting and book illustration and then wrote poetry, which persuaded her to exchange an artistic for a literary career. She worked as a reporter for *The Times* and the *Daily Mail* and reviewed for the *TLS* and the *English Review.* During the First World War she worked in the Ministry of Information. She was one of the few women to report from the front, a role which she later noted was 'not considered decent' for a woman. *The Sword of Deborah,* subtitled 'first-hand impressions of the British Women's Army in France', was only released for publication in 1919. The success of her story 'The Mask' in 1912 paved the way for the publication of her first novel, *The Milky Way* (1913), which she considered 'a very bad book'. A request by the dramatist Harold Marsh Harwood (1874–1959) to adapt 'The Mask' for the stage led to a successful collaboration and in 1918 to a secret marriage. She and her husband collaborated on several plays, including *The Pelican* (1916, published 1926), *Billeted* (1917), and *How to be Healthy though Married* (1930). She wrote two plays by herself, *Quarantine* (1922) and *Anyhouse* (1925), and in 1921 published *The White Riband,* her first mature novel, which was praised by Conrad, among others. *Tom Fool* (1926), a historical novel set in Cornwall, *Moonraker; or The French Pirate and her Friends* (1927), a subversion of a traditional adventure story with a female pirate captain, and *The Lacquer Lady* (1929), about the early days of Burmese independence, inspired by a visit to the country, are among her best novels. Her other professional interest was criminology. 'My chief passion is murder,' she was fond of saying. Her main contribution to criminal theory was the suggestion, in *Murder and its Motives* (1924), that there were born 'murderees' as well as born murderers. She edited a number of cases for the Notable British Trials series and based her novel *A Pin to See the Peep Show* (1934) on the notorious Thompson–Bywaters case of 1922 in which a bored young wife was convicted of the murder of her husband, a murder which had in fact been committed by her lover. A subsequent stage adaptation was not a success. *London Front* (1940) and *While London Burns* (1942) were letters written by Jesse and her husband to friends in America. Her last two novels, *The Alabaster Cup* and *The Dragon in the Heart*, were published in 1950 and 1956. She also published *The Happy Bride* (1920), a book of poems, and two collections of stories, *Beggars on Horseback* (1915) and *Many Latitudes* (1928). *The Story of Burma* (1946) was a travel book. She became a fellow of the Royal Society of Literature in 1947. At one point she lost the fingers of her right hand and learned to write with her left. Rebecca *West's obituary described her as 'a skilful, amusing, clandestine sort of feminist, never tired of getting in an adroit plea for the dignity and independence of womankind'. Her secretary wrote her biography. *See* Joanna Colenbrander, *A Portrait of Fryn* (1984).

Jewsbury, Geraldine (Ensor), novelist (b. Measham, Derbyshire, 22 August 1812, d. London, 23 September 1880).

Geraldine Jewsbury was the daughter of Thomas Jewsbury, a Manchester merchant and insurance agent. Her mother died when she was 6, and she was brought up by her elder sister *Maria Jane, who was also a novelist. When Maria married in 1832 Geraldine took charge of the household, and after her father's death in 1840 became housekeeper for her brother Frank. In 1841 she met Thomas and Jane *Carlyle, who were to become two of the most formative intellectual influences on her life. She became closely attached to Jane Carlyle and in 1854, the year after her brother's marriage she moved to Chelsea to be near her. She rapidly became the centre of a literary and artistic circle. Jewsbury's first novel, *Zoe*, published in 1845, shocked its readers with its religious and sexual heterodoxy, and was considered to have been overly influenced by the novels of George Sand. Like most of her novels, it reflected her strongly feminist views about the position of women and the limitations of marriage. *The Half Sisters* (1848), her next work, was written as a challenge to conventional views about female submissiveness and also showed the influence of Sand. Its story of two contrasting half-sisters, one a woman of genius and the other brought up to be a good wife and mother, owed much to Madame de Staël's **Corinne*, a novel which also influenced Maria Jane Jewsbury. The accurate picture of industrial life in Manchester presented in *Marian Withers* (1851), her next novel, caused it to be linked with Elizabeth

*Gaskell's *Mary Barton*, and like its predecessors it reinforced its author's critical views on the position of women in society. Other novels included *Constance Herbert* (1855), which was dedicated to Carlyle, *The Sorrows of Gentility* (1856), and *Right or Wrong* (1859). Jewsbury also wrote children's books, including *The History of an Adopted Child* (1852) and *Angelo; or The Pine Forest in the Alps* (1856), and contributed to periodicals like *Douglas Jerrold's Shilling Magazine*, Mrs S. C. *Hall's *Juvenile Budget*, and Dickens's *Household Words*. Her influence on her contemporaries was felt not through her fiction, but in her capacity as a prolific reviewer of fiction for the *Athenaeum* between 1849 and 1880, and as a reader of fiction for the house of Bentley from 1858 until her death. Rhoda *Broughton satirized her in *A Beginner* (1894) as Miss Grimshaw, reviewing for the *Porch* 'with a tomahawk'. She moved from London to Kent in 1866 after Jane Carlyle's death and died of cancer in 1880. *See Selections from the Letters of Geraldine Jewsbury to Jane Welsh Carlyle*, ed. Mrs A. Ireland (1892); Virginia Woolf, 'Geraldine and Jane', *The Common Reader: Second Series* (1932); Suzanne Howe, *Geraldine Jewsbury: Her Life and Errors* (1935); Monica Fryckstedt, *Geraldine Jewsbury's Athenaeum Reviews: A Mirror of Mid-Victorian Attitudes to Fiction* (1986); Norma Clarke, *Ambitious Heights: Writing, Friendship, Love: The Jewsbury Sisters, Felicia Hemans and Jane Welsh Carlyle* (1990).

Jewsbury, Maria Jane, novelist (b. Measham, Derbyshire, 25 October 1800, d. Poona, India, 4 October 1833).

Maria Jane Jewsbury was the eldest of the six children of Thomas Jewsbury, a Derbyshire cotton merchant who removed to Manchester in 1818. Her mother Maria, née Smith, died the following year and she assumed the responsibility for her younger siblings, including *Geraldine, who also became a novelist. She had been sent to a school at Shenstone in Derbyshire until she was 14 but had to be withdrawn because of ill health. The poet Alaric Watts, then editor of the *Manchester Courier*, spotted a poem she had published in the *Manchester Gazette* and encouraged her to contribute to various *annuals or albums, and also persuaded the publishers Hurst & Robinson to publish a collection of her verse and prose, *Phantasmagoria* (1825). The work was dedicated to Wordsworth and initiated a friendship with the poet and also with members of his family. He in turn addressed his poem 'Liberty' (1829) to her. Convalescence after a long illness in 1826 gave her the opportunity to write. She published periodical articles, more fiction for albums, a collection of poetry, *Lays of Leisure Hours* (1829), dedicated to Felicia *Hemans, and *Letters to the Young* (1828), based on letters of advice written to Geraldine at school, which went into three editions. In 1830 she published her best-known and longest work, a collection of stories under the title *The Three Histories: The History of an Enthusiast, The History of a Nonchalant,* and *The History of a Realist. The History of an Enthusiast* was a response to Madame de Staël's novel **Corinne* (1807), a tale of two heroines, one of whom aspires to literary fame while her friend seeks to fulfil the more conventional woman's role. The novel differs in certain ways from Madame de Staël's model, and also differs interestingly from Geraldine Jewsbury's *The Half Sisters* (1848), which was also influenced by *Corinne. The Three Histories* went into three editions and established her reputation. She contributed some of her most perceptive writing to the *Athenaeum* in 1831. In 1832 she married the Revd William Kew Fletcher, a chaplain in the East India Company. She took her manuscripts with her to India and planned future projects, but died of cholera at Poona fourteen months after her marriage, aged 33. *See* Eric Gillett, *Maria Jane Jewsbury: Occasional Papers* (Oxford, 1932), which has a memoir; Suzanne Howe, *Geraldine Jewsbury: Her Life and Errors* (1935); Joanne Wilkes, *Australasian Victorian Studies Association, Armidale Conference Papers* (1988); Norma Clarke, *Ambitious Heights: Writing, Friendship, Love: The Jewsbury Sisters, Felicia Hemans and Jane Welsh Carlyle* (1990).

Jhabvala, Ruth Prawer, novelist, short story writer, and script writer (b. Cologne, 7 May 1927).

Ruth Prawer Jhabvala is the younger of the two children and only daughter of Marcus Prawer, a Polish-Jewish solicitor, and his German-Jewish wife Eleonora Cohn. The family fled to England from Germany as refugees in 1939 and she became a naturalized British subject in 1948. She attended segregated Jewish schools in Germany and then Stoke Park Secondary School in Coventry, followed by Hendon County School in outer London, 1940–5. She took a BA and then in 1951 an MA in English literature from Queen Mary College, University of London, and in the same year married Cyrus S. H. Jhabvala, an Indian architect. They have three daughters. She lived in India from 1951 until 1975. Having written in German on religious subjects when very young, she recalled that within months of arriving in England she began to write stories in English about the English lower middle classes in whose midst she found herself. Similarly on her arrival in India she began immediately to write about Indian society, taking as the 'central fact' of her work that she was a European living permanently in India. Her novels, she once claimed, are not a balanced or authoritative view of India 'but only one individual European's attempt to compound the puzzling process of living in it'. Her first book, *To whom she Will* (1955, published in New York as *Amrita*, 1956), was followed by *The Nature of Passion* (1957), *Esmond in India* (1958), *The Householder* (1960), *Get Ready for Battle* (1963), *A Backward Place*

(1965), *A New Dominion* (1972, published in New York as *Travellers*, 1973), and *Heat and Dust* (1975), which won the Booker Prize. The novels underline the contrasts of Indian society, the ruthless social mobility of the emergent middle classes versus the old caste system, materialism and snobbery set against traditional mysticism, intellectual progress and enlightenment in opposition to superstition. Her penetrating social observation and the inherent comedy of her novels have prompted comparisons with Jane *Austen. As well as novels Jhabvala has published collections of short stories, notably *Like Birds, Like Fishes* (1963), *A Stronger Climate* (1969), *An Experience of India* (1972), and *How I Became a Holy Mother* (1976). She has also written screenplays, including *Shakespeare Wallah*, with James Ivory, (1965), *The Guru* (1968), *Bombay Talkie* (1970), and *Autobiography of a Princess*, with James Ivory and John Swope (1975). In 1975 she moved to New York, where she now lives. *In Search of Love and Beauty* (1983) deals with wealthy expatriates living in New York, and *Three Continents* (1987) with a disastrous meeting of East and West. Her recent film work, much of it written in conjunction with the partnership of James Ivory and Ismail Merchant, includes screenplays for Henry James's *The Bostonians* and *The Europeans*, E. M. Forster's *Room with a View*, Bernice Rubens's *Madame Sousatska*, and *Quartet*, based on the novel by Jean *Rhys. Her film work marks a shift away from Indian themes and an increasing preoccupation with the rootless or displaced individual in Europe and America. *See* H. M. Williams, *The Fiction of Ruth Prawer Jhabvala* (1973); Vasant A. Shahane, *Ruth Prawer Jhabvala* (1976); Yasmine Gooneratne, *Silence, Exile and Cunning: The Fiction of Ruth Prawer Jhabvala* (1983); Laurie Sucher, *The Fiction of Ruth Prawer Jhabvala: The Politics of Passion* (1989).

Johnson, Pamela Hansford, novelist, dramatist, and critic (b. Clapham, London, 29 May 1912, d. London, 18 June 1981).

Pamela Hansford Johnson was the elder daughter of Reginald Kenneth Johnson, a colonial administrator who served in the Gold Coast, and of Amy Clotilda Howson, whose father the actor C. E. Howson had been treasurer to the actor-manager Henry Irving. She went to Clapham County Secondary School but left at 16 to learn shorthand and typing and then to work in a bank. She never regretted her decision, which had been caused in part by her father's death, declaring that 'a course in Eng. Lit. has rotted many a promising writer'. She later claimed that Aldous Huxley's *Texts and Pretexts* (1933) had been the key to her 'higher education' in both English and French literature. She published poetry first at the age of 14 and won a poetry prize in 1934 for *Symphony for Full Orchestra*. She fell in love with Dylan Thomas, who won the same *Sunday Referee* prize the following year. They contemplated marriage but then parted amicably. In 1936 she married Gordon Neil Stewart, an Australian journalist by whom she had a son and a daughter. They divorced in 1949 and in 1950 she married the novelist C. P. Snow, later Lord Snow (1905–80). They had one son. Her first novel, *This Bed thy Centre*, published in 1935, won critical approval but also notoriety due to its openness about sexuality. Her next five novels were undistinguished, until in 1940 she wrote *Too Dear for my Possessing*, the first of a trilogy, followed by *An Avenue of Stone* (1947) and *A Summer to Decide* (1949). Her marriage to Snow resulted in a formidable literary partnership and inaugurated the major phase of her career. Of her thirty-one novels, ten of the best were written after 1950. These included *Catherine Carter* (1952), the only book with a theatrical setting, *An Impossible Marriage* (1954), which had an autobiographical novelist/narrator, and the so-called 'Dorothy Merlin' trilogy, which satirized literary life: *The Unspeakable Skipton* (1959), based on Frederic Rolfe, Baron Corvo, *Night and Silence—Who is Here?* and *Cork Street, Next to the Hatter's* (1965). Other titles included *The Humbler Creation* (1959), *An Error of Judgement* (1962), and *The Honours Board* (1970). She also wrote six radio plays based on reconstructions of Proust commissioned by the BBC in 1958, seven plays, and a book on the implications of the infamous Moors Murders case, *On Iniquity* (1967). She was a regular reviewer for the *Sunday Times* and early in her career reviewed for *John o' London's*, the *Daily Telegraph*, and the *Sunday Chronicle*. She also wrote a British Council pamphlet on Ivy *Compton-Burnett (1951). A sufferer from migraine for over thirty years, she helped to found the Migraine Trust in 1969. She became a fellow of the Royal Society of Literature and was appointed CBE in 1975. A book of memoirs, *Important to Me*, was published in 1974, and her last novel, *A Bonfire* (1981), appeared two months before her death. *See* Isabel Quigly, *Pamela Hansford Johnson* (1968); Ishrat Lindblad, *Pamela Hansford Johnson* (1982).

Johnstone, Christian Isobel ('Margaret Dods'), novelist and journalist (b. Fifeshire, 1781, d. Edinburgh, 26 August 1857).

Little is known of the early life of Christian Johnstone, a pioneering woman editor. She was born in Scotland, married a Mr M'Leish, whom she then divorced, and in 1812 married John Johnstone, a schoolmaster in Dunfermline. Johnstone later became proprietor and editor of the *Inverness Courier*, an enterprise in which Christian assisted, particularly by writing extensively on literary topics. Johnstone eventually sold the *Courier* and moved to Edinburgh, where he opened a printing office and bought the copyright of the *Edinburgh Weekly Chronicle*. Christian again helped to edit the magazine, which eventually became *Johnstone's Edinburgh Magazine* and was then incorporated with *Tait's Edinburgh Magazine* in 1834. She was installed as editor of *Tait's* and given a half-share in the property as co-proprietor until her retirement in 1846. She was thus the first woman to edit a major journal before the 1860s, when Bessie Rayner *Parkes, Mary Elizabeth *Braddon, Mrs Henry *Wood, Emily *Faithfull, and others made it a common practice. As well as editing *Tait's*, Johnstone contributed over 400 articles during the twelve years of her editorship, almost 20 per cent of the total. She also strongly encouraged the work of other women writers in the magazine, notably Harriet *Martineau, Catherine *Gore, Eliza Lynn *Linton, Mary Russell *Mitford, Amelia *Opie, Mary *Howitt, Frances Brown, Sarah Fry, Hannah Lawrance, Eliza Meteyard, and (possibly) Lady *Blessington. Johnstone also took a personal interest in reviewing the work of almost every new woman writer of the 1830s and 1840s. De Quincey cited her, along with Joanna *Baillie and Mary Russell Mitford, as examples of women 'cultivating the profession of authorship with absolutely no sacrifice or loss of feminine dignity'. Apart from her journalism, the most popular of her works was *The Cook and Housewife's Manual* (1826), written under her pseudonym Margaret Dods, which reached its tenth edition in 1854 and realized a steady income for her after she retired from *Tait's*. Others works included *Clan Albin: A National Tale* (1815), a novel which John Wilson of *Blackwood's* compared favourably with the work of Susan *Ferrier, and *Elizabeth de Bruce* (1827), another novel. *Edinburgh Tales* (1845–6) consisted of three volumes of stories collected from the various periodicals she edited, some written by herself, and others by Anne *Marsh, Catherine Gore, Catherine *Crowe, Mary Russell Mitford, and Mary and William Howitt. Johnstone also published some popular historical works. She attributed her low profile as a professional woman writer to the fact that she did not fit the stereotype of a woman of letters. She was divorced and had remarried, was childless, and had worked throughout her career as a paid, full-time journalist. 'I know that the woman who turns her talents to any profitable use, is, in some occult sense . . . in our Society, *degraded*,' a character in one of her stories declares ('Violet Hamilton', *Edinburgh Tales*, II (1845–6). *See The Wellesley Index to Victorian Periodicals*, ed. W. E. Houghton *et al.*, iv (1987).

Julian of Norwich, mystic (b. Norwich *c.*1343, d. Norwich, *c.*1413).

Julian of Norwich, commonly regarded as the first Englishwoman of letters, was probably a Benedictine nun of the house of Carrow, near Norwich. She later became an anchorite or hermit, enclosed in a cell attached to the church of St Julian and St Edward at Conisford, from which she derived her name. During an illness in 1373 she experienced a series of sixteen visions which she described later in her *Revelations of Divine Love*. This was the so-called 'short' version of the text, which was revised and expanded twenty years later in the light of further meditation and reflection. The longer version demonstrated her developing skills as a writer and her grasp of the complexities of Christian theology. T. S. Eliot quoted from her in 'Little Gidding', the last of *Four Quartets* (1942). Her claim to be 'unlettered' and merely an amanuensis dependent upon God, part of the tradition of female piety, has tended to obscure her extensive learning and the originality of her work. Her reputation spread during her lifetime. She was visited by Margery *Kempe and her writings copied and read abroad by English recusants. The longer version of the *Revelations* was first published in 1670, ed. R. F. S. Cressy. The first critical edition of both the 'short' and 'longer' versions is by Edmund Colledge and James Walsh, *A Book of the Showings to the Anchoress Julian of Norwich* (1978), and is based on the manuscripts and the 1670 text. The same editors have produced a modernized version, *Showings/Julian of Norwich* (1978). The longer version was first modernized by Walsh (1961) and C. Wolters (1966), and the shorter by Anna Maria Reynolds (1958). *See* P. Molinari, *Julian of Norwich: The Teaching of a Fourteenth Century Mystic* (1958); R. K. Stone, *Middle English Prose Style: Margery Kempe and Julian of Norwich* (1970); Edward Ingram Watkin, *On Julian of Norwich and in Defense of Margery Kempe* (1979); Jennifer P. Heimmel, *'God is our Mother': Julian of Norwich and the Medieval Image of Christian Feminine Divinity* (1982).

K

Katherine of Sutton, playwright (d. 1376).

The first recorded woman playwright in England, Katherine of Sutton, abbess of Barking nunnery, in Essex, was probably a noblewoman by birth, and, by virtue of her office as abbess of Barking, a baroness in her own right. Between 1363 and 1376 she rewrote the Easter dramatic offices in order to stimulate more devotion and engagement in the services during this important festival. Her adaptations of the liturgical plays were unusually lively, particularly her *elevatio crucis*, which contained a representation of the harrowing of hell. In her *visitatio sepulchri* the roles of the three Marys were played, not by priests, as was the custom, but by nuns, one of the early instances of medieval women participating in the theatre. Katherine of Sutton's works are said to resemble rather the sophisticated French liturgical drama of the period than its more simplistic English counterpart. The Barking plays were published by Karl Young in 1910 and included in his *Drama of the Medieval Church* (2 vols., 1933). J. B. L. Tolhurst edited the entire Ordinale in the Henry Bradshaw Society Publications (1927–8). *See* Eileen Power, *Medieval English Nunneries* (1922); Nancy Cotton, *Women Playwrights in England c.1363–1750* (1980).

Kavanagh, Julia, novelist and biographer (b. Thurles, County Tipperary, 1824, d. Nice, 28 October 1877).

Julia Kavanagh was the daughter of Morgan Peter Kavanagh (1800–1874), a novelist, poet, and philologist from whom she became estranged when he ascribed his inferior novel *The Hobbies* to their joint authorship in 1857. Her childhood was spent in London and in Paris, where she settled with her parents. Much of her time was devoted to the care of her invalid mother, who became a close companion, particularly after the rift with her father, and with whom she published a volume of fairy-tales, *The Pearl Fountain* (1876). The family returned from Paris to London in 1844. Kavanagh's first notable publication was *The Three Paths* (1848), a book for children. Her first novel was *Madeleine* (1848), which, like much of her early fiction, had a French setting. *Nathalie* (1850), its successor, was admired by Charlotte *Brontë. *Rachel Grey* (1856) was given an English setting and, like many of her novels, centred on a strong, independent woman as its heroine. Other novels include *Adele* (1858), *Beatrice* (1865), *Silvia* (1870), and *John Dorrien* (1875). Kavanagh is possibly better known for a series of biographical volumes about women, *Woman in France during the Eighteenth Century* (1850), *Women of Christianity* (1852), *French Women of Letters* (1862), and *English Women of Letters* (1863), which she wrote to redress what she saw as the omission of women from historical writing, and to highlight their achievements. Her last publication was a collection of short stories, *Forget-me-Nots* (1878). She returned to France towards the end of her life and died at Nice. *See* A. Sergeant (ed.), *Women Novelists of Queen Victoria's Reign* (1897).

Kaye-Smith, Sheila, novelist (b. St Leonard's-on-Sea, Sussex, 1887, d. Northiam, Sussex, 14 January 1956).

Sheila Kaye-Smith was the daughter of Edward Kaye-Smith, a prominent physician and surgeon, and his wife (née de la Condamine). She was educated at home, and then at Hastings and St Leonard's Ladies' College. In 1924 she married the Revd Theodore Penrose Fry, later Sir Penrose Fry, vicar of St Leonard's. In 1929 they converted to Roman Catholicisim. Fry resigned his living and they bought and worked a farm in the Sussex countryside. Sheila Kaye-Smith published her first novel, *The Tramping Methodist*, in 1908. Most of her other early works were historical romances, but in 1916 she established herself with *Sussex Gorse*, which, like most of her subsequent novels, had a Sussex setting. The pronounced regionalism of her novels earned her a comparison with Hardy on the one hand, and an association with the novels debunked by Stella *Gibbons in *Cold Comfort Farm* (1932) on the other. Along with *Sussex Gorse*, her best novels, out of a total of thirty-one, include *Little England* (1918), *Green Apple Harvest* (1920), and *Joanna Godden* (1921). For her admirers, her novels evoke a feeling for landscape and also a feeling for working the land. Her strengths include her study of rural communities, farmers, and their families, and her handling of rural dialects. She has, however, been accused of repetition and of writing too much. Her Sussex, it is alleged, lacks the universality of Wessex and her novels are said to be as regional in interest as they are regional in setting. She was influenced by the novelist W. L. George, who taught her to plan her novels, which helps to explain their at times mechanical and formulaic quality. Katherine *Mansfield commented on her want of curiosity, her reluctance to explore what her characters speak, feel, or think: 'The plot's the thing—and having decided upon it she gets her team together and gives out the parts.' Kaye-Smith was for a time best known for two studies of Jane *Austen, written collaboratively with her friend the novelist Gladys Bertha *Stern, *Talking of Jane Austen* (1943) and *More Talk about Jane Austen* (1950). She wrote three volumes of unconventional autobiography, *Three Ways Home* (1937), about her conversion, *Kitchen-Fugue* (1945), described as an 'informal cookbook-autobiography', and *All the Books of my Life* (1956), organized around her reading at important times in her life. *See* Glen Cavaliero, *The Rural Tradition in the English Novel* (1977); Dorothea Walker, *Sheila Kaye-Smith* (1980); Katherine Mansfield's *Critical Writings*, ed. Clare Hanson (1987).

Keane, 'Molly' (Mary Nesta, also 'M. J. Farrell'), novelist and playwright (b. Ballyrankin, County Kildare, 20 July 1905).

Mary Nesta Skrine, as she was born, was one of the five children of Walter Clarmont Skrine, a member of the Anglo-Irish gentry of County Kildare, and his wife Agnes Shakespeare (Nesta) Higginson, who wrote poetry under the pseudonym **Moira O'Neill**. Her mother was also the model for various distant and powerful matriarchs in Keane's fiction. She was taught at home by her mother and by governesses and went briefly to a boarding school near Dublin. She began to write under the bedclothes when home from school with flu. Her first novel, *The Knight of the Cheerful Countenance*, was published by Mills and Boon in 1928, under the pseudonym M. J. Farrell, a name she took from a pub in order to conceal her identity from her friends in hunting circles. She published several others in succession, *Young Entry* (1928), *Taking Chances* (1929), *Mad Puppetstown* (1931), all sardonic comedies about the decaying country house society of her youth. *Devoted Ladies* (1934) introduced a lesbian theme. *Full House* (1935) dealt with mental illness and *Two Days in Aragon* (1941) confronted the wider political context of Irish life. In 1938 she married Robert Lumley Keane, by whom she had two children. In the same year she published *Spring Meeting*, the first in a series of successful plays written in collaboration with John Perry. *Ducks and Drakes* (1941), *Guardian Angel* (1944), which she wrote alone, and *Treasure Hunt* (1949), directed by John Gielgud and starring Sybil Thorndike, followed. Her husband's death in 1946 as the result of an operation was the prelude for a nearly thirty-year gap in her writing. *Loving without Tears* (1951) and *Treasure Hunt* (1952), a rewriting of her play, brought to an end her first phase of fiction writing. She began to write again in the 1970s with *Good Behaviour* (1981) which was turned down by Collins, her original publisher, because the comedy was too black. André Deutsch published it under her own name and it was short-listed for the Booker Prize. *Time after Time* (1983) followed, and was adapted for television in 1986. The subjects of her later work, including her latest, *Loving and Giving* (1988), are the same as the earlier fiction, the blackly comic, bizarre, class-ridden world of the Anglo-Irish ascendancy, the vanished world of her childhood, presented this time with a more cutting edge. *See* Bridget O'Toole, in *Across a Roaring Hill: The Protestant Imagination in Modern Ireland*, ed. Gerald Dawe and Edna Longley (1985); Mary Chamberlain (ed.), *Writing Lives* (1988); Shusha Guppy, *Looking Back* (1992).

Kelly, Isabella, later Hedgeland, novelist and poet (*c.*1758–*c.*1857).

Isabella Kelly was born in the Scottish Highlands, the daughter of William Fordyce, an army officer and later a courtier, and his wife Elizabeth Fraser. In 1789 she married Colonel Robert Kelly, a feckless cavalry officer. The preface to her *Collection of Poems and Fables*, published by subscription in 1794, referred to 'a child's death and other troubles', and she later said that her poems were 'too personal to please in general'. They nevertheless went into a second edition in 1807, but by that time she had established herself as a productive novelist with William Lane's *Minerva Press. The titles of her first books are indicative of their *Gothic preoccupations: *Madeleine; or The Castle of Montgomery* (1794), *The Abbey of St. Asaph* (1795), and *The Ruins of Avondale Priory* (1796). Most of the available knowledge about her life is deduced from the prefaces to her works. That to *Joscelina; or The Rewards of Benevolence* (1797) claimed she wrote in order to extricate her husband from financial distress and to provide for her children. According to Montague Summers, the novelist M. G. Lewis, author of *The Monk* (1796), fell in love with Kelly's eldest son, and through this connection assisted Isabella in her literary work by introducing her to his publisher John Bell, who published *The Baron's Daughter* in 1802. Mr Kelly later died in Trinidad, leaving her with three children. She married a Mr Hedgeland for a brief period until 'speculation lost his fortune and broke his heart'. According to an application she made to the Royal Literary Fund in 1832, she wrote ten novels as well as pedagogical works. The latter included a French grammar for children (1805), and *Instructive Anecdotes for Youth* (1819), the preface to which states that she was educating her daughters herself at her home in Chelsea. According to Summers she opened a school at Chelsea. One of her daughters also wrote. *See* Montague Summers, *The Gothic Quest* (1938; repr. 1964).

Kelly, Sophia *see under* SHERWOOD, Mary Martha

Kemble, Adelaide *see under* KEMBLE, Fanny

Kemble, Fanny (Frances Anne), afterwards Butler, diarist, poet, and actress (b. London, 27 November 1809, d. London, 15 January 1893).

Born into a theatrical family, Fanny Kemble was the daughter of the actor and manager Charles Kemble and his actress wife Marie Thérèse Kemble. She made her first appearance on the stage at Covent Garden in 1829, playing Juliet to her father's Mercutio and her mother's Lady Capulet, and followed this with a series of theatrical triumphs which cleared the debt from her father's management of Covent Garden and launched her theatrical career. She accompanied her father on a highly successful American tour in the autumn of 1833 and in January 1834 married Pierce Butler, a southern planter. The marriage was not a success, and they divorced in 1848, leaving Butler the custody of their two daughters. Her *Journal of a Residence in America* (1835) joined the ranks of travel literature critical of American institutions, particularly slavery, and extracts from its powerful sequel, *Journal of a Residence on a Georgian Plantation in 1838–9* (1863), were reprinted by supporters of emancipation during the Civil War. Fanny Kemble's other early works included several plays, *Francis the First* (1832), *The Star of Seville* (1837), and a collection of *Plays* translated from Schiller and Dumas (1863). She also published a collection of *Poems* (1844), and a travel book, *A Year of Consolation* (1847), a record of a journey to Italy. She returned briefly to the stage in 1847, and in 1848 inaugurated a series of readings from Shakespeare which she undertook both in England and America for the next twenty years. After her separation from her husband she resumed her maiden name and lived for two decades in Lennox, Massachusetts, and later in Philadelphia near her married daughters. She returned to England in 1877 and continued the writing of her autobiography *Records of a Girlhood*, published in 1878, and its sequels *Records of Later Life* (1882) and *Further Records 1848–83* (1890). These caused some offence in theatrical circles because of their critical picture of theatrical life. A new collection of her poems was published in 1866 and a revised edition in 1883. She also published *Notes upon Some of Shakespeare's Plays* (1882) and a novel, *Far Away and Long Ago* (1889). Fanny Kemble's acting talents and readings earned her a wide circle of admirers. John Wilson, 'Christopher North' of *Blackwood's Magazine*, among others equated her with her aunt Mrs Siddons. Macready declared her 'one of the most remarkable women of the present day' and G. H. Lewes pronounced her readings 'an intellectual delight'. Her sister **Adelaide Kemble,** later **Sartoris** (1816–

79), a singer, published several volumes of short stories. *See* Henry James, *Essays in London and Elsewhere* (1893); Una Pope-Hennessy, *Three English Women in America* (1929); Dorothy Marshall, *Fanny Kemble* (1977); J. C. Furnas, *Fanny Kemble: Leading Lady of the Nineteenth Century Stage* (1982).

Kempe, Anna Eliza *see* BRAY, Anna Eliza

Kempe, Margery, autobiographer and mystic (b. King's Lynn, Norfolk, *c.*1373, d. *c.*1439).

Margery Kempe was the daughter of John Brunham, one-time mayor of Lynn, now King's Lynn, in Norfolk. Around 1393 she married John Kempe, a civic official, also of Lynn. Possibly during the difficult birth of the first of her fourteen children she experienced a vision of Christ and an ensuing spiritual crisis. Eventually she gave up her brewing and milling business and she and her husband swore mutual vows of chastity in order to free her for a somewhat unorthodox religious life. She refused to be enclosed as an anchorite or nun, and instead dressed in white and undertook pilgrimages to the Holy Land, and travelled in England and Europe, flamboyantly endeavouring to enact Christ's teachings in her life. Her fits of hysterical weeping alienated some and she was accused of charlatanry and tried for Lollardy. In 1420 she dictated to two amanuenses a manuscript known as the 'Book of Margery Kempe'. Although she wrote of herself in the third person and for the glory of God, the book presents an honest, direct account of her experiences, both psychological and physical. It has come to be regarded as the first autobiography in English by a woman. The original manuscript has been lost. A portion of it was printed by Wynken de Worde in *A Short Treatyse of Contemplacyon* in 1501. The first full critical edition was published by the Early English Text Society in 1940 (ed. Sanford B. Meech and Hope Emily Allen). A modernized translation was published by W. Butler-Bowden in 1936 (2nd edn. 1954), and by Barry A. Windeatt in 1985. *See The Medieval Mystics of England*, ed. E. Colledge (1962, modernized excerpts); Clarissa W. Atkinson, *Mystic and Pilgrim: The 'Book' and the World of Margery Kempe* (1983); Marion Glasscoe (ed.), *The Medieval Mystical Tradition in England* (1984); Katharina M. Wilson (ed.), *Medieval Women Writers* (1984); Sarah Beckwith, in *Medieval Literature: Criticism, Ideology and History*, ed. David Aers (1986).

Kennedy, Margaret Moore, novelist, playwright, and critic (b. London, 23 April 1896, d. Adderbury, Oxfordshire, 31 July 1967).

Margaret Moore Kennedy was the eldest of the four children of Charles Moore Kennedy, a barrister of Irish extraction, and his wife Elinor Marwood. She was educated at home by governesses, along with her siblings, and then went to Cheltenham Ladies' College. She read history at Somerville College, Oxford, where Dorothy L. *Sayers and Vera *Brittain were contemporaries, and took a second-class honours degree in 1919. By her own account she had written and destroyed five novels and three plays before going up to Oxford. Her first book, however, was a historical study, *A Century of Revolution* (1922), on the impact of the French Revolution in France. Her first novel to be published was *The Ladies of Lyndon* (1923). The following year she published *The Constant Nymph,* the book which established her reputation. Loosely based on the circle surrounding the painter Augustus John, the novel's exploration of the conflict between bohemia and bourgeois society and the price paid for artistic and personal freedom won praise from Arnold Bennett, Thomas Hardy, H. G. Wells, and A. E. Housman, among others, and became a best seller. She co-authored the stage adaptation (1926), which played in both London and New York with Noel Coward and later John Gielgud in the leading role. Four film versions followed. The clash between unconventionality and bourgeois constraints and respectability was a recurrent theme in Kennedy's novels, particularly in *The Game and the Candle* (1926) and *The Oracles* (1955). Another preoccupation was the anatomizing of family relationships, particularly the pain suffered by children through divorce and remarriage. With interruptions from the war and in spite of suffering from Bell's palsy from 1939 onward she produced sixteen novels in all. *The Fool of the Family* (1930) was a sequel to *The Constant Nymph. The Feast* (1950) was a Literary Guild choice in the United States and along with *Lucy Carmichael* (1951) was a UK Book Society choice. *Troy Chimneys* (1953) won the James Tait Black Memorial Prize. As well as the dramatization of *The Constant Nymph* Kennedy wrote several plays, including *Escape Me Never!* (1933) and *Autumn* (with Gregory Ratoff, 1937). She also wrote a study of Jane Austen (1950) and *The Outlaws on Parnassus* (1958), on the art of the novel and its place in contemporary culture. *The Mechanized Muse* (1942) was about screen-writing, in which she was also engaged. In 1925 she married David Davies, a barrister, later Sir David and a county court judge, by whom she had a son and two daughters, one of whom, **Julia Birley**, is also a novelist. Kennedy wrote at home in the manner of nineteenth-century women writers, usually on the drawing-room table or in her bedroom. Her last novel appeared in 1964, the year of her husband's death and three years before her own. *See* Violet Powell, *The Constant Novelist* (1983); Billie Melman, *Women and the Popular Imagination in the Twenties* (1988).

Killigrew, Anne, poet and painter (b. London, 1660, d. London, 16 June 1685).

Anne Killigrew was the daughter of Sir Henry Killigrew, prebendary of Westminster and chaplain to the Duke of York, later James II. She was well educated for her time and sex, and early demonstrated a talent for painting. Through her father's influence she was given the post of Maid of Honour to Mary of Modena, Duchess of York, where one of her companions was Anne *Finch, later Countess of Winchilsea. She died of smallpox when not quite 25. Her father arranged for the posthumous publication of her *Poems* in 1686, prefaced by Dryden's ode 'To the Pious Memory of the Accomplished Young Lady, Mrs. Anne Killigrew, Excellent in the Two Sister Arts of Poesy and Painting'. Dryden particularly admired her two portraits of James II and Queen Mary. Her poems reflect the sombre mood of the court, advocate piety, and reject courtly love. Her conventional style prompted accusations of plagiarism, which she ruefully acknowledged, 'The envious age, only to me alone, | Will not allow what I do write my own', continuing, 'I willingly accept Cassandra's fate, | To speak the truth, although believed too late.' Dryden's ode is highly complimentary:

Art had she none, yet wanted none;
For nature did that want supply,
So rich in treasures of her own,
She might our boasted stores defy:
Such noble vigour did her verse adorn,
That it seem'd borrow'd where 'twas only born.

Her poems were included in **Poems by Eminent Ladies* (1755). *See* Ann Messenger, *His and Hers: Essays in Restoration and Eighteenth-Century Literature* (1986); Elaine Hobby, *Virtue of Necessity: English Women's Writing 1649–1688* (1988).

Kingscote, Adelina Georgina Isabella *see under* NEW WOMAN

Kingsley, Mary (Henrietta), travel writer (b. Islington, London, 13 October 1862, d. Simon's Town, near Cape Town, 3 June 1900.

Mary Kingsley was the eldest child and only daughter of Dr George Henry Kingsley, a medical doctor with an interest in science and travel, and his wife Mary Bailey. The novelists Charles and Henry Kingsley were her uncles, and Mary St Leger Kingsley Harrison (Lucas *Malet) was her first cousin. She had no formal education, but was left to her own devices in the family home at Highgate, with access to her father's library. She developed an interest in natural history, ethnography, and anthropology, and read books of travel. She also cared for her invalid and depressive mother. She was allowed German lessons so that she could translate scientific articles which interested her father. The family moved to Cambridge when her younger brother became a student, and she benefited from wider intellectual association, but remained a shy, reclusive young woman. Virginia *Woolf used her as an example of a daughter's education sacrificed in the interest of her brothers, the 'Arthur's Education Fund' syndrome wittily expounded in *Three Guineas* (1938). Her parents' deaths within six weeks of each other in 1892 released her from domestic duties at the age of 30, and instead of studying medicine, as she had at first intended, she resolved to travel and to pursue her scientific interests. On her first journey to West Africa in 1893 she explored the coast from what is now Sierra Leone to Luanda, and travelled inland along the Congo River. In 1894 she set out again, this time for a year, exploring the interior, travelling in unmapped territories, discovering a new genus of fish, an unknown snake, and a rare lizard, and making the most extensive ethnological field studies of West Africa to date. She learned to trade with rubber and oil, trekked through jungles, canoed down rapids, made the first ascent of Mount Cameroon by the north-east face, and brought home an important collection of insects, shells, plants, reptiles, and fish. On her return she was in demand as a lecturer and writer. Her first travel book, *Travels in West Africa* (1897), a narrative of both her journeys, was an immediate success. The raciness and exuberance of her style, combined with her humour, made it a classic. She wrote passionately of the need for Europeans to understand African peoples and was critical of missionaries and colonialists alike. A second book, *West African Studies* (1897), continued these themes and a third, *The Story of West Africa* (1899), was part of a History of Empire series. She also wrote a memoir of her father, prefixed to his *Notes on Sport and Travel* (1900). She died of a fever, brought on by overwork and declining health, aged 38, at Simon's Town, near Cape Town, South Africa, where she had gone to nurse during the Boer War. *See* S. Gwynn, *The Life of Mary Kingsley* (1933); Katherine Frank, *A Voyager Out: The Life of Mary Kingsley* (1986); Valerie Grosvenor Myer, *A Victorian Lady in Africa: The Story of Mary Kingsley* (1989); Dea Birkett, *Mary Kingsley: Imperial Adventuress* (1992).

Kingsley, Mary St Leger *see* MALET, Lucas

L

'**Lake,** Claude' *see* BLIND, Mathilde

Lamb, Lady Caroline, née Ponsonby, novelist and poet (b. 13 November 1785, d. London, 26 January 1828).

Caroline Lamb was the fourth child and only daughter of Frederick Ponsonby, third Earl of Bessborough, and his wife Lady Henrietta Frances Spencer, the daughter of the first Earl Spencer. As a small child she was so highly strung a doctor advised her parents that formal schooling would be dangerous to her nervous system. Instead she was sent to her aunt, the Duchess of Devonshire, to be brought up with her children. Neuroses and mental instability of varying degrees of severity were to dominate the rest of her life. In 1805 she married William Lamb, later Lord Melbourne and Prime Minister and ten years her senior. Their twenty-year marriage was troubled, loving, disrupted, and eventually terminated. Their only child, born mentally retarded, died in 1836 at the age of 29. In 1812 Caroline Lamb met Lord Byron, with whom she fell passionately in love, confiding to her diary the now famous phrase that he was 'mad, bad and dangerous to know'. Her violent response to Byron's ending of their brief relationship in 1813 led her husband to seek a formal separation, but a reconciliation took place at the last minute. In 1816 Lady Caroline published her first novel, *Glenarvon*, a *roman à clef* written secretly in the middle of the night, and containing thinly disguised portraits of Byron and other members of London society. Byron's response, in a letter to the poet Thomas Moore, was that 'if the authoress had written the truth ... the romance would not only have been more romantic but more entertaining. As for the likeness, the picture can't be good. I did not sit long enough.' On hearing that Byron had laughed at her novel, Lamb ceremoniously burned all his letters. The novel was translated into Italian the following year and reprinted as late as 1865 as *The Fatal Passion. A New Canto* was written to Byron's *Don Juan* and published anonymously in 1819. Her next novel, the realistic *Graham Hamilton* (1822), was written after she had received the advice to 'write a book which will offend nobody; women cannot afford to shock'. Her third novel and her own favourite, the exotic *Ada Reis* (1823), incorporated a South American setting and a sojourn in Hades. In 1824 she accidentally met Byron's funeral procession on its way to Newstead, the shock of which was so unsettling it led eventually to William Lamb's decision to separate permanently from her. She lived for the remainder of her life at Brocket, the Lambs' country estate in Hertfordshire, and died of dropsy at the age of 42, at Melbourne House, Whitehall, with her husband at her bedside. Vain, excitable, clever, and generous, Caroline Lamb featured in the novels of two of her contemporaries, Bulwer-Lytton and Disraeli. Sydney Owenson, Lady *Morgan, was a friend. She wrote poetry for various *annuals, some of which was set to music by Isaac Nathan, who collected her *Fugitive Pieces and Reminiscences of Lord Byron* together with some of her poetry, letters, and recollections (1829). *See* Elizabeth Jenkins, *Lady Caroline Lamb* (1932); Lord David Cecil, *The Young Melbourne* (1939; repr. 1948); Henry Blyth, *Caro: The Fatal Passion: The Life of Lady Caroline Lamb* (1972).

Lamb, Mary Ann, prose writer (b. the Temple, London, 3 December 1764, d. St John's Wood, London, 20 May 1847).

The second of seven children of John Lamb, a lawyer's clerk and servant, and Elizabeth Field, the daughter of a domestic servant, Mary Ann Lamb went to a day school in Fetter Lane, near her home, along with her younger brother Charles. After the death of Samuel Salt, their father's employer, the family moved to Holborn, where Mary and Charles supported their ageing mother and increasingly senile father, Mary by needlework and Charles with a clerkship in the East India Company. On 22 September 1796, while worn down by overwork, Mary became irritated with a young apprentice and pursued her round the room with a knife. Her mother intervened and was accidentally stabbed to death. A verdict of temporary insanity was given by the court and Mary was put into her brother's custody rather than being sent to a lunatic asylum. There was a family history of mental instability, and this incident triggered off periods of insanity which occurred sporadically for the rest of Mary Lamb's life. Her brother devoted himself selflessly to her care, and the close relationship between brother and sister was remarked upon by many of their contemporaries. 'I am wedded, Coleridge, to the fortunes of my sister and my poor old father,' Charles wrote to his close friend. Their father died shortly after the tragic incident and brother and sister set up home together. They moved frequently, as Mary's condition made it difficult to remain for long in any lodgings. In 1807, at the suggestion of William Godwin, who had established himself as a publisher of children's books, Mary and Charles published *Tales from Shakespeare*, Mary undertaking the major portion of the work with the comedies, and Charles the tragedies. Mary's name did not appear on the publication. The work was constantly reprinted throughout the century and was translated into many languages. In 1809 she published *Mrs. Leicester's School; or The History of Several Young Ladies*, a collection of short stories, with Charles contributing three of the ten. Several have autobiographical elements. The same year they jointly published *Poetry for Children*, again with Godwin, hoping to capitalize on the popularity of children's verse begun by Isaac Watts and others. Charles, meanwhile, was making his literary reputation, writing for the *London Magazine* under the pseudonym Elia. The portrait of Bridget Elia in 'Mackery End in Hertfordshire' was his affectionate commemoration of his sister. The couple adopted a young orphan, Emma Isola, whom they brought into their home and educated. She later married the publisher Edward Moxon. Mary's attacks became more frequent, as did her consequent absences from home. Lamb retired from the East India House in 1825 on receipt of a pension, and devoted himself full time to his writing. The removals continued, from Pentonville, to Holborn, the Temple, Covent Garden, Islington, Enfield, and eventually to Edmonton as Mary required increased nursing care. Charles died in 1834, and Mary survived him for thirteen years. She wrote little after *Poetry for Children*, apart from some verses in 1828. Her essay 'On Needlework' in the *British Ladies' Magazine* (1815) showed a shrewd perception of the condition of working women. In her periods of lucidity Mary Lamb endeared herself to many literary associates and friends, who paid tribute to her acuity and originality. *The Letters of Charles and Mary Lamb* have been edited by E. W. Marrs (1975–8). *See also* A. Gilchrist, *Mary Lamb: A Biography* (1883); W. C. Hazlitt, *The Lambs: Their Lives, their Friends and their Correspondence* (1897); H. R. Ashton, *I had a Sister* (1937); E. C. Ross, *The Ordeal of Bridget Elia* (1940); Jane Aaron, in *Romanticism and Feminism*, ed. Anne K. Mellor (1988); Jane Aaron, *A Double Singleness: Gender and the Writings of Charles and Mary Lamb* (1991).

Lamb, Mary Montgomerie *see* FANE, Violet

Landon, Laetitia Elizabeth (L.E.L.), poet (b. Chelsea, London, 14 August 1802, d. Cape Coast Castle (now Ghana), 15 October 1838).

The eldest of the three children of John Landon, a partner in an army agency, and Catherine Jane Bishop, Laetitia Landon was educated in a school in Chelsea attended later by Mary Russell *Mitford and also by Lady Caroline *Lamb. The family was said to have lost its money in the South Sea Bubble fiasco and subsequent generations, including Laetitia's grandfather, had been mainly clergymen. When still a child Landon met William Jerdan, the editor of the *Literary Gazette*, who was struck by her precocity and encouraged her to write poetry. Her first poem, 'Rome', was published in the *Gazette* in 1820, when she was only 18, under the signature 'L'. She was soon reviewing for Jerdan as well as publishing a stream of volumes of poetry, including *The Fate of Adelaide* (1821), *The Improvisatrice* (1824), *The Troubadour* (1825), *The Golden Violet* (1827), *The Venetian Bracelet* (1828), and *The Vow of the Peacock* (1835). *Traits and Trials of Early Life* (1836), stories with poems interspersed, is supposedly autobiographical. She was a frequent contributor to gift books and *annuals, and edited *Fisher's Drawing-Room Scrap Book* (1832–9), *Heath's Book of Beauty* (1833), and the *New Juvenile Keepsake* (1838). She also contributed a metrical version of the Odes to Isabel Hill's important translation of Madame de Staël's **Corinne* (1833). Landon wrote several novels, including *Romance and Reality* (1831), *Francesca Carrara* (1834), *Ethel Churchill* (1837), a historical novel generally acknowledged to be her best, and *Duty and Inclination* (1838). At her peak she earned an estimated £2,500 a year, much of which went to support her family, impoverished by her father's speculations in agricultural schemes. Her own name was frequently the subject of scandal in literary circles, occasioned partly by her imprudent behaviour and also by gossip encouraged by William Maginn, the dissolute editor of *Fraser's Magazine*, with whom she had a liaison. As a result, her engagement to John Forster, a rising man of letters and later the biographer of Dickens, was broken and shortly after, in July 1838, she married George Maclean, newly appointed Governor of Cape Coast Castle, who was rumoured to have a wife living in Africa. On 15 October she was discovered lying in her room with an empty bottle of prussic acid in her hand. Whether the cause of death was accidental (she had taken the drug for many years to control muscular spasms in her hand) or suicide was never satisfactorily resolved. *The Zenana and Other Poems*, mainly collected from annuals, appeared after her death in 1839 and also *Lady Anne Granard* (1842), a novel. Much anthologized, 'L.E.L.', as she signed herself, was one of the most popular women poets of the nineteenth century. Collected editions of her works appeared regularly after her death, one as late as 1873, edited by William Bell Scott. Her poetry was fashionable in its themes and notable more for its quantity, fluency, and sentiment than for its quality. *See* S. L. Blanchard, *Life and Literary Remains of L.E.L.* (1841); H. Ashton, *Letty Landon* (1951); Kathleen Hickok, *Representations of Women: Nineteenth-Century British Women's Poetry* (1984); Angela Leighton, *Victorian Women Poets: Writing against the Heart* (1992).

Lanyer, or Lanier, Aemilia, poet (b. London, 1569, d. London, April 1645).

Aemilia Lanyer was one of two daughters of Baptist Bassano, an Italian musician at the English court, and his common-law wife Margaret Johnson. Her father died when she was 7 and her mother in 1587. She was for a time the mistress of Henry Carey, first Lord Hunsden (1524?–1596), Lord Chamberlain to *Elizabeth I and forty-five years her senior. When she became pregnant by him in 1592 she was hastily married to Captain Alfonso Lanyer, whose family had served as court musicians for several generations. Their financially precarious life possibly led Lanyer to publish her one volume of poems, *Salve Deus Rex Judaeorum* ('Hail God King of the Jews') in 1611. It contained a central poem on Christ's passion accompanied by shorter poems addressed to noble ladies, possibly to attract patrons, and a 200–line poem, 'The Description of Cooke-ham', one of the earliest 'country house' poems. The tone of the poems is strongly feminist, particularly an address to 'the Vertuous Reader'. At the same time her feminism is informed by her belief in women's pivotal importance in Christianity. She stressed women's spirituality, chastity, and virtue, in other words, the traditional feminine attributes, but also their learning, knowledge, and wisdom. According to Elaine Beilin, Lanyer was 'the first woman seriously and systematically to write epideictic poetry, the poetry of praise about women'. Lanyer's last years were spent in near poverty, which Alfonso Lanyer's legacy of a licence for the weighing of hay and straw in London failed to alleviate. She opened a school in St Giles-in-the-Fields between 1617 and 1618, and spent much time in lawsuits. Much of the information about her derives from the 'casebooks' of Simon Forman, the astrologer, whom she consulted in 1597. A. L. Rowse's allegation that she was the 'Dark Lady' of Shakespeare's sonnets is generally agreed to be without foundation. *See The Poems of Shakespeare's Dark Lady*, ed. A. L. Rowse (1978); Barbara Lewalski, in *Silent but for the Word: Tudor Women as Patrons, Translators and Writers of Religious Works*, ed. Margaret Hannay (1985); Elaine V. Beilin, *Redeeming Eve: Women Writers of the English Renaissance* (1987); Tina Krontiris, *Oppositional Voices: Women as Writers and Translators in the English Renaissance* (1992).

Lawless, the Honourable Emily, novelist and poet (b. County Kildare, 17 June 1845, d. Gomshall, Surrey, 19 October 1913).

The Honourable Emily Lawless was the eldest of the eight children of Edward Lawless, third Baron Cloncurry, and his wife Elizabeth Kirwan, a famous society beauty. Despite their privileged position as members of the Anglo-Irish gentry tragedy dogged the family. Her father committed suicide when Emily was 14 and two of her sisters followed suit. She led a sheltered, almost reclusive life, most of it spent on the family's estates, her mother's in County Galway and her father's in County Kildare, where, according to her *Who's Who* entry, her recreations were 'dredging, mothing, gardening and geologizing'. Her novels were mainly studies of Irish peasant life, as in *Hurrish* (1886), set in County Clare in the 1870s, prior to the agitation for Home Rule. It was dedicated to her friend Margaret *Oliphant and won praise from Gladstone for shedding light on the Irish problem. *Major Lawrence FLS* (1887) was the story of an English officer returned from India and *With Essex in Ireland* (1890), a documentary-style novel of the kind popularized by Anne *Manning, was a fictionalized 'account' by a private secretary of Essex's 1599 expedition which initially was thought to be a genuine document. *Grania* (1892), set on the Island of Aran, was Lawless's most popular novel and brought her to the attention of Mrs Humphry *Ward, who became a close friend. Other novels included *Maelcho* (1894), the story of the Desmond rebellion of 1579, and *The Race of Castlebar* (1913), about a threatened French invasion, written in collaboration with Shan F. Bullock, who completed the book after her death. Lawless published several collections of poems, many with Irish themes, including her best known, *With the Wild Geese* (1892), *The Point of View* (1909), poems and prose, and *The Inalienable Heritage* (1914), published posthumously. She wrote a history of Ireland (1887) and a biography of her countrywoman and fellow novelist Maria *Edgeworth (1904) in the English Men of Letters series. She left Ireland in her later years, disenchanted, it was said, with the turn taken by contemporary Irish politics, and with her mental and physical health deteriorating. She never married and died in Surrey at the age of 68. *See* the introd. to her *Collected Poems*, ed. Padraic Fallon (1965).

Lead, Jane, mystic, poet, and autobiographer (b. Norfolk, 1623 or 1624, d. 19 August 1704).

Jane Lead was the daughter of Schildknap Ward, a member of an established Norfolk family. Her education was typical for one of her sex and class, centring on domestic accomplishments and basic literacy. When she was 15 she experienced a vision in the midst of Christmas festivities, an experience which influenced the later direction of her life. She spent some time among radical religious sects in Cromwellian London and after refusing several suitors selected by her parents married William Lead, a distant relation six years her senior. They had four daughters. Lead's death in 1670 left her a widow at 46 and released to follow her chosen 'life of Spiritual Virginity'. She was greatly influenced by the German idealist philosopher and Protestant theologian Jacob Boehme (1575–1624), and joined a congregation organized by Dr John Pordage, one of his Anglican disciples. In 1681, at the age of 57, she published her first book, *The Heavenly Cloud now Breaking*, a spiritual guide, and two years later, in 1683, a commentary on the Apocalypse, *The Revelation of Revelations*, followed by *The Enochian Walks with God* (1694). Her journal, begun in 1670 and continued up to 1686, was published in the form of a spiritual autobiography, *A Fountain of Gardens*, in four volumes (1697–1701). A series of other works followed, all of them risking prosecution under the stringent laws against sectarian publications after the Restoration. Jane Lead's work was better known on the Continent, particularly in Germany and The Netherlands, than in England. When she became blind at the age of 71 she was assisted by Dr Francis Lee, a disciple and former Oxford don, who later married her widowed daughter Barbara. Lee acted as her editor and secretary and helped her to form a congregation known as the Philadelphian Society, philosophically based in Boehme's ideas. Her *Message to the Philadelphian Society* (1696) was directed to the group. Jane Lead wrote in a combination of prose and poetry. Her style was at times ungrammatical and her imagery elaborate. Her writings prefigured the self-defining and confessional mode recognizable in the work of the English Romantics. She spent her last years in near poverty, helped by a German sympathizer. She died in an almshouse at the age of 80. The manuscript of Francis Lee's 'The Last Hours of Jane Lead, by an Eye and Ear Witness' is in Dr Williams' Library, London. *See* articles by Catherine F. Smith in *Shakespeare's Sisters: Feminist Essays on Women Poets* ed. Sandra Gilbert and Susan Gubar (1979); in *Poetic Prophecy in Western Literature*, ed. Jan Wojcik and Raymond-Jean Frontain (1984); and in *Virginia Woolf and Bloomsbury: A Centenary Celebration*, ed. Jane Marcus (1987).

Leapor, Mary, poet (b. Marston St Lawrence, Northamptonshire, 26 February 1722, d. Brackley, Northamptonshire, 12 November 1746).

Mary Leapor's father Philip was a gardener on the estate of Sir John Blencowe, a judge. He later moved to Brackley, where he set up his own nursery and continued to work on local estates. Mary had no formal education but learned to read and write at an early age, although her mother Anne discouraged her early efforts to write poetry. These were largely imitations of Dryden and Pope, whose works she possessed. After her mother's death in 1742 she acted as her father's housekeeper and continued her reading and writing. She was employed for a time as a cook-maid in a nearby great house where, according to legend, she wrote 'while the jack was standing still and the meat scorching'. Her poetry attained some celebrity in Northamptonshire and came to the attention of Bridget Fremantle, the daughter of a former vicar, who sought to encourage what she perceived to be Leapor's very considerable talents. She organized local worthies in raising a subscription and encouraged Leapor to send a play and a sample of her poetry to London to obtain advice on publication. Leapor was made uneasy by this process, although her patron appears to have acted tactfully and with genuine admiration for her work. She died suddenly of measles before any plans for publication could reach fruition, expressing the wish before she died that her poems should be published for her father's benefit after her death. The subscribers were organized and *Poems upon Several Occasions* was published in 1748, with an address 'To the Reader' by Fremantle. One of her poems had been published previously in the *London Magazine* in January 1747, and the volume was noticed in the *Monthly Review*. Samuel Richardson became interested in Leapor and with Isaac Hawkins Browne printed and edited a new volume of *Poems* containing a memoir by Bridget Fremantle in 1751. Leapor's subscribers and supporters included Mary *Delany, Elizabeth *Montagu, Colley Cibber, Stephen Duck, the farm labourer poet, and Christopher Smart, who published one of her poems in the *Midwife* (1750). The *Monthly Review* gave the second volume a long notice, the *London Magazine* reprinted several poems, John Duncombe praised her in *The *Feminiad* (1754), and a selection of her work was included in **Poems by Eminent Ladies* (1755). The strong influence of Pope is apparent in all of Leapor's verse. *See* Donna Landry, *The Muses of Resistance: Laboring-Class Women's Poetry in Britain, 1739–1796* (1990); Richard Greene, *Mary Leapor: A Study in Eighteenth Century Women's Poetry* (1993).

Lee, Harriet, novelist and playwright (b. London, 1757, d. Clifton, near Bristol, 1 August 1851).

Harriet Lee was the daughter of John Lee, an actor, and the sister of Sophia *Lee, also a novelist and dramatist. Their mother, an actress, died early, and after their father's death in 1781 the family moved to Bath, where Sophia set up a girls' school, assisted by Harriet. In 1786 Harriet published her first novel, *The Errors of Innocence* (1786), epistolary in form and in five volumes, which criticized novelists' conceptions of female chastity, vulnerability, and sensibility. She followed this in 1787 with a comedy, *The New Peerage*, performed nine times at Drury Lane, and by *Clara Lennox* (1797), a two-volume novel which was translated into French. Her major and best- known work was *The Canterbury Tales* (1797–1805), a series of twelve stories in five volumes related by travellers thrown together by an accident. Sophia Lee contributed two of the stories but Harriet's major contribution is generally regarded as superior. One of her stories, 'Kruitzner', greatly influenced Byron, who dramatized it as *Werner* (1823), acknowledging his indebtedness to her in the preface. Lee's own dramatization of the story was *The Three Strangers*, performed at Covent Garden in 1825 and published in 1826. In 1798 she published a three-act play, *The Mysterious Marriage; or The Heirship of Rosalva*, which was never performed. William Godwin, then the recent widower of Mary *Wollstonecraft, proposed marriage to her in 1798, but she declined. She remained unmarried for the rest of her life, dying at the age of 94, and surviving her sister by 26 years. *See* Montague Summers, *The Gothic Quest* (1938; repr. 1964); Jane Spencer, *The Rise of the Woman Novelist: From Aphra Behn to Jane Austen* (1986).

'Lee, Holme' (Harriet Parr), novelist (b. York, 31 January 1828, d. Shanklin, Isle of Wight, 18 February 1900).

Holme Lee was the daughter of William Parr, a traveller in silks, satins, and other luxury goods, and his wife Mary Grandage. She was educated in York and from an early age claimed to regard literature as a profession. Her first novel, *Maude Talbot* (1854), a story of mill life with some sensational elements in the plot, was published under the pseudonym Holme Lee. The second, *Gilbert Massinger* (1855), was originally sent to Dickens, who was impressed by it but pronounced it too long for *Household Words*. It was subsequently translated into Italian (1869). *Thorney Hall* (1855), her next work, was translated into French. Parr published over thirty novels between 1854 and 1882 under her pseudonym, helped by the patronage of Charles Edward Mudie, proprietor of the famous circulating library, who approved of the moral tone and also the sentimentality of her fiction. Other titles included *Kathie Brand* (1856), *Against Wind and Tide* (1859), *Annie Warleigh's Fortunes* (1863), *Her Title of Honour* (1871), *Straightforward* (1878), and *A Poor Squire* (1882). Her most substantial work was a life of Joan of Arc (1866), published under her own name. She also published a collection of *Legends from Fairyland* (1860), and several children's stories. She never married and died at Shanklin, on the Isle of Wight, at the age of 72.

Lee, Sophia, novelist and playwright (b. London, 1750, d. Clifton, near Bristol, 13 March 1824).

Sophia Lee was one of six children of John Lee, an actor manager, and his wife, also an actress. Her younger sister *Harriet, with whom she collaborated, was also a novelist and playwright. Her mother died when the children were young and Sophia took her place, looking after her younger siblings while still managing to write a three-act opera, *The Chapter of Accidents.* On advice she expanded it into a five-act comedy, performed with great success at the Haymarket in August 1780, and published the same year. It went into several editions the following year, as well as French and German translations, and remained a popular production for several seasons at Drury Lane and Covent Garden. After her father's death in 1781 Sophia used the proceeds of *A Chapter of Accidents* to establish a girls' school at Bath, assisted by Harriet, which also became a home for their sisters. In 1785 she published *The Recess,* a three-volume historical novel based on the supposed twin daughters of Mary Queen of Scots, born of a secret marriage. The novel's underlining of women's 'lost' lives or invisibility in history, its treatment of madness and oppression, and its use of Gothic conventions have attracted the attention of contemporary critics who link it to better known *Gothic novels by Ann *Radcliffe, who very much approved of it, and others. It went through several editions and was translated into French and Portuguese. Sophia Lee also published *A Hermit's Tale* (1787), a long ballad. Her blank-verse tragedy *Almeyda, Queen of Grenada* was produced at Drury Lane in April 1796, with a cast which included Sarah Siddons and John Philip and Charles Kemble, but it ran for only four nights. She also wrote the initial frame story and two of the twelve tales in Harriet Lee's collection *The Canterbury Tales* (1797–1805). In 1803 she gave up her school and the following year published *The Life of a Lover,* a six-volume semi-autobiographical epistolary novel. A comedy, *The Assignation,* produced at Drury Lane in 1807 was not a success. Her last work was a three-volume novel, *Ormond; or The Debauchee* (1810). After leaving Bath she lived for a while near Tintern Abbey in Monmouthshire and later settled at Clifton, near Bristol, where she died at the age of 74. *See* Montague Summers, *The Gothic Quest* (1938; repr. 1964); Jane Spencer, *The Rise of the Woman Novelist: From Aphra Behn to Jane Austen* (1986).

'**Lee,** Vernon' (Violet Paget), novelist and critic (b. Château St Léonard, near Boulogne, 14 October 1856, d. Il Palmerino, San Gervasio, Florence, 13 February 1935).

Vernon Lee's father Henry Ferguson Paget was an Anglicized Polish *émigre* who took part in the Warsaw insurrection of 1848 and was forced to flee the country. He adopted the name Paget from his first wife. He became tutor to Eugene Lee-Hamilton (1845–1907), a chronic invalid and later a minor poet, and in 1855 married the boy's widowed mother Matilda Lee-Hamilton, née Adams. Violet Paget was the only child of this marriage and her half-brother became an important intellectual influence in her early years. She adopted part of his name in her pseudonym, anticipating that she would only be taken seriously if she wrote as a man. As a child she travelled widely in Europe and in 1880, at the age of 24, published her best-known book, *Studies of the Eighteenth Century in Italy*. She made her first visit to England in 1881, when she was painted memorably by John Singer Sargent. She published a number of travel books, including *Genius Loci* (1899), *The Spirit of Rome* (1906), and *The Sentimental Traveller*, which were much admired by Aldous Huxley. She also wrote novels, which ranged from *Miss Brown* (1884), a satire on aestheticism, which Henry James pronounced 'a deplorable mistake', to historical fiction including *Ottilie* (1883), *Penelope Brandling* (1903), and *Louis Norbert* (1914). Vernon Lee made a significant contribution to the study of aesthetics. *The Beautiful* (1913) explored the psychological effects of beauty, and *The Handling of Words* (1923) applied her ideas to literary texts. Her impact on other writers has yet to be acknowledged. The novelist and critic Maurice Baring (1874–1945) pronounced her 'by far the cleverest person I ever met'. Lee's fervent pacifism, powerfully represented in *Satan the Waster* (1920), won her enemies during the First World War. *See* Peter Gunn, *Vernon Lee: Violet Paget 1856–1935* (1964); Burdett Gardner, *The Lesbian Imagination: Victorian Style* (1987).

Lafanu, Alicia (1753–1817), Alicia (1795–1826), and Elizabeth *see under* SHERIDAN, Frances

Lehmann, Rosamond (Nina), novelist (b. Bourne End, Buckinghamshire, 3 February 1901, d. London, 14 March 1990).

Rosamond Lehmann was the second daughter of Rudolph Chambers Lehmann, sportsman, barrister, one-time Liberal MP, and a long-serving contributor to *Punch*, and his American wife Alice Marie Davis. Her brother John (1907–87) was a poet, editor, and publisher and one of her sisters, Beatrix, was an actress. The children grew up at Fieldhead, the family home in the Thames Valley. She wrote poetry as a child, published a poem in the *Cornhill Magazine* when she was 16, and won a scholarship to Girton College Cambridge, in 1919. She married Leslie Runciman in 1922, and in 1927 published her first novel, *Dusty Answer*, about a young girl's development from childhood to maturity. It was an immediate success and identified one of her major preoccupations and also one of her strengths as a writer, the articulation of the complex psychology of young women. The novel's frank treatment of female sexuality gave it a *succès de scandale* and it became something of a cult book in the inter-war period. *A Note in Music* (1930), which followed, also created a stir, this time because of its treatment of homosexuality. Her first marriage ended in divorce and in 1928 she married the painter Wogan Philipps, by whom she had a son and a daughter. *Invitation to the Waltz* (1932), considered by some to be her best novel, returned to the subject of a young girl's sudden awakening to adult perceptions. *The Weather in the Streets* (1936) took the same characters several years on, to a failed marriage, adultery, and an abortion. *The Ballad and the Source* (1944), her most ambitious novel and the most elaborate in structure, was the story of three generations of women, much of which is presented through the consciousness of a young girl. The same characters reappeared in a much later sequel, *The Sea-Grape Tree* (1976). *The Echoing Grove* (1953) was technically her most intricate novel, dealing with the relationships of two sisters and the man who is the husband of one and the lover of the other. Lehmann published a collection of stories, *The Gipsy's Baby* (1946). Her only play, *No More Music*, was produced in London in 1939 with her sister Beatrix in the lead. She undertook a translation of Jacques Lemarchand's *Geneviève* in 1947, which won the Denyse Clairouin Prize in 1948, and of Jean Cocteau's *Les Enfants terribles* (1955). Her second marriage ended in 1942. She had a love affair with the poet C. Day Lewis which came to an end after nine years, and in 1958 suffered an acute loss in the death of her daughter from polio. Her subsequent spiritual experiences and her 'personal discovery' that 'death does not extinguish life' led to *The Swan in the Evening: Fragments of an Inner Life* (1967) and *Letters from our Daughters* (1972), written with Cynthia Sandys and published by the College of Psychic Studies. *Rosamond Lehmann's Album* (1985) outlined a further novel sequence which was never completed. Lehmann was for a time president of the English Centre of PEN and an international vice-president. She was also a member of the council of the Society of Authors and a co-director of her brother's publishing firm. She was appointed CBE in 1982. *See* John Lehmann, *The Whispering Gallery* (1951) and *I am my Brother* (1960); Diana E. LeStourgeon, *Rosamond Lehmann* (1965); Sydney Janet Kaplan, *Feminine Consciousness in the Modern British Novel* (1975); Gillian Tindall, *Rosamond Lehmann: An Appreciation* (1985); Mary Chamberlain (ed.) *Writing Lives* (1988); Ruth Siegel, *Rosamond Lehmann: A Thirties Writer* (1989); Judy Simons, *Rosamond Lehmann* (1992); Shusha Guppy, *Looking Back* (1992).

Leigh Smith, Barbara *see* BODICHON, Barbara

L. E. L. *see* LANDON, Laetitia Elizabeth

Lennox, Charlotte, novelist, playwright and poet (b. Gibraltar(?) 1729(?), d. London, 4 January 1804).

Charlotte Lennox was the daughter of James Ramsay an army officer who served in a regiment in Gibraltar, where she was probably born, and near Albany, New York, where she spent some of her childhood. Her father died when she was about 15 and she was sent back to England to be looked after by an aunt who turned out to be senile or insane, leaving her virtually without support. She was brought to the attention of the Countess of Rockingham and of her sister Lady Isabella Finch, who became the dedicatee of her *Poems on Several Occasions* (1747). In the same year she married Alexander Lennox, a ne'er-do-well who was said to have been employed by the printer William Strahan. They eventually had two children but Charlotte was always the breadwinner and the family relied almost entirely on her exertions. She had a brief and unsuccessful career on the stage between 1748 and 1750. A literary career seemed a better prospect, particularly as she had begun to assemble a group of powerful supporters, including Dr Johnson, who hosted a much publicized party to celebrate the publication of her first novel, *The Life of Harriot Stuart* (1750), at which she was crowned with laurel. Through Johnson she met Samuel Richardson, and they together organized the publication of her next and most popular novel, *The Female Quixote* (1752), a satire on the reading of romances in which the heroine's world is constructed from French fiction of the previous century. The novel was reviewed enthusiastically by Fielding, who joined her circle of admirers, as did John Boyle, Earl of Orrery. She undertook a series of French translations, including the memoirs of the Duke de Sully, the Countess of Berci, and Madame de Maintenon, as well as a three-volume work on Shakespeare's source materials, *Shakespear Illustrated* (1753–4). Johnson was tireless in his support, writing dedications, reviewing her work, and creating publicity. He cited her in the entry on 'Talent' in his *Dictionary*. Another novel, *Henrietta*, published in 1758, formed the basis of a comedy, *The Sister*, performed once at Covent Garden in 1769, with an epilogue by Goldsmith. Despite the failure it was translated into German in 1776 and, according to the *DNB*, Sir John Burgoyne stole three characters from it for his successful play *The Heiress* (1786). Lennox edited eleven numbers of the monthly *Lady's Museum* (1760–1), contributing most of its contents, including a novel, *Sophia*, on the sense and sensibility theme, published separately in 1762. In financial terms, translations, journalism, and novels meant drudgery with only meagre rewards. The success of a heavily subscribed volume of poetry or a theatrical triumph eluded her. The Duchess of *Newcastle secured her husband a post in the customs office and a London flat, but she continued to write of her great 'distress'. In 1775 her *Old City Manners*, based on *Eastward Hoe* by Chapman, Marston, and Jonson, was produced at Drury Lane by Garrick and secured a long run together with a benefit. Her last novel, the epistolary

Euphemia, was published in 1790. Like her first, *Harriot Stuart*, it drew on her American childhood for some of its scenes. Although *The Female Quixote* was an undoubted success, Charlotte failed to capitalize on it, in part, it was alleged, due to her outspoken remarks and her bad manners. *Harriot Stuart* contained a satirical portrait of Lady Isabella Finch, her patron. Stories of her chaotic household, her tactlessness, and her lack of personal cleanliness proliferated, as did supposedly consequent refusals of patronage by eminent literary and titled ladies. Mrs *Piozzi once remarked that 'tho her books are generally approved, nobody likes her'. Johnson's plans for a collected edition of her works did not materialize. His death in 1784 was a personal blow, coming as it did after that of her 18–year-old daughter. Her son George was dispatched to America after she and her husband separated in 1792. Her reputation took an upturn when the publication of Boswell's *Life of Johnson* in 1791 revealed that he had ranked her above Elizabeth *Carter, Hannah *More, and Fanny *Burney, but it brought no financial relief. An application on her behalf to the newly established Royal Literary Fund proved successful. She died, after a hard-working life as a professional woman of letters, in Dean's Yard, Westminster, in 1804. *See* M. R. Small, *Charlotte Lennox: An Eighteenth Century Lady of Letters* (1935); Patricia Meyer Spacks, in *Fetter'd or Free? British Women Novelists 1670–1815*, ed. Mary Anne Schofield and Cecilia Macheski (1986); Janet Todd, *The Sign of Angellica: Women, Writing and Fiction, 1660–1800* (1989); Katherine Sobba Green, *The Courtship Novel 1740–1820: A Feminised Genre* (1991).

Lessing, Doris (May) ('Jane Somers'), novelist, short story writer, and playwright (b. Kermanshah, Iran, 22 October 1919).

Born in what was then known as Persia, Doris Lessing is the daughter of Captain Alfred Cook Tayler, a bank manager and First World War amputee, and his wife Emily Maude McVeagh. When she was 5 the family moved to a remote farm in Rhodesia, where she had a solitary childhood and first experienced physical freedom. She also first observed racial inequality and the blinkered perspectives of middle-class whites in Africa. At 7 she was sent to a convent school in Salisbury, which she hated. Partly to anger her ambitious mother she left school at 14 and worked as an *au pair* and then as a telephone operator. She wrote two bad novels (her own assessment), which remained unpublished, and at 19 married Frank Charles Wisdom, a civil servant, by whom she had a son and a daughter. They divorced in 1943 and in 1945 she married Gottfried Anton Nicholas Lessing, a German-Jewish refugee who shared her communist sympathies. She worked as a secretary for the Rhodesian government and engaged in radical politics through a Marxist group who were fighting for black liberation. She left Lessing in 1949 and, taking their son, moved to London. Her first book, *The Grass is Singing* (1950), about the relationship of a white farmer's wife and her black servant, drew on her African childhood and her observations of black and white relations and of sexual conflict. Two collections of short stories, *This was the Old Chief's Country* (1951) and *Five: Short Novels* (1953), which won the Somerset Maugham Award, also reflected her African experience. The 'Children of Violence' quintet which followed (*Martha Quest* (1952), *A Proper Marriage* (1954), *A Ripple from the Storm* (1958), *Landlocked* (1965), *The Four-Gated City* (1969)) has an autobiographical foundation, taking the heroine from an African childhood to post-war England, challenging her left-wing politics and ending apocalyptically in AD 2000. But it was her experimental novel *The Golden Notebook* (1962) with its woman writer protagonist that brought her to prominence, both as a major innovative writer of fiction and as a figure in the women's movement. Her heroine Anna Wulf attempts to control her fragmented life by writing variously of her experiences in a series of notebooks, in the fifth of which, the 'golden', the barriers which she has set up between different aspects of her life break down, to make way for new meanings and configurations. Later novels, *Briefing for a Descent into Hell* (1971), *The Summer before the Dark* (1973), and *Memoirs of a Survivor* (1975), further explore mental breakdown, emotional crisis, and the breakdown of society. In 1979 Lessing began a new fictional sequence, *Canopus in Argus: Archives* (5 vols., 1979–83), which broke away dramatically from her previous work, and engaged in anti-realist, 'speculative' fiction or fantasy to create a fictional universe with epic and mythic events. In 1983, under the pseudonym 'Jane Somers', she published *The Diary of a Good Neighbour* and *If the Old Could . . .*, about a fashion magazine editor and an old woman, which were reprinted under her own name in 1984. *The Good Terrorist* (1985), which won the W. H. Smith Literary Award, questions revolutionary idealism, and *The Fifth Child* (1988) the ideology of the family. Lessing's fiction is concerned with left-wing politics, with sexual conflict, with the position of women, and with the dangers of the domination of technology, concerns which are also reflected in her *Collected African Stories* (1973) and her *Collected Stories* (1978). Latterly she has become interested in Sufi thought. She has published two plays, *Each to his Own Wildernesses* (1959) and *Play with a Tiger* (1962), and a collection of essays about a return visit to Africa, *Going Home* (1957). The mildly satirical *In Pursuit of the English* (1960) was adapted for the stage in 1990. *London Observed* (1992) is a series of short stories set in the London of the 1980s. *See* Jenny Taylor (ed.), *Notebooks/Memoirs/Archives: Reading and Rereading Doris Lessing* (1982); Claire Sprague and Virginia Tiger (eds.), *Critical Essays on Doris Lessing* (1986); Claire Sprague, *Rereading Doris Lessing: Narrative Patterns of Doubling and Repetition* (1987); Carey Kaplan and Ellen Cronan Rose (eds.), *Doris Lessing: The Alchemy of Survival* (1988); Ruth Whittaker, *Doris Lessing* (1988); Claire Sprague (ed.), *In Pursuit of Doris Lessing: Nine Nations Reading* (1990).

Leverson, Ada, novelist (b. London, 10 October 1862, d. London, 30 August 1933).

Nicknamed 'the Sphinx' by her friend Oscar Wilde, Ada Leverson was born into a wealthy and cultivated upper middle-class London family. Her father Samuel Beddington was a property investor and her mother Zillah Simon a talented amateur pianist. She was educated at home and at 19, against her parents' wishes, married Ernest Leverson, a gambler and speculator. The marriage was not happy, but, fearful of scandal, the couple remained together until 1900 when Ernest, by then bankrupt, emigrated to Canada. They had two children, a son who died early and a daughter, Violet Wyndham, who later wrote Leverson's biography. Ada Leverson's first publications were articles, sketches, and parodies which she published in *Punch, Black and White*, and the *Yellow Book*. Her parody of *The Picture of Dorian Gray*, entitled 'An Afternoon Party', published in the *Yellow Book* in 1892 brought her to the attention of Wilde, who later became a close friend. She was particularly supportive during his trial and was one of a small group of friends who met him on his release from gaol. The friendship in turn brought her membership in an 1890s coterie which included Aubrey Beardsley, George Moore, and Max Beerbohm. Her parody of Wilde's *The Sphinx* in 1894 earned her the sobriquet. She began to write novels only after her husband's departure. Her first, *The Twelfth Hour*, was published in 1907, the year after Wilde's death. All six novels were written in bed, dictated to a typist, and published by Grant Richards, who first encouraged her to write. The novels are comedies of manners, dealing with marriage among the Edwardian upper middle classes. *Love's Shadow* (1908), *Tenterhooks* (1912), and *Love at Second Sight* (1916) form a trilogy about a married couple, Edith and Bruce Ottley, the latter supposedly based on Ernest Leverson, which was later reprinted as *The Little Ottleys* (1962). The plots of the others, including *The Twelfth Hour, The Limit* (1911), and *The Bird of Paradise* (1914), revolve around marital jealousy, absent or preoccupied husbands, and potentially erring wives. Leverson's dialogue, remarked upon by most critics, was said to have been influenced sometimes by Wilde, and sometimes by Jane *Austen. At the end of her life she joined a circle dominated by the *Sitwells, grew increasingly deaf, and was known for her kindness to young authors. She was also famous for her sayings, which, as Osbert Sitwell remarked in *The Times* (1 September 1933), are recorded in the memoirs of her contemporaries. Her *Letters to the Sphinx from Oscar Wilde with Reminiscences of the Author* (1930) contains a vivid account of the opening night of *The Importance of Being Earnest*, first published in the *Criterion* (1926), and a picture of Wilde in the 1890s, 'The Importance of Being Oscar'. Leverson also wrote weekly columns for the *Referee* (1903–5) under the name Elaine. *See* Osbert Sitwell, *Noble Essences; or Courteous Revelations* (1950); *The Letters of Oscar Wilde*, ed. Rupert Hart-Davies (1962); Violet Wyndham, *The Sphinx and her Circle: A Biographical Sketch of Ada Leverson 1862–1933* (1963); V. S. Pritchett, *The Living Novel* (1964); Charles Burkhart, *Ada Leverson* (1973).

Levy, Amy, poet and novelist (b. Clapham, 10 November 1861, d. London, 10 September 1889).

Amy Levy was the second daughter of Lewis Levy, an editor, and his wife Isabelle Levin, both from cultivated and orthodox Jewish families who encouraged her precocious literary talent. Her first poem was published at 13. She was educated at Brighton, and later went to Newnham College, Cambridge, becoming the first Jewish girl to matriculate. She was a contemporary of Constance *Garnett at Cambridge. Garnett's sister, the novelist Clementina Black, was a friend, as were Vernon *Lee and Olive *Schreiner. Her strongly feminist views were clearly stated in her first volume of poetry, *Xantippe and Other Poems* (1881), the title poem being a defence of Socrates' reputedly shrewish and much-maligned wife. It was followed by *A Minor Poet and Other Verses* (1884), which included most of the poems in the first volume, and then by *A London Plane Tree* (1889), a collection of lyrics. Accounts of her life conflict. She may have worked in a factory, lived in a garret, taught in a London school, or spent a winter in Florence. Whatever the facts, her contemporary reputation rested not on her poetry, but on a single novel, *Reuben Sachs*, which presented an unflattering picture of London Jewish life and created something of a furore when it was published in 1888. A subsequent novel, *Miss Meredith* (1889), about a governess who falls in love with the son of an Italian household, may have been written earlier. *The Romance of a Shop* (1888), a shorter novel, was well received. Levy's poetry was characterized by melancholy. She was herself a depressive, and the subject of 'A Minor Poet' eerily prefigured her own death by suicide in 1889, shortly after correcting the proofs of *A London Plane Tree*. Oscar Wilde, to whose *Women's World* she contributed, called her 'a girl of genius'. *See* Linda G. Zatlin, *The Nineteenth Century Anglo-Jewish Novel* (1981); Edward Wagenknecht, *Daughters of the Covenant: Portraits of Six Jewish Women* (1983).

Lindsay, Lady Anne *see* BARNARD, Lady Anne

Linton, Eliza Lynn, née Lynn, novelist and journalist (b. Keswick, Cumberland, 10 February 1822, d. London, 14 July 1898).

Eliza Lynn Linton was the twelfth and last child of the Revd James Lynn, vicar of Crosthwaite, Cumberland, and of Charlotte Goodenough, daughter of the Bishop of Carlisle. Her childhood was lonely and unhappy, exacerbated by her mother's early death and her father's indifference. She was entirely self-taught, and read French, Italian, German, and Spanish as well as some Latin and Greek. At the age of 23 she persuaded her father to support her for a year in London, where she determined to launch herself upon a career as a professional writer. Her first novel, *Azeth the Egyptian* (1846), was based on background reading in the British Museum and won some critical praise. Its successor *Amymone* (1848) was another historical novel, this time with a Greek setting, and a strong advocacy of women's rights. *Realities* (1851), the next novel, was criticized for supposed indecencies, and as a result Lynn abandoned fiction and turned to journalism. She worked for the *Morning Chronicle* and then as a newspaper correspondent in Paris. She published a collection of *Witch Stories*, first in *All the Year Round* and then issued separately in 1861. By this time she had begun to move in literary circles, becoming friendly with Walter Savage Landor, whom she regarded as a second father, and with Dickens, to whom she sold Gad's Hill, in Kent, the house she inherited from her father. In 1858 she married William James Linton, a well-known engraver with radical political convictions, whose wife had recently died, leaving him with a large family. The marriage was not a success. The couple parted amicably. They never divorced, and Lynn retained her husband's name, becoming known as Eliza Lynn Linton. She returned to writing fiction, more confident, more pugnacious, and based on her own experience of the world. *Grasp your Nettle* (1865), *Sowing the Wind* (1867), *The Mad Willoughbys and Other Tales* (1875), and *The Atonement of Leam Dundas* (1877) all confront the problems of women. *Joshua Davidson* (1872), her most successful novel in terms of sales, was a recasting of the life of Christ in a modern setting, and was intensely critical of the Church of England. *Under which Lord?* (1879) was an attack on ritualism in the Church. But undoubtedly her most celebrated if notorious work began as a series of articles in the *Saturday Review*. 'The Girl of the Period' (14 March 1868) was an opportunistic attack on the modern emancipated woman, paradoxical in that it was written by a woman who had established herself as a professional writer, separated from her husband, and a one-time advocate of women's rights. It won her enemies among her own sex but secured her financial success as a writer. The series was republished as *The Girl of the Period and Other Essays* (1883) and produced counter-attacks, including Sarah *Grand's

'The Man of the Moment'. Two late novels continued the assault on the modern woman. *The One Too Many* (1894) attacked higher education for women and the cult of the so-called Girton girl. *In Haste and at Leisure* (1895) further condemned the so-called *New Woman. As a final fling, she wrote a nicely barbed 'appreciation' of George *Eliot in Hurst and Blackett's collection of essays *Women Novelists of Queen Victoria's Reign* (1897). Lynn Linton wrote several autobiographical novels including *Patricia Kemball*, based on her childhood (1874), *The Rebel of the Family* (1880), and, most interestingly, *The Autobiography of Christopher Kirkland* (1885), in which she cast herself as a man. Her actual autobiography, *My Literary Life*, was published posthumously in 1889. *See* G. S. Layard, *Eliza Lynn Linton: Her Life, Letters and Opinions* (1901); Herbet van Thal, *Eliza Linn Linton* (1979); Nancy Fix Anderson, *Woman against Women in Victorian England: A Life of Eliza Lynn Linton* (1987).

Lively, Penelope (Margaret), novelist and children's writer (b. Cairo, Egypt, 17 March 1933).

The daughter of Roger Low and Vera Greer, Penelope Lively lived in Egypt until she was 12, when she was sent to a boarding school in Sussex. She read history at St Anne's College, Oxford, and in 1957 married Jack Lively, a political scientist. They have two children. What links her children's books, with which her writing career began, with her mainstream adult fiction is her obsession with history, with the connections between the past and the present. In her children's books time travel integrates past and present as historical characters impinge on the present day. The title figure of *The Ghost of Thomas Kempe* (1973), a Jacobean sorcerer, reappears in a contemporary setting. The book won the Carnegie Medal for children's literature. The anthropologist great-grandfather of the main character in *The House in Norham Gardens* (1974) is connected to the present through his relics, still preserved in the house. The Victorian child in *A Stitch in Time* (1976), which won the Whitbread Award, becomes alive for the contemporary heroine through a sampler hanging on the wall. The past impinges variously on the present in her adult fiction. The archaeologist hero of *Treasures of Time* (1979), which won the National Book Award, finds that the past can disturb the present. The eponymous biographer in *According to Mark* (1984) discovers connections between his own life and that of his historical subject. The female popular historian in *Moon Tiger* (1987), which won the Booker Prize, constructs her own history while on her death-bed, only to find that it is different from the one she has remembered. Illness and death act as catalysts to historical reconstructions in Lively's work, as with the contrasting female protagonists of *Perfect Happiness* (1983) or the middle-aged brother and sister of *Passing On* (1989), who are released by the death of their tyrannical mother. *City of the Mind* (1991) uses the London of both past and present as a backdrop to the story of a modern architect and also makes use of the time travel technique of her early work in a series of narrative vignettes. Lively's work to date includes nine novels and over twenty works for children. She has also published several collections of stories, including *Nothing Missing but the Samovar* (1976), *Corruption and Other Stories* (1984), and *Pack of Cards* (1986).

Llangollen, the Ladies of, diarists and letter writers: Lady Eleanor Butler (b. County Kilkenny, 1739, d. Plas Newydd, Llangollen, North Wales, 1829) and Sarah Ponsonby (b. Ireland, 1755, d. Plas Newydd, 1831).

Lady Eleanor Butler was the daughter of the *de jure* sixteenth Earl of Ormonde, a Catholic family prominent in the Anglo-Irish ascendancy. (The title was restored to her brother in 1792.) Sarah Ponsonby was an orphan, the ward of the equally well-connected Sir William and Lady Elizabeth Fownes, of Woodstock, in County Kilkenny, twelve miles from Lady Eleanor's family home. In a celebrated escapade in May 1778 the two women fled their parental homes, Butler under threat of being sent to a convent, and Ponsonby to escape the unwelcome advances of her guardian. In spite of fierce opposition from both families they settled together at Plas Newydd in North Wales, where they lived for the next fifty years. Despite gossip to the contrary, the relationship was probably best described as a 'romantic friendship'. The German Prince Puckler-Muskau called them 'the two most celebrated virgins in Europe'. With almost no financial resources the women created a Gothic cottage in the fashion of the day, a garden with grottoes and waterfalls, and a Gothic cowshed for their single cow. They were visited by many eminent literary figures, who publicized their rural retreat and their self-conscious experiment in living. Anna *Seward celebrated them in her poem *Llangollen Vale* (1795). Wordsworth and Southey visited them, and each sent poems, which in Wordsworth's case were not well received. Other visitors and correspondents included Hester Lynch *Piozzi, Madame de Genlis, Maria *Edgeworth, Sir Walter Scott, Hannah *More, and Lady Caroline *Lamb. The Duke of Wellington, Charles Darwin, Sir Humphry Davy, and Josiah Wedgwood also made their acquaintance. By the early nineteenth century their life-style, which had been shaped by a combination of Gothic modishness and the late eighteenth-century cult of rural 'retirement', grew increasingly eccentric. They died within two years of each other, their lives spanning the period from the Jacobite Rebellion of 1745 to the Great Reform Bill. Their letters and diaries reflect the cult of sensibility of which they were a part, although Butler's journals at their best have been compared with those of Dorothy *Wordsworth. Selections from her diaries have been published as *The Hamwood Papers of the Ladies of Llangollen and Caroline Hamilton*, ed. G. H. Bell (1930). *Life with the Ladies of Llangollen*, ed. Elizabeth Mavor (1984), is a selection from the letters and journals of both. *See* Elizabeth Mavor, *The Ladies of Llangollen: A Study in Romantic Friendship* (1971); M. C. Bradbrook, in *Women and Literature 1779–1982* (1982).

'Lovechild, Mrs Solomon' *see* FENN, Lady Eleanor

Lowndes, Marie Adelaide Belloc *see* BELLOC-LOWNDES, Marie Adelaide

'Loy, Mina' (Mina Gertrude Lowy), poet and playwright (b. London, 1882, d. Aspen, Colorado, 1966).

Mina Loy was the daughter of a Hungarian-Jewish father, Sigmund Lowy, and an English Protestant mother, Julia Brian. She left school at 17, studied art for two years in Munich, and returned to London in 1901 to continue her art studies with Augustus John, among others. While a student she met the English painter Stephen Haweis, whom she married in 1903, changing her name to Loy instead of taking his name. They lived in Paris and later Florence and had three children, one of whom died in infancy. They frequented Gertrude Stein's Paris salon and became part of the Anglo-American colony in Florence which included Stein, Alice B. Toklas, and Mabel Dodge, later Luhan (1879–1962), an American journalist and patron of the arts who became one of Loy's closest friends. Loy became involved with the Italian Futurist movement led by Filippo Tomasino Marinetti, with whom she had an affair. Her 'Aphorisms on Futurism' were published in the magazine *Camera Work* in 1914 and her poems, 'Love Songs to Johannes', in the new poetry magazine *Others* in 1915. She broke with the Futurists when they moved towards Fascism and embraced feminism, writing her unpublished 'Feminist Manifesto', which urged women to 'leave off looking to men to find out what you are *not*. Seek within yourselves to find out what you are.' The manifesto also proposed the 'unconditional' surgical destruction of virginity at puberty. Her unpublished play *The Pamperers*, written in 1915–16, satirized the masculinity of the Futurists. In 1916 she left her children in Florence with a nurse and sailed to New York, where she continued to publish her work in little magazines, acted with the Provincetown Players, and was chosen as a representative 'modern woman' by the *New York Evening Sun*. In 1917 she divorced Haweis and married Arthur Craven, an arch publicist, boxer, forger, and one-time writer who disappeared before the birth of their daughter in 1919. The circumstances of his presumed death were never resolved. Loy settled for a while in New York, where she published a poem in Ezra Pound's *Little Review*, in the same issue as an instalment of Joyce's *Ulysses* which was then seized by the US Post Office as obscene. In New York she met the American poet H(ilda) D(oolittle), her friend *Bryher, and the latter's husband Robert McAlmon, whose Paris-based Contact Press later published her work. She flitted between expatriate circles in Florence, Berlin, and Paris with her two daughters (her son by Haweis had also died) and eventually set up a business designing and making lampshades in Paris. She continued to write poetry and became a well-known figure in the literary circle which included the American poets Nathalie Barney, Djuna Barnes, and Harriet Monroe as well as Gertrude Stein. Robert McAlmon published *Lunar Baedecker* (1923), her only book until *Lunar Baedecker and Time-Tables*, a collection of her work from many sources, appeared belatedly and unremarked in 1958. Parts of her autobiographical poem 'Anglo-Mongrels and the Rose' were published in the *Little Review* in 1923 and in McAlmon's *Contact Collection of Contemporary Writers* in 1925. She published little in the 1930s and moved again to New York in 1936, where she remained until 1953. She published a few poems in the 1940s but Random House rejected her proposed 'Selected Poems'. She turned her attention to the derelicts of New York's Bowery, assembling her 'Constructions' or montages, which were exhibited in 1959, as well as writing some moving poems. Her last years were spent in Aspen, Colorado, where she lived as a virtual recluse, a local literary curiosity from another age. She died there at the age of 84. The highly experimental nature of Loy's work and its sexual honesty have been used to account for her disappearance from print in the 1930s. Partly because of the fragmented nature of her publications, which were sprinkled in little magazines, it went unnoticed in the 1940s and 1950s, despite the introductions by William Carlos Williams, Denise Levertov, and others to *Lunar Baedecker and Time-Tables* in 1958. Although her work was admired by Williams, Pound, Eliot, and the critic Ivor Winters, she became one of the 'lost voices' of modernism, partly resurrected by the publication of *The Last Lunar Baedecker*, her collected poems, edited by Roger Conover in 1982. *See* Virginia M. Kouidis, *Mina Loy: American Modernist Poet* (1980); Gillian Hanscombe and Virginia L. Smyers, *Writing for their Lives: The Modernist Women 1910–1940* (1987); Bonnie Kime Scott (ed.), *The Gender of Modernism* (1990).

'**Lucas**, Victoria' *see* PLATH, Sylvia

Lumley, Lady Jane or Joanna, translator (*c.*1537–1576).

Jane Lumley was the eldest daughter and co-heiress of Henry Fitzalan, twelfth Earl of Arundel, and his wife Katherine Grey. Lady Jane Grey was her cousin. She was fortunate in her father, whose extensive library gave her early access to Latin and Greek literature, in which languages she became fluent, and in her husband John, Baron Lumley (1534?–1609), who possessed one of the largest private libraries in England. The Arundel library was later added to his, as was that of Thomas Cranmer, and at his death it was purchased by James I for his son Henry, Prince of Wales. Lumley was a Catholic, like his wife, and also an astute courtier, who managed to remain in favour throughout the reigns of Mary, *Elizabeth, and James I. The couple had three children, all of whom died in infancy. They shared an interest in classical literature, and in translation. Lumley translated Erasmus' *Institutio principis Christiani* (*The Education of a Christian Prince*) while Jane translated various orations of Isocrates from Greek to Latin. She is best known for her translation into English of Euripides' *Iphigenia*, which she completed around 1555, probably working from Erasmus' Latin version. This is the earliest extant English translation of a Greek play. It was published by the Malone Society in 1909 as *Iphigenia in Aulis*, edited by Harold H. Child. Jane Lumley's sister Mary, later Duchess of Norfolk, left some Latin manuscripts. *See* Myra Reynolds, *The Learned Lady in England, 1650–1760* (1920); Nancy Cotton, *Women Playwrights in England* c.*1363–1750* (1980); Elaine V. Beilin, *Redeeming Eve: Women Writers of the English Renaissance* (1987).

'**Lyall**, Edna' (Ada Ellen Bayly), novelist (b. Brighton, 25 March 1857, d. Eastbourne, Sussex, 8 February 1903).

Edna Lyall was the youngest of the four children of Robert Bayly, a barrister, who died when she was 11, and his wife Mary Winter, who died three years later. Being delicate, she was educated at home, then at the home of an uncle who became her guardian, and finally at private schools in Brighton. Her entire adult life was spent in the homes of her two sisters, both of whom married clergymen, at Lincoln, London, and Eastbourne. She was a committed Christian and politically a liberal, both convictions which informed her fiction. Under the pseudonym Edna Lyall, concocted from nine letters in her three names, she published her first book, *Won by Waiting* (1879), a girl's story, which went unnoticed until her subsequent reputation prompted over thirteen editions. *Donovan* (1882), with its agnostic hero who returns to faith, won Gladstone's approval and attracted the attention of the radical free-thinker Charles Bradlaugh, who became a friend, despite their religious differences. She lent financial support to his election campaigns and after his death in 1891 subscribed six months' royalties to his memorial fund. The hero of *We Too* (1884), the sequel to *Donovan*, bore a strong resemblance to Bradlaugh, and the novel itself established her reputation. *In the Golden Days* (1885), set in the seventeenth century, was her first truly popular work. Ruskin read it on his death-bed. It was a measure of her fame that in 1886 someone anonymously claimed to be the real 'Edna Lyall', and a rumour also circulated that 'Edna Lyall' had been confined to a lunatic asylum. Ada Bayly fought these by publicly announcing her identity and defending herself in *Autobiography of a Slander* (1887), a work which was translated into French, German, and Norwegian. *Doreen* (1894), a pro-Irish Home Rule novel whose hero was modelled on the Irish nationalist leader Michael Davitt, won a second commendation from Gladstone. *The Autobiography of a Truth* (1896) championed the Armenians against the Turks and *The Hinderers* (1902) opposed the Boer War. Her novels with a purpose were less popular with her public than her romances, both historical and contemporary, which included titles like *Wayfaring Men* (1897), *Hope the Hermit* (1898), *In Spite of All* (1901). Edna Lyall contributed the chapter on Mrs Gaskell to Hurst and Blackett's collection of essays *Women Novelists of Queen Victoria's Reign* (1897). *The Burges Letters* (1902) was an autobiography. She suffered from heart disease and died at Eastbourne at the age of 46. Before her death she donated three bells to her church at Eastbourne, named Donovan, Erica, and Hugo, after the main characters in her three best-known books. *See* J. M. Escreet, *The Life of Edna Lyall* (1904)

M

m m m m m m m m m m

Macaulay, Catherine, historian (b. Olantigh House, Wye, Kent, 2 April 1731, d. Binfield, Berkshire, 22 June 1791).

Catherine Macaulay was the second daughter of John Sawbridge, a Kentish landowner, and his wife Elizabeth Wanley, the heiress of a London banker. Her mother died when she was 2 and by her father's wish she was educated at home with her brother, who later became a supporter of the radical John Wilkes. In 1760 she married Dr George Macaulay, a Scottish physician who was in charge of a London lying-in hospital. He died six years later, leaving her well off and with a 6-year-old daughter. Prior to his death she had begun to write her major work, *The History of England from the Accession of James I to that of the Brunswick Line.* The eight volumes, which covered the period up to 1688, were published over the twenty years between 1763 and 1783. The anti-monarchical thrust of her history and her known radical sympathies made her reputation controversial from the beginning. She was praised by Horace Walpole, the poet Thomas Gray, and reportedly by William Pitt in the House of Commons. Mary *Wollstonecraft spoke of her as 'the woman of the greatest abilities that this country has ever produced'. Others less sympathetic attacked her private life, which invited comment. She shared the Bath residence of an elderly admirer, Dr Thomas Wilson, rector of St Stephen's, Walbrook, who erected a statue of her in the church. (It is now in Warrington Town Hall.) When in 1778, at the age of 57, she married William Graham, aged 21, the younger brother of a well-known quack doctor, various satires circulated in London, including a spurious letter from

Catherine to the Revd Wilson. Undeterred by the unfavourable publicity she entered vigorously into many of the major debates of her age, responding to Hobbes in her *Loose Remarks* (1767), arguing for copyright in 1774, attacking the Quebec Act and the taxation of the North American colonies in 1775, responding to Burke's pamphlet *Thoughts on the Cause of the Present Discontents* in 1770, and to his *Reflections on the French Revolution* in 1790. Her *Letters on Education* (1790) put forward strongly feminist views on the need for equality of the sexes in education and on the importance of women choosing their husbands. The last work was said to have greatly influenced Mary Wollstonecraft. One volume of a projected sequel to her history, 'From the Revolution to the Present Time', appeared in 1778 but was not a success. Her republican views made Macaulay much more popular in France and America than in England. She met many of the leading French republicans on a visit to Paris in 1777. The memoirist Madame Roland (1754–93) reportedly confessed to the ambition of becoming 'la Macaulay de son pays'. Her history was translated into French in 1791–2. She visited and later corresponded with George Washington and created a large following on a trip to North America in 1784–5. One indication of her contemporary celebrity was the number of paintings of her done during her lifetime, including one by Gainsborough and another by Joseph Wright of Derby. Another, less flattering, was the allegation that she had been banished from the British Museum for tearing four leaves from one of the documents she had consulted when writing her *History*, a charge successfully refuted by her husband after her death. Despite her high profile during the second half of the eighteenth century her work was virtually forgotten in the nineteenth, despite the praise of the historian W. E. L. Lecky (1838–1903). Reviewing the first two volumes of Thomas Babington Macaulay's *History of England* in the *Quarterly Review* for 1849, John Wilson Croker reminded readers that Catherine Macaulay had made 'quite as much noise' in her day as her namesake 'does in ours'. *See* Lucy M. Donnelly, *The Celebrated Mrs. Macaulay* (1949, reprinted from the *William and Mary Quarterly*); Bridget Hill, *The Republican Virago* (1992).

Macaulay, Dame (Emilie) Rose, novelist, travel writer, journalist, and critic (b. Rugby, Warwickshire, 1 August 1881, d. London, 30 October 1958).

Rose Macaulay was the second of the seven children of George Campbell Macaulay, an assistant master at Rugby School, later a university lecturer in English at Cambridge, and his wife Grace Conybeare, whose family had produced several generations of intellectual clergymen. Thomas Babington Macaulay was her grandfather's first cousin. She was brought up in Italy, where the family had gone in search of a cure for her mother's tuberculosis, and taught by her parents until their return to England, when she went to Oxford High School. With the help of a generous uncle she read history at Somerville College, Oxford, and was awarded an *aegrotat* in 1903. Her writing career began with contributions to the *Westminster Gazette* and several early novels, *Abbots Verney* (1906), *The Furnace* (1907), *Views and Vagabonds* (1912), and *The Lee Shore* (1912), which won a Hodder & Stoughton novel competition. She also published two volumes of poetry during these early years, *The Two Blind Countries* (1914) and *Three Days* (1919). She worked as a civil servant throughout the First World War, an experience recorded in *What Not* (1918). *Potterism* (1920) was the first in a line of witty, ironic, and sometimes satirical works which opened up a new vein of talent in the middle period of her career. *Dangerous Ages* (1921), a comedy about stages in women's lives, won the Femina Vie Heureuse Prize. *Told by an Idiot* (1923) was compared with Virginia *Woolf's *Orlando* (1928). Other novels during this period included *Keeping up Appearances* (1928) and *Staying with Relations* (1930). *They were Defeated* (1932), her one historical novel, was based on the poet Robert Herrick and the pre-Civil War period in Cambridge. She also wrote several books of criticism, including *Some Religious Elements in English Literature* (1931) and studies of Milton (1934) and E. M. Forster (1938). She endured two severe personal blows during the Second World War, the destruction of her London flat and her books by bombing, and the death from cancer, in 1942, of Gerald O'Donovan, a writer with whom she had had a liaison since 1918. O'Donovan, a civil servant, was married and an ex-priest. Their relationship was kept secret from most of her friends and from O'Donovan's wife. Two travel books written after the war, *They Went to Portugal* (1946), on the English penchant for that country, and *Fabled Shore* (1949), established her as a serious practitioner of the genre. *The Pleasure of Ruins* (1953), another travel book, identified a theme which also manifested itself in her fiction, the contrast of civilization and barbarism, highlighted in *Orphan Island* (1924), *Crewe Train* (1926), and in the more mature novel of her last phase, *The World my Wilderness* (1950). She wrote in all twenty-three novels over a period of nearly fifty years. Her last was her best known and probably her best, the semi-autobiographical *The Towers of Trebizond* (1956), which won the James Tait Black Memorial Prize. She was working on a new novel, *Venice Besieged*, at the time of her sudden death in 1958, the year in which she was created a DBE. Rose Macaulay was also an energetic and prolific journalist, writing during her last years for the *TLS*, the *Spectator*, the *New Statesman*, the *Observer*, and the *Listener*, even though there was no longer the financial necessity for this level of commitment. Three collections of letters exist. *Letters to a Friend 1950–2* and *Last Letters to* *a Friend 1952–8*, edited by her cousin Constance Babington Smith (1961–2), were written to a spiritual confessor following her return to the Church of England after the estrangement brought about by her relationship with Gerald O'Donovan. *Letters to a Sister*, also edited by Smith (1964), were written to Jean Macaulay and include the fragment of *Venice Besieged*. *See* Constance Babington Smith, *Rose Macaulay: A Biography* (1972); Jane Emery, *Rose Macaulay: A Writer's Life* (1991).

McCorquodale, Barbara *see* CARTLAND, Barbara

McFall, Frances Elizabeth *see* GRAND, Sarah

Mackintosh, Elizabeth ('Gordon Daviot', 'Josephine Tey'), playwright and novelist (b. Inverness, 1896 or 1897, d. London, 13 February 1952).

The names Gordon Daviot, a modestly successful playwright of the 1930s and 1940s, and Josephine Tey, the author of eleven novels and detective stories, have virtually eclipsed that of Elizabeth Mackintosh, whose personal life was intensely private. She was the daughter of Colin Mackintosh, a greengrocer, and his wife Josephine Horne, a former teacher. She grew up in Inverness, went to the Royal Academy (a high school), and then refused to go on to university, the expected procedure ('I stuck my toes in and refused to continue what I had been doing for the previous twelve years'). Instead, she went to Anstey Physical Training College in Birmingham. She worked as a physical education teacher in various parts of England, but gave it up in order to return to Scotland to look after her father after her mother's death. She wrote stories for the *English Review* and other periodicals and in 1929 published her first novel, *The Man in the Queue*, using the pseudonym Gordon Daviot. It introduced her gentlemanly detective hero Alan Grant, who bore a family resemblance to the sleuth heroes of Agatha *Christie, Dorothy L. *Sayers, Margery *Allingham, and Ngaio *Marsh, the current queens of detective fiction. She retained the pseudonym for a series of plays based on historical or biblical figures which began with the successful *Richard of Bordeaux* (1933), starring and directed by John Gielgud. Laurence Olivier played in the less successful *Queen of Scots* (1934), produced in the same year as her notorious flop, *The Laughing Woman*, a dramatization of the relationship between the sculptor Henri Gaudier and Sophia Brzeska. Her other well-known play, *The Stars Bow Down* (1939), the story of Joseph and his brothers, was produced at the Malvern Festival. As Josephine Tey, the name of her great-great-grandmother, she launched a series of detective novels, beginning with *A Shilling for Candles* (1936), which was adapted for film by Alfred Hitchcock as *Young and Innocent* (1937). The series culminated in her best-known and most original book *The Daughter of Time* (1951), a re-examination of the case of Richard III and the Princes in the Tower, with her contemporary detective hero in hospital this time, working on historical evidence. Several of her detective novels were without Alan Grant, including *Miss Pym Disposes* (1948), set in a girls' school, *The Franchise Affair* (1948), based on an eighteenth-century kidnapping, and *Brat Farrar* (1949). Two of her novels, *Kif: An Unvarnished History* (1929) and *The Expensive Halo* (1931), were published as by Gordon Daviot. Her last Alan Grant story, *The Singing Sands*, was published posthumously in 1952. Elizabeth Mackintosh died of cancer at the age of 55. Her *Plays* were collected in 1953–4 with a foreword by John Gielgud. *See* Jessica Man, *Deadlier than the Male* (1981); E. F. Bargainnier, *10 Women of Mystery* (1981); Alison Light, in *The Progress of Romance: The Politics of Popular Fiction*, ed. Jean Radford (1986).

'Malet, Lucas' (Mary St Leger Kingsley, later Harrison), novelist (b. Eversley, Hampshire, 4 June 1852, d. Tenby, Dyfed, 27 October 1931).

Lucas Malet was the younger daughter of the novelist Charles Kingsley (1819–75) and his wife Frances Grenfell. Henry Kingsley (1830–76), another novelist, was her uncle. As a girl she studied at the Slade School of Fine Art but abandoned the idea of a career in the art world when she married the Revd William Harrison, who was shortly afterwards appointed vicar of Clovelly, in north Devon. The marriage was an unhappy one and the two eventually separated, but she began to write in the early years of her marriage. It was to avoid a connection with the famous Kingsley name that she adopted the pseudonym Lucas Malet, drawn from two other family names, when she published her first novel, *Mrs. Lorimer* (1882). Her reputation was made with her second, *Colonel Enderby's Wife* (1885), the story of an unhappy marriage between a middle-aged man and a younger woman. *The Wages of Sin* (1891), which again revolved around a painful misalliance, was one of her best-known works. *The Carissima* (1896) was the story of a destructive relationship with a macabre twist at the end, and *The Gateless Barrier* (1900) a sophisticated ghost story. Possibly the best known of all was *Sir Richard Calmady* (1901), the hero of which was hideously deformed. Physical deformities, the grotesque, and the macabre featured in Lucas Malet's fiction, and her 'Meredithian' style was often commented upon. Five years after her husband's death in 1897 she was received into the Roman Catholic Church. She bought a house in Eversley, her father's old parish, and adopted her cousin Gabrielle Vallings as her daughter. She travelled extensively in France, lived in London during the First World War, and eventually settled in Montreux. She was a prominent member of literary circles in France and England, a friend of Henry James, among others, and received a civil-list pension the year before she died. *See* W. L. Courtney, *The Feminine Note in Fiction* (1904; repr. 1973).

Mallowan, Agatha Maria Clarissa *see* CHRISTIE, Dame Agatha

Manley, (Mary) Delarivier, playwright, novelist, satirist, and autobiographer (b. 7 April 1663, d. London, 11 July 1724).

Delarivier Manley (the frequently used Mary is incorrect) was one of the five children of Sir Roger Manley, a Royalist soldier and historian, by his Dutch wife. She may have been born in Holland, where her father served after the Restoration with an English regiment, or, as the *DNB* suggests, in Jersey or at sea between Jersey and Guernsey. Her father died in 1688, leaving her £200 and a share in his estate. She was tricked into a bigamous marriage by her cousin John Manley and bore an illegitimate child. When Manley returned to his first wife, Delarivier was befriended for a short time by the Duchess of Cleveland, former mistress of Charles II, who then accused her of seducing her son. She moved to Devon, where she started to write. In 1696 she published *Letters Written by Mrs. Manley* in imitation of Madame d'Aulnoy, based on actual correspondence, and itself much imitated in later decades. She then returned to London to make her theatrical début with two plays, *The Lost Lover; or The Jealous Husband*, a comedy, written in seven days and an acknowledged failure, and *The Royal Mischief*, a highly successful tragedy. *The Lost Lover* was produced at Drury Lane in 1696, during the period of her liaison with Sir Thomas Skipwith, the theatre manager. Quarrels within the company over its production prompted her to take *The Royal Mischief* to Lincoln's Inn Fields in the same year, where it had a successful run with an all-star cast. Along with Mary *Pix and Catharine *Trotter she was satirized by 'W.M.' in *The *Female Wits*, produced at Drury Lane in 1697, in itself a measure of her impact on the theatre. The ending of a six-year relationship with the warden of the Fleet Prison prompted another withdrawal to the country, after which she returned in 1705 to try her hand at political satire, with *The Secret History of Queen Zarah and the Zarazians*, aimed at Sarah, Duchess of Marlborough, and the Whigs. The following year she produced her first novel, *The Lady's Paquet Broke Open*, and in 1709 created a stir when she brought out her *Female Tatler*, edited by 'Mrs. Crackenthorpe, a lady that knows everything'. In the same year she published her most controversial and best-known work, the scandalous *Secret Memoirs and Manners of Several Persons of Quality . . . from the New Atlantis*, known by its short title, *The New Atlantis*, a blend of fact and fiction, politics, scandal, and autobiography which was immensely popular. It went through at least seven editions by

1736. A second volume followed within months and Mrs Manley, the publisher, and the printer were promptly arrested. The latter were discharged, and the author eventually acquitted, causing Lady Mary Wortley *Montagu to lament, 'Miserable is the fate of writers! If they are agreeable they are offensive, and if dull, they starve.' Undeterred, Mrs Manley immediately brought out volumes iii and iv, under the titles *Memoirs of Europe towards the Close of the Eighth Century* (1710) and *Court Intrigues* (1711), the latter a version of *The Lady's Paquet.* Her appetite whetted for political satire, she produced several on behalf of the Tories, and in June 1711 succeeded Swift as editor of the *Examiner.* She wrote two further tragedies, *Almyna; or The Arabian Vow,* produced at the Haymarket in 1707, and *Lucius, the First Christian King of Britain,* performed to great acclaim at Drury Lane in 1717. *The Adventures of Rivella* (1714) was a fictionalized autobiography which commented on the sexual double standard and on women's writing. *The Power of Love: In Seven Novels* (1720) adapted traditional stories. The last was a notable financial success, earning her 600 guineas. For the last years of her life she lived with the printer John Barber, who later, as Alderman Barber, became Lord Mayor of London. She died at his printing house in Lambeth Hill in 1724. *See* Fidelis Morgan (ed.), *A Woman of No Character: An Autobiography of Mrs. Manley* (1986); Constance Clark, *Three Augustan Women Playwrights* (1986); Ros Ballaster, *Seductive Forms: Women's Amatory Fiction 1684–1740* (1992).

Manning, Anne, novelist (b. London, 17 February 1807, d. Tunbridge Wells, Kent, 14 September 1879).

Anne Manning was the eldest of the large family of William Oke Manning, an insurance broker for Lloyd's, and Joan Whatmore Gibson, daughter of the principal surveyor of the London Docks and a distant cousin of Charles and Mary *Lamb. Her paternal grandfather was a Unitarian minister and several members of the family became distinguished lawyers. She was taught by her mother, an accomplished scholar, knew several foreign languages, some science, including astronomy, and won a Royal Academy medal for her painting. Living in Chelsea aroused her interest in history. Her first publication, *A Sister's Gift: Conversations on Sacred Subjects* (1826), written for her siblings when she was 19, succeeded largely because of her grandfather's energetic advertising of it. *Village Belles* (1838), her first novel, was a conventional story of village life. She was best known for a series of historical novels, written in diary form, imitating archaic style and spelling and printed with 'antique' typography and layout. The heroine and diarist of *The Maiden and Married Life of Mary Powell* (1849) was the future Mrs John Milton. Its popularity led to a sequel, *Deborah's Diary* (1858), supposedly written by

Milton's daughter. *The Household of Sir Thomas More* (1851) was the fictional diary of More's daughter Margaret *Roper. Like her first novel, it was published in *Sharpe's London Magazine* and went through several editions in volume form as well as French and German translations. *Cherry and Violet: A Tale of the Great Plague* (1853) was another pseudo-historical diary. *The Lincolnshire Tragedy: Passages in the Life of the Faire Gospeller, Mistress Anne *Askew* (1866) was based on the life of the sixteenth-century martyr and autobiographer. The novels were attacked as 'spurious antiques' in *Fraser's Magazine* (1855) and the public warned against accepting them as authentic diaries. The Archbishop of Canterbury and Cardinal Manning, on the other hand, praised their historical accuracy. All of Manning's work was published anonymously, usually 'by the author of *Mary Powell*'. *The Ladies of Bever Hollow* (1858) was her most successful non-historical novel. She lived the retired life of a Victorian spinster with her mother and later with her sisters in Reigate and Tunbridge Wells. Her autobiographical 'Passages in an Authoress's Life' (1872) was being serialized in the magazine *Golden Hours*, to which she was a regular contributor, when she became ill. It was never completed. *See* Charlotte *Yonge, in *Women Novelists of Queen Victoria's Reign*, ed. A. Sergeant (1897).

Manning, Olivia ('Jacob Morrow'), novelist (b. Portsmouth, 2 March 1908, d. Ryde, Isle of Wight, 23 July 1980).

Olivia Manning was the elder of the two children of Lieutenant-Commander Oliver Manning, a retired naval officer, and his second wife Olivia Morrow, of Northern Irish and American descent. Her brother Oliver was killed in the Second World War. Straitened financial circumstances and domestic disharmony made for a painful childhood. She went to Portsmouth Grammar School, where she wrote four 'lurid serials' under the pseudonym Jacob Morrow, for which she was paid £12 each. She moved to London when she was 18, working in the office of a department store during the day and writing during the evenings and into the night. The firm of Jonathan Cape encouraged her and published her first novel, *The Wind Changes* (1937), set in Dublin during the Troubles. In 1939 she married Reginald (Reggie) Donald Smith (d. 1985), then a British Council lecturer in Bucharest, later a BBC drama producer and a professor of English. They returned to Romania just as the Second World War broke out and escaped to Greece before the Italian invasion. These experiences formed the substance of her best and also her best-known work, *The Balkan Trilogy* (1981; televised 1987), which describes the emotional lives of individuals caught up in great events. Harriet and Guy Pringle, the main characters, were acknowledged, if partial, portraits of herself and her husband. *The Great Fortune* (1960), *The Spoilt City* (1962), and *Friends and Heroes* (1965) charted the development of their relationship and those of other foreign onlookers in the early years of the war, first in disintegrating Romania, and then in Greece. A second trilogy, *The Levant* (1982), was based on the next stage of the couple's wartime experiences, when Manning was press officer at the US Embassy in Cairo and then press assistant at the public information office in Jerusalem. Egypt, Jerusalem, and Syria are the settings of *The Danger Tree* (1977), *The Battle Lost and Won* (1978), and *The Sum of Things*, published posthumously in 1980. Between her first novel and the trilogies she published *The Remarkable Expedition* (1947), an account of Stanley's rescue of the Emir Pasha, and several other novels, *Artist among the Missing* (1949), *School for Love* (1951), *A Different Face* (1953), and *The Doves of Venus* (1955). *The Playroom* (1969), like so much of her work, contained autobiographical elements. *The Rain Forest* (1974) is about unhappily married writers. She wrote for *Horizon*, the *Spectator*, the *New Statesman*, as well as *Vogue* and *Punch*. Sketches from the last were collected in *My Husband Cartwright* (1956). Other collections of stories included *Growing Up* (1948) and *A Romantic Hero* (1967). She was appointed CBE in 1976 and died of a stroke while on holiday in 1980. *See* Walter Allen, *Tradition and Dream* (1964); G. S. Fraser, *The Modern Writer and his World* (1964); Kay Dick, *Friends and Friendship* (1974); H. Mooney, in *Twentieth-Century Women Novelists*, ed. Thomas Staley (1982); Robert K. Morris, in *British Novelists since 1900*, ed. Jack I. Biles (1987).

'**Mansfield,** Katherine' (Kathleen Mansfield Beauchamp), short story writer (b. Wellington, New Zealand, 14 October 1888, d. Fontainebleau, France, 17 October 1923).

Katherine Mansfield was the third of the six children of Harold Beauchamp, a partner in a shipping company who later became chairman of the Bank of New Zealand and Sir Harold, and his wife Annie Burnell Dyer. Her early childhood was spent in a village near Wellington, where she went to the local primary school. Later she went to Wellington Girls' High School and to Miss Swainson's private school, where she wrote stories for the school magazine. From 1903 to 1906 she and her two sisters were sent to London, to Queens' College in Harley Street, where she met Ida Baker, or LM, as she was known, who became her lifelong companion. She reluctantly went back to New Zealand but in 1908 persuaded her father to let her return to London on a small allowance, which she attempted to supplement by her writing. She had an affair with Garnet Trowell, a New Zealand violinist, by whom she became pregnant, impulsively married George Bowden, left him the same day, and fled to a spa in Bavaria, where she miscarried. *In a German Pension* (1911), her first collection of short stories, was based on these experiences. In 1910 she began to publish stories in A. R. Orage's periodical the *New Age.* The next year she met the critic John Middleton Murry (1889–1957), then an Oxford undergraduate in charge of the magazine *Rhythm,* to which she also contributed, as well as to its successor the *Blue Review* (1911–13) and *Signature* (1915). *Novels and Novelists,* a collection of her essays from the *Athenaeum,* which Murry also edited from 1919 to 1921, was published in 1930. They lived together from 1912 on and off for the rest of her life, marrying in 1918 when she was able to obtain a divorce from Bowden. The death of her brother Leslie in France in 1915 and the onset of then undefined ill health triggered a series of short stories based on her New Zealand childhood, including *Prelude* (1918), published by the Hogarth Press, and *Je ne parle pas français* (1919), privately printed. *The Aloe,* the original, longer version of *Prelude,* written in 1916, was eventually published in 1930. *Bliss and Other Stories,* published in 1920 and which included the earlier stories, established her reputation. *The Garden Party and Other Stories* (1922), also New Zealand stories, was the last volume published in her lifetime. She and Murry travelled to the south of France in 1915–16 in an attempt to alleviate the symptoms of tuberculosis which had begun to take hold. They spent time in Cornwall in 1916 with D. H. Lawrence and his wife Frieda, and in 1916 she met Virginia *Woolf, who after her death confessed that Mansfield's was the only writing of which she had ever been jealous. Her remaining years were spent writing and travelling, sometimes with Murry, sometimes with Ida Baker, in search of a cure or at least relief from her illness. She died at the Gurdjieff Institute near Fontainebleau, where she had gone for a new form of treatment. Mansfield's writing transformed the short story in English. In the words of one biographer, she was 'a true modernist who changed the rules'. Her work was compared with that of Chekhov in its absorption with the everyday and the sensitivity of its perceptions but there was much about her writing that was unique. Two collections of stories were published posthumously, *The Dove's Nest* (1923) and *Something Childish* (1924). Her *Journal,* edited by Murry in 1927, and her letters, a selection of which he published in 1928, according to the *DNB,* 'belong to the permanent literature of self-revelation'. Virginia Woolf said of the journal, 'we feel that we are watching a mind which is alone with itself'. *The Collected Letters of Katherine Mansfield* are being edited by Vincent O'Sullivan and Margaret Scott (1984–). Her *Poems,* first collected in 1923, have been edited by Vincent O'Sullivan (1988) and her *Critical Writings* by Clare Hanson (1987). *See* Virginia Woolf, *Granite and Rainbow* (1958); Antony Alpers, *The Life of Katherine Mansfield* (1980); Cherry A. Hankin, *Katherine Mansfield and her Confessional Stories* (1983); Kate Fullbrook, *Katherine Mansfield* (1986); Claire Tomalin, *Katherine Mansfield: A Secret Life* (1987); Paulette Michel and Michel Dupuis, *The Fine*

Instrument: Essays on Katherine Mansfield (1989); Brownlee Jean Kirkpatrick (ed.) *A Bibliography of Katherine Mansfield* (1989).

'Marchant, Catherine' *see* COOKSON, Catherine

Marryat, Augusta, Blanche, and Emilia *see under* MARRYAT, Florence

Marryat, Florence, novelist (b. Brighton, 9 July 1838, d. London, 27 October 1899).

Florence Marryat was the sixth daughter and eleventh child of Captain Frederick Marryat (1792–1848), the novelist and children's writer, and his wife Catherine Shairp. Her grandfather Shairp had been consul-general at the court of Russia. She had governesses but later in her life claimed to have 'read everything I could find . . . . I may be said to have educated myself, and probably I got more real learning out of this mode of procedure than if I had gone through the regular routine of the schoolroom.' When she was 16 she married Captain Ross Church of the Madras Staff Corps, with whom she travelled across India and by whom she had eight children. They divorced, although Marryat passed herself off as a widow, and in 1879 she married Colonel Francis Lean of the Royal Marines. Her first novel, *Love's Conflict*, was written after her return to England in 1865, as a distraction while nursing children with scarlet fever. She wrote over ninety novels in all, many of which were translated into German, French, Swedish, Flemish, and Russian. Much of the proceeds went towards the education of her children. She wrote quickly and rarely revised. Most were *sensation novels, with melodramatic plots, turning on the conflict of love and duty. Some of the titles are indicative of content: *Too Good for him* (1865), *Her Lord and Master* (1871), *A Crown of Shame* (1888), *On Circumstantial Evidence* (1889), *A Fatal Silence* (1891), *A Passing Madness* (1897), *A Rational Marriage* (1899). At one point in her career the sexual adventurousness of her plots marked her out as the writer of fiction unsuitable for young readers. Although a Roman Catholic, Marryat was fascinated by spiritualism, and wrote several books on the subject. *There is no Death* (1891), in particular, received considerable attention and she was deluged with letters from readers. She was also at one time a comedy actress, performing in her own plays, a singer with the D'Oyly Carte company, a public lecturer, the producer of her own one-woman show, the manager of a school of journalism, and a dog breeder. She edited the monthly *London Society* from 1872 to 1876 and in 1872 published *The Life and Letters of Captain Marryat* (1872). Several of her sisters were also novelists, including **Augusta, Blanche,** and **Emilia (Norris)**. *Fighting the Air* (1875) supposedly gives a portrait of Augusta and herself. *See* Helen C. Black, *Notable Women Authors* *of the Day* (1893); Elaine Showalter, *A Literature of their Own: British Women Novelists from Brontë to Lessing* (1977).

Marsh, Anne, née Caldwell, later Marsh-Caldwell, novelist (b. Linley Wood, Staffordshire, 1791, d. Linley Wood, 5 October 1834).

The daughter of James Caldwell, JP, recorder of Newcastle under Lyme and Deputy Lieutenant of Staffordshire, and his wife Elizabeth Stamford, Anne Caldwell married Arthur Cuthbert Marsh, the son of a partner in a London banking firm, in 1817. They had seven children. Her husband was ruined financially by a notorious swindler in 1824, and at the suggestion of her friend Harriet *Martineau she began to write, publishing *Two Old Men's Tales*, 'The Deformed' and 'The Admiral's Daughter', in 1834. These launched her on a successful writing career during which she became one of the most popular novelists of her generation. *Mount Sorel* (1845) and *Emilia Wyndham* (1846), two early novels, are among her best known. The heroine of the latter has to cope when her father is swindled out of his estate, an indirect reflection of Marsh's own experience. Her husband died in 1849, leaving her the sole support of their children. *Lettice Cooper* (1850), *The Wilmingtons* (1850), and *Ravenscliffe* (1851), produced in rapid succession, were followed regularly by others, over twenty-five in total, earnest and often didactic in tone, and mainly based on the lives of the upper middle classes and the aristocracy. *Chronicles of Dartmoor* (1866) portrays the life of a small country town similar to Elizabeth *Gaskell's *Cranford.* On the death of her brother she succeeded to the family estate in 1858, resuming the surname of Caldwell and publishing as Anne Caldwell, Mrs Marsh, and Mrs Marsh-Caldwell. Later novels included *Heathside Farm* (1863) and *Chronicles of Dartmoor* (1866), both stories of country life. Many of her novels were translated, particularly into German. They were collected in fifteen volumes in Hodgson's Parlour Library (1857). In addition she published two historical works, a translation of the *Song of Roland* (1854), and a number of children's books. *See Harriet Martineau's Autobiography*, with memorials by Maria Weston Chapman (1877); Sally Mitchell, *The Fallen Angel: Chastity, Class and Women's Reading 1835–1880* (1981).

Marsh, (Edith) Ngaio, detective writer (b. Christchurch, New Zealand, 23 April 1899, d. Christchurch, 18 February 1982).

Ngaio (pronounced Ny-o) Marsh was the only child of English-born Henry Esmond Marsh, who emigrated to New Zealand and became a bank clerk, and his wife Rose Elizabeth Seager, a New Zealander. 'Ngaio' is the Maori name for an indigenous flowering tree. She went to St Margaret's College and later to Canterbury School of Art in Christchurch, intent on becoming a painter. Deflected by a growing interest in the theatre, she joined the professional Allan Wilkie Shakespeare Company, then touring Australasia, in 1920, as an actress and a producer. She spent four years in London from 1928 working as an interior decorator, and according to her autobiography *Black Beech and Honeydew* (1968; rev. 1981) read a detective novel one rainy Sunday and decided to write one herself. Her first novel, *A Man Lay Dead* (1934), introduced her hero, Detective Chief Inspector Roderick Alleyn, named after the Elizabethan actor-manager who founded Dulwich College, her father's old school. Not quite as well known as the detective heroes of her colleagues Margery *Allingham, Agatha *Christie, and Dorothy L. *Sayers, the tall, handsome Old Etonian Alleyn featured in all thirty-two of her detective novels, later with his wife Agatha Troy, a painter. Four of Marsh's novels were set in New Zealand, *Vintage Murder* (1937), *Colour Scheme* (1943), *Died in the Wool* (1944) and *Photo-Finish* (1980). Most of the others have tranquil upper-class English settings, disturbed only by the bizarre and brutal quality of her murders. Several of her books are set in the theatre, including *Enter a Murderer* (1935), *Opening Night* (1951), and *Death at the Dolphin* (1967, published in the USA as *Killer Dolphin*, 1966), and almost all contain references to Shakespeare. Marsh divided her time between England and New Zealand, between writing and work in the theatre. She was a driver for the Red Cross in New Zealand during the Second World War and worked as a producer with the D. D. O'Connor Theatre Company between 1944 and 1952. In 1950 she founded the British Commonwealth Theatre Company, which toured Australia and New Zealand, and in the same year directed Pirandello's *Six Characters in Search of an Author* at the Embassy Theatre, London. The Ngaio Marsh Theatre was founded at the University of Canterbury in 1962. As well as her autobiography Marsh published two travel books about New Zealand and some short stories. She was appointed DBE in 1966, and awarded the Grand Master Award of the Mystery Writers of America in 1977. Her last novel, *Light Thickens*, was published after her death in 1982. She died in the house built by her father overlooking Christchurch at the age of 82. *See* M. Shadbolt, *Love and Legend: Some 20th Century New Zealanders* (1976); L. L. Panet, *Watteau's Shepherd: The Detective Novel in Britain, 1914–1940* (1979); E. F. Bargainnier, *10 Women of Mystery* (1981); A. C and L. J. Dooley, in *Art in Crime Writing: Essays on Detective Fiction*, ed. Bernard Benstock (1983).

'**Martin,** Stella' *see* HEYER, Georgette

Martin, Violet *see* ROSS, Martin; *see also* SOMERVILLE, Edith Oenone

Martineau, Harriet, novelist, journalist, and writer on political economy (b. Norwich, 12 June 1802, d. Ambleside, Westmorland, 27 June 1876).

Harriet Martineau was the third daughter and sixth of the eight children of Thomas Martineau, a Norwich fabric manufacturer, and Elizabeth Rankin, the daughter of a sugar refiner. The family were of Huguenot descent and were active members of the Unitarian community at Norwich. Probably her closest relationship was with her younger brother James (1805–1900), later a leading Unitarian theologian. Their subsequent estrangement, largely due to diverging religious beliefs, was particularly painful to her. She suffered from ill health most of her life, and her deafness, which became apparent when she was 16, was a serious disability. The collapse of the family business and the death of her father in 1826 meant that she had to support herself by her writing from an early age. She began with an article in the Unitarian *Monthly Repository* under the editorship of the influential W. J. Fox. Her reputation was made by a series of instructive tales, *Illustrations of Political Economy* (1832–4), followed by *Poor Laws and Paupers Illustrated*, and the sequel *Ilustrations of Taxation*, which she wrote for the Society for the Diffusion of Useful Knowledge. Martineau was at this point an enthusiastic exponent of the views of the Philosophical Radicals. A tour of America in 1834–5 produced two successful travel books, *Society in America* (1837) and the even more popular *A Retrospect of Western Travel* (1838), both highly critical of American society. While in America she became an active supporter of the abolitionist cause and also a campaigner for international copyright. Her first novel, *Deerbrook*, which she thought her best work, a tale of community life sometimes regarded as a precursor of George *Eliot's *Middlemarch*, was published in 1839. It was followed by *The Hour and the Man* (1841), *The Playfellow* (1841), a series of children's stories, from which the best known, *The Crofton Boys*, was separately published in 1856, and *Forest and Game-Law Tales* (1845–6). *Life in the Sickroom* (1844) and *Letters on Mesmerism* (1845) were the result of a lengthy illness (an ovarian cyst) and attempts to find cures. Her advocacy of mesmerism was a source of embarrassment in some quarters and also brought about a breach with some of her family. Her health restored, she moved to Ambleside in 1844, where she built herself a house, ran a small farm, and enjoyed domesticity. Her writing was undertaken with renewed energy. A trip to the Middle East produced another popular travel book, *Eastern Life, Past and Present* (1848). She was persuaded to write a popular *History of England during the Thirty Years' Peace 1816–1846* (1849–50) by Charles Knight of the Society for the Diffusion of Useful Knowledge. With H. G. Atkinson she published *Letters on the Laws of Man's Nature and*

Development (1851), the anti-theological stance of which exacerbated her growing quarrel with her brother. In the following year she published a condensed translation of Auguste Comte's *Philosophie positive* (1852–3), which was highly influential in introducing English readers to his work. Martineau contributed regularly to many periodicals, including *Household Words*, the *Westminster Review*, to which she at one time gave financial support, and later the *Edinburgh Review*. Between 1852 and 1866 she wrote regularly for the *Daily News*. Some of her articles for the last, a series of sometimes acerbic portraits of her contemporaries, were collected in *Biographical Sketches* (1869, enlarged 1877). Towards the end of her life she took an active role in the campaign for the repeal of the Contagious Diseases Acts. At the onset of heart disease in 1855 she wrote her engaging *Autobiography*, which was published posthumously in 1877. Martineau was a formidable mid-Victorian woman of letters, for whom no single category, whether novelist, journalist, philosopher, or historian, is appropriate. A collection of her essays, *Harriet Martineau on Women*, was edited by Gayle Graham Yates in 1985. *Harriet Martineau's Letters to Fanny Wedgwood* were published in 1983 (ed. Elizabeth S. Arbuckle) and her *Selected Letters* (ed. Valerie Sanders) in 1990. *See* R. K. Webb, *Harriet Martineau: A Radical Victorian* (1960); Valerie K. Pichanick, *Harriet Martineau: The Woman and her Work 1802–1876* (1980); Valerie Sanders, *Reason over Passion: Harriet Martineau and the Victorian Novel* (1986); Deirdre David, *Intellectual Women and Victorian Patriarchy* (1987); Susan Hoecker-Drysdale, *Harriet Martineau: First Woman Sociologist* (1993).

Mathers, Helen, later Reeves, novelist (b. Misterton, near Crewkerne, Somerset, 26 August 1853, d. London, 11 March 1920).

Helen Mathers was the third daughter and one of twelve children of Thomas Mathers, a country gentleman, and his wife Maria Buckingham. The children were educated by a governess in a regimen which included lots of outdoor sports and harsh paternal discipline. At 13 she went to Chantry School, Frome, where she worked so hard she injured her health, resulting in partial deafness which remained for the rest of her life. She began to write when young, and at 16 sent a poem to Dante Gabriel Rossetti, who was encouraging. The novelist George Augustus Sala sent one of her stories to M. E. *Braddon's *Belgravia*, which launched her career as a writer of fiction. Her first full-length novel was her greatest success. The autobiographical *Comin' thro' the Rye* (1875), written secretly and much influenced by the work of Rhoda *Broughton, sold over 35,000 copies for Mathers's publisher Richard Bentley, to whom she had sold the copyright. The story drew on her own painful progress from adolescence to maturity and its sexual reference was considered 'advanced' for its time. Other novels also derived their titles from popular songs, as in *Cherry Ripe!* (1878), *Land o' the Leal* (1878), *As he Comes up the Stair* (1878), and *My Lady Greensleeves* (1879). Mathers wrote several *sensation novels with melodramatic plots as in *Murder or Manslaughter* (1885). In 1876 she married Henry Albert Reeves, who became an eminent orthopaedic surgeon. They had one son. Mathers professed to write her books on slips of paper in intervals between domestic duties. Her *Who's Who* entry listed her recreation as needlework. *See* Helen C. Black, *Notable Women Authors of the Day* (1893); Elaine Showalter, *A Literature of their Own: British Women Novelists from Brontë to Lessing* (1977).

Mayor, F(lora) M(acdonald) ('Mary Strafford'), novelist (b. Kingston upon Thames, Surrey, 20 October 1872, d. Hampstead, London, 28 January 1932).

F. M. Mayor was the fourth child and the younger of identical twins born to the Revd Joseph Mayor, professor of classics and later of moral philosophy at King's College, London, and his wife Jessie Grote, an accomplished musician and linguist. Eminent academics and clergymen proliferated on both sides of the family. Jessie Mayor, who was in her forties when the twins were born, translated Icelandic sagas into English. Flora was educated at Surbiton High School and then at Newnham College, Cambridge, her only lengthy separation from her twin sister Alice. At Cambridge she incurred parental disapproval by engaging in a 'rapturous' social life and amateur dramatics as well as reading forbidden novelists, like Olive *Schreiner. She took a third in history and returned home, publishing her first novel, *Mrs. Hammond's Children*, in 1901 under the pen-name Mary Strafford. Despite parental opposition she sought work in the theatre, using Mary Strafford as her stage name, but met with little success. In 1903 she became engaged to a young architect, Ernest Shepherd, whose death from a fever nine months later left her prostrate with asthma and heart trouble. She remained a semi-invalid for the rest of her life, which was never lived apart from members of her family. She spent periods with each of her elder brothers, with her elderly parents, and eventually with her sister in Hampstead, dying of pneumonia at the age of 60. Mayor's novels chronicled lives which were variations of her own, the seemingly wasted existence of Edwardian spinsters in the period before and after the First World War. She claimed that Jane *Austen's *Persuasion* had influenced her rendering of the emotional life more than any other work. She was also sympathetic to the cause of women's suffrage. In *The Third Miss Symons* (1913), according to Merryn Williams, she was the first to write a 'clinical study of spinsterhood'. That novel prepared the ground for her best work, *The Rector's Daughter* (1924), the story of a dutiful unmarried daughter whose one chance of love evaporates when her lover chooses someone young and beautiful. The book was published by Leonard and Virginia *Woolf. *The Squire's Daughter* (1929) looked back nostalgically to the period before the war, but was not a success. *The Room Opposite* (1935) is a posthumous collection of stories. Rebecca *West, E. M. Forster, and John Masefield were among Mayor's admirers, but such was her contemporary reputation that Masefield's *Times* obituary note was not even printed. Recent critical studies and reprints of her novels have redressed the balance for a writer who Williams claims, has been 'of all distinguished English novelists' perhaps 'the least valued'. *See* Sybil Oldfield, *Spinsters of this Parish* (1984); Merryn Williams, *Six Women Novelists* (1987).

Meeke, Mary ('Gabrielli'), novelist (d. Staffordshire, 1816).

Mary Meeke's posthumous reputation was in part due to the enthusiasm of her most famous admirer, the historian Thomas Babington Macaulay, who once claimed to 'all but know her books by heart'. She may have been the wife of Frances Meeke, a Staffordshire clergyman who died in 1801. She used several pseudonyms, including Gabrielli, under which she wrote four novels, but speculation as to her possible Italian origins has been proved groundless. In the preface to *Midnight Weddings* (1802) she ingenuously suggests that the aspiring author should consult his or her publisher as to how best to satisfy the prevailing public taste. She herself appeared to have had little difficulty in this respect, publishing thirty-four works, twenty-eight of them with William Lane's *Minerva Press and many with alluring titles: *Which is the Man* (1801), *What Shall Be, Shall Be* (1801), '*There's a Secret: Find it out*' (1808), *Matrimony the Height of Bliss or Extreme of Misery* (1811). Others had more conventionally *Gothic associations: *The Abbot of Clugny* (1795), *Ellen, Heiress of the Castle* (1807), and *The Veiled Protectress; or The Mysterious Mother* (1819). Despite his enthusiasm, Macaulay acknowledged her to be only second rate. 'My tastes are, I fear, incurably vulgar', he wrote to his sister, 'as you may perceive by my fondness for Mrs. Meeke's novels.' Her books were, he agreed with his sister, 'one just like another, turning on the fortunes of some young man in a very low rank of life who eventually proves to be the son of a duke'. Most of Meeke's novels did in fact turn on a basic inheritance plot by which the suffering and virtuous hero was rewarded with his missing title and social position, set against an exotic background and enlivened with elements of Gothic and sentimental fiction. *Midnight Weddings*, one of her best-known novels, affected to reverse the popular convention by beginning with the hero's wedding, only to have the ceremony interrupted and then abandoned by the discovery that he is not the nobleman he claimed to be. The reading of popular Gothic fiction, of which she was an adept practitioner, was, Meeke claimed in her preface, 'a very innocent, if not a very profitable recreation'. She translated a number of works from French and German and completed Mary *Collyer's translation of Klopstock's *Messiah* (1811). Mary Russell *Mitford was another of her admirers. *See* Dorothy Blakey, *The Minerva Press, 1790–1820* (1939).

Melville, Elizabeth, Lady Colville of Culross, poet (b. Halhill, Scotland, 1571(?)).

Elizabeth Melville was the daughter of Sir James Melville of Halhill, a courtier and diplomat and the author of the well-known *Memoirs of his Own Life*, published by the Bannatyne Club in 1683. Her mother was Christina Boswell. She married John Colville of Culross, later Lord Culross, the son of a Scottish judge. Their eldest son Alexander Colville became an eminent Scottish Episcopalian cleric and Hebrew scholar. Elizabeth Melville was celebrated by her fellow Presbyterians as a 'faithfull and vertuous Ladie', a woman 'unwearied in religious exercises' who was also able to 'delite in poesie'. In 1603 she published a long poem in *ottava rima*, *Ane Godlie Dreame Compylit in Scottis Meter*, 'be M.M. Gentelwoman in Culros at the requeist of her freindis'. The M.M. is assumed to stand for Mistress Melville. Unlike her fellow poets Isabella *Whitney and Anne *Dowriche, Melville made no attempt to disguise her sex or to apologize for it. Her own persona is at the centre of the three movements of the Calvinist *Dreame*, the first of which emotionally professes the poet's sinfulness and misery. The next movement is a vivid dream sequence in which Christ appears to guide the pilgrim through worldly afflictions to a heavenly reward, and the third is an exhortation to readers to learn from the dream and to prepare for their end. Ten further editions of the poem appeared between 1606 and 1737, and three more in the nineteenth century. Elizabeth Melville also left letters and a sonnet. *See* Elaine V. Beilin, *Redeeming Eve: Women Writers of the English Renaissance* (1987); Germaine Greer *et al.* (eds.), *Kissing the Rod: An Anthology of Seventeenth-Century Women's Verse* (1988).

Meysey-Wigley, Caroline *see* CLIVE, Caroline

Mew, Charlotte, poet (b. London, 15 December 1869, d. London, 24 March 1928).

Charlotte Mew was the third of the seven children of Frederick Mew, an architect, and Anne Kendall, the daughter of Henry Edward Kendall, also an architect. Two of the seven children died in infancy, another died at 5, and two were confined to mental asylums. The spectre of insanity and the resulting drain on family finances were the cause of much anxiety. Charlotte Mew's life was outwardly one of extreme uneventfulness, prompting comparisons with Emily *Brontë and Emily Dickinson. She lived in the Bloomsbury area of London throughout her life, and in the family house in Gordon Square for over thirty years, went to a private school, and attended lectures at University College London. She was closely attached to her mother and to her sister Anne. She began to write poetry and also prose when she was young and published regularly in the magazine *Temple Bar* between the ages of 20 and 30. A short story, 'Passed', appeared in the *Yellow Book* in 1894. She also published poems, essays, and short stories at intervals in the *Nation*, the *New Statesman*, the *Englishwoman*, and the *Chap-Book*. Only one volume of poetry was published in her lifetime, *The Farmer's Bride*, published by Harold Monro's Poetry Bookshop in 1916 (and in New York with eleven new poems as *Saturday Market*, 1921). It brought her immediate recognition. Thomas Hardy in particular admired her work and together with John Masefield and Walter de la Mare secured her a civil-list pension in 1922. A second volume, *The Rambling Sailor*, was published posthumously in 1929. Mew's poetry was technically innovative, often written in rhyming free verse. Her subjects included lost childhood, dead lovers, renunciation, sexual and religious passion. Some of her poems were cast as dramatic monologues, demonstrating her psychological insight into complex situations, as in 'Madeleine in Church' and 'In Nunhead Cemetery'. Her sexual inclinations appear to have been lesbian, Ella *D'Arcy, and May *Sinclair numbering among her infatuations, but the outward facts of her life reveal little. In 1927 her sister Anne died of cancer. Charlotte Mew took her own life in a nursing home in March 1928. Her *Collected Poems* were published in 1953 with a memoir by Alida Monro, and her *Collected Poems and Prose* were edited by Val Warner in 1981. *Friends of a Lifetime: Letters to S. C. Cockerell*, Viola Meynell (1940), includes some of Mew's letters. *See* Harold Monro, *Some Contemporary Poets* (1920); Penelope Fitzgerald, *Charlotte Mew and her Friends* (1984); Angela Leighton, *Victorian Women Poets: Writing against the Heart* (1992).

Meynell, Alice (Christiana), poet and essayist (b. Barnes, Surrey, 17 August 1847, d. London, 22 November 1922).

Alice Meynell was educated almost entirely by her father, Thomas James Thompson, a Cambridge graduate of independent means and literary tastes. Her mother Christiana Weller was a concert pianist, and her sister Elizabeth, later Lady Butler, was a painter of considerable reputation. The sisters travelled extensively in France, Switzerland, and Italy with their parents and Alice was fluent in French and Italian. At the age of 20 she became a convert to Roman Catholicism, preceded by her mother, and followed by her sister and, much later, her father. Her first volume of poems, *Preludes* (1875), was praised by Ruskin, Rossetti, and also George *Eliot. Through the Catholic poet Aubrey de Vere she was introduced to Tennyson and gradually made the acquaintance of other literary figures, including Coventry Patmore, George Meredith, and Francis Thompson, to whom she was a great support, both practical and moral. In 1877 she married the Catholic journalist and literary critic Wilfred Meynell. They had eight children. She helped her husband with the editing of various periodicals, including the *Pen* (1880), the *Weekly Register* (1881–98), and *Merry England* (1883–95), while writing herself for a number of others. An accomplished essayist, her work at its best equals that of Virginia *Woolf in its range, poise, and style. Her early collections of essays *The Rhythm of Life* (1893) and *The Colour of Life* (1896) were largely drawn from her journalism and her later work was also collected and republished. The austere lyricism of her poetry prompted comparisons with Christina *Rossetti, and by the end of her life she was linked with Emily *Brontë, Elizabeth Barrett *Browning, and Rossetti as a major woman poet. Her verse is suffused both with her strong religious faith and latterly by her increasingly fervent feminism. *Poems* (1893) was comprised mainly of the contents of *Preludes*, but was followed by *Other Poems* (1896), *Later Poems* (1902), *A Father of Women and Other Poems* (1917), and the posthumous *Last Poems* (1923). As well as her prolific journalism she compiled several anthologies of poetry and wrote prefaces to over a dozen selections from the work of other writers, including Jean *Ingelow, Rossetti, and Charlotte *Yonge, and a biography of Ruskin (1900). In 1901–2 she undertook a lecture tour of the United States. Meynell was a strong supporter of the campaign for women's suffrage, although never a militant, and professed strong pacifist sentiments during the First World War. Her daughter **Viola** (1886–1956), who became a novelist and poet, published a *Memoir* (1929) and her son Francis, a journalist, was instrumental in promoting the publication of her poetry. *See* A. K. Tuell, *Mrs. Meynell and her Literary Generation* (1925); June Badeni, *The Slender Tree: A Life of Alice Meynell* (1981); Angela Leighton, *Victorian Women Poets: Writing Against The Heart* (1992).

Meynell, Viola *see under* MEYNELL, Alice

Mill, Harriet *see* TAYLOR, Harriet

Milton, Frances *see* TROLLOPE, Frances

Minerva Press.

The Minerva Press was a publishing house established in Leadenhall Street, London, by William Lane (1745?–1814), a former poulterer. The press was a prolific producer of 'Novels, Tales, Adventures and Romances' in the period of its heyday, 1790–1820, and at its peak a barometer of public taste. Between 1795 and 1810 more than a third of the annual output had *Gothic titles. Lane paid lip-service to the morally improving quality of his publications, rejecting any which contained violence and emphasizing instead sentimentality and fantasy and in many instances including moral prefaces and conclusions. He published a sufficient quantity of popular fiction to stock the system of circulating libraries which he founded in 1791 and which outlived his press. Latterly the 'Minerva Press' became an epithet of contempt, synonymous with pulp fiction or trashy novels, 'those scanty intellectual viands of the whole female reading public', as Charles Lamb once described them. Lane published almost twice as many women novelists as men, most of them writing anonymously or pseudonymously. They included Anna Maria *Bennett, Elizabeth *Bonhote, Frances *Brooke, Fanny *Burney (an edition of *Evelina*, 1815), Elizabeth *Griffith, Susannah *Gunning, Elizabeth *Hamilton, Barbara *Hofland, Isabella *Kelly, Mary *Meeke, Mary Ann *Radcliffe, and Regina Maria *Roche. His associate Anthony King Newman carried on the publishing side of the business after his death. *See* Dorothy Blakey, *The Minerva Press, 1790–1820* (1939); Coral Ann Howells, *Love, Mystery and Misery: Feeling in Gothic Fiction* (1978).

Minifie, Margaret *see under* GUNNING, Susannah

Minifie, Susannah *see* GUNNING, Susannah

Mitchell, Gladys (Maude Winifred) ('Stephen Hockaby', 'Malcolm Torrie'), detective writer (b. Cowley, Oxfordshire, 19 April 1901, d. Corfe Mullen, Dorset, July 1983).

Gladys Mitchell was the daughter of a Scots father, James Mitchell, and his wife Annie Julia Maude Simmonds. She was educated at the Green School, Isleworth, in Middlesex, and at Goldsmith's College and University College London. Professionally she was a schoolmistress, teaching English, history, and games from her college days until 1966, when she finally retired. At the same time she produced a novel a year from 1929 onwards, totalling over sixty books. (She wrote in the staff room during breaks.) Her first, *Speedy Death* (1929), introduced her detective heroine Mrs Beatrice Adela Lestrange Bradley, later Dame Beatrice, a psychoanalyst as well as sleuth, many of whose socially progressive views were shared with her creator, whose mouthpiece she frequently became. Mrs Bradley remained the central character of nearly all sixty detective novels. Many of the books, such as *Death at the Opera* (1934) and *Laurels are Poison* (1942), were set in the tension-laden and enclosed worlds of girls' schools and colleges which Mitchell knew well. She was a member of the famous Detection Club, along with Dorothy L. *Sayers and Agatha *Christie, a survivor of the so-called golden age of detective writing who carried on writing into the 1970s. Many of her novels reversed the conventions of the genre. She was fond of black comedy and mild spoofs. In the course of the double murder plot of *Speedy Death* Beatrice Bradley actually commits the second offence for which she is tried and found not guilty, only to confess to her defence counsel, who is also her son by her first marriage. Meanwhile the very masculine corpse which results from the first murder turns out to be that of a female. Her interest in exotic folklore and witchcraft often spilled over into her books, as did her passion for ancient buildings and architectural history. Mitchell also wrote under the masculine pseudonyms Stephen Hockaby and Malcolm Torrie, the latter series having a detective hero Timothy Herring, who is later joined by his wife. She contributed to several well-known collections of detective stories and received the Silver Dagger Award of the Crime Writers' Association in 1976. She published her last novel in 1979 at the age of 78.

Mitchison, Naomi (Margaret), novelist, short story writer, and writer for children (b. Edinburgh, 1 November 1897).

Naomi Mitchison is the daughter of the late John Scott Haldane, a philosopher and physiologist, and Kathleen Trotter, an active suffragist. She and her brother J. B. S. Haldane (1892–1964), the scientist and writer, were sent to the Dragon School, Oxford, which then took mainly boys. Later she had a governess while he went to Eton. The war interrupted her studies for a science degree as a home student at St Anne's College, Oxford, and she became a VAD (Voluntary Aid Detachment) nurse. In 1916 she married G. Richard Mitchison (d. 1970), a barrister and later a Labour MP (he became Lord Mitchison in 1964). They had four sons, one of whom died, and two daughters. From the beginning Naomi Mitchison's career combined literature and politics. She was active in the establishment of the first birth control clinics in London, visited Russia and Austria in the 1930s, and, as a native Scot who settled permanently in Argyllshire in 1937, became involved in local and national affairs. She stood unsuccessfully as a Labour candidate for the Scottish Universities in 1935 and between 1963 and 1989 was a tribal mother (Mmarona) to the Bakgatla of Botswana. Her more than eighty books range from fiction and short stories to plays, travel, children's books, biography, and fantasy. Her early novels were historical but also explored contemporary issues. *The Conquered* (1923) is set in Gaul at the time of Julius Caesar's conquest, *Cloud Cuckoo Land* (1925) is about the inhabitants of an Aegean island in the fourth century BC, and *The Corn King and the Spring Queen* (1931) contrasts three ancient civilizations. *The Blood of the Martyrs* (1939), set against the background of the persecution of the early Christians, is one of several novels which considers early socialist experiments, while *The Bull Calves* (1947) uses its historical context, the aftermath of the 1745 Jacobite Rebellion, as a parallel for the reconstruction of Scottish society and the involvement of women after the Second World War. *We have been Warned* (1935), which drew on her observations of communism in Russia, was rejected by several publishers because of sexual explicitness. Her later fiction has moved in the direction of science fiction: *Memoirs of a Spacewoman* (1962), *Solution Three* (1975), a post-nuclear fantasy, and *Not by Bread Alone* (1983). She has written several volumes of autobiography, *Small Talk: Memoirs of an Edwardian Childhood* (1973), *All Change Here: Girlhood and Marriage* (1975), and *You May Well Ask: A Memoir 1920–1940* (1979), supplemented by two volumes of diaries, *Vienna Diary* (1974) and *Among you Taking Notes: The Wartime Diary of Naomi Mitchison, 1939–45* (1985). *Mucking Around* (1981) describes her travels over five decades. She published two further historical novels in 1991, at the age of 93. *Sea-Green Ribbons*, set during the period of Cromwell and the Levellers, examines patriarchy and the position of women. *The Oath Takers*, set in the Frankish empire after Charlemagne, explores power and morality. Mitchison's *Who's Who* entry lists 'surviving so far' under 'Recreation'. *See* Mary Chamberlain (ed.), *Writing Lives* (1988); Jill Benton, *Naomi Mitchison: A Century of Experiment in Life and Letters* (1990).

Mitford, Jessica *see under* MITFORD, Nancy

Mitford, Mary Russell, essayist and dramatist (b. Alresford, Hampshire, 16 December 1787, d. Swallowfield, Berkshire, 10 January 1855).

The daughter of George Mitford or Midford, an improvident member of an old Northumberland family, who had some medical training but never practised, and of Mary Russell, the independently wealthy daughter of a Hampshire clergyman, Mary Mitford won a £20,000 prize in a lottery at the age of 10, which enabled her father to build a house at Reading and to send her to school at Mrs St Quintin's, Hans Place, London, where both Lady Caroline *Lamb and Laetitia *Landon (L.E.L.) were also educated. Mary was a precocious child and a voracious reader. She published her first volume of *Poems* in 1810, followed by *Christina, the Maid of the South Seas* (1811) and *Watlington Hill* (1812), both long poems, and *Narrative Poems on the Female Character* (1813). In 1820, when her father's improvidence had reduced the family to virtual poverty, they moved to a cottage in the village of Three Mile Cross in Berkshire, on the main road between Reading and Basingstoke. The need for an income led Mitford to begin a series of sketches for the little-known *Lady's Magazine* in 1819. The immediate success of 'Our Village' increased the magazine's sales from 250 to 2,000 and made Mary Russell Mitford's reputation. Her friend Elizabeth Barrett (later *Browning) pronounced her 'a sort of prose Crabbe in the sun'. *Our Village* was collected in five volumes (1824–32). It was republished frequently throughout the century and the 1893 edition was edited by Anne Thackeray *Ritchie, with illustrations by Hugh Thomson. Meanwhile she tried her hand at the writing of tragedy, persuaded that her real talents lay in that direction. *Julian* (1823) was produced at Covent Garden with Macready in the title role. It was followed by *Foscari* (1826), with Charles Kemble, and the best of her plays, *Rienzi*, which was produced at Drury Lane in 1828. Another, *Charles I* (1834), played at the Victoria Theatre, south of the Thames. She also wrote *Mary Queen of Scots* (1831), in verse, and an opera libretto, *Sadak and Kalasrade* (1835). Her plays were collected in 1854, but although admired by her friends, were generally pronounced dull. *Bedford Regis; or Sketches of a Country Town*, based on Reading, appeared in 1835, and although it went into three editions, it did not equal the success of *Our Village*. Miss Mitford by this time had become a celebrity, largely as a result of *Our Village*. Her large number of friends and acquaintances, among them Harriet *Martineau, Felicia *Hemans, and Amelia *Opie, are affectionately presented in *Recollections of a Literary Life* (1852). Her last work, *Atherton* (1854), a novel, won Ruskin's approbation, but fiction was not her genre. Mitford was a lively conversationalist and an attractive letter writer. Her letters were collected by A. G. L'Estrange in *The Life of Mary Russell Mitford* (1870), and again in *The Friendships of Mary Russell Mitford in Letters from her Literary Correspondents* (1882). A second series of her letters was edited by H. F. Chorley (1872). *Elizabeth Barrett to Miss Mitford: Unpublished Letters* was edited by Betty Miller in 1954. *See* Harriet Martineau, *Biographical Sketches* (1877); Virginia *Woolf, *The Common Reader* (1925); Shelagh Hunter, *Victorian Idyllic Fiction: Pastoral Strategies* (1984); P. D. Edwards, *Idyllic Realism from Mary Russell Mitford to Hardy* (1988).

Mitford, Nancy (Freeman), novelist and biographer (b. Chelsea, London, 28 November 1904, d. Versailles, 30 June 1973).

Nancy Mitford was the eldest of the six daughters and a son of David Bertram Ogilvy Freeman-Mitford, second Baron Redesdale, and his wife Sydney Bowles. One grandfather, the first Baron, had been a diplomat, traveller, and a close friend of Edward VII. The other, Thomas Gibson Bowles, was a brilliant but eccentric back-bencher and the founder of the magazine *Vanity Fair*. Her childhood was spent in various houses in the Cotswolds. Her father refused to send her to school, maintaining that education was unnecessary for daughters (their brother went to Eton). She became an avid reader of biographies, memoirs, and letters, but grew up, she claimed, 'as ignorant as a owl'. She blamed her parents for her lack of education, and caricatured her father affectionately as the lowbrow Uncle Matthew of her novels. After a finishing school in Gloucestershire and a brief period at the Slade School of Art she went to Paris, which was the beginning of a lifelong love affair with all things French. She returned to London as a débutante, where she met Henry Green, Evelyn Waugh, John Betjeman, Robert Byron, Maurice Bowra, and Harold Acton, among others, and lived for a while with Waugh and his first wife Evelyn Gardner until the break-up of their marriage. She began to write for *Vogue* and *Harper's Magazine* and in 1931 published her first novel, *Highland Fling*, followed by *Christmas Pudding* (1932) and, in 1935, *Wigs on the Green*, intended as a spoof on the British Fascist movement. In 1933 she married Peter Murray Rennell Rodd, younger son of the first Baron Rennell. The marriage was childless and unhappy, and they were eventually divorced in 1958. She became an ARP driver during the war and helped to turn a fashionable Curzon Street bookshop into a wartime refuge for intellectuals. Her fourth novel, *Pigeon Pie*, about the phoney war, was published in 1940, but it was her next book, *The Pursuit of Love* (1945), which sold over a million copies and turned her into a popular writer. It drew on her affair with Gaston Palewski, a member of the Free French and later adviser and minister under de Gaulle, and also on her own upper-class family life. She returned to Paris immediately after the war, and followed up her success with *Love in a Cold Climate* (1949) and *The Blessing* (1951). In the 1950s she turned to biography, of which the first, *Madame de Pompadour* (1954), was the liveliest and her best. *Voltaire in Love* (1957), the lavishly illustrated *The Sun King* (1966), on Louis XIV, and *Frederick the Great* (1970) followed. One final novel, *Don't Tell Alfred* (1960), was based on her observations of diplomatic life, and continued the story of the main character in *The Pursuit of Love* and *Love in a Cold Climate*, and her Radlett relations. An essay on 'The English Aristocracy', published in *Encounter* in 1955, sparked off a heated debate on 'U' (upper-class) and 'non-U' speech and was reprinted with other essays in *Noblesse Oblige*, co-edited with A. S. C. Ross. She translated Madame de Lafayette's *The Princesse de Clèves* (1950) and Alfred Roussin's farce *The Little Hut* (1951). She wrote regularly for the *Sunday Times* in the 1950s. *The Water Beetle*, a collection of essays, was published in 1962, and *A Talent to Annoy: Essays, Journalism and Reviews* (ed. Charlotte Mosley) appeared posthumously in 1986. Through her mother she was connected with the Stanleys, famous for their theologians, and edited two volumes of their correspondence, *The Ladies of Alderley* (1938) and *The Stanleys of Alderley* (1939). 'Essentially a child of the twenties', as James Lees-Milne's *DNB* entry suggests, she remained a witty, elegant, and glamorous figure to the end of her life, photographed by Cecil Beaton, painted by William Acton and others. She was awarded the Légion d'honneur in 1972, and appointed CBE. She died in Versailles, where she had moved in 1967. Her sister **Jessica Mitford** (b. 1917), a critic of American social and political life, has written of the Mitford family life in *Hons and Rebels* (1960). *See* Harold Acton, *Nancy Mitford: A Memoir* (1975); Selina Hastings, *Nancy Mitford* (1985).

Molesworth, Mary Louisa ('Ennis Graham'), novelist and children's writer (b. Rotterdam, 1839, d. London, July 1921).

Mary Louisa Molesworth was the elder daughter of Scottish parents, Charles Augustus Stewart, a merchant, and his wife Agnes Janet Wilson. In 1841 the family moved from Rotterdam to Manchester, where she was taught at home by her mother and wrote stories to amuse herself. *The Carved Lions* (1895) drew on her early childhood. She was taught writing by the Revd William Gaskell, husband of Elizabeth *Gaskell, and went to school briefly in Switzerland. In 1861 she married the well-connected Major Richard Molesworth, an officer in the Dragoons. A head wound sustained in the Crimean War left him with 'a very violent temper' and financially irresponsible. The couple had four children but later separated, Mrs Molesworth living for several years in France and Germany until 1883, when she settled permanently in London. Her husband died in 1900. Ill-matched couples featured prominently in her early novels, written under the pseudonym Ennis Graham, the name of a deceased friend. When these proved unsuccessful she was encouraged to write children's books. *Tell me a Story* (1875), a collection of tales, was followed by her well-known children's novel *Carrots* (1876), about a red-haired boy who finds it hard to adjust to the grown-up world, and by *The Cuckoo Clock* (1877), her first book to make use of fantasy and the first to be published under her own name. Other successful books for children included *The Tapestry Room* (1879), another fantasy, set in France, *The Adventures of Herr Baby* (1881), based on her youngest son, and *Hoodie* (1882), a portrait of her daughter. Some of her critics complained of her characters' use of baby talk but others commended her realistic picture of children's lives. She herself believed that children's stories should be real ('save in an occasional flight to fairyland') and also moral, without becoming didactic. She produced over a hundred titles, and her books had many admirers including Swinburne, who ranked her next to George *Eliot. *See* Marghanita Laski, *Mrs. Ewing, Mrs. Molesworth and Mrs. Hodgson Burnett* (1950); R. L. Green, *Mrs. Molesworth* (1961).

Monck, Mary, poet (b. *c*.1678, d. Bath, 1715).

Mary Monck was the second daughter of Robert Molesworth, later Viscount Molesworth, a diplomat, politician, and writer with estates in County Dublin and also in Yorkshire, and his wife Laetitia, daughter of Richard, Lord Coote of Coloony. One of seventeen children, only nine of whom survived to adulthood, she was more or less self-educated, and taught herself Latin, Italian, and Spanish, as well as reading widely in English literature. She became the first wife of George Monck of Dublin, Member for Philipstown in the Irish Parliament between 1703 and 1713. He apparently suffered from a series of mental disorders and the couple lived apart for some time, Mary taking their children with her. She died at Bath in 1715 around the age of 37. Her father published a volume of her poems and translations in 1716, dedicated to the Princess of Wales, later Queen Caroline, and under the title *Marinda*, describing them in the preface as 'the Product of the leisure Hours of a Young Gentlewoman lately Dead, who in a Remote Country Retirement, without any Assistance but that of a good Library, and without omitting the daily Care due to a large Family, not only perfectly acquired the several Languages here made use of, but the good Morals and Principles contain'd in those Books'. They had been found in her desk, 'written with her own hand, little expecting, and as little desiring the Publick shou'd have any Opportunity of Applauding or Condemning them'. Some of her poems were published in George Colman and Bonnell Thornton's collection **Poems by Eminent Ladies* (1755), including possibly her best known and frequently anthologized 'Verses Written on her Death-Bed at Bath to her Husband in London'.

Montagu, Elizabeth, essayist, letter writer, and literary hostess (b. York, 2 October 1720, d. London, 25 August 1800).

Elizabeth Montagu was the elder daughter and fourth child of wealthy and well-connected parents. Her father Matthew Robinson was a Yorkshire landowner and her mother Elizabeth Drake a Cambridgeshire heiress. Her sister Sarah *Scott became a well-known novelist. Their early education was supervised by Dr Conyers Middleton, a Cambridge scholar who was her maternal grandmother's second husband. In 1742 she married Edward Montagu, grandson of the Earl of Sandwich, a man nearly thirty years her senior, who owned estates in Yorkshire and Berkshire and coal mines in Northumberland and who later became a Whig MP. Their only son died soon after his birth, and she channelled her energies into creating a literary salon at her London house in Hill Street, Mayfair. She was a talented hostess and insisted that intellect took precedence over social eminence at both her breakfast parties and later her evening 'conversation parties'. Literature was the main topic of conversation and card-playing was forbidden. Her parties became a centre for the the *Bluestocking Circle, which included her friend the Duchess of Portland, formerly Lady Margaret Cavendish Harley, Elizabeth *Carter, Catherine *Talbot, Elizabeth *Vesey, Mary *Delany, Frances Boscawen, Anna *Seward, and Hester *Chapone. There were other hostesses, including Mrs Vesey, the Duchess of Portland, and Mrs Fulke Greville, but Mrs Montagu was dubbed 'Queen of the Blues' because of the splendour of her entertainments as well as the sharpness of her intellect. In 1760 she contributed three dialogues to her friend Lord Lyttleton's *Dialogues of the Dead*, a satire on modern society, and in 1769 published *An Essay on the Writing and Genius of Shakespeare*, ostensibly to refute Voltaire's depreciation of the poet. Her friendship with Dr Johnson was damaged by his disparaging comments on both these works but in general her reputation for learning and intellect was enhanced by their publication. She inherited her husband's fortune after his death in 1775 and in 1782 built Montagu House, in Portman Square, a lavishly decorated mansion where her parties continued on a grand scale for over ten years. She was generous to her friends, especially to Elizabeth Carter, on whom she bestowed an annuity, and patronized younger writers, including the poet James Beattie, the philosopher Richard Price, Hannah *More, and Fanny *Burney. She was also generous to her tenants and employees, and entertained London chimney sweeps every year on May Day on the lawns of her house. A woman of strong opinions, she evoked strong, sometimes hostile reactions in her contemporaries, but her contribution to the general acceptance of women as intellectuals was tacitly acknowledged. Her letters are the best reflection of her engaging personality. *See The Letters of Mrs. Elizabeth Montagu*, ed. M. Montagu (4 vols., 1809–13); *Elizabeth Montagu, the Queen of the Bluestockings: Her Correspondence from 1720[1732]–1761*, ed. Emily J. Climenson (2 vols., 1906); *Mrs. Montagu, 'Queen of the Blues': Her Letters and Friendships from 1762–1800* (2 vols., 1923); Sylvia H. Myers, *The Bluestocking Circle* (1990).

Montagu, Lady Mary Wortley, poet and letter writer (b. Thoresby, Nottinghamshire, 1689, d. London, 21 August 1762).

Lady Mary Wortley Montagu was the eldest of the four children of Evelyn Pierrepont, fifth Earl of Kingston, later Marquis of Dorchester and first Duke of Kingston, and Lady Mary Fielding, daughter of the third Earl of Denbigh. The novelist Henry Fielding was a cousin. Her mother died when she was 13, and she was educated by governesses who she once said were like those of Clarissa Harlowe, in Richardson's novel, who filled her head with 'superstitious tales and false notions'. Much of her education was gained from reading in her father's libraries and she also taught herself Latin. As a girl she acted as her father's hostess and through him met Addison, Steele, Gay, Congreve, and other literary figures. In 1712 she married Edward Wortley Montagu, a Whig politician and MP for Huntingdon who was eleven years her senior. Her father objected to the match on the grounds of the inadequacy of the marriage settlement and Mary eloped with Montagu to avoid marriage to a candidate of her father's choice. Montagu was appointed a treasury commissioner in 1714 and Mary became a prominent figure at court and in London society, widely celebrated as a beauty and a wit. Pope in particular professed his admiration for her. Her first publication was an essay in the *Spectator*, and she wrote a critique of Addison's *Cato*, to which the author responded by adopting some of her suggestions. Her *Court Poems*, later retitled *Town Eclogues*, were published without her permission in 1716. In the same year her husband was appointed ambassador to Turkey. Some of her best letters record the long journey to Constantinople, and her responses to Turkish life and culture. Montagu was recalled in 1718, and they returned to England with their two children, maintaining a house in London and another in Twickenham, near Pope. Mary had suffered seriously from smallpox in 1715 and had had her son inoculated against the disease while abroad. On her return she was active in promoting inoculation and was largely responsible for its introduction into England. Her friend Mary *Astell encouraged her to publish her so-called 'Embassy Letters', compiled from her letters and journals written while abroad, but she refused. Her relations with Pope soured in or around 1728 when he satirized her in *The Dunciad*. The exact cause was unknown although the most likely was her rebuff of a declaration of love. A vicious print warfare ensued, with Pope making scarcely veiled references and lampoons of her in a stream of works. She in turn was assumed to be the joint author, with Lord Hervey, of *Verses Addressed to the Imitator of... Horace* (1733). In 1737–8 she wrote *The Nonsense of Common Sense*, nine issues of a weekly pro-Walpole newspaper, in response to the Opposition journal *Common Sense; or The Englishman's Journal*, edited by the Earl of Chesterfield. In 1736 she fell in love with Francesco Algarotti, a bisexual Italian writer, for whose favours she competed with various men, including Lord Hervey and later Prince Frederick of Prussia. She left England in pursuit of him three years later, but the affair cooled. She and her husband maintained an amicable correspondence, but chose not to meet again. She travelled in France and Italy for a period of over twenty years, settling in various centres, including Avignon, Brescia, and eventually Venice. Her letters to friends and family, and especially to her daughter Lady Bute, later wife of the Prime Minister, give witty and perceptive comments on contemporary life, literature, and social issues. Horace Walpole's letters, in turn, described her as 'old, dirty, tawdry, and painted', after their encounter in

Florence in 1740. He nevertheless published her *Six Town Eclogues: With Some Other Poems* (1747). Despite her social position, she was reluctant to play a full part in literary life, but instead showed her poems to friends. She once reflected that the use of knowledge in her sex, besides the amusements of solitude, was to moderate the passions and learn to be contented at a small expense. She returned to London in January 1762, after her husband's death, and died of cancer in August of that year. Before her death she arranged for the posthumous publication of the *Embassy Letters*, which appeared in 1763. Her *Poetical Works* were published in 1768 and her collected *Works*, including letters, poems, and essays, in 1803 (5 vols., ed. J. Dallaway). Her great-grandson Lord Wharncliffe produced an edition of her *Letters and Works* in 1837, with an introduction by her granddaughter Lady Louisa Stuart. The first modern edition of *The Complete Letters of Lady Mary Wortley Montagu* was published by Robert Halsband (3 vols., 1965–7). Halsband also edited her *Selected Letters* (1970). A new edition of *Essays and Poems and Simplicity: A Comedy* by Robert Halsband and Isobel Grundy was published in 1977. Her *Turkish Embassy Letters* have been edited by Anita *Desai (1992). *See* Robert Halsband, *Life of Lady Mary Wortley Montagu* (1956); Patricia Meyer Spacks, in *The Private Self: Theory and Practice of Women's Autobiographical Writings*, ed. Shari Benstock (1988).

The Monument of Matrones.

The Monument of Matrones: Conteining Seven Severall Lamps of Virginitie, or Distinct Treatises . . . Compiled . . . by Thomas Bentley of Graies Inne Student (1582) was a compendium of sacred writings, mainly by women, designed to aid women in their private devotions. The writers included Queen *Elizabeth I, Catherine Parr (1512–48), Lady Jane Grey (1537–54), Lady Elizabeth Tyrwhitt, Lady Frances Abergavennie, and many anonymous gentlewomen as well as women of the Bible, both real and allegorical. *See* Elaine V. Beilin, *Redeeming Eve: Women Writers of the English Renaissance* (1987).

Moodie, Susanna *see under* STRICKLAND, Agnes

More, Cecilia and Elizabeth *see under* ROPER, Margaret

More, Hannah, poet, playwright, and religious writer
(b. Stapleton, Gloucestershire, 2 February 1745, d. Clifton, near Bristol, 7 September 1833).

Hannah More was the fourth of the five daughters of Jacob More, the headmaster of a free school at Fishponds, near Stapleton in Gloucestershire. Her mother was Mary Grace, a farmer's daughter. More was High Church and Tory in his affiliations, and determined that his daughters should be educated in order to earn their own living. Hannah was precocious and clever. Her father taught her Latin and mathematics, and she learned French, Italian, and Spanish at a school established by her elder sisters. Her first publication was a pastoral drama, *The Search after Happiness* (1762), intended for the instruction of 'young persons', particularly young ladies. The next, *The Inflexible Captive* (1774), which derived from a Latin translation, was performed at the Theatre Royal, Bath. She met most of the members of the literary and scientific circle in and around Bristol, and in 1822 suffered a broken engagement which made her resolve never to entertain another. She paid a visit to London with her sisters and obtained introductions to most of the eminent literary and theatrical figures of the day. She became a close friend of David Garrick and his wife, met Burke, Joshua Reynolds, and Dr Johnson, and was also a friend of Horace Walpole. She knew Elizabeth *Montagu and most of the other members of the *Bluestocking Club, which she celebrated in her long poem *The Bas Bleu* (1786). Her friendship with Garrick inspired her two major dramas, *Percy* (1778), a verse tragedy, and *The Fatal Falsehood* (1779). Garrick's death in 1779 signalled the gradual waning of More's asociation with metropolitan literary and artistic circles and a widening of her acquaintance with religious and philanthropic figures, particularly her friendship with William Wilberforce and later Zachary Macaulay and other members of the Clapham Sect of Evangelicals. The didactic *Sacred Dramas* (1782) indicated the new direction of her work. She lived for a time with Mrs Garrick, to console her, and then removed to Cowslip Green, near Bristol. Her first serious work of a philosophical nature, *Thoughts on the Importance of the Manners of the Great to General Society*, was published in 1788 and also *Slavery: A poem*. The following year Hannah and her sisters established Sunday schools, friendly societies, and also weekly schools in parishes around Cowslip Green to raise the educational level and the standard of living of the poor. More's ideas about education for the lower orders were practical and patrician. They were taught the Bible and Catechism and 'such coarse works as may fit them for servants. I allow of no writing for the poor,' she wrote to Wilberforce. The writing of tracts also became an important activity. She had been encouraged to write one to counter the heady propaganda of the French Revolution in 1792. *Village Politics by Will Chip* (1792) was distributed by the government in thousands to Scotland and Ireland. *Remarks on the Speech of M. Dupont* (1793) was written in response to the professed atheism of the French government. She and her sisters wrote a series of penny tracts containing moral tales, instructive ballads, and Bible stories, which were collected as *Cheap Repository Tracts* (1795–8). The circulation in the first year was said to have reached two million, and the organization which was created for their distribution led to the formation of the Religious Tract Society. The best known of the tracts was *The Shepherd of Salisbury Plain* (1795). Several of More's works treated the subject of education, particularly for women. She favoured practical education as opposed to accomplishments, as in her *Strictures on the Modern System of Female Education* (1799), which went through thirteen editions, but she was no advocate of women's rights. 'Rights of women! We shall be hearing of the Rights of Children next!' she supposedly commented in response to Mary *Wollstonecraft. More's most popular work, and her only novel, *Coelebs in Search of a Wife* (1808), set out the duties of a model wife who is sensibly educated, but who nevertheless adheres to the traditional womanly sphere. She continued to write tracts in prose and verse. *The Feast of Freedom* (1819), a poem in celebration of the abolition of slavery in Ceylon, was set to music by Charles Wesley. *Moral Sketches*, her last significant work, appeared in 1819. Her four sisters predeceased her. She herself suffered a series of illnesses and died in 1833. *See* W. Roberts, *Memoirs of the Life and Correspondence of Hannah More* (1834); Charlotte *Yonge, *Hannah More* (1888); Mitzi Myers, in *Fetter'd or Free? British Women Novelists 1670–1815*, ed. Mary Anne Schofield and Cecilia Macheski (1986); Elizabeth Kowaleski-Wallace, *Their Fathers' Daughters: Hannah More, Maria Edgeworth, and Patriarchal Complicity* (1991); Kathryn Sutherland, in *Revolution in Writing: British Literary Responses to the French Revolution*, ed. Kelvin Everest (1991).

Morgan, Sydney, Lady Morgan, née Owenson, novelist
(b. Dublin, 25 December 1783, d. London, 14 April 1859).

Sydney Morgan was the daughter of an Irish actor, Robert MacOwen (1744–1812), who changed his name to Owenson, and Jane Mill, the daughter of a Shrewsbury tradesman. Her date of birth was the subject of some speculation as she inclined to put it forward, and her detractors maliciously put it back as far as 1775. She attended schools in Dublin but spent much of her youth backstage in her father's theatrical company. She inherited his extrovert talents and could sing, dance, and also play the harp. She may also have appeared on stage in her youth. She became a governess at an early age in order to help extricate her father from financial difficulties and published her first volume of *Poems* in 1801. She wrote verses to accompany a number of Irish melodies, and published these as *Twelve Original Hibernian Melodies* in 1805. Meanwhile she determined to write novels, hoping to emulate the earnings of Fanny *Burney. Her first attempts, *St. Clair* (1803) and *The Novice of St. Dominick* (1805), were popular romances supposedly modelled on Goethe's *Sorrows of Werther*, but her third, *The Wild Irish Girl* (1806), which contained strongly nationalistic sentiments, established her reputation. It was as a novelist of Irish life, particularly peasant life, that she was best known. In 1807 she wrote a modestly successful opera, *The First Attempt* (1807), as well as two volumes of *Patriotic Sketches of Ireland*, and in 1809 another novel, *Woman; or Ida of Athens*, which contained some advanced theories of education for women. As a result of her local celebrity she took up residence as a member of the household of the Marquis of Abercorn. Partly at the insistence of Lady Abercorn she married the Marquis's surgeon Sir Thomas Charles Morgan in 1812. There were no children of the marriage. *O'Donnel: A National Tale*, published in 1814, was praised by Sir Walter Scott but also subjected to personalized attacks in Tory periodicals, particularly by J. W. Croker in the *Quarterly Review* and in *Blackwood's Magazine*. Another Irish novel, *Florence M'Carthy*, was also savagely reviewed, as was her popular and successful book on France (1815). A similar work on Italy (1821) was praised by Byron as 'fearless and excellent' but won official disfavour. *The O'Briens and the O'Flahertys* (1827), which professed strong views in favour of Irish emancipation, continued the run of severe reviews. Lady Morgan responded vigorously to many of these in various periodicals. A second visit to France produced *France in 1829–30* (1830), which like its predecessor was written in conjunction with her husband. She also wrote a series of autobiographical sketches, *A Book of the Boudoir* (1829), collected her articles from the *New Monthly Magazine* under the title *Absenteeism* (1827), and embodied her observations of Belgium in a novel, *The Princess* (1835). In 1837 she became the first woman to receive a pension for 'services to the world of letters' and in 1839 moved from Dublin to London, where she became a prominent figure in social circles. *Woman and her Master* (1840) asserted the equality of the sexes, and the superiority of women in some respects. She assisted her husband in *A Book without a Name* (1841), a collection of magazine pieces, but this was her last major publication. She engaged in a brief pamphlet war with Cardinal Wiseman in 1851 and published *Passages in my Autobiography* with the help of Geraldine *Jewsbury in 1859, the year of her death. Hepworth Dixon, the editor of the *Athenaeum* and her literary executor, edited her *Memoirs: Autobiographies, Diaries and Correspondence* (1862). *See* W. J. Fitzpatrick, *Lady Morgan: Her Career Literary and Personal* (1860); Lionel Stevenson, *The Wild Irish Girl: The Life of Sydney Owenson, Lady Morgan* (1936), Mary Campbell, *Lady Morgan: The Life and Times of Sydney Owenson* (1988); James Newcomer, *Lady Morgan the Novelist* (1990).

Morrell, Lady Ottoline (Violet Anne), literary hostess (b. London, 16 June 1873, d. Tunbridge Wells, Kent, 21 April 1938).

Lady Ottoline Morrell was the only daughter and youngest child of Lieutenant-General Arthur Cavendish-Bentinck and his second wife Augusta Mary Elizabeth Browne, later Baroness Bolsover in her own right. Lady Ottoline's title was granted to her and her siblings by Queen *Victoria when her half-brother became Duke of Portland in 1879. She was educated by her mother at Welbeck Abbey, the family seat, and as a child rebelled against the orthodoxies of upper-class society. In 1902 she married Philip Edward Morrell, a Liberal MP, first for South Oxfordshire and then for Burnley, who shared her political views and also her aesthetic interests. They had a son who died in infancy and a daughter. Their London home in Bedford Square became the centre of an intellectual circle which included Henry James, Bertrand Russell, Yeats, Walter de la Mare, Eliot, Augustus John, Lytton Strachey, Virginia *Woolf, Siegfried Sassoon, Aldous Huxley, and D. H. Lawrence. Both Lawrence and Huxley drew her unflatteringly, in *Women in Love* and *Crome Yellow*, and possibly in *Lady Chatterley's Lover*, *Those Barren Leaves*, and *Point Counter Point*. The twelve-year rift caused by *Women in Love* was only just patched up in 1928. Both Morrells were pacifists and their house became a refuge for conscientious objectors during the war. Garsington Manor in Oxfordshire became the centre of their hospitality from 1913, and after the war the circle revived and expanded to include a new generation of artists, writers, and intellectuals: Maynard Keynes, Katherine *Mansfield, Mark Gertler, *Carrington, and others. According to Lord David Cecil's *DNB* entry, Ottoline Morrell was 'a character of Elizabethan extravagance and force', whose powerful personality expressed itself in her conversation, her dress, even the decoration of her houses. She was a fierce champion and generous patron, but her friendships were often punctuated by violent quarrels. Augustus John and Bertrand Russell were her lovers. Her role in the literary and artistic life of her time is underlined by her regular appearance in the letters and memoirs of her contemporaries. Her own *Memoirs*, ed. Robert Gathorne-Hardy (2 vols., 1963, 1974), in turn reflect a literary and cultural era. *See* Sandra Johnson Darroch, *Lady Ottoline Morrell* (1975); Miranda Seymour, *Ottoline Morrell: Life on the Grand Scale* (1992).

'Morrow, Jacob' *see* MANNING, Olivia

Muir, 'Willa' (Wilhelmina Johnstone, also 'Agnes Neill Scott'), novelist, poet, and translator (b. Montrose, 13 March 1890, d. London, 22 May 1970).

The daughter of Peter Anderson, a Montrose draper, and his wife, both natives of Unst, in the Shetlands, Willa, as she was known, could speak several dialects as a child. She attended a board school and later Montrose Academy and took a first in classics at the University of St Andrews in 1910. She moved to London, where she became a lecturer and then vice-principal of Gipsy Hill Training College. She was forced to resign her post after her engagement to the writer and poet Edwin Muir (1887–1959), whose atheist principles offended her superiors. They were married in 1919 and lived in Glasgow, where Edwin worked as an office clerk. She taught school for a while and in 1921 they left for Europe, living in Prague, Dresden, Hellerau, and in Italy and Austria between 1921 and 1924, a period which was crucial to Edwin's recovery from a nervous breakdown. They then spent several years in the south of France, where they began to work together as translators, Willa, the better linguist, undertaking the bulk of the work. Between 1924 and 1940 they produced more than forty volumes of translations, many of them of contemporary German authors including Sholem Asch, Hermann Broch, Lion Feuchtwanger, and, most importantly, Franz Kafka, whose work became widely known in the 1930s largely due to their translations. Some of Willa Muir's translations were published under her own name, some under the pseudonym Agnes Neill Scott, and some jointly with her husband. They returned in 1927 to England, where their son was born the same year, and lived in London and the Home Counties until 1935, when they moved to Scotland. Her first novel, *Imagined Corners*, was published in 1931, followed by *Mrs. Ritchie* (1933). Her strongly held views about women's position in a patriarchal society were reflected in these and in her earlier essay *Women: An Enquiry* (1925), published by Leonard and Virginia *Woolf in their Hogarth Essay series. *Mrs. Grundy in Scotland* (1936) was a companion work to Edwin Muir's *Scott and Scotland* (1936), both reflecting the resurgence of interest in Scottish culture in the 1920s and 1930s. The Muirs lived again in Prague between 1945 and 1948 and in Rome in 1949–50, where Edwin worked for the British Council. They were in Edinburgh between 1950 and 1955, spent a year at Harvard in 1955–6, and then settled in Cambridge. Willa edited Edwin's *Collected Poems* (1960), published the year after his death, and completed *Living with Ballads* (1965), a book which he had begun. Her *Laconics, Jingles and Other Verses* was published in 1969, and *Belonging: A Memoir* in 1968. *See* E. W. Mellown, *Bibliography of the Writings of E. Muir* (rev. edn. 1966), which lists the Muirs' translations.

Mulock, Dinah Maria *see* CRAIK, Dinah Maria

Mulso, Hester *see* CHAPONE, Hester

Murdoch, (Jean) Iris, novelist and philosopher (b. Dublin, 15 July 1919).

Iris Murdoch is the only child of Wills John Hughes Murdoch, an Irish-born civil servant, and his wife Irene Alice Richardson, a singer, a close family group she later described as 'a perfect trinity'. She grew up in London, was educated at the Froebel Educational Institute, London, Badminton School, and Somerville College, Oxford, where she took a first in Greats in 1942. After university she became a civil servant in the Treasury and then worked with the United Nations Relief and Rehabilitation Administration (UNRRA) during the war. She held a studentship in philosophy at Newnham College, Cambridge, and returned to Oxford as a fellow and tutor in philosophy at St Anne's College from 1948 to 1963. She lectured at the Royal College of Art from 1963 to 1967. In 1956 she married John Bayley, Oxford don and literary critic. *Under the Net* (1954), her first novel to be published but the sixth she wrote, embodied some of the philosophical preoccupations which were to become a hallmark of her fiction. Its successors, which followed rapidly and prolifically, have won most of the prestigious contemporary literary prizes: *Flight from the Enchanter* (1956), *The Sandcastle* (1957), *The Bell* (1958), *A Severed Head* (1961, dramatized 1963), *An Unofficial Rose* (1962), *The Unicorn* (1963), *The Italian Girl* (1964, dramatized 1967), *The Red and the Green* (1965), *The Nice and the Good* (1968), *Bruno's Dream* (1969), *A Fairly Honourable Defeat* (1970), *The Black Prince* (1973, James Tait Black Memorial Prize, dramatized 1989), *The Sacred and Profane Love Machine* (1974, Whitbread Prize), *A Word Child* (1975), *Henry and Cato* (1976), *The Fire and the Sun* (1977), *The Sea, the Sea* (1978, Booker Prize), *The Philosopher's Pupil* (1983), *The Good Apprentice* (1985), *Acastos* (1986), *The Book and the Brotherhood* (1987), *The Message to the Planet* (1989). In two essays on the writing of fiction, 'The Sublime and the Beautiful Revisited' (1960) and 'Against Dryness' (1961), Murdoch allied herself with the humanist-realist school of novelists as opposed to the 'clear, crystalline work', the 'simplified fantasy myth' of those devoted to 'the consolations of form'. Her work embodies both traditions. She writes usually of the intellectual and professional middle classes, their sexual relationships and search for love, subjects explored in inventive, highly patterned, and symbolic plots which embrace the comic, the absurd, and the unexpected. Her characters often devise strategies by which to define their lives, roles to play, quests, theories to live by, and find that reality alters these structures. She is concerned with the nature of good and evil, with the search for freedom, and the power of language. Several of her novels have male narrators. She has written three plays, *The Servants and the Snow* (1970), *The Three Arrows* (1972), and *Art and Eros* (1980), and a book of poems, *A Year of Birds* (1978). Her philosophical work includes a book on Sartre (1953) *The Sovereignty of Good* (1970), and *Metaphysics as a Guide to Morals* (1992). She was created DBE in 1987. *See* A. S. *Byatt, *Degrees of Freedom: The Novels of Iris Murdoch* (1965); Richard Todd, *Iris Murdoch* (1984); John Haffenden (ed), *Novelists in Interview* (1985); Peter Conradi,

Iris Murdoch: The Saint and the Artist (1986); Deborah Johnston, *Iris Murdoch* (1987); Lorna Sage, *Women and the House of Fiction: Post-War Women Novelists* (1992).

n n n n n n n n n n n n n

N

Nairne, Carolina, Baroness, song writer (b. Gask, Perthshire, 16 August 1766, d. Gask, 16 October 1845).

The daughter of Laurence Oliphant, a member of an ardent Jacobite family, and Margaret Robertson, the daughter of the chief of the clan Donnochy, Carolina Nairne was named after Prince Charles Stuart. In 1806 she married her cousin Major William Murray Nairne, whose peerage was restored by George IV in 1824, making his wife Baroness Nairne. They had one son. She began to write lyrics at an early age, and became interested in Burns's adaptation of old Scottish songs, persuading her brother to subscribe to the 1786 edition of his poems. In 1792 she produced a new version of 'The Pleuchman' (ploughman) for her brother to sing at a local gathering, and in 1797 sent a friend a copy of her 'The Land o' the Leal' to console her on the death of a child. She kept her writing secret, even from her husband, and between 1821 and 1824 contributed to R. A. Smith's *The Scottish Minstrel*, a collection of Scottish songs, under the pseudonym Mrs Bogan of Bogan. On the death of her husband in 1829 she moved with her son to Clifton, near Bristol, and from there to Dublin. Her son's delicate health persuaded her to travel extensively on the Continent. She continued her travels after his death in 1837, eventually returning to Scotland in 1843. She agreed to the publication of her anonymous poems just before her death, and *Lays from Strathearn* by Carolina, Baroness Nairne, appeared posthumously in 1846. A collection of her *Songs* was published in 1902 and again in 1911 and 1912. Like Burns she utilized traditional tunes to which she added new words, and her familiarity with lowland Scots enabled her to strike a chord with Scottish readers. Her ballads, Jacobite verses, and sentimental songs had a far wider appeal and included 'Charlie is my darling', 'Will ye no' come back again?', 'The Hundred Pipers', 'Laird o'Cockpen', and 'Caller Herrin'. The last has several well-known musical settings. Her *Life and Songs*, ed. Charles Rogers (1869), included lyrics by her niece Caroline Oliphant (1807–31). *See* C. Rogers, *The Life and Songs of the Baroness Nairne* (1869).

Nesbit, E(dith), children's writer (b. London, 19 August 1858, d. Jesson St Mary's, New Romney, Kent, 4 May 1924).

E. Nesbit was the sixth child and youngest daughter of John Collis Nesbit, head of an agricultural college in Kennington, south London, who died when she was 3, and his wife Sarah. The family spent a period abroad for her elder sister's health, and she was educated in convents, which she hated, in France and Germany and later Brighton. They eventually settled in a large country house in Kent where she lived for most of her life. The setting and the Kent landscape were reflected in much of her writing. She published her first story in the *Sunday Magazine* in 1876. In 1880, seven months pregnant, she married Hubert Bland, a young bank employee whose socialist sympathies she shared, and by whom she had two daughters and two sons. They were both politically active, and involved in the formation of the Fabian Society in 1884. The failure of Bland's brush-making business and his subsequent smallpox early in their marriage threw the burden of income on her, and she began to write professionally. She wrote a number of novels, published collections of poems and short stories, and wrote verses for and decorated greeting cards, all of which brought much-needed income. Bland gradually developed a career as a journalist and edited *To-Day*, in which George Bernard Shaw's early fiction appeared. The couple became friendly with Sidney and Beatrice *Webb, Shaw, and H. G. Wells, and under the pseudonym 'Fabian Bland' co-operated on a novel, *The Prophet's Mantle* (1885). In the 1890s, when in her forties, Nesbit began to achieve considerable success with children's fiction. *The Story of the Treasure Seekers* (1899), a chronicle about the Bastable family, was followed by the *Would-be-Goods* (1901) and *The New Treasure Seekers* (1904) and established her as the creator of a new form of children's fiction, without moralizing and with believable children. Another group of stories involved fantasy and time travel, later to become a familiar feature of children's writing. These included *Five Children and It* (1902), *The Phoenix and the Carpet* (1904), and *The Story of the Amulet* (1906). Most of the books were serialized first in the *Pall Mall Gazette* and the *Strand, London*, and *Windsor* magazines. *The Railway Children* (1906) is probably her best-known book, its popularity revived by a film version in 1970. The story of an absent father, a determined writer-mother, and plucky, resourceful children is thought to have contained elements of both autobiography and wish fulfilment. Later books included *The Enchanted Castle* (1907), *The House of Arden* (1908), and its sequel, *Harding's Luck* (1909). She also published a collection of fairy stories, *The Old Nursery Tales* (1908), *The Magic City* (1910), and her last children's books, *The Wonderful Garden* (1911) and *Wet Magic* (1913). She wrote 'adult' novels as well as children's fiction, of which the best known was *The Red House* (1902). Her domestic life was far from tranquil. She brought up her own four children and two illegitimate children of Bland's, while condoning other infidelities. She herself had several affairs. H. G. Wells gave a somewhat malicious picture of their bohemian family life in *Experiments in Autobiography* (1934). Bland died in 1914. Nesbit edited a collection of his newspaper essays for publication, many of them about marriage. Her income was reduced as a result of the war and in 1915 she was granted a civil-list pension for services to literature. In 1917 she married Thomas Terry Tucker, a marine engineer and a fellow socialist who collaborated in a collection of stories, *Five of Us and Madeline*, published posthumously in 1925. She died of cancer in 1924 at Jesson St Mary's, near New Romney in Kent, where she had moved after Bland's death. Her reminiscences, *Long Ago when I was Young*, were published in 1966. *See* Doris Langley Moore, *E. Nesbit: A Biography* (1933); Noel *Streatfeild, *Magic and Magicians: E. Nesbit and her Children's Books* (1958); Julia Briggs, *A Woman of Passion: The Life of E. Nesbit: 1858–1924* (1987).

Newcastle, Margaret Cavendish, Duchess of, poet, playwright, and woman of letters (b. St John's, near Colchester, Essex, 1623, d. London, 1674).

Margaret Cavendish, Duchess of Newcastle, was the youngest of the eight children of Sir Thomas Lucas, a wealthy Essex landowner, and his wife Elizabeth Leighton. Her father died when she was an infant. Under her mother's aegis, family life was relaxed and indulgent, education undisciplined, and Margaret's penchant for flamboyant dress encouraged, a characteristic for which she was notorious in later life. She was to regret her lack of rigorous education, advocating more of it for women in her plays and elsewhere. Her lack of knowledge of grammar and her total inability to revise were serious impediments in her writing which could be traced back to her imperfect schooling. At the age of 20 she resolved to become Maid of Honour to Queen Henrietta Maria, following the Queen into exile in France in 1645. There she met the exiled William Cavendish, Marquess, later Duke, of Newcastle, a widower thirty years her senior, a patron of writers and artists and a minor poet and playwright. They married in Paris the same year, an unusually happy and productive union. Cavendish encouraged her writing during their period abroad until the Restoration. She published *Poems and Fancies* and *Philosophicall Fancies* (1653). The latter was revised as part of *Philosophical and Physical Opinions* (1655 and 1663), and as *Grounds of Natural Philosophy* (1668). Her interests were eclectic, sometimes maverick, her work impulsive and undisciplined. Contemporary science, natural history, the natural world, human behaviour, language, all were grist to her mill. Her strong feminist views surfaced in her plays, two volumes of which were published but never performed. *Plays* (1662) and *Plays never before Printed* (1668) contained heroines who become soldiers, raise armies, receive a masculine education, write poetry, and address assemblies of learned men. Structurally they are incoherent and virtually unperformable. She none the less sent the sumptuously produced volumes, designated as 'written by the thrice noble, illustrious and excellent Princess the Lady Marchioness of Newcastle', to friends and protégés, and to the libraries of the universities. She also wrote a utopian fiction, *The Description of a New World Called the Blazing World* (1666), in which the oppression of women was addressed. The first edition of *Nature's Pictures* (1656) contained an autobiography, 'A True Relation of my Birth, Breeding and Life', and she also published a biography of her husband (1667), the work for which, ironically, she was best known after her death. 'Know it is fame I covet,' one of her heroines proclaims. It was an appropriate epithet for the Duchess, extravagant in her appearance, cushioned against ridicule by her social position, and convinced that literature was the only means by which a woman could achieve renown. Virginia *Woolf wrote about her sympathetically in *The Common Reader* (1925). Her two stepdaughters, **Lady Jane Cavendish** (1621–69) and **Lady Elizabeth Brackley** (*c.*1626–63), the children of Elizabeth Bassett, the Duke's first wife, collaborated on an unpublished volume, 'Poems, Songs and a Pastoral', which included a play, and wrote a second play, *The Concealed Fansyes* (published 1931). *See* Douglas Grant, *Margaret the First: A Biography of Margaret Cavendish, Duchess of Newcastle 1623–1673* (1957); Sara Heller Mendelson, *The Mental World of Stuart Women: Three Studies* (1987); Elaine Hobby, *Virtue of Necessity: English Women's Writing 1649–1688* (1988); Moira Ferguson, in *Women Writers of the Seventeenth Century*, ed. Katharina M. Wilson and Frank J. Warnke (1989); Janet Todd, *The Sign of Angellica: Women, Writing and Fiction, 1660–1800* (1989); Kate Lilley (ed.), *The Description of the New Blazing World and Other Writings* (1992).

New Woman.

The New Woman was a stereotypical emancipated woman prominent in the fiction of the 1890s, which in turn reflected late nineteenth-century debates over sexual double standards, women's occupations, and the vote. The term was supposedly coined by Sarah *Grand to describe a modern type of woman, independent, sexually autonomous, educated or at least well read, characterized by short hair, 'rational' dress, a nervous temperament, smoking, drinking, the practice of birth control, and other forms of 'advanced' behaviour. The most publicized 'New Woman' novelists were Grant Allen (1848–99), author of the notorious and successful *The Woman who Did* [shun a conventional marriage] (1895), and Thomas Hardy, whose character Sue Bridehead in *Jude the Obscure* (1895) is a complex portrait of a New Woman. Allen's novel produced two responses by women, *The Woman who Didn't* (1895) by **'Victoria Crosse' (Vivian Cory)** and *The Woman who Wouldn't* by **'Lucas Cleeve' (Adeline Georgina Isabella Kingscote,** 1850?–1908). As well as Sarah Grand, the women writers who contributed to the stereotype included George *Egerton, Mona *Caird, and **'Iota' (Kathleen Mannington Caffyn,** 1855?–1926). Eliza Lynn *Linton and Margaret *Oliphant entered the lists against the New Woman, the latter with a famous article on the 'Anti-Marriage League' in *Blackwood's Magazine* (January 1896). The work of George Meredith and George Gissing contributed to the debate as did the production of Henrik Ibsen's *The Doll's House* and *Hedda Gabler* in London in the early 1890s. The furore over the New Woman was largely an 1890s phenomenon but interest in the type influenced the literary representation of women by both male and female writers until well into the next century. *See* Lloyd Fernando, *'New Women' in the Late Victorian Novel* (1977); Gail Cunningham, *The New Woman and the Victorian Novel* (1978); Lyn Pykett, *The 'Improper' Feminine: The Women's Sensation Novel and the New Woman Writing* (1992).

Nichols, Grace, poet, novelist, and children's writer (b. Georgetown, Guyana).

Grace Nichols was educated at St Stephen's Scots School, the PPI High School, and the University of Guyana. From 1967 to 1970 she taught school in Guyana, then worked for the Georgetown *Chronicle* and the government information service and in 1977 emigrated to Britain. She is married to the poet John Agard and has a daughter. Her powerful sequence of poems *i is a long memoried woman* links the experience of African women during slavery to earlier oppressions of Amerindian and Caribbean women. It won the Commonwealth Poetry Prize in 1983. *The Fat Black Woman's Poems* (1984), comic, rueful, and angry, sets a stereotypical figure against her ideal 'thin' European counterpart: 'Look at de frozen thin mannequins | fixing her with grin | and de pretty face salesgals | exchanging slimming glances | thinking she don't notice.' The poems included in *Lazy Thoughts of a Lazy Woman and Other Poems* (1989) combine Creole and standard English, reflecting her immersion in Caribbean culture. Her novel *Whole of a Morning Sky* (1986) is based on her childhood. Nichols's children's books, which integrate multicultural myths and legends, include *Trust You Wriggly* (1981), *Leslyn in London* (1984), and *Baby Fish and Other Stories. Come on into my Tropical Garden* (1988) is a poetry anthology for children. Other anthologies which she has edited include *No Hickory, No Dickory, No Dock* (1991), a collection of Caribbean nursery rhymes, edited with John Agard, *Black Poetry* (1988), and *Can I Buy a Slice of Sky* (1991), a collection by black, Asian, and Amerindian poets. Her own poetry is frequently anthologized. *See* Lauretta Ngcobo (ed.), *Let it be Told: Essays by Black Women in Britain* (1987).

Nightingale, Florence, nursing reformer (b. Florence, 12 May 1820, d. London, 13 August 1910).

Named after the city of her birth, Florence Nightingale was the younger daughter of William Edward Nightingale, a landowner and country gentleman with Whiggish and Unitarian affiliations, and his wife Frances Smith, the daughter of a noted abolitionist. She grew up in the family's two country houses, Lea Hurst in Derbyshire and Embley Park in Hampshire, where she and her sister received a liberal education from their father. She was taught history, mathematics, classical languages, and philosophy. She also studied modern languages and read widely in English literature. Her resentment of the enforced idleness of country house society, the tyranny of upper-class family life, and the barriers erected against women leading fruitful lives is reflected in the autobiographical fragment 'Cassandra', written in 1852 (published in Ray Strachey, *The Cause* (1928)). Her friend John Stuart Mill used some of her arguments in his *The Subjection of Women* (1869). Despite her family's objections she undertook the unladylike task of hospital visiting, through which she came to recognize the need for professional nursing. A period spent at the Institute of Protestant Deaconesses at Kaiserwerth in Germany reinforced her belief that nursing could become a vocation for middle-class women. She subsequently visited hospitals in London, Edinburgh, Dublin, and Paris and in 1853 was appointed to the unpaid post of Superintendent of the Hospital for Invalid Gentlewomen in London. The publicity surrounding the state of hospital facilities in the Crimea after the outbreak of war in 1854 led her friend Sidney Herbert, then Secretary of State for War, to ask her to undertake the overall supervision of nursing in the Crimea. She became Superintendent of the Female Nurses in the Hospitals in the East, or more popularly 'The Lady-in-Chief', and later the legendary 'Lady with a Lamp' described in Longfellow's poem 'Santa Filomena' (1857). Her achievements in the Crimea between 1854 and 1856 won her national recognition and royal admiration. She gave her sanction to the founding of a School for Nurses at St Thomas's Hospital in London and exerted her influence on a Royal Commission to improve sanitary conditions in the army and later in the Indian army. She was instrumental in improving the nursing service in civilian hospitals and in remedying hospital provision in India following the Indian Mutiny of 1857. Nightingale's role as the founder of modern nursing has been given fuller treatment elsewhere. As a writer her efforts were largely channelled into her reports to various public bodies concerned with the reform of medical facilities. Her best-known work was her *Notes on Nursing: What it is, and what it is not* (1860), which sold 15,000 copies in its first month of publication. 'Cassandra' ranks with Mill's *Subjection* as one of the most forceful Victorian polemics on the need for women's education and entry into professional life. Her unpublished treatise 'Suggestions for Thought to Searchers after Truth among the Artisans of England', a massive, disorganized religious and philosophical work of which 'Cassandra' formed a part, was written in 1852 and revised and put together after her return from the Crimea. Mill urged her to publish it but Benjamin Jowett, another influential friend, dissuaded her. It was privately printed in 1860. Extracts from it, including 'Cassandra', have been edited by Mary Poovey (1992). She also compiled an anthology on the writings of medieval mystics, 'Notes from Devotional Authors of the Middle Ages'. *Una and the Lion* (1868) was a eulogy of her colleague and former student Agnes Jones, who died while nursing in a workhouse. Her *Selected Writings* were published in 1954 (ed. Lady Ridgeley Seymer), and her *Selected Letters* (ed. M. Vicinus and B. Nergaard) in 1990. Much of Nightingale's life after the Crimea was spent as a semi-invalid, confined to her bedroom, where she wrote her reports and her books, with her family kept safely at a distance but at her service. She was the first woman to be given the Order of Merit, in 1907, and only the second to have the Freedom of the City of London conferred on her, in 1908. Despite her rejection of marriage and the feminine role constructed for women, and her support for married women's property rights, she disliked the modern notion of women's rights and felt uneasy with the suffrage campaign, which was mounting in strength at the time of her death in 1910. *See* E. T. Cook, *The Life of Florence Nightingale* (1913); Lytton Strachey, *Eminent Victorians* (1918); Cecil Woodham-Smith, *Florence Nightingale* (1950); Mary Poovey, *Uneven Developments: The Ideological Work of Gender in Mid-Victorian England* (1988); Elaine Showalter, in *Tradition and the Talents of Women*, ed. Florence Howe (1991).

Nine Muses, *The.*

The Nine Muses; or Poems Written by so many Ladies upon the Death of the

Famous John Dryden, Esq. (1700) was a collection of elegies by 'severall ladies', but not nine, despite the title, including Sarah Fyge *Egerton, Delarivier *Manley (the editor), Lady Piers, Mary *Pix, Catharine *Trotter, and possibly Susanna *Centlivre. Each 'Muse' in turn mourns the death of the poet, who died in 1700.

Norton, Caroline (Elizabeth Sarah), novelist and poet (b. London, 22 March 1808, d. London, 15 June 1877).

Caroline Norton was one of the three daughters of Thomas Sheridan and granddaughter of the dramatist Richard Brinsley Sheridan (1751–1816). Her mother was **Caroline Henrietta Callander,** afterwards Campbell, a celebrated beauty who was also a novelist. Thomas Sheridan died in 1817 while in the Colonial Service, and the family were given a grace and favour residence at Hampton Court. The three Sheridan sisters were well known in London society for their extraordinary beauty, and in the case of Caroline for cleverness and wit as well. In 1827 she married the Honourable George Chapple Norton, brother of the third Lord Grantley, a young barrister of modest means and a violent temper. The marriage was miserable from the beginning. Caroline had begun to write at the age of 13 and in 1829 published her first book of poems, *The Sorrows of Rosalie*, followed in 1830 by *The Undying One*, a long poem based on the story of the Wandering Jew. In addition she wrote for various *annuals, and from 1831 edited *La Belle Assemblée*. She estimated that in a single year she earned at least £1,400 from her literary activities. Her husband exploited her friendship with Lord Melbourne in order to secure a minor appointment, and then, possibly at the instigation of some of his Tory friends, brought an action for adultery against Melbourne. The trial, which supposedly provided Dickens with the idea for 'Bardell versus Pickwick' in *Pickwick Papers*, resulted in the acquittal of the accused, but Mrs Norton's reputation was stained. She and her husband remained estranged, and she continued to write in order to support herself and their three sons. Two long poems dealing with contemporary social conditions, *A Voice from the Factories* (1836) and *A Child of the Islands* (1845), were widely acclaimed, as was *The Dream* (1840), which prompted H. N. Coleridge in the *Quarterly Review* to pronounce her 'the Byron of poetesses'. Mrs Norton's continued battles with her husband over finances (he at one point claimed the earnings from her writing) and the custody of their children resulted in some powerful pamphlet warfare, which influenced both the Infant Custody Act of 1839 and the Matrimonial Causes (Divorce) Act of 1857. Mrs Norton's novels frequently contained autobiographical elements, as in *Stuart of Dunleath* (1851), *Lost and Saved* (1863), and *Old Sir Douglas* (1863), which was serialized in *Macmillan's Magazine*, all three of which dealt with marital discord. Norton died in 1875, and in 1877 Caroline Norton married Sir William Stirling-Maxwell, an old friend. She died four months later. Two of her three sons predeceased her and the third died in the same year. Caroline Norton's work was celebrated more for the aura surrounding its author than for its intrinsic merits. Her story inspired George Meredith's *Diana of the Crossways* (1885). James O. Hoge and Jane Marcus have edited *Selected Writings* (1978). *See* A. S. Acland, *Caroline Norton* (1948); David Cecil, *Young Lord Melbourne* (1939) and *Lord Melbourne* (1954); Margaret *Forster, *Significant Sisters* (1984); Mary Poovey, *Uneven Developments: The Ideological Work of Gender in Mid-Victorian England* (1988); Alan Chedzoy, *A Scandalous Woman* (1992).

Norton, Mary, children's writer (b. London, 10 December 1903, d. Hartland, Devon, 29 August 1992).

Mary Norton was the daughter of Reginald Spencer Pearson, a doctor, and his wife Mary (Minnie) Savile Hughes. Her childhood in the family's Georgian manor house in Bedfordshire is reflected in the setting of many of her books for children. She was convent educated and then worked briefly as an actress with the Old Vic Company until her marriage in 1927 to shipping magnate Robert Norton, by whom she had four children. They lived for a while in Portugal and returned to England at the beginning of the war, where she worked for the BBC. When her husband joined the navy, she moved with her children to New York, where she wrote her first children's book, *The Magic Bed-Knob* (1943), about four children and a music teacher who is an amateur witch. She returned to London and the Old Vic towards the end of the war and wrote the sequel, *Bonfires and Broomsticks* (1947). The two were combined in the successful *Bedknob and Broomstick* (1957), which was later made into a Walt Disney film. But it was *The Borrowers* (1952; televised 1992), the first of a sequence about minute people who live in the houses of humans from whom they 'borrow', which established her as one of the leading children's writers of the post-war period. The book won the Carnegie Medal and the Hans Christian Andersen Award. It was followed by *The Borrowers Afield* (1955), *The Borrowers Afloat* (1959), *The Borrowers Aloft* (1961), and *The Borrowers Avenged* (1982), which chart subsequent adventures of the borrowers as they are ejected from various refuges. Human follies and delusions and the impermanence of the human condition are echoed in the plight and the reactions of the miniature characters, who present an ingenious view of the human world from the height of six inches. Norton also wrote *Are All the Giants Dead?* (1975), a humorous story about the retired heroes and heroines of classic fairy-tales. In 1970 she married

Lionel Bonsey (d. 1989) and in 1972 they moved to County Cork. They eventually settled in north Devon, where she died in her 90th year. *See* John Rowe Townsend, *Written for Children* (1965; rev. 1974).

O

O'Brien, Edna, novelist, short story writer, and screen-writer (b. Tuamgraney, County Clare, 15 December 1932).

Edna O'Brien is one of the four children of Michael O'Brien, a farmer in the west of Ireland, and his wife Lena Cleary. Her childhood was solitary, dominated by fear of her father and the intensity of a Roman Catholic upbringing. She went to a National School at Scariff, then to a convent in County Galway, and from there to the Pharmaceutical College of Ireland in Dublin, where she qualified as a Licentiate. In 1952 she married Ernest Gebler, a novelist, by whom she had two sons. The marriage was dissolved in 1967. They moved to London after their marriage, and it was only there that O'Brien began to write. Her first three novels are a loosely autobiographical trilogy about two contrasting Irish girls' maturation into life, love, and eventual disillusion. The first, *The Country Girls* (1960), her own favourite ('it came like a song . . . it was effortless'), won the Kingsley Amis Award. She wrote the screenplay in 1983. It was followed by *The Lonely Girl* (1962), for which she also wrote the screenplay, with the title *The Girl with Green Eyes*, in 1964. The third novel, *Girls in their Married Bliss*, was published in 1964. She added an epilogue when the trilogy was collected in 1987, taking the story up to the death of one of the main characters. *August is a Wicked Month* (1965) and *Casualties of Peace* (1967) present two young women's resilience in the face of failure to find happiness in love, a recurring O'Brien theme. Others are the inevitable conflicts between men and women, and the loneliness, guilt, and sense of loss which form part of women's experience.

Her frankness in treating female sexuality has been celebrated and condemned. Several of her books are banned in Ireland. She experimented with narrative in *A Pagan Place* (1970), recollections of a nun's childhood and adolescence in rural Ireland during the Second World War, presented in the second person, and in *Nights* (1972), a first-person reverie of a middle-aged Irish divorcee living in England. *Johnny I Hardly Knew you* (1977) is narrated by a woman who has been imprisoned for murdering her lover. *The High Road* (1988) involves failed love, jealousy, and another crime of passion. *Time and Tide* (1992) is a story of mother love, of the heroine's for her two sons, and of her memories of her own mother. O'Brien's six volumes of short stories, of which the latest is *Lantern Slides* (1990), play to her strengths and avoid the weaknesses of plot which mar some of her novels. She has written several screenplays, including *Time Lost and Time Remembered* (1966), based on her own short story 'A Woman at the Seaside'. Her plays include *Virginia*, performed in 1980, derived from *Woolf's diaries, and *Madame Bovary*, produced in 1987, based on Flaubert's novel. She has written books for children, including *James and Nora* (1981), on the Joyce marriage. She has also produced several books about Ireland, which she regards as 'the only place I belong to', including the autobiographical essay *Mother Ireland* (1976) and *Tales for the Telling* (1986), a collection of Irish folk- and fairy-tales. She lives in London. *See* Nell *Dunn (ed.), *Talking to Women* (1965); Grace Eckley, *Edna O'Brien* (1974); Darcy O'Brien, in *Twentieth-Century Women Novelists*, ed. Thomas Staley (1982); Lorna Sage, *Women in the House of Fiction: Post-War Women Novelists* (1992).

O'Brien, Kate, novelist, playwright, and critic (b. Limerick, 3 December 1897, d. Canterbury, 13 August 1974).

Kate O'Brien was born in Limerick, the 'Mellick' of her fiction, the fourth daughter and sixth of the nine children of Thomas O'Brien, a horse dealer, and his wife Catherine Thornhill, who died when Kate was 5. She was educated at Laurel Hill Convent, Limerick, and at University College, Dublin. After her degree she worked for the foreign languages department of the *Manchester Guardian*, taught in a Hampstead convent, and worked as a secretary for her brother-in-law in the United States and as a governess in Spain. Spain was to become the setting for several of her novels, including *Mary Lavelle* (1936), whose heroine is an Irish governess working in that country. In 1932 she returned to England, where she married Gustaaf Renier, a Dutch journalist from whom she separated after a few months. She wrote in her spare time, while working in London, contributing stories and articles to periodicals. After her successful first play, *Distinguished Villa* (1926), she published her first novel, *Without my Cloak* (1931), a family saga of upper middle-class Irish life, set in 'Mellick', which won both the Hawthornden and James Tait Black Memorial prizes. *The Anti-Room* (1934), her second novel, had a similar setting and emphasized what was to become a constant theme of her work, the conflict between Catholicism and the artistic or liberal temperament. *The Land of Spices* (1941), a novel about convent life, was banned in Ireland. *That Lady* (1946), a historical novel set in Spain in the period of Philip II, was recognized as a major work, although a dramatized version, tried out in New York in 1949, was not a success. She wrote a biography of Teresa of Ávila (1951), books of travel, several plays, including dramatizations of her own novels, and the autobiographical *Presentation Parlour* (1963). She returned to Ireland at the end of the Second World War, but spent the last ten years of her life in Kent, living in relative obscurity after her early literary celebrity. *See* Lorna Reynolds, *Kate O'Brien* (1986); John Hildebidle, *Five Irish Writers: The Errand of Keeping Alive* (1989).

O'Keefe, Adelaide, poet (b. Dublin, 5 November 1776, d. *c.* 1855).

Adelaide O'Keefe was the only daughter and third child of the Irish dramatist John O'Keefe (1747–1833), who moved to London in 1780 and wrote comic operas and farces for the Haymarket, Covent Garden, and Drury Lane theatres. Adelaide O'Keefe's first publication is possibly still her best known, a group of thirty-four poems which she contributed to Ann and Jane *Taylor's *Original Poems for Infant Minds* (1804). Her contributions were signed 'Adelaide'. Poetry written specifically for children continued to occupy her. She published *Original Poems Calculated to Improve the Mind of Youth* (1808), *National Characters Exhibited in 40 Geographical Poems* (1808), and, much later, *Poems for Young Children* (1849). Other work included *Patriarchal Times; or The Land of Canaan* (1811), which had a sixth edition in 1842, *Zenobia, Queen of Palmyra* (1814), *Poems* (1819), and two narratives, *Dudley*, a three-volume novel (1819), and *The Broken Sword: A Tale* (1854). Most of her middle years, if not most of her life, were spent caring for her father, first in London, and then in Southampton, where he died in 1833. Adelaide O'Keefe was still living in Southampton in 1848, and died probably in 1855.

'Oliphant, Margaret' (Margaret Oliphant Wilson), novelist, biographer, and historical writer (b. Wallyford, Musselburgh, near Edinburgh, 4 April 1828, d. Windsor, Berkshire, 25 June 1897).

Margaret Oliphant was the daughter of Francis Wilson, a minor customs official, and his wife Margaret Oliphant. Her childhood was spent at Lasswade, near Edinburgh, then in Glasgow and Liverpool, as the family moved with their father's work. Francis Wilson was a remote, ineffectual father, and the family revolved around their energetic, intelligent mother. Religious controversy figured largely in family life as the Oliphants adhered to the newly formed Free Church of Scotland after the Disruption of 1843, the background to which was reflected in Margaret Oliphant's first novel, *Passages in the Life of Mrs. Margaret Maitland* (1849). Scottish scenes figured in the early fiction, the most notable of which were *Caleb Field* (1851), *Merkland* (1851), and *Katie Stewart* (1853). In 1852 she married her cousin Francis Wilson Oliphant, a stained-glass artist. The couple settled in London, and Mrs Oliphant began a connection with *Blackwood's Magazine* and the firm of Blackwood which was to last for the rest of her life. Frank Oliphant developed consumption and his death in 1859 left his wife with three young children, in debt, and without an obvious source of income. She returned to Edinburgh, where John Blackwood and his brother promised financial support. After a humiliating interview in which her latest offering for the *Magazine* was refused but the promise of financial support renewed, she sat up all night, according to her *Autobiography*, and wrote the first of the series which was to establish her reputation, *The Chronicles of Carlingford* (*1862–76*). *The Rector and The Doctor's Family*, two stories published in one volume, was followed by *Salem Chapel* (1863), *The Perpetual Curate* (1864), *Miss Marjoribanks* (1866), and *Phoebe Junior: A Last Chronicle of Carlingford* (1876), each serialized in *Blackwood's* and then separately published. The books were modelled on Trollope's 'Barsetshire' novels, even to echoes in plotting, and a similar final title, but were less wide ranging in their social perspective and centred more on questions of vocation, doctrinal disputes, and church politics. Mrs Oliphant's industry was phenomenal. Full-length novels were written in parallel with a regular stream of articles for *Blackwood's*, as well as a number of biographies, including an outstanding and sympathetic *Life of Edward Irving* (1862), another of her friend John Tulloch (1888), one of Thomas Chalmers (1893), and one of Laurence Oliphant (1891) (no relation). She wrote a *Literary History of England* (1882) and *The Victorian Age of English Literature* (1892), the latter with her son Frank. The novels continued, over a hundred in total, many of them clear-eyed accounts of unhappy or disappointing marriages, strong women supporting weak or ineffectual husbands, fathers, and brothers. *The Greatest Heiress in England* (1879), *Hester* (1883), *The Ladies Lindores* (1883), *Kirsteen* (1890), and *Sir Robert's Fortune* (1895) are among the best. She also found stories of the supernatural a sympathetic mode, and wrote *A Beleaguered City* (1880), *A Little Pilgrim in the Unseen* (1882), and *Stories of the Seen and Unseen* (1885). She edited a series of Foreign Classics for Blackwood, and wrote a number of general historical works and books of travel. Of her non-fiction probably the most important is her *Annals of a Publishing House* (1897), a detailed and loving account of the publishing business of which she was a faithful supporter. Mrs Oliphant's three children predeceased her. Her daughter Maggie died prematurely in 1864, and she supported her feckless sons until their deaths, and also three of her brother's children. Her *Autobiography*, published in 1899, and edited by her friend Mrs A. L. Coghill, is a moving account of the life of a truly professional woman of letters. It has been edited by Q. D. Leavis (1974) and by Elisabeth Jay (1990), among others. *See* V. and R. A. Colby, *The Equivocal Virtue* (1966); John Stock Clarke, *Margaret Oliphant: A Bibliography*, Victorian Fiction Research Guides 11 (1986); Merryn Williams, *Margaret Oliphant: A Critical Biography* (1986).

Olivier, Edith (Maud), novelist (b. Wilton, Wiltshire, 1879(?), d. Wilton, 10 May 1948).

Edith Olivier was one of the ten children of the Revd Canon Dacres Olivier, rector of Wilton, in Wiltshire, and chaplain to the Earls of Pembroke. She was taught by her mother, the daughter of a bishop, who knew sufficient Latin to prepare her sons for public school, and then by governesses. She won a scholarship for study at St Hugh's Hall, Oxford, which she took up for four unconsecutive terms, her health preventing her from remaining in Oxford during the winter months. Her upbringing in a late Victorian clerical household, strict, regimented, and presided over by a benevolent but stern paterfamilias, determined the rest of her life. Suitors were discouraged and the theatrical career she had hoped for proved impossible. The ironic title of her autobiography, *Without Knowing Mr. Walkley* (1938), ruefully reflected her unfulfilled ambition, Arthur Walkley being the then dramatic critic of *The Times*. Instead she 'trained the choir, conducted the choral society, managed the girls' club, acted in private theatricals', activities which befitted the rector's unmarried daughter. During the First World War she helped to organize the Women's Land Army in Wiltshire. She wrote her first novel, *The Love-Child* (1927), about a lonely girl and her imaginary companion, after the deaths of her father and one of her sisters, waking up one night with the idea and writing four chapters straight off, a practice she repeated for many of her books. *As Far as Jane's Grandmother's* (1928), the story of an ineffectual struggle against a dominating personality, was, she said, 'a symbolic picture of life in my father's house'. Other novels included *The Triumphant Footman* (1930), subtitled 'a farcical fable', *Dwarf's Blood* (1931), and *The Seraphim Room* (1932), set in a cathedral close. She published a collection of stories set in Wiltshire, *Moonrakings* (1930), several volumes of local history and reminiscences, and two biographies, of Mary Magdalen (1934) and of Alexander Cruden (1934), the compiler of an eighteenth-century biblical concordance. She lived all her life in and near Wilton, serving as the town's mayor for several terms. Despite the seeming remoteness of her rural life she had links with literary and artistic circles. The artist Rex Whistler was a friend and confidant and provided the decorations for several of her books. Other friends included Sylvia Townsend *Warner, the novelist David Garnett, son of Constance *Garnett, and the American poet Elinor Wylie. Olivier died in her home on the Earl of Pembroke's estate in 1948, her age uncertain, as she carefully refused to reveal her date of birth.

Olliffe, Florence *see under* BELL, Gertrude

'O'Neill, Moira' *see under* KEANE, Molly

Opie, Amelia, née Alderson, novelist and poet (b. Norwich, 12 November 1769, d. Norwich, 2 December 1853).

Amelia Opie was the only child of James Alderson, a Norwich physician with strong humanitarian principles, a radical in politics and a Unitarian, and his wife Amelia Briggs. She was haphazardly educated in the traditional feminine accomplishments of music, dancing, and French. Her mother died when she was 15 and she took charge of her father's household, acting as his hostess and entering local society. She began to write poems which were published in newspapers and magazines, and when she was 18 wrote 'Adelaide', a tragedy in which she took the leading role. She visited London in 1794 and was introduced into radical intellectual circles whose members included Horne Tooke, the painter Thomas Holcroft, William Godwin, and Mary *Wollstonecraft. She professed great admiration for the last, declaring that everything she saw for the first time disappointed her except Mary Wollstonecraft. Despite the popular story, William Godwin did not propose to her. She did, however, meet the painter John Opie, recently divorced from his first wife, who had eloped with another man. They were married in 1798. Opie reportedly did not share his wife's love of society, and encouraged her writing as a way of keeping her at home. She had published her first novel, *The Dangers of Coquetry*, anonymously in 1790. Her next was a sentimental domestic story, *The Father and Daughter* (1801), which was printed with a poem, *The Maid of Corinth*. Scott was said to have wept over it, *Agnese*, an opera by Paer, was based on it, and it went to ten editions by 1844. Her next novel, *Adeline Mowbray; or The Mother and Daughter* (1804), was loosely based on the life of Wollstonecraft, but rather than endorsing her views, it constituted an attack on Godwinian attitudes to marriage. *Simple Tales* was published in 1806. John Opie died in 1807, and Mrs Opie then returned to Norwich, where she continued to write, but also retained her connections with fashionable literary circles. Byron, Scott, and Wordsworth were numbered among her friends. She contributed a memoir to her husband's *Lectures* *on Painting* (1809) and published another novel, *Valentine's Eve*, in 1816. At Norwich she gradually engaged with the Society of Friends and formally became a Quaker in 1825. This meant an end to her novel writing. *Madeline* was published in 1822 but another novel on the stocks was abandoned despite the prospect of a considerable sum from her publishers, who had already advertised the work. She now turned to improving works including *Illustrations of Lying* (1825) and *Detraction Displayed* (1828) and contributed to periodicals. She also wrote poetry. Her first collection, *Poems* (1802), included two of her best-known poems, 'The Orphan Boy' and 'The Felon's Address to his Child'. Another, 'There is a voice in every gale', was often anthologized as a hymn. Other volumes were *The Warrior's Return* (1808), *The Black Man's Lament* (1826), reflecting her interest in the Anti-Slavery Society, and her last work, *Lays for the Dead* (1834). She had a striking physical presence as well as considerable charm and vivacity, and sat to several eminent artists, including David d'Angers and Benjamin Haydon. Despite her new-found Quakerdom she retained her love of society and good living and continued to visit London and also Paris, alternating this fashionable life with charitable work. She died at the age of 84, after only a few months of declining health. *See* C. L. Brightwell, *Memorials of the Life of Amelia Opie* (1854); Julia *Kavanagh, *English Women of Letters* (1863); Harriet *Martineau, *Biographical Sketches* (1877); Anne Thackeray *Ritchie, *A Book of Sibyls* (1883); J. Menzies-Wilson and H. Lloyd, *Amelia: The Tale of a Plain Friend* (1937).

Orczy, Emma Magdalena Rosalia Maria Josepha Barbara, Baroness, novelist (b. Tarna-Ors, Hungary, 23 September 1865, d. London, 12 November 1947).

Baroness Orczy was the daughter of Baron Felix Orczy, a talented musician and the scion of an ancient landowning Hungarian family, and his wife Emma, Comtesse Wass. When the Baron's agricultural experiment led to a peasant revolt he abandoned farming and turned to a musical career in Budapest. Baroness Orczy was convent educated and, as her father opposed university education for women, she studied painting at the West London School of Art and then at the Heatherley School of Art, where she met her husband, the artist Henry George Montagu Barstow, the son of a clergyman. They were married in 1894 and their only son was born in 1899. Baroness Orczy illustrated children's stories and published translations, short stories, and also detective stories in London magazines. The central character of one series, *The Old Man in the Corner* (1909), published in the *Royal Magazine*, is credited with originating the armchair detective. The female detective who featured in *Lady Molly of Scotland Yard* (1910) was less successful. But it is for her novel *The Scarlet Pimpernel* (1905), the story of an English nobleman who rescued French aristocrats from the guillotine during the Reign of Terror, that she remains best known. Written in 1902, the novel was rejected by twelve publishers before being turned into a play produced first in Nottingham and then in London. This sparked off the phenomenal popularity of the tale, which culminated in a film version produced by Orczy's countryman Alexander Korda in 1933. Orczy wrote scores of historical romances, sometimes as many as three in one year, including sequels to *The Scarlet Pimpernel*, none of which remotely equalled it in popularity. All of her novels were written in English, although she did not encounter the language until the age of 15. She and her husband settled in Monte Carlo after the First World War. Montagu Barstow died in 1943 and Orczy returned to London, where she died in 1947. Her autobiography *Links in the Chain of Life* was published in 1947.

'Orinda' *see* PHILIPS, Katherine

Osborne, Dorothy, letter writer (b. Chicksands Priory, Bedfordshire, 1627, d. Moor Park, near Farnham, Surrey, 1695).

Dorothy Osborne was the youngest of the eleven children of Sir Peter Osborne (1584–1653), an eminent Royalist, and his wife Lady Dorothy Danvers. In 1648, when she was 21, she met Sir William Temple (1621–99), also a Royalist, later a diplomat, statesman, and writer. Their seven-year courtship was conducted largely by letter and in the teeth of opposition from both families. They eventually married in 1655, despite the ravages of an attack of smallpox which she suffered during the courtship. Several of their children died in infancy. A daughter, Diana, survived to the age of 14, and a son, John Temple, became secretary-at-war and committed suicide by throwing himself from a boat near London Bridge, to the grief of his parents. Dorothy Osborne was her husband's confidante, supporter, and helpmeet during their forty years of marriage, acting as a diplomat, and later as an ambassador's wife in Brussels, the Hague, Ireland, as well as London. She was commended by Charles II for her bravery during a sea battle against the Dutch in 1671, and her friendship with the future Queen Mary aided Temple's negotiations over the royal marriage. Dorothy Osborne died at Moor Park, the Temple estate in Surrey, at the age of 68. Her letters came to public attention by an indirect route. Those written to Temple during their courtship, 1652–4, were published by T. P. Courtenay in his *Memoirs of the Life, Works and Correspondence of Sir William Temple* (1836). They were commended enthusiastically by Macaulay in a review essay for the *Edinburgh Review* in October 1838: 'To us surely it is as useful to know how the young ladies of England employed themselves a hundred and eighty years ago, how far their minds were cultivated, what were their favourite studies, what degree of liberty was allowed to them, what use they made of that liberty, what accomplishments they most valued in men and what proofs of tenderness delicacy permitted them to give to favoured suitors as to know all about the seizure of Franche Comté and the treaty of Nimeguen.' Macaulay linked her with the seventeenth-century memoirist Lucy *Hutchinson. E. A. Parry published the complete series of seventy letters from Osborne to Temple in 1888, and another edition, by G. C. Moore Smith, was published in 1928. In her review of the latter Virginia *Woolf praised Osborne's skills as a letter writer: 'The *Letters*, like the letters of all born letter-writers . . . make us feel that we have our own seat in the depths of Dorothy's mind.' Woolf noted too that had she been born in 1827 Osborne would have written novels, and had she been born in 1527, she would never have written at all. *Dorothy Osborne: Letters to Sir William Temple* has been edited by Kenneth Parker (1987). *See* Virginia Woolf, 'Dorothy Osborne's Letters', *The Common Reader: Second Series* (1932); Lord David Cecil, *Two Quiet Lives: Dorothy Osborne, Thomas Gray* (1948).

'Ouida' (Marie Louise de la Ramée), novelist
(b. Bury St Edmunds, Suffolk, 1 January 1839, d. Viareggio, Italy, 25 January 1908).

'Ouida' was derived from a childish mispronunciation of Louise, and 'de la Ramée' was a more glamorous version of her Guernsey-born father's surname, Ramé. Louis Rame was a teacher of French in Bury St Edmunds. His wife Susan Sutton was English. Ouida's father was the greatest influence on her education, encouraging her love of reading and her general precocity. He moved to Paris and in the late 1850s the rest of the family moved to London, where Marie was introduced to Harrison Ainsworth, then editor and proprietor of *Bentley's Miscellany*. He published her first story, 'Dashwood's Drag; or The Derby and what Came of it', in *Bentley's* in 1859 and then her first full-length novel, *Granville de Vigne*, in the *New Monthly Magazine* (1861–3), which he also edited. It was subsequently published in three volumes by Tinsley, under the new title *Held in Bondage* (1863), and was the first occasion on which she used her pseudonym. *Held in Bondage* already had some of the trademarks of the Ouida novel, an aristocratic hero with sporting and military inclinations, whose love intrigues involved hidden identity, class differences, revenge, and bigamy. It was followed by *Strathmore* (1865), helpfully parodied in *Punch* as 'Strapmore! a Romance by "Weeder"', which ensured its popular success. The most successful of all her novels, *Under Two Flags*, was published in 1867. It sold millions of copies and in the twentieth century was made into a Hollywood film. There was also at least one stage version. *Idalia*, which she had written when she was 16, was also published in 1867, and the vogue for her novels was reinforced by an attack in the *Pall Mall Gazette*. From 1860 Ouida paid regular visits to Italy, establishing herself in expensive London hotels on her return, and consciously cultivating the image of a glamorous and successful writer. She was the subject of much public attention, not all of it flattering, although Bulwer-Lytton declared *Folle-Farine* (1871) a triumph of modern English romance. In 1874 she settled permanently near Florence, living in considerable style, surrounded by dogs, to which she was devoted. The novels continued, including *Two Little Wooden Shoes* (1874) and *Signa* (1875), both of which spawned operatic versions, the sentimental *A Dog of Flanders and Other Tales* (1872), *Moths* (1880), a social satire on which a play was based, and *The Massarenes* (1897), which vigorously satirized the English aristocracy. Ouida's novels, forty-four in all, were best suited to the three-volume format. The decline in her popularity followed the emergence of the single-volume novel in the mid-1890s. At the end of her career she abandoned fiction, and wrote for the *Fortnightly Review*, the *Nineteenth Century*, and the *North American Review* on literary subjects and on some of the causes about which she felt passionately, including the anti-vivisection campaign, the campaign against women's suffrage, and the Boers' struggle in South Africa. Some of these essays were collected in *Views and Opinions* (1895) and *Critical Studies* (1900). She remained in Italy after the death of her mother, living in near destitution. Her extravagant life had eaten up her earnings and she had sold her copyrights, a practice common to many women writers. Friends secured her a civil-list pension in 1906, which her pride almost made her refuse. She died of pneumonia in 1908 and was buried in the English cemetery at Bagni di Lucca. *See* E. Lee, *Ouida: A Memoir* (1914); Yvonne ffrench, *Ouida* (1938); E. Bigland, *Ouida: The Passionate Victorian* (1950); Monica Stirling, *The Fine and the Wicked: The Life and Times of Ouida* (1957); Olivia *Manning's introd. to *Under Two Flags* (1967).

Owenson, Sydney *see* MORGAN, Sydney

pppppppppppppp

P

Paget, Violet *see* LEE, Vernon

'Parker, Leslie' *see* THIRKELL, Angela

Parkes, Bessie Rayner, later Belloc, feminist, poet, and essayist (1829–1925).

Bessie Rayner Parkes was the daughter of Joseph Parkes (1796–1865), a Birmingham solicitor and Unitarian with radical connections, and his wife Elizabeth Priestley, the eldest daughter of Joseph Priestley, the Unitarian scientist and political Radical. Her father's friends included Jeremy Bentham, George Grote, and John Stuart Mill, as well as many eminent Whigs. She grew up in an atmosphere of reformist ideals and political ferment on both a local and national level as the family moved between Birmingham and London. She taught herself to read and had an early ambition of becoming a poet. In 1846 she met Barbara Leigh Smith (later *Bodichon), a feminist and reformer who became a lifelong friend. Both were interested in the reform of women's education and legal rights and in 1858 they established the **English Woman's Journal* to advance their ideas. Barbara Leigh Smith provided the money and Bessie Rayner Parkes became both editor and a frequent contributor. Leigh Smith's marriage in 1859 to Eugène Bodichon meant that she spent part of each year in Algeria, leaving Parkes in charge of the journal and of the circle of women involved in it, known as the Langham Place Group. In 1854 Parkes published *Remarks upon the Education of Girls* and in 1865 she wrote her *Essays on Women's Work*, a plea for better education and more employment opportunities, particularly for 'surplus' single women. Women's employment was her main concern, but she also supported the right of married women to property and earnings and to the vote. Her views were qualified, however. She did not believe in complete equality of the sexes, seeing women's 'delicate' organization of both brains and bodies as preventing equal competition and therefore separating herself from the more advanced views of contemporaries like Bodichon, Emily Davies, and Elizabeth Garrett Anderson. Between 1861 and 1864 she converted to Roman Catholicism, partly due to her interest in the work of the Irish Sisters of Mercy and Sisters of Charity. The death of her friend Adelaide *Procter, also a convert to Catholicism, may have been a contributing factor. In 1867, after an unsatisfactory love affair, she went on holiday to France, where she met Louis Belloc, two years her junior, the son of a French painter and an Irish-French writer and a chronic invalid. Their five years of marriage, pursued in the teeth of opposition from both families as well as from Barbara Bodichon, were idyllically happy. Their two children, Hilaire Belloc (1870–1953) and Marie *Belloc-Lowndes, both became writers. Louis Belloc's sudden death from sunstroke left her distraught. She returned with her children to London, suffered a severe financial loss through a rash investment, and was reduced to near poverty. She removed with the children to Slindon, in Sussex. Her friendship with Barbara Bodichon survived the rift caused by her marriage, but her links with the active women's movement were not renewed. She was never more than an approving bystander in the campaigns of the 1880s and 1890s or the renewed suffrage campaign after 1900. Ironically, neither of her children followed in her early footsteps. Marie Belloc-Lowndes remained studiedly aloof from the women's movement and Hilaire Belloc became a leading anti-feminist, disapproving both of women's suffrage and of higher education for women. Parkes published *Poems* (1852) and several other volumes, including *Summer Sketches and Other Poems* (1854), *Gabriel: A Poem* (1856), and *Ballads and Songs* (1863). Many of her poems were collected in *In Fifty Years* (1904). Her collected essays included *In a Walled Garden* (1895) and *A Passing World* (1897). *See* Marie Belloc-Lowndes, *I too have Lived in Arcadia* (1941); Hester Burton, *Barbara Bodichon 1827–91* (1949); Robert Speaight, *The Life of Hilaire Belloc* (1957).

Parr, Harriet *see* LEE, Holme

Parsons, Eliza, novelist and dramatist (b. 1748(?), d. Leytonstone, Essex, 5 February 1811).

Eliza Parsons was the only daughter of a Plymouth wine merchant named Phelps. At an early age she married a Mr Parsons, a turpentine merchant of Stonehouse, near Plymouth. Parsons moved his business to London in pursuit of better trade after losses in the American War of Independence and built extensive warehouses and workmen's lodgings. A fire in 1782 destroyed the premises, including the workmen's lodgings, which Eliza Parsons instructed should be pulled down to prevent the fire from spreading. As a result, Parsons gave up the business and secured an appointment in the Lord Chamberlain's office, where Eliza was also granted a place. After her husband's death in 1790 she wrote in order to provide for her eight children, producing more than nineteen works, of which the first, *The History of Miss Meridith* (1790), an epistolary novel, included the Prince of Wales, Mrs Fitzherbert, Horace Walpole, and Elizabeth *Montagu among its subscribers. Several of her novels were published by William Lane's *Minerva Press, known for its production of popular *Gothic fiction, including *The Errors of Education* (1791), *Woman as she Should Be* (1793), *Lucy* (1794), and *The Girl of the Mountains* (1797). *The Mysterious Warning* (1796), also a Minerva Press book, was an adaptation of *Hamlet*, a moral fable about the destructive effects of the passions on man's hopes for salvation. The dedication to the Prince of Wales read, 'I have never written a line tending to corrupt the heart, sully the imagination, or mislead the judgment of my young readers.' Jane *Austen listed *The Castle of Wolfenbach* (1793) and *The Mysterious Warning* among the novels of terror read by Isabella Thorpe in *Northanger Abbey*. Montague Summers named Parsons as one of a handful of Gothic novelists (the others included Ann *Radcliffe, Charlotte *Smith, and Isabella Hedgeland *Kelly) who continued to be widely read until the middle of the Victorian period. Parsons translated Molière's two-act farce *The Intrigues of a Morning*, which was produced at Covent Garden for two separate benefits in 1792, and in 1804 published six tales from La Fontaine as *Love and Gratitude*. She received several small sums from the Royal Literary Fund and on one occasion narrowly escaped debtors' prison. Only four of her eight children were still alive at her death in 1811. *See* Montague Summers, *The Gothic Quest* (1938; repr. 1965); Dorothy Blakey, *The Minerva Press, 1790–1820* (1939); Coral Ann Howells, *Love, Mystery and Misery: Feeling in Gothic Fiction* (1978).

Pearce, (Ann) Philippa, children's writer (b. Great Shelford, Cambridgeshire, 1921).

Philippa Pearce is one of the four children of Ernest Alexander Pearce, a flour miller, and his wife Gertrude Alice Ramsden. She grew up in the mill house on the River Cam where her father had been born and recreated the setting and the surrounding landscape in many of her stories. She went to the Perse Girls' School in Cambridge and then read English and history at Girton College. She worked as a civil servant during the Second World War and then became a script writer and producer in the BBC schools service. She moved into publishing in 1958 as an editor in the education department of Oxford University Press and in 1960 became children's editor for André Deutsch. She married Martin Christie (d. 1965) in 1963 and has a daughter. Pearce's first book, *Minnow on the Say* (1955), written while convalescing from tuberculosis, was an adventure story set in Great and Little Barley (Great Shelford) on the River Say (Cam), about two boys of differing social backgrounds whose involvement in a treasure hunt changes one of their lives. It was runner-up for the Library Association's Carnegie Medal, which she won with her next book, *Tom's Midnight Garden* (1958), widely acclaimed as a classic of children's literature and one of the best children's novels produced since the war. The story of a bored and lonely child and his relationship with the Victorian girl who once lived in the house, the novel embodies several of Pearce's themes, the relationship of old and young, loneliness, and the resulting creation of a fantasy world. *A Dog so Small* (1962) explores loneliness, relationships between generations, fantasy, and longing. She wrote the texts for various picture-books and adapted a story written for adults by Major Sir Brian Fairfax-Lucy, *The Children of the House* (1968), about four neglected children growing up in an Edwardian country house. It was reissued as *The Children of Charlcote* (1989). She has published several collections of stories, *The Elm Street Lot* (1969), about a working-class street, *What the Neighbours Did* (1972), about children's everyday lives, and *The Shadow-Cage and Other Tales of the Supernatural* (1977), a series of ghost stories for children. *The Battle of Bubble and Squeak* (1978), about a family row over gerbils, won the Whitbread Award. Later books include the acclaimed *The Way to Sattin Shore* (1983), about a fatherless girl, and *Who's Afraid* (1986), another collection of supernatural stories. Pearce's work has been praised for its restrained style, the eschewal of melodrama and other props in children's writing, the creation of believable characters, and her 'severe' realism. *See* John Rowe Townsend, *A Sense of Story* (1971).

Pembroke, Mary Herbert, Countess of, poet and translator (b. Penshurst, Kent, 1561, d. London, 25 September 1621).

Mary Herbert, Countess of Pembroke, was born Mary Sidney, third daughter of Sir Henry Sidney and Mary Dudley, daughter of the Duke of Northumberland. The poet Sir Philip Sidney was her brother and Lady Mary *Wroth her niece. She was taught Latin and Greek, and spent her childhood at Ludlow Castle, her father's official residence as President of The Marches of Wales. After the deaths of her sisters she spent a period at court as Maid of Honour to *Elizabeth I, and when she was 15 became the third wife of Henry Herbert, second Earl of Pembroke, twenty-five years her senior, by whom she had four children. She turned their home, Wilton House, near

Salisbury, into a haven for poets, the first beneficiary being her brother, who wrote the initial version of his prose romance *Arcadia* there, and dedicated it to her. After his death in 1586 she acted as his literary executor, issuing corrected editions of his works, revising and completing the *Arcadia* (from book iii) for publication in 1593, and helping to revise and complete a metrical version of the Psalms, of which he had finished only forty-three. These remained unpublished until 1823, but were known and admired by Ben Jonson, Donne, and George Herbert, among others. Ruskin, a later admirer, made a selection in 1877 under the title *Rock Honeycomb*, and a complete edition was published in 1963. In 1592 she published a translation of Philippe de Mornay's *A Discourse of Life and Death* and a Senecan tragedy, based on Robert Garnier's *Antonius* (published separately in 1595 as *Antonie*). She also translated Petrarch's *Triumph of Death* (published 1912; ed. G. F. Waller, 1977). Her elegy to her brother, 'To the Angell Spirit of Sir P. Sidney', was published with Samuel Daniel's works in 1623. Another poem, 'A Dialogue between Two Shepherds, Thenot and Piers in Praise of Astrea', written in honour of the Queen's visit to Wilton, was included in an anthology in 1602. Among the poets who enjoyed her patronage were Samuel Daniel, Nicholas Breton, and Thomas Moffet. Thomas Nashe, Gabriel Harvey, Sir John Harrington, Donne, and Ben Jonson publicly acknowledged her work. After her husband's death in 1601 she was granted a royal manor in Bedfordshire by James I and built Houghton House, where she lived for the remainder of her life. She died of smallpox in 1621. *See* F. B. Young, *Mary Sidney Countess of Pembroke* (1912); G. F. Waller, *Mary Sidney, Countess of Pembroke* (1979); Margaret P. Hannay (ed.), *Silent but for the Word: Tudor Women as Patrons, Translators and Writers of Religious Works* (1985); Margaret P. Hannay, *Philip's Phoenix: Mary Sidney, Countess of Pembroke* (1990); Mary Ellen Lamb, *Gender and Authorship in the Sidney Circle* (1990); Anne M. Haselkorn and Betty S. Travitsky (eds.), *The Renaissance Englishwoman in Print: Counterbalancing the Canon* (1990). *See* T. S. Eliot, 'Apology for the Countess of Pembroke' (1932).

'**Percy,** Charles Henry' *see* SMITH, Dodie

'Perdita' *see* ROBINSON, Mary

Pfeiffer, Emily Jane, poet (b. 26 November 1827, d. Putney, London, January 1890).

Emily Jane Pfeiffer was the daughter of R. Davis, an army officer with considerable property in Oxfordshire, and also an interest in art. Her mother (née Tilsley) was the daughter of a prosperous Montgomeryshire banker. The failure of the family bank, in which her father was implicated, brought financial hardship and a grim home life, and prevented her from receiving any formal education. Her father, however, encouraged the study and practice of both painting and poetry. In 1853 she married Jurgen Edward Pfeiffer, a German banker resident in London. Her first book, *Valisneria; or A Midsummer Night's Dream*, a fantasy, was published in 1857 and prompted comparisons with Sara *Coleridge's *Phantasmion.* After *Margaret; or The Motherless* (1861), a long poem, she wrote virtually nothing for the next sixteen years but instead educated herself through reading. She began publication in earnest in her mid-forties, with *Gerard's Monument and Other Poems* (1873). This inaugurated a stream of works: *Poems* (1876), *Glan-Alarch: His Silence and Song* (1877), *Sonnets and Songs* (1880), *The Wynnes of Wynhavod* (1881), a verse drama, and *Under the Aspens* (1882), many of which reflected her feminist concerns and her self-awareness as a woman artist. *The Rhyme of the Lady of the Rock and how it Grew* (1884) was a complex narrative in prose and verse which addressed social issues affecting women and the anxieties of a woman poet. *Flying Leaves from East and West* (1885) was a travel book based on a round-the-world journey. Pfeiffer was interested in developments in work for women and her articles on the subject were reprinted in *Women and Work* (1887). She was also an advocate of more practical female dress. Her husband's death in 1889 was a severe blow. She published a final book of poems, *Flowers of the Night* (1889), but died the following year, leaving money for the establishment of an orphanage, a drama school, and a hall for women students at University College, Cardiff. Pfeiffer's main strength as a poet, despite her many long poems, was her use of the sonnet form. In her practice of both she was often compared with Elizabeth Barrett *Browning. In 1880 she wrote 'The Lost Light', a eulogy on George *Eliot, whom she greatly admired. *See* E. S. Robertson, *English Poetesses* (1883); V. *Sackville-West, 'The Women Poets of the Seventies', in *The Eighteen-Seventies*, ed. Harley Granville-Barker (1929); Kathleen Hickok, *Representations of Women: Nineteenth-Century British Women's Poetry* (1984).

Philips, Katherine ('Orinda'), poet and translator (b. London, 1 January 1632, d. London, 22 June 1664).

Known to her contemporaries as 'the matchless Orinda', Katherine Philips was the daughter of John Fowler, a London merchant, and his wife Katherine Oxenbridge. According to John Aubrey she had read the Bible through before she was 4. When she was 8 her father sent her to a fashionable boarding school in Hackney run by a Mrs Salmon, which probably encouraged her strong Royalist views. There she met the first of her intimate female friends, Mary Aubrey, the 'M. A.' of several poems, who was to be a formative influence on her writing. After her father's death her mother married Hector

Philips and moved to his estate in Cardiganshire. Two years later, in 1648, Katherine married James Philips, his son by a previous marriage and a prominent Parliamentarian. She was 17 and he was 54. They had two children, a son who died in infancy and a daughter. Katherine Philips gathered around her a group of mainly female friends, forming what became known as her Society of Friendship. Each was given a classical name. Hers was Orinda. Mary Aubrey's was Rosania, James Philips's, Antenor. Anne Owen, another close friend, was Lucasia. Dr Jeremy Taylor (Palemon) addressed his 'Letter on the Measures and Offices of Friendship' to her in 1657. The inner circle of the group was exclusively female and Philips's friendships with women were intense and emotional. She began to write poems which circulated among the coterie. Some were prefixed to Henry Vaughan's *Poems* in 1651, and others were printed in the posthumous edition of the plays of William Cartwright in the same year. Her reputation had flourished sufficiently by 1662 that, when the couple moved to Dublin in that year, she was fêted by literary society in the city. Robert Boyle, Earl of Orrery, persuaded her to translate Corneille's *Pompey* and to adapt it for the English stage. Her version, which contained songs linking the acts, was produced to wide acclaim in Dublin in 1663, and printed in both Dublin and London. Charles II reportedly asked for a copy. Philips took pains to ensure that her name was not attached to *Pompey* and was therefore distressed when in 1664 an unauthorized version of her *Poems* was published, declaring she had 'never writ a line in my life with intention to have it printed . . . sometimes I think that to make verses is so much above my reach, and a diversion so unfit for the sex to which I belong that I am about to resolve against it forever'. She began work in secret on a translation of Corneille's *Horace* which was never completed. Returning to London in 1664 she caught smallpox and died suddenly, aged 33. Her collected *Poems*, including Pompey and the unfinished *Horace*, were published in 1667, and her *Letters from Orinda to Poliarchus* (Sir Charles Cotterel, Master of Ceremonies at Charles II's court) were published in 1705. Her poems were included in **Poems by Eminent Ladies* (1755), and some of her letters published with *Familiar Letters Written by the Late Earl of Rochester* (1697). Among her later admirers was Keats, who commended and quoted her 'To Mrs. M. A. at parting' in a letter to J. H. Reynolds in 1817. *See* P. W. Souers, *The Matchless Orinda* (1931); Elizabeth H. Hageman, in *Women Writers of the Renaissance and Reformation*, ed. Katharina M. Wilson (1987); Elaine Hobby, *Virtue of Necessity: English Women's Writing 1649–1688* (1988); Maureen E. Mulvihill, in *Curtain Calls: British and American Women and the Theater 1660–1820*, ed. Mary Anne Schofield and Cecilia Macheski (1991).

Pilkington, Laetitia, poet and playwright (b. Dublin, 1708(?), d. Dublin, 29 August 1750).

Laetitia Pilkington was the second of the three children of Dr John van Lewen, a Dutch physician and obstetrician who had settled in Dublin. Her mother (née Meade), a great granddaughter of the Earl of Kilmallock, discouraged her reading, but her father indulged her writing of poetry. In 1725 she married Matthew Pilkington (*1701–74*), vicar of Donabate and Portrahan, near Dublin, who was also a minor poet. They had three children. Through her friend Constantia *Grierson, who had been her father's pupil, she was introduced to Dr Patrick Delany, a friend of Swift, which provided an entrée to the Swift circle for both Pilkingtons. She became a particular favourite, and Swift in turn corrected Matthew's *Poems on Several Occasions* (1730) and secured his appointment as chaplain to the Lord Mayor of London, hoping to use him as his London agent. Pope and Bolingbroke reported unfavourably on Pilkington, Pope pronouncing him 'an intolerable coxcomb', and as stories of his immorality surfaced, Swift's good opinion altered. Relations between the couple deteriorated when Laetitia arrived in London, and rumours of the extra-marital affairs of both reached Dublin. Literary as well as sexual rivalry was instanced as a cause of disharmony by mutual friends. Pilkington obtained a divorce and Laetitia settled in London, where she turned to writing. She published *The Statues; or The Trial of Constancy: A Tale for the Ladies* (1739) and *An Excursory View on the Present State of Men and Things: A Satire* (1739), but her output was not sufficient for financial independence and her fortunes rapidly declined. Gossip surrounding her dubious relationships with various men increased and for a time she lived with the painter James Worsdale, a relationship first encouraged by her husband. She was imprisoned in the Marshalsea for debt, befriended by Colley Cibber, and opened a print shop in St James's, where she wrote letters and pamphlets to order. She also for a time became a friend of Samuel Richardson. In 1748 she returned to Dublin, where she published the first volume of her spirited and frank *Memoirs*, which, among other things, presented a unique and intimate view of the domestic life of Swift during the period of their early friendship. A second volume followed in 1749 and a third, augmented by her son John Carteret Pilkington, was published posthumously in 1754. Her unflattering portrait of her husband in the *Memoirs* resulted in a minor pamphlet war between them, Matthew Pilkington issuing *Seasonable Advice to the Publick Concerning a Book of Memoirs Lately published* (1748) followed by her *An Answer to Seasonable Advice to the Publick . . .* (1748). A comedy, *The Turkish Court; or The London 'Prentice*, acted in Dublin in 1749 but never published, was said to have been hers. She died in Dublin in 1750. Matthew Pilkington assumed new respectability after her death, and in 1770 published *The Gentleman's and Connoisseur's Dictionary of Painters*, which remained a standard reference work until well into the next century. Laetitia Pilkington's reputation for wit was reflected in the publication of *The Celebrated Mrs. Pilkington's Jests; or The Cabinet of Wit and Humour* (1764). Her poems were included in **Poems by Eminent Ladies* (1755). But the odour of impropriety never quite left her, as evidenced by the *DNB*'s designation of her as an 'adventuress' rather than a writer. Virginia *Woolf described her as 'a very extraordinary cross between Moll Flanders and Lady *Ritchie' in a sympathetic portrait in 'Lives of the Obscure', *The Common Reader: Second Series* (1932). *See* Diana M. Relke, in *Gender at Work: Four Women Writers of the Eighteenth Century*, ed. Ann Messenger (1990).

Piozzi, Hester Lynch Thrale, woman of letters, bluestocking (b. Bodwell, near Pwllheli, Caernarvonshire, 16 January 1741, d. Clifton, near Bristol, 2 May 1821).

Hester Thrale Piozzi was the daughter of John Salusbury, an impoverished Welsh landowner, and Hester Maria Cotton, his cousin. Salusbury's patron Lord Halifax, then President of the Board of Trade, sent him to Nova Scotia, and his wife and young daughter lived first with her family, and then with Salusbury's brother Sir Thomas Salusbury at Offley Hall, Hertfordshire. Hester's cleverness was apparent from an early age. She learned Latin and modern languages and wrote articles for the *St. James's Chronicle* before she was 15. During her father's absence, and against her wishes, her uncle arranged a marriage for her with Henry Thrale, the son of a wealthy local brewer, in 1763. The marriage was not unhappy, despite their divergent interests and Thrale's occasional infidelities, and they had twelve children, of whom four survived to adulthood. Thrale became MP for Southwark from 1765 to 1780 and due to Mrs Thrale's literary interests their house at Streatham Park became the focus of a lively intellectual circle which included Edmund Burke, Charles and Fanny *Burney, Garrick, Goldsmith, Sir Joshua Reynolds, and Samuel Johnson, who became a semi-permanent resident from 1765. Mrs Thrale was active in her husband's political career and also in his business, which was sold for £135,000 after his death in 1781, leaving her financially independent. Her subsequent marriage in 1784 to Gabriel Piozzi, an Italian musician and a Roman Catholic, scandalized society and alienated her eldest daughter and also Dr Johnson, who completely severed his connection with her. Her second marriage marked the beginning of her literary career. The couple moved to Florence, where Mrs Piozzi became friendly with Robert Merry, the founder of the so-called Della Cruscan poets, and contributed to and wrote the preface for his *Florence Miscellany* (1785).

She published her most important and best-known book, the perceptive and non-adulatory *Anecdotes of the Late Samuel Johnson* (1786), and prepared her two-volume edition of Johnson's letters, which was published in 1788 after her return to England. The couple settled at Streatham Park, where Mrs Piozzi was received once again into literary circles. Other works included a travel book, *Observations and Reflections Made in the Course of a Journey through France, Italy and Germany* (1789), *British Synonymy* (1798), intended to help foreigners with the language, and *Retrospection* (1801), a popular world history, which was badly received. She wrote some poetry, most of which was collected in *Thraliana*, her lively and detailed journal of her life from 1776 to 1809, first published in 1942 (ed. K. C. Balderston). The best known of her poems, 'Three Warnings', first appeared in *Miscellanies*, published by Dr Johnson's companion Anna *Williams in 1766. In 1795 the Piozzis moved to Wales, where Gabriel Piozzi died in 1809. Hester Piozzi died in 1821, aged 81, leaving her estate to a nephew of Piozzi's whom the couple had adopted. Her life in Bath, which she frequented in later years, is described in *Piozziana; or Recollections of Mrs Piozzi*, by E. Mangin (1833). Her *Autobiography, Letters and Literary Remains* (1861, ed. A. Hayward) was based in part on *Thraliana*. Other accounts of Mrs Thrale and her circle are given in Boswell's *Life of Johnson* and Fanny Burney's *Autobiography*. *The Piozzi Letters: Correspondence of Hester Lynch Piozzi 1784–1821* is being edited by Edward A. and Lillian D. Bloom (1989–). *See* J. L. Clifford, *Hester Lynch Piozzi* (1941; expanded 1968); Mary Hyde, *The Impossible Friendship: Boswell and Mrs Thrale* (1972); William McCarthy, *Hester Thrale Piozzi: Portrait of a Literary Woman* (1985).

Pitter, Ruth, poet (b. Ilford, Essex, 7 November 1897, d. Long Crendon, near Aylesbury, 29 February 1992).

Ruth Pitter was the eldest of the three children of George Pitter and his wife Louisa Murrell, both elementary school teachers in the East End of London, 'of the superior artisan class, intelligent, idealistic, country-lovers, poetic, altruistic', as she described them. She went to a local elementary school, then to the Coburn School in Bow. After a spell in the War Office during the First World War she escaped to Suffolk to work as a painter in an arts and crafts firm which made pottery and furniture. She and her life-long companion Kathleen O'Hara, a painter, later established their own business in Chelsea, Deane & Forester. She began to write poetry from the age of 5 and published her first poem in A. R. Orage's *New Age* when she was 13. 'From the very first I realized there was no money in poetry and determined not to write for money,' she later recalled. 'By commercial slavery and continued anxiety, I have avoided patronage and the meal-ticket marriage, and am (as a writer) independent of politics, publishers and jobbery.' Her *First Poems* (1920) was followed by *First and Second Poems 1912–1925* (1927), with a preface by Hilaire Belloc, who along with David Cecil and George Orwell was one of her early supporters. Other books included *Persephone in Hades* (1931), *A Mad Lady's Garland* (1935), and *A Trophy of Arms* (1936), which won the Hawthornden Prize. During the war she and O'Hara gave up the business and took war jobs in offices. Pitter worked in a machine shop at night ('lousy dump, but lovely people'). In 1952 they settled in Long Crendon in Buckinghamshire. She continued to write and the honours accumulated. *The Ermine: Poems 1942–52* (1953) won the Heinemann Award and in 1955 she became the first woman to receive the Queen's Gold Medal for Poetry. *Poems 1926–1966* appeared in 1968, published in the USA as *Collected Poems* (1969). *The End of Drought* (1975) and *A Heaven to Find* (1987) were incorporated into *Collected Poems* (1990), published at the age of 93, with a foreword by Elizabeth *Jennings. Pitter has been regarded as an anti-modernist poet, working in the late nineteenth-century tradition. As *The Times* obituary (3 March 1992) commented, 'her poetry behaves as if all the literary movements of the past century, from Georgianism to Concrete Poetry, had simply never happened'. Yet James Stephens, introducing *A Trophy of Arms*, saw her as the best living poet after Yeats. Others have seen her both as a mystical religious poet (she was converted to Anglicanism in her forties) and as a poet of the natural world in the modern tradition stretching from Edward Thomas to Ted Hughes. Her language is concrete, precise, the detail often grotesque. Many of the poems are humorous. Her works include what she has termed her 'profane poems', *The Rude Potato* (1941), on gardening, and *Pitter on Cats* (1947). She was appointed Companion of Literature in 1974 and CBE in 1979. Her name was mentioned as a possible successor to the Poet Laureateship after C. Day-Lewis's death in 1972. An injury to her eye caused by hot enamel resulted in total blindness in her last years. She died in her 95th year. *See* Arthur Russell (ed.), *Ruth Pitter: Homage to a Poet* (1969); and her own preface to *Poems 1926–66* (1968).

Pix, Mary, playwright (b. Nettlebed, Oxfordshire, 1666, d. London(?) *c.*May 1709).

Mary Pix was the daughter of the Revd Roger Griffith, vicar of Nettlebed, Oxfordshire, and his wife Lucy Berriman, who claimed descent from Oxfordshire gentry. In 1684 she married George Pix, a London merchant tailor. They had one child, who died in 1690. Mary Pix came to prominence in 1696 with a tragedy, *Ibrahim the Thirteenth Emperour of the Turks* (she had meant Ibrahim the twelfth), performed at Drury Lane. A novel, *The Inhuman Cardinal*, and a farce, *The Spanish Wives*, appeared in the same year, launching her on a successful career as a dramatist which was more productive than that of any other woman playwright other than Aphra *Behn. Comedy was her province, and her successes included *The Innocent Mistress* (1697), *The Beau Defeated* (1700), *The Different Widows* (1703), and *The Adventures in Madrid* (1706). One comedy which was not a success, *The Deceiver Deceived* (1697) led to a pamphlet war when Mrs Pix suspected that the actor–dramatist George Powell, who had starred in *The Innocent Mistress* and had seen the manuscript of *The Deceiver Deceived*, had appropriated some of the lines for his own play *Imposture Defeated* (published 1698). Congreve entered the lists in her defence. Pix's tragedies were laboured and overblown. *Queen Catherine*, produced at Lincoln's Inn in 1698, *The False Friend* (1699), also at Lincoln's Inn, *The Double Distress* (1701), *The Czar of Muscovy* (1701), and *The Conquest of Spain* (1705) did little to enhance her reputation. Her comedies contained shrewd observations of the mercantile classes and sharp comedy on marital infidelity. She also adapted a long poem from Boccaccio, *Violenta; or The Rewards of Virtue* (1704), and contributed to the volume of elegies published by women poets to mark Dryden's death, *The *Nine Muses*, published in 1700. Satirized along with the equally successful Delarivier *Manley and Catharine *Trotter in an anonymous play *The *Female Wits* by W. M. (performed 1696, published 1704), Pix was popularly remembered for her fatness and her penchant for wine. *See* Fidelis Morgan, *The Female Wits: Women Playwrights on the London Stage 1660–1720* (1981); Constance Clark, *Three Augustan Women Playwrights* (1986); Juliet McLaren, in *Gender at Work: Four Women Writers of the Eighteenth Century*, ed. Ann Messenger (1990); Mary Anne Schofield and Cecilia Macheski (eds.) *Curtain Calls: British and American Women and the Theater, 1660–1820* (1991).

'**Plaidy,** Jean' *see* HIBBERT, Eleanor

Plath, Sylvia ('Victoria Lucas'), poet and novelist (b. Jamaica Plain, Massachusetts, 27 October 1932, d. London, 11 February 1963).

Sylvia Plath was the daughter of Otto Emil Plath, professor of biology at Boston University and an authority on bees, and his wife Aurelia Schober. She grew up in Winthrop, Massachusetts, but after her father's death in 1940 the family moved to Wellesley. With her father's death and the resulting end of her seaside childhood, those parts of her life, in her words, 'sealed themselves off like a ship in a bottle'. She worked remorselessly for academic and social success at High School in Wellesley, and later at Smith College, to which she won a scholarship in 1950. While at Smith she published stories and poems in the college literary magazine and won a fiction contest sponsored by *Mademoiselle* magazine. A month as guest editor of the special college issue of *Mademoiselle* in 1952 precipitated a severe depression and a suicide attempt for which she was hospitalized. These experiences were later reflected in her only novel, *The Bell Jar*, published in 1963 (filmed 1979) under the pseudonym Victoria Lucas. The bell jar of the title referred to the private vacuum in which her madness had confined her. She returned to Smith in the autumn of 1953 and graduated *summa cum laude* in 1955. She won a Fulbright Fellowship to Newnham College, Cambridge, where she met the English poet Ted Hughes, whom she married in June 1956. She submitted forty-three poems as Part II of the Cambridge English tripos and took a second BA in 1957. Only six of the poems were later included in her first published collection, but they were an early revelation of her interest in psychic states and the spirit world. Plath and Hughes returned to the United States, where she taught in the English department at Smith for a year but found she had little time for writing. The following year they moved to Boston, where she attended the poetry seminars of Robert Lowell and met the poet Anne Sexton, all three sharing an interest in nervous disorders, domestic difficulties, and mental breakdowns. In the autumn of 1959 Plath and Hughes received a fellowship to Yaddo, a writers' colony at Saratoga Springs, New York, where she completed the poems which formed her first collection, *The Colossus* (1960). While at Yaddo she experimented with meditation, under Hughes's influence, and read African folk-tales and the poetry of Theodore Roethke, all of which encouraged her to deal more openly with her own psychological condition in her work. They returned to England at the end of 1959. Their first child, a daughter, was born in 1960. Plath won the Cheltenham Festival Award for *The Colossus* and a Eugene F. Saxton writing fellowship, but also suffered a miscarriage followed by an appendectomy. In September 1961 the couple moved to Devon, where Plath settled into country life and took up bee-keeping and horse riding. Their second child, a son, was born in January 1962. She suffered severe writing blocks but wrote relentlessly, widening her range of subjects to include her experiences as a hospital patient, a mother, and even a bee-keeper. The discovery of Hughes's infidelity led to their separation in the late summer of 1962. She took the children back to London to live in a flat in Fitzroy Road once inhabited by Yeats. The almost frenetic burst of writing continued, with Plath working between four o'clock and seven in the morning before the children woke, producing sometimes as many as two or three poems a day in what A. Alvarez called 'one of the most astonishing creative outbursts of our generation'. The poems also constituted the work for which she is best remembered. She suffered from recurrent bouts of flu and from the harshness of one of the coldest winters of the century. *The Bell Jar* was published in January 1963. Less than a month after its publication, and after a final period of intense creativity, she committed suicide in February 1963. *Ariel*, her second collection, comprised mainly of the poems written during the last months of her life, was finally published in 1965. Of them the critic George Steiner wrote that 'no group of poems since Dylan Thomas's *Deaths and Entrances* has had as vivid an impact on English critics and readers'. The furious, intimate, destructive, and revelatory nature of the poems combined with the nature of her death have lent both a notoriety and a legendary quality which is not altogether positive. Two more collections of poems, *Crossing the Water* (1971) and *Winter Trees* (1971), which included her radio play *Three Women: A Monologue for Three Voices*, written in 1962, have appeared, and a collection of short stories, *Johnny Panic and the Bible of Dreams* (1979). *Letters Home: Correspondence 1950–1963* (1975) was edited by Aurelia Schober Plath. Ted Hughes edited her short stories and diary excerpts (1979), her *Collected Poems* (1981), her *Journals* (1982, with Frances McCullough), and *Selected Poems* (1985). The manuscript of a second novel, provisionally titled *Double Exposure*, disappeared in 1970. *See* Linda W. Wagner (ed.), *Critical Essays on Sylvia Plath* (1984); Stephen Tabor (ed.), *Sylvia Plath: An Analytical Bibliography* (1987); Linda Wagner-Martin, *Sylvia Plath: A Biography* (1988); Linda Wagner (ed.), *Sylvia Plath: The Critical Heritage* (1988); Anne Stevenson, *Bitter Fame: A Life of Sylvia Plath* (1989); Ronald Hayman, *The Death and Life of Sylvia Plath* (1991); Pat Macpherson, *Reflecting on 'The Bell Jar'* (1991); Jacqueline Rose, *The Haunting of Sylvia Plath* (1991).

Poems by Eminent Ladies (London: R. Baldwin, 1755).

This was a two-volume anthology of women poets, edited by George Colman the elder (1732–94) and Bonnell Thornton (1724–68), whose literary partnership began with their joint proprietorship of a weekly paper, the *Connoisseur*, published between January 1754 and September 1756. *Poems by Eminent Ladies* included selections from the work of some eighteen women, 'particularly Mrs. *Barber, Mrs. *Behn, Miss [Elizabeth]*Carter, Lady *Chudleigh, Mrs. *Cockburn, Mrs. *Grierson, Mrs. Jones, Mrs. *Killigrew, Mrs. *Leapor, Mrs. Madan, Mrs. Masters, Lady M. W. *Montagu, Mrs. *Mon[c]k, Dutchess of *Newcastle, Mrs. K. *Philips, Mrs. *Pilkington, Mrs. *Rowe, Lady *Winchelsea'. According to the preface the volumes were compiled 'as a standing proof that great abilities are not confined to the men, and that genius often glows with equal warmth, and perhaps with more delicacy, in the breast of a female'. The collection, it was emphasized, was 'not inferior to any miscellany compiled from the works of men'. Each selection was prefixed by a short biographical account of the writer. The anthology was publicized fancifully in the *Connoisseur* and a second edition published in 1773. Like George *Ballard's *Memoirs of Several Ladies of Great Britain who* *have been Celebrated for their Writings* (1752) and John Duncombe's *The *Feminiad* (1754) it helped to establish a mid-eighteenth-century canon of women writers.

Ponsonby, Sarah *see* LLANGOLLEN, Ladies of

Porter, Anna Maria, novelist (b. Durham, 1780, d. Montpellier, near Bristol, 21 September 1832).

Anna Maria Porter was the youngest of the five children of William Porter, an army surgeon, who died before she was born, and Jane Blenkinsop. Her elder sister *Jane also became a novelist, and her brother Sir Robert Ker Porter (1777–1842) was a well-known historical painter and traveller. Her mother moved to Edinburgh after her husband's death and sent the girls to a school run by a Mr George Fulton. The young Walter Scott was a neighbour. Another neighbour, the elderly 'Luckie Forbes', fascinated the children with fairy stories and tales of Scottish history. The two girls regarded a literary career as a serious possibility from an early age. Together with their brother Robert they collaborated on a literary magazine, the *Quiz*, in 1797. When she was 13 Anna began her *Artless Tales*, published in two volumes in 1793–5. *Walsh Colville* and *Octavia* appeared anonymously in 1797 and 1798. A move to London around 1803 introduced the family to literary circles, to the artist friends of their brother, to their father's military and naval associates, and to the theatre, where Robert for a time painted scenery. Anna's *The Fair Fugitive*, a 'musical entertainment', was performed at Covent Garden in May 1803 but never printed. Her first major work was *The Hungarian Brothers* (1807), a historical romance about the French Revolutionary War which went through several editions, and was translated into French in 1818. A series of others followed rapidly, many of them historical romances: *Don Sebastian; or The House of Braganza* (1809); *The Recluse of Norway* (1814), *The Knight of St. John* (1817), *The Fast of St. Magdalen* (1818), *The Village of Mariendorpt* (1821), *Roche-Blanche; or The Hunters of the Pyrenees*, *O'Hara; or 1798* (1825), *Honor O'Hara* (1826), and her last novel, *The Barony* (1830). *Tales of Pity on Fishing, Shooting and Hunting* (1814) reflected her long-held sympathy with animals. She also wrote *Tales round a Winter Hearth* (1826), and *Coming Out* (1828) with her sister. The two lived together with their mother in London and in Esher, in Surrey, until the latter's death in 1831. Neither married. By far the more prolific of the two, Anna Maria Porter's works have not lasted as well as the highly successful works of her sister. Both writers, however, were translated into French and German, and were also popular in America. They helped to create the vogue for historical fiction which was begun by Maria *Edgeworth and capitalized upon by Scott with *Waverley* (1814) and successive works. Anna Maria Porter was also a contributor to *annuals and other periodicals. She died suddenly of typhus at the age of 52.

Porter, Jane, novelist (b. Durham, 1776, d. Bristol, 24 May 1850).

Jane Porter was one of five children of William Porter, an army surgeon with a distinguished family background who died when she was 3, and of Jane Blenkinsop of Durham. One of her brothers was Sir Robert Ker Porter (1777–1842), a well-known historical painter, diplomat, and traveller. Her closest sibling was her younger sister *Anna Maria, with whom she lived for most of her life and with whom she worked in close association. Their striking and also contrasting physical appearance led the journalist Samuel Carter Hall, for whose periodicals they wrote, to dub the blonde Anna 'L'Allegro' to the brunette Jane's 'Il Penseroso'. After their father's death the younger children moved to Edinburgh with their mother, where they were sent to a school run by a Mr George Fulton. Jane was said to rise at four in the morning in order to read *The Faerie Queene*, Sidney's *Arcadia*, and tales of chivalry. In 1797 Robert, Jane, and Anna Maria collaborated on a short-lived illustrated periodical, the *Quiz*, published with the help of the bibliophile Thomas Frognall Dibden. A move to London provided an introduction to literary circles which included Hannah *More and Anna Laetitia *Barbauld, to artist friends of their brother, to military friends of their father, and to a number of political refugees from the Continent who were currently making their home in England. It was the last which provided the background to Jane's first and immediately successful novel, *Thaddeus of Warsaw* (1803), which went through many editions and won her the commendation of the Polish patriot General Kosciusko. The tenth edition of 1819 was dedicated to him, and reprints, translations, and American editions continued until 1868. Her next novel, *The Scottish Chiefs* (1810), was based on the story of William Wallace and was particularly admired by the poet Thomas Campbell, who had helped her with sources, Mary Russell *Mitford, and Joanna *Baillie, who claimed to have been helped by it in her poem on Wallace in *Metrical Legends* (1821). Like its predecessor the novel went through many editions and its success contributed to the vogue for historical novels begun by Maria *Edgeworth and others, and which culminated in Scott's *Waverley* (1814). *The Pastor's Fireside* (1815) was based on the later Stuarts, and the subject of *Duke Christian of Luneburg; or Traditions of the Harz* (1824) was said to have been suggested to her by George IV, who requested that she write on his ancestor. She claimed that her last work, *Sir Edward Seaward's Narrative of his Shipwreck* (1831), was based on an actual diary and 'edited' by her, but it, too, was a work of fiction. She published *Tales round a Winter Hearth* (1826) and *Coming Out* (1828) with Anna Maria. Her success with novels was not repeated with her excursion into the theatre. *Egmont; or The Eve of St. Alyne* was neither printed nor performed. *Switzerland* (1819) was withdrawn from Drury Lane although Charles Kean was in the principal role, and *Owen, Prince of Powys* (1822), also with Kean, was a failure. Despite the undoubted popularity of her novels, Jane Porter's last days were dogged by financial difficulties. The publisher of *The Scottish Chiefs* made her an additional payment in 1842, and she also received a pension from the Royal Literary Fund. She lived with her mother in Surrey until the latter's death in 1831, after which she moved to London with her sister, who died the following year. Her 'beloved and protecting brother' Robert died in 1842. Although her last work was published in 1831 she remained a prominent figure in the literary world and died in 1850 at the age of 74.

Potter, (Helen) Beatrix, writer and illustrator of children's books (b. South Kensington, London, 28 July 1866, d. Sawrey, Lancashire, 22 December 1943).

Beatrix Potter was the elder of the two children of Rupert Potter, a qualified barrister who never practised, and his wife Helen Leech. Both parents were Unitarians, and both had inherited substantial fortunes derived from the Lancashire cotton industry. Her childhood was solitary and oppressive, spent in the nursery of a large house in Bolton Gardens, 'my unloved birthplace', as she later referred to it, until the birth of her brother five years later. She was taught by governesses until she was 15, and occupied herself by reading Maria *Edgeworth, Scott, Lewis Carroll, and Edward Lear. She also smuggled into the house a menagerie of small animals, which she studied and drew, sometimes adding clothes and anthropomorphic activities to amuse visiting children. Her brother was sent to Charterhouse, but she had no formal education after the age of 15 and lived at home, a dutiful, unmarried daughter. One of her governesses had encouraged her drawing and she spent some time sketching in the Natural History Museum. Her father took her to Royal Academy exhibitions. In her mid-twenties she began to write story-letters containing illustrations to entertain the sick child of one of her governesses, developing anecdotes about her pets. Encouraged by Canon H. D. Rawnsley, one of the co-founders of the National Trust and a friend of her father's whom she had met while in the Lake District, she approached publishers, who were unhelpful. In 1901 she had *The Tale of Peter Rabbit* privately printed, followed in 1902 by *The Tailor of Gloucester.* Frederick Warne & Company became interested, republished both stories, and over the next thirty years published twenty-four of her books. The association was personal as well as professional. Despite her parents' disapproval she became engaged to Norman Warne, one of the publisher's three sons. He died of leukaemia several months later but Potter used the opportunity to separate herself from her parents by buying Hill Top Farm at Sawrey, in the Lake District, where her family had once stayed while on holiday. *The Pie and the Patty Pan* was a celebration of Sawrey village and also the farm, which was illustrated on the frontispiece. The period between 1906 and 1913 represented the peak of her creativity, and many of the stories grew out of details of local life. The tales of *Jeremy Fisher* (1906), *Tom Kitten* (1907), *Jemima Puddleduck* (1908), *The Roly-Poly Pudding* (1908), *Ginger and Pickles* (1909), *Mr. Tod* (1912), and *Pigling Bland* (1913) all had Hill Top or Lake District associations. In their humorous treatment of social nuance and the niceties of behaviour her stories reflected the burden of her late Victorian upbringing. Despite the cosy domesticity of their settings, they also demonstrated the inherent dangers of life and the omnipresence of death. Once ensconced in the Lake District Potter systematically studied the techniques of farming and gradually became engaged in the running of Hill Top. In 1913, at the age of 47, and against her parents' wishes, she married William Heelis, an Ambleside solicitor. Her life as a writer effectively came to an end, and she put all her energies into sheep farming, becoming an expert on the breeding of Herdwicks. She published *Apple Dapply's Nursery Rhymes* (1917), which she had compiled in 1905, *The Tale of Johnny Town-Mouse* (1918), *Cecily Parsley's Nursery Rhymes* (1922), and in 1930 *The Tale of Little Pig Robinson*, but nothing else of substance. Enthusiastic American readers persuaded her to produce *The Fairy Caravan* in 1929 for the American market (published in England in 1952), but it was not a success. She died at Sawrey in 1943 and left her extensive property and her house to the National Trust. Her stories have been translated into French, German, Dutch, Japanese, Welsh, and Latin. *The Journal of Beatrix Potter 1881–9* was decoded and edited by Leslie Linder (1966) and a selection of her letters edited by Judy Taylor (1989). *See* Margaret Lane, *The Tale of Beatrix Potter* (1946) and *The Magic Years of Beatrix Potter* (1978); Graham Greene, 'Beatrix Potter', in *Collected Essays* (1969); Leslie Linder, *The History of the Writings of Beatrix Potter* (1971); Ulla Hyde Parker, *Cousin Beatie* (1981); Ruth Macdonald, *Beatrix Potter* (1986); Judy Taylor, *Beatrix Potter: Artist, Storyteller and Countrywoman* (1986).

'**Powerscourt,** Sheila' *see* WINGFIELD, Sheila

'**Preedy,** George R.' *see* BOWEN, Marjorie

Procter, Adelaide (Anne), poet (b. London, 30 October 1825, d. London, 2 February 1864).

Adelaide Procter was the eldest daughter and first of the six children of Bryan Waller Procter, a London solicitor better known as the poet Barry Cornwall, and his wife Anne Skepper. She published her first poems at the age of 18 in the *annual *Heath's Book of Beauty*, in 1843. In 1853 she sent some poems under the pseudonym Mary Berwick to her father's friend Charles Dickens, then the editor of *Household Words*. Dickens was enthusiastic, and published most of her subsequent poetry in *Household Words* and *All the Year Round*. The poems were collected in two volumes as *Legends and Lyrics* in 1858, and a second series issued in 1861. Adelaide Procter was an active campaigner on women's issues. She was a central figure in the Langham Place Group of feminists along with Bessie Rayner *Parkes and Barbara *Bodichon, who founded the **English Woman's Journal* in 1858, and she became the journal's most prominent poet. She was also at the forefront of the debates conducted in the journal. In 1859 she was appointed to a committee charged with considering ways of providing employment for women. This became the Society for Promoting the Employment of Women, on which Procter served as secretary. Bessie Parkes, Emily *Faithfull, and Jessie Boucherett (who reviewed *Legends and Lyrics* for the *English Woman's Journal*) were among her associates. In 1861 she edited a volume of prose and verse, *The Victoria Regia*, which was set up in type by women compositors at Emily Faithfull's Victoria Press and included among its contributors Tennyson, Thackeray, Harriet *Martineau, and Arnold. She continued her combination of literature and philanthropy by publishing *A Chaplet of Verses* in 1862, the proceeds of which went to support a Catholic night shelter for women. (She had converted to Roman Catholicism in 1851, along with two of her sisters.) Her health had always been poor, and she died of consumption in February 1864. Procter was one of the most popular poets of her day and a decade after her death the demand for her verse, which was much anthologized, was said to be greater than that for any contemporary poet except Tennyson. Her best-known lyric, 'The Lost Chord', was set to music by Sir Arthur Sullivan. She wrote narrative poetry as well, including 'Homeward Bound', which had the same story as Tennyson's 'Enoch Arden'. Despite her popularity, she remained modest, insisting, 'Papa is a poet. I only write verses.' Dickens contributed a memoir to the posthumous edition of her *Legends and Lyrics* in 1866 and Bessie Rayner Parkes included reminiscences of her in *In a Walled Garden* (1895), a portrait which, interestingly, ignored Procter's contribution to the women's movement. *See* [Bryan Waller], *Procter: An Autobiographical Fragment* (1877; repr. 1936); Kathleen Hickok, *Representations of Women: Nineteenth-Century British Women's Poetry* (1984).

Pym, Barbara (Mary Crampton), novelist (b. Oswestry, Shropshire, 2 June 1913, d. Oxford, 11 January 1980).

Barbara Pym was the elder daughter of Frederick Crampton Pym, a solicitor, and his wife Irene Spenser Thomas. She went to Huyton College, a boarding school near Liverpool, and then to St Hilda's College, Oxford, where she took a second in English in 1934. She determined on a writing career as a schoolgirl, wrote for the school magazine, and completed a first novel, '*Young Men in Fancy Dress*' (unpublished), when she was 16. She finished a second novel in 1934, but it too remained unpublished. After Oxford she lived mostly at home, apart from a period teaching in Poland, which came to an end in 1938. During the war she worked as a postal censor in Bristol and then in Naples with the Women's Royal Naval Service. On her return to London she joined the International African Institute, first as a research assistant and then as assistant editor of the journal *Africa* between 1958 and 1974. Her first published novel, *Some Tame Gazelle* (1950), which had been originally rejected, was followed by *Excellent Women* (1952), *Jane and Prudence* (1953), *Less than Angels* (1955), *A Glass of Blessings* (1958), considered by many to be her best, and in 1961 *No Fond Return of Love*. The unsensational subject-matter of her novels, middle-class, middle-aged, unmarried people associated with the Church or academic life, and the accompanying social comedy and mild irony, attracted a small but loyal following. Publishers, however, were not enthusiastic and the 1960s and early 1970s marked a period of painful neglect and a decline in her reputation. In 1977 the *Times Literary Supplement* published a symposium on the most over- and underrated writers of the previous three-quarters of a century. The critic Lord David Cecil and the poet Philip Larkin both nominated Pym as the most underrated writer, which led to a re-evaluation and a burgeoning of reprints of her work in both Britain and America. A new novel, *Quartet in Autumn*, was published in 1977 and short-listed for the Booker prize, followed by *The Sweet Dove Died* (1978), which had been written earlier. *A Few Green Leaves*, completed just before her death, and *Crampton Hodnet*, another early novel, were published posthumously in 1980 and 1985. *An Unsuitable Attachment*, written in the 1960s but rejected by publishers, was published in 1982. In retirement Pym lived with her sister in a village near Oxford, the quiet, middle-class rural life of 'church, gardening, local history and country walks', as she described it, which is reflected in some of her novels. Her last years saw some recompense for earlier neglect in the form of press, television, and radio interviews, and a fellowship of the Royal Society of Literature. She died of cancer in 1980. *A Very Private Eye: The Diaries, Letters and Notebooks of Barbara Pym* was published in 1984, and a further novel, *An Academic Affair*, was assembled from two unrevised drafts in 1986. *See* Diane Benet, *Something to Love: Barbara Pym's Novels* (1986); Robert Emmet Long, *Barbara Pym* (1986); Dale Salwak (ed.), *The Life and Work of Barbara Pym* (1987); Janice

Rossen (ed.), *Independent Women: The Function of Gender in the Novels of Barbara Pym* (1988); Annette Weld, *Barbara Pym and the Novel of Manners* (1992).

R

r r r r r r r r r r r r r r r

Radcliffe, Ann, novelist (b. London, 9 July 1764, d. London, 7 February 1823).

Ann Radcliffe was the daughter of William Ward, a haberdasher, and Ann Oates. Her uncle Thomas Bentley (her mother's brother-in-law) was a partner of Josiah Wedgwood, the potter, and probably through this connection the family moved to Bath in 1772, where her father managed a china shop. In 1787 she married William Radcliffe, a graduate of Oxford and a law student, who earned his living primarily through journalism. He edited the *Gazette* between 1791 and 1793, and although admitted to the Middle Temple, he seems not to have pursued a legal career, but eventually assumed the editorship of the *English Chronicle.* There were no children, but the marriage was apparently a happy one, with Radcliffe an admiring and supportive husband as his wife's writing career began to flourish. It was alleged by more than one biographer that she began to write in the evenings to keep herself occupied while Radcliffe was busy with his newspapers. Her first two novels, *The Castles of Athlin and Dunbayne* (1789) and *A Sicilian Romance* (1790), were journeyman efforts at romantic fiction. It was with *The Romance of the Forest* (1791), quickly followed by *The Mysteries of Udolpho* (1794) and *The Italian* (1797), that her reputation as one of the most accomplished practitioners of the *Gothic novel was made. Her strengths were in the creation of evocative settings, striking incidents, and the extremes of emotion produced by terror. Her plots were thought to be wild and her characters improbable, but the unprecedented payments made for *The Mysteries of Udolpho* and for *The Italian* (£500 and £800) were indicative of her phenomenal popularity.

She wrote a sixth novel, *Gaston de Blonville*, in 1802 (published posthumously in 1826). Despite her success she refused to enter literary society, remaining diffident about her writing and shunning the approaches made by her contemporaries. She preferred domestic life with her husband and their travels together, which she recorded in *A Journey Made in the Summer of 1794 through Holland and the Western Frontier of Germany* (1795). Parts of her later travel journals were published posthumously. So reclusive was her later life that there were rumours that she had either gone mad from contemplating Gothic horrors or had died. Latterly she suffered from both asthma and depression, and died suddenly after an asthma attack in 1823, at the age of 59. Several of her novels contained verse, and after *Gaston de Blonville*, which included a long narrative poem, she wrote mainly poetry. Her poems were collected in *Poetical Works* (1834), but an unauthorized collection of *Poems* taken from the novels was published in 1815. Scott wrote an introduction to her novels for Ballantyne's Novelists' Library in 1824, and Sergeant Talfourd contributed a memoir to the first edition of *Gaston de Blonville* (1826). *See* R. Kiely, *The Romantic Novel in England* (1972); Elizabeth MacAndrew, *The Gothic Tradition in Fiction* (1979); David Punter, *The Literature of Terror* (1980); Juliann E. Fleenor (ed.), *The Female Gothic* (1983); Kenneth W. Graham (ed.), *Gothic Fictions: Prohibition/Transgression* (1989); Janet Todd, *The Sign of Angellica: Women, Writing and Fiction, 1660–1800* (1989).

Radcliffe, Mary Ann, feminist, autobiographer, and novelist (*c.*1746–*post* 1810).

Scottish born Mary Ann Radcliffe was the only child of a Catholic mother and a much older Anglican father who died when she was 2. At the age of 14, and as a Protestant heiress of considerable fortune, she secretly married Joseph Radcliffe, a Catholic some twenty years her senior, by whom she had eight children. Her husband's failed business ventures soon depleted her inheritance and his penchant for drink and inactivity left her disenchanted and eventually in sole charge of their children. She took jobs as a lady's companion and housekeeper, acted as governess to the children of a friend, and ran a shoe shop in Oxford Street and later a school in Kennington. *The Female Advocate; or An Attempt to Recover the Rights of Women from Male Usurpation* (1799) was written out of personal bitterness and frustration at the difficulties of a middle-class woman without male protection and in need of work. In it she paid tribute to the 'Amazonian' spirit of her predecessor in polemic, Mary *Wollstonecraft, but her emphasis was more practical. She argued for the alleviation of the 'unremitted oppression' of women by more opportunities for work and quoted Hester *Chapone's warnings on the dangers of vulnerable women falling into prostitution. *The Female Advocate* was republished as part of *The Memoirs of Mrs. Mary Ann Radcliffe in Familiar Letters to her Female Friend* (1810), which also contained warnings against precipitous marriages. Various novels were attributed to Mary Ann Radcliffe, some confusing her with the more eminent Ann *Radcliffe, an error which she may have regarded as an advantage. *The Fate of Velina de Guidova* and *Radzivil*, both published in 1790 by William Lane's *Minerva Press, were listed as by Mrs. [Ann? or Mary Ann?] Radcliffe, and only later identified as being by the author of *Manfrone; or The One-Handed Monk* (1809). The last, a lurid and melodramatic *Gothic fiction showing the influence of both Ann Radcliffe and Matthew Lewis, was acknowledged as hers when it was published. The novel's explicit treatment of sexual neurosis and violence led William Lane to decline it initially. His successor offered the Minerva imprint for a second edition in 1819, once it had been generally accepted. Mary Ann Radcliffe compiled the short-lived *Radcliffe's New Novelist's Pocket Magazine*, which specialized in Gothic fiction, in 1802. She spent her final years in Edinburgh, in poor health and living on the charity of friends. *See* Coral Ann Howells, *Love, Mystery and Misery: Feeling in Gothic Fiction* (1978); Moira Ferguson (ed.), *First Feminists: British Women Writers 1578–1799* (1985).

'**Raimond,** C. E.' *see* ROBINS, Elizabeth

Raine, Kathleen (Jessie), poet and critic (b. Ilford, Essex, 14 June 1908).

Kathleen Raine's father George Raine, a miner's son, was a secondary schoolmaster and Nonconformist preacher. Her mother Jessie was a Scot. She was born and spent her early years in Ilford, a London suburb which she loathed. She regarded her wartime refuge with an aunt in Northumberland as her natural home. 'Since the age of ten, when I finally returned to the suburb, I have lived in exile,' she later wrote. She went to Ilford County High School and then won a scholarship to Girton College, Cambridge, where she read natural sciences and published poems in *Experiment*, an undergraduate magazine. She married the writer Hugh Sykes Davies, divorced him, and married the poet and sociologist Charles Madge, by whom she had a son and a daughter. She later left him and returned to the Scottish border, where she wrote the poems which were to form her first book, *Stone and Flower* (1943), illustrated by Barbara Hepworth. This, and her next books, *Living in Time* (1946) and *The Pythoness* (1949), more metrically formal than her later work, have sometimes been regarded as her best. *The Year One* (1952) marked a shift to freer metres. Raine's work has been influenced by the symbolic language of the Romantics and later poets, many of whose works she has edited and written about (Blake, Coleridge, Shelley, Yeats, David Jones). A failed love affair with the writer Gavin Maxwell was the inspiration for *The Hollow Hill* (1965) and also informed *The Lost Country* (1971) and *On a Deserted Shore* (1973). *The Oval Portrait* (1977) contained poems written to her deceased mother. Her Neoplatonic mysticism, her anti-materialism, and her talent for natural observation are reflected in her *Collected Poems 1935–1980* (1981). Her *Selected Poems* was published in 1988. Raine has written three volumes of autobiography, *Farewell Happy Fields* (1973), *The Land Unknown* (1975), and *The Lion's Mouth* (1977). *Autobiographies* was published in 1992. She is perhaps best known as a critic, particularly for her books on Blake and Yeats, *Blake and Tradition* (1968; abridged 1974), *Blake and the New Age* (1979), *Yeats, the Tarot and the Golden Dawn* (1972), and *Yeats the Initiate* (1986). Her work as a translator, particularly of Balzac, is highly regarded, and she co-edits the arts magazine *Temenos*. *See* Ralph J. Mills, *Kathleen Raine* (1967); Erika Duncan, *Unless Soul Clap its Hands: Portraits and Passages* (1984).

Ramée, Marie Louise de la *see* OUIDA

Reeve, Clara, novelist and poet (b. Ipswich, 1729, d. Ipswich, 3 December 1807).

Clara Reeve was the eldest daughter of the eight children of William Reeve, rector of Freston and of Kerton, in Suffolk, and perpetual curate of St Nicholas, Ipswich. Her mother Hannah Smithies was the daughter of George I's goldsmith and jeweller. One of her brothers became a vice-admiral, and another was rector of Brockley, Suffolk, and Master of Bungay grammar school. She later claimed that she learned all she knew from her father. He encouraged her to read at an early age, including Parliamentary Debates, Rapin's *History of England*, Cato's *Letters*, Plutarch, and Greek and Roman history on her reading list. Her *Original Poems on Several Occasions* (1769), published with a long list of subscribers, included a 'prologue to a play that was never acted, which remains unacknowledged and unanswered', and the libretto for an oratorio whose composer, she claimed, commissioned another text before she had finished it. Despite these early set-backs she went on to publish a translation of John Barclay's Latin novel *Argenis* (1621) under the title *The Phoenix* (1772), not surprising, given the rigour of her early training, and then, in 1777, *The Champion of Virtue: A Gothic Story*, better known from the 1778 edition onwards as *The Old English Baron*. She acknowledged the influence of Horace Walpole's *Gothic novel *The Castle of Otranto* (1765) but claimed its machinery was so violent the effects were destroyed. He in turn found her novel 'insipid', and claimed that 'any trial for murder at the

Old Bailey would make a more interesting story'. It was to become her best-known work, going through numerous editions, plus French and German translations. The 1780 edition was dedicated to Richardson's daughter Mrs Bridgen, who corrected and revised it. *The Progress of Romance* (1785) was a criticism of current fiction in the form of a dialogue, which was attacked in the *Gentleman's Magazine* (1786) by Anna *Seward, who objected, among other things, to Reeve's praise of *Pamela*. Reeve's other works included *The Two Mentors* (1783), which also had French and German translations, and *The Exiles* (1788), both epistolary novels, *The School for Widows* (1791) and its continuation *Plans of Education* (1792), *Memoirs of Sir Roger de Clarendon* 1793), a Gothic novel with a medieval setting, and *Destination; or Memoirs of a Private Family* (1799), the last a didactic story on the subject of education, one of Reeve's particular interests. Scott wrote a memoir of Reeve for Ballantyne's Novelists' Library (1823). *See* Elizabeth MacAndrew, *The Gothic Tradition in Fiction* (1979); David Punter, *The Literature of Terror* (1980).

Reeves, Helen Buckingham *see* MATHERS, Helen

'**Renault, Mary**' (Eileen Mary Challans), novelist (b. West Ham, London, 4 September 1905, d. Cape Town, 13 December 1983).

Mary Renault was the elder daughter of Frank Challans, a London doctor of Huguenot stock, and his wife Clementine Mary Newsome Baxter, who claimed descent from the seventeenth-century Nonconformist divine Richard Baxter. She was treated as an 'honorary boy' at her co-educational prep school and regretted the transition to Clifton High School in Bristol, a traditional girls' school, although she was consoled by the 'huge collection of books' she found there. She read Malory and the whole of *The Faerie Queene* and came to regard the medieval period as a golden age. She then read English at St Hugh's College, Oxford, where she wrote poetry and took a third in 1928. She declined to take the usual path into teaching ('it digs too deep into the sources of creation') but instead trained as a nurse at the Radcliffe Infirmary. She attempted her first novel, about cowboys, at 8 but left it unfinished. The heroine of *The Friendly Young Ladies* (1944), not coincidentally, was a writer of westerns. Hospitals and medical personnel featured in her first novel, *Purposes of Love* (1939), for which she adopted the pseudonym Mary Renault, fearing the disapproval of nursing authorities for her extra-curricular activity and drawing the name from her reading in medieval French. During the Second World War she met Julie Mullard, with whom she lived for the rest of her life. Their relationship is partially reflected in *The Friendly Young Ladies. Return to Night* (1949) won the Metro-Goldwyn-Mayer prize of £40,000, which enabled her to give up her job and become a full-time writer, although the film rights on the novel were never taken up. She and Julie Mullard emigrated to South Africa in 1948 and made their permanent home in Cape Town. *The Charioteer* (1953), last of a group of six early novels, all dealing with aspects of love, was a study of the homosexual relationships of a group of servicemen during the Battle of Britain. After that novel Renault changed direction and began a series of novels set in ancient Greece, based on detailed research, which won both critical and popular acclaim. *The Last of the Wine* (1956), set during the third Peloponnesian War, was followed by *The King Must Die* (1958), her most celebrated novel, based on the Theseus legend. The story of Theseus was continued in *The Bull from the Sea* (1962), which was less successful. *The Lion in the Gateway* (1964) was a children's book about the wars between the Greeks and the Persians. *The Mask of Apollo* (1966) was set in Syracuse and Athens in the fourth century BC. A trilogy of novels about Alexander the Great, *Fire from Heaven* (1969), *The Persian Boy* (1972), and *Funeral Games* (1981), together with her study *The Nature of Alexander* (1975), generated controversy among classical scholars over her interpretation of Alexander, the criticism turning on the fact that she read her sources in translation and did not know Greek. The fuss did little to dampen enthusiasm for her books. While living in South Africa Renault was a member of the Progressive Party and became president of the South African branch of PEN. She was elected a fellow of the Royal Society of Literature but never returned to Britain. She died in South Africa at the age of 78. *See* Peter Wolfe, *Mary Renault* (1969); Carolyn G. Heilbrun, in *From Parnassus*, ed. Dora B. Weiner and William R. Reylor (1976).

Rendell, Ruth ('Barbara Vine'), novelist and crime writer (b. London, 17 February 1930).

Ruth Rendell is the daughter of two teachers, Arthur and Ebba Elise Grasemann. She was educated at Loughton High School in Essex, and then worked as a reporter and subeditor for Express and Independent Newspapers in west Essex between 1948 and 1952. In 1950 she married Donald Rendell, also a journalist. They have one son. They divorced, and later remarried in 1977. Rendell's fiction divides into two groups, the 'Kingsmarkham' series of detective novels, with her main character, the middle-aged, tolerant Detective Chief Inspector Reginald Wexford and his supportive family, and a number of crime novels which stand independently of a series. The first 'Wexford' novel was *From Doon with Death* (1964). Its successors like *The Best Man to Die* (1969), *No More Dying then* (1971), *Some Lie and Some Die* (1973), *Shake Hands Forever* (1975), and *A Sleeping Life* (1978) contain sub-plots involving Wexford's corps of family, friends, and associates, a focus of normality set against the world of crime. By her own admission Rendell's chief interest as a writer is in the creation of character, to which are added carefully defined settings and sharply observed social criticism. Her non-Wexford novels are more sombre, often involving aberrant circumstances which lead to horrific crime. The focus in these too is on character, the crimes becoming a means of exploring the character. *The Face of Trespass* (1974) centres on an impoverished young author, *A Demon in my View* (1976) on a psychotic would-be murderer of women, *A Judgement in Stone* (1977) on a mass murderer, *Live Flesh* (1986) on a rapist, *Talking to Strange Men* (1987) on a child molester. *Unkindness of Ravens* (1985) parodies contemporary feminists, and *Heartstones* (1987) focuses on anorexia. Rendell's *Collected Stories* appeared in 1987. *Suffolk* (1989) is an evocation of the county which forms the setting for many of her novels. As Barbara Vine Rendell has published a number of novels which are closer to mainstream fiction, although still involving murder, among them *A Dark-Adapted Eye* (1986) and *House of Stairs* (1988). *See* Jane S. Bakerman, in *10 Women of Mystery*, ed. Earl F. Bargainnier (1981).

'**Rhys**, Jean' (Ella Gwendolen Rees Williams), novelist and short story writer (b. Roseau, Dominica, 24 August 1890, d. Exeter, 14 May 1979).

Jean Rhys was the fourth of the five children and the second daughter of William Rees Williams, a medical doctor of Welsh descent who had a government post on Dominica, in the West Indies, and his wife Minna Lockhart, whose family had been sugar planters on the island for several generations. As a child she was lonely, and wrote poetry and plays, a process which was to continue into her maturity, that of 'writing out' unhappiness, of ordering her life through writing. Gwen, as she was known, was sent to a convent school on the island and then, at the age of 16, dispatched to the Perse School, Cambridge, which she disliked and which she left after a term. She persuaded her father to let her go to the Academy of Dramatic Art in London, which she then tried hard to leave, again after a term, when he died. She declined to return to the West Indies but instead took various jobs, in the chorus of a company performing musicals, as a model, and as a ghost writer for a book on furniture. She also changed her name several times, eventually deciding on Jean Rhys. Her first love affair, with a stockbroker twenty years her senior, ended when he paid her off with an allowance on which she managed to live, supplemented by some occasional theatre work, until her first marriage in 1919. The affair formed the basis of a manuscript which she kept in a suitcase until 1934, when it was published as *Voyage in the Dark*. Her first husband was Jean Lenglet, a Dutch song-writer and journalist with whom she lived in Paris, and by whom she had a son, who died in infancy, and a daughter. In 1923 Lenglet was imprisoned for disobeying an extradition order, leaving her penniless. Rhys was befriended by Ford Madox Ford, who encouraged her to write, published her sketches and short stories, set in Montparnasse of the 1920s, in the *Transatlantic Review*, and wrote an introduction to them when they were republished as *The Left Bank* (1927). Her first novel, *Postures* (1928), later retitled *Quartet*, was based on her relationship with Ford. After her divorce from Lenglet in 1932 she married Leslie Tilden Smith, a publisher's reader. He died in 1945 and in 1947 she married his cousin Max Hamer, a poet and retired naval officer. They were extremely hard up financially and in 1952 Hamer was imprisoned for misappropriating funds from his employers. After his release they lived in Bude, in Cornwall, and then Cheriton Fitzpaine, Devon, where Rhys remained after Hamer's death in 1964. There are autobiographical elements in many of Rhys's novels, heroines, many with West Indian backgrounds, who wander through London and Paris, vulnerable and victimized, particularly by men. *After Leaving Mr. Mackenzie* (1931), *Good Morning Midnight* (1939), as well as *Voyage in the Dark* have recognizable 'Rhys' heroines and a distinctively spare style which was praised by critics but left little impression on the reading public. Her work was virtually forgotten until in 1957 the BBC placed an advertisement in a weekly newspaper asking for information about her in preparation for a dramatization of *Good Morning Midnight*. Rhys was then working on a novel which was to revitalize her reputation, *Wide Sargasso Sea*, published in 1966 and inspired by the character of Bertha Mason, Rochester's mad wife in Charlotte *Bronte's *Jane Eyre*. The novel traces the life of Bertha or rather 'Antoinette' Mason from a West Indian childhood to her incarceration in the attic at Thornfield. The novel won the W. H. Smith Award for 1966, an Arts Council bursary, and the Heinemann Award of the Royal Society of Literature. Rhys's novels were reprinted along with a selection of her stories, *Tigers are Better Looking* (1968), and critical recognition and financial security were assured. She was appointed CBE in 1978. Success had almost come too late. She spent her last years in Devon, lonely, but still writing while in her eighties. *Sleep it off, Lady*, a collection of short stories, was published in 1976, and *Smile Please: An Unfinished Autobiography* was published in 1979, the year of her death. Her *Letters 1931–1966* was published in 1984 (ed. Francis Wyndham and Diana Melly), and her *Collected Short Stories* in 1986. The novelist David Plante portrayed her unflatteringly in old age in *Difficult Women* (1983). *See* Edwin Wendell Mellown, *Jean Rhys: A Descriptive and Annotated Bibliography of Works* (1984); Teresa F. O'Connor, *Jean Rhys: The West Indian Novels* (1986); Nancy R. Harrison,

Jean Rhys and the Novel as Women's Text (1988); Carole Angier, *Jean Rhys: Life and Work* (1990); Coral Ann Howells, *Jean Rhys* (1991).

Richardson, Dorothy (Miller), novelist (b. Abingdon, Berkshire, 17 May 1873, d. Beckenham, Kent, 17 June 1957).

Dorothy Richardson was the third of the four daughters of Charles Richardson, a self-styled 'gentleman of no occupation', and his wife Mary Miller Taylor. Her childhood, she recalled, was spent in 'secluded surroundings in late Victorian England' in which Southborough House, a day school in Putney, provided a link with 'the world'. Her father's bankruptcy in 1893 and her mother's suicide in 1895 threw her on her own resources. She became a pupil-teacher in Germany, then a governess in England, and later moved to London as a dentist's receptionist. Her brief affair with H. G. Wells transformed itself into a lasting friendship, and in 1917, at the age of 43, she married Alan Odle, a young artist and illustrator whose health was delicate. She wrote first for periodicals, the *Saturday Review*, the unconventional monthly *Ye Crank*, the *Adelphi*, the *Little Review*, and dental magazines, and in 1912 began to write fiction. *Pointed Roofs*, the first of thirteen parts of her major work *Pilgrimage*, was published in 1915. Through her rendering of the interior life of its autobiographical heroine Miriam Henderson, Richardson put into practice her belief that a literary work 'remains essentially an adventure of the stable contemplative human consciousness'. The individual parts of *Pilgrimage* after *Pointed Roofs* were *Backwater* (1916), *Honeycomb* (1917), *Interim* (1919), *The Tunnel* (1919), *Deadlock* (1921), *Revolving Lights* (1923), *The Trap* (1925), *Oberland* (1927), *Dawn's Left Hand* (1931), *Clear Horizon* (1935), *Dimple Hill* (1938), and the posthumously published *March Moonlight* (1967). May *Sinclair was the first woman writer to champion her work, coining the phrase 'stream of consciousness' in a review of *Pointed Roofs* (*The Egoist*, April 1918). Richardson thought the term, which has come to be closely associated with her work, a 'perfect imbecility', marginally preferring the American variant 'interior monologue'. Other female contemporaries were cautious. After pronouncing *The Tunnel* 'better in its failure than most books in their success' (*TLS* 13 February 1919), Virginia *Woolf declared in a notice of *Revolving Lights* (*TLS* 19 May 1923) that Richardson had developed what 'we might call the psychological sentence of the feminine gender. . . . It is a woman's sentence, but only in the sense that it is used to describe a woman's mind by a writer who is neither proud nor afraid of anything that she may discover in the psychology of her sex'. Richardson coined the phrase 'feminine prose' in her introduction to the 1938 collected edition of *Pilgrimage*. Katherine *Mansfield's review of *The Tunnel* (*Athenaeum*, 4 April 1919) was more qualified: 'There is no plot, no beginning, no middle or end. Things just "happen", one after another with incredible rapidity and at break-neck speed. There is Miss Richardson, holding out her mind, as it were, and there is Life, hurling objects into it as fast as she can throw.' *Bryher, however, whom she met in 1923, became a friend and also gave her financial support. As well as *Pilgrimage* Richardson published a book on the Quakers (1914) and another on their founder George Fox (1914), and also poems and French and German translations. She and Odle lived alternately in Cornwall and London until his death in 1948. The writer who she thought best understood her work was Ford Madox Ford, who called her 'the most abominably unknown contemporary writer', a situation not altogether remedied later in the century, as witnessed by her exclusion from the *DNB*. *See* John Rosenberg, *Dorothy Richardson: The Genius they Forgot* (1973); Gloria G. Fromm, *Dorothy Richardson: A Biography* (1977); Gillian E. Hanscombe, *The Art of Life: Dorothy Richardson and the Development of Feminist Consciousness* (1982); Jean Radford, *Dorothy Richardson* (1991).

'Richardson, Henry Handel' (Ethel Florence Lindesay Richardson), novelist (b. Melbourne, Australia, 3 January 1870, d. Fairlight, near Hastings, Sussex, 20 March 1946).

Henry Handel Richardson was the elder of two daughters of Walter Lindesay Richardson, a Dublin-born doctor who emigrated to Australia during the 1850s gold-rush, and his English wife Mary Bailey. The family led a peripatetic existence, as her father lost money through speculation and then died when she was 9. Her childhood was solitary, and filled by reading and by writing. ('I had scribbled stories ever since I could hold a pen.') Her mother took a job as a postmistress and sent her to the élite Presbyterian Ladies' College in Melbourne, an experience she later wrote about in her autobiographical novel *The Getting of Wisdom* (1910). She studied piano for three years at the Leipzig Conservatorium but abandoned the idea of a musical career in the face of family opposition and in 1895 married John George Robertson, a Scottish philologist and German scholar whom she met in Leipzig. Between 1896 and 1904 they lived in Strasbourg, where he was professor of English and she began her first novel, *Maurice Guest* (1908), based on her Leipzig experiences and, for its time, remarkably frank in its treatment of sexuality. They moved to London in 1904 on his appointment to a chair of German at London University. She remained in England for the rest of her life, apart from a visit to Leipzig in 1907 to refresh her memory while writing *Maurice Guest* and a two-month visit to Australia in preparation for her best work, the trilogy *The Fortunes of Richard Mahoney* (1930). Based loosely on the lives of her parents, and drawing on their letters and diaries, the three novels, *Australia Felix* (1917), *The Way Home* (1925), and

Ultima Thule (1929), chart the progress of the hero from his beginnings in a mining settlement through a prosperous medical career and an even more successful financial one to bankruptcy and death. The sequence manages to convey not only a portrait of the hero but also a picture of the growth and emergence of modern Australia and its search for identity. The success of the trilogy, particularly the third volume, which became a best seller, established her international reputation and won her a nomination for a Nobel Prize in 1932. Richardson was meticulous in the creation of authentic backgrounds to her novels, the legacy of her earlier reading of French, German, and Russian realist fiction. This was particularly true of her last novel, *The Young Cosima* (1939), based on the life of Cosima Wagner. She also published a collection of stories, *The End of Childhood* (1934). The high point of her life was her years on the Continent. Although most of her writing was done in England her time there, according to Leonie Kramer's *DNB* entry, was 'in the nature of a retirement'. Her contribution to Australian literature in the form of the trilogy has been widely and handsomely acknowledged, but according to Kramer she wrote as an expatriate and her sympathies were with Europe. After her husband's death in 1933 she moved to Sussex, where she died at the age of 76. Her autobiography *Myself when Young* (1948) was unfinished at her death and was completed by her friend Olga Roncoroni. *See* Nettie Palmer, *Henry Handel Richardson: A Study* (1950); K. McLeod, *Henry Handel Richardson: A Critical Study* (1985); Axel Clark, *Henry Handel Richardson* (1990).

Riddell, Mrs J. H. (Charlotte Eliza Lawson Riddell, née Cowan, also 'F. G. Trafford'), novelist (b. Carrickfergus, County Antrim, 30 September 1832, d. Hounslow, London, 24 September 1906).

Mrs Riddell was the daughter of James Cowan, High Sheriff of County Antrim, and his English wife Ellen Kilshaw. Her father died when she was young, and his property passed out of the immediate family. She looked after her invalid mother in Ireland, and in 1856 moved to London, hoping to make a living by writing. Her first two books disappeared without trace, but her third, *The Moors and the Fens* (1858), published under the pseudonym F. G. Trafford and with a writer heroine, was a modest success, and launched her literary career. Her marriage in 1857 to Joseph Hadley Riddell, a civil engineer, provided her with an insider's view of the City of London which was to become the background for her most successful novels. She is best remembered for titles like *City and Suburb* (1861), *Mitre Court* (1885), and *The Head of the Firm* (1892), all of them focusing on the London financial world. The most popular of all, *George Geith of Fen Court* (1864), about a clergyman who leaves his wife and his parish to become a City accountant, was made into a successful play, and rivalled M. E. *Braddon's *Lady Audley's Secret* as the publisher William Tinsley's best seller of the period. In 1867 Riddell became editor of the *St. James's Magazine*, established in 1861 by Mrs Samuel Carter *Hall. Her later work included the autobiographical *A Struggle for Fame* (1883), which drew on her efforts to establish herself as a writer, *Weird Stories* (1882), a collection of ghost stories, which became one of her specialities, and *Above Suspicion* (1876), a *sensation novel. Despite her background she avoided Irish settings in her later work, apart from *Berna Boyle* (1882). Her husband died in 1880, heavily in debt. Mrs Riddell undertook to pay off his creditors by her writing, publishing more than thirty books by the time of her death. She was the first writer to receive a pension from the Society of Authors, in 1901. *See* Helen C. Black, *Notable Women Authors of the Day* (1893); Nigel Cross, *The Common Writer: Life in Nineteenth-Century Grub St.* (1985).

Ridler, Anne (Barbara), née Bradby, poet (b. Rugby, Warwickshire, 30 July 1912).

Anne Ridler is the only daughter of Henry Christopher Bradby, a housemaster at Rugby School, and his wife Violet Milford. She went to Downe House School, in Berkshire, spent six months in Florence and Rome, and then took a diploma in journalism at King's College, London, in 1932. She worked as a secretary and reader for the publishing house of Faber & Faber between 1935 and 1940 and in 1938 married Vivian Ridler, later Printer to the University of Oxford, by whom she has two sons and two daughters. Ridler's eleven volumes of poetry, published over a period of nearly fifty years and written in traditional forms and metres, deal with love, separation, domesticity, faith, the growth and maturing of children, and a sense of place. *Poems*, her first collection, was published in 1939, *New and Selected Poems*, her latest, in 1988. 'It was Eliot who first made me despairing of becoming a poet; Auden . . . who first made me think I saw how to become one,' she once wrote. The influence of Donne, Marvell, Herbert, and other metaphysicals can also be detected in her work. The poems in the wartime volume *The Nine Bright Shiners* (1943) anticipate motherhood, *The Golden Bird* (1951) the separation brought about by war, and *A Matter of Life and Death* (1959) the emotions evoked by a child's growing up and away. The combination of domestic and religious themes has led some critics to compare her with Coventry Patmore. Her verse dramas carry on the tradition revived by Eliot: *Cain* (1943), *Henry Bly* (1947), and *The Trial of Thomas Cranmer* (1956), the last produced in Oxford on the 400th anniversary of his death. She has translated opera libretti and edited the work of James Thomson, Charles Williams, Walter de la Mare, Thomas Traherne, George Darley, and William Austin, as well as compiling anthologies of poetry. She published *Ten Poems* with E. J. *Scovell in 1984. Fellow poets Kathleen *Raine and Elizabeth *Jennings have praised her work. *See* William V. Spanos, *The Christian Tradition in Modern British Verse Drama* (1967); Elizabeth Jennings, in *Poetry Today*, 61 (1961).

Rigby, Elizabeth *see* EASTLAKE, Elizabeth

Riley, Joan, novelist (b. St Mary, Jamaica, 1958).

Joan Riley is the youngest of eight children. She spent her childhood in Jamaica, then emigrated to Britain, where she took a degree at the University of Sussex in 1979 and an MA from the University of London in 1984. She teaches black history and culture and works in a drugs advisory agency. Her fiction treats of the dislocation of immigrant life in Britain and of the often painful conjunction of the old culture and the new as in *A Kindness to the Children* (1992). Her first novel, *The Unbelonging* (1985), is about an 11-year-old Jamaican girl's coming to terms with life in Britain, with racist hostility, isolation, and the threat of incest, a sense of displacement which a visit to the Caribbean does not resolve. *Waiting for Twilight* (1987) is about an old woman, now stroke-ridden, who looks back on her life in Jamaica in the 1950s and in Britain in the 1960s. *Romance* (1988) treats of two contrasting sisters, one with a successful career and the other a wife and mother, who are forced to rethink their lives by a visit of Jamaican grandmothers, and a glimpse of a matriarchal culture. Riley has been blamed for what are seen by black readers, notably Maud *Sulter, as negative attitudes. She is the single parent of a daughter and campaigns on behalf of single parents. *See* Lauretta Ngcobo, (ed.), *Let it be Told: Essays by Black Women in Britain* (1987).

Ritchie, Anne Isabella, née Thackeray, Lady Ritchie, novelist, essayist, and biographer (b. London, 9 June 1837, d. Freshwater, Isle of Wight, 26 February 1919).

Anne Thackeray Ritchie, or Anny, as she was known, was the elder of William Makepeace Thackeray's two daughters. Their mother Isabella Gethin Shawe was mentally ill from their childhood onward, and they were sent to their grandparents in Paris in 1840. Thackeray brought them back to London in 1847 where, as the daughters of a celebrated novelist, they mingled with the Dickens children, and met most of the major literary figures of the day. Anny also acted as her father's amanuensis. After his death her circle of friends expanded to include Tennyson, the *Brownings, Ruskin, Swinburne, and George *Eliot. She began to publish essays in the *Cornhill Magazine*, first under her father's editorship and later under that of her brother-in-law Leslie Stephen. She published her first novel, *The Story of Elizabeth* (1863), derived from her youthful experiences of Paris, when she was 26. Her second, *The Village on the Green* (1867), and *Old Kensington* (1873) were the two novels for which she was best known, both of them domestic stories set in places familiar to her. *Miss Angel* (1875) was based on the life of the eighteenth-century painter Angelica Kauffmann, and *Mrs. Dymond* (1885), her fifth novel, was set against the background of the Franco-Prussian war. In 1877, at the age of 40, she married her second cousin Richmond Thackeray Willoughby Ritchie, seventeen years her junior. He first proposed to her while still a schoolboy at Eton. Despite the disparity of age it was an extremely happy marriage. They had a son and a daughter, and Ritchie rose in the Indian civil service to be created KCB in 1907, hence her subsequent style, Lady Ritchie. Most of Anne Thackeray's fiction was written before her marriage. Later, she drew on her wide acquaintance and her gift for memoir writing to publish a series of essays and biographies: *Madame de Sévigné* (1881), *A Book of Sibyls* (1883), on English women writers, *Records of Tennyson, Ruskin, and Robert and Elizabeth Browning* (1892), and *Lord Tennyson and his Friends* (1893). Two collections of her essays are among her best-known titles, *Blackstick Papers* (1908) and *From the Porch* (1913). She contributed introductions to the Biographical Edition of her father's works (1898–9) and was commemorated by her niece Virginia *Woolf as Mrs Hilbery in *Night and Day* (1919). She was elected a fellow of the Royal Society of Literature in 1903, and was president of the English Association in 1912–13. *See Letters of Anne Thackeray Ritchie*, ed. H. Ritchie (1924); V. Woolf, 'The Enchanted Organ: Anne Thackeray', in *The Moment and Other Essays* (1947); Winifred Gerin, *Anne Thackeray Ritchie: A Biography* (1981).

Robertson, E(ileen) Arnot (Arbuthnot), novelist and film critic (b. Holmwood, Surrey, 1903, d. London, 21 September 1961).

E. Arnot Robertson was the daughter of G. A. Robertson, a doctor. She was educated at Sherbourne Girls' School, of which she later wrote, 'nothing could make me so unhappy again', and in Paris and Switzerland. She travelled extensively in Africa, the West Indies, Europe, and the United States, none of which was helpful in the settings of her fiction, she claimed, finding it easier to be convincing about unfamiliar places. Singapore, Malaya, Greece, Zanzibar, and Hong Kong formed the increasingly exotic locations of her novels. In 1927 she married Henry Turner (later Sir Henry), then general secretary of the Empire Press Union, by whom she had a son. As a child she wrote stories to compensate for the lack of sporting and musical talents much prized by her family. *Cullum* (1928), her first novel, was about a girl's affair with a philandering novelist. *Three Came Unarmed* (1928) set down three children brought up in Borneo in the midst of 'civilized' England for the first time. *Four Frightened People* (1931), her first novel to receive wide attention, reversed the process and placed four middle-class English characters in the Malayan jungle. *Ordinary Families* (1933), a best seller filmed by Cecil B. de Mille in 1934, was about the dynamics of a middle-class family devoted to sailing, as was Robertson's. Her later books, none of which equalled the early successes, included the illustrated *Thames Portrait* (1937), *Summer's Lease* (1940), *The Signpost* (1943), *Devices and Desires* (1954), *Justice of the Heart* (1958), and the posthumous *Strangers on my Roof* (1964). After the Second World War she turned her energies to film reviewing, and became involved in a celebrated libel suit against MGM, who banned her from screenings because of hostile reviews. The House of Lords overturned her initial victory. Her husband drowned in a boating accident in the spring of 1961 and Robertson committed suicide five months later. *See* P. Devlin's introd. to reprints of *Four Frightened People* and *Ordinary Families* (1972).

Robins, Elizabeth ('C. E. Raimond'), novelist and actress (b. Louisville, Kentucky, 1862, d. Henfield, Sussex, 8 May 1952).

American-born Elizabeth Robins was one of eight children of Charles E. Robins, a banker. Her childhood was spent in a country house on Staten Island, New York, and she was educated at Putnam Seminary in Zanesville, Ohio. She left school at 16 to go on stage under an assumed name, due to her father's disapproval, and joined a touring company. Her husband George Richmond Parks, an actor, committed suicide shortly after their marriage in 1887. On a trip to London in 1889 she was befriended by Oscar Wilde, who secured her an introduction to the London theatre world. She played Mrs Errol in the dramatization of Frances Hodgson *Burnett's *Little Lord Fauntleroy* and through an acquaintance with Henry James had a part in the dramatization of *The American*. She made her name, however, in a series of Ibsen roles, beginning with *Hedda Gabler* (1891) and including most of the first English productions of Ibsen's plays. She published several novels under the pseudonym C. E. Raimond. *The Magnetic North* (1904), influenced by a visit to the Klondike, became a best seller, and *My Little Sister* (1913) was based on the white slave-trade. Undoubtedly her most interesting novel was *George Mandeville's Husband* (1894), a denunciation of pseudo-intellectual women novelists and a satire on George *Eliot. Her later novel *Way Stations* (1913) addressed the contemporary feminist debate about women's relations to work and to the family. Robins was a charismatic and vigorous crusader for the cause of female suffrage. Her play *Votes for Women* (1907), which she later made into a novel, *The Convert*, has been called by Elaine Showalter 'the most influential piece of literary propaganda to come out of the suffrage movement' and by Samuel Hynes 'a dispatch from the front [of the sex war], fiercely partisan and militant'. She was a founder of the Actresses' Franchise League and in 1908 became president of the *Women Writers' Suffrage League. Her pamphlet *Woman's Secret* was a challenge to women not to imitate the point of view of men, but to write as women. Her memoirs are included in *Ibsen and the Actress* (1932), *Theatre and Friendship* (1932), *Both Sides of the Curtain* (1940), and *Raymond and I* (1956). *See* Samuel Hynes, *The Edwardian Turn of Mind* (1968); Elaine Showalter, *A Literature of their Own: British Women Novelists from Brontë to Lessing* (1977); Wendy Mulford, in *Re-Reading English*, ed. P. Widdowson (1982); Catherine Wiley, in *Women in Theatre*, ed. James Redmond (1989).

Robinson, Mary, née Darby, poet and novelist (b. Bristol, 27 November 1758, d. Windsor Park, Berkshire, 26 December 1800).

Mary Robinson's father was the captain of a Bristol whaling ship, born in America, and inclined only erratically to domestic life. He embarked on a scheme to establish a whale fishery on the coast of Labrador when Mary was young, leaving her mother (née Seys) with five children to support. Mary was sent to the school in Bristol kept by Hannah *More's sisters, and when the family moved to London, to a school in Chelsea run by a Mrs Lorrington, whom she was later to claim the most formative influence on her early life. When the latter's drunkenness forced the school's closure, Mary was sent to another school in Chelsea, until the family's financial circumstances made it impossible for her to continue. She and her mother then set up a girls' school, as a way of meeting their debts. Her father put an end to this enterprise and she was dispatched to a finishing school in Marylebone where, through the dancing master, she was introduced to David Garrick. Attracted by her striking appearance Garrick proposed that she play Cordelia to his Lear, but her theatrical début was deferred due to her marriage in 1774 to Thomas Robinson, an articled clerk whom her parents mistakenly considered a good match. She led a fashionable life, neglected by her husband and surrounded by his rakish friends, until his imprisonment for debt in 1775. She shared his ten months in prison along with their infant daughter, and wrote a volume of *Poems* which were published in 1775 and attracted the patronage of the Duchess of Devonshire. A second daughter died in infancy the following year. On their release from prison she reapplied to Garrick, who launched her on a successful stage career in 1776. For the next four seasons she performed regularly at Drury Lane and in 1780 her role as Perdita in *The Winter's Tale* attracted the attentions of the 17-year-old Prince of Wales, later George IV. His bond of £20,000 was subsequently offered in recognition of her position as a Royal Mistress, an arrangement which ended within a year.

The bond was unpaid, the scandal unpleasant, and Mary felt unable to resume her theatrical career. Her name was linked with several other famous men, including Charles James Fox, who secured her a government pension of £500 in return for surrendering the Prince's bond. She then established a long-term relationship with Colonel, later Sir Banastre, Tarleton, an English army officer, later MP for Liverpool and a minor military historian. It was while travelling in pursuit of him that she suffered a miscarriage which resulted in partial paralysis of her legs. The relationship ended in 1798 when he married an heiress. Virtually crippled, with the resumption of a stage career impossible, and in need of money, she turned her energies to writing. She had published *Captivity: A Poem* and *Celadon and Lydia; A Tale* in 1777. In 1788 she began to contribute to the Della Cruscan poetical correspondence, led by the poet Robert Merry, along with Hannah *Cowley and Hester *Piozzi. Other more substantial enterprises followed. Her *Poems* (1791) had 600 subscribers, many of them eminent. In 1793 she published a second volume of *Poems, Modern Manners,* which included a satire on William Gifford's attacks on the Della Cruscans, and *Sight: The Cavern of Woe and Solitude.* A collection of sonnets, *Sappho and Phaon,* and *The Sicilian Lover: A Tragedy* appeared in 1796. Her most financially successful works were a series of novels, the sales of which were promoted by her notoriety and their supposedly autobiographical elements. *Vancenza* (1792), *The Widow* (1794), *Angelina* (1796), *Hubert de Sevrac,* a *Gothic novel (1796), *Walsingham* (1797), *The False Friend* (1799), and *The Natural Daughter* (1799) brought her a steady profit as her health declined. She contributed poetry to the *Morning Post,* along with Southey, using names such as Tabitha Bramble, Bridget, and Laura. Coleridge, who also contributed to the newspaper, admired her work. The title of her *Lyrical Tales* (1800) demonstrated the early influence of *Lyrical Ballads.* Encouraged by her friendship with Mary *Wollstonecraft and William Godwin she published, as Anne Frances Randall, *A Letter to the Women of England on the Injustice of Mental Subordination* (1799), reflecting her disillusion with marriage. Her autobiography was unfinished at her death in 1800 at the age of 42. Her daughter **Mary Elizabeth Robinson** wrote one novel, *The Shrine of Bertha* (1794), and edited her mother's *Memoirs with Some Posthumous Pieces* (1801) and her *Poetical Works* (1806). Today Mary Robinson is as much remembered for her portraits by Romney, Gainsborough, Reynolds, and others, painted at the height of her fame as an actress, as for her writing. *See* Stanley V. Makower, *Perdita: A Romance in Biography* (1908); Robert D. Bass, *The Green Dragoon: The Lives of Banastre Tarleton and Mary Robinson* (1957); M. Steen, *The Lost One* (1937); Stuart Curran, in *Romanticism and Feminism,* ed. Anne K. Mellor (1988).

Robinson, Mary Elizabeth *see under* ROBINSON, Mary

Roche, Regina Maria, novelist (b. County Wexford, 1764? d. Waterford, 17 May 1845).

Little is known of Regina Maria Roche's life. She was born Regina Dalton, the daughter of Captain Blundel Dalton, and brought up in Dublin. Books were an early passion and she began to write, she claimed, almost before 'I could well guide a pen'. She published a total of sixteen novels, two under her maiden name, *The Vicar of Lansdowne; or Country Quarters* (1789) and *The Maid of the Hamlet* (1793). Sometime around 1794 she married Ambrose Roche (d. 1829) and moved to England. It was her next novel, *The Children of the Abbey* (1796), which made her name. It went through ten editions by 1825 and was still in print as late as 1882. Its combination of domestic realism and a contemporary British setting with Gothic feeling and a conventional plot involving a lost inheritance gave it a distinctive tone among *Gothic novels. Harriet Smith in Jane *Austen's *Emma* had read the novel, leading to the supposition that Austen herself may have done so. Roche wrote fifteen other novels, most of which, like *Children of the Abbey*, were published by William Lane's *Minerva Press, and most were still in print in the 1830s. Several were translated into French. *Clermont* (1798) was one of the 'horrid' novels listed by Austen in *Northanger Abbey*. Roche was one of the stalwarts of the Minerva Press. The unprecedented success of *The Children of the Abbey* mirrored the phenomenal popularity of the publishing house as a whole, which reached its peak in the 1790s. Michael Sadleir in his pamphlet *Northanger Novels* (1927) described Roche as 'an out and out sensibility writer but with a Gothic accent'. Roche and her husband were cheated out of estates in Ireland by a dishonest lawyer. She spent her last years in retirement on the Mall in Waterford, where she died at the age of 81. *See* Coral Ann Howells, *Love, Mystery and Misery: Feeling in Gothic Fiction* (1978).

Roper, Margaret, née More, translator and woman of letters (1505–44).

Margaret Roper was the eldest of the four children, three daughters and a son, of Sir Thomas More and his first wife Jane Colt. Her father paid particular attention to his daughters' education, believing that women could benefit from learning, but that their virtues should be private and domestic. Margaret, his favourite, lived her life according to these principles. More's biographers, who included her husband William Roper, whom she married in 1521, have emphasized the extent of her learning and accomplishments and also her devotion to her father, her husband, and their five children. She had an extensive knowledge of philosophy, theology, and astronomy and was fluent in both Latin and Greek. She wrote Latin poems and a treatise on the Four Last Things, and translated Eusebius from Greek to Latin, none of which works survive. Her one published work was an English translation of Erasmus' *Treatise upon the Paternoster* (1524, published 1526). On the strength of this, and from contemporary accounts of her prodigious scholarship, she gained the reputation, along with Anne Cooke, Lady *Bacon, of being one of the outstanding women of letters of the sixteenth century. The legend that after her father's execution she brought his head from the Tower of London, kept it until her death, and was buried with it in her arms serves to emphasize the persistent and powerful influence of her father on her life. Some of her letters to him during his imprisonment were published in *The Correspondence of Sir Thomas More*, ed. E. F. Rogers (1947). Margaret Roper was commemorated in Tennyson's 'Dream of Fair Women' and Anne *Manning wrote an imaginary diary, *Margaret More's Tagebuch* (1870). Her daughter **Mary,** later **Clarke,** and then **Bassett** (1507?–72), wrote Latin and Greek orations, and translated her mother's Latin translation of Eusebius into English. Margaret Roper's sisters **Elizabeth Dancy** (b. 1506?) and **Cecilia Heron** (b. 1507?) were also celebrated for their learning, particularly in languages. Their Latin style was commended by Erasmus, with whom they corresponded. *See* Ernest E. Reynolds, *Margaret Roper* (1960); Elaine V. Beilin, *Redeeming Eve: Women Writers of the English Renaissance* (1987); Rita M. Verbrugge, in *Silent but for the Word: Tudor Women as Patrons, Translators and Writers of Religions Works* ed. Margaret P. Hannay (1985); Elizabeth McCutcheon, in *Women Writers of the Renaissance and Reformation*, ed. Katharina M. Wilson (1987).

Roper, Mary *see under* ROPER, Margaret

'Ross, Martin' (Violet Florence Martin), of Somerville and Ross, novelist (b. Ross, County. Galway, 11 June 1862, d. Cork, 21 December 1915).

Violet Florence Martin was the eleventh and youngest daughter of James Martin, Deputy Lieutenant of Galway, and a member of an old Anglo-Irish family, distinguished in both literature and the law. Her mother Anna Selina Fox was the granddaughter of Charles Kendal Bushe, Lord Chief Justice of Ireland at the time of Union, a measure which he had vigorously opposed. There were painters and poets on both sides of the family. Her father left the family estate at Ross to recoup his fortunes by a career in journalism in London, later returning and dying there in 1872. Violet Martin spent her childhood in Dublin, and was educated at home and at Alexandra College. In 1886 she met her second cousin Edith Oenone *Somerville, with whom she formed an immediate attachment. Both were interested in their family history, in their respective estates, and in hunting. Neither cousin married, although Violet apparently had a long love affair with Warham St Leger, a minor poet. Their literary collaboration began in 1887, and their first novel, *An Irish Cousin* (1889), was published as by Martin Ross (after the estate) and Geilles Herring. Edith Somerville soon dropped the pseudonym and the partnership became generally known as 'Somerville and Ross'. *Naboth's Vineyard* (1891), *The Real Charlotte* (1894), which drew heavily on Violet Martin's childhood, and *The Silver Fox* (1897) culminated in what became their best-known work, a series of twelve stories entitled *Some Experiences of an Irish RM* (1899), RM standing for Resident Magistrate. There were two sequels, *Further Experiences* (1908) and *Mr. Knox's Country* (1915), and another novel, *Dan Russel the Fox* (1911). Somerville and Ross's fiction offers a perceptive and satirical view of Anglo-Irish society and its absurdities. Violet Martin, generally regarded as the more intellectual and literary of the two cousins, was an ardent feminist and also a keen churchgoer. Two books of essays, *Some Irish Yesterdays* (1906) and *Stray-Aways* (1920), contain much of her writing, and are autobiographical. She was injured in a riding accident in 1898, from which she never fully recovered. She died in 1915. Edith Somerville maintained that she could still communicate with her cousin and the joint publications continued after her death. She was awarded a posthumous doctorate of letters by Trinity College, Dublin, in 1932. *See* John Cronin, *Somerville and Ross* (1972); Hilary Robinson, *Somerville and Ross: A Critical Appreciation* (1980).

Rossetti, Christina (Georgina), poet (b. London, 5 December 1830, d. London, 29 December 1894).

Christina Rossetti was the younger daughter of Gabriele Rossetti, an Italian scholar, poet, and political refugee who became professor of Italian at King's College, London. Her mother was Frances Mary Lavinia Polidori, the sister of the novelist Dr John William Polidori (1795–1821), Byron's one-time physician and secretary. She was educated at home by her mother, and was slow in learning to read but precocious in her writing, producing poems in both English and Italian. Her first published poem was written for her mother's birthday in 1842, privately printed by her maternal grandfather. She published a volume of poems in 1847, at the age of 16, again privately printed, and in 1850 contributed several poems under the pseudonym Ellen Alleyne to the Pre-Raphaelite journal the *Germ*, edited by her brother Dante Gabriel Rossetti (1828–82). The decline in their father's health which began in the 1840s reached an acute stage in 1850, when he was threatened with blindness. The main source of financial support was Christina's brother William Michael Rossetti (1829–1919), a critic, editor, and translator who was also a clerk in the Inland Revenue. Christina and her mother opened a day school in north London and another in Frome, in Somerset, where the family moved briefly in 1853. Neither was successful. In 1854 they returned to London where Gabriele Rossetti died. Religion was a vital element in Christina Rossetti's life. Initially she followed her mother's Evangelical leanings but gradually moved towards a High Church or Anglo-Catholic position. In 1848 she became engaged to James Collinson, a young painter on the fringes of the Pre-Raphaelite circle. She had refused his initial offer because he was a Roman Catholic but accepted him when he returned to the Church of England. She broke off the engagement on his reconversion to Roman Catholicism in 1850. More lasting in its effect was her later relationship with Charles Bagot Cayley, a translator and scholar, which again foundered on religious grounds. Cayley was a non-believer and Christina refused to marry anyone who could not share her religious beliefs. They remained friends none the less and his death in 1883 was a severe blow. Rossetti's reputation was made in 1862 with the publication of *Goblin Market and Other Poems*, which contained two illustrations by D. G. Rossetti. The title poem, a disturbing fairy-tale about two sisters, one of whom succumbs to the temptations of the goblins and is saved by the other sister, has attracted the interest of feminist critics and has been central to the renewed critical interest in and the revaluation of Rossetti in the twentieth century. Her next volume, *The Prince's Progress and Other Poems* (1866), had a title-page and frontispiece as well as binding designed by her elder brother, who also played a large part in the selection of poems for inclusion. She published *Sing-Song: A Nursery Rhyme Book* in 1872 with a second edition in 1893, and in 1875 Macmillan published the first collected edition of her work, *Goblin Market, the Prince's Progress and Other Poems*, which contained thirty-seven poems previously published in periodicals, including 'Christmas Carol', better known by its first line, 'In the bleak mid-winter'. This edition was subsequently reprinted several times. In 1881 she published *A Pageant and Other Poems*, which contained a sonnet sequence, 'Monna Innominata', love poems which Rossetti claimed in a note were variations on Elizabeth Barrett *Browning's 'Sonnets from the Portuguese', the kind of poems the latter might have written had she been unhappy rather than happy. The volume contained a second sonnet cycle, 'Later Life'. A new collected edition, *Poems* (1890), added *A Pageant and Other Poems* plus seven new poems to the 1875 edition. Rossetti also published a number of devotional volumes, *Called to be Saints* (1881), *Time Flies: A Reading Diary* (1885), and *The Face of the Deep* (1892), for the Society for the Diffusion of Useful Knowledge, the poems from which were collected in *Verses* (1893). The themes of many of the poems in the *Goblin Market* volume, lost love and happiness, a longing for death, resignation, mutability, isolation, as well as sisterly relationships, were constant preoccupations of Rossetti's work as a whole. She made attempts to widen the concerns of her poetry to include some social issues which occupied her in various charitable activities, notably a home for fallen women, prostitutes, and unmarried mothers, but later abandoned the idea. 'It is not in me and therefore it will never come out of me to turn to politics or philanthropy with Mrs. Browning', she wrote to D. G. Rossetti. Her one significant fictional work, *Maude: A Story for Girls*, written in 1850 and published posthumously in 1897, canvasses various possible lives for women, including that of a writer. Rossetti's health had never been robust. In 1871 she contracted Graves' disease, a thyroid disorder, and in 1892 she was diagnosed as suffering from cancer. Her later years were clouded by the deaths of most of her family, Dante Gabriel in 1882, and her mother in 1886. Her elder sister **Maria Francesca** (b. 1827), who published a number of devotional works as well as a highly regarded essay on Dante in 1871, died in 1876, having previously joined an Anglican sisterhood. Christina died in 1894. Her only surviving sibling William Michael became in effect her literary executor, editing *New Poems* (1894), some of which were republished from periodicals, and others which had never been published. In 1904 he effected the publication of her *Poetical Works*, which had been in preparation since 1899, the standard edition of her poetry until the recent *Complete Poems of Christina Rossetti*, ed. Rebecca W. Crump (3 vols., 1979–90). W. M. Rossetti also edited her *Family Letters* (1908). Lona M. Packer's speculative biography *Christina Rossetti* (1963) has been largely discredited. *See* Virginia Woolf, *The Common Reader: Second Series* (1932); Jerome J. McGann, in *The Beauty of Inflections* (1985); Cora Kaplan, *Sea Changes* (1986); Antony H. Harrison, *Christina Rossetti in Context* (1988); David A. Kent, (ed.), *The Achievement of Christina Rossetti* (1989); Kathleen Jones, *Learning Not to be First: The Life of Christina Rossetti* (1992); Angela Leighton, *Victorian Women Poets: Writing against the Heart* (1992).

Rossetti, Maria Francesca *See under* ROSSETTI, Christina

Rowe, Elizabeth, poet (b. Ilchester, Somerset, 11 September 1674, d. Frome, Somerset, 20 February 1737).

Elizabeth Rowe was the eldest of the three daughters of Walter Singer, a Nonconformist minister who had at one time been imprisoned for his beliefs, and Elizabeth Portnell, whom he met when she was a prison visitor. He later became a prosperous merchant in Frome, in Somerset. Elizabeth received a religious education, probably at a local boarding school, together with the usual accomplishments of music and drawing. She also wrote poetry from an early age, some of which was published anonymously in John Dunton's *Athenian Mercury* (*1694–5*). In the next year (1696) Dunton published her *Poems on Several Occasions: Written by Philomela*, including many reprinted from the *Mercury*, and later reprinted more of her early poems in his *Athenian Oracle* (1704). In his *Life and Errors* (1705) he praised her as 'the richest genius of her Sex'. Through her writing she became friendly with the family of Lord Weymouth at nearby Longleat, and particularly with his son Henry Thynne, who taught her Italian and French and read Latin with her. Thynne's daughter Frances, Countess of Hertford and later Duchess of Somerset, was to become Rowe's lifelong friend. The non-juring Bishop Thomas Ken, then resident at Longleat and also known to her father, was another formative influence on her. Matthew Prior met her in 1703 at Longleat and reportedly fell in love with her. She rebuffed his advances but used his influence to publish two Latin translations in Tonson's *Poetic Miscellanies*, v (1704). Prior praised her work in the preface to his *Poems* (1709). Isaac Watts was a fervent admirer of her poetry, and addressed a poem to her in his *Horae Lyricae* (1709). In 1709 she met Thomas Rowe (1687–1715), a young classical scholar thirteen years her junior and also the son of a Nonconformist minister. They married the following year. Rowe died of consumption in 1715, and Elizabeth spent the rest of her life in virtual seclusion at Frome, undertaking charitable work, and in 1728 publishing *Friendship in Death in Twenty Letters from the Dead to the Living*. It went through numerous editions, was translated into French and German, and became her most popular work. *Letters Moral and Entertaining* (3 parts, 1727–33) followed, and like its predecessor was pious and moralizing in intent. *The History of Joseph* (1736) was a long poem in eight books, based on the biblical story. Elizabeth Rowe died of apoplexy in Frome in February 1737. At her request Isaac Watts edited a collection of her prayers, *Devout Exercises of the Heart* (1737), which went through several editions, including one published in America in 1792. Her brother-in-law Theophilus Rowe edited her *Miscellaneous Works* (1739), which included a memoir, prefatory verses by Elizabeth *Carter, the Countess of Hertford, and others, some poems by Thomas Rowe, and some of her letters to the Countess. Her work was widely read and influential during her lifetime and after. It was frequently reprinted well into the nineteenth century and several volumes had French and German translations. Johnson claimed Mrs Rowe was the first English writer to combine successfully 'the ornaments of romance in the decoration of religion'. Isaac Watts insisted that she had rescued 'the honour of Poetry . . . from the Scandal which has been cast upon it, by the abuse of Verse to loose and profane Purposes'. Her poems appeared in various miscellanies during her lifetime and after, including *Divine Hymns and Poems* (1704) and **Poems by Eminent Women* (1755). Her *Poems on Several*

Occasions was reissued under her own name in 1737, and her *Miscellaneous Works* went through several editions including a four-volume enlarged one in 1796. *See* Henry Stecher, *Elizabeth Singer Rowe: The Poetess of Frome* (1973); Madeleine Forell Marshall, *The Poetry of Elizabeth Singer Rowe* (1987); Madeleine Forell Marshall in *Teaching Eighteenth Century Poetry*, ed. Christopher Fox (1990).

Rowson, Susanna, novelist, playwright, and actress
(b. Portsmouth, 1762, d. Boston, Massachusetts, 2 March 1824).

Susanna Rowson's mother Susanna Musgrave died at her birth. Her father William Haswell, a lieutenant in the British navy, took her to New England, where he had settled, in 1766. He later remarried and had three sons. Susanna read at an early age (Dryden's Virgil, Pope's Homer, Shakespeare, and Spenser) and became the protégé of the famous American lawyer James Otis, who reportedly imbued her with democratic principles. At the outbreak of the War of Independence her father's property was confiscated and the family confined as prisoners of war. They returned to England in 1778, where Susanna became a governess until her marriage in 1786 to William Rowson, a feckless hardware merchant and trumpeter in the Royal Horse Guards. In the same year she published *Victoria*, an epistolary 'seduction novel' whose characters were taken from real life. It was dedicated to Georgina, Duchess of Devonshire (1757–1806), herself the author of two epistolary novels. Through this connection she secured an introduction to the Prince of Wales and a pension for her father. Her next novel was *The Inquisitor; or Invisible Rambler* (1788), followed in 1790 by her greatest popular success, *Charlotte: A Tale of Truth*, later known as *Charlotte Temple*, another story of seduction, supposedly based on fact, and a *Minerva Press best seller. It had several American editions and in 1835 was translated into German. Other fiction included *Mentoria* (1791) and the autobiographical *Rebecca; or The Fille de Chambre* (1792). William Rowson went bankrupt shortly after the publication of *Charlotte Temple* and Susanna went on stage to augment their income. They toured England with a theatre company and in 1793 emigrated to the United States, where they joined the Philadelphia New Theatre and later companies in Annapolis and Baltimore. She ended her theatrical career in 1797 in Boston with the Federal Street Theatre, where she played in her own comedy, *Americans in England*. After leaving the stage she opened a successful girls' school in Boston, which continued until her retirement in 1822. Rowson published another epistolary novel, *Trials of the Human Heart* (1795), in the preface to which she explained her feelings for her new country, and a four-volume family saga, *Reuben and Rachel; or Tales of Old Times* (1798), which she had begun much earlier. A sequel to *Charlotte Temple*, *Charlotte's*

Daughter; or The Three Orphans, appeared posthumously in 1828. She also wrote seven pieces for the stage, including an operetta, *Slaves in Algiers* (1794), and several farces. She edited the *Boston Weekly Magazine* 1802–5 and published several school textbooks. Her *Miscellaneous Poems* was published in Boston in 1804. Although most of her fiction was first published in England, Rowson has come to be regarded as an early American novelist and playwright. Not all the attention her work received was flattering. William Cobbett attacked her coarsely in *A Kick for a Bite* (1795). She died and was buried in Boston. *See* Cathy N. Davidson (ed.), *Reading in America: Literature and Social History* (1989); Mary Anne Schofield, in *Modern American Drama: The Female Canon*, ed. June Schlueter (1990); Doreen A. Saar, in *Curtain Calls: British and American Women and the Theater 1660–1820* ed. Mary Anne Schofield and Cecilia Macheski (1991).

Ruck, 'Berta' (Amy Roberta), popular novelist (b. Murree, India, 2 August 1878, d. Aberdovey, Merioneth, Wales, 11 August 1978).

Berta Ruck was the eldest of the eight children of Arthur Ashley Ruck, a British army officer serving in India, and his wife Elizabeth Eleanor D'Arcy, whose family were also military. She was brought up in Wales from the age of 2, living with her paternal grandmother in Merionethshire until her father was appointed Chief Constable of Caernarvonshire in 1888. She went to St Winifred's School at Bangor, worked briefly as an *au pair* in Germany, and then went to the Lambeth School of Art with the intention of becoming a book illustrator. She won a scholarship to the Slade School of Art and spent a year at Calorossi's (art college) in Paris. She began work by illustrating stories in the *Idler* and the short-lived *Jabberwock* and then contributed short stories to magazines like *Home Chat.* In 1909 she married a fellow student, later a novelist, Oliver Onions (1873–1961; he changed his name to George Oliver), by whom she had two sons. In 1912 a *Home Chat* serial, 'His Official Fiancée', attracted the eye of a publisher, who asked her to turn it into a book. Its instant success the following year in both Britain and the United States launched her long career as a popular novelist. She published as many as three books a year, beginning with *The Courtship of Rosamond Fayre* (1915), *The Lad with Wings* (1915), and the collection of short stories *Khaki and Kisses* (1916), and ending in 1967 with *Shopping for a Husband*, which she published at the age of 89. Most of her books have a predictable Cinderella plot, involving a neglected or impoverished heroine who is eventually rewarded with a wealthy and adoring husband. She published several volumes of autobiography, beginning with *A Story-Teller Tells the Truth* (1935), parts of which were incorporated into *A Smile for the Past* (1959), *A Trickle of Welsh Blood* (1967), *An Asset to Wales* (1970), and *Ancestral Voices* (1972). The publication in 1920 of a *Berta Ruck Birthday Book* attested to her early and considerable popularity. Virginia *Woolf probably inadvertently put her name (as Bert*h*a Ruck) on a tombstone in *Jacob's Room* (1922), causing an exchange of solicitors' letters and their eventual, congenial meeting. Ruck's popularity continued throughout the Second World War, during which she lectured to the troops and afterwards broadcast on Welsh radio and on BBC television. She attributed her longevity (she died at the age of 100) to open-air swimming all year round.

Rumens, Carol, poet and novelist (b. Lewisham, London, 10 December 1944).

Carol Rumens is the daughter of Arthur Lumley and Marjorie May Mills. She was educated at convent schools in London and Croyden and read philosophy at Bedford College, University of London. She married David Rumens in 1965 and has two daughters. She worked as a publicity assistant and copy-writer and was the poetry editor of *Quarto* and then of the *Literary Review* as well as a regular reviewer for the *Observer*. She has also been a creative writing fellow at the University of Kent. Her collections of poetry began with *Strange Girls in Bright Colours* (1973), which dealt with the dilemmas of married women, followed by *A Necklace of Mirrors* (1978), which looked at women's lives in history. Many of her poems treat of the sufferings and horrors of twentieth-century European history, particularly that of Russia and Eastern Europe, as in *Direct Dialling* (1985) and *From Berlin to Heaven* (1989). 'I do not belong to that school of thought which says in the face of extreme horror, suffered by others, one should be silent,' she once wrote. 'On the contrary, I believe that all the forces of imagination should be employed to speak of their suffering.' Other volumes include *Unplayed Music* (1981), *Scenes from the Gingerbread House* (1982), autobiographical poems about childhood, *Star Whisper* (1983), and *The Greening of Snow Beach* (1988). Her *Selected Poems* was published in 1987. Rumens has written a novel, *Plato Park* (1987), and a study of Jean *Rhys (1985), and has edited *Making for the Open: The Chatto Book of Post-Feminist Poetry 1964–1984* (1985), a selection from fifty-six women poets.

S

Sackville-West, 'Vita' (Victoria Mary), novelist, poet, and biographer (b. Knole, near Sevenoaks, Kent, 9 March 1892, d. Sissinghurst, Kent, 2 June 1962).

Vita Sackville-West was the only child of Lionel Sackville-West, later third Baron Sackville, and his wife (and cousin) Victoria Sackville-West. She grew up at Knole, the ancestral home of the Sackvilles, which she loved and which, as a female, she was unable to inherit. She was educated by governesses until she was 13, and then sent to a day school in London. Her childhood was essentially solitary. She was fond of her father, but her relationship with her mother, the illegitimate daughter of the second Baron Sackville and the Spanish flamenco dancer Pepita de Oliva, was ambivalent, and at times anguished. She spent much of her time reading, and also writing, and immersed herself in the countryside surrounding Knole. By the time she was 18 she had written eight novels (one in French) and five plays, all on historical subjects, and also many poems. In 1913 she married Harold Nicolson, a young diplomat, later a politician and writer, by whom she had two sons (a third was stillborn). They bought Long Barn, near Knole, which she used as the family home and a base for her writing, while Harold worked either in London or abroad. The marriage was unconventional, but in its way successful. Both partners were essentially homosexual. Vita's passionate affair with Violet Keppel (later Trefusis), a childhood friend, between 1918 and 1921 did not end the marriage, nor did the ensuing close relationships with other women, including Virginia *Woolf. Common interests, mutual support, and genuine affection kept them together. In 1929 Harold resigned from the

Foreign Office to become a journalist. Long Barn was sold and in 1930 they bought Sissinghurst Castle, also in Kent, which they planned to restore, and to create a garden. Writing and gardening became equally her passions. She was immensely prolific, producing over forty books in all, novels, poetry, biography, and books of travel. Her writing developed from its adolescent phase to maturity in the period immediately after her marriage. She wrote *Knole and the Sackvilles* (1922), a history of her home and her family. The setting of *The Edwardians* (1930), a best-selling novel reflecting English society before the First World War, again drew on Knole. The strongly feminist *All Passion Spent* (1931) showed the impact of Woolf's *A Room of One's Own* (1929), which she first heard as Cambridge lectures. *Seducers in Ecuador* (1924) was written for Woolf and was reciprocated by Woolf's *Orlando* (1928). Her last novel, *Signposts in the Sea*, was published in 1961, the year before she died. Her poetry, which she valued most, was varied in form. *Poems of West and East* (1917) consisted of short lyrics. *The Land* (1926), which won the Hawthornden Prize, was a long poem in the manner of the *Georgics*, as was *The Garden* (1946). *Sissinghurst* (1931) celebrated the newly emerging garden. Her *Collected Poems* was published in 1933. She wrote several biographies: of her grandmother and her mother, in *Pepita* (1937); of Aphra *Behn (1929), of Joan of Arc (1936), of the Duchesse de Montpensier, in *Daughter of France* (1959), and possibly the most distinguished, *The Eagle and the Dove* (1943), a study of St Teresa of Ávila and St Thérèse of Lisieux. She edited a portion of her ancestor Lady Anne *Clifford's *Diary* (1923), and wrote an introduction to the work of Alice *Meynell (1947). She also published travel books, most notably *Twelve Days* (1928), based on a trip to Persia when Harold was posted there in 1925. The creation of the garden at Sissinghurst, the joint work of the Nicolsons, was in its way as distinguished an achievement as their literary output. Collections of her gardening columns, which she wrote for the *Observer* between 1946 and 1961, were frequently reprinted as books, as were her 'Country Notes' in the *New Statesman* 1938–41. As well as these, she wrote book reviews regularly for the *Listener*, the *Nation*, and the *Athenaeum*. She died at Sissinghurst in 1962. *See* Harold Nicolson, *Diaries and Letters*, ed. Nigel Nicolson (3 vols., 1966–8); Nigel Nicolson, *Portrait of a Marriage* (1973); Michael Stevens, *Vita Sackville-West: A Critical Biography* (1974); Victoria Glendinning, *Vita: The Life of Vita Sackville-West* (1983); *The Letters of Vita Sackville-West to Virginia Woolf*, ed. L. DeSalvo and M. A. Leaska (1984); Suzanne Raitt, *Vita and Virginia: The Work and Friendship of V. Sackville-West and Virginia Woolf* (1993).

Sayers, Dorothy L(eigh), novelist, playwright, essayist, and translator (b. Oxford, 13 June 1893, d. Witham, Essex, 17 December 1957).

Dorothy Sayers was the only child of the Revd Henry Sayers, headmaster of Christ Church Choir School, Oxford, and later rector of Bluntisham, Huntingdonshire, and his wife Helen Mary Leigh. Percival Leigh, one of the early contributors to *Punch*, was her great-great-uncle. She was educated at the Godolphin School, Salisbury, and won a scholarship to Somerville College, Oxford, where she took a first in modern languages in 1915. (Women were not admitted to degrees until 1920.) She published a volume of poems, *Opus I* (1916), edited *Oxford Poetry* (1917–19), and taught for a year at Hull High School for Girls. She then became a copy-writer for a London advertising agency, a job which she held until 1931. In 1924 she had a son, and in 1926 she married Oswald Atherton Fleming, a war correspondent. Shortly after 1920 she determined to earn her living by writing detective stories, methodically applying herself to the task of studying the genre from Wilkie Collins onward. (She later wrote an introduction for a 1944 edition of *The Moonstone*.) Most of her fiction was written in little more than a decade. *Whose Body?* (1923), her first novel, introduced her aristocratic detective hero Lord Peter Wimsey and his manservant Bunter. Eight further books appeared in nine years, including *Clouds of Witness* (1926), *Unnatural Death* (1927), *The Unpleasantness at the Bellona Club* (1928), *Strong Poison* (1930), in which Harriet Vane, a woman detective story writer, first appeared, and *The Five Red Herrings* (1931). Subsequent titles showed a deepening of her talents and a wider range. *Murder Must Advertise* (1933) utilized her experience in advertising. *The Nine Tailors* (1934), regarded by many as her best book, drew on her East Anglian childhood and a knowledge of campanology, and *Gaudy Night* (1935) on her Oxford years. The last continued the story of Harriet Vane, who became the focus of Sayers's explorations of the social and intellectual role of women and eventually married Wimsey in *Busman's Honeymoon* (1937), originally a play written with Muriel St Clare Byrne (1936). *Busman's Honeymoon* was the last Lord Peter Wimsey novel and Sayers's last detective novel. She edited three anthologies of detective stories, *Great Short Stories of Detection, Mystery and Horror* (1928, 1931, 1934), and *Tales of Detection* (1936). The introduction to the first volume provided an important account of the development and an assessment of the genre. In 1940 her work abruptly changed direction. Two plays with Christian themes written for the Canterbury Festival, *The Zeal of thy House* (1937) and *The Devil to Pay* (1939), were preludes to a larger project, *The Man Born to be King*, a cycle of radio plays broadcast between December 1941 and October

1942. She published collections of essays and speeches and studies on literature, popular theology, and social questions. In 1949 she produced the first part of her translation of Dante's *Divine Comedy*, the *Inferno*, followed in 1955 by the *Purgatorio*. She was working on the *Paradiso* at the time of her death in 1957. It was completed by Barbara Reynolds in 1962 and the three parts published by Penguin. Sayers was co-founder and then president of the Detection Club 1949–57, and president of the Modern Language Association 1939–45. *See* Janet Hitchman, *Such a Strange Lady* (1975); Margaret P. Hannay, *As her Whimsey Took her: Critical Works on the Work of Dorothy L. Sayers* (1979); James Brabazon, *DLS: A Biography* (1981); Patricia Craig and Mary Cadogan, *The Lady Investigates* (1981); Barbara Reynolds, *The Passionate Intellect: Dorothy L. Sayers' Encounter with Dante* (1989); Catherine Kenney, *The Remarkable Case of Dorothy L. Sayers* (1990).

'Scarlett, Susan' *see* STREATFEILD, Noel

Schreiner, Olive (Emilie Albertina) ('Ralph Iron'), novelist (b. Wittebergen, Basutoland, 24 March 1855, d. Cape Town, 11 December 1920).

Olive Schreiner was the sixth of the twelve children (ten survived) of Gottlob Schreiner, a Methodist missionary of German descent, and his English wife Rebecca Lyndall. She was entirely self-educated and brought up under strict parental discipline in an atmosphere of Calvinistic gloom. She pronounced herself a free-thinker at 12, after the death of a sister. She had considered studying medicine, then impossible for a woman, adjusted her ambition to nursing, and when thwarted by ill health (a chest condition which developed into asthma) she became a governess. She lived with various of her brothers and sisters between posts and began draft manuscripts of three novels, *Undine*, begun in 1873–4 and published posthumously in 1928, *The Story of an African Farm*, her best and also her best-known work, begun in 1874–5 and published in 1883, and the unfinished *From Man to Man*, begun in 1875 and published posthumously, in 1926. Her father died in 1876 and her mother converted to Catholicism. She saved enough money to book a passage to England in 1881, taking the manuscript of *The Story of an African Farm* with her. It was rejected by Macmillan but George Meredith accepted it for Chapman & Hall and it was published under the pseudonym Ralph Iron. Her reputation was made and for the most part rested on this highly idiosyncratic feminist novel, parts of which were autobiographical. *The Story of an African Farm* anticipated much of the *New Woman fiction of the 1890s and produced a critical debate which brought her an introduction to avant-garde circles. Eleanor Marx, the political theorist and writer, became a close friend, as did Edward Carpenter and the mathematician and eugenicist Karl Pearson. Havelock Ellis was another intimate friend, although probably not her lover, and introduced her to Fabian socialism. Schreiner was a compulsive but neurotic writer who found enormous difficulty in completing her work. She revised, abandoned, and reinstated her various manuscripts. She began work on her second major novel, *From Man to Man*, but the only other publication to emerge from her London period (1881–9) was *Dreams* (1891), a collection of allegories. A further collection, *Dream Life and Real Life*, appeared in 1893, also under the signature Ralph Iron. She returned to South Africa at a period of intense political ferment. Her brother was a member of the Cape Colony Parliament and a minister in Cecil Rhodes's government. An initial infatuation with Rhodes changed to disillusion, particularly after the Jameson Raid of 1896. In anticipation of the Boer War, which she vehemently opposed, she wrote the allegory *Trooper Peter Halket of Mashonaland* (1897). In 1894 she married Samuel Cron Cronwright, a politician and farmer eight years her junior. Their daughter was born the following year but died almost immediately. The loss left Schreiner both physically and emotionally drained. Although the couple later became estranged, Cronwright, who took the name Cronwright-Schreiner, devoted much time and energy to promoting her career. She became a prominent voice in the women's movement from the 1890s onward. Her *Women and Labour* (1911) was regarded as a seminal work. She returned to England in 1913, leaving her husband in South Africa until 1920, when he joined her briefly. They returned almost immediately to South Africa, where she died of a heart attack. Cronwright edited her letters and wrote a biography (both 1924) as well as introductions for her two remaining novels. Schreiner's influence on other women writers has been considerable. Virginia *Woolf, Dorothy *Richardson, and Doris *Lessing were among her professed admirers. *From Man to Man* has been seen by critics to anticipate *Woolf's *A Room of One's Own* (1929) in its exploration of the crisis of the woman artist. Yet admirers and critics alike have viewed her work as depressing and claustrophobic, and have seen in Schreiner, as in her heroines, an overwhelming sense of frustration and of talents wasted. Elaine Showalter sees her as writing out of a 'double colonialism', that of the new woman and that of a writer isolated from the cultural mainstream. *See The Letters of Olive Schreiner*, ed. Richard Rive (1988–); Virginia Woolf, *Women and Writing*, ed. Michele Barrett (1979); Elaine Showalter, *A Literature of their Own* (1977); Ruth First and Ann Scott, *Olive Schreiner* (1980); Joyce Avrech Berkman, M. V. Smith, and D. Maclennan (eds.), *Olive Schreiner and After* (1983); Joyce Avrech Berkman, *The Healing Imagination of Olive Schreiner: Beyond South African Colonialism* (1989); Gerald Monsman, *Olive Schreiner's Fiction* (1992).

'Scott, Agnes Neill' *see* MUIR, Willa

Scott, Sarah, novelist and historian (b. West Layton, Hutton Magna, Yorkshire, 1723, d. Catton, near Norwich, 30 November 1795).

Sarah Scott was the younger daughter of Matthew Robinson, a Yorkshire landowner, and his wife Elizabeth Drake. The *Bluestocking Elizabeth *Montagu was her elder sister and their physical similarity, 'as like as two peas', led to her family nickname 'The Pea'. In 1752 she made, according to Mrs *Delany, the 'foolish choice' of marriage to George Lewis Scott, a mathematician and one-time tutor to the Prince of Wales, later George III. The couple soon separated, 'through disagreement of tempers'. After the separation she lived with Lady Barbara Montagu (no relation) until the latter's death in 1765, engaging in philanthropic activities. She determined on writing as a means of earning a living. Her first novel, *The History of Cornelia* (1750), written before her marriage, was published anonymously, as were all her subsequent novels. *Agreeable Ugliness* (1754), loosely based on a novel by Pierre Antoine LaPlace, foreshadowed the 'sense and sensibility' theme of later eighteenth-century fiction. In *A Journey through Every Stage of Life* (also 1754) a female character demonstrates that a woman can live independently and then promptly marries. Her best-known book, *A Description of Millenium Hall* (1762), presents life stories of women living a utopian existence in a secular convent. The book took a month to write, a return of a guinea a day, Scott reckoned. The eponymous hero of *The Man of Real Sensibility; or The History of Sir George Ellison* (1765), later *The History of Sir George Ellison* (1766), improves slaves' lives in Jamaica and then spends a period in England emulating Millenium Hall. The novel went through several editions, including some in America. The epistolary *The Test of Filial Duty* (1772) contrasts two sisters and attacks clandestine marriages. Scott also published a biography of Gustavus Ericson, King of Sweden (1761), as by Henry Augustus Raymond, a history of the House of Mecklenburgh (1762), and a life of Théodore Agrippa d'Aubigné (1772). She died 'in obscurity', according to the *DNB*, at Catton near Norwich. Her letters and papers were burned after her death, by her instruction. *See* Walter Marion Crittenden, *The Life and Writings of Mrs. Sarah Scott, Novelist* (1932); Jane Spencer's introd. to *Millenium Hall* (1986); Janet Todd, *Women's Friendship in Literature* (1980).

Scovell, Edith Joy, poet (b. Sharow, West Yorkshire, 9 April 1907).

A clergyman's daughter, Edith Joy Scovell was educated at Casterton School, Westmorland, and then read classics and English at Somerville College,

Oxford. She took her degree in 1930 and interspersed the writing of poetry with secretarial work in London, while also reviewing occasionally for the feminist weekly *Time and Tide*. She married Charles Elton, an ecologist, in 1937, and accompanied him as a field assistant on research projects in Central and South America. They have two children. Her first volume of poetry, *Shadows of Chrysanthemums*, was published in 1944, when she was 37. *The Midsummer Meadow* followed, and in 1956 *The River Steamer*, a retrospective collection which contained some new work. Twenty-six years later she published *The Space Between* (1982), and then *Listening to Collared Doves* (1986). Her *Collected Poems* was published in 1988. The subjects of Scovell's quietly meditative poems are birth, motherhood, nature, and the process of ageing, but her poetry is neither domestic nor 'women's poetry', as early reviewers alleged. *Poetry Review* (1986) entitled her 'a visionary in sensible shoes', which better reflects her subtle and complex talent. As the critic Philip Hobsbawm noted, 'it is not the imagery alone but what is behind the imagery which forms her subject matter, as in the title poem of *The Space Between*: "It is not the flowers' selves only, webbed in their skies of green | It is the depth they grant to sight, it is the space between."' She wrote of her own work in 1956, 'I should like the surface to be entirely clear, and the meaning entirely implicit.' Once compared with Barbara *Pym in the degree of critical neglect and the justification for reassessment, Scovell was championed by the poet Geoffrey Grigson, who anthologized her in 1949, and more recently by Carol *Rumens. *Poetry Review* called her 'probably the best neglected poet in the country'. *Selected Poems* (1992) includes seven new poems.

Second Sex*, *The *see* BEAUVOIR, Simone de

sensation novels.

A sub-genre of mid-Victorian fiction, particularly prevalent in the 1860s and practised by Dickens, Wilkie Collins, Charles Reade, and a number of women novelists, notably Mary Elizabeth *Braddon and Mrs Henry *Wood. Sensation novels were characterized by adventuresome plots involving, in some cases, the journalistic 'sensations' of the day, notorious cases of bigamy, arson, forcible incarceration in lunatic asylums, and other crimes which became the inspiration for outlandish plots. Another source was Victorian stage melodrama with its blatant contrast between the forces of good and evil, which greatly influenced the work of Braddon and also Wood, whose novel *East Lynne* (1861) was in turn adapted for the stage. Mrs *Oliphant, who disliked sensation fiction, attributed its emergence to the 'violent stimulation of serial publication', the need to entice readers by surprise endings, unexpected twists in the plot, mystery, and disguise. The opportunity of subverting realist conventions made the genre particularly attractive to women writers, who could push their heroines to the extremes of moral and sexual behaviour, seduction, bigamy, adultery, even murder, thus registering a protest against the absolute moral and behavioural codes which governed women's lives. Sensation plots became a means of acknowledging female sexuality. Critics have traced links between the *Gothic conventions of late eighteenth- and early nineteenth-century women's writing and the sensation novels of the 1860s. Other practitioners of sensation fiction include *Ouida, Mrs J. H. *Riddell, Amelia B. *Edwards, Florence *Marryat, Helen *Reeves and Rhoda *Broughton. *See* Winifred Hughes, *The Maniac in the Cellar: Sensation Novels of the 1860s* (1980); Lyn Pykett, *The 'Improper' Feminine: The Women's Sensation Novel and the New Woman Writing* (1992).

Seward, Anna, poet (b. Eyam, Derbyshire, 12 December 1742, d. Lichfield, Staffordshire, 25 March 1809).

Anna Seward was the elder of the two surviving daughters of Thomas Seward (1708–90), rector of Eyam, in Derbyshire, and later canon of Lichfield and Salisbury, and Elizabeth Hunter, whose father had been headmaster of Lichfield Grammar School and the teacher of Dr Johnson. Thomas Seward was a man of literary inclinations and some modest talents. He co-edited the works of Beaumont and Fletcher, and contributed several poems to Robert Dodsley's *Collection of Poems* (1748–58), including one on 'The Female Right to Literature'. He encouraged Anna's taste for literature, claiming she could recite 'L'Allegro' at the age of 3, while her mother disapproved, and ordered that needlework be substituted for poetry in the daily routine. The family moved to Lichfield in 1754, where Anna met Dr Erasmus Darwin, the physician and poet, who encouraged her literary activities, while she in turn provided some introductory lines which grew into his long poem *The Botanic Garden* (1789–91). Despite several suitors, she never married, and devoted herself to the care of her father after her mother's death in 1780. Her only sister died in 1764, and was replaced in her affections by a companion, Honoria Sneyd, who later became the second wife of Richard Lovell Edgeworth and the stepmother of Maria *Edgeworth. She became a frequent contributor to the *Gentleman's Magazine* and through occasional visits to London widened her circle of literary acquaintances. Her early poetry received the patronage of Anne, Lady Miller (1741–81), at 'poetical assemblies' at her villa Bath-Easton, near Bath. She was also a friend of William Hayley (1745–1820), a popular poet of the day. Anna Seward's dislike and disapproval of Dr Johnson was well known, and was the subject of a series of letters in the *Gentleman's Magazine* under the signature Benvolio. She published elegies on Garrick and on Captain Cook (1780), and a 'Monody on the unfortunate Major André' (1781), Honoria Sneyd's suitor who had been executed by the Americans during the Revolutionary War. The latter work reportedly brought her an apology from General Washington. Her 'poetical novel' *Louisa*, the work in which she took most pride, was published in 1784. Her poem *Llangollen Vale* (1796) described a visit she made to Lady Eleanor Butler and Sarah Ponsonby, the Ladies of *Llangollen, and her *Original Sonnets* (1799) demonstrated some success with that form. Despite her confined and provincial life, Anna Seward was a prominent figure in late eighteenth-century literary circles, and a vigorous promoter of young writers, as well as an outspoken critic of many of her female contemporaries. Her *Memoirs of the Life of Dr. Darwin* (1804) described the cultural life of Lichfield, of which she was a central figure, as her sobriquet 'The Swan of Lichfield' suggested. Her work was criticized for sentimentality, affectation, and obscurity, but her admirers included Wordsworth and Scott. She persuaded the latter to publish her collected *Poetical Works*, which appeared posthumously in 1810. He declined to publish her twelve-volume manuscript collection of letters, which she had carefully revised for publication. These were eventually published in six volumes by Archibald Constable (1811). She died at the Bishop's Palace, Lichfield, which had been her home since 1754. *See* E. V. Lucas, *A Swan and her Friends* (1907); Margaret Ashmun, *The Singing Swan* (1931); H. Pearson, *The Swan of Lichfield* (1936), includes a selection of her letters.

Sewell, Anna, novelist (b. Yarmouth, Norfolk, 30 March 1820, d. Old Catton, Norfolk, 25 April 1878).

Anna Sewell was the daughter of Isaac Sewell, a bank manager, and his wife **Mary Wright Sewell**, a writer of popular didactic poetry and moral tales for children. (Her sentimental ballad *Mother's Last Words*, published in 1860, reportedly sold over a million copies.) The family were Quakers and Anna and her brother Philip, two years her junior, were brought up in a household where philanthropy and good works were held in high regard. (They gave up a seaside holiday to send money to famine victims in Ireland.) Their father's lack of success in business meant that the family moved frequently. For a while he kept a shop in London, then travelled for a Nottingham lace factory, and eventually in 1835 became a bank manager in Brighton. When she was 14 an injury to her ankle which was subsequently badly set left her lame for the rest of her life. She used a pony and trap, and after a year's treatment in Marienberg, in Germany, was able to walk temporarily. She lived all her life under the care of her devoted mother, moving with the family from Brighton to various towns in Sussex until her father's retirement, when they settled at Wick, near Bristol and Bath, and then at Old Catton, in

Norfolk. In 1871 she began to write the single work on which her fame rests. *Black Beauty ('The Autobiography of a Horse, Translated from the Original Equine')* was published in 1877, the year before her death. The story of a once beautiful and valued horse who becomes a drudge, subjected to cruelty and hardship by inconsiderate masters, was at once a classic animal story and propaganda for the emergent animal cruelty movement. Its potential was immediately recognized by the founders of the RSPCA. Sewell received £20 from her mother's publisher for the book but died before its full impact was felt. It nevertheless sold 100,000 copies by the time of her death at the age of 58. *See* M. Bayly, *The Life and Letters of Mrs. Sewell* (1889); M. J. Baker, *Anna Sewell and Black Beauty* (1956); Susan Chitty, *The Woman who Wrote Black Beauty* (1971).

Sewell, Elizabeth Missing, novelist and children's writer (b. Newport, Isle of Wight, 19 February 1815, d. Bonchurch, Isle of Wight, 17 August 1906).

Elizabeth Missing Sewell was one of the twelve children of Thomas Sewell, a solicitor, and his wife Jane Edwards. One of her brothers became the first premier of New Zealand, another was the Warden of New College, and a third became an eminent lawyer. William Sewell (1804–74), a leading figure in the Tractarian movement and also a novelist (he wrote the fiercely anti-Catholic *Hawkstone* (1845)), had a strong influence on her religious views. Through him she was introduced to Newman, Keble, and other leading figures in the Oxford Movement. She went to a day school in Newport and later to a boarding school at Bath. In 1840 she published *Stories, Illustrative of the Lord's Prayer*, the first of many works of a pietistic nature, and like many of her early books, published as 'edited' by William. When their father died in 1842, deeply in debt as a result of two bank failures, his children resolved to pay off his creditors. A portion of her literary earnings was regularly used for this purpose until the debt was cleared. She also undertook the care of her younger siblings, jeopardizing her own chances of marriage. The rewards of the spinster's life are a recognizable theme in her fiction and romantic love is notable for its absence. *Katharine Ashton* (1854) is a somewhat cheerless picture of the life of a religious woman, devoted to usefulness. *Amy Herbert* (1844), intended for young girls, emphatically embodied staunch High Church views and stressed religious duty. *Laneton Parsonage*, published in three parts in 1846–8, was written for children, on the use of the Catechism. William Sewell's fierce reaction to Newman's conversion to Roman Catholicism in 1845 was reflected in the anti-Catholic thrust of *Margaret Percival* (1847). *The Experience of Life* (1853), Sewell's most popular work, was based on her own childhood. Most of her enthusiastic following in England and America at the height of her popularity in the 1840s and 1850s were young female readers. Her career and outlook in many ways resembled that of her contemporary Charlotte *Yonge, to whose *Monthly Packet* she contributed. To augment the income from her writing she and one of her sisters took pupils in their home and in 1866 she established a girls' school at Ventnor to put into practice her liberal ideas on women's education, most of which were outlined in her *Principles of Education* (1865). She was an enthusiastic traveller later in life and published several travel books as well as devotional works and school textbooks. She died at the age of 91. *See The Autobiography of Elizabeth M. Sewell*, ed. Eleanor M. Sewell (1907); Shirley Foster, *Victorian Women's Fiction* (1985).

Sewell, Mary Wright *see under* SEWELL, Anna

'Shearing, Joseph' *see* BOWEN, Marjorie

Shelley, Mary Wollstonecraft, née Godwin, novelist (b. Somers Town, London, 30 August 1797, d. London, 1 February 1851).

Mary Godwin was the only child of Mary *Wollstonecraft and the radical philosopher William Godwin (1756–1836). Her mother died within days of her birth and she was brought up by her father and his second wife, a Mrs Clairmont, whom he married in 1801. 'Neither Mrs. Godwin nor I have leisure enough for reducing modern theories of education to practice,' her father was recorded as saying. None the less she was raised in an intellectual household through which passed many of the leading literary figures of the day. She could read Latin and Greek and knew French and Italian. She detested her stepmother, idolized her dead mother, and sought love from her reserved and distant father. In May 1814 she met the poet Percy Bysshe Shelley, one of her father's admirers, who was then estranged from his wife Harriet Westbrook. In July Shelley and Mary, accompanied by Mary's half-sister Claire Clairmont, eloped to Switzerland. *A History of a Six Weeks' Tour*, one result of the adventure, was written by Mary with Percy's assistance and published in 1817. Mary was also pregnant, and in February 1815 gave birth prematurely to a daughter, who died soon after. A son, William, was born in January 1816. In June of 1816 Shelley, Mary, and Claire Clairmont joined Byron and his physician Dr Polidori at the Villa Diodati near Geneva. A ghost story competition was the alleged inspiration for her first novel, *Frankenstein; or The Modern Prometheus*, begun the same month and completed the following May, after their return to England. Her journal for 1815 records a formidable reading programme of Romantic poetry, eighteenth- and early nineteenth-century fiction, including *Gothic novels, travel books, history, classical literature, and a small amount of contemporary science, much of which found its way indirectly into *Frankenstein*. The novel was published in March 1818. The writing was interrupted by the deaths by suicide of her half-sister Fanny Imlay, and of Harriet Shelley, who drowned herself in the Serpentine in December 1816. Shelley and Mary were married in the same month. A daughter, Clara, was born in September 1817. After the publication of *Frankenstein* in 1818, Mary and Shelley returned to Italy, where they were to remain until Shelley's death by drowning in 1822. Clara died in Venice in 1818, followed by William in 1819. Their fourth and only surviving child Percy was born in November 1819. Mary immersed herself in Shelley's circle of friends, which included Byron, Leigh Hunt, Peacock, Thomas Jefferson Hogg, and Edward J. Trelawny. Claire Clairmont, who had a daughter by Byron, was also an intimate and, from Mary's viewpoint, an unwelcome member of the group. William Godwin made repeated financial demands on the couple, some of which were met by Shelley. Mary sent him some of the proceeds of her second novel, *Valperga*, written between 1820 and 1822, and published in 1823. After Shelley's death Mary and the 3-year-old Percy returned to England. Her relations with Shelley's family were strained, and her finances precarious. She resisted her father-in-law's demands that Percy be turned over to his care and managed to send him to Harrow and then to Cambridge on her slender income, most of which derived from her writing. Their situation improved after the death of Shelley's last child by Harriet, which left Percy the heir to his grandfather's baronetcy and estate. Mary edited Shelley's *Posthumous Poems* (1824), which were suppressed by his father. Her next novel, *The Last Man* (1826), which ends apocalyptically with the destruction of humanity by a plague, contained a fictional portrait of Shelley. *Perkin Warbeck* (1830), a historical novel, was followed by the partly autobiographical *Lodore* (1835), and *Falkner* (1837). Her novel *Matilda*, which dealt with a father's incestuous desire for his daughter, completed in 1819, was not published until 1959. She wrote for the *annuals, contributed to Dion Lardner's *Cabinet Cyclopaedia*, and prepared a four-volume edition of Shelley's *Poetical Works*, with a preface and notes, for publication in 1839. She published his *Essays, Letters from Abroad, Translations and Fragments* the following year. She and Percy travelled on the Continent between 1840 and 1843, and she published *Rambles in Germany and Italy* in 1844. At the death of Sir Timothy Shelley in 1844 the title and the estate passed to Percy, and their financial future was secure. She never completed her projected biography of Shelley, and died in London in her 54th year. Despite her subsequent novels and her devoted editing of her husband's work, she remains known for a novel which she began at the age of 19, a work about which, as she recorded in the preface to the 1831 edition, she was constantly asked 'How I, then a young girl, came to think of, and to dilate upon, so very hideous an idea'. *The Letters of Mary Wollstonecraft Shelley* have been edited by Betty T. Bennett (3 vols., 1980–8) and her *Journals* by Paula R. Feldman and Diana Scott-Kilvert (2 vols., 1987). An edition of *The Works of Mary Shelley* is in progress, edited by Nora Crook *et al.* (1995–). *See* Ellen Moers, *Literary Women* (1977); U. C. Knoepflmacher and George Levine, *The Endurance of Frankenstein* (1979); Mary Poovey, *The Proper Lady and the Woman Writer* (1984); Chris Baldick, *In Frankenstein's Shadow: Myth, Monstrosity, and Nineteenth-Century Writing* (1987); Anne K. Mellor, *Mary Shelley: Her Life, her Fiction, her Monsters* (1990).

Sheridan, Caroline Elizabeth Sarah *see* NORTON, Caroline

Sheridan, Frances, novelist and dramatist (b. Dublin, 1724, d. Blois, France, 26 September 1766).

Frances Sheridan was the youngest of the five children of the Revd. Dr Philip Chamberlaine, an Irish churchman, and his wife Anastasia Whyte. Her mother died shortly after her birth. Her father disapproved of women being taught to write, although he reluctantly agreed that she could be taught to read. She was secretly taught writing and Latin by her eldest brother and botany by another. At the age of 15 she wrote a romance, 'Eugenia and Adelaide', and two sermons. The former was later adapted for the stage by her daughter Alicia. The theatre was another activity forbidden by her father, and in 1745 she took advantage of his increasing infirmity to accompany her brothers to various Dublin productions. Her active support for the actor-manager Thomas Sheridan (1719–88), whose management of a Dublin theatre had made him the centre of controversy, led to their meeting and eventual marriage in 1747. The couple had six children, the third of whom was Richard Brinsley Sheridan (1751–1816), the dramatist. Their daughters **Alicia** (later **Lefanu**) (1753–1817) and **Elizabeth** (also later **Lefanu**) (1758–1837) both wrote. Further controversy involving Sheridan's theatre dictated a move to London in 1758, where Frances Sheridan met Samuel Richardson, who encouraged the publication of her first novel, *Memoirs of Miss Sidney Biddulph* (1761). The novel, which owed much to *Pamela*, achieved a phenomenal success, including a French adaptation and a German translation. It was followed by a comedy, *The Discovery* (1763), produced at Drury Lane by Garrick with him and Thomas Sheridan in leading roles. *The Dupe* (published 1764) was less successful and was withdrawn after three performances at Drury Lane in December 1763. Financial set-backs forced the family to move to France. They settled at Blois, where Mrs Sheridan wrote the second part of *Sidney Biddulph* (1767) and a comedy, *A Trip to Bath* (1765), which remained unpublished until 1902, and which contained a forerunner of Mrs Malaprop in her son's *The Rivals*. She also wrote a novel with a fashionable oriental setting, *The History of Nourjahad* (1767), published after her sudden death in 1766. Her granddaughter **Alicia Lefanu** (*c*.1795–*c*.1826), also a novelist, edited her *Memoirs* (1824). *See* Margaret Anne Doody, in *Fetter'd or Free? British Woman Novelists 1670–1815*, ed. Mary Anne Schofield and Cecilia Macheski (1986); Janet Todd, *The Sign of Angellica: Women, Writing and Fiction, 1600–1800* (1989).

Sherwood, Mary Martha, children's writer (b. Stanford, Worcestershire, 6 May 1775, d. Twickenham, London, 20 September 1851).

Mary Martha Sherwood was the elder daughter of Dr George Butt, rector of Stanford, Worcestershire, and chaplain to George III, and his wife Martha Sherwood. She was sent to a school at Reading Abbey which, when it later moved to London, numbered Mary Russell *Mitford and Laetitia *Landon among its pupils. She was good at Latin and wrote stories and plays, including *The Traditions* (1795), published by subscription to help the school. *Susan Gray* (1802), written to encourage religious principles in the poor, was a surprising success, and went through many pirated editions until the copyright was returned to her in 1816. In 1803 she married her cousin Henry Sherwood, an army officer whose regiment was posted to India shortly afterward. She left her daughter behind and threw herself into charitable work for soldiers' orphans in India. While in India she met and was greatly influenced by Henry Martyn, the evangelical missionary. Her story *Little Henry and his Bearer* (1814), published anonymously and sold to her publisher for £5, has been compared to Harriet Beecher Stowe's *Uncle Tom's Cabin* in popularity. It went through nearly a hundred editions, was translated into Hindustani, Assamese, Chinese, Sinhalese, French, and German, and effectively began her career as a writer of moral stories for children. *The Indian Pilgrim*, an allegory based on Bunyan's *Pilgrim's Progress*, was published in 1818, and in the same year she wrote the first part of what was to become her best-known and most influential work, *The History of the Fairchild Family*, 'a child's manual . . . calculated to show the importance and effects of religious education', as the title-page explained. In the most celebrated of the stories the Fairchilds' father shows them a rotting corpse hanging from a gibbet as a warning against family quarrels. Despite the heavy-handed moral, the children are believable, and the shock and suspense of some of the scenes makes them unintentionally attractive. It went through fourteen editions between 1818 and 1842, when a second part was published. A third appeared in 1847, and new editions continued into the twentieth century. According to the *DNB*, most children of the English middle class born in the first quarter of the nineteenth century were brought up on *The Fairchild Family*. The Sherwoods returned to Worcestershire with a family of five and three adopted orphans. Mrs Sherwood became a prison visitor and studied Hebrew in order to write a dictionary of the prophetic books of the Bible, which she completed shortly before her death. It was never published. She wrote over 300 stories and tracts, mainly directed to the young. A selection was published as *The Juvenile Library* in 1880. Her works were particularly popular in America and a collected edition was published in 1855, four years after her death. She kept a journal for most of her life, used by her daughter Sophia in her *Life of Mrs Sherwood* (1854; enlarged F. J. H. Darton 1910). **Sophia** (first **Streeten**, afterwards **Kelly**), was a co-author with her mother of several of her publications, and published a novel, *The Anchoret of Montserrat*. Mrs Sherwood's sister **Lucy Littleton Cameron**, née Butt (1781–1858) was also a voluminous and popular children's writer, whose best-known works were *The History of Margaret Whyte*, written in 1798, and *The Two Lambs* (1821). Her son Charles Cameron's *Life of Mrs. Cameron* (1862) incorporates some autobiography. *See* M. Nancy Cutt, *Mrs. Sherwood and her Books for Children: A Study* (1974).

Sidney, *see* PEMBROKE, Mary Herbert, Countess of

Simcox, Edith (Jemima), journalist and autobiographer (21 August 1844–15 September 1901).

Edith Simcox was the third child and only daughter of George Price Simcox, described variously as a merchant and a gentleman, and his wife Jemima Haslope. Both her brothers went to Oxford and both became fellows of Queen's College. Edith knew French and German, which she learned at school, some Italian, and could read Latin and basic Greek. She was also well read in English literature and philosophy. Her wide intellectual and social interests were reflected in her reviews and articles on art, literature, history, moral philosophy, economics, education, women's suffrage, and trade unions for periodicals like the *Academy*, *Fraser's Magazine*, and the *Nineteenth Century* as well as *The Times* and the *Manchester Guardian*. Her interest in women's employment led her to establish a shirt manufacturing company in Soho between 1875 and 1884 with her friend Mary Hamilton, to employ women under humane and unsweated conditions. From there she took an active interest in the trade union movement, organizing workers, speaking at meetings, writing in the press, and representing English trade unions at international labour congresses on the Continent. She was also an elected member of the London School Board 1879–82, campaigning for compulsory secular education for all children. Simcox is best known, however, for her intense, emotional friendship with George *Eliot, whom she first met in December 1872, shortly after the publication of *Middlemarch*, which she reviewed for the *Academy*. She was 28 and Eliot 53. Her passionate devotion to the novelist is recorded in a manuscript journal entitled 'Autobiography of a Shirt Maker' which she kept between May 1876 and January 1900. After Eliot's death in 1880 Simcox travelled to Warwickshire to observe the scenes of her early life and to interview people who had known her, but her ambition to write Eliot's biography was thwarted by John Cross's assumption of the task. Her 'George Eliot: A Valedictory Article' was published in the *Nineteenth Century* in May 1881. Simcox published three books, *Natural Law: an Essay in Ethics* (1877), *Episodes in the Lives of Men, Women and Lovers* (1882), and *Primitive Civilizations* (1894), a prelude to an unrealized project for a history of ownership or appropriation. All three were written in varying degrees under the inspiration of George Eliot, but the *Episodes* in particular, although fictional, reflect her love for the novelist and the emotional stresses which this caused. The 'Autobiography' remains unpublished in the Bodleian Library, Oxford. *See* K. A. McKenzie, *Edith Simcox and George Eliot* (1961).

Simpson, Helen *see under* DANE, Clemence

Sinclair, Catherine, novelist and children's writer (b. Edinburgh, 17 April 1800, d. London, 6 August 1864).

Catherine Sinclair was the fourth of the six daughters of Sir John Sinclair, a politician and agriculturalist, by his second wife Diana Macdonald. Two of her brothers became eminent clergymen. She acted as her father's secretary from the age of 14 until his death in 1835 and published her first book the following year. The preface to *Modern Accomplishments; or The March of Intellect* (1836), a study of female education, acknowledged that it had been corrected by 'a venerated parent, now no more'. She began to write children's books in order to entertain a nephew, and these alternated with adult fiction; *Modern Flirtations; or A Month at Harrowgate* (1841), *Jane Bouverie; or Prosperity and Adversity* (1846), *Sir Edgar Graham; or Railway Speculators* (1849), a topical subject for the 1840s, and *Cross Purposes* (1855), an anti-Catholic novel, also topical, were representative of her fiction. Of her children's books, *Holiday House* (1839) was her most successful and longest lived. 'Uncle David's Nonsensical Story', which forms a story within a story in the book, is regarded as the beginning of the modern fairy-tale. *Frank Vansittart; or The Model Schoolboys* (1853) and *Charlie Seymour; or The Good and Bad Choice* (1856) were also popular. She wrote works of non-fiction, including *Shetland and the Shetlanders* (1840), *Scotland and the Scotch* (1840), which was published in America and translated into several languages, *Modern Superstition*, and *Popish Legends; or Bible Truths* (1852), an appropriate subject for one of her evangelical leanings. She was well known in Edinburgh for her indefatigable philanthropy, establishing soup kitchens, drinking fountains, a mission station, and seats for pedestrians on busy roads. She did not marry, and lived in Edinburgh all her life. Her niece Lucy *Walford, also a novelist, gives an attractive picture of her in her *Recollections of a Scottish Novelist* (1910). *See also* John Rowe Townsend, *Written for Children* (1965; rev. 1974); F. J. Harvey Darton, *Children's Books in England* (3rd edn. 1982).

Sinclair, 'May' (Mary Amelia St Clair), novelist (b. Rock Ferry, Cheshire, 1863, d. Aylesbury, Buckinghamshire, 14 November 1946).

May Sinclair was the sixth child and only daughter of William Sinclair, a Scot and at one time a prosperous Liverpool shipowner, and his wife Amelia. The failure of his business in 1870 and Sinclair's intermittent alcoholism brought about the disintegration of the family. May lived with her mother until the latter's death in 1901, with sole responsibility for the family after the death of her father and four of her brothers in the 1880s. Apart from a formative year at Cheltenham Ladies' College, she was impressively self-educated, particularly in the classics, German philosophy, and English literature. Dorothea Beale, the headmistress of Cheltenham, encouraged her interest in philosophy and introduced her to the work of T. H. Green, which she later espoused in two books, *A Defense of Idealism* (1917) and *The New Idealism* (1922). She encountered the work of Freud while working at a London clinic and became interested in psychoanalysis, which she was later to explore in her fiction. Her first publication was a volume of poems, *Essays in Verse* (1891). Her novel *Audrey Craven* (1897) has been seen as an early modernist text. *The Divine Fire* (1904) won critical acclaim in America, where her reputation remained higher than in England. She met the Imagists H(ilda) D(oolittle), Richard Aldington, and Ezra Pound, who greatly influenced her. In England she became a friend and supporter of Lawrence, Eliot and Dorothy *Richardson, in a review of whose work she was the first to use the phrase 'stream of consciousness'. The best of Sinclair's twenty-four novels describe the struggles of women to escape from sexual repression and intolerable domestic confinement, which reflected her own experience. *Mary Olivier: A Life* (1919) and *Life and Death of Harriet Frean* (1922) were autobiographical. Others included *Mr and Mrs Nevill Tyson* (1898), *The Helpmate* (1907), *The Creators* (1910), and *The Tree of Heaven* (1917). She wrote a book on the *Brontës (1912), and also a fictionalized version of their lives, *The Three Sisters* (1914), regarded as one of her best works. She was an active suffragette before the First World War, working with the Women's Freedom League and for the *Women Writers' Suffrage League. She drove an ambulance at the front in the war, even though she was in her fifties, and wrote an account of it in *A Journal of Impressions in Belgium* (1915). Her later novels, written in the 1920s and 1930s, are generally regarded as less interesting, and overly preoccupied with psychoanalysis. Her reputation as one of the most significant of modernist writers declined abruptly after the early 1920s and she has not been adequately reassessed. She suffered from Parkinson's disease in the last decades of her life. *See* T. E. M. Boll, *Miss May Sinclair, Novelist* (1973); H. D. Zegger, *May Sinclair* (1976); Sydney Janet Kaplan, *Feminine Consciousness in the Modern British Novel* (1975).

'Singleton, Mary' *see* BROOKE, Frances

Singleton, Mary Montgomerie *see* FANE, Violet

Sitwell, Edith (Louisa), poet (b. Scarborough, Yorkshire, 7 September 1887, d. London, 9 December 1964).

Edith Sitwell was the eldest of the three children of Sir George Reresby Sitwell and Lady Ida Emily Augusta Denison, daughter of the Earl of Londesborough. She grew up at Renishaw Hall near Chesterfield, the family seat, where she was privately educated, most notably by Helen Rootham, who became her governess in 1903 and also her companion until her death in 1938. According to her autobiography *Taken Care of* (1965) her childhood was unhappy, due in part to her interests in music and literature, which ran counter to those of her parents, and because of her unique physical appearance, utterly unlike that of a classic Edwardian beauty. The similar interests of her two brothers Osbert (1892–1969) and Sacheverell (1897–), later her collaborators in various literary projects, compensated for parental disregard. A reading of Swinburne's *Poems and Ballads* when she was 17 persuaded her that she wanted to write poetry. She published her first poems, 'Drowned Suns' in the *Daily Mirror* in 1913 and her first book of poems, *The Mother*, in 1915 when she was 28. *Twentieth Century Harlequinade* (1916), published collaboratively with Osbert, contained seven of her poems and in the same year all three Sitwells helped to launch an annual anthology, *Wheels*, intended as an attack on *Georgian Poetry*, the official organ of the poetry 'establishment' which she and her brothers despised and against which they saw their own work as directed. *Wheels* continued until 1921 and counted as one of its major successes the publication in 1919 of seven of Wilfred Owen's war poems as well as poems by Nancy Cunard, Iris Tree and Aldous Huxley. But it was the first 'performance' in 1923 of *Façade*, the joint work of Sitwell and William Walton, then an unknown young composer, that brought her into the limelight and also brought critical abuse. Sitwell 'spoke' her poems behind a curtain painted with a female figure, eyes closed and mouth open, to demonstrate her theory that poetry should emphasize musical cadence and dissociate itself from the personality of the poet. Her highly original poems, witty and technically innovative, made use of dance music in order to expose 'the rhythmical flaccidity, the verbal deadness, the dead and expiated patterns of some of the poetry immediately preceding us'. They laid her challenge to the Georgian poets and placed her firmly in the camp of the modernists, although she returned to an earlier elegiac and romantic vein in *The Sleeping Beauty* (1924) and *Troy Park* (1925). *Gold Coast Customs* (1929), her next long poem, combined the technical virtuosity displayed in *Façade* with grim satire in juxtaposing the savagery of ancient African tribal life with contemporary European civilization. A period of silence was broken by *Street Songs* (1942), followed by *Green Song* (1944), *The Song of the Cold* (1945), and in 1947 *The Shadow of Cain.* Sitwell wrote a number of prose works in the intervals between books of poems. Some she regarded as pot-boilers. Others, such as *The English Eccentrics* (1933) and two historical works, *Fanfare for Elizabeth* (1946) and *The Queens and the Hive* (1962), had considerable success. Her only novel, *I Live under a Black Sun* (1937), based on the life of Swift, attracted little attention from the critics until her four volumes of poetry during the Second World War created a new climate of critical acclaim. She undertook lecture tours in America after the war but in the 1950s her poetry was regarded as unfashionable. Her last collections of poetry were *Gardeners and Astronomers* (1953) and *The Outcasts* (1962). She also edited numerous anthologies of poetry. Sitwell accented her unique physical features and her near six foot height by highly individualistic and stylized dressing when she appeared in public. Her portrait was painted by Wyndham Lewis, b y Roger Fry, and by her friend the Russian *émigré* artist Pavel Tchelitchev. She was also photographed by Cecil Beaton. She became a Roman Catholic in 1955. She was appointed DBE in 1954 and died in London in 1964, aged 77. Her *Who's Who* entry listed 'silence' among her recreations. *See Selected Letters 1919–64*, ed. John Lehmann and Derek Parker (1970); E. Salter, *The Last Years of a Rebel* (1967); John Lehmann, *A Nest of Tigers* (1968); John Pearson, *Façades: Edith, Osbert and Sacheverell Sitwell* (1978); V. Glendinning, *Edith Sitwell: A Unicorn among Lions* (1981).

Smedley, Menella Bute, poet and novelist (b. 1819 or 1820, d. London, 25 May 1877).

Menella Bute Smedley was the daughter of the Revd Edward Smedley, an encyclopaedia editor and poet as well as a clergyman, and his wife Mary Hume. She was educated at home by her father and later acted as his amanuensis. The family, which included several other children, lived in London until their father's illness forced a retirement to Dulwich, where he died in 1836. She began to publish didactic stories in her thirties, including *The Maiden Aunt* (1849), *The Use of Sunshine* (1852), and *Nina: A Tale for the Twilight* (1853). Her main talent, however, was for poetry. She published a collection of narrative poems, *Lays and Ballads from English History* (1856), *Poems Written for a Child* (1868, with Mrs E. A. Hart), and a longer narrative poem, *The Story of Queen Isabel* (1863). Her collected *Poems* were published in 1868 and included an unacted verse drama, *Lady Grace.* Her novels included *Twice Lost* (1863), *A Mere Story* (1865), and *Linnet's Trial* (1871). Smedley never married. Later in life she undertook philanthropic work among pauper children, editing a report on *Boarding-out and Pauper Schools Especially for Girls* (1875).

Smith, Barbara Leigh *see* BODICHON, Barbara

Smith, Charlotte, née Turner, poet and novelist (b. London, 4 May 1749, d. Tilford, near Farnham, Surrey, 28 October 1806).

Charlotte Smith was the eldest daughter of Nicholas Turner of Stoke House, Surrey, and later Bignor Park, Sussex, and his wife Anna Towers. Her mother died when she was 3 and she was brought up by her aunt, who sent her to indifferent schools at Chichester and then Kensington. Her father remarried when she was 15, and as a matter of convenience her own marriage was arranged with Benjamin Smith, the son of a wealthy West Indian merchant and a director of the East India Company. The marriage was not happy, despite the birth of twelve children, and the situation was exacerbated by Smith's wild extravagances and general fecklessness in business. At her father-in-law's death in 1776 his estate was left to his grandchildren but the will proved so complicated that Charlotte Smith spent much of her life in frustrating litigation. Benjamin Smith was imprisoned for debt in 1783, and after sharing his incarceration for several months Charlotte determined on a writing career. A collection of poems, *Elegiac Sonnets*, was published in 1784 by James Dodsley, with the help of her friend the poet William Hayley (1745–1820). Subsequent editions proved increasingly popular, particularly the expanded fifth edition (1789), which included Cowper, Charles James Fox, Horace Walpole, Thomas and Joseph Warton, and Mrs Siddons among its subscribers. Coleridge, Wordsworth, and Burns were among those who paid tribute to her sonnets. A move to France in the mid-1780s to escape creditors enabled her to translate Prévost's *Manon Lescaut* (1785) and *The Romance of Real Life* (1787), based on French criminal trials. After their return to England the couple separated, although not legally, and Charlotte gave her husband financial assistance up to his death in Berwick gaol in 1806. She considered herself to be primarily a poet, but in 1788 published *Emmeline; or The Orphans of the Castle*, the first of a series of novels by which she gained a considerable reputation as a writer of the sentimental school. It was praised by Sir Walter Scott in particular and was followed by *Ethelinde* (1789), *Celestina* (1791), *Desmond* (1792), and *The Old Manor House* (1793), which Scott considered her best work. Several of her novels, including *Emmeline*, *The Old Manor House*, and *Montalbert* (1795), contained *Gothic elements and, it was claimed, influenced the work of Ann *Radcliffe. Many contained autobiographical and contemporary references. Charlotte Smith had strong pro-Republican sympathies at the beginning of the French Revolution which she then revised in response to the Terror. Her poem *The Emigrants* (1793), dedicated to Cowper, marked the change in her views. She also wrote a series of stories, *The Letters of a Solitary Wanderer* (1799), and several children's books, including *Rural Walks in Dialogues for Young Persons* (1795) and *Conversations, Introducing Poetry* (1804). Her sister **Catherine Ann Dorset** (1750(?)–1817(?)) became a noted writer of children's books. Charlotte Smith died shortly after her husband in 1806, survived by eight of their children. *Beachy Head, with Other Poems* was published posthumously in 1807, unfinished. *See* memoir by Catherine Ann Dorset in Walter Scott, *Miscellaneous Prose Works* (1829); F. M. A. Hilbish, *Charlotte Smith: Poet and Novelist* (1941); Diana Bowstead, in *Fetter'd or Free? British Women Novelists 1670–1815*, ed. Mary Anne Schofield and Cecilia Macheski (1986); Stuart Curran in *Romanticism and Feminism*, ed. Anne K. Mellor (1988).

Smith, 'Dodie' (Dorothy Gladys) ('C. L. Anthony', 'Charles Henry Percy'), playwright, novelist, and children's writer (b. Whitefield, Lancashire, 3 May 1896).

One of the most successful women playwrights of the first half of the twentieth century, Dodie Smith is the daughter of Ernest Smith, who died when she was a baby, and his wife Ella Furber, who had once wanted to become an actress. She was brought up by her maternal grandparents William and Margaret Furber in Old Trafford, Manchester. After her mother's remarriage in 1910 she moved to London, where she went to St Paul's Girls' School and later to the Royal Academy of Dramatic Art. While there she sold a play, *Schoolgirl Rebels*, written under the pseudonym Charles Henry Percy, for a film script. She toured with various repertory companies until 1923, when she gave up the stage and went to work for Heal & Son, the furniture store. Her one-act play *British Talent* was performed at the Three Arts Club, an amateur theatre, in 1924 but her first professional success was with a romantic comedy, *Autumn Crocus* (1931), written under the pseudonym

C. L. Anthony. Her next play, *Service* (1932), about the repercussions of bankruptcy in a family department store, drew on her experience with Heal's. *Touch Wood* (1934) sustained her initial success. *Call it a Day* (1935), about a middle-class family, a favourite subject, was the first to use the name Dodie Smith and the first production to transfer to New York and later to Europe. *Bonnet over the Windmill* (1937) was not a success but *Dear Octopus* (1938), which starred Dame Marie Tempest and John Gielgud in the first production, became the best known of all her plays. The octopus of the title was the family ('that dear octopus from whose tentacles we never quite escape, nor, in our inmost hearts, ever quite wish to'). In 1939 she married Alec Macbeth Beesley, a long-time friend and her business manager. They moved to the United States, where they remained for fifteen years. While there she wrote film scripts, one play, *Lovers and Friends*, produced in New York in 1943, and her first novel, *I Capture the Castle* (1948), about an adolescent girl's awakening to love and maturity, which became a best seller. She wrote a second novel, *Letter from Paris* (1952), based on Henry James's *The Reverberator*, on her return to London and adapted *I Capture the Castle* for the stage in 1954 to critical scorn but popular approval. Smith wrote five other novels and several books for children, of which *The Hundred and One Dalmatians* (1956) was the best known, its success reinforced by a Walt Disney film in 1961. *Dear Octopus* was revived in 1967 to general critical acclaim. Her last two plays, *These People, Those Books* (1958) and *Amateur Means Lover* (1961), were not a success. She published her autobiography in four volumes: *Look Back with Love* (1974), *Look Back with Mixed Feeling* (1978), *Look Back with Astonishment* (1979), and *Look Back with Gratitude* (1985).

Smith, Sarah *see* STRETTON, Hesba

Smith, 'Stevie' (Florence Margaret), poet and novelist (b. Hull, 20 September 1902, d. Devon, 7 March 1971).

Stevie Smith was the daughter of Charles Ward Smith, a shipping agent, and his wife Ethel Spear. When the family business failed Charles Smith joined the merchant navy, rendering himself only an intermittent presence in his daughter's life. She was brought up in Palmers Green, London, by her mother, who died when she was 16, and an adored aunt, the 'lion aunt' who later figured in much of her work. She spent three years in a sanatorium recovering from tuberculosis and then went to Palmers Green High School and to the North London Collegiate School for Girls. After school she took a secretarial course and obtained her first and only job as a secretary with the publishing house of Newnes, where she worked for over thirty years. She wrote her first novel on the firm's yellow copying paper. *Novel on Yellow*

Paper (1936) was followed by *Over the Frontier* (1938) and *The Holiday* (1949), all three autobiographical in content. It was with her poetry, however, that her originality was immediately apparent. She published eight volumes, beginning with *A Good Time was Had by All* (1937). Her verse, witty, caustic, at times enigmatic, contemporary in idiom, and containing vivid imagery, dealt with much the same subject-matter as her fiction, personal relationships, social manners, loneliness, love, and death. According to Anthony Thwaite she was 'primarily a poet of the odd, the disconcerting, the unexpected'. Other volumes included *Tender Only to One* (1938), *Mother, What is a Man?* (1942), *Harold's Leap* (1950), *Not Waving but Drowning* (1957), the title poem of which is probably her best-known work, *The Frog Prince and Other Poems* (1966), *The Best Beast* (1969), and *Scorpion and Other Poems* (1972). Many of the poems were illustrated by her own line drawings. The publication of her *Selected Poems* in 1962 and a selection in the Penguin Modern Poets series in the early 1960s first gave her a substantial audience. She was well known as a reader of her own work, both on recordings and at poetry readings, which flourished in the 1960s. In 1969 she received the Queen's Gold Medal for Poetry. She died of a brain tumour at the age of 68. Her poems were posthumously gathered in *The Collected Poems of Stevie Smith* (1975). Jack Barbera and William McBrien edited *Me Again: Uncollected Writings of Stevie Smith* (1981). Rosamond *Lehmann, Naomi *Mitchison, and Sylvia *Plath were among the admirers of her work. *See* Kay Dick (ed.), *Ivy* [Compton-Burnett] *and Stevie* (1971); Jack Barbera and William McBrien, *Stevie* (1985); Frances Spalding, *Stevie Smith: A Critical Biography* (1988).

'Somers, Jane' *see* LESSING, Doris

Somerville, Edith (Anna Oenone), of Somerville and Ross ('Geilles Herring'), novelist (b. Corfu, 2(?) May 1858, d. Drishane, Castlehaven, Country Cork, 8 October 1949.

Edith Somerville was the eldest of the eight children of Thomas Henry Somerville, an army officer, and his wife Adelaide Eliza Coghill. Both families were prominent in the Anglo-Irish ascendancy. Eight generations of Somervilles had lived in the eighteenth-century Drishane House, County Cork, where Edith Somerville grew up. She was educated by governesses, with a brief spell at Alexandra College, Dublin. She also studied painting in London, Düsseldorf, and Paris, and had several one-man shows in London and New York. Her other main interest was riding. It was while working as an artist for the *Graphic* that she met her second cousin Violet Martin ('Martin *Ross'). The two were immediately attracted to each other, sharing an interest in family genealogy, in riding, and in writing. They began work on their first novel, *An Irish Cousin* (1889), in which Violet Martin supplied most of the text and Somerville the illustrations. It was published under the pen-names Martin Ross and Geilles Herring. Somerville then dropped her pseudonym, and the partnership became known as Somerville and Ross. *Naboth's Vineyard* (1891), their next novel, presented a harsh view of Catholic Ireland, and contained a melodramatic plot. In 1894 they wrote what is generally regarded as their best work, *The Real Charlotte*, about an older woman who corrupts a young girl. *The Silver Fox* (1897) was set in the west of Ireland, with numerous hunting scenes. Their most successful and most reprinted work was a collection of comic stories, *Some Experiences of an Irish RM* (1899), RM standing for Resident Magistrate. *Further Experiences* (1908) and a second sequel, *Mr. Knox's Country* (1915), capitalized on the early success. *Dan Russel the Fox* (1911) again had hunting as a background. After her mother's death in 1895 Somerville took over the running of the family estate, and, like Violet Martin's house at Ross, it ate into most of her income. Both women learned Irish in response to growing nationalism, and both supported the suffragettes, but without militancy. Somerville became chairman of the Munster Women's Franchise League and was also a cautious advocate of independence for Ireland, criticizing the government's suppression of the 1916 uprising. Neither of the cousins married. They lived on their respective estates, communicating by letter, travelling often in England, Ireland, and Europe, and writing up their travels in books like *Through Connemara in a Governess Cart* (1893), *In the Vine Country* (1893), and *Beggars on Horseback* (1895). Ross became a virtual invalid after a riding accident in 1898 and died in 1915. Somerville maintained that she was still in touch with her and published further titles by Somerville and Ross, including *Irish Memories* (1917), *Mount Music* (1919), and *The Big House of Inver* (1925). She was given an honorary doctorate of letters by Trinity College, Dublin, in 1932, and continued to publish fiction into the 1940s. She farmed her estate, with the help of a brother and a sister, until 1946, was a local Master of Fox Hounds, and published her last book in 1949, the year of her death. The Somerville and Ross partnership produced fourteen books before Violet Martin's death, books which collectively present an acute, often satirical perspective on Anglo-Irish life before 1916. Molly *Keane edited a selection of their letters (1989). *See* John Cronin, *Somerville and Ross* (1972); Hilary Robinson, *Somerville and Ross: A Critical Appreciation* (1980).

Somerville, Mary, writer on science (b. Jedburgh, 26 December 1780, d. Naples, 29 November 1872).

The daughter of Admiral, later Sir William, Fairfax and his second wife

Margaret Charters, Mary Somerville was brought up in the home of her aunt and later mother-in-law Martha Somerville, at Burntisland, near Edinburgh. Her father was absent on foreign service for much of her childhood, but at one point instructed that she should read a chapter of the Bible and an article from the *Spectator* each day. Her formal education was at an indifferent boarding school at Musselburgh. At an early age she read Hester *Chapone's *Letters on the Improvement of the Mind* and followed the course of study it recommended. She taught herself Latin and read for two hours every morning before breakfast with her uncle, despite the disapproval of her aunt. Her interest in mathematics was kindled when she discovered some algebra in a puzzle at the back of a book of fashion. Her brother bought her a copy of Euclid and of Bonnycastle's *Algebra*. In 1804 she married Samuel Greig, a naval officer and the Russian consul for Britain. While not encouraging, her husband did not prevent her from studying mathematics. Greig died in 1807, leaving her with two young sons, and in 1812 she married her cousin Dr William Somerville, who actively sympathized with her intellectual interests. She was particularly keen that the two daughters of this marriage should have as complete an education as their brothers. In 1816 they moved to London, where she attended lectures at the Royal Institution and met eminent members of the intellectual and scientific community including Brougham, Melbourne, Macaulay, Herschel, Lyell, and Whewell. She also corresponded with Humboldt, Arago, and Laplace. She presented her first scientific paper to the Royal Society in 1826 and in 1827 Brougham asked her to write a book for the Society for the Diffusion of Useful Knowledge on Laplace's *Le Mécanique céleste*. Its publication in 1831 raised her to the first rank in scientific circles. Her next work, *The Connection of the Physical Science* (1834), a summary of research into physical phenomena, went through several editions. *Physical Geography*, which followed in 1848, was delayed in part by her husband's illness and subsequent travel, but like its predecessor went through many editions. Her final work, *Molecular and Microscopic Science*, was published in 1869, in her 89th year. Mary Somerville's ability to grasp all aspects of scientific research and to write about them intelligibly made her one of the most remarkable women of her generation. Henry Morley claimed she was the first to shake man's comfortable faith in the incapacity of women for scientific thought. She left her library to Girton College, Cambridge. Somerville Hall, later College, Oxford, was named after her. *See Personal Recollections of Mary Somerville*, ed. Martha Somerville (1873); Elizabeth C. Patterson, *Mary Somerville and the Cultivation of Science 1815–1840* (1983).

'Somerville and Ross' *see* SOMERVILLE, Edith Anna Oenone, *and* Ross, Martin

Southcott, Joanna, prophetic writer (b. Gittisham, Devon, April 1750, d. London, 27 December 1814).

Joanna Southcott was the fourth daughter of William Southcott, a small farmer, and his wife Hannah. She rejected several suitors and worked as a domestic and also as an upholsterer in and around Exeter until she was over 40. Although scantily educated she read the Bible regularly and was a communicant of the established Church. In 1791 she joined the Wesleyans, and on Easter Monday 1792 claimed to have had an apocalyptic vision. She then issued a series of sealed prophecies, challenging a group of local clergy to testify as to the truth of her forecasts. Only one supported her. In 1801 she paid for the printing of *The Strange Effects of Faith*, the printer including a bill of 2*s.* 6*d.* 'for correcting the spelling and grammar of the prophecies'. Several clergymen now became her followers and urged her move to Paddington, where she began to 'seal' her followers, entering their names on the list of the elect and gaining over 140,000 adherents, the nucleus of a powerful millenarian movement. Her writings were subjected to three separate 'trials', and in 1802 she predicted she would give birth to Shiloh, the second Christ. She showed symptoms of pregnancy in the spring of 1814 and went into seclusion, where she died in December. No evidence of pregnancy was found. Her disciples constituted a strong religious force even after her death, and her return was predicted as late as 1874. Joanna Southcott's writings were numerous and their ephemerality makes them bibliographically complicated. Estimates run as high as sixty-five separate works, and many unpublished manuscripts have been discovered. Two books of verse, *Song of Moses and the Lamb* (1804) and *Hymns or Spiritual Songs* (1807), were collected from her writings. Her *Life* and *Memoirs* were published in 1814. *See* James K. Hopkins, *A Woman to Deliver her People* (1982).

Southey, Caroline Anne *see* BOWLES, Caroline Anne

Spark, Muriel, novelist, poet, and short story writer (b. Edinburgh, 1 February 1918).

Muriel Spark was born in Edinburgh of Anglo-Jewish parents, Bernard Camberg, an engineer, and his wife Sarah Elizabeth Maud Uezzell. Of her native city she once wrote, 'Edinburgh is the place that I, a constitutional exile, am essentially exiled from.' She went to James Gillespie's School for Girls, the inspiration for the setting of her best-known novel *The Prime of Miss Jean Brodie* (1961), and then to Heriot Watt College. She spent some time in southern Africa between 1937 and 1944, an experience reflected in *The Go-away Bird and Other Stories* (1958). In 1937 she married Sydney Oswald Spark, whom she later divorced, and had one son. She worked in the political intelligence department of the Foreign Office during the war, later recalled in *The Hothouse by the East River* (1973), and then as a journalist. She became secretary of the Poetry Society, edited *Poetry Review* from 1947 to 1949, and established the short-lived literary magazine *Forum* (1949–50). Her first books were literary studies, of Mary *Shelley (1951; revised 1988), of Emily *Brontë (jointly with Derek Sandford, 1953), and of John Masefield (1953). She edited a collection of essays on Wordsworth (1950, with Derek Sandford), selections of Emily Brontë's poems (1952), Mary Shelley's letters (1953), the Brontës' letters (1954), and Newman's letters (1957, with Derek Sandford). In 1951 she won a short story competition organized by the *Observer*. Spark became a Roman Catholic in 1954 and shortly after, encouraged by Macmillan's, her publishers, redirected her literary energy to the writing of fiction. Her first novel, *The Comforters* (1957), published at the age of 39, was praised by Evelyn Waugh, whose influence on her work, particularly its satirical vein, was to become more pronounced. *Robinson* (1958), about a Catholic convent, was followed by *Memento Mori* (1959), a macabre and witty story about a group of old people and the first novel to receive substantial critical attention. It was adapted for the stage in 1964. *The Ballad of Peckham Rye* and *The Bachelors*, both published in 1960, demonstrated her fondness for juxtaposing the supernatural with prosaic actuality. *The Prime of Miss Jean Brodie*, about a charismatic Edinburgh teacher, remains her best-known work and was adapted for the stage in 1966, for the cinema in 1969, and for television in 1978. *The Girls of Slender Means* (1963), set in a wartime hostel for women, was adapted for radio in 1964 and for television in 1975. *The Mandelbaum Gate* (1965), an uncharacteristic and technically innovative work set in Jerusalem, won the James Tait Black Memorial Prize. Subsequent novels, *The Public Image* (1968), *The Driver's Seat* (1970), *Not to Disturb* (1971), *The Abbess of Crewe* (1974), *The Takeover* (1976), *Territorial Rights* (1979), *Loitering with Intent* (1981), *The Only Problem* (1984), *A Far Cry from Kensington* (1988), and *Symposium* (1990), variously combine the real with the illusory, the comic with the macabre, the uncanny with the rational. As critics have noted, Spark is fascinated by the bizarre underpinnings of superficially conventional lives. Her Catholicism works itself out in her fiction by her preoccupation with the nature of good and evil. She published *The Fanfarlo and Other Verse* (1952), *Collected Poems I* (1967), and *Going up to Sotheby's and Other Poems* (1982). Her short stories were collected in 1967 and 1987. She has written one play, *Doctors of Philosophy* (1963), several radio plays, and two books for children. Her autobiography *Curriculum Vitae* was published in 1992. A study by her one-time collaborator Derek Sandford (1963), according to Spark, is not reliable. *See* Patricia Stubbs, *Muriel Spark* (1973); Peter Kemp, *Muriel Spark* (1974); Ruth Whittaker, *The*

Faith and Fiction of Muriel Spark (1982); Alan Bold (ed.), *Muriel Spark: An Odd Capacity for Vision* (1984); Judy Sproxton, *The Women of Muriel Spark* (1992).

Speght, Rachel, polemicist and poet (b. London, 1597).

Rachel Speght was the daughter of the Revd James Speght, rector of St Mary Magdalene, Milk St., and then of St Clement in Eastcheap, and not, as is sometimes suggested, of Thomas Speght, the editor of Chaucer. Rachel Speght was the first to reply to Joseph Swetnam's notorious *An Araignment of Lewde, Idle, Froward and Unconstant Women* (1613). Her *A Mouzell for Melastomus: The Cynicall Bayter of, and Foule Mouthed Barker against Evahs Sex* was published in 1617. Dedicated to 'all vertuous Ladies Honourable or Worshipfull and to all other of Hevahs sex fearing God', it used Scripture to emphasize women's traditional virtues and to restore their character. She carefully separated her argument for women's spiritual equality from her acceptance of their social and political inferiority. The dedication to Speght's second work, an allegorical poem, *Mortalities Memorandum, with a Dreame Prefix'd, Imaginarie in Manner, Reall in Matter* (1621), showed her sensitivity to accusations that her first work had been written by her father and her determination to disprove them. In 'The Dream', a psychodrama, she produced a counter-myth to that of the Garden of Eden by detailing a pilgrimage from natural ignorance to divine knowledge. The characters Thought, Experience, Knowledge, Industrie, and Disswasion participate in the process which brings the central female character to a state of true knowledge which will lead to full humanity and then to immortality. Little is known of Speght's life after the publication of her two works, except that she married William Procter, a gentleman, in 1621 at the age of 24 and had two children. *See* Simon Shepherd, *The Women's Sharp Revenge* (1985); Elaine V. Beilin, *Redeeming Eve: Women Writers of the English Renaissance* (1987); Mary Nyquist and Margaret Ferguson (eds.), *Re-membering Milton* (1987).

'Speranza' *see* WILDE, Jane Francesca Elgee, Lady

Stanhope, Lady Hester (Lucy), traveller (b. Chevening, Kent, 12 March 1776, d. Djouni, Syria, 23 June 1839).

The eldest daughter of Charles, Viscount Mahon, later third Earl of Stanhope, and his first wife Hester Pitt, sister of William Pitt (the younger), Hester Stanhope and her sisters received an indifferent education, largely ignored by their socializing and abstracted parents. She lived for a while with her grandmother and from 1803 until his death in 1806 kept house for her famous uncle. She acted as his hostess and became a trusted confidante despite numerous indiscretions. Pitt once confided, 'I let her do as she pleases;

for if she were resolved to cheat the devil she could do it.' She declared that the pension of £1,200 which he bequeathed to her would not keep her in an appropriate style, and set out in 1810 for the Middle East, accompanied by her physician Charles Lewis Meryon and a small retinue. After a love affair with Michael Bruce, the son of a Scots nobleman and eleven years her junior, and a shipwreck off Rhodes, she settled at Djouni, on the slopes of Mount Lebanon, in Syria, building a fortress-like encampment from which she held court to European visitors, intrigued against British consular officials, and presided over her 'domain' as a self-styled and increasingly eccentric empress. Lamartine and Sir Arthur Kinglake as well as numerous other travellers visited her and recorded their impressions of her masculine Eastern dress and her lengthy conversations in which she harangued her visitors often for hours on end. Her generosity to the poor and her prodigal life-style eventually resulted in substantial debts. Lord Palmerston, then Foreign Secretary, appropriated the bulk of her pension to settle them and Lady Hester in turn wrote abusive letters to him and to the Queen in protest. In the end she shut herself up in her house, walled up the gate, refused to see any visitors, and died in isolation. Charles Meryon prepared the *Memoirs of Lady Hester Stanhope* 'as related by herself in conversations with her Physician' for publication in 1845 (repr. 1985), followed by the *Travels of Lady Hester Stanhope* 'forming the completion of her memoirs' in 1846 (repr. 1983). *See Life and Letters of Lady Hester Stanhope*, ed. C. L. W. Primrose, Duchess of Cleveland (1897); Lytton Strachey, in *Books and Characters: French and English* (1922); Joan Haslip, *Lady Hester Stanhope* (1934); J. B. Watney, *Travels in Araby of Lady Hester Stanhope* (1975); *The Essays of Virginia Woolf I* (1986).

Stannard, Mrs Arthur *see* WINTER, John Strange

Stark, Freya (Madeline), travel writer, autobiographer (b. Paris, 31 January 1893).

Freya Stark is the elder of the two daughters of Robert Stark, a painter and sculptor, and his wife Flora Stark, also his cousin, a pianist and portrait painter. Her childhood alternated between her father's home near Dartmoor, Asolo, near Venice, and Piedmont, in northern Italy, where her mother had grown up. As a child she had almost no formal education. Between 1912 and 1914 she read English and then changed to history at Bedford College, where her mentor was the scholar and critic W. P. Ker, then Quain Professor of English, later professor of poetry at Oxford. She nursed in Italy during the First World War and in 1921 began to learn Arabic, studying briefly at the School of Oriental Studies in London. Despite recurring ill health she persisted with her study of Arabic and sailed for Beirut and extensive travels in the Middle and Near East in 1927. Her more than twenty travel books, beginning in 1933 with *Baghdad Sketches*, mediate the Arab world for the European reader and are firmly based in historical sources, supplemented by first-hand accounts of her extensive and intrepid travels. Many are illustrated by her near-professional photographs. They include *The Valleys of the Assassins* (1934), *The Southern Gates of Arabia* (1936), *Seen in the Hadramaut* (1938), *A Winter in Arabia* (1940), *Letters from Syria* (1942), *East is West* (1945), and *Perseus in the Wind* (1948). Her travels won medals from the Royal Asiatic Society, the Royal Scottish Geographical Society, and the Royal Geographical Society. During the Second World War she was used by the British government to help woo the Arabs to the allied cause. In 1947 she married Stewart Henry Perowne, an English diplomat and expert on the Middle East. The first volume of her engaging four-volume autobiography *Traveller's Prelude* (1950) charts her late Victorian childhood, which straddled English middle-class country life, bohemian London, and Anglo-Italian cultural circles. It ends with her departure on her travels. Further volumes, *Beyond Euphrates* (1951), *The Coast of Incense* (1953), and *Dust in the Lion's Paw* (1961), take the story to the end of the war. *The Journey's Echo* (1963) collects excerpts from the travel books and the autobiography. Eight volumes of her *Letters* (1914–80) have been edited by Lucy and Caroline Moorehead (1974–82). *Over the Rim of the World: Selected Letters* was published in 1988. She was appointed DBE in 1972. *See* Caroline Moorehead, *Freya Stark* (1985).

Stead, Christina (Ellen), novelist (b. Rockdale, Sydney, Australia, 17 July 1902, d. April 1983).

Christina Stead's parents David George Stead and Ellen Butters were both Australian-born children of, in her words, 'youthful English immigrants of poor origin'. Her father was a naturalist in the government fisheries department and later the architect of the New South Wales state trawling industry. He was also a Fabian socialist. Her mother died when she was 2 and her father remarried shortly after, producing six half-brothers and sisters whom she helped to raise and to whom she told partly remembered, partly invented stories. These experiences later formed the background of *The Man who Loved Children* (1940). She went in succession to St George High School, Sydney Girls' High School, and Sydney Teachers' College. Although she qualified as a teacher she disliked teaching (her voice was not strong enough), and she took a course in business studies and then worked at a series of office jobs in order to save enough money to go to Europe. *For Love Alone* (1944) reflects this part of her life and also her ideas about love and female sexuality. She arrived in London in 1928, took a job with a grain merchant, and the following year went to Paris, where she found a secretarial job in a bank. In 1929 she met William Blake, an American banker with Marxist leanings and also a writer of historical romances and books on economics. They spent the period between 1929 and 1937 in France and Spain. *The Salzburg Tales* (1934), a collection of stories told by persons of different backgrounds gathered in Salzburg for the annual festival, was begun before she left Australia and published in 1934. Three major novels followed; *Seven Poor Men of Sydney* (1934), regarded as one of the first Australian modernist novels and set in the depression years, *The Beauties and the Furies* (1936), about student life in Paris, and *The House of All Nations* (1938), a study of the world of international finance, also set in Paris, and her longest novel. In 1937 Stead and Blake moved to the United States, where she worked for a while (uncongenially) as a script writer for Metro-Goldwyn-Mayer and briefly as an instructor at New York University. Several more novels were written in America, including *Lettie Fox: Her Luck* (1946), which, like *For Love Alone*, examined female sexuality, *A Little Tea, a Little Chat* (1948), set in New York with a monstrous egoist as protagonist, and *The People with the Dogs* (1952), about an American family. *I'm Dying Laughing*, posthumously published in 1987, about an old-style American communist couple, also drew on her years in the United States, particularly on her period in Hollywood. In 1953 Stead and Blake, who were married in 1952, settled in Surbiton, in Surrey, where they remained until Blake's death in 1968. Her last three novels focused on English characters. The effects of post-war poverty are brutally portrayed in *Cotter's England* (1967), originally published as *The Dark Places of the Heart* (1966). *The Little Hotel* (1973) satirizes English expatriates in Switzerland and *Miss Herbert* (1976) is a study of an Englishwoman. *The Puzzleheaded Girl* (1967), a collection of four novellas, was also published during her years in England. After Blake's death in 1968 Stead returned to Australia to a fellowship in creative arts at the Australian National University at Canberra, a post she held until her retirement in 1980. She remained in Australia until her death in her 81st year. *Ocean of Story*, another collection of stories, was published posthumously in 1986. Greatly neglected during the early and middle part of her career, with her works largely out of print, Stead's reputation grew steadily during the 1960s and 1970s. The American poet and critic Randall Jarrell introduced a new edition of *The Man who Loved Children* in 1966. She received the Patrick White Award in 1974 and was several times nominated for the Nobel Prize for Literature. Much earlier a perceptive Rebecca *West named her 'one of the few people really original we have produced since the [First World] War'. Of herself Stead once wrote, 'I am not puritan, nor party . . . nor political but on the side of those who have suffered oppression, injustice, coercion, prejudice and have been harried from birth.' *See* Ron

Geering, *Christina Stead* (1969); Diana Brydon, *Christina Stead* (1987); Susan Sheridan, *Christina Stead* (1988); Chris Williams, *Christina Stead: A Life of Letters* (1989); Mary Lynn Broe and Angela Ingram (eds.), *Women's Writing in Exile* (1989); Judith Kegan Gardiner, *Rhys, Stead, Lessing and the Politics of Empathy* (1989).

Stern, G(ladys) B(ertha), novelist (b. London, 17 June 1890, d. 19 September 1973).

G. B. Stern (she later adopted the name Bronwyn in place of Bertha) was the second daughter of Albert Stern and his wife Elizabeth Schwabacher. The family, who were involved in the gem industry, lost their money in a financial crash when she was 14, and they spent the next ten years living in a series of hotels, boarding houses, and flats. She left Notting Hill High School at 16 to travel with her parents in Germany and Switzerland, attended schools in both countries, and eventually spent two years at the Academy of Dramatic Art. She wrote her first play, for production in the billiard room, at 7, and her first poem, published in a periodical, at 17. The first of her forty novels, *Pantomime* (1914), was written when she was 20. *Twos and Threes* (1916) was the first to attract serious critical attention, followed by *Children of No Man's Land* (1919). But it was her series of novels about the large, idiosyncratic, and Jewish Rakonitz family, loosely based on her own ('half truth, half invention'), for which she was best known: *The Tents of Israel* (1924), reissued as *The Matriarch* (1948), *A Deputy was King* (1926), *Mosaic* (1930), *Shining and Free* (1935), and *The Young Matriarch* (1942). The first was dedicated to John Galsworthy, a tacit acknowledgement of the influence of the *Forsyte Saga*. The first three were collected as *The Rakonitz Chronicles* in 1932 and an omnibus edition, *The Matriarch Chronicles*, was published in 1936. Mrs Patrick Campbell starred in a stage version of *The Matriarch* in 1929. The matriarch of the title was Stern's despotic great-aunt Anastasia, who was reportedly 'looking for Gladys with a gun' when the novels were first published. Toni, the 'young matriarch', bears some resemblance to Stern herself. In 1919 she married Geoffrey Lisle Holdsworth, a New Zealand journalist whom she met through her friend Noel Coward, but they were later divorced. Stern wrote several plays, as well as two books on Jane *Austen with her friend Sheila *Kaye-Smith, and a study of Robert Louis Stevenson. She began a series of autobiographical reminiscences in her forties: *Monogram* (1936), *Another Part of the Forest* (1941), *Trumpet Voluntary* (1944), *Benefits Forgot* (1949), and *A Name to Conjure with* (1953). She converted to Roman Catholicism in 1947 and described the experience in *All in Good Time* (1954).

'Strafford, Mary' *see* MAYOR, F. M.

Streatfeild, (Mary) Noel ('Susan Scarlett'), novelist and writer for children (b. Amberley, Sussex, 24 December 1895, d. 11 September 1986).

Noel Streatfeild was one of the five children of the Revd William Champion Streatfeild, vicar of St Leonards-on-Sea and later Suffragan Bishop of Lewes, and his wife Janet Venn. Elizabeth Fry, the prison reformer, was her great-great-grandmother. Their strict late Victorian clerical household and her resentment of her sisters turned her into a rebel. (She once found her father on his knees praying for guidance as to how to deal with his difficult daughter.) She went to St Leonard's Ladies' Academy, where she was taught by Sheila *Kaye-Smith but later expelled, and then to Laleham School, Eastbourne. She and her sisters performed in parish plays and concerts as children and after war work at the Woolwich Arsenal she went to the Academy of Dramatic Art. She acted professionally for nearly ten years, touring England, South Africa, Australia, and New Zealand as 'Noelle Sonning', but after her father's death in 1929 gave up the theatre in order to write. Her first novel, *The Whicharts* (1931), the story of three young girls struggling in the world of show business, was later recast as *Ballet Shoes* (1936), an unsentimental view of children working professionally in the theatre and probably the best known of all her books. It originated a sub-genre of career-orientated children's books. *Tennis Shoes* (1937), her own favourite, was about a difficult and conceited younger sister who eventually becomes a star player. Streatfeild spent several months on tour with a circus to research the background for *The Circus is Coming* (1938), the story of two orphans who run away to a circus to join their uncle, which won the Carnegie Medal. During the Second World War she worked as an air-raid warden and organized food distribution centres for the Women's Voluntary Service. She continued to write adult fiction, addressing illegitimacy, divorce, prostitution, and homosexuality in *Caroline England* (1937) and *The Winter is Past* (1940), and in *Aunt Clara* (1952) upholding religion and family bonds. She published twelve novels under the pseudonym Susan Scarlett between 1939 and 1951. She continued to write for children during the war, with *The House in Cornwall* (1940) and *The Children of Primrose Lane* (1941), both run-of-the-mill adventure stories, and *Party Frock* (1945), about a village pageant. Popular later books included *White Boots* (1951), about professional skating, *The Growing Summer* (1966), set in Ireland, *Thursday's Child* (1970), about an Edwardian orphan, and *The Boy Pharaoh, Tutankhamen* (1972), a historical biography written for children. Various short series were written around the Bell family (1954–60), the Maitlands (1978–9), and Gemma, a child film star (1968–9). Streatfeild became, as she once said ruefully, 'a national institution' in the world of children's books, reviewing, lecturing, campaigning against horror comics, and appearing on children's book programmes. Several of her books were serialized on television. Her output and sales were prodigious and included plays, a biography of E. *Nesbit (1958), and three volumes of fictionalized autobiography, *A Vicarage Family* (1963), *Away from the Vicarage* (1965), and *Beyond the Vicarage* (1965). *See* Barbara Ker Wilson, *Noel Streatfeild* (1961); Angela Bull, *Noel Streatfeild: A Biography* (1984).

'Stretton, Hesba' (Sarah Smith), children's writer, novelist, and tract writer (b. Wellington, Shropshire, 27 July 1832, d. Ham, Surrey, 8 October 1911).

Sarah Smith was the third daughter and fourth of the eight children of Benjamin Smith, a provincial bookseller and publisher, and Ann Bakewell, a fervent evangelical who died when Sarah was 8. She attended a local day school but received most of her education from reading the books in her father's shop. In 1859 her sister Elizabeth sent one of her stories to Dickens, who published 'The Lucky Leg' in *Household Words* and sent her a cheque for £5. She subsequently published a story in every Christmas number of *All the Year Round*, the successor to *Household Words*, until 1866, including 'The Travelling Post Office' in *Mugby Junction* in December 1866. Thinking her name not sufficiently interesting for an author, she changed it to Hesba Stretton. Hesba comprised the first letters of the names of each of her remaining brothers and sisters in order of age and Stretton from the village of All Stretton in Shropshire. Her first successful story, *Jessica's First Prayer* (1867), published initially in the magazine *Sunday at Home*, became a legend in publishing history. It sold over a million and a half copies and was translated into most European as well as Asian and African languages. It was the story of a street urchin or 'street arab' and demonstrated Stretton's first-hand knowledge of slum conditions and the life of destitute children in large cities. (She and her sister lived in Manchester for several years before moving to London.) Tsar Alexander II ordered a copy to be placed in every Russian school. *Little Meg's Children* (1868) and *Alone in London* (1869) together sold three-quarters of a million copies. Stretton published fifty volumes between 1866 and 1906, most of them religious and moral tales published by the Religious Tract Society, for which she became a favourite author. Later in her career she wrote full-length novels, including *The Clives of Burcot* (1866), *Paul's Courtship* (1867), *David Lloyd's Last Will* (1869), *The Doctor's Dilemma* (1872), *Hester Morley's Promise* (1873), and *Through a Needle's Eye* (1879). These were written in a less didactic vein, and directed at older readers. Stretton devoted much of her energy to charitable activities. Child abuse was a particular concern. Along with Angela Burdett Coutts she helped to found the London Society for the Prevention of Cruelty to Children in 1884. She also organized the collection of £1,000 for the relief of peasants in the Russian famine of 1892. She led an austere personal life, eschewing the theatre and an interest in personal possessions, despite her relative financial success. She was housebound due to ill health for four years before her death in 1911. *See* Margaret Maison, *Search your Soul, Eustace* (1961); R. L. Wolff, *Losses and Gains* (1977); J. S. Bratton, *The Impact of Victorian Children's Fiction* (1981).

Strickland, Agnes, historian and novelist (b. London, 19 August 1796, d. Southwold, Suffolk, 13 July 1874).

Agnes Strickland was one of the nine children of Thomas Strickland, who worked for a shipping company, and his second wife Elizabeth Homer. Six of the Strickland children became writers. **Elizabeth** (1794–1875) substantially assisted Agnes in her historical works. **Jane Margaret** (1800–88) published a history of Rome (1854), edited by Agnes. Samuel (1809–1867) emigrated to Canada and recorded his experiences in *Twenty-Seven Years in Canada* (1853), also edited by Agnes. **Catherine Parr Traill** (1802–99), another emigrant to Canada, became an accomplished naturalist as well as a writer of juvenile fiction, and published sketches and essays about settler life. **Susanna** (later **Moodie**) (1803–85) emigrated to Canada after marriage and wrote several books about Canada as well as sentimental novels. Their father took charge of the education of Agnes and Elizabeth, teaching them Greek, Latin, and mathematics and encouraging their interest in history. The family fortunes, however, were in steady decline throughout most of their childhood, and Strickland's death from gout in 1818 was in part the result of anxiety over his financial difficulties. Publishing became a virtual necessity. Agnes published several volumes of poetry and some translations of Petrarch, wrote for the *annuals, and co-edited *Fisher's Juvenile Scrapbook.* She and Elizabeth wrote several successful children's books and together planned a series of biographies of female sovereigns, obtaining permission to dedicate the work to the young Queen *Victoria. The first two volumes of *The Lives of the Queens of England* appeared in 1840 with only Agnes's name on the title-page, despite Elizabeth's extensive contribution. Agnes undertook exhaustive research for the books in official records and in private manuscript collections. When Lord John Russell refused her permission to consult state papers, as a woman, she circumvented him by lobbying Lord Normanby. The French historian Guizot was so impressed by her work that he arranged for her to have access to the French official archives. The twelfth and final volume of *The Lives of the Queens* was published in 1848. Meanwhile in 1842–3 she published the *Letters of Mary, Queen of Scots,* dedicated to Jane *Porter, whose father had helped her with Russian sources. Helped by Elizabeth, she published the *Lives of the Queens of Scotland* (1850–9), *Lives of the Bachelor Kings of England* (1861), *Lives of the Seven Bishops Committed to the Tower in 1688* (1866), and in 1868 *Lives of the Tudor Princesses*. In the course of her career she also wrote four novels: *Alda, the British Captive* (1841), *How Will it End?* (1865), and two historical novels, *Guthred, the Widow's Slave* (1875) and *The Royal Brothers* (1875). Her last historical work, *Lives of the Last Four Princesses of the Royal House of Stuart*, was published in 1872. She was granted a civil-list pension in 1870, suffered partial paralysis after a fall in 1872, and died in 1874. Strickland's most successful work, *The Lives of the Queens of England*, passed entirely as her own, despite the substantial number of entries done by Elizabeth. In 1863 the sisters managed to purchase the copyright from Henry Colburn's executrix prior to a six-volume edition, published in 1864–5, which sold over 11,000 copies. It continued to have a steady sale throughout the later decades of the century. Strickland's strength as a historian was her phenomenal energy in locating and using original sources. Her popularity rested on her eye for domestic and gossipy detail, but her work was uncritical and her objectivity marred by her innate Toryism. Her sister Jane wrote her biography. *See* J. M. Strickland, *Life of Agnes Strickland* (1887); Una PopeHennessey, *Agnes Strickland: Biographer of the Queens of England 1796–1874* (1940).

Strickland, Elizabeth and Jane Margaret *see under* STRICKLAND, Agnes

'Struther, Jan' (Joyce Anstruther, later Placzek), journalist, short story writer, and poet (b. 6 June 1901, d. New York, 20 July 1953).

Jan Struther's pen-name was an adaptation of her family name of Anstruther. Her father Henry Torrens Anstruther was a magistrate, one-time MP, and Lord of the Treasury. Her mother Eva, daughter of the fourth Baron Sudeley, was a writer and was created DBE for her work as Director of the Camps Library, set up in 1914 to supply books to the troops. Jan was educated privately in London and in 1917 began her long career as a journalist. She contributed verses, articles, and short stories to various publications including the *London Mercury*, *Punch*, the *Spectator*, the *New Statesman* and *The Times*. In 1923 she married Anthony Maxtone Graham, an insurance broker, by whom she had two sons and a daughter. Her first collection of poems, *Betsinda Dances*, was published in 1931, followed by *Sycamore Square* (1932), *The Modern Struwwelpeter* (1936), a collection for children, and *The Glass-Blower* (1940). She is chiefly known, however, for the creation of a single character, Mrs Miniver, a middle-class English housewife, plucky, patriotic, and conventional, who, with her husband, family, and the neighbours, first appeared in a series of articles on the court page of *The Times* in 1937. The paper's management saw the articles as a means of attracting female readers whose own lives Mrs Miniver was intended to reflect. The articles were so popular they were collected as a book (1939), which was only modestly successful in Britain but which became a Book of the Month Club choice and a best seller in America. To American readers Mrs Miniver symbolized a particular kind of British fortitude during the early years of the war. The book was the origin of a Hollywood film (1942) which, it was later acknowledged, substantially aided the British cause. The Minivers were constantly confused with Struther's own family. She moved to America in 1940 with two of her children, where she lectured and undertook propaganda work. Her first marriage was dissolved and in 1948 she married A. K. Placzek, a Columbia University librarian. She also published a collection of her articles from *Punch* and the *Spectator, Try Anything Twice* (1938), and edited another collection, *Women of Britain* (1941). She died in New York. *See* Alison Light, *Forever England: Femininity, Literature and Conservatism between the Wars* (1991).

Stuart-Wortley, Lady Emmeline (Charlotte Elizabeth), poet and travel writer (b. 2 May 1806, d. Beirut, November 1855).

Born into a privileged background, Emmeline Stuart-Wortley was the second daughter of John Henry Manners, fifth Duke of Rutland, and his wife Lady Elizabeth Howard, daughter of the Earl of Carlisle. Her brother Lord John Manners (1818–1906) was one of the leaders of the 'Young England' movement, a group of aristocratic young Tories who later associated with Disraeli. Her father was the author of several books of travel. In 1831 she married the Honourable Charles Stuart-Wortley, by whom she had three children. She began to publish poetry after her marriage, beginning with *Poems* (1833) and progressing to a volume a year for the next eleven years. Several were the result of her travels on the Continent, including *Travelling Sketches in Rhyme* (1835), *Impressions of Italy* (1837), and *Sonnets* (1839), written during a tour which extended as far as Hungary and Turkey. Many of her poems appeared first in Blackwood's Magazine. She was reviewed by H. N. Coleridge in the *Quarterly*, and others, perhaps tongue in cheek, compared her work in quality and quantity to that of the Duchess of *Newcastle and Laetitia *Landon. She edited two issues of the well-known *annual the *Keepsake* in 1837 and 1840, which brought her into contact with metropolitan literary circles which included Caroline *Norton, the Countess of *Blessington, and the elderly Mary *Shelley. Tennyson contributed a poem to one of her issues. Stuart-Wortley became an intrepid traveller, producing a three-volume account of her *Travels in the United States* in 1851 and another in 1853. While on a tour of the Middle East in 1855 she broke a leg after being kicked by a mule but insisted on continuing her journey from Beirut to Aleppo and returning across the Lebanon. She died on her return to Beirut.

Sullivan, Arabella *see under* DACRE, Lady

Sulter, Maud, poet and journalist (b. Glasgow, 1960).

Born in Scotland of mixed races, Maud Sulter began to write from the age of 3, when in bed with measles. She was brought up by her white working-class grandfather, who shared writing sessions at the kitchen table, and her mother, 'who took care of putting food on the table, clothes on my back and paying the rent'. As president of her students' union she campaigned in 1979 for civil rights issues and against the anti-abortion bill, and wrote of her own abortion in her story 'On Bleecker' (1985). Her poem 'As a Blackwoman' politicizes the act of bearing a black child after centuries of rape and persecution: 'As a blackwoman | the bearing of my child | is a political act.' It won the Vera Belle Prize in 1984, was praised by Grace *Nichols, and became the title poem of her first collection (1985), dedicated to her grandfather. Sulter's work has appeared in various anthologies, including *Watchers and Seekers*, ed. Rhonda Cobham and Merle Collins (1987), and in the feminist magazine *Spare Rib.* She writes in Glaswegian English in 'Thirteen Stanzas' about a friend who died from a hysterectomy, and in 'Under Attack' about violence toward women: 'The stigmata on my smooth | blackskinned thigh | appeared | not by divine | intervention | but | at the end | of a pair of | twelve inch shears.' As a journalist Sulter has campaigned for publishing opportunities for black women in a white publishing establishment. *Passion* (1990), which she edited, is a collection of discourses on black women's creativity. Other work includes *Zabat: Narratives* (1989) and *Necropolis* (1990). She has also edited *Echo: Works by Women Artists 1850–1940* (1991). She writes about her work in Lauretta Ngcobo (ed.), *Let it be Told: Essays by Black Women in Britain* (1987).

Sutcliff, Rosemary, novelist and children's writer (b. West Clandon, Surrey, 14 December 1920, d. 23 July 1992).

Rosemary Sutcliff was the daughter of a naval officer and spent her first ten years in various postings before settling in Devon. When she was 2 she contracted Still's disease, an arthritic condition which eventually confined her to a wheelchair. Disabilities and scars, both physical and mental, and the adjustment to them feature prominently in her fictional worlds. She was taught at home by her mother, who read aloud to her frequently, and went to school for the first time at the age of 9. The work of Kipling was a formative influence from this early period as were the real adventure stories told by her father and his naval friends. She left school 'mercifully early' at 14 and then went to Bideford School of Art, where she excelled at miniature painting, but was told that larger-scale work would be impossible because of her handicap. She began to write, working on the retelling of legends from British history. Oxford University Press, after refusing one manuscript, suggested she tackle the Robin Hood legend. *The Chronicle of Robin Hood* was published in 1950, the first of a series of historical novels for children and adults which emphasized the continuity of past and present and the contiguity of peoples, Picts, Scots, Romans, Saxons, and Normans, from which modern Britain developed. *The Eagle of the Ninth* (1954), serialized on the BBC's *Children's Hour*, initiated a sequence set in Roman Britain which included *The Silver Branch* (1957), *The Lantern Bearers* (1959), winner of the Carnegie Medal, and, much later, *Frontier Wolf* (1980). An actual and a symbolic link between the stories, a ring passed from father to son, stressed the continuity of history. *The Mark of the Horse Lord* (1965), about a freed Roman gladiator who impersonates a North British chief, was set in the same period and is often regarded as her best book. Other favoured periods were the Dark Ages, the setting for *Outcast* (1955) and *Dawn Wind* (1961), the Bronze Age, the scene of *Warrior Scarlet* (1958), as well as Norman and Viking Britain. *Blood Feud* (1977), set against the Viking excursions to the Black Sea, was filmed for television in 1991. The legend of King Arthur formed the background for another sequence beginning with *Sword at Sunset* (1963), followed by *Tristan and Iseult* (1971), *The Light beyond the Forest* (1979), and *The Sword and the Circle* (1981). Sutcliff's early books were criticized for their stilted and artificial dialogue, but latterly her characters' carefully adapted speech came to be regarded as one of her strengths. Her books have fictional rather than historical characters, frequently male adolescents on the brink of adulthood who undergo testing circumstances and conflicts of loyalty. Meticulously researched backgrounds, a sense of place, and a remarkable understanding of military tactics have been instanced as reasons for her success as a historical novelist, her works totalling fifty-three volumes. She claimed not to distinguish between books for children and those for adults: 'I have very little idea what makes the difference between one of my children's books and one of my adult books . . . I don't write for adults, I don't write for children . . . I write for some small, inquiring thing in myself.' She was appointed CBE in 1992 and was a fellow of the Royal Society of Literature. Her autobiography *Blue Remembered Hills: A Recollection* (1983) concentrates on her early years. *See* Margaret Meek, *Rosemary Sutcliff* (1962); John Rowe Townsend, *A Sense of Story* (1971).

tttttttttttttttt

T

Talbot, Catherine, essayist, letter writer, and bluestocking (b. Berkshire, May 1721, d. London, 9 January 1770).

Catherine Talbot was the only child of Edward Talbot, a fellow of Oriel College, Oxford, who, upon his marriage to Mary Martyn, the daughter of a prebendary of Lincoln Cathedral, resigned his fellowship to become Archdeacon of Berkshire. Edward Talbot's father had been Bishop of Durham, and his brother became Lord Chancellor. His early death in 1720, some months before Catherine's birth, left his widow in straitened circumstances. She and her young child were given a home by one of her husband's protégés, Edward Secker, and his wife. Secker became successively Bishop of Oxford, Dean of St Paul's, and Archbishop of Canterbury. Mrs Talbot and Catherine remained members of his household until his death in 1768, associating with prominent members of society, both clerical and literary, while Catherine took charge of his charitable activities. Secker supervised her early education in the Scriptures and in modern languages. She knew French, Italian, German, and a little Latin. She was also tutored in geography and astronomy, and became a proficient water-colourist. Through her astronomy tutor she was introduced to Elizabeth *Carter, who became a lifelong friend and correspondent. Catherine wrote miscellaneous essays and poems in a commonplace book which became known as 'The Green Book'. Despite the encouragement of her friends, she did not publish in her lifetime, confining her work to her 'considering drawer', apart from one paper in Dr Johnson's *Rambler* (no. 30, June 1750). She was instrumental, however, in urging Elizabeth Carter to publish her translation of Epictetus. The two were particularly friendly with Samuel Richardson, who discussed the development of his novel *Sir Charles Grandison* with them and sent them parts of it to read before publication. Catherine suffered from poor health for much of her adult life and eventually died of cancer at the age of 49. After her death Elizabeth Carter arranged for the publication of her collection of religious and moral essays *Reflections on the Seven Days of the Week* (1770), which went through more than ten editions. A two-volume collection, *Essays on Various Subjects* (1772), followed. Several editions of her collected *Works* were published from 1772, but she is best known for her lively letters to Elizabeth Carter between their meeting in 1741 and her death in 1770, which were published by the latter's nephew in 1809. *See* M. Pennington, *Memoirs of the Life of Mrs. Elizabeth Carter* (1807); Sylvia H. Myers, *The Bluestocking Circle* (1990).

Taylor, Ann, née Martin, writer of conduct books (b. 20 June 1757, d. Ongar, Essex, 4 June 1830).

Ann Martin married Isaac Taylor, engraver and later Congregational minister of Colchester and then of Ongar, in 1781. She participated fully with him in the education of their children, of whom six of the original eleven survived to adulthood. The method of education was based on a series of instruction booklets and charts, and Ann Taylor supplemented this by reading aloud. She corresponded assiduously with her children when they were away from home, and the correspondence became the nucleus of a series of conduct books. She was encouraged to write and then to publish by the literary success of her two elder daughters *Ann and *Jane. Like all the family's publications, the books had a widespread sale. Titles included *Advice to Mothers* (n.d.), *Maternal Solicitude for a Daughter's Best Interests* (1813), *Practical Hints to Young Females* (1815), *The Present of a Mistress to a Young Servant* (1816), and *Reciprocal Duties of Parents and Children* (1818). Ann Taylor also published *The Family Mansion* (1819), *Retrospection: A Tale* (1821), *The Itinerary of a Traveller in the Wilderness* (1825), and *Correspondence between a Mother and her Daughter at School* (1817). She died at Ongar less than a year after her husband, and six years after her daughter Jane. *See* Isaac Taylor, *The Family Pen* (1867); D. M. Armitage, *The Taylors of Ongar* (1938), C. Duff Stewart, *The Taylors of Ongar: An Analytical Bio-Bibliography* (1975).

Taylor, Ann, afterwards Gilbert, poet (b. Islington, London, 30 January 1782, d. Nottingham, 20 December 1866).

Ann Taylor, as she was best known, was the eldest of the eleven children of Isaac Taylor of Ongar (1759–1829) and his wife Ann Martin *Taylor, prominent members of the Nonconformist community in Essex. Isaac Taylor was a skilled engraver as well as a Congregational minister, and several of his children, particularly *Jane and her brother Isaac (1787–1865), later known as Isaac Taylor of Stanford Rivers, began to write collectively from an early age, a family enterprise which eventually encouraged their parents to write. The children were taught the techniques of engraving and the girls in particular assisted in their father's productions. Ann was the first to publish, contributing to an *annual, *The Minor's Pocket Book*, published by the firm of Darton & Harvey, from 1798. It was the publishers who encouraged Ann and Jane to produce their first notable work, the two-volume *Original Poems for Infant Minds* (1804–5), which went through many editions during the nineteenth century, and won the admiration of Keats, Southey, and Scott, among others. It was primarily the work of Ann (49 poems), and Jane (43), but there were contributions from Isaac Taylor (father and brother), from Bernard Barton, a Quaker poet, and Adelaide *O'Keefe (1776–1855), who contributed a quarter of the whole. This was followed by *Rhymes for the Nursery* (1806), by Ann and Jane, which was equally successful, and remained in print until 1907, with five American editions and a German translation. Their third joint publication was *Hymns for Infant Minds* (1810), which acknowledged the influence of Isaac Watts and modestly professed to emulate his *Divine Songs*. The reputations of both sisters rested on these three publications. *Original Poems* went through fifty-two editions by 1881, *Rhymes for the Nursery* forty-four by the same date, and there were fifty-six editions of the *Hymns* by 1886. The sisters also wrote *Rural Scenes* (1805) and *City Scenes* (1806), sketches in prose and verse with some contributions from their brother Isaac and illustrations by their father. *Limed Twigs to Catch Young Birds* (1808) was a reading manual, *Signor Topsy-Turvey's Wonderful Magic Lantern* (1810) a series of rhymes based on role reversals. In 1813 Ann Taylor married the Revd Josiah Gilbert, classical and mathematics tutor at the Congregational college at Masborough near Rotherham, who proposed marriage before he met her on the strength of having read her poems. They lived first in Rotherham, then Hull, and eventually Nottingham, with his various ministerial callings, and raised a large family. Jane died in 1824. Ann survived to emend some of the subsequent editions of the *Songs* and *Hymns*, to contribute to a collection of *Original Hymns* in 1842, and to write a *Memoir* of her husband in 1853. She also published *The Wedding among the Flowers* (1808), an imitation of William Roscoe's children's work *The Butterfly's Ball and Grasshopper's Feast*, which appeared in the same year and prompted numerous imitations. The relative merits of Ann and Jane Taylor were a popular subject of discussion among their contemporaries, and the authorship of individual poems was not always clear. Ann is best known for 'My Mother' and 'The Notorious Glutton', and for her hymn 'I thank the goodness and the grace'. The influence of Isaac Watts on the work of the Taylors is clear. There are links too with Blake's *Songs of Innocence and Experience.* Ann Taylor's *Autobiography* was published posthumously in 1874. *See* Isaac Taylor, *The Family Pen* (1867); D. M. Armitage, *The Taylors of Ongar* (1938); C. Duff Stewart, *The Taylors of Ongar: An Analytical Bio-Bibliography* (1975).

Taylor, Elizabeth, novelist and short story writer (b. Reading, Berkshire, 3 July 1912, d. Penn, Buckinghamshire, 19 November 1975).

Elizabeth Taylor was the daughter of Oliver Coles and his wife Elsie Fewtrell. She went to the Abbey School, Reading, where she wrote secretly and determined on becoming a novelist. After leaving school she worked as a governess and as a librarian and in 1936 married John William Kendall Taylor, a confectionery manufacturer. They had a daughter and a son. They settled in the village of Penn, in Buckinghamshire, which, Jane *Austen-like, she considered a more accommodating setting for a writer than London: 'Village-life, with its wider differences—in every social sense—seems a better background for a woman novelist and certainly more congenial to me.' Her witty and penetrating novels of middle-class life and manners in the prosperous Thames Valley commuter belt have often been compared to those of Austen and Elizabeth *Bowen. Her first, *At Mrs. Lippincote's*, was published in 1945, when she was 34. *Palladian* followed in 1946 and after that she published a novel more or less every two years. *A Wreath of Roses* (1949) became a best seller. Others included *A Game of Hide and Seek* (1951), *The Sleeping Beauty* (1953), *Angel* (1957), which some consider her best, and which the Book Marketing Council named as one of the 'Best Novels of our Time', *In a Summer Season* (1961), *The Soul of Kindness* (1964), *The Wedding Group* (1968), and *Mrs. Palfrey at the Claremont* (1971). The last, a study of old age, was adapted for television. Many of her short stories were published in the *New Yorker* as well as in *Harper's Magazine* and *Harper's Bazaar*, which won her a large American following. Her collections of stories, *Hester Lilly* (1954), *The Blush* (1958), *A Dedicated Man* (1965), and *The Devastating Boys* (1972), are characterized by what the novelist Angus Wilson styled 'warm heart, sharp claws and exceptional powers of formal balance'. She died at the age of 63. *See* Robert Liddell, *Elizabeth and Ivy* [Compton-Burnett] (1986).

Taylor, Harriet, feminist writer (b. London, 1807, d. Avignon, France, 1858).

Harriet Taylor was the fourth of the seven children of Thomas Hardy, a London surgeon, and his wife Harriet Hurst. At 18 she married John Taylor, a wholesale druggist eleven years her senior, allegedly to escape her domineering father and an unhappy home life. They had two sons and a daughter. John Taylor was an active Unitarian and associated with the parliamentary Radicals. The couple were members of a circle which included the eminent Unitarian preacher W. J. Fox, Sarah Flower *Adams, and Harriet *Martineau. Through the Fox circle Harriet Taylor met John Stuart Mill, then recovering from a nervous breakdown, in 1830. Their attraction was immediate, Mill enjoying the company of a clever woman and Harriet finding the intellectual stimulus lacking in her marriage. After attempts to end the sexually innocent but intense relationship John Taylor agreed to an arrangement whereby Harriet spent much of her time at a house at Walton-on-Thames where she was visited by Mill, while outward appearances of normal married life were maintained. Two years after Taylor's death from cancer in 1849 Mill and Harriet Taylor were married. Their long and unorthodox relationship had made them inevitably the subject of gossip and as a result they tended to shun society after their marriage, a situation which irritated many of Mill's friends. Harriet Taylor was a crucial influence on Mill's thinking and writing. Their essays on marriage, which they exchanged in 1831–2, reveal her views to be the more advanced of the two on the subject, advocating women's financial independence within marriage and their responsibility for children. Taylor contributed reviews and poems to the Unitarian *Monthly Repository* but much of her intellectual energy was directed towards suggestions and revisions of Mill's work. She had a substantial influence on his *Principles of Political Economy* (1848), on the essay *On Liberty* (1859), and on his *Autobiography* (1873), all of which went unacknowledged. An appreciative dedication of the *Principles of Political Economy* was withdrawn on John Taylor's objection. Her most important influence, however, was on Mill's developing feminism. An article on 'The Enfranchisement of Women' in the *Westminster Review* in 1851 was largely written by Harriet Taylor, but, as was usual for quarterly reviews, was published anonymously. They jointly wrote an article on brutality within the family in the *Morning Chronicle* in August 1851, which appeared under Mill's name. It was reproduced for private distribution in 1853. Taylor was undoubtedly an inspiration behind Mill's *Subjection of Women*, published after her death in 1869, although the ideas expressed in it were distinctly his. She died from tuberculosis while they were travelling in France in 1858, after a marriage of only seven years. Harriet Taylor remained a controversial figure among Mill's friends even after her death, many resenting her influence over him, as well as their secluded life. Assessments of her intellectual ability as well as her input into Mill's work were exaggerated, negatively by Mill's friends and positively by Mill himself, particularly during his years of mourning. Feminist historians of late have come to regard her work as an important influence on the women's movement of the 1850s. Her daughter Helen Taylor (1831–1907) took over her mother's role as a companion to Mill and *The Subjection of Women* was published partly due to her encouragement. Helen Taylor in turn became a crucial figure in the movement for women's rights. *See John Stuart Mill and Harriet Taylor: Their Correspondence and Subsequent Marriage*, ed. F. A. Hayek (1951); Alice S. Rossi (ed.), *Essays on Sex Equality: John Stuart Mill and Harriet Taylor* (1970); Malcolm Hardman, *Six Victorian Thinkers in Context* (1991).

Taylor, Jane, poet (b. London, 23 September 1783, d. Ongar, Essex, 13 April 1824).

Jane Taylor was the second of the eleven children of Isaac Taylor of Ongar, an engraver and Nonconformist minister, and his wife Ann Martin *Taylor. The family became known as 'The Taylors of Ongar', a kind of literary collective, which had its beginning when *Ann, the eldest, began to contribute to the *annual *The Minor's Pocket Book* in 1798. Jane Taylor's first contribution was 'The Beggar's Boy', and at the encouragement of the publishers Darton & Harvey the sisters went on to write *Original Poems for Infant Minds* (1804–5), *Rhymes for the Nursery* (1806), and *Hymns for Infant Minds* (1810), all of which were phenomenally successful and established their reputation as poets for the young. Jane Taylor's best-known contribution was 'Twinkle twinkle little star'. *Rural Scenes* (1805) and *City Scenes* (1806), *Limed Twigs to Catch Young Birds* (1808), *Signor Topsy-Turvey's Wonderful Magic Lantern* (1810) and *Original Hymns for Sunday Schools* (1812) were interspersed with the major publications. The co-operative ventures ended in 1813 with Ann Taylor's marriage to the Rev Josiah Gilbert. Jane and her brother Isaac moved to Devon for two years and then to Cornwall, where she wrote *Display: A Tale for Young People* (1815) and *Essays in Rhyme on Morals and Manners* (1816). Her contributions to the *Youth's Magazine* between 1816 and 1822 were collected as the *Contributions of Q. Q.* (1824). Jane Taylor's health had always been precarious. She devoted herself to parish work with her parents at Ongar, and died prematurely of cancer in 1824 at the age of 40. Robert Browning was a known admirer of Jane Taylor's prose, and Walter Scott of her poetry. Her *Memoirs and Correspondence* were published in 1825. *See* H. C. Knight, *Jane Taylor: Her Life and Letters* (1880); Isaac Taylor, *The Family Pen* (1867); D. M. Armitage, *The Taylors of Ongar* (1938); C. Duff Stewart, *The Taylors of Ongar: An Analytical Bio-Bibliography* (1975); Stuart Curran, in *Romanticism and Feminism*, ed. Anne K. Mellor (1988).

'Teachwell, Mrs' *see* FENN, Lady Eleanor

Tennant, Emma (Christina) ('Catherine Aydy'), novelist and journalist (b. London, 20 October 1937).

Emma Tennant is the daughter of Christopher Grey Tennant, second Baron Glenconner, and his wife Elizabeth Powell. She was born in London but evacuated at the age of 2 to a decrepit baronial castle near Peebles, where she went to the village school and treasured her rural isolation. When the family returned to London she was sent to St Paul's Girls' School; she left at 15 and went instead to an idiosyncratic finishing school in Oxford, 'the most exciting and informative period of my life'. She studied art history briefly in Paris and returned to London to become a débutante. She worked as the travel correspondent of *Queen* and then the features editor of *Vogue*, contributed to the *Listener* and the *New Statesman*, and in 1975 founded *Bananas*, a literary magazine to encourage new writing, which she edited until 1978. Her first novel, *The Colour of Rain*, about young upper-class London and influenced by her then father-in-law Henry Green, was published under the pseudonym Catherine Aydy in 1964. Alberto Moravia reportedly found it 'a symbol of the decadence of English writing today', resulting in a nine-year silence before she published *The Time of the Crack* (1973, republished as *The Crack* (1978)), a futuristic fable about a fissure in the Thames which combined black humour, satire, and apocalyptic vision and invited comparisons with H. G. Wells, Orwell, and Evelyn Waugh. It was published under her own name, as is all her subsequent fiction. *The Last of the Country House Murders* (1974) was also set in the future, and parodied the country house party detective fiction of the 1930s and 1940s. Fantasy and reality, dreams and fictions, blend in *Hotel de Dream* (1976), one of whose characters is a romantic novelist. Tennant's fiction consciously reworks earlier novels and styles, as in *The Bad Sister* (1978), which is modelled on James Hogg's *Confessions of a Justified Sinner* (1824), and exchanges modern sexual politics for the Scottish Calvinism of the original. *Queen of Stones* (1982) similarly reworks William Golding's *Lord of the Flies* (1954) from a female perspective and, like *The Bad Sister*, has female protagonists. *Woman beware Woman* (1983), its title a deliberate echo of Middleton's *Women beware Women*, deals with treachery on both a public and private level among its three female protagonists. *The Adventures of Robina, by Herself* (1987) is a pastiche of Defoe which draws on her experiences as a débutante. *Two Women of London: The Strange Case of Ms. Jekyll and Mrs. Hyde* (1989) is a crime novel loosely based on Stevenson's original. *The Magic Drum* (1989) both parodies an Agatha *Christie-style detective novel and appropriates the legend of Sylvia *Plath. The world of childhood was a central theme in Tennant's early fiction, particularly in two highly experimental works, *Wild Nights* (1979) and *Alice Fell* (1980), which blend realism and fantasy and eschew conventional plots. *Black Marina* (1985) is her most explicitly political novel, with direct bearing on events in Grenada in the early 1980s. As the title suggests, like the story of Shakespeare's *Pericles* it is about a daughter's search for a father. 'The Cycle of the Sun' is the overall title of a series of novels intending to explore contemporary English life from the 1950s to the 1980s, of which two have so far appeared: *House of Hospitalities* (1987) and *A Wedding of Cousins* (1988). *Sisters and Strangers: A Moral Tale* (1990) is a retelling of the story of Eve, within a fairy-tale format. *Faustine* (1991) is a contemporaty satirical version of *Faust*, involving three generations of women in one family. She also wrote the film script for *Frankenstein's Baby* (1990). Tennant is the general editor of *In Verse*, and editor of Penguin's 'Lives of Modern Women' series. She has two daughters and a son and lives in London. *See* John Haffenden (ed.), *Novelists in Interview* (1985).

'Tey, Josephine' *see* MACKINTOSH, Elizabeth

Thackeray, Anne Isabella *see* RITCHIE, Anne Isabella

Thirkell, Angela (Margaret) ('Leslie Parker'), novelist (b. Kensington, London, 30 January 1890, d. Bramley, Surrey, 29 January 1961).

Angela Thirkell was the eldest child of John William Mackail (1859–1945), a classical scholar and later professor of poetry at Oxford, and his wife Margaret Burne-Jones, the only daughter of the painter Edward Burne-Jones. The family's London home was a meeting-place for literary, artistic, and political figures. Sir Edward Poynter, the painter, was a great-uncle. Stanley Baldwin, later Prime Minister, and Rudyard Kipling were her mother's cousins. Kipling encouraged her early attempts at poetry. Her brother Denis Mackail (1892–1971) also became a novelist. She went to St Paul's Girls' School, where she was a prefect, a prize winner, and a star gymnast and pianist, but left at 16 for finishing school in Paris. In 1911 she married James Campbell McInnes, a singer, by whom she had two sons, and a daughter who died in infancy. Her son Colin McInnes (1914–76) became a writer. She divorced McInnes for cruelty and adultery in 1917 and the following year married an Australian engineer, George Launcelot Allnutt Thirkell, by whom she had a third son. They left England for Australia (the harrowing journey is graphically described in *Trooper to the Southern Cross* (1934), published under the pseudonym Leslie Parker), where she found life culturally as well as financially impoverished. She wrote articles, short stories, and scripts for Australian radio, but in 1930 she left Australia and her husband for good. She returned to England and began to write for a living as well as acting as a publisher's reader. *Three Houses* (1931), which drew on her late Victorian childhood amidst famous Victorians, was followed by the autobiographical *Ankle Deep* (1933) and *Wild Strawberries* (1934), considered one of her best novels. The revival of interest in Trollope in the 1930s possibly sparked off her own neo-'Barsetshire' novels, loosely modelled on the originals, chronicles of genteel, snobbish, late nineteenth-century rural life. Even the titles are reminiscent of Trollope: *Pomfret Towers* (1938), *The Brandons* (1939), *Cheerfulness Breaks in: A Barsetshire War Survey* (1940), *Northbridge Rectory* (1941), *Marling Hall* (1942), *The Duke's Daughter* (1951). The 'Barsetshire' novels fitted the mood of the 1930s better than that of the post-war years, when Thirkell's popularity declined and her work seemed faintly anachronistic and her humour acid. She continued to write into her seventies, producing a total of thirty-three novels, children's stories, and a biography of Harriette Wilson (1936), the eighteenth-century courtesan. She also wrote introductions for reprints of works by Jane *Austen, Elizabeth *Gaskell, Thackeray, and Trollope. Her last novel, *Three Score and Ten* (1961), was unfinished at her death, and was completed by C. A. Lejeune. *See* her son Graham McInnes's memoir in *The Road to Gundagai* (1965); Margot Strickland, *Angela Thirkell: Portrait of a Lady Novelist* (1977).

Thomas, Elizabeth ('Corinna'), poet (b. 1675, d. London, 5 February 1731).

Elizabeth Thomas was the daughter of Emmanuel Thomas of the Inner Temple and his wife Elizabeth Osborne. Her father died when she was 2, leaving her mother in financial difficulty. She claimed to have had nine months' tutoring in Latin, writing, mathematics, pharmacy, and chemistry, but otherwise taught herself. She corresponded with John Norris of Bemerton, the Cambridge Platonist, through whom she came to know Mary *Astell, whose work she admired and to whom she addressed a poem, 'To Almystrea, on her Divine Words'. Mary *Chudleigh was also a correspondent whose feminist views she shared. In 1699 she sent two of her poems to Dryden, who professed to see similarities with Orinda (Katherine *Philips), and suggested she adopt the pen-name Corinna. She contributed a poem to *Luctus Britannici* (1700), a collection of elegies in Dryden's honour, which attracted the attention of Richard Gwinnett, a lawyer and writer, who courted her for nearly sixteen years before proposing marriage. She was also a friend of Henry Cromwell, a minor writer in Pope's circle, although probably not his mistress, as had been thought. Her mother's illness prevented marriage to Gwinnett, who died in 1717, leaving her a small legacy. Legal difficulties over this and her mother's debts plunged her into poverty and seclusion. She published her *Miscellany Poems* (1722), which were reissued in 1726 and 1727, and sold some letters of Pope, given to her by Henry Cromwell, to the notorious publisher Edmund Curll, who promptly published them (1726). This earned her some savage lines as 'Curll's Corinna' in *The Dunciad* in 1728, and contributed to her unflattering reputation in subsequent years. In 1727 she was confined to the Fleet Prison for debt, where she continued to write and to receive intermittent charity from various notable figures. *Codrus; or The Dunciad Dissected* (1728) may have been written by her and Curll. An inaccurate account by her of Dryden's death and funeral appeared in *Memoirs of William Congreve* (1730), published by Curll, and in the same year she published *The Metamorphosis of the Town; or A View of the Present Fashions.* Her correspondence with Gwinnett, published posthumously as *Pylades and Corinna* in 1731–2 (vol. ii is titled *The Honourable Lovers*), was prefaced by a highly unreliable autobiography, the 'Life of Corinna' which she was writing at her death. As well as enduring poverty and imprisonment she suffered for many years from the effects of swallowing a chicken bone in 1711, a celebrated case which was presented to the College of Physicians in 1730. She was eventually released from prison and died in lodgings in Fleet St. in 1731.

Thompson, Flora, autobiographer, essayist, poet (b. Juniper Hill, near Brackley, Oxfordshire, 5 December 1876, d. Brixham, Devon, 21 May 1947).

Flora Thompson was the eldest of the six surviving children of Albert Timms, a stone mason, and his wife Emma Lapper, a nursemaid. Family life was 'somewhat harsh and restricted' due to poverty, maternal discipline, and her father's drinking, but not unhappy. She walked three miles to school and back every day between the ages of 5 and 12. Her insatiable desire to read and also to write persuaded her mother not to send her into service at 12, the usual pattern for village girls, but instead she became a post office clerk at the village of Fringford and then at Greyshott, in Surrey, where she met her husband John Thompson, also a post office clerk. They married in 1900 and moved to Bournemouth, where two children were born. She read and wrote secretly to avoid the disapproval of her husband and in-laws, won a prize for an essay on Jane *Austen, and published an article and a short story in a local paper. Encouraged by this modest success, she then wrote 'small sugared love stories' to earn money for her children's education. In 1920 she began a monthly column of notes on nature and country life for the *Catholic Fireside* which continued until 1927; these were later titled *The Peverel Papers.* She also wrote essays for the *Daily News* and for various women's magazines and worked as a ghost writer for a big game hunter whose work appeared in *Chambers's*

Journal, the *Scottish Field*, and various African papers. The family then moved from Bournemouth to Liphook in Hampshire, where her third child was born when she was 41. Urged by her friend the Scottish poet Ronald Campbell Macfie, she published a collection of poems, *Bog-Myrtle and Peat*, in 1921, the lukewarm reception of which persuaded her she ought not to become a poet. Through the pages of the *Catholic Fireside* she founded the Peverel Society, a correspondence club for aspiring writers to whom she offered constructive criticism and encouragement for nearly eighteen years while also working in her husband's post office. In 1937 she began a series of sketches about her childhood. 'Old Queenie' was published in the *Lady* and 'May Day' in the *Fortnightly Review*. They were expanded to form part of *Lark Rise*, the first of her autobiographical trilogy, published in 1939. *Over to Candleford* was written in 1940 and published the following year and, like the first volume, was an immediate success. The death of her younger son in 1940, when his convoy was torpedoed, was a shock from which she never fully recovered. *Candleford Green*, written reluctantly in nine months and published in 1943, gave her little pleasure, although it was the most popular of the three. They were collected as *Lark Rise to Candleford* in 1945 and a fourth volume, *Still Glides the Stream*, was completed shortly before her death in 1947, at the age of 70. Another autobiographical volume, *Heatherley*, was written between *Candleford Green* and *Still Glides the Stream* but was not published until 1976. The three volumes of *Lark Rise to Candleford* are part fiction, part autobiography, part social history, although none of the categories alone is adequate. According to Margaret Lane they form a genre of their own, a unique view of a passing rural society, remembered from a child's experience and written by a 'creative mind . . . at work on the bedrock level'. Comparisons have been made with Mary Russell *Mitford's *Our Village* but Thompson, in Lane's view, does not have Mitford's genteel detachment. Instead she writes the annals of the poor totally without sentiment and from the position of one of their number. *A Country Calendar and Other Writings*, ed. Margaret Lane (1979), contains selections from the *Catholic Fireside* articles. *The Peverel Papers* were reprinted, ed. Julian Shuckburgh (1986). *See* Margaret Lane, *Flora Thompson* (1957; repr. 1976); Gillian Lind *Flora Thompson: The Story of the Lark Rise Writer* (1990).

Tighe, Mary, poet (b. Dublin, 9 October 1772, d. Woodstock, County Kilkenny, 24 March 1810).

Mary Tighe was the daughter of the Revd William Blachford, a wealthy Irish clergyman who was also a librarian, and his wife Theodosia Tighe, a prominent supporter of the Methodist movement in Ireland. Her father died shortly after her birth, and she was given an education appropriate to a gentlewoman by her mother, who was a granddaughter of the Earl of Darnley and a descendant of the first Earl of Clarendon. Latin and Greek, modern languages, and large amounts of English poetry, however, also featured in the programme. In 1793 she married her cousin Henry Tighe, a Member of the Irish Parliament, a historian, and a Latin poet. The marriage was not happy and to add to her misery she developed consumption, to which her family was susceptible. Partly to console herself at the prospect of continuing ill health she wrote a long poem, in Spenserian stanzas, on the legend of Cupid and Psyche (Spenser had been an admired poet in her youth). *Psyche; or The Legend of Love* was privately printed in 1805, and published in 1811, the year after her premature death at the age of 38. The profits went to build a wing of an orphan asylum in Wicklow. The poem was constantly republished in the nineteenth century, including at least one American edition, and was widely admired by, among others, Thomas Moore, who wrote 'To Mrs. Henry Tighe on Reading her "Psyche"', and later by Felicia *Hemans, who wrote 'The Grave of a Poetess' and also 'I stood where the life of song lay low' after visiting Mrs Tighe's grave. Keats was probably familiar with the edition of 1811. *Mary: A Series of Reflections during Twenty Years* was privately printed by her brother-in-law in 1811, and a novel, *Selena*, remained unpublished. *See also* E. V. Weller, *Keats and Mary Tighe* (1928); P. Henchy, *The Works of Mary Tighe* (1957, pamphlet).

Time and Tide (1920–79).

An 'Independent-Non Party Weekly Review' founded by Margaret Haig, Viscountess Rhondda (1883–1958), a wealthy former suffragette and businesswoman who determined that the review should change the 'nation's habit of mind' and establish a fresher, more liberal climate of opinion. Under its first editor Helen Archdale (1920–6) the review was closely connected with the Six Point Group, the feminist organization which included among its six goals equal pay and opportunities for women and various legal and administrative reforms. The review attracted a large number of women writers as reviewers and contributors. Winifred *Holtby was a key figure in the early stages. At her death in 1935 Lady Rhondda wrote that 'she had as large a share in building [*Time and Tide*] as it is today as anyone in the world'. Other prominent figures were Rebecca *West and Cicely *Hamilton. Stella *Benson, E. *Nesbit, Viola Meynell, Katherine *Mansfield, and Sylvia Townsend *Warner contributed short stories, Vita *Sackville-West and Dorothy L. *Sayers published poems. Book reviewers included Rose *Macaulay, Vera *Brittain, Ethel Smyth, G. K. Chesterton, Aldous Huxley, Bertrand Russell, and G. B. Shaw. Extracts from Virginia *Woolf's *A Room of One's Own* appeared in 1929 and E. M. *Delafield's *Diary of a Provincial Lady* was serialized in 1930. Under Lady Rhondda's editorship (1926–58) the review moved into its major phase, shifting its emphasis in the 1930s from feminism to politics in general and creating a forum for discussion of European and American as well as domestic affairs. Poetry, stories, and book reviews continued as major features. D. H. Lawrence, W. H. Auden, Walter de la Mare, T. S. Eliot, and E. M. Forster all published in the review, and the number of women contributors also remained high. The historian C. V. Wedgwood was literary editor between 1944 and 1952. New contributors included Storm *Jameson, Gertrude Stein, Pamela Hansford *Johnson, Rumer *Godden, Kathleen *Raine, Stella *Gibbons, Edith *Sitwell, and Stevie *Smith. Lady Rhondda's death in 1958 marked the end of the review as originally conceived. Her successors merged it temporarily with *John o' London's* and then redesigned it as a news magazine on the model of the American *Time Magazine.* Ironically the last subtitle of the once ardently feminist publication in 1977 was 'The Businessman's Weekly Newspaper'. It ceased publication in 1979. *See* Margaret Haig, Viscountess Rhondda, *This was my World* (1933) and *Notes on the Way* (1937); Vera Brittain, *Testament of Friendship* (1940) and *Testament of Experience* (1957); E. M. Delafield (ed.), *Time and Tide Album* (1932).

Tonna, Charlotte Elizabeth ('Charlotte Elizabeth'), novelist and journalist (b. Norwich, 1 October 1790, d. Ramsgate, 12 July 1846).

Charlotte Elizabeth Tonna, or 'Charlotte Elizabeth', as some of her works were signed, was the daughter of Michael Browne, rector of St Giles's, Norwich, and minor canon of Norwich Cathedral. In 1813 she married Captain George Phelan, an officer of the 60th Norwich regiment, and spent two years with him in Nova Scotia before returning to his estate near Kilkenny, in Ireland. The marriage was unhappy and the couple separated around 1824. Charlotte went to live with her brother at Clifton, near Bristol, where she met Hannah *More. Phelan died in 1837 and in 1841 she married Lewis Hippolytus Joseph Tonna, secretary of the Royal United Service Institution and a writer of ultra-Protestant polemical works. During her first marriage she wrote tracts for Protestant religious societies under the signature Charlotte Elizabeth. She published an abridged version of Foxe's *Book of Martyrs* and wrote two popular poems, 'The Maiden City' and 'No Surrender', specifically for the Orange cause. Her Evangelical background prompted an interest in social conditions which in turn led to a series of early, heavily documented social problem novels for which she is best known. *The System* (1827) reflected the Evangelical campaign against slavery. *Combination* (1832) was one of the first novels to deal (apprehensively) with trade unions and strike action. *Helen Fleetwood: Tale of the Factories* (1841), her most popular book, was written in support of the Ten Hours Movement. The polemical and influential *Perils of the Nation* (1843) used documentary evidence to emphasize working conditions in factories and urged that 'the mighty engine of female influence' be used more effectively in the reform movement. The four stories of *The Wrongs of Women* (1843–4) focused on trades which employed women and children, supported by evidence from the Second Report of the Children's Employment Commission of 1843. Tonna edited successively the *Protestant Annual*, the *Christian Lady's Magazine* and the *Protestant Magazine*, which she used as a vehicle for her own work, both fiction and non-fiction. She published a series of essays on the factory system in 1838 and again in 1842. Others of her novels include *Conformity* (1841) and *Falsehood and Truth* (1841). Harriet Beecher Stowe wrote an introduction to her *Collected Works* (1844), which contained her *Personal Recollections*, first published in 1841. They were continued 'to the close of her life, 1847' in the fourth edition of the works in 1854. *See* Joseph A. Kestner, *Protest and Reform: The British Social Narrative by Women 1827–1867* (1985).

'Torrie, Malcolm' *see* MITCHELL, Gladys

'Trafford, F. G.' *see* RIDDELL, Mrs J. H.

Traill, Catherine Parr *see under* STRICKLAND, Agnes

Trapnel, Anna, prophetic writer (*fl.* 1642–60).

Anna Trapnel was the daughter of William Trapnel, a shipwright of Poplar. On New Year's Day 1642, the day after her mother's death, she was 'seized with the spirit of the Lord' while listening to a sermon by the Baptist preacher John Simpson of St Botolph's Church in Aldgate. After that occasion she frequently experienced visions, uttering prophecies and sometimes falling to the ground. She gave her possessions to the Parliamentarian army and went to live with a series of women friends. Possibly under Simpson's influence she joined the Fifth Monarchists, a radical political and religious sect prominent during the 1650s, which preached the imminent Kingdom of Christ on earth and the overthrow of the existing government. In January 1654, while attending the trial of Vavasour Powell, a Welsh Fifth Monarchist detained for prophesying the end of the Protectorate, she was again 'seized by the spirit' and burst out singing and dancing and uttering prophecies, a state which lasted for twelve days. Her words, or those which were comprehensible, a mixture of verses and prophetic utterances in prose, were taken down and published as *The Cry of a Stone; or A Relation of Something Spoken in Whitehall by Anna Trapnel . . . Uttered in Prayers and Spiritual Songs, by an Inspiration Extraordinary, and Full of Wonder* (1654). Now disenchanted with Cromwell, to whom she referred as the 'little horn' on the head of the Beast, she was used by the Fifth Monarchists in their propaganda campaign in the West Country in 1654 until she was arrested and imprisoned, first in Plymouth and then in Bridewell. She refused to promise to stop her public prophecies and appeared in Cornwall again in 1655. *A Legacy for Saints: Being Several Experiences of the Dealings of God with Anna Trapnel* (1654) was a record of her conversion, written while in prison. *Anna Trapnel's Report and Plea; or A Narrative of her Journey from London into Cornwal* (1654) was a narrative of her experiences prior to her imprisonment. *Strange and Wonderful Newes from White-Hall* (1654) was her own account of her Whitehall trance. Another trance in 1657 which lasted for ten months was recorded in her *Voice for the King of Saints.* Like *The Cry of a Stone* it was an account of her words, apparently published with her approval. After 1658 her prophecies appear to have ceased, and there is no record of her involvement in the failed Fifth Monarchist uprising of 1661. She may possibly have married in 1661. *See* Bernard S. Capp, *The Fifth Monarchy Men* (1972); Germaine Greer *et al.* (eds.), *Kissing the Rod: An Anthology of Seventeenth-Century Women's Verse* (1988); Elaine Hobby, *Virtue of Necessity: English Women's Writing 1649–88* (1988).

Travers, P(amela) L(yndon), poet, critic, and children's writer (b. Queensland, Australia, 1906).

P. L. Travers is the daughter of a Scots-Irish mother and an Irish father who settled in Australia. She was educated privately and came to England when she was 17, where she worked as a dancer and an actress and also wrote poetry. She was encouraged by AE (George Russell) to submit her poems to the *Irish Statesman* and became a regular contributor in the 1920s. She was a drama critic for the *New English Weekly* in the 1930s and also contributed poetry, travel essays, and film reviews. While recovering from an illness in the early 1930s she wrote the first of her 'Mary Poppins' books, about a quintessential English nanny who believes in magic. Set in the cosy world of the English nursery between the wars (the Walt Disney film transposed it to the Edwardian period), the original *Mary Poppins* (1934) was followed by *Mary Poppins Comes Back* (1935), and by six others, the last in 1989. Travers has also written other stories for children, including *I Go by Sea, I Go by Land* (1941), about two English children evacuated to America during the Second World War, *The Fox at the Manger* (1963), and *Friend Monkey* (1971), the last two combining her interest in mythology and religion. She has lived in the United States at various periods, working for the British Ministry of Information during the Second World War and as a writer in residence at various colleges between 1965 and 1970. She is currently a consulting editor for *Parabola: The Magazine of Myth and Tradition. See* Staffan Bergsten, *Mary Poppins and Myth* (1978); Jonathan Cott, *Pipers at the Gates of Dawn* (1983); Shusha Guppy, *Looking Back* (1992).

Trimmer, Sarah, children's writer and writer on education (b. Ipswich, 6 January 1741, d. Brentford, London, 15 December 1810).

Sarah Trimmer was the only daughter of John Joshua Kirby, an artist and engraver who specialized in architectural drawings, and his wife Sarah Bull. She was sent to a boarding school in Ipswich and later moved with her family to London, where she was introduced into literary and artistic circles by her father, who thought she might have a talent for writing. She impressed Dr Johnson with her early interest in Milton, and a friendship developed. In 1759 the family moved to Kew, where her father had been appointed Clerk of Works and where she met James Trimmer, whom she married in 1762. The couple had twelve children, six sons and six daughters, whom they educated at home, with some help with classics for their sons from a local clergyman. When Mrs *Barbauld published her *Lessons for Children* (1778) friends persuaded Mrs Trimmer similarly to make use of the materials she had assembled for her children's education, and she published her *Easy Introduction to the Knowledge of Nature and Reading the Holy Scriptures* (1780), which reached its eleventh edition by 1802. Other didactic works for children followed, of which the most famous was *Fabulous Histories* (1786), popularly known in numerous nineteenth-century editions by its subtitle *The History of the Robins*, and later as *The Robins*. It concerned a group of children who encountered a family of robins and other animals which were given human traits in order to encourage their proper treatment. Mrs Trimmer was active in the establishment of Sunday schools for poor children, and also 'schools of industry' which taught them practical skills. She published *The Economy of Charity* (1787) on their management and promotion. Influenced by Madame de Genlis, the French educationalist, she pioneered the use of illustrations to accompany texts in teaching young children, and published several editions of *New and Comprehensive Lessons* between 1814 and 1830, which made the technique more widely available. Several of her works, including *The Two Farmers* (1786) and *The Servant's Friend* (1787), were published by the Society for the Diffusion of Useful Knowledge, thus ensuring a large circulation over a long period. She also produced the *Family Magazine* (1778–89), with factual information and didactic fiction, some of which was published separately as *Instructive Tales* (1810). Disapproving of fairy-tales and keen to promote only wholesome and instructive works for children she established the *Guardian of Education* (1802–6), which reviewed current children's books and attacked the influence of Rousseau ('the greatest injury the youth of this nation ever received was from the introduction of Rousseau's system'). Mrs Trimmer published a number of other educational works aimed at children and servants, some, like *Sacred History* (1782), on religious subjects, and others, like *The Charity School Spelling Book* (1800) and *The Teacher's Assistant*, of a more practical nature. She offered an assessment of the monitorial system of education proposed by Joseph Lancaster in *A Comparative View of the New Plan of Education* (1805). Elizabeth *Carter and Hannah *More were admirers of her work. *See Some Account of the Life and Writings of Mrs. Trimmer* (1814); D. M. Yarde, *The Life and Works of Sarah Trimmer, a Lady of Brentford* (1972); F. J. Harvey Darton, *Children's Books in England* (3rd edn. 1982).

Trollope, Cecilia *see under* TROLLOPE, Frances

Trollope, Frances, novelist (b. Stapleton, near Bristol, 10 March 1780, d. Florence, 6 October 1863).

The daughter of William Milton, afterwards vicar of Heckfield, Hampshire, and Frances Gresley, who died early, Frances Milton spent her early years keeping house for her brother Henry, a civil servant in the War Office. In 1809 she married Thomas Anthony Trollope, an unsuccessful barrister with a talent for unfortunate financial speculation. The couple had seven children, of whom three became novelists, Thomas Adolphus (1810–92), Anthony (1815–82) and **Cecilia** (1816–49), later **Tilley,** who wrote one novel. Thomas Anthony Trollope's temperamental unsuitability for the legal profession was exacerbated by a run of financial misfortune which led Mrs Trollope to attempt a rescue by establishing a bazaar or department store selling fancy goods in Cincinnati, Ohio. This too was a spectacular failure, and in desperation she wrote her first work, *Domestic Manners of the Americans* (1832), which brought her immediate success and fame at the age of 52, catering as it did for the enormous interest in America in the early 1830s, and presenting the seemingly vulgar and eccentric habits of the Americans in a comical if spiteful light. The book was probably the most celebrated of a cluster of travel books on America in the 1830s and 1840s and launched its author on a full-time literary career. Like most of the other travel books it was highly critical of the institution of slavery. The death of one of her sons in 1834 followed by that of her husband in 1835 reinforced Frances Trollope's literary ambitions. She wrote two further travel works, one on Belgium (1833) and one on Paris (1835), but these were inferior to the American book. Another on *Vienna and the Austrians* was published in 1838. Her real talent was for fiction. Her two best-known novels, *The Vicar of Wrexhill* and *Widow Barnaby*, were published in 1837 and 1839. Sequels to the latter, *The Widow Married* (1840) and *The Barnabys in America* (1843), followed, interspersed by a stream of other titles, sometimes as many as three in one year. *The Life and Adventures of Michael Armstrong, the Factory Boy* (1840) was one of the earliest industrial novels. Mrs Trollope's contemporaries were quick to fasten on the vulgarity and coarseness of her characters and the tone of her fiction, to which they attributed her success and her distinctiveness. R. H. Horne said of her work: 'she cannot go out of herself: she serves up everything with the same sauce: the predominant flavour is Trollope still.' It was nevertheless a winning style. Mrs Trollope's energy was unflagging. Like her junior colleague Margaret *Oliphant she combined the role of mother with that of a professional writer, and often wrote into the early hours of the morning. Beginning her career at the age of 52 she published a total of thirty-five novels. *See* A. Trollope, *Autobiography* (1883); T. A. Trollope, *What I Remember* (1887); Frances Eleanor Trollope (daughter-in-law), *A Memoir of Frances Trollope* (1895); Helen Heineman, *Mrs. Trollope: the Triumphant Feminine in the Nineteenth Century* (1979); Johanna Johnston, *Fanny Trollope* (1979).

Trotter, Catharine, later Cockburn, playwright and philosopher (b. London, 16 August 1679, d. Long Horsley, Northumberland, 11 May 1749).

Catharine Trotter was one of two daughters of Captain David Trotter, a naval officer who died of plague while on a mission to Turkey in 1684, and his wife Sarah Ballenden. Catharine was precocious from her childhood: she taught herself to write and also learned French without a teacher, although she had tuition in Latin and logic. The family were members of the Church of England, but friendship with several old Catholic families persuaded her to become Roman Catholic. She published a short novel, *Olinda's Adventures* (1693), and began to write poetry at 14. At 16 she adapted Aphra *Behn's translation of a French short story, *Agnes de Castro*, for a production at Drury Lane (published 1696). In 1697 she sent verses to Congreve in celebration of his tragedy *The Mourning Bride*, which won her his enthusiastic patronage. He acted as chief adviser for her next play, *The Fatal Friendship*, a tragedy performed with great success at Lincoln's Inn Fields in 1698. George Farquhar was so taken with it that he sent her a copy of his *Love in a Bottle*, asking for her comments. It was a measure of her success that she was one of several women poets asked to write a verse tribute on Dryden's death in 1700, published under the title *The *Nine Muses*. Another was her inclusion, along with Delarivier *Manley and Mary *Pix, as the object of the satire *The *Female Wits* by W. M., performed at Drury Lane in 1696. Her comedy *Love* *at a Loss; or Most Votes Carry it* was performed at Drury Lane in 1700 (published 1701), followed in 1701 by *The Unhappy Penitent*, in her more congenial form of tragedy. The published version of the latter contained a preface on play-writing. Having written four successful plays she left London at the age of 22, settling in Salisbury with her sister, where she met Bishop Burnet and his wife Elizabeth. After reading Locke's *Essay Concerning Human Understanding* (1690) and the subsequent attacks upon it she wrote her *A Defence of Mr. Locke's 'Essay of Human Understanding'*, which was published anonymously in 1702. Locke, in a letter, claimed she had 'not only vanquished my adversary, but reduced me also absolutely under your power'. She returned to the theatre to write what was to be her last play, *The Revolution of Sweden* (1706), another tragedy for which Congreve supplied both support and criticism. While acting as a lady's companion in Surrey she abandoned Catholicism for the Church of England, writing *A Discourse Concerning a Guide in Controversies* (1707) on the problems of denominational Christianity. Having previously decided on a clergyman husband, she accepted Patrick Cockburn, the son of a Scottish theologian and vicar of Nayland in Suffolk, in 1708. They had two sons and a daughter. The exchange of the world of London theatre for clerical penury and rural isolation proved a mortal blow to her writing. Cockburn felt unable to take the Oath of Abjuration, renouncing the Stuarts, required of all public servants after the accession of George I in 1714, and consequently had to leave the Church. After twelve years in a teaching post he was eventually persuaded to take the Oath in 1726 and appointed minister of the Episcopalian Church in Aberdeen, and also to the living of Long Horsley near Morpeth in Northumberland. Catharine rewrote *Love at a Loss* under the title *The Honourable Deceivers*, which was never published, and also wrote several more philosophical tracts, one in defence of Dr Samuel Clarke, the Cambridge metaphysician (1747). She died four months after her husband in 1749, aged 70. A two-volume edition of her works was published in 1751 which included only one play, *The Fatal Friendship*, as the editor felt her prose works were 'of more general and lasting use to the world'. Edmund Gosse in his 1916 biography pronounced them 'so dull that merely to think of them brings tears into one's eyes'. Catharine Trotter also wrote some poetry, which is included in the *Works*. *See Works of Mrs. Catharine Cockburn*, ed. T. Birch (1751, includes a memoir); Nancy Cotton, *Women Playwrights in England c.1365–1750* (1980); Fidelis Morgan (ed.), *The Female Wits: Women Playwrights of the Restoration* (1981); Constance Clark, *Three Augustan Women Playwrights* (1986); Mary Anne Schofield and Cecilia Macheski (eds), *Curtain Calls: British and American Women and the Theater 1660–1820* (1991).

Tucker, Charlotte Maria ('A.L.O.E.', i.e. 'A Lady of England'), children's writer (b. Barnet, London, 8 May 1821, d. Amritsar, India, 2 December 1893).

Charlotte Tucker was the sixth child and third daughter of Henry St George Tucker, an Indian civil servant and financier, and Jane Boswell, the daughter of an Edinburgh lawyer. The Tucker family had been colonial civil servants for several generations, in both India and the Bermudas. At the family home in London, where she was privately educated, she met many notable political figures of the day, including the Duke of Wellington. She began to write verses and plays at an early age as well as undertaking charitable work among London's poor, but she did not begin to write seriously until after her father's death in 1851. *Claremont Tales; or Illustrations of the Beatitudes* (1852), her first book, was a series of moralizing tales for the young. Encouraged by their success she published on average one or two books a year, giving the proceeds to charity. *The Rambles of a Rat* (1854), *Wings and Stings* (1855), *Old Friends with New Faces* (1858), *The Story of a Needle*, and *The Giant Killer* (1868) were some of the best among the 140-odd titles published between 1854 and 1893. Her work was strongly allegorical, and included Bible stories, adventure stories, animal fables, and homilies. In 1875, at the age of 54, she taught herself Hindustani, and went to India as a member of the Church of England Zenana Society, visiting high-caste Indian women living in enforced seclusion. She settled in Batala, north of Lahore, which she made the centre of her missionary activities, involving herself in the education and conversion of Indian boys and writing booklets for translation into vernacular dialects. Many of the books were published by the Christian Literary Society and the Punjab Religious Book Society. She suffered a serious illness in 1885 from which she never fully recovered, and died eight years later at Amritsar. As she requested in her will she was buried at Batala, without a coffin, and at a cost of no more than five rupees. *See* Agnes Giberne, *A Lady of England: The Life and Letters of Charlotte Maria Tucker* (1895); A. Sergeant (ed.), *Women Novelists of Queen Victoria's Reign* (1897).

Tynan, Katharine, poet and novelist (b. Clondalkin, County Dublin, 23 January 1861, d. Wimbledon, London, 2 April 1931).

Katharine Tynan was the fourth daughter of Andrew Cullen Tynan, an Irish farmer and cattle trader who was active in the Irish Nationalist movement, and his wife Elizabeth O'Reilly. Her puritanical mother, an invalid, forbade dances, the theatre, and the reading of fiction, but she read in secret, 'everything' from Rossetti and William Morris to M. E. *Braddon and Eugène Sue. An attack of measles affected her eyesight and curtailed her schooling at the Sienna Convent in Drogheda. She joined the Ladies' Land

League and like her father was a strong supporter of Parnell, although she declined active involvement in politics. Her first publication was a poem printed in a Dublin penny paper in 1878. Her first book of poems, *Louise de la Vallière* (1885), was published with financial help from her father. It brought her to the attention of Wilfred and Alice *Meynell, W. M. Rossetti, and his sister *Christina, as well as to members of the Irish literary renaissance including Yeats and George Russell (AE). *The Way of a Maid* (1895), her first novel, paved the way for a prolific career as a popular romantic novelist. She published six or seven titles a year over a twenty-five-year period, more than a hundred in total. Her collections of poems, eighteen in all, many of them strongly Catholic in their preoccupation, gained critical approval and kept her a place at the centre of the Irish literary movement. In 1893 she married Henry Albert Hinkson, a barrister and also a novelist, who converted to Roman Catholicism. They had two sons and a daughter and lived in England until Hinkson's appointment as a Resident Magistrate in County Mayo in 1911. After his death in 1919 she lived for a time on the Continent and then partly in England and partly in Ireland. Her poem 'Sheep and Lambs', better known by its opening line 'All in the April morning', was praised by Yeats, who was a particular friend. His letters to her were published in 1953. Some of her better-known novels include *The Dear Irish Girl* (1899), *The Handsome Brandons* (1899), *She Walks in Beauty* (1899), and *Betty Carew* (1910). *A Union of Hearts* (1901) and *Her Ladyship* (1907) dealt with Irish social problems, as did a late work, *The Playground* (1930). Tynan was a prolific journalist, writing for English, Irish, and American publications during her years in England after her marriage. She also wrote a five-volume autobiography, *Twenty-Five Years: Reminiscences* (1913), *The Middle Years* (1916), *The Years of the Shadow* (1919), *The Wandering Years* (1922), and *Memories* (1924), which offers an interesting perspective on the period. Her *Collected Poems*, with a foreword by AE, were published in 1930. Her daughter **Pamela Hinkson** was also a novelist. *See* Marilyn Gaddis Rose, *Katherine Tynan* (1974).

u u u u u u u u u u u u u u

U

Uttley, 'Alison' (Alice Jane), children's writer and novelist (b. Cromford, Derbyshire, 17 December 1884, d. High Wycombe, Buckinghamshire, 7 May 1976).

Alison Uttley was the elder child and only daughter of Henry Taylor, a Derbyshire farmer, and his wife Hannah Dickens, a former lady's maid. Country life at Castle Top Farm, which she knew intimately as a child, was to inform all her adult writing. She was educated at home, then at a local board school, the Lear School in Holloway, where she became interested in science, and finally at Lady Manners Grammar School, Bakewell, where she won a scholarship and several school prizes. She became the second woman honours graduate of Manchester University, taking a B.Sc. in physics in 1906, and then went to training college (later Hughes Hall) in Cambridge. She taught physics at Fulham Secondary School and became interested in socialism, developing a friendship with Ramsay Macdonald, later Labour Prime Minister, and his wife. In 1911 she married James Arthur Uttley, a civil engineer. Their only son was born in 1915. Her husband, who had become a depressive as a result of his First World War experiences, killed himself in 1930, leaving her as the sole support of their son. She had begun to write before his death, despite his discouragement, and had published magazine articles and a children's book, *The Squirrel, the Hare and the Little Grey Rabbit* (1929), written to amuse her son. Over thirty 'Little Grey Rabbit' titles followed, and more than a hundred books in total, stories of Sam Pig, Tim Rabbit, Brock the Badger, Fuzzypeg the Hedgehog, all Uttley perennials, and all inhabiting a Victorian farming community based on her childhood.

The autobiographical *The Country Child* (1931) was her first book directed at an adult readership. It was followed by *Ambush of Young Days* (1937), *The Farm on the Hill* (1941), and two relatively unsuccessful novels, *High Meadows* (1938) and *When All is Done* (1945). Her most original and possibly her best work was *A Traveller in Time* (1939), a fantasy based again on her rural childhood, but also drawing on careful research into a local plot to rescue Mary Queen of Scots in 1569. The book reflected Uttley's interest in dreams, discussed in her autobiographical essay *The Stuff of Dreams* (1953). The early 'Little Grey Rabbit' books were illustrated by Margaret Tempest, later ones by Katherine Wigglesworth, and many of her books about the countryside by C. F. Tunnicliffe. After her husband's death she made her home in Buckinghamshire, near Beaconsfield, where she died at the age of 91. Manchester University gave her an honorary D.Litt. in 1970. Her only son, with whom she had an intense and later painful relationship, committed suicide in 1978. *See* Denis Judd, *Alison Uttley: The Life of a Country Child 1884–1976* (1986).

v v v v v v v v v v v v v v

V

'V' *see* CLIVE, Caroline

Vesey, Elizabeth, also Handcock, bluestocking and letter writer (b. 1715(?), d. London, 1791).

Elizabeth Vesey was the second daughter of Thomas Vesey, Bishop of Ossory, a nd his wife Mary Muschamp of Horsley in Surrey. She married first William Handcock, MP for Fore, and secondly, in 1746, her cousin Agmondesham Vesey, an Irish MP who later became Account-General of Ireland. She met Elizabeth *Montagu in 1755 and through her and also through her second husband's extensive connections gradually gained entry to literary and political circles. Agmondesham Vesey assisted George Lyttelton in his *Life of Henry II* (1767–71), and through his friendship with Edmund Burke was made a privy councillor in Ireland and a member of 'The Club', a masculine literary circle founded by Dr Johnson in 1763–4. Elizabeth Vesey used her natural social gifts in the organization of London parties which became a focus for members of the *Bluestocking Circle, vying with Mrs Montagu, Mrs Boscawen, and the Duchess of Portland as the group's most prominent hostess. Her parties, which were at their peak between 1770 and 1784, took place on the evenings members of The Club dined together, and the group joined her salon afterwards. Mrs Vesey's wit and vivacity earned her the sobriquet of 'The Sylph', while Horace Walpole described her parties as 'Babels'. She was a valued friend and correspondent of many literary women of the period. Hannah *More's poem *The Bas bleu* (1786) was addressed to her and began, 'Vesey, of verse the judge and friend'. Elizabeth

*Carter's letters to her (1763–87) were edited by Carter's nephew Montagu Pennington (1809). Some of her own letters were published in R. Brimley Johnson, *Bluestocking Letters* (1926). *See* Sylvia H. Myers, *The Bluestocking Circle* (1990).

Victoria, Queen, memoirist and letter writer (b. Kensington Palace, London, 24 May 1819, d. Osborne, Isle of Wight, 22 January 1901).

The granddaughter of George III and only child of his fourth son Edward, Duke of Kent, and Mary Louisa Victoria of Saxe-Coburg, the widow of Prince Ernest Charles of Leiningen, Victoria acceded to the throne in 1837. In 1840 she married Prince Albert of Saxe-Coburg-Gotha (d. 1861). An energetic correspondent, particularly with members of her own family, she also kept a journal from the age of 13 until shortly before her death, amassing a total of over a hundred volumes. The only portions published during her lifetime were *Leaves from a Journal of our Life in the Highlands 1848–1861*, published in 1868, with editorial assistance from Arthur Helps. Plainly written and practical in outlook they conveyed the Queen's love of Scotland and the details of a happy and domestic family holiday. *More Leaves*, covering the year 1862–3, appeared in 1883. Both were instant best sellers. Various collections of the Queen's letters have been published since her death. Three official series of *The Letters of Queen Victoria* were published with royal approval. The first, covering 1837–61, was edited by A. C. Benson and Reginald B. B. Esher (1907); the second, 1862–78, by George Earle Buckle (1926); the third, 1886–1901, also edited by Buckle, was published in 1930. More recently, five volumes of selected letters between the Queen and members of her immediate family, particularly her eldest daughter, have been published, the first four edited by Roger Fulford: *Dearest Mama: Letters between Queen Victoria and the Crown Princess of Prussia, 1861–4* (1968); *Your Dear Letter, 1865–71* (1971); *Darling Child, 1871–8* (1976); *Beloved Mama, 1878–85* (1981). *Beloved and Darling Child: Last Letters between Queen Victoria and her Eldest Daughter 1886–1901* was edited by Agatha Ramon (1990). Among the Queen's many biographers have been Edith *Sitwell, *Victoria of England* (1936), and Lettice *Cooper, *The Young Victoria* (1961). *See* Lytton Strachey, *Queen Victoria* (1921); Elizabeth Longford, *Victoria R.I.* (1964); Cecil Woodham-Smith, *Queen Victoria: Her Life and Times* (1972); Dorothy Thompson, *Queen Victoria: Gender and Power* (1990).

Victoria Magazine (May 1863–June 1880).

The *Victoria Magazine* was founded by Emily *Faithfull, who had established the Victoria Press to extend the range of technological jobs open to women. The monthly magazine represented a similar attempt to foster women's literary aspirations. The first number appropriately contained Christina *Rossetti's 'To L.E.L. [Laetitia *Landon], "Whose heart was breaking for a little love"'. Not all the contributors were women. They included Thomas Adolphus Trollope, brother of Anthony and son of Frances *Trollope, the novelist George Macdonald, critics R. H. Hutton, Nassau Senior, and F. D. Maurice, as well as the poet Adelaide *Procter. The magazine became a vociferous advocate of women's rights, including the ownership of property and entry into higher education, and it pressed for improvement in conditions and opportunities for employment. It published Frances Power *Cobbe's spirited response in support of John Stuart Mill's petition for the extension of the franchise to women in June 1866. The magazine covered all matters dealing with health and welfare, particularly in relation to women. Its 'Miscellanea' section summarized articles bearing on women's issues in other periodicals. A correspondence column provided an opportunity for women to make their views known, as did another feature, 'the Victoria Discussion Society'. The 'Literature of the Month' section focused on books related to women's concerns. Another column, 'Women and Work—a Guide to Employment for Women', begun in November 1876, was designed to help women to find work. The magazine ceased publication in June 1880.

Victoria Press *see* FAITHFULL, Emily

'Vine, Barbara' *see* RENDELL, Ruth

'Voleur, Le' *see* CAREY, Rosa Nouchette

Voynich, Ethel (Lilian), novelist (b. Cork, 1864, d. New York, 1960).

Ethel Voynich's reputation rests on the strength of a single novel. Born Ethel Lilian Boole, the daughter of George Boole, an eminent mathematician, and his wife Mary Everest, a feminist philosopher, she was educated in Irish schools and later in Berlin. She also travelled to Russia. In 1891 she married a young Polish exile, Habdank-Woynicz (1865–1930), who became a naturalized British subject and Anglicized his name to Wilfrid Michael Voynich. Voynich had been arrested for his participation in the Polish nationalist movement against the Tsar in 1885, was sent to Siberia, and escaped to England in 1890. The background to Ethel Voynich's first novel *The Gadfly* (1897) drew heavily on her husband's political experience and its strength, according to the Marxist critic Arnold Kettle, lay in her sympathy with his revolutionary idealism. The strongly anti-clerical novel is set in the

Italy of the Risorgimento. As well as the revolutionary hero, the 'gadfly' of the title, the novel contains a sympathetic portrait of a young Englishwoman, also a revolutionary. The novel went through eight impressions in four years and received extensive critical attention in Eastern Europe and in the Soviet Union, where it was made into a film in 1955. Voynich published three more novels before moving with her husband to the United States in 1916: *Jack Raymond* (1901), the story of a rebel and a misfit whose personal suffering is alleviated by the sympathetic widow of a Polish patriot, *Olive Latham* (1904), an autobiographical story about an English nurse who falls in love with a Russian revolutionary, and *An Interrupted Friendship* (1910), which picks up the story of the hero of *The Gadfly*. Voynich's later novels are characterized by an obsessive interest in physical pain and violence and none is considered equal to her first. She published two translations of Russian stories, *Stories from Garshin* (1893) and *The Humour of Russia* (1895), and a translation of Chopin's letters (1931). A last novel, *Put off thy Shoes* (1945), was published in America. *See* W. L. Courtney, *The Feminine Note in Fiction* (1904; repr. 1973); Arnold Kettle, in *Essays in Criticism*, 7 (1957).

W

Wakefield, Priscilla, née Bell, children's writer (b. Tottenham, London, 31 January 1751, d. Ipswich, 12 September 1832).

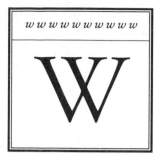

Priscilla Wakefield was born into a family of energetic and committed Quakers. Her father was Daniel Bell of Stamford, Middlesex, and her mother Catherine Barclay was the granddaughter of an eminent Quaker apologist. Elizabeth Fry, the prison reformer, was her niece and Edward Gibbon Wakefield, the Radical politician and colonial administrator, her grandson. In 1771 she married Edward Wakefield, a London merchant, by whom she had two sons and a daughter. As a young wife she engaged in philanthropic activities, in particular promoting savings banks, known as 'frugality banks', and establishing a charity for lying-in women in Tottenham. When the family's fortunes declined in the 1790s she began to write instructive books for children, specializing in natural history and in books of travel. Several became extremely popular and went through multiple editions both during her lifetime and after her death. *Juvenile Anecdotes founded on Facts* (2 vols., 1795–8) went into eight editions by 1825. *The Juvenile Travellers* (1801), the story of an imaginary tour of Europe, reached its nineteenth edition by 1850. *An Introduction to Botany in a Series of Familiar Letters* (1796) was translated into French, and extended to eleven editions by 1841. Other works included *Leisure Hours; or Entertaining Dialogues* (1794–6), *A Family Tour through the British Empire* (1804), and her one work addressed to an adult audience, *Reflections on the Present Condition of the Female Sex, with Suggestions for its Improvement* (1798), which advocated the extension of education and vocational opportunities for women to include science, teaching, with the training to be undertaken by women instructors, serving in shops, portrait painting, and farming. Although a member of the Society of Friends, Priscilla Wakefield did not conform to its strictures on either dress or amusements. Her portrait, together with her sister, was painted by Gainsborough.

Walford, Lucy (Bethia), novelist (b. Portobello, near Edinburgh, 17 April 1845, d. London, 11 May 1915).

Lucy Walford was the daughter of John Colquhoun, sportsman, author, and former army officer, and his wife Frances Sara Fuller-Maitland. The family were well-connected, stern Presbyterians and moved in Edinburgh society. Her grandfather was a baronet, and the novelist Catherine *Sinclair was her aunt. She was educated at home by governesses and by her own account read avidly from the age of 7. The work of Charlotte *Yonge was an important early influence, and when in 1868 she read Jane Austen for the first time she claimed the experience was 'to exercise an abiding influence over all my own future efforts'. In 1869 she married Alfred Saunders Walford (d. 1907) of Cranbrook Hall, Ilford, Essex, by whom she had two sons and five daughters. She began to write secretly after her marriage, contributing sketches and stories, often with Edinburgh settings, to *Blackwood's Magazine.* Her first book, *Mr. Smith: A Part of his Life* (1874) took several years to complete, and was immediately successful. Her family disapproved, but Queen *Victoria was one of the book's professed admirers. Her talent for light-hearted domestic comedy was reflected in *Pauline* (1877), *The Baby's Grandmother* (1884), *Cousins* (1885), *The History of a Week* (1886), *A Mere Child* (1888), *A Stiff-Necked Generation* (1889), *The Havoc of a Smile* (1890), *The Mischief of Monica* (1892), and *Sir Patrick the Puddock* (1899). *The Matchmaker* (1893) was the last three-volume novel to be accepted by Mudie's Circulating Library. Walford wrote forty-five books in all, her last, *David and Jonathan on the Riviera,* published in 1914 in her 70th year. She served as London correspondent for the New York *Critic* between 1889 and 1893 and wrote for various London magazines, including Edmund Yates's *World. Four Biographies from Blackwood's* (1888) included Jane *Taylor, Hannah *More, and Mary *Somerville. Her autobiography *Recollections of a Scottish Novelist* (1910) gives a vivid account of her early life and *Memories of Victorian London* (1912) is a rich source of contemporary literary gossip.

Ward, Mary Augusta, née Arnold (Mrs Humphry Ward), novelist (b. Hobart Town, Tasmania, 11 June 1851, d. London, 24 March 1920).

Mary Ward was the eldest of the eight children of Thomas Arnold (the second son of Dr Thomas Arnold, headmaster of Rugby) and Julia Sorell, whom he met while farming in Tasmania. The poet Matthew Arnold was her uncle. Thomas Arnold's religious crises dominated and damaged his family's life, leading ultimately to his estrangement from his wife. His conversion to Roman Catholicism in 1856 ended his inspectorate of schools in Tasmania and the family returned to England, while Arnold taught in Catholic educational establishments in Dublin and Birmingham. Mary was educated at indifferent boarding schools during this period. Her father's return to the Church of England meant a welcome move to Oxford in 1867, where Arnold taught and Mary began to read voraciously in the Bodleian Library, becoming expert in Spanish history and literature and thriving on her exposure to university circles. In 1872 she married Thomas Humphry Ward, a young fellow of Brasenose, and subsequently became involved in the movement to admit women to the university. She became the first secretary of Somerville College in 1879 and at the same time contributed extensively to the *Dictionary of Christian Biography* on early Spanish churchmen. Her marriage and the birth of a son and two daughters together with her increased academic activity cushioned the blow of her father's reconversion to Roman Catholicism in 1876. In 1881 the Wards moved to London, where Humphry Ward became a leader writer and art critic for *The Times*. Mary Ward contributed to the paper as well but had also begun to write fiction. Her first novel, *Miss Bretherton*, was published in 1884 and the next year she published an important translation of Henri-Frédéric Amiel's *Journal intime*. Her own religious beliefs had undergone a profound change, due in part to her association with Oxford intellectuals like T. H. Green, Benjamin Jowett, and Mark Pattison. She moved to a liberal, anti-dogmatic position expressed in her 1881 pamphlet *Unbelief and Sin* and most fully reflected in her best-selling novel *Robert Elsmere* (1888), the story of the loss of faith of its sensitive clergyman hero. The book captured the intellectual and spiritual dilemma of a generation of readers. Gladstone's review in the *Nineteenth Century* helped its already buoyant sales, and the novel became a legendary best seller in both Britain and America. Ward's next novel, *David Grieve* (1892), was not a success. Her third, *Marcella* (1894), was one of the last three-deckers, and like its sequel *Sir George Tressady* (1896) reflected her interest in social concerns. She had become involved in the establishment of a settlement house for the poor in Bloomsbury, later the Passmore Edwards Settlement. Her particular interest in play centres for children and in helping physically handicapped children developed into the Mary Ward Centre, which still exists. At risk to her already precarious health she pursued both her writing and her philanthropy. The one-volume *Story of Bessy Costrell* (1895) was followed by her other major novel dealing with a religious crisis, *Helbeck of Bannisdale* (1898), which presented the strains of a Protestant–

Catholic relationship sympathetically, and drew on her perceptions of her father for the main character. Though her fame was at its peak, her later novels represented a falling-off of her talents: *Eleanor* (1900), *Lady Rose's Daughter* (1903), *The Marriage of William Ashe* (1905), *The Case of Richard Meynell* (1911), a sequel to *Robert Elsmere*, and *Delia Blanchflower* (1915). The last presented an unsympathetic picture of a suffragette, a cause which Mary Ward steadfastly opposed. Despite her fervent belief in higher education for women, she just as fervently opposed their direct involvement in political and public life, feeling that their influence could best be effected from within the domestic sphere. In 1908 she organized the Women's Anti-Suffrage League. She was an active propagandist during the First World War, and was encouraged by Theodore Roosevelt to write *England's Effort* (1916), and later *Towards the Goal* (1917) and *Fields of Victory* (1919) to promote the American war effort. Shortly before she died in 1920, she was appointed one of the first seven women magistrates. She published her autobiographical *A Writer's Recollections* in 1918, and her daughter Janet Trevelyan published a *Life* in 1923. *See* William S. Peterson, *Victorian Heretic* (1976); John Sutherland, *Mrs. Humphry Ward: Eminent Victorian, Pre-eminent Edwardian* (1990).

Waring, Anna (Laetitia), hymn writer (b. Plas-y-Velin, Neath, Glamorganshire, 19 April 1820, d. Clifton, Bristol, 10 May 1910).

Anna Waring was the second daughter of Elijah and Deborah Waring, both active members of the Society of Friends. Her uncle Samuel Miller Waring (1792–1827) was a hymn writer and like him she left the Friends in order to join the Church of England. She learned Hebrew in order to study the poetry of the Old Testament and made a practice of reading the Hebrew Psalms daily. She began to write hymns at an early age, and continued to write regularly until near her death at the age of 90. One of her best known, 'Father, I know that all my life', was written in 1846, when she was 23. Her *Hymns and Meditations* (1850) went through many editions in the nineteenth century and into the twentieth, including some American reprints, with hymns being added to successive editions. The first contained nineteen hymns, while that of 1863 was enlarged to thirty-eight. Other well-known hymns included 'Go not far from me, O my Strength' and 'My heart is resting, O my God'. She published *Additional Hymns* (1858), *Days of Remembrance* (1886), a calendar of Bible texts, and wrote extensively for the *Sunday Magazine*. She never married. *See* M. S. Talbot, *In Remembrance of Anna Laetitia Waring* (1911).

Warner, Sylvia Townsend, novelist and poet (b. Harrow, Middlesex, 6 December 1893, d. Maldon Newton, Dorset, 1 May 1978).

Sylvia Townsend Warner was the only child of George Townsend Warner, a master at Harrow School, and his wife Nora Hudleston. She was educated privately, worked in a munitions factory during the First World War, and between 1918 and 1928 became an editor of the ten-volume *Tudor Church Music*, published by Oxford University Press (1923–9). She began to write after the war, publishing *Espalier*, a collection of poems, in 1925. Her first novel, *Lolly Willowes* (1926), a supernatural story about a woman who realizes her vocation as a witch, became the first American Book of the Month and was nominated for the Prix Femina. The following year she became guest critic of the *New York Herald Tribune* and began a long association with the *New Yorker*, which published more than 140 of her short stories in the next four decades. Through the novelist T. F. Powys, an important influence on her writing, she met the poet **Valentine Ackland,** who became her lifelong companion. *Whether a Dove or a Seagull* (1934), another collection of poems, was written jointly with Ackland. From the early 1930s Warner became a committed writer of the Left. She and Ackland went to Spain to work for the Red Cross and joined the Communist Party in 1935. She attended the congress of anti-Fascist writers in Spain, was associated with the *Left Review*, and became a member of the Association of Writers for Intellectual Liberty. *Time Importuned* (1928), her second book of poems, was published in 1928, and *Opus* 7, a novel in verse, in 1931. Neither had a large audience. Warner was best known for her novels, seven in all, and her collections of short stories. *Mr. Fortune's Maggot* (1927), about a bank clerk turned South Seas missionary, was followed by several novels with historical settings: *The True Heart* (1929), set in Victorian Essex, *Summer will Show* (1936), which marked her growing political awareness, and was set during the Paris Revolution of 1848, and her own favourite, *The Corner that Held them* (1948), a recreation of life in a fourteenth-century English convent. *After the Death of Don Juan* (1938) was a satirical political fable. *The Flint Anchor* (1954), her last novel, contained some sharp social observations about a nineteenth-century English family, reminiscent of Jane *Austen. Despite her prolific output of short stories, few were anthologized or made their mark on the genre. Notable collections included *Some World Far from ours* (1929), *Elinor Barley* (1930), *The Salutation* (1932), *More Joy in Heaven* (1935), *The Cat's Cradle-Book* (1940), *A Garland of Straw* (1943), *The Museum of Cheats* (1947), *A Stranger with a Bag* (1966), *The Innocent and the Guilty* (1971), and *Kingdoms of Elfin* (1977), a return to the folklore themes of *Lolly Willowes*. She worked on for a long time but never completed a biography of T. F. Powys, but wrote a study of T. H. White (1967) and translated Proust's *Contre Sainte-Beuve* (1958). Her poetry has been compared to that of Hardy. She herself admired Emily Dickinson, Emily *Brontë, and Christina *Rossetti. *Twelve Poems* was published posthumously in 1980 and her *Collected Poems* in 1982. She resisted writing her autobiography, 'because I'm too imaginative', but the posthumous *Scenes of Childhood* (1981) drew on her Edwardian upbringing. A selection of her letters was published in 1982 (ed. William Maxwell). She won the Prix Menton in 1969, and was a fellow of the Royal Society of Literature and an honorary member of the American Academy of Arts and Letters. *See* special issue of *PN Review*, 23 (1981), ed. Claire Harman; Wendy Mulford, *This Narrow Place: Sylvia Townsend Warner and Valentine Ackland: Life, Letters and Politics 1930–51* (1988); Claire Harman, *Sylvia Townsend Warner: A Biography* (1989).

Webb, Beatrice, née Potter, political and social writer, autobiographer, and diarist (b. Standish House, near Gloucester, 22 January 1858, d. Passfield Corner, near Liphook, Hampshire, 30 April 1943).

Beatrice Webb was the eighth of the nine daughters of Richard Potter, a railway magnate and financier, and his wife Laurencina Hayworth, the daughter of a Liverpool merchant. Both her grandfathers were Liberal Members of Parliament and supporters of the free trader John Bright. She once described herself and her husband as belonging to 'the B's of the world—bourgeois, bureaucratic and benevolent'. She was educated at home by governesses, by extensive Continental travel undertaken with her parents, and by a wide range of serious reading. Her chief mentor in her youth was the philosopher Herbert Spencer, a friend of her father's, who likened her to George *Eliot in both her intellectual stamina and her imaginative capacity. She came out at 18 as was customary for one of her social background but refused to conform to the pattern of a débutante ('dissipation doesn't suit me, morally or physically', she wrote in her diary), developing instead a passionate concern for philosophical and social problems. After her mother's death in 1882 she ran her father's household and was closely involved in his business affairs. Her awareness of social conditions was extended when she began to help Charles Booth, her cousin's husband, in the investigations which led to his monumental *Life and Labour of the People in London* (1889–91). She published the results of her own investigations into London dock life in an article in the *Nineteenth Century* in 1887. After a four-year infatuation with the politician Joseph Chamberlain and in the course of her work for her first book, *The Co-operative Movement in Britain* (1891), she met Sidney Webb (1859–1947), the self-educated son of a London clerk and a minor civil servant. Six months after her father's death in 1892 they were married and what Beatrice called 'the firm of Webb' came into existence. 'We are both of us second-rate minds; but we are curiously combined,' she noted. The Webbs worked so much in concert that it became fashionable to treat them collectively on the grounds that it was impossible to separate or to distinguish their work. G. B. Shaw commented wittily that 'the Webbs can exchange gloves, shoes and lectures at a moment's notice'. 'The firm' were dedicated to social reform on a broad front, to alleviating poverty, extending the level of education, promoting trade unionism, and improving local government. Together they wrote a history of trade unionism (1894), a two-volume work on industrial democracy (1897), and a major nine-volume history of English local government (1906–29). Both were active in the Fabian Society, later in the Labour Party, and were instrumental in the establishment of the London School of Economics. Beatrice served on the Royal Commission on the Poor Laws (1905–9) and both wrote for and were involved in the founding of the *New Statesman* (1913). Beatrice's combative pamphlet *The Wages of Men and Women: Should they be Equal?* (1919), written as a minority report of a government committee on the pay of women war workers, did much to rectify her one-time opposition to women's suffrage. (She had signed Mrs Humphry *Ward's manifesto against the enfranchisement of women in 1909.) She refused to accept the title (Lady Passfield) which came with Sidney's peerage in 1929. Their trip to Russia in 1932 was the result of a long-term interest in that country. *Soviet Communism: A New Civilization?* (1935) shocked many by its enthusiastic support for the Soviet Union. Beatrice Webb's literary reputation rests not on her social and economic works but on her two-volume autobiography *My Apprenticeship* (1926) and *Our Partnership* (1948), and on the extensive diaries which she wrote daily from her girlhood onward. The first volume takes the story of her life up to her marriage and the second, published posthumously, covers the period to 1911. Both make use of her diaries, from which selections were published in 1952 and 1956, edited by Margaret Cole. A four-volume edition, edited by Norman and Jean Mackenzie, was published in 1982–5. F. R. Leavis in his introduction to *Mill on Bentham and Coleridge* (1950) noted her latent talents as a novelist, a genre to which she confessed she 'was tempted from time to time'. Like Spencer he compared her in intellectual range with George Eliot and saw her autobiography, in terms of nineteenth-century thought, as carrying on where John Stuart Mill's had left off. Less flatteringly, H. G. Wells described the Webbs in *The New Machiavelli* (1911) as the Baileys, 'two active self-centred people, excessively devoted to the public service . . . the most formidable and distinguished couple conceivable'. *The*

Letters of Sidney and Beatrice Webb have been edited by Norman Mackenzie (3 vols., 1978). *The Webbs in Asia: The 1911–12 Travel Diary* has been edited by George Feaver (1992). *See* Margaret Cole, *Beatrice Webb* (1946); Lisanne Radice, *Beatrice and Sidney Webb: Fabian Socialists* (1984); Deborah E. Nord, *The Apprenticeship of Beatrice Webb* (1985); Barbara Caine, *Destined to be Wives: The Sisters of Beatrice Webb* (1986); Carolyn Seymour-Jones, *Beatrice Webb: Woman of Conflict* (1992).

Webb, (Gladys) Mary, née Meredith, novelist, essayist, and poet (b. Leighton-under-the-Wrekin, Shropshire, 25 March 1881, d. St Leonard's, Sussex, 8 October 1927).

Mary Webb was the eldest of the six children of George Edward Meredith, head of a boys' prep. school in Shropshire, and his wife Sarah Alice Scott, an Edinburgh doctor's daughter whose family were connected with Sir Walter Scott. She was educated at home by governesses and briefly at a finishing school in Southport. At 14 she was running the household after her mother had been injured in a hunting accident. At 20 she contracted Graves' disease, a thyroid deficiency which gave her a goitre and staring eyes, and which was to recur throughout her life. While convalescing she wrote essays, which were later collected along with her poems in *The Spring of Joy* (1917). Her father's death in 1909 was followed by a period of intense grief. In 1912, at the age of 31, she married Henry Bertram Law Webb, a schoolmaster. The marriage was not happy and there were no children. They lived in Weston-super-Mare and after two years returned to Shropshire, where they supplemented their income by market gardening. Under the stimulus of the Shropshire countryside, with which she felt a keen affinity, she began to write again, producing in only three weeks her first, strongly autobiographical, novel, *The Golden Arrow*, which contained a character modelled on her father. It inaugurated an intense eight-year period in which she wrote four more novels, *Gone to Earth* (1917), *The House in Dormer Forest* (1920), *Seven for a Secret* (1922), dedicated to Thomas Hardy, and her best-known work *Precious Bane* (1924). Her fiction displayed an almost mystical reverence for nature. The novels were set in the past, and emphasized nature's power, beauty, and also cruelty. Her plots revealed tragic lives and several of her characters had physical deformities. Although *Precious Bane* won the Femina Vie Heureuse Prize in 1925 and others were praised by reviewers, the novels were published in small runs and attracted only a modest readership. Stanley Baldwin, then Prime Minister, wrote to express his admiration for *Precious Bane*, but it was not until he spoke enthusiastically of her work at a Royal Literary Fund dinner in 1928, the year after her death, that she became famous. Her novels were reprinted with introductions by Baldwin, John

Buchan, H. R. L. Sheppard, Robert Lynd, and G. K. Chesterton. Her poems were published with an introduction by Walter de la Mare, and *The Spring of Joy* was reprinted in 1928. An unfinished historical novel, *Armour wherein he Trusted*, was issued in 1929. Webb's reputation has had a difficult passage since the early 1930s. The initial posthumous acclaim was damaged by Stella *Gibbons's parody of regional novels, *Cold Comfort Farm* (1932), in which Webb's sombre plots and use of rural dialects and characters found ready satire. But a second wave of appreciation occurred from the mid-1970s onwards. Her *Collected Prose and Poems* were edited by G. M. Coles in 1977, and her *Selected Poems*, also by Coles, in 1981. *See* Glen Cavaliero, *The Rural Tradition in the English Novel* (1977); Gladys Mary Coles, *The Flower of Light: A Biography of Mary Webb* (1978); Erika Duncan, *Unless Soul Clap its Hands: Portraits and Passages* (1984); M. A. Barale, *Daughters and Lovers: The Life and Writing of Mary Webb* (1986).

Webster, Augusta ('Cecil Home'), poet, playwright, and translator (b. Poole, Dorset, 30 January 1837, d. Kew, London, 5 September 1894).

Augusta Webster was the daughter of George Davies, a naval officer, later Vice-Admiral, and his wife Julia Augusta Hume. Her maternal grandfather Joseph Hume (1767–1843) a translator of Dante, was a friend of Hazlitt, Lamb, and William Godwin. Her childhood was spent successively on board a ship in Chichester harbour, at Banff Castle, at Penzance, and eventually in Cambridge where her father was Chief Constable of Cambridgeshire. She attended classes at the Cambridge School of Art, learnt French during brief spells in Paris and Geneva, taught herself Greek in order to help a younger brother, and also learned Italian and Spanish. Her first book, *Blanche Lisle and Other Poems* (1860), was published under the pseudonym Cecil Home, followed by *Lilian Gray* (1864), a poem, and *Lesley's Guardians* (1864), her only novel. In 1863 she married Thomas Webster, a fellow of Trinity College, Cambridge, and later a law lecturer and solicitor. They had one daughter. In 1870 they moved to London, where Webster practised law. From her marriage onward she published under the name Augusta Webster, beginning with a translation of Aeschylus' *Prometheus Bound* (1866) and Euripides' *Medea* (1868), which established her as a serious translator. Her first important volume of poems was *Dramatic Studies* (1866), a collection of eight dramatic monologues showing the influence of both Robert and Elizabeth Barrett *Browning. Three of the speakers were women. 'She has caught Mr. Browning's style with an accuracy that at times makes us almost believe that she has borrowed his words', one reviewer noted. *A Woman Sold and Other Poems* (1867), a longer book with a variety of poetic forms, again showed the influence of the Brownings as well as of Tennyson's *Poems 1842*. *Portraits* (1870), a collection of thirteen monologues, went into a second edition in the same year and a third in 1893. One of the monologues, 'A Castaway', spoken by a prostitute, was compared with D. G. Rossetti's 'Jenny' and later praised by Vita *Sackville-West. Several of the monologues addressed women's predicaments, particularly marriage choices and the plight of the single woman. Webster wrote very little poetry after 1870. *A Book of Rhyme* (1881) introduced the Italian stanza form known as a 'risputti' or 'stornelli' into English poetry. *Mother and Daughter*, a sonnet sequence published posthumously in 1895, edited by W. M. Rossetti, expressed the varying moods and experiences of motherhood, none of them overly idealized. Later in her career she wrote for the theatre. Two plays, *The Auspicious Day* (1872), a melodrama, and *Disguises* (1879), a romantic comedy, were not performed, but a third, *In a Day* (1882), was produced in 1890 with her daughter in the leading role. *The Sentence* (1887), a three-act tragedy about Caligula, was highly regarded by some of her contemporaries, including Christina *Rossetti. W. M. Rossetti pronounced it extravagantly 'the one supreme thing amid the work of *all* British poetesses . . . one of the masterpieces of European drama'. Webster twice stood successfully for election to the London School Board, where she campaigned for the introduction of technical training and for better education for women. *A Housewife's Opinions*, a collection of essays on issues related to married women, were reprinted from the *Examiner* in 1878. Her *Examiner* essays on women's suffrage were reissued by the Women's Suffrage Union (1878). A selection of her poetry was published in 1893, the year before her death at the age of 57. *See* V. Sackville-West, 'The Women Poets of the Seventies', in *The Eighteen-Seventies*, ed. Harley Granville-Barker (1929); Kathleen Hickok, *Representations of Women: Nineteenth-Century British Women's Poetry* (1984); Angela Leighton, *Victorian Women Poets: Writing Against the Heart* (1992).

Weldon, Fay, novelist and playwright (b. Alvechurch, Worcester, 22 September 1933).

Fay Weldon is the daughter of Frank Thornton Birkinshaw, a doctor, and his wife Margaret Jepson, a writer. After her parents' divorce in 1937 she lived with her mother, grandmother, and sister in Christchurch, New Zealand, where she went to a girls' school and grew up believing 'the world was peopled by females'. Relationships between women, particularly mothers and daughters, are a prominent theme in her writing. She and her mother returned to London, where she went to South Hampstead High School and then to the University of St Andrews, where she read economics and psychology. She worked as an advertising copy-writer (the slogan 'Go to work on an egg' was hers), became a single parent (of a son), and in 1960 married Ronald Weldon, an antique dealer, by whom she had three more sons. Her writing career began in the mid-1960s, when she wrote more than thirty television plays, radio scripts, and eight plays for the stage. Her first novel, *The Fat Woman's Joke* (1967, published in the USA as *And the Wife Ran away*), first appeared as a television play of the same title in 1966. Her novels include *Down among the Women* (1971), *Female Friends* (1975), *Remember me* (1976), *Little Sisters* (1978, published in the USA as *Words of Advice*), *Praxis* (1978), *Puffball* (1980), *The President's Child* (1982), *The Life and Loves of a She-Devil* (1984; televised 1986, filmed 1990), *The Shrapnel Academy* (1986), *Leader of the Band* (1988), *The Cloning of Joanna May* (1989), *Moon over Minneapolis* (1991), and *Life Force* (1992). Weldon's feminism is central to her work, which deals with women's troubled relationships with one another, with their children, and with the men who ultimately control and dominate their lives. The extravagant use of black comedy and the supernatural sometimes pushes the fiction to the limits of realism. Her experience as a dramatist is reflected in the deliberate adoption of dialogue which she then subjects to a 'translation', showing what the characters actually meant. She has also published two collections of short stories, *Watching me, Watching you* (1981), which includes her first novel, and *Polaris and Other Stories* (1985). *Letters to Alice on First Reading Jane Austen* (1984), a manifesto on reading the classics, reflects *Austen's own letters to her niece Cassandra. Weldon has also published a study of Rebecca *West (1985), and a polemic against censorship, *Sacred Cows* (1989). *The Heart of the Country* (1987) was her first original television serial. She wrote the film script for Christina *Stead's *For Love Alone*. *See* Margaret Crosland, *Beyond the Lighthouse: English Women Novelists in the 20th Century* (1981); John Haffenden (ed.), *Novelists in Interview* (1985); Olga Kenyon, *Women Novelists Today* (1988); Lorna Sage, *Women in the House of Fiction: Post-War Women Novelists* (1992).

Wellesley, Dorothy (Violet), poet (b. White Waltham, Berkshire, 20 July 1889, d. Withyham, Sussex, 11 July 1956).

Dorothy Wellesley was the only daughter of Robert Ashton, of Croughton, Cheshire, and his wife Lucy Cecilia Dunn Gardner. In 1914 she married Lord Gerald Wellesley, who became the seventh Duke of Wellington in 1943. They had two children, a son and a daughter. As was customary with those of her social background she was educated at home, mainly by foreign governesses, a serious disadvantage to her when she came to write and when, as her friend Vita *Sackville-West pointed out in her *DNB* entry, she needed the intellectual stimulus and discipline of school and university. She began to write poetry at an early age, and from the beginning was a self-styled rebel and a romantic, proclaiming herself an agnostic, a hater of convention, and a free spirit. Sir George Goldie, later the founder of Nigeria, whose biography she wrote in 1934, claimed to have examined her scalp and to have found the bumps of temper, pride, and combativeness highly developed at the age of 11. Her first volume, *Early Poems*, was published in 1913. Others followed at regular intervals, including *Poems* (1920), *Pride and Other Poems* (1923), *Genesis* (1926), *Matrix* (1928), *Jupiter and the Nun* (1932), *Lost Planet and Other Poems* (1942), *Desert Wells* (1946), and *Rhymes for Middle Years* (1954). Her collected poems, *Early Light*, were published in 1955. Her best poetry was characterized by an intense, detailed, and personal vision of nature, what Yeats, who greatly admired her work, called her 'passionate precision'. He introduced a selection of her work published in 1936 and his *Letters on Poetry*, written to her, were published in 1940. A new edition in 1964 was edited by Kathleen *Raine. Yeats and Wellesley together edited the 1937 series of Cuala Press broadsides. She also edited the first series of Hogarth Living Poets and The English Poets in Pictures series, 1941–2. According to Sackville-West, Dorothy Wellesley's poetry was marred by carelessness, a refusal to revise, or to pay attention to grammar and syntax. She also attempted to combine it with amateurish philosophy, history, and archaeology, to give it, in Sackville-West's words, 'a weight it should never have been asked to carry'. She published her autobiography *Far Have I Travelled* in 1952.

West, Jane, novelist and poet (b. London, 30 April 1758, d. Little Bowden, Northamptonshire, 25 March 1852).

Jane West was the only child of John and Jane Iliffe. The family moved to Desborough, in Northamptonshire, when she was 11. She was entirely self-educated, and began to write poetry at the age of 13, later claiming to her friend and patron the antiquarian Thomas Percy that 'the catalogue of my compositions previous to my attaining twenty would be formidable. Thousands of lines flowed in very easy measure. I scorned correction, and never blotted.' She married Thomas West, a farmer from Little Bowden in Northamptonshire whose family had been rectors of the parish for a century and a half, and who were proud of their connection with the minor poet Gilbert West (1703–56). They had three sons. Jane West was persistent in bringing her work to the attention of influential men and women of letters, acquiring a steady list of subscribers while at the same time self-consciously stressing her devotion to domestic duties in the prefaces to *Miscellaneous Poetry* (1786) and *Miscellaneous Poems and a Tragedy* (1791). Her first two novels, *The Advantages of Education; or The History of Maria Williams* (1793) and *A Gossip's Story* (1796), anticipated Jane *Austen's *Sense and Sensibility* as novels of the anti-sensibility school. West's innate Toryism was reflected in her next novel, *A Tale of the Times* (1799), proclaimed as an anti-Jacobin work, and regarded as an implicit attack on William Godwin's *Political Justice.* In 1797 she published *An Elegy on the Death of Edmund Burke. The Infidel Father* (1802) attacked the tenets of atheism, and *The Loyalists* (1812), her first historical novel, set during the English Civil War, reflected her conservatism. *Alicia de Lacey* (1814), a historical romance, may have capitalized on Scott's popularization of this genre, while her final novel, *Ringrove,* published in 1827, when she was 70, derived from the instructive Evangelical tales of writers like Hannah *More. Her *Poems and Plays* were collected in four volumes (1799–1805). West also wrote several popular conduct books, *Letters to a Young Man* (1801) and *Letters to a Young Lady* (1806), the latter dedicated to the Queen and advocating more education for women to fit them for their social and moral responsibilities. Her husband predeceased her in 1823, and she died at Little Bowden in 1852. *See* Marilyn Butler, *Jane Austen and the War of Ideas* (1975, 1987); Patricia Meyer Spacks, in *Fetter'd or Free? British Women Novelists 1670–1815,* ed. Mary Anne Schofield and Cecilia Macheski (1986).

'West, Dame Rebecca' (Cicily Isabel Fairfield, later Andrews), novelist and journalist (b. London, 21 December 1892, d. London, 15 March 1983).

Rebecca West was the youngest of three daughters of Charles Fairfield, one-time army officer and itinerant journalist, and his wife Isabella Campbell Mackenzie. Fairfield abandoned his family in 1901, and his wife returned to her native Edinburgh, where she had been a governess. He died in 1906 without seeing them again. West was given a bursary to attend George Watson's Ladies' College, where she won the school essay prize and at 15 had a letter on 'Women's Electoral Claims' published in the *Scotsman.* A brief period at the Academy of Dramatic Art in London proved unfruitful but she began to write for a new feminist weekly, the *Freewoman,* later the *New Freewoman.* Her pseudonym Rebecca West was taken from a character in Ibsen's *Rosmersholm.* West soon proved a witty, iconoclastic, and ascerbic journalist, writing for the *Clarion,* the *Star,* the *Daily News,* the *New Statesman,* as well as the American *Bookman, New Republic, Vanity Fair,* and the *New York Herald Tribune.* Her irreverent criticism of H. G. Wells's novel *Marriage* led to their meeting in 1913 and to a ten-year affair which was to prove the most intense and also the most destructive aspect of her personal life. Their son Anthony was born in 1914. The troubled relationship of mother and son which evolved into legal as well as emotional battles was another source of unhappiness. In 1930 West married Henry Maxwell Andrews, a banker, who provided her with a stable background until his death in 1968. Her first book was a critical study of Henry James (1916). Her early novels, *The Return of the Soldier* (1918) and *The Judge* (1922), drew on her own emotional experiences, and were the first of eight. Her favourite was *Harriet Hume* (1929) but probably the best was *The Fountain Overflows* (1957), a family saga intended as the first of a trilogy, in which the family portraits were scarcely disguised. *The Birds Fall down* (1966), the last of her novels to be published before her death, contained a character based on her father. Three novels were published posthumously: *This Real Night* (1984), *Cousin Rosamund* (1985), and the unfinished *Sunflower* (1986), dedicated to G. B. *Stern, which drew on her relationship with Wells. In mid-career it was for her trenchant reportage of the Nuremberg trials, described in *The Meaning of Treason* (1949; revised 1965), and the post-war British treason trials, in *A Train of Powder* (1955), that West was justly famous. Probably her most distinguished book was *Black Lamb and Grey Falcon* (1937), a historical travel book and cultural study based on a journey through Yugoslavia, which reflected her love affair with that country or, more specifically, with Serbia. Her disapproval of the totalitarian regime which replaced the Nazi occupation in Yugoslavia hardened into a vociferous anti-communism which possibly had an effect on her later reputation, obscuring the ardent feminism which had remained since her youth. She continued to write and to publish to within months of her death at the age of 90. She was created DBE in 1959. Some of her journalism has been collected in *The Young Rebecca: Writings of Rebecca West 1911–17*, ed. Jane Marcus (1982). Marcus has also edited her *Writings 1911–1917* (1989). *See also* Gordon N. Ray, *H. G. Wells and Rebecca West* (1974); Harold Orel, *The Achievement of Rebecca West* (1986); Victoria Glendinning, *Rebecca West: A Life* (1987, the authorized biography); Joan Garrett Packer, *Rebecca West: An Annotated Bibliography* (1991).

'**Westmacott,** Mary' *see* CHRISTIE, Dame Agatha

Weston, Elizabeth Jane, scholar and poet (b. London, 2 November 1582, d. Prague, 23 November 1612).

Elizabeth Jane Weston's father was thought to have been a member of an old family living at Sutton, in Surrey. The loss of his property, as a result of either Catholicism or political rebellion, forced the family to leave England for the Continent, where they eventually settled at Brux, in Bohemia. Weston's love of high living occasioned further debts in Prague, where he died suddenly in 1597. His widow, son, and daughter found themselves destitute and also badly served by his creditors. Elizabeth Jane and her mother went to Prague in the hope of enlisting the sympathy of the Emperor, Rudolph II. Her scholarly accomplishments (she spoke and wrote English, German, Greek,

Latin, Italian, and Czech), as well as her beauty, won her some powerful advocates and a successful lawsuit. She had already begun to write Latin verses and to correspond with some of the leading scholars of her day in England and in Europe. She spoke mainly German and always wrote, whether prose or poetry, in Latin. Her poems were collected and printed at Frankfurt an der Oder by a Silesian nobleman, Georg Martin von Baldhoven, as *Parthenicon Elisabethae Joannae Westoniae, virginis nobilissimae, poetriae florentissimae, linguarum plurimarum peritissimae.* The third book contained a list of learned women, ending with Weston. Other editions were printed in 1605 or 1606 at Prague, in 1609 at Leipzig, in 1712 in Amsterdam, and at Frankfurt in 1723. Many of her poems were addresses to princes, including James I, who was said to have assisted her suit to the Emperor. She also wrote epigrams, epistles to friends, and a Latin poem in praise of typography, and translated some of Aesop's Fables into Latin verse. English scholars thought highly of her work, and ranked her with Sir Thomas More and the best Latin poets of her day. Her reputation on the Continent was, if anything, higher. Around 1602 she married a lawyer, Johann Leon, agent at the imperial court for the Duke of Brunswick and the Prince of Anhalt, by whom she had four sons, all of whom predeceased her, and three daughters. She died at Prague in 1612 and was buried there. *See* George *Ballard, *Memoirs of Several Ladies of Great Britain* . . . (1752; ed. Ruth Perry, 1985).

Wharton, Anne, poet (b. Ditchley, Oxfordshire, 1659, d. Adderbury, Oxfordshire, 29 October 1685).

Anne Wharton was the second daughter and co-heiress of Sir Henry Lee, a wealthy landowner, and his wife Anne Danvers. Her father died of the plague before she was born, and her mother in childbirth. She was raised at Ditchley in Oxfordshire by her grandmother Anne Wilmot, mother of John Wilmot, Earl of Rochester. In 1673, at the age of 14, she was married to Thomas Wharton, afterwards Marquis of Wharton, who was to become leader of the Whig faction in Parliament and also, according to the *DNB*, to acquire the reputation of being the greatest rake in England. She brought a substantial dowry and a large annual income to the union, which was childless and unhappy. Apart from a year in Paris in 1680–1 for her health, she spent her time in retirement at her husband's country seat, reading and writing. She knew and corresponded with Rochester's mentor Gilbert Burnet, later Bishop of Salisbury, who counselled her against leaving her husband and circulated her poems to Edmund Waller, and also to his female friends. She died at Rochester's home at Adderbury at the age of 26, of a pox caught from her husband, according to her grandmother. She was one of the best-known women poets of the Restoration, although her poetry remained unpublished at her death. Much of it circulated privately and won the commendation of Dryden, Edmund Waller, and Aphra *Behn, among others. Her poems, mainly lyrics, were posthumously published in various miscellanies. Her 'Elegy on the Death of the Earl of Rochester' was published in *Poems by Several Hands*, edited by Nahum Tate in 1685. Some of her poems and others written to her were appended to the poet Edward Young's *Idea of Christian Love* (1688), and more were printed in a miscellany appended to Behn's *Lycidus; or The Lover in Fashion* (1688) and in Dryden's *Miscellany Poems* (1702). Her paraphrase of the Book of Jeremiah along with her praise of Behn appeared in *A Collection of Poems* (1693), reissued as *The Temple of Death* (1695). It was also printed in *Whartoniana* (1727). She left an unpublished blank-verse tragedy, *Love's Martyr; or Witt above Crowns*, and a version of Ovid's *Epistles*, 'Penelope to Ulysses'. Dryden's *Eleonora* (1692) was dedicated to the memory of Wharton's elder sister, the Countess of Abingdon.

Wheeler, Rosina *see* BULWER-LYTTON, Rosina

'**White,** Antonia' (Eirene Adeline Botting), novelist, translator, and journalist (b. London, 31 March 1899, d. London, 10 April 1980).

Antonia White was the only child of Cecil George Botting, senior classics master at St Paul's School, London, and his wife Christine Julia White. Her parents converted to Roman Catholicism when she was 7 and she was then baptized into that faith. By her own account she 'read voraciously' as a child, wrote stories, and published a newspaper which included favourable reviews of her own imaginary books. She was sent to the Convent of the Sacred Heart at Roehampton when she was 9, where she won prizes and from which she was expelled at 14 for writing an *Ouidaesque novel. Her convent experience formed the basis of her first and best-known novel, *Frost in May* (1933), which became a best seller. She attended St Paul's Girls' School for two years, leaving against her father's wishes to become in turn a governess, a teacher in a boys' school, a civil servant, and an advertising copy-writer. She also spent a year at the Royal Academy of Dramatic Art, followed by a brief period as an actress in provincial repertory. Her first marriage in 1921 was annulled on the grounds of non-consummation in 1924. It precipitated a mental breakdown and a nine-month stay in a mental hospital, which provided the material for the third novel of an autobiographical trilogy, *Beyond the Glass* (1954). In 1924 she married for a second time. This marriage was also annulled and in 1930 she married the novelist and journalist Tom Hopkinson, by whom she had a daughter. During this period she became fashion editor of the *Daily Mirror* and drama critic of **Time and Tide*. Her mental instability recurred in 1934, but she recovered through Freudian analysis. She worked again as an advertising copy-writer and then became fashion editor of the *Sunday Pictorial.* During the Second World War she was employed as a writer by the BBC and worked in the political intelligence department of the Foreign Office. Her reputation as a writer was made and rests on *Frost in May*, which she once referred to as 'a kind of legend, the perfect thing I brought off once and never will again'. The first volume of her trilogy, *The Lost Traveller*, was published in 1950, followed by *The Sugar House* (1952) and completed by *Beyond the Glass*, all of which were based on her early life between the ages of 9 and 23. None received the critical acclaim or acquired the popularity of *Frost in May.* White lapsed from Catholicism in 1926, but returned to the Church in 1940, giving an account of the process in a series of letters, *The Hound and the Falcon* (1965). During the last three decades of her life, beginning in 1949, she became a prolific translator, publishing over thirty translations of the work of Colette, de Maupassant, and Marguérite Duras among others. She received the Clairouin Prize for translation in 1950 and became a fellow of the Royal Society of Literature in 1957. She died in London in 1980. White had two daughters, one of whom, Susan Chitty, has edited her *Diaries 1926–1979* (1991–2) and written an introduction to White's unfinished autobiography *As Once in May* (1983), a fragment covering her life up to the age of 6. Both daughters have published memoirs expressing frank and ambivalent feelings about their mother, Chitty in *Now to my Mother* (1985), and Lyndall Hopkinson in *Nothing to Forgive* (1988). White published a play, *Three in a Room* (1947), two children's stories, and *Strangers* (1954), a collection of short stories. Her four novels formed the basis of a television series, *Frost in May*, in 1982. *See* Merryn Williams, *Six Women Novelists* (1987); Paulina Palmer, in *Feminist Criticism: Theory and Practice*, ed. Susan Sellers (1991).

Whitney, Isabella, poet (*fl.* 1567–75).

Isabella Whitney was born into a family of minor gentry consisting of four daughters and two sons. The family home was at Coole Pilate near Nantwich, in Cheshire. Three of her sisters went to London, probably into some form of genteel service, and her brother Geoffrey Whitney (1548?–1601?) was sent to Magdalene College, Cambridge, which he left before taking a degree. His well-known work *A Choice of Emblemes* was published in 1586. Isabella Whitney's writing suggests that she was familiar with some contemporary literature, with the classics, which she may have read in translation, and with Scripture. Her work consists of two poems published by Richard Jones in 1567, *The Copy of a Letter*, 'lately written in meeter, by a younge Gentilewoman: to her unconstant Lover. With an Admonition to al yong Gentilwomen, and to all other Mayds in general to beware of mennes flattery', and a collection of poems, *A Sweet Nosegay or Pleasant Posye, 'Contayning a hundred and ten Phylosophicall flowers', published in* 1573. The work contains metrical versions of maxims from Sir Hugh Platt's *The Floures of Philosophie* (1572), for which she vaguely apologized in her preface, adding that although she had stepped into 'anothers garden for these Flowers' yet 'they be of my owne gathering and makeing'. As well as the 'flowers' or poems the latter work contained 'Certain Familier Epistles and Friendly Letters by the Auctor: With Replies' and a fictional 'Wyll and Testament' addressed to the City of London. *The Copy of a Letter* upheld women's traditional virtues through the persona of a woman betrayed, emphasizing female piety and chastity and condemning male lust and fickleness. Whitney drew on a range of classical betrayed women from Dido to Ariadne and exhorted her readers to protect their virtue. The poems of *A Sweet Nosegay*, written in the ballad metre, had a moral mission, to warn against sin and folly in the contemporary materialist world symbolized by London. Women in particular were at risk, and Whitney wrote humorously of the temptations and snares of the worldly city as opposed to the heavenly one which awaited, a world of infection and pestilence, the flowers from her metaphorical garden offering a cure and a protection from worldly temptations. The 'Wyll and Testament' implicitly asked all Christians to examine their worldliness in the face of death. She may have contributed poems to miscellanies printed by Richard Jones in 1566 and 1578. Little is known of her personal life. She may also have married and changed her name to Eldershae, and possibly had two children. *See* Elaine V. Beilin, *Redeeming Eve: Women Writers of the English Renaissance* (1987); Ann Rosalind Jones, in *The Ideology of Conduct: Essays on Literature and the History of Sexuality*, ed. N. Armstrong and L. Tennenhouse (1987); Tina Krontiris, *Oppositional Voices: Women as Writers and Translators in the English Renaissance* (1992).

'Whyte, Violet' *see* WINTER, John Strange

'Wickham, Anna' (Edith Alice Mary Hepburn, née Harper), poet (b. Wimbledon, London, 1884, d. Hampstead, London, 1947).

Anna Wickham derived her pen-name from Wickham Terrace, Brisbane, where at the age of 10 she promised her father that she would be a poet. Her father Geoffrey Harper was a music salesman and piano tuner, and her flamboyant mother Alice Whelan had trained as a teacher. Her parents took her to Australia at the age of 6, where she attended a succession of schools and eventually Sydney High School. After their return to England she studied singing in Paris, but abandoned her musical ambitions in 1905 when she married Patrick Hepburn, a solicitor and also an astronomer, whose middle-class background and conventional notions about marriage became an immediate source of friction. They had four sons. She wrote poetry to relieve the frustrations and tensions of her domestic life. Her first collection, *Songs of John Oland* (1911), was published in the teeth of her husband's opposition (he had her confined to a lunatic asylum for six weeks after a row). The pleasures of motherhood, on the other hand, were a constant consolation. Alida and Harold Monro of the Poetry Bookshop published nine of her poems in their collection *Poetry and Drama* (1914), followed by two volumes of poems, *The Contemplative Quarry* (1915) and *The Little Old House* (1921). Grant Richards published her third, *The Man with a Hammer* (1916). A New York edition of *The Contemplative Quarry* and *The Man with a Hammer* in 1921 contained an introduction by the poet and critic Louis Untermeyer, who linked the vital feminist elements in her work with the work of May *Sinclair, Virginia *Woolf, Rebecca *West, Dorothy *Richardson, and the American Willa Cather. Untermeyer described her as 'a magnificent gypsy of a woman, wayward, ironic, spontaneous . . . gnarled in her own nervous protests'. After the sudden death of her third son from scarlet fever in 1922 Wickham went to Paris, where she met the American poet and patron of the arts Natalie Barney (1876–1972), through whom she was introduced to a number of English and American as well as French writers. Barney became a regular correspondent and a source of support both emotional and even financial for over ten years, although she appears not to have returned Wickham's passionate devotion. Patrick Hepburn secured a two-year judicial separation in 1926 but the family were reunited in 1928. He died as a result of a mountaineering accident in 1929. Wickham continued to write exuberantly feminist, often erotic poems, emotionally charged, sardonic, compulsive, sometimes experimental in form, as in the lines she said must preface all her books: 'Here is no sacrificed I | Here are more I's than yet were in one human | Here I reveal our common mystery: | I give you *woman*.' Most of her poems were more closely linked to the late nineteenth century than to the world of Auden in which she found herself. She in fact published no major collections in later years. Thirty-six of her poems were included in Richards's Shilling Selections, edited by John Gawsworth, who also included her in the anthologies *Edwardian Poetry* (1937) and *Neo-Georgian Poetry* (1937). She was estimated to have written 1,400 separate poems at the time of her death. Much of her correspondence and possibly many of her manuscripts were destroyed when a firebomb fell on her house in Parliament Hill in 1943. Wickham hanged herself in 1947. Her *Selected Poems*, edited by David Garnett, were published in 1971. *See* introd. by R. D. Smith to *The Writings of Anna Wickham, Free Woman and Poet* (1984), which includes the previously unpublished 'Fragment of an Autobiography: Prelude to a Spring Clean' and her essay 'The Spirit of the Lawrence Women', first published in 1966.

Wilde, Jane Francesca Elgee, Lady ('Speranza'), poet and essayist (b. Wexford, 27 December 1821, d. London, 3 February 1896).

Lady Wilde was the daughter of Charles Elgee, an Anglo-Irish lawyer, and the granddaughter of a rector and archdeacon in the Church of Ireland. Her mother Sarah Kingsbury was the daughter of a clergyman, also of the established Church. As a young woman she involved herself in the nationalist cause, contributing inflammatory prose and verse under the pseudonym Speranza to the Irish journal the *Nation.* It was her article in 1848, 'Jacta alea est' ('The Die is Cast'), urging young Irishmen to take up arms against the British that was used by the prosecution in an unsuccessful attempt to convict the nationalist leader Charles Gavan Duffy of sedition. Speranza claimed her authorship publicly and insisted on her right to speak at the trial. The case brought about the suppression of the journal. At 30 she married William Robert Wills Wilde, later Sir William, an eminent Irish surgeon and also a distinguished antiquary. Their home in Merrion Square, Dublin, became a literary salon frequented by intellectuals, bohemians, and Irish nationalists. It was in this atmosphere that their two sons William C. K. Wilde (1852–1899), later a journalist, and the poet and dramatist Oscar Wilde (1854–1900) grew up. A third child, a daughter died at the age of 10. Lady Wilde was an eccentric figure, nearly six feet tall, fond of outlandish clothes and extravagant headdresses. She was also known for epigrammatic witticisms similar to those of her younger son, and she shared with him a facility for languages. She published several translations from German and French, notably works by Lamartine and Dumas. Her first volume of *Poems* (1864) contained forceful nationalist verse. A second series was published in 1867 and a reissue of both in 1871. After her husband's death she moved to London in 1879, where she conducted a more raffish literary salon with Oscar Wilde as the central figure. Her friends included *Ouida, Marie *Corelli, and Violet *Hunt. She edited two collections of essays on Irish legends and customs begun by her husband (1887 and 1890), and published several volumes of her own essays, including *Notes on Men, Women and Books* (1891) and *Social Studies* (1893). In an essay on 'The Bondage of Women' included in *Social Studies* she wrote: 'We have now traced the history of women from Paradise to the nineteenth century, and have heard nothing through the long roll of the ages but the clank of their fetters.' Oscar Wilde's early journalism includes two reviews of his mother's books which he admitted were flagrant puffs. Despite some assistance from her son Lady Wilde's finances dwindled drastically. She received a grant from the Royal Literary Fund in 1888 and a civil-list pension in 1890 in recognition of her late husband's services to statistical science and literature. She none the less died impoverished during Oscar Wilde's imprisonment in 1896. *See* H. Wyndham, *Speranza: A Biography of Lady Wilde* (1951); Richard Ellmann, *Oscar Wilde* (1987).

Williams, Anna, poet (b. Rosemarket, near Milford Haven, 1706, d. London, 6 September 1783).

Anna Williams's father Zachariah Williams (1673(?)–1755) was a physician and inventor who thought he had discovered a new method of ascertaining longitude at sea. He came to London in the 1720s, accompanied by his daughter, hoping to receive the £20,000 prize which had been instituted for the discovery, but his hopes were disappointed, and he was eventually admitted as a pensioner to the Charterhouse. Anna Williams was well educated, knew French and Italian, and helped to support herself and her father through needlework. At the Charterhouse she met the scientist Stephen Grey and assisted him in his experiments with electricity, witnessing, as she later recorded, 'the emission of the electrical spark from a human body'. She suffered from cataracts which led to the severe reduction of her sight. She continued with her needlework, and also made some money from a translation of de la Bléterie's *Life of the Emperor Julian* (1746). When the Williamses were expelled from the Charterhouse (it was against the rules to have one's family live there) they were befriended by Dr Johnson and his wife. He arranged for an operation on her eyes, conducted at his house, which unfortunately resulted in her total blindness. Her father died in 1755, leaving her in a financially precarious position. Garrick gave her a benefit with Aaron Hill's play *Merope* in 1756, which raised £200. Soon after the death of Johnson's wife she moved into his house and from that time until the end of her life lived either with or near him. Subscriptions for the proposed publication of her *Miscellanies in Prose and Verse* had been instigated by Johnson as early as 1750, but whether he doubted their quality, or whether the project was simply postponed, they were not published until 1766. Johnson contributed a preface, and Hester Thrale (later *Piozzi) a poem. The publication realized a little over £300, the interest on which, together with an annual allowance of £10 from Elizabeth *Montagu from 1775 onward, allowed her to live in reasonable comfort. Her health deteriorated in 1776 and she grew increasingly bad-tempered. She died at Johnson's house in 1783 and at his suggestion left her money to a home for deserted females. Anna Williams features prominently in Boswell's writing, where he recorded Johnson's high regard for her.

Williams, Helen Maria, political writer, poet, and novelist (b. London, 1762, d. Paris, 15 December 1827).

Helen Maria Williams was the daughter of Charles Williams, an army officer of Welsh descent, and Helen Hay, a Scot. She was brought up in Berwick-upon-Tweed after her father's death, and educated by her mother. The family, which included her mother and her only sister, moved to London in 1781, where she published her *Edwin and Eltruda: A Legendary Tale* (1782) with the help of a family friend. The poem was well received, and reprinted in a collection of old ballads in 1784. Its success gave her an entrée to literary circles, where her acquaintances included Fanny *Burney, Dr Johnson, Elizabeth *Montagu, Anna *Seward, Hester *Piozzi, Samuel Rogers, and Charlotte *Smith. *An Ode on the Peace* (1783), *Peru* (1784), her *Collected Poems* (1786), which were generously subscribed, and her *Poem* on the Slave Bill (1788) cemented her reputation as a fashionable poet with liberal opinions. Her acquaintances now included members of Dissenting and radical circles. A poem on 'The Bastille' which was included in her novel *Julia* (1790) previewed her enthusiasm for the French Revolution, which she was soon to witness at first hand. She arrived in France in the summer of 1790, at the invitation of an aristocratic French family, determined to be impressed by what she saw. Her *Letters Written in France in the Summer of 1790* (1790) were widely read in England, as were the subsequent four volumes *Letters from France* (1792–6). Her salon in Paris in 1793 was a meeting place for many expatriate sympathizers with the Revolution, including Thomas Paine, Mary *Wollstonecraft, and Gilbert Imlay. Williams was a particular friend and supporter of Madame Roland, the Girondist leader and writer, who was executed in the summer of 1793. She was herself imprisoned by Robespierre in 1793. Despite the increasing atrocities of the Terror her enthusiasm for the Revolution never wavered. This attitude lost her the support of many of her friends in England and many of her readers. Rumours of her extra-marital liaison with the Unitarian radical John Hurford Stone accelerated the decline in her reputation. Horace Walpole dismissed her as a 'scribbling trollop', and another contemporary described her as 'an intemperate advocate of Gallic licentiousness'. Mrs Piozzi noted in her diary that her 'friends are all ashamed of her'. Others of her critics maintained that she had misjudged the real situation in France, and was easily swayed by partisan witnesses. Her *Letters from France* were continued by *A Tour in Switzerland* (1798), an account of six months' residence there with Stone in 1794, *Sketches of the State of Manners and Opinions in the French Republic* (1801), and the forged *Political and Confidential Correspondence of Louis XVI* (1803), which she 'edited', believing it to be genuine. In 1815 she published *A Narrative of the Events which have*

Taken Place in France from the Landing of Napoleon Bonaparte . . . to the Restoration of Louis XVIII (1815) and in 1819 *Letters on the Events which have Passed in France since the Restoration.* Most of her energies went into her letters and narratives about France, but while in prison she translated Saint-Pierre's *Paul et Virginie* and later von Humboldt's travels. Her second novel, *Perourou, the Bellows-Mender* (1801), was better known in its stage version, *The Lady of Lyons*, by Bulwer-Lytton. Her *Poems* were collected in 1791, before she left permanently for France, and her *Poems on Various Subjects* was published in 1823. She reopened her salon in Paris after the Restoration. Stone died in 1818. She lived for a while in Amsterdam with her nephew, and died in Paris in 1827. *See* L. D. Woodward, *Une Anglaise amie de la Révolution française: Hélène-Maria Williams et ses amies* (1930); Janet Todd, introd. to *Letters from France 1790–5* (1976).

Williams, Peggy Eileen Arabella *see* EVANS, Margiad

Winchilsea, Anne Finch, Countess of *see* FINCH, Anne

Wingfield, Sheila (Claude) ('Sheila Powerscourt'), poet (b. Hampshire, 23 May 1906).

Sheila Wingfield is the only daughter of Colonel Claude Beddington, a landowner who fought in both the Boer War and the First World War, and his wife Frances Ethel Homan-Mulock. She went to Roedean, passed the entrance exam for Cambridge at 15, but was prevented by her mother from going to university. In 1932 she married the Honourable Mervyn Patrick Wingfield, later Viscount Powerscourt, by whom she had a daughter and two sons. By her own account she determined to become a poet 'in the nursery', but literature was a 'hole and corner' affair because of her parents' disapproval and later her husband's dislike of literary circles. Her first collection, *Poems* (1938), published when she was 32, demonstrated her professed interests, 'the Irish and English countryside and country ways in general . . . history, archaeology, folklore, and the superb economy of the classical Greeks'. Its spare, economical style prompted comparisons with the early Imagist works of H(ilda) D(oolittle) and Ezra Pound. *Beat Drum, Beat Heart* (1946), a long meditative poem in four linked sections, 'Men and War', 'Men at Peace', 'Women in Love', 'Women at Peace', contrasted military and personal experience, and explored the effects of war. *A Cloud across the Sun* (1949) contained poems mainly about Ireland, where she and her husband lived at Powerscourt, the family's country house in County Wicklow, until its destruction by fire in 1974. She has published several retrospective collections: *A Kite's Dinner: Poems 1938–54* (1954), a Poetry Book Society choice, *The Leaves Darken* (1964), *Her Storms: Selected Poems 1938–77* and *Admissions: Poems 1974–77* (both 1977). Her *Collected Poems* was published in 1983. She has also written two unconventional volumes of memoirs, *Real People* (1952), which John Betjeman described as 'a new kind of autobiography, a selfless one . . . a series of reminiscences written with a poet's care for the sound and sense of words and all about other people', and *Sun too Fast* (1974), a collection of autobiographical fragments. The latter, published under the name Sheila Powerscourt, appeared in the same year as the destruction of her country house and a year after her husband's death. She has suffered from ill health in the intervening years and now lives in Switzerland. *See* prefaces by G. S. Fraser to *Her Storms* (1977) and *Collected Poems* (1983).

Winkworth, Catherine, poet and translator (b. Holborn, London, 13 September 1827, d. Monnetier, near Geneva, 1 July 1878).

Catherine Winkworth was the fourth daughter of Henry Winkworth, a silk merchant and the son of an Evangelical clergyman, and of Susanna Dickenson, the daughter of a Kentish farmer. The family moved to Manchester in 1829, where Catherine was taught at home by governesses but also by two eminent Unitarian clergymen, the Revd William Gaskell, later the husband of Elizabeth *Gaskell, and the Revd James Martineau, brother of Harriet *Martineau. The Winkworth family became close friends with the Gaskells and Catherine later claimed that she owed her knowledge and appreciation of English literature to William Gaskell. Her mother died in 1841, and in 1845, the year of her father's remarriage, she went to live for a year with an aunt in Dresden as governess to her daughters. The year in Germany stimulated an intense interest in German language and literature. In 1855 she published the first series of her *Lyra Germanica*, translations of commonly used German hymns, which went into more than twenty editions, and was followed in 1858 by a second series, and by a selection in 1859. The translations did more to influence the use of German hymns in England than any other source. At the suggestion of Baron Bunsen, a former German ambassador, they were published with music as *The Chorale Book for England* in 1862. In the same year the family suffered a financial set-back and moved to Clifton, near Bristol, where Catherine immersed herself in the movement to promote higher education for women. She organized a series of successful lectures followed by classes to prepare women for Cambridge examinations, and helped in the establishment of Bristol University College, later Bristol University. After her death two scholarships for women were founded in her memory. She was also a governor of the Red Maid's School, Bristol, a promoter of the Clifton High School for Girls, and a member of the council of Cheltenham Ladies' College. She published translations of German prose as well as hymns, *Veni Sancti Spiritus* (1865), a collection of Latin and English hymns, and *Christian Singers of Germany* (1869), a series of biographical sketches. She died of a heart attack in 1878. *See* M. J. Shaen, *Memorials of Two Sisters: Susanna and Catherine Winkworth* (1908).

Winkworth, Susanna, translator (b. London, 13 August 1820, d. Clifton, Bristol, 25 November 1884).

Susanna Winkworth received much the same education as her younger sister *Catherine. Both moved in Manchester Unitarian circles and were friendly with William and Elizabeth *Gaskell. In 1850 Susannah confided her wish to translate the life of the German historian Niebuhr to Elizabeth Gaskell, who arranged for her to spend time in Bonn with Baron Bunsen, then the German ambassador to England. She stayed in Bonn, acting as Bunsen's secretary for a year in 1850–1, while working on the translation. So much new material was added to the *Life* in the form of letters and essays that the translation was virtually an original work, published by Chapman & Hall in 1851–2. At the suggestion of Bunsen, who had become her literary mentor, she published an important translation of the *Theologia Germanica* (1854), first discovered and published by Luther in 1516. The translation contained a preface by Charles Kingsley. In 1855 Winkworth completed a Life of Luther begun by Julius Charles Hare. She translated Bunsen's *Signs of the Times* (1856), his *God in History* (1868–70), the Life and sermons of the German theologian John Tauler (1857), and Max Muller's *German Love from the Papers of an Alien* (1858). When the family moved to Bristol she became active in a campaign to secure better housing for the poor and shared her sister Catherine's interest in education for women. *See* M. J. Shaen, *Memorials of Two Sisters: Susanna and Catherine Winkworth* (1908).

'**Winter,** John Strange' (Henrietta Eliza Vaughan, Mrs Arthur Stannard, also 'Violet Whyte'), novelist (b. York, 13 January 1856, d. Putney, London, 13 December 1911).

John Strange Winter was the only daughter of Henry Vaughan Palmer, rector of St Margaret's, York, and a former officer in the Royal Artillery, and his wife Emily Catherine Cowling. She was educated at Bootham House School, York, and in 1874 began a ten-year engagement with the *Family Herald*, publishing novels and stories under the pseudonym Violet Whyte. The long-standing family tradition of army service was reflected in *Cavalry Sketches* (1881) and *Regimental Legends* (1883), published under the masculine pseudonym John Strange Winter, thought more appropriate to the subject-matter. She retained the name to the end of her career. In 1884 she married Arthur Stannard, a civil engineer, by whom she had a son and three daughters. In 1885 she published her best-known work, *Bootles' Baby: A Story of the Scarlet Lancers*, serialized first in the *Graphic*, which reportedly sold two million copies in the ten years after publication. There was also a successful dramatized version. Military life continued to be the main setting for over one hundred novels which followed, leading Ruskin, a friend and regular correspondent, to pronounce her 'the author to whom we owe the most finished and faithful rendering ever yet given of the character of the British soldier'. Her novels included *Army Society* (1886), *Pluck* (1886), *Mignon's Husband* (1887), *Beautiful Jim of the Blankshire Regiment* (1888), *A Soldier's Children* (1892), *That Mrs. Smith* (1893), and *Grip* (1896). In 1891 she founded a penny weekly magazine, *Golden Gates*, later retitled *Winter's Weekly*, which continued until 1895. Mrs Stannard's professionalism was reflected in her presidencies of the Writers' Club (1892) and of the Society of Women Journalists (1901–3). It combined with an equally fervent domesticity, according to contemporary sources. In 1896 the ill health of her husband and youngest daughter led the family to remove to Dieppe, which formed the background for many of her later works. She was intensely fond of animals and also interested in women's dress and grooming. At the end of her career she developed and sold a number of toiletries for the hair and complexion. She died as a result of an accident at the age of 55. Despite her various commercial successes she left little more than £500. *See* Helen C. Black, *Notable Women Authors of the Day* (1893); Oliver Bainbridge, *John Strange Winter: A Volume of Personal Record* (1916).

Winterson, Jeanette, novelist (b. Manchester, 1959).

Jeanette Winterson is the adopted daughter of Pentecostal Evangelists John William Winterson, a factory worker, and his wife Constance Brownrigg. Conditioned for evangelistic service, she wrote sermons at 8, attended Accrington Girls' Grammar School, and prepared to become a preacher. A love affair with a woman when she was 15 brought parental and community opprobrium and she left home. She kept up her academic studies at Accrington FE College while working variously as an ice-cream van driver, a make-up assistant in a funeral parlour, and a domestic in a mental home. After reading English at St Catherine's College, Oxford, 1978–81, she worked at the Roundhouse Theatre, London, and in publishing 1983–7. She has been a full-time writer since 1987. Her autobiographical first novel *Oranges Are not the Only Fruit* (1985) brought her some critical attention and the television version in 1990 widened her audience. The *Bildungsroman*, satiric, comic, angry, yet affectionate, chronicles her upbringing in the close but censorious

Lancashire community, the emergence of a lesbian identity, and her adolescent struggles with her mother. It won the Whitbread Award for a first novel. *Boating for Beginners* (1985) presents a conjunction of modern capitalism, feminism, and publicity techniques with the biblical story of Noah. *The Passion* (1987) juxtaposes the story of a French peasant who is chef to Napoleon with that of an androgynous Venetian girl from a fishing community. The novel, which won the John Llewellyn Rhys Memorial Prize, combines fantasy, dream, and ideas about history, narrative, and passion. *Sexing the Cherry* (1989) is a historical novel, rich in literary allusion, which sets its two seventeenth-century characters against twentieth-century counterparts. The narrative is repeatedly interrupted by digressions. The rewriting of the fairy-tale of the twelve dancing princesses, which forms one of the many interludes, is reminiscent of the work of Angela *Carter. *Written on the Body* (1992) is about a triangular relationship in which the gender of the main character is unspecified. The possibilities as well as the constrictions of narrative and fantasy underpin all of Winterson's novels. In *Oranges Are not the Only Fruit* the narrator proclaims: 'I could have been a priest not a prophet. The priest has a book with the words set out. Old words, known words, words of power, words that are always on the surface. . . . The prophet has no book. The prophet is a voice that cries in the wilderness, full of sounds that do not always set into meaning.' Winterson has written an alternative fitness guide, *Fit for the Future* (1986), a radio play, *Static* (1988), and has edited *Passion Fruit: Romantic Fiction with a Twist* (1986). She lives in London. *See* Susan Rubin Suleiman, in *Femmes Frauen Women*, ed. Françoise van Rossum-Guyon (1990); Rebecca O'Rourke, in *Feminist Criticism: Theory and Practice*, ed. Susan Sellers (1991).

Wollstonecraft, Mary, later Godwin, novelist and essayist (b. Spitalfields, London, 27 April 1759, d. London, 10 September 1797).

Mary Wollstonecraft was the eldest of the three daughters and the second of the six children of Edward John Wollstonecraft, a one-time farmer who dissipated a large inheritance from his father, a Spitalfields manufacturer, in various unsuccessful commercial and agricultural schemes, and his Irish wife Elizabeth Dixon. Her mother's favouritism towards her elder brother, the strictness of the parental regime, and her father's increasing drunkenness and violence (Mary reportedly lay on the landing outside her parents' bedroom to prevent him beating her mother) made for an unhappy childhood. Mary spent two years as a lady's companion in Bath, and after their mother's death in 1780 she and her sisters left home permanently. In 1783 she set up a school in Newington Green with her sister Eliza and a friend, Fanny Blood.

Thoughts on the Education of Daughters (1787), her first publication, was prompted by these experiences, and published with the help of Joseph Johnson, the radical bookseller of St Paul's Churchyard. After a journey to Lisbon to comfort Fanny Blood, who later died as a result of childbirth, Wollstonecraft took a post in Ireland as governess to the children of Lord Kingsborough, later the Earl of Kingston. The following year she returned to London, where Johnson published her novel *Mary: A Fiction* (1788), a collection of *Original Stories from Real Life* (1788), a later edition of which was illustrated by Blake, and a selection of texts for girls, *The Female Reader* (1789). Johnson employed her as a reader and translator for the next five years, during which time she translated Lavater's *Physiognomy*, Jacques Necker's *Of the Importance of Religious Opinions* (1788), and C. G. Salzmann's *Elements of Morality* (1790), and contributed several articles to Johnson's *Analytical Review*. In 1791 she impulsively wrote a response to Burke's *Reflections on the Revolution in France* (1790), published by Johnson as *A Vindication of the Rights of Men*. She had by this time begun to move in radical circles, meeting William Godwin unpropitiously in 1791, when he considered that she dominated the conversation in a group which included Thomas Paine. She published her most famous work, *A Vindication of the Rights of Woman*, a powerful plea for a change in society's perceptions of the function and potential of women, in 1792. It met with some success, and was translated into French, but its full impact was to be posthumous. She had meanwhile fallen passionately in love with Henry Fuseli (1741–1825), a Swiss artist who had settled in London, and who did not return her affections. In December 1792 she went to Paris to distance herself from Fuseli, and to view the impact of the Revolution at first hand. Her impressions were recorded in her *Historical and Moral View of the French Revolution* (1794). In Paris she met Helen Maria *Williams and Gilbert Imlay, an American *émigré* writer and veteran of the recent Revolutionary War, with whom she lived as his common-law-wife. In May 1794 she bore him a daughter, Fanny. In 1796 she travelled to Scandinavia to assist Imlay's business interests, publishing some of her *Letters Written during a Short Residence in Sweden, Norway and Denmark* (1796). The cooling of Imlay's affections and his liaison with another woman prompted an unsuccessful attempt to drown herself by jumping into the Thames. She eventually broke off the relationship, resumed her friendship with Johnson, and began to move again in literary society. Godwin had been impressed by her *Letters from Sweden*, declaring later, 'if ever there was a book calculated to make a man in love with its author, this appears to be the book', and renewed his acquaintance with her at the home of Mary *Hays. They began to live together in September 1796 and Mary's pregnancy prompted them to marry in March 1797. Godwin took an additional apartment further down the street in order to work. Mary died of complications during the birth of their daughter Mary (later *Shelley) in September 1797. Her unfinished novel *The Wrongs of Woman; or Maria*, in many ways a sequel to her earlier feminist work, was published together with other *Posthumous Works*, including letters and a *Memoir* by Godwin, in 1798. Her reputation during her life was controversial, due both to her radical and 'unfeminine' political views and to the circumstances of her private life. It declined dramatically after her death, remained low through much of the nineteenth century, but has been restored in the twentieth through the attention given to her works by feminist critics and the women's movement. A selection of her letters was published in 1979 (ed. Ralph M. Wardle). Her complete *Works* were published in 1989 (ed. Janet Todd and Marilyn Butler). *See* George *Eliot, 'Margaret Fuller and Mary Wollstonecraft', *The Essays of George Eliot*, ed. T. Pinney (1963); Virginia *Woolf, 'Mary Wollstonecraft', *The Common Reader: Second Series* (1932); Claire Tomalin, *The Life and Death of Mary Wollstonecraft* (1974); Janet Todd (ed.), *Mary Wollstonecraft: A Bibliography* (1976); Mary Poovey, *The Proper Lady and the Woman Writer* (1984); Cora Kaplan, *Sea Changes* (1986); Janet Todd, *The Sign of Angellica: Women, Writing and Fiction, 1660–1800* (1989); Gary Kelly, *Revolutionary Feminism: The Mind and Career of Mary Wollstonecraft* (1992).

Women Writers' Suffrage League.

Founded in 1908 by journalists Cicely *Hamilton and Bessie Hatton as an auxiliary of the National Union of Women's Suffrage Societies, with the object of obtaining 'the Parliamentary Franchise for women on the same terms as it is, or maybe, granted to men'. The prospectus stated that its methods were 'the methods proper to writers—the use of the pen'. The qualification for membership was the publication or production of a book, article, story, poem, or play for which the author had received payment and an annual subscription of *2s. 6d.* Women writers were encouraged to join the League. 'A body of writers working for a common cause cannot fail to influence public opinion,' the prospectus urged. League members were expected to write letters to newspapers, to contribute to suffrage periodicals, and to write essays, stories, and plays publicizing the demand for the vote. On the whole they did not engage in militancy. Elizabeth *Robins was the League's first president. According to Elaine Showalter her play *Votes for Women* (1907) was one of the most influential pieces of literary propaganda to come out of the suffrage movement. Other activists in the League were Beatrice *Harraden, Violet *Hunt, May *Sinclair, Olive *Schreiner, Sarah *Grand, Gertrude Warden, Alice *Meynell, Flora Annie Steel, Mrs Israel Zangwill, Mrs Havelock Ellis, and Evelyn Sharp. The literature produced by

League members included Charlotte Despard and Mabel Collins's *Outlawed: A Novel on the Woman Suffrage Question* (1908), Evelyn Sharp's short stories *Rebel Women* (1910), and Elizabeth Gibson's collection of poems *From the Wilderness* (1910). Theatrical productions included Cicely Hamilton's comedy *How the Vote was Won* (1909), Beatrice Harraden's skit *Lady Geraldine's Speech*, Bessie Hatton's *Before Sunrise*, and *A Pageant of Great Women*, starring Ellen Terry, which opened at the Scala Theatre in November 1909. The Anti-Suffrage League also attracted women writers, notably Mrs Humphry *Ward, who became its first president in 1908. Marie *Corelli and Pearl *Craigie ('John Oliver Hobbes') also expressed anti-suffrage sentiments. The suffrage campaign was attacked from the Left as well as from the Right. Opposition from the Left formed around a group who were mainly anarchistic socialists, friends of the Fabian Society, and contributors to the *New Age* magazine. Their chief organ was the *Freewoman*, later the *New Freewoman* (1911–13), a periodical edited by Dora Marsden, succeeded by the *Egoist* (1914–19), edited by Harriet Shaw Weaver. Marsden dissociated the *New Freewoman* from the suffrage campaign at an early stage, claiming that the periodical was not for 'the advancement of Woman, but for the empowering of individuals, men and women'. *See* Elaine Showalter, *A Literature of their Own: British Women Novelists from Brontë to Lessing* (1977); Karmela Belinki, *Women's Fiction and Suffrage in England* 1905–1914 (1984).

Wood, Mrs Henry (Ellen, née Price), novelist (b. Worcester, 17 January 1814, d. London, 10 February 1887).

Mrs Henry Wood was the daughter of Thomas Price, a cultivated Worcester glove manufacturer, and his wife Elizabeth Evans. She lived with her grandmother during her early years, and developed a curvature of the spine which remained with her for the rest of her life. Much of her writing was done in a reclining chair with her manuscript on her knees. In 1836 she married Henry Wood, a banker and former consular official. They lived in France with their children for twenty years until a reversal in her husband's fortunes necessitated a return to London and the supplementing of the family income by her writing. She had begun to write while in France, contributing to *Bentley's Miscellany* and to Henry Colburn's *New Monthly Magazine*. Her first novel, *Danesbury House* (1860), was written in less than a month in response to the offer of a prize by the Scottish Temperance League. Her next novel, *East Lynne* (1861), a *sensation novel advocating marital fidelity, made her reputation, and remained her best-known work. Wood sold the copyright to her publisher Richard Bentley for £600. The novel was subsequently translated into several European languages, and the various dramatized versions became stock items in the repertoire of theatrical companies both in Britain and abroad. Mrs Wood received no royalties for these or for the hundreds of thousands of copies which were sold in her lifetime. It is in the dramatized version, not the novel, that Isabel Vane, the disguised heroine, watches the death of her son and utters the lines 'Dead! dead! and never called me mother.' *East Lynne* was followed by two family sagas, *Mrs Halliburton's Troubles* (1862) and *The Channings* (1862), both involving her characteristic plotting devices of crime and detection. In 1867 she brought Alexander Strahan's magazine the *Argosy*, which she modelled on Elizabeth *Braddon's *Belgravia* and used as an outlet for her own fiction. Her best contributions to the magazine are thought to be her 'Johnny Ludlow' stories, based on memories of her Worcestershire childhood, and republished in volume form in 1874–89. Wood often used autobiographical material and local colouring in her fiction. She was an orthodox churchwoman and a strong conservative. Her fiction invokes stern retribution for all who transgress the codes of Victorian family morality. The unflattering picture of trade union activity in *A Life's Secret* (1867), published by the Religious Tract Society in the *Leisure Hour*, resulted in a demonstration outside the society's offices. Mrs Wood's favourite work was the uncharacteristic *Shadow of Ashlydyat* (1863), a ghost story with *Gothic elements. Other novels included *Lord Oakburn's Daughters* (1864), *Mildred Arkell* (1865), a story of a Victorian spinster, *Anne Hereford* (1868), *Roland Yorke* (1869), the sequel to *The Channings, Bessy Wells* (1875), and *Court Netherleigh* (1881). By the end of her career Wood had published over thirty full-length novels and over 300 short stories. She died of heart failure in 1887. Her son Charles, who had helped to edit the *Argosy*, published *Memorials of Mrs Henry Wood* (1894). *See* A. Sergeant (ed.), *Women Novelists of Queen Victoria's Reign* (1897); Winifred Hughes, *The Maniac in the Cellar: Sensation Novels of the 1860s* (1980); Sally Mitchell (ed.), *Mrs Henry Wood's East Lynne* (1984).

Woodbridge, Mercy *see under* BRADSTREET, Anne

Woolf, (Adeline) Virginia, novelist and critic (b. London, 25 January 1882, d. Rodmell, Sussex, 28 March 1941).

Born at Hyde Park Gate, London, Virginia Woolf was the third of the four children of Leslie Stephen, later Sir Leslie (1832–1904), Victorian philosopher and man of letters, and his second wife Julia Duckworth (1847–95). Both parents had been married before. Stephen's first wife Harriet (Minny) was the daughter of W. M. Thackeray, making Anne Thackeray *Ritchie her 'aunt' by a former marriage. Family life alternated between London and a house near St Ives in Cornwall. She was taught at home by both parents and given the run of her father's library. She read voraciously but none the less resented her brothers' easy access to a university education, a theme she expanded in her feminist polemic *Three Guineas* (1938). She endured the sexual harassment of her two half-brothers and in 1895 the death of her mother. This, together with the deaths of a half-sister in 1897, her father's in 1904, and her brother Thoby's in 1906, precipitated the first in a series of mental breakdowns which were to increase in severity, together with the ensuing repugnant treatments. After their parents' deaths, Virginia, her sister, the painter Vanessa Bell (1879–1961), and her brother Adrian, together with Duckworth half-brothers and a sister, lived in a series of houses in Bloomsbury, which eventually became the nucleus of the so-called 'Bloomsbury Group' of writers, artists, and intellectuals dedicated to opposing Victorian orthodoxy and promoting a refined modern culture. Other members of the 'group' included Roger Fry, John Maynard Keynes, Lytton Strachey, E. M. Forster, and Clive Bell (husband of Vanessa). Virginia had begun to write regularly for the *Times Literary Supplement* in 1905. In 1912 she married Leonard Sidney Woolf (1880–1969), the Cambridge-educated son of a Jewish barrister, recently returned from a stint as a colonial civil servant in Ceylon. Leonard Woolf tailored his own career as a writer and social reformer to bolster Virginia's precarious mental health and to act as a buffer to the outside world. She recovered from a severe breakdown in 1914 after a year's convalescence. In 1917, partly as a form of therapy, the Woolfs set up the Hogarth Press, publishing *Two Stories* by 'L. and V. Woolf'. The unexpected success of the venture led to a series of publications advertised as by 'the best and most original' of young authors. These included Katherine *Mansfield's *Prelude* (1918), T. S. Eliot's *Poems* (1919), and E. M. Forster's *The Story of the Siren* (1920). Vanessa Bell designed the distinctive dust-jackets and provided occasional woodcut illustrations. Virginia had meanwhile begun to write fiction. *The Voyage Out*, her first novel, published in 1915 but written earlier, was followed in 1919 by *Night and Day*. But it was a trio of highly original novels, *Jacob's Room* (1922), *Mrs Dalloway* (1925), and *To the Lighthouse* (1927), which established her as a writer in the forefront of the modernist movement. Their use of the stream of consciousness or interior monologue, the absence of conventional plot or action, and the lyrical intensity of the novels marked Woolf out from her Edwardian and Georgian contemporaries. An essay, 'Mr. Bennett and Mrs. Brown', published in the *Nation and Athenaeum* (1923) set out her opposition to her 'materialist' or realist predecessors (Wells, Galsworthy, and Arnold Bennett) and outlined her own highly individual principles of fiction-writing. The works of Joyce, William James, Bergson, and Freud were important early influences. *The Waves* (1931) was the most complete realization of the stream of consciousness technique. *Orlando* (1928), a fantasy/history with an androgynous hero/heroine, was inspired by her relationship with Vita *Sackville-West. *Flush* (1933) was the 'biography' of Elizabeth Barrett *Browning's dog. *The Years* (1937) was a more conventional family chronicle. *Between the Acts* (1941), her last novel, marked a return to experimental fiction and bridged the time gap between Woolf's Victorian childhood and her twentieth-century adulthood. She wrote meanwhile a stream of perceptive, elegant, and highly individualistic literary criticism for various weekly reviews. Many of her essays included shrewd personal responses to and reassessments of long-forgotten women writers of all periods. Some were collected in *The Common Reader* (1925) and *The Common Reader: Second Series* (1932). Her most forceful contribution to the cause of women's writing was the polemical *A Room of One's Own* (1929 manuscript versions ed. S P Rosenbaum 1992), based on lectures she gave at Girton College, Cambridge, followed in 1938 by a sequel, *Three Guineas.* In 1941, after completing Between the Acts, but before its publication, fearing the onset of another mental breakdown, she drowned herself in the River Ouse near her home in Sussex. Several collections of her essays were published posthumously: *The Death of the Moth* (1942), *The Moment and Other Essays* (1947), *The Captain's Death Bed* (1950), and *Granite and Rainbow* (1958). Leonard Woolf edited *A Writer's Diary* in 1953 and four volumes of her *Collected Essays* (1966–7). *A Haunted House* (1943) collected previously unpublished short stories. Her *Letters* have been edited by Nigel Nicolson and Joanne Trautmann (6 vols., 1975–80), her *Diaries* by Anne Olivier Bell and Andrew McNeillie (5 vols., 1977–84), and her early journals by M. A. Leake (1990). Susan Dick has edited *The Complete Shorter Fiction* (1985, rev. 1989); and *Moments of Being*, ed. Jeanne Schulkind (1976, rev. 1985), collects unpublished autobiographical writings. Andrew McNeillie is editing her *Essays* (1986–). The centrality of Woolf's work to contemporary (post-1970) feminist criticism and the ending of her copyright in 1991 have prompted numerous new editions of her novels, the introductions to which reflect the range of critical approaches to her work. A Shakespeare Head Press edition of her works is in preparation. *See* Quentin Bell, *Virginia Woolf: A Biography* (2 vols., 1972); Robin Majumdar and Allen McLaurin (eds.), *Virginia Woolf: The Critical Heritage* (1975); B. J. Kirkpatrick, *A Bibliography of Virginia Woolf* (3rd edn. 1980); Jane Marcus (ed.), *New Feminist Essays on Virginia Woolf* (1981); Lyndall Gordon, *Virginia Woolf: A Writer's Life* (1984); Angelica Bell, *Deceived with Kindness* (1984); Rachel Bowlby, *Virginia Woolf: Feminist Destinations* (1988); John Mepham, *Virginia Woolf: A Literary Life* (1992); Suzanne Raitt, *Vita and Virginia* (1993).

Wordsworth, Dorothy, diarist and letter writer (b. Cockermouth, 5 December 1771, d. Rydal, Cumberland, 25 January 1855).

Dorothy Wordsworth was the third of the five children of John Wordsworth, law-agent to Sir James Lowther, later first Earl of Lonsdale, and his wife Ann Cookson, the daughter of a Penrith linen draper. The poet William Wordsworth was an older brother and Christopher Wordsworth (1774–1846), later Master of Trinity College, Cambridge, a younger. The death of their mother in 1778 and of their father in 1783 left the children virtually without financial support. The Earl of Lonsdale's debt to John Wordsworth was not settled until his death in 1802. The boys were either sent to Cambridge or established in professional careers, while Dorothy was sent to live first with her mother's cousin in Halifax, where she briefly attended a boarding school and then a day school, then to her maternal grandparents in Penrith, and eventually, and more congenially, to her uncle the Revd William Cookson, at Forncett, in Norfolk. In 1795 she and William settled at Racedown Lodge, north Dorset, where William had a tutoring post, and where Dorothy acted as his amanuensis, housekeeper, and literary helpmeet. It was the beginning of their life together which ended only with Wordsworth's death in 1850. In 1797 they took a house at Alfoxden to be near Coleridge, who wrote of the new relationship, 'we are three people . . . but only one soul'. Dorothy's now famous Journals were begun at Alfoxden in 1798, 'to give William pleasure'. They recorded their daily life together and presented a rare combination of domestic detail and powerful and poetic observations of nature and rural life. They were also uniquely influential in Wordsworth's own creative process, as a comparison of some of his poems with passages in the Journals demonstrates. Dorothy and William made a tour of Germany in 1798, settling for a time at Goslar. On their return in 1799 they discovered Dove Cottage, at Town End, Grasmere, to which they moved in December 1799 and where Dorothy wrote her important 'Grasmere Journals' (1800–3). William's marriage to Mary Hutchinson in 1802 made no outward change in her domestic life. The remainder of it was uneventful, consisting of travels and visits, and the births, deaths, and marriages of her family. She and William went on a walking tour of Scotland in 1803. A second tour in 1822 prompted revisions to her *Recollections of a Tour Made in Scotland AD* 1803, which had been widely circulated in manuscript, but was not published until 1874. Parts of her Journal written during walks in Patterdale in 1805 were incorporated with alterations in William's *Guide to the Lakes* (1820). William, Mary, Dorothy, and the children moved to Allan Bank, Grasmere, in 1808, and eventually, in 1813, settled at Rydal Mount, which was to be their home for the rest of their lives.

A tour with William and Mary of Switzerland, the Italian Lakes, and Paris in 1820 produced her 'Journal of a Tour on the Continent'. A few short visits to friends in 1826 and a trip to the Isle of Man in 1828 were her last absences from home. A serious illness in 1829 was a prelude to the onset of arteriosclerosis from which she never recovered. She lived at Rydal until 1855, with intermittent periods of lucidity, cared for by William and his family. Dorothy also wrote poems, some of which were published anonymously with William's, in her lifetime. Her *Narrative Concerning George and Sarah Green* was published in 1936 (ed. E. de Selincourt), and reissued in 1987 as *The Greens of Grasmere* (ed. Hilary Clark). The complete edition of the *Journals* was published in 1941 (ed. E. de Selincourt), a selection in 1971 (ed. Mary Moorman), and the *Grasmere Journals* (ed. Pamela Woof) in 1991. *The Letters of William and Dorothy Wordsworth* (2nd edn. C. L. Shaver, A. G. Hill, and Mary Moorman) was published in 1967–88, and a selection of Dorothy's *Letters* (ed. A. G. Hill) in 1981 (repr. 1985). *See* Ernest de Selincourt, *Dorothy Wordsworth: A Biography* (1933; repr. 1950); Margaret Homans, *Women Writers and Poetic Identity* (1980); Robert Gittings and Jo Manton, *Dorothy Wordsworth* (1985); Susan M. Levin, *Dorothy Wordsworth & Romanticism* (1987); Anne K. Mellor (ed.), *Romanticism and Feminism* (1988).

Wroth, Lady Mary, poet and prose writer (b. Penshurst Place, Kent, 1586–77, d. 1651–3).

Lady Mary Wroth was the eldest daughter of Sir Robert Sidney, later Earl of Leicester, and his wife Barbara Gamage. Sir Philip Sidney was her uncle and Lady Mary Herbert, Countess of *Pembroke, her aunt. In 1604 she married Sir Robert Wroth, an Essex landowner by whom she had one son but with whom she had little in common. Lady Mary was a prominent figure in court circles after her marriage, known as a poet and as a patroness of literature. She acted in one of Ben Jonson's masques, and he in turn dedicated *The Alchemist* to her in 1610. Chapman prefaced a sonnet addressed to her to his translation of the *Iliad* and George Wither apostrophized her as 'Arts Sweet Lover' in an epigram. Her husband's death in 1614 left her with substantial debts which she struggled to repay. Her son James died two years later. Possibly as a means of securing an income she published a prose romance, *The Countesse of Montgomerie's Urania* (1621), modelled on Sir Philip Sidney's *Arcadia*. The work contained a set of sonnets in three sequences entitled *Pamphilia to Amphilanthus* and, as in the *Arcadia*, various songs were interspersed with the prose and sonnets. Many of the characters were thinly veiled satirical portraits of prominent figures in court circles, and as a result of strong protests the work was withdrawn six months after publication. Lady Mary was admonished to imitate her 'vertuous and learned Aunt' rather than to publish 'lascivious tales and amarous toyes', ironic in that the Countess of Pembroke had encouraged her to imitate Sidney's works. An unfinished sequel remained unpublished. She also wrote a verse play, *Loves Victorie*, which was partly published in 1853. In both of her works the pains of courtly love are seen from a woman's perspective. The Amphilanthus, 'Lover-of-two', of the sonnets is likely to have been her cousin William Herbert, third Earl of Pembroke, one of the dedicatees of Shakespeare's First Folio, who became her lover and by whom she had two illegitimate children. She eventually retired from the court and spent the last part of her life in the country. The exact date of her death is unknown. *The Poems of Lady Mary Wroth*, ed. Josephine A. Roberts, were published in 1983. *See* Elaine V. Beilin, *Redeeming Eve: Women Writers of the English Renaissance* (1987); Margaret P. Hannay, in *Women Writers of the Renaissance and Reformation*, ed. Katharina M. Wilson (1987); Mary Ellen Lamb, *Gender and Authorship in the Sidney Circle* (1990); Anne M. Haselkorn and Betty S. Travitsky (eds.) *The Renaissance Englishwoman in Print: Counterbalancing the Canon* (1990); Naomi J. Miller and Gary Waller (eds.), *Reading Mary Wroth: Representing Alternatives in Early Modern England* (1991).

yyyyyyyyyyyyyyy

Y

Yearsley, Ann, poet and playwright (b. Clifton, near Bristol, 1752, d. Melksham, Wiltshire, 8 May 1806).

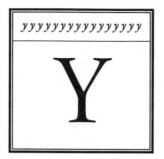

Ann Yearsley's father John Cromartie was a labourer, and his wife Ann had a milk round which her daughter later inherited. She had no formal education, but was taught to write by her brother, and began to read at an early age. In 1774 her parents persuaded her to marry John Yearsley, an illiterate labourer, who was thought to be a sound financial prospect with an estate of £6 a year. They had six children in seven years, one of whom died, but the marriage was not happy. In the hours remaining after work and when her children were in bed Yearsley read, and began to write poetry. She was introduced to Hannah *More, who lived nearby, through her cook, who had provided her with pigswill. More gave her a grammar, a spelling book, and a dictionary, helped her to revise her work, and with the aid of Elizabeth *Montagu secured more than a thousand subscribers for her first volume, *Poems on Several Occasions*, which was published in 1785 with a prefatory letter from More to Montagu, extolling Yearsley's literary qualities. The book's supporters included eminent clerics, titled ladies, and prominent members of the literary and artistic world like Sir Joshua Reynolds, Horace Walpole, and Dr Charles Burney. The proceeds were invested by More, with Mrs Montagu and herself as trustees, to provide a modest income with which it was intended Ann Yearsley should run a school. At first flattered and grateful to her patron, Yearsley came to resent what she felt was More's high-handedness and the dependence it sought to establish. Her 'Autobiographical Narrative', added to the fourth edition of her *Poems* in 1786, gave her side of the story, which had become a public row, while More and her supporters lamented Yearsley's 'ingratitude' and 'malice'. Yearsley found sympathy and support in Anna *Seward and a new patron in Frederick Hervey, Bishop of Derry and Earl of Bristol, who helped her to publish the fourth edition of her *Poems*. She reprinted her 'Narrative' in her new volume, *Poems on Various Subjects* (1787), making it clear that the new collection was all her own work, and not, as rumour had it regarding its predecessor, only publishable because of More's revisions. Her later work embraced large issues, as in her *Poem on the Inhumanity of the Slave Trade* (1788), and also local ones, as in her *Stanzas of Woe* (1790), attacking a local mayor for punishing her children, who had trespassed on his property. She wrote *Earl Goodwin* (1791), a verse tragedy, which was produced in Bath and also in Bristol, and in 1795 *The Royal Captives*, a historical novel based on the story of the Man in the Iron Mask. Her eldest son William was apprenticed to an engraver and provided the frontispiece to *The Rural Lyre* (1796), her last collection of poems. The quarrel with More was never completely healed, but her poems won enthusiastic praise from Anna Seward, who linked her with Burns, from Horace Walpole, and Southey. She opened a circulating library in Bristol Hot Wells, with help from Joseph Cottle, the Bristol bookseller and publisher who was another of her admirers. Her health failed and, depressed by the deaths of two of her sons and her husband, she spent her later years in virtual seclusion. She died at Melksham, in Wiltshire, where she had moved to be near another of her sons. *See* R. Southey, *Lives of the Uneducated Poets* (1836; ed. J. S. Childers 1925); J. M. S. Tompkins, *Polite Marriage* (1938); Donna Landry, *The Muses of Resistance: Laboring-Class Women's Poetry in Britain, 1739–1796* (1990).

Yonge, Charlotte Mary, novelist (b. Otterbourne, near Winchester, 11 August 1823, d. Otterbourne, 24 March 1901).

Charlotte Yonge was the daughter of William Crawley Yonge, an ardent churchman and magistrate who retired from the army in order to marry Frances Mary Bargus, a vicar's daughter whose mother objected to military men. Her only sibling was a brother, seven years her junior. Charlotte was taught mathematics, Latin, and Greek by her father, who, according to the *DNB*, believed in higher education for women, but 'deprecated any liberty for them'. She was taught modern languages by tutors, and had a good knowledge of botany and also conchology. Her father was a formative influence on her life, and, following his example, she taught Sunday school for seventy-one years, beginning at the age of 7. The most significant event in her youth was the appointment of John Keble to the adjacent parish of Hursley in 1835. He encouraged her to use her by then obvious literary talents to inculcate Christian principles through fiction. Keble kept a close eye on her work, revising and excising what he thought were inappropriate details. Before she published her first novel, *The Abbey Church; or Self Control and Self Conceit* (1844), her family decided it would be wrong for her to earn money from writing, unless it was donated to a good cause. Consequently the proceeds of her first successful novel, *The Heir of Redclyffe* (1853), were donated to a fund to purchase a schooner for the Melanesian mission. The admirers of *The Heir of Redclyffe*, with its story of repentance and Christian self-sacrifice, included William Morris and Dante Gabriel Rossetti, and the book launched her on a literary career of prodigious proportions, with more than 150 titles to her credit. It was followed by a series of novels for adults and children, the best known of which included *Heartsease* (1854), *The Lances of Lynwood* (1855), *The Daisy Chain* (1856), a chronicle of the May family, regarded as her best work, which had a sequel in *The Trial* (1864), *Dynevor Terrace* (1857), and *The Pillars of the House* (1873), another saga about a large family, a subject about which she wrote convincingly. She wrote numerous works for children, both fiction and non-fiction. Of the former the most popular were *The Little Duke; or Richard the Fearless* (1854), *The Dove in the Eagle's Nest* (1866), and *The Chaplet of Pearls* (1868), all with historical settings. She wrote intelligently about women's predicaments in *Hopes and Fears; or Scenes from the Life of a Spinster* (1860) and *The Clever Woman of the Family* (1865). She edited the *Monthly Packet*, aimed at younger members of the Church of England, from 1851 until 1890, one of the longest-serving editorships of any Victorian periodical, and edited and contributed to other periodicals as well. Her long list of publications included popular historical works, Bible studies, biography, and didactic books for children. Her father died in 1854, her mother in 1868, and her brother in 1892, increasing her isolation in her last years. She surrounded herself with a small circle of friends, which included Christabel Coleridge, her successor as editor of the *Monthly Packet* and her biographer, the novelist Frances Mary Peard (1835–1923), and, for a short time, Mrs Humphry *Ward. She died of pleurisy in 1901, aged 77. The Charlotte Yonge Society was founded by Lettice *Cooper, Elizabeth Jenkins, and Marghanita Laski. *See* Christabel R. Coleridge, *Charlotte Mary Yonge: Her Life and Letters* (1903); G. Battiscombe, *C. M. Yonge: The Story of an Uneventful Life* (1943); M. Mare and A. C. Percival, *Victorian Best Seller: The World of Charlotte Yonge* (1947); G. Battiscombe and M. Laski, *A Chaplet for Charlotte Yonge* (1965).

Young, E(mily) H(ilda), novelist (b. Northumberland, 1880, d. Bradford-on-Avon, Wiltshire, 8 August 1949).

E. H. Young was the daughter of William Michael Young, a Northumberland shipowner, and his wife Frances Jane Young. She was educated at Gateshead High School and then at Penrhos College, a girls' boarding school at Colwyn Bay in North Wales. In 1902 she married J. A. H. Daniell, a Bristol solicitor, and went to live in that city, which, with the adjoining Clifton, became the Radstowe and Upper Radstowe of her novels. Daniell enlisted for active service in the First World War, although over the official age limit, and was killed at Ypres in 1917. Young worked in a munitions factory and as a groom during the war and after her husband's death moved to London. She formed a *mènage à trois* with her lover Ralph Henderson, headmaster of Alleyn's School, and his wife, keeping the name Mrs Daniell for respectability. From 1940 until her death they lived in Bradford-on-Avon in Wiltshire. Young wrote thirteen novels, as E. H. Young, most of them subtle studies of marriages or relationships governed by class divisions and strict codes of behaviour. *A Corn of Wheat* (1910), *Yonder* (1912), and *Moon Fires* (1916), written while she lived in Bristol, were followed by *The Bridge Dividing* (1922), reprinted in 1927 as *The Misses Mallett*, the first of her London novels, in which the heroine marries a man she has rejected thirty years earlier, believing she was 'meant for something better'. In *William* (1925) a conventional father defends his daughter's desertion of her unloved husband in order to elope with another man. The novel was a Reader's Club first choice in the USA when it was reissued in 1941. *Miss Mole* (1930), which won the James Tait Black Memorial Prize, is the story of a spinster housekeeper to a Nonconformist minister. *Jenny Wren* (1932) and its sequel *The Curate's Wife* (1934) focus on two contrasting daughters of a gentleman who married beneath him. *The Times* obituarist celebrated Young's sympathy with 'normal' characters and experience, her depiction of 'ordinary or seemingly ordinary personal relationships', and her 'delicately astringent humour'. More recent critics have remarked on the 'subversiveness' of this apparently conventional writer, an observation particularly relevant to *Chatterton Square* (1947), her last novel, in which a middle-aged wife moves toward liberation and criticism of her morally tyrannical and egocentric husband. Young also wrote two novels for children, *Caravan Island* (1940) and *River Holiday* (1942). *See* M. Lawrence, *We Write as Women* (1937).

SELECT BIBLIOGRAPHY

1. Pre-1920

The following is a list of works published before 1920 which either deal exclusively with women writers or give substantial reference to them.

BALLARD, GEORGE, *Memoirs of Several Ladies of Great Britain who have been Celebrated for their Writings or Skill in the Learned Languages, Arts and Sciences* (1752, 1775), ed. Ruth Perry (Detroit, 1985).

BARBAULD, ANNA LAETITIA, *The British Novelists: With an Essay and Prefaces, Biographical and Critical*, 50 vols. (London, 1810).

BETHAM, MARY MATILDA, *A Biographical Dictionary of the Celebrated Women of Every Age and Country* (London, 1804).

BETHUNE, GEORGE W., *The British Female Poets* (Philadelphia, 1848).

Biographium Femineum: The Female Worthies; or Memoirs of the Most Illustrious Ladies of All Ages and Nations (London, 1766).

BLACK, HELEN C., *Notable Women Authors of the Day* (Glasgow, 1893).

CAREY, ROSA NOUCHETTE, *Twelve Notable Good Women of the Nineteenth Century* (London, 1899).

CHORLEY, H. F., *The Authors of England: A Series of Medallion Portraits* (1838, 1861).

CIBBER, THEOPHILUS, *The Life of the Poets of Great Britain and Ireland to the Time of Dean Swift*, 5 vols. (London, 1753).

COLMAN, GEORGE, and THORNTON, BONNELL (eds.), *Poems by Eminent Ladies*, 2 vols. (London, 1755, 1773).

COSTELLO, LOUISA STUART, *Memoirs of Eminent English Women*, 4 vols. (London, 1844).

COURTNEY, W. L., *The Feminine Note in Fiction* (London, 1904; repr. 1973).

CRAIK, GEORGE LILLIE, *The Pursuit of Knowledge under Difficulties Illustrated by Female Examples* (London, 1847).

——*Sketches of the History of Literature and Learning in England from the Norman Conquest to the Accession of Elizabeth, with Specimens of the Principal Writers*, 6 vols. (London, 1844–5).

CUNNINGHAM, ALAN, *Biographical and Critical History of British Literature of the Last Fifty Years* (Paris, 1834).

DORAN, J., *Their Majesties' Servants: Annals of the English Stage*, ed. R. W. Lowe (London, 1888).

DUNCOMBE, JOHN, *The Feminiad; or Female Genius: A Poem* (London 1751).

DYCE, ALEXANDER, *Specimens of British Poetesses* (London, 1825).

ELWOOD, Mrs E. K., *Memoirs of the Literary Ladies of England from the Commencement of the Last Century*, 2 vols. (London, 1843).

Eminent Women series, ed. J. H. Ingram (Allen & Co., London, 1883–). Titles include Mathilde Blind, *George Eliot* (1883); Agnes Mary France Robinson, *Emily Brontë* (1883); J. H. Ingram, *Elizabeth Barrett Browning* (1888).

GENEST, JOHN, *Some Account of the English Stage from ... 1660 to 1830*, 10 vols. (London, 1832).

GRANGER, JAMES, *A Biographical History of England*, 3 vols. (1769–74); 2nd edn., 4 vols. (London, 1775).

HALE, SARAH JOSEPHA BUELL, *Woman's Record; or Sketches of All Distinguished Women from the Creation to 1854 ad. in Four Eras with Selections from Female Writers of Every Age* (New York, 1855).

HAMILTON, C. J., *Women Writers: Their Works and Ways*, 2 series (London, 1892–3).

HAYS, MARY, *Female Biography; or Memoirs of Illustrious and Celebrated Women of All Ages and Countries* (London, 1803).

HOPE, EVA, *Queens of Literature of the Victorian Era* (London, 1886).

——*Famous Women Authors* (London, 189?).

HOWITT, WILLIAM, *Homes and Haunts of the Most Eminent British Poets*, 2 vols. (London, 1847).

HUNT, LEIGH, 'Specimens of British Poetesses', in *Men, Women and Books: A Selection of Sketches, Essays and Critical Memoirs from his Uncollected Writings*, vol. ii (London, 1847).

JOHNSON, R. BRIMLEY, *The Women Novelists* (London, 1918).

——*Some Contemporary Novelists: Women* (London, 1920).

KAVANAGH, JULIA, *English Women of Letters*, 2 vols. (London, 1863).

MARTINEAU, HARRIET, *Biographical Sketches* (1869, 1877).

MAYER, GERTRUDE TOWNSHEND, *Women of Letters*, 2 vols. (London, 1894).

'PASTON, GEORGE' [Emily Morse Symonds], *Little Memoirs of the Eighteenth Century* (London, 1901).

——*Little Memoirs of the Nineteenth Century* (London, 1902).

REYNOLDS, MYRA, *The Learned Lady in England, 1650–1760* (Boston, 1920).

RITCHIE, ANNE THACKERAY, *A Book of Sibyls; Mrs. Barbauld, Mrs. Opie, Miss Edgeworth, Miss Austen* (London, 1883).

——*Blackstick Papers* (London, 1908).

ROBERTSON, ERIC SUTHERLAND, *English Poetesses* (London, 1883).

ROWTON, FREDERICK, *The Female Poets of Great Britain* (London, 1848).

——*Cyclopaedia of Female Poets* (Philadelphia, 1874).

SERGEANT, ADELINE (ed.), *Women Novelists of Queen Victoria's Reign: A Book of Appreciations* (London, 1897).

'TYTLER, SARAH' [Henrietta Keddie], and Watson, J. L. (eds.), *The Songstresses of Scotland*, 2 vols. (London, 1871).

WALPOLE, HORACE, *A Catalogue of the Royal and Noble Authors of England, Scotland and Ireland*, 5 vols. (London, 1806).

WILLIAMS, JANE, *The Literary Women of England*, including a biographical epitome of all the most eminent to the year 1700 and sketches of the poetesses to the year 1850 with extracts from their works and critical remarks (London, 1861).

2. Post-1920

ABEL, ELIZABETH, HIRSCH, MARIANNE, and LANGLAND, ELIZABETH, *The Voyage In: Fictions of Female Development* (Hanover, NH, 1983).

ACKLEY, KATHERINE ANNE, *Women and Violence in Literature: An Essay Collection* (New York, 1990).

ANDERSON, LINDA, *Plotting Change: Contemporary Women's Fiction* (London, 1990).

——*Remembered Futures: Women and Autobiography in the Twentieth Century* (Hemel Hempstead, 1992).

ARMITT, LUCIE (ed.), *Where no Man has Gone before: Women and Science Fiction* (London, 1990).

ASHFIELD, ANDREW, *Romantic Women Poets, 1770–1838: An Anthology* (Manchester, 1993).

AUERBACH, NINA, *Communities of Women: An Idea in Fiction* (Cambridge, Mass., 1978).

——*Woman and the Demon: The Life of a Victorian Myth* (London, 1982).

BAKER, NIAMH, *Happily Ever After? Women's Fiction in Postwar Britain 1945–1960* (Basingstoke, 1989).

BAKERMAN, JANE S., *And then there Were Nine . . . More Women of Mystery* (Bowling Green, Oh., 1985).

BALD, M., *Women-Writers of the Nineteenth Century* (Cambridge, 1923).

BANKS, OLIVE, *A Biographical Dictionary of British Feminists*, i: *1800–1930;* ii: *1900–1945* (Hemel Hempstead, 1985, 1990).

BARGAINNIER, EARL F., *10 Women of Mystery* (Bowling Green, Oh., 1981).

BARKER, FRANCIS, BERNSTEIN, JAY, COOMBES, JOHN, HULME, PETER, STONE, JENNIFER, and STRATTON, JON (eds.), *1642: Literature and Power in the Seventeenth Century* (Colchester, 1981).

BASCH, FRANÇOISE, *Relative Creatures: Victorian Women in Society and the Novel 1837–1867* (London, 1974).

BEAUMAN, NICOLA, *A Very Great Profession: The Woman's Novel 1914–1939* (London, 1983).

BEER, PATRICIA, *Reader I Married him* (London, 1974; repr. 1986).

BEILIN, ELAINE V., *Redeeming Eve: Women Writers of the English Renaissance* (Princeton, NJ, 1987).

——'Current Bibliography of English Women Writers, 1500–1640', in Anne M. Haselkorn and Betty S. Travitsky (eds.), *The Renaissance Englishwoman in Print: Counterbalancing the Canon* (Amherst, Mass., 1990).

BELL, MAUREEN, PARFITT, GEORGE, and SHEPHERD, SIMON, *A Biographical Dictionary of English Women Writers,* 1580–1720 (Hemel Hempstead, 1990).

BENSTOCK, SHARI, *Women of the Left Bank: Paris 1900–1940* (London, 1987).

——(ed.), *The Private Self: Theory and Practice of Women's Autobiographical Writings* (Chapel Hill, NC, 1988).

BLAIN, VIRGINIA, CLEMENTS, PATRICIA, and GRUNDY, ISOBEL (eds.), *The Feminist Companion to Literature in English: Women Writers from the Middle Ages to the Present* (London, 1990).

BLAKE, KATHLEEN, *Love and the Woman Question in Victorian Literature* (Brighton, 1983).

BLODGETT, HARRIET, *Centuries of Female Days: Englishwomen's Private Diaries* (New Brunswick, NJ, 1988).

BRANT, CLARE, and PURKISS, DIANE (eds.), *Women, Texts and Histories 1575–1760* (London, 1992).

BREEN, JENNIFER, *In her Own Write: Twentieth Century Women's Fiction* (Basingstoke, 1990).

BRINK, J. R. (ed.), *Female Scholars: A Tradition of Learned Women before 1800* (Montreal, 1980).

BROE, MARY LYNN, and INGRAM, ANGELA, *Women's Writing in Exile* (Chapel Hill, NC, 1989).

BROWN, PENNY, *The Poison at the Source: The Female Novel of Self-Development in the Early Twentieth Century* (Basingstoke, 1991).

BROWNE, ALICE, *The Eighteenth Century Feminist Mind* (Brighton, 1987).

CARR, HELEN (ed.), *From my Guy to Sci-Fi: Genre and Women's Writing in the Postmodern World* (London, 1989).

CHAMBERLAIN, MARY (ed.), *Writing Lives: Conversations between Women Writers* (London, 1988).

CLARK, SUZANNE, *Sentimental Modernism: Women Writers and the Revolution of the Word* (Bloomington, Ind. 1991).

COBHAM, RHONDA, and COLLINS, MERLE (eds.), *Watchers and Seekers: Creative Writing by Black Women in Britain* (London, 1987).

COLBY, VINETA, *The Singular Anomaly: Women Novelists of the Nineteenth Century* (New York, 1970).

COPPER, HELEN M., MUNICH, ADRIENNE AUSLANDER, and SQUIER, SUSAN MERRILL (eds.), *Arms and the Woman: War, Gender, and Literary Representation* (Chapel Hill, NC, 1989).

CORBETT, MARY JEAN, *Representing Femininity: Middle-Class Subjectivity and Victorian Women's Autobiographies* (Oxford, 1992).

COSSLETT, TESS, *Woman to Woman: Female Friendships in Victorian Fiction* (Brighton, 1988).

COTTON, NANCY, *Women Playwrights in England c.1363–1750* (London, 1980).

CRAIG, PATRICIA, and CADOGAN, MARY, *The Lady Investigates: Women Detectives and Spies in Fiction* (London, 1981).

CROSLAND, MARGARET, *Beyond the Lighthouse: English Women Novelists in the 20th Century* (1981).

CROSS, NIGEL, *The Common Writer: Life in Nineteenth-Century Grub Street* (Cambridge, 1985).

CUNNINGHAM, GAIL, *The New Woman and the Victorian Novel* (London, 1978).

DAVIDSON, C. N., and BRONER E. M., *The Lost Tradition: Mothers and Daughters in Literature* (New York, 1980).

DRONKE, PETER, *Women Writers of the Middle Ages* (Cambridge, 1984).

DUPLESSIS, RACHEL BLAU, *Writing beyond the Ending: Narrative Strategies of Twentieth-Century Women Writers* (Bloomington, Ind., 1985).

——*The Pink Guitar: Writing as Feminist Practice* (London, 1990).

FADERMAN, LILLIAN, *Surpassing the Love of Men: Romantic Friendship and Love between Women from the Renaissance to the Present* (London, 1981).

FERGUSON, MOIRA (ed.), *First Feminists: British Women Writers 1578–1799* (New York, 1985).

——*Subject to Others: British Women Writers and Colonial Slavery, 1670–1834* (London, 1992).

FOSTER, SHIRLEY, *Victorian Women's Fiction: Marriage, Freedom and the Individual* (London, 1985).

——*Across New Worlds: Nineteenth-Century Women Travellers and their Writings* (Hemel Hempstead, 1990).

FRIEDMAN, ELLEN G., and FUCHS, MIRIAM (eds.), *Breaking the Sequence: Women's Experimental Fiction* (Princeton, NJ, 1989).

FULLBROOK, KATE, *Free Women: Ethics and Aesthetics in Twentieth-Century Women's Fiction* (Hemel Hempstead, 1990).

GILBERT, SANDRA, and GUBAR, SUSAN, *The Madwoman in the Attic: The Woman Writer and the Nineteenth-Century Literary Imagination* (London, 1979).

————(eds.), *Shakespeare's Sisters: Feminist Essays on Women Poets* (London, 1979).

————*No Man's Land: The Place of the Woman Writer in the Twentieth Century*, i: *The War of Words*; ii: *Sexchanges* (New Haven, Conn., 1988, 1989).

GOLDBERGER, AVRIEL H. (ed.), *Woman as Mediatrix: Essays on Nineteenth-Century Women Writers* (London, 1987).

GOLDMAN, DOROTHY (ed.), *Women and World War I: The Written Response* (London, 1992).

GREEN, KATHERINE SOBBA, *The Courtship Novel 1740–1820: A Feminised Genre* (Lexington, Ky, 1991).

GREENE, GAYLE, *Changing the Story: Feminist Fiction and the Tradition* (Bloomington, Ind., 1992).

GREER, GERMAINE, HASTINGS, SUSAN, MEDOFF, JESLYN, and SANSONE, MELINDA, *Kissing the Rod: An Anthology of Seventeenth-Century Women's Verse* (London, 1988).

GRUNDY, ISOBEL, and WISEMAN, SUSAN (eds.), *Women, Writing History: 1640–1740* (London, 1992).

HANLEY, LYNN, *Writing War: Fiction, Gender, and Memory* (Amherst, Mass., 1991).

HANNAY, MARGARET PATTERSON (ed.), *Silent but for the Word: Tudor Women as Patrons, Translators and Writers of Religious Works* (Kent, Oh., 1985).

HANSCOMBE, GILLIAN, and SMYERS, VIRGINIA L., *Writing for their Lives: The Modernist Women 1910–1940* (London, 1987).

HASELKORN, ANNE M., and TRAVITSKY, BETTY S. (eds.), *The Renaissance Englishwoman in Print: Counterbalancing the Canon* (Amherst, Mass., 1990).

HENDERSON, KATHERINE USHER, MCMANUS, BARBARA F., *Half Humankind: Contexts and Texts of the Controversy about Women in England 1540–1640* (Urbana, Ill., 1985).

HICKOK, KATHLEEN, *Representations of Women: Nineteenth-Century British Women's Poetry* (London, 1984).

HIGONNET, MARGARET RANDOLPH, JENSON, JANE, MICHEL, SONYA, and WEITZ, MARGARET COLLINS (eds.), *Behind the Lines: Gender and the Two World Wars* (New Haven, Conn., 1989).

HOBBY, ELAINE, *Virtue of Necessity: English Women's Writing 1649–1688* (London, 1988).

HOMANS, MARGARET, *Women Writers and Poetic Identity: Dorothy Wordsworth, Emily Brontë and Emily Dickinson* (Princeton, NJ, 1980).

——*Bearing the Word: Language and Women's Experience in Nineteenth Century Women's Writing* (London, 1986).

HUGHES, WINIFRED, *The Maniac in the Cellar: Sensation Novels of the 1860s* (Princeton, NJ, 1980).

HUMM, MAGGIE, *Border Traffic: Strategies of Contemporary Women Writers* (Manchester, 1991).

JACKSON, J. R. DE J., *Romantic Poetry by Women: A Bibliography 1770–1835* (Oxford, 1993).

JACOBUS, MARY (ed.), *Women Writing and Writing about Women* (London, 1979).

JAY, KARLA, GLASGOW, JOANNE, and STIMPSON, CATHERINE, *Lesbian Texts and Contexts: Radical Revisions* (New York, 1990).

JONES, LIBBY FALK, and GOODWIN, SARAH WEBSTER (eds.), *Feminism, Utopia, and Narrative* (Knoxville, Tenn., 1990).

JOUVE, NICOLE WARD, *White Woman Speaks with Forked Tongue: Criticism as Autobiography* (London, 1991).

KAPLAN, CAREY, and CRONAN, ROSE ELLEN, *The Canon and the Common Reader* (Knoxville, Tenn., 1990).

KAPLAN, SYDNEY JANET, *Feminine Consciousness in the Modern British Novel* (Urbana, Ill., 1975).

KENYON, OLGA, *Women Novelists Today: A Survey of English Writing in the Seventies and Eighties* (Brighton, 1988).

KHAN, NOSHEEN, *Women's Poetry of the First World War* (Hemel Hempstead, 1988).

KING, MARGARET L., *Women of the Renaissance* (Chicago, 1992).

KRONTIRIS, TINA, *Oppositional Voices: Women as Writers and Translators in the English Renaissance* (London, 1992).

LANDRY, DONNA, *The Muses of Resistance: Laboring-Class Women's Poetry in Britain, 1739–1796* (Cambridge, 1990).

LEIGHTON, ANGELA, *Victorian Women Poets: Writing against the Heart* (Hemel Hempstead, 1992).

LIGHT, ALISON, *Forever England: Femininity, Literature and Conservatism between the Wars* (London, 1991).

LIONNET, FRANÇOISE, *Autobiographical Voices: Race, Gender, Self-Portraiture* (Ithaca, NY, 1989).

LONSDALE, ROGER (ed.), *Eighteenth-Century Women Poets: An Oxford Anthology* (Oxford, 1989).

LOVELL, TERRY, *Consuming Fiction* (London, 1987).

MACCARTHY, BRIDGET, *Women Writers: Their Contribution to the English Novel 1621–1744; The Later Women Novelists 1744–1818* (Cork, 1944, 1947).

MAHL, MARGARET, and KOON, HÉLÈNE (eds.), *The Female Spectator: English Women Writers before 1800* (Bloomington, Ind., 1977).

MELLOR, ANNE, K. (ed.), *Romanticism and Feminism* (London, 1988).

MESSENGER, ANN, *His and Hers: Essays in Restoration and Eighteenth-Century Literature* (Lexington, Ky., 1986).

——*Gender at Work: Four Women Writers of the Eighteenth Century* (Detroit, 1990).

MEWS, HAZEL, *Frail Vessels: Women's Role in Novels from Fanny Burney to George Eliot* (London, 1969).

MILLS, SARA, *Discourses of Difference: An Analysis of Women's Travel Writing and Colonialism* (London, 1991).

MITCHELL, SALLY, *The Fallen Angel: Chastity, Class and Women's Reading 1835–1880* (Bowling Green, Oh., 1981).

MOERS, ELLEN, *Literary Women* (London, 1977).

MONTEITH, MOIRA (ed.), *Women's Writing: A Challenge to Theory* (Brighton, 1986).

MORGAN, FIDELIS (ed.), *The Female Wits: Women Playwrights on the London Stage 1660–1720* (London, 1981).

MORGAN, JANICE, HALL, COLLETTE T., and SNYDER, CAROL L. (eds.), *Redefining Autobiography in Twentieth-Century Women's Fiction: An Essay Collection* (New York, 1991).

MYERS, SYLVIA HARCSTARK, *The Bluestocking Circle: Women, Friendship, and the Life of the Mind in Eighteenth-Century England* (Oxford, 1990).

NATHAN, RHODA B., *Nineteenth-Century Women Writers of the English-Speaking World* (New York, 1986).

NESTOR, PAULINE, *Female Friendships and Communities: Charlotte Brontë, George Eliot, Elizabeth Gaskell* (Oxford, 1985).

NEWTON, JUDITH LOWDER, *Women, Power and Subversion: Social Strategies in British Fiction 1778–1860* (London, 1986).

NGCOBO, LAURETTA (ed.), *Let it be Told: Black Women Writers in Britain* (London, 1987).

PALMER, PAULINA, *Contemporary Women's Fiction: Narrative Practice and Feminist Theory* (Brighton, 1989).

PERRY, RUTH, *Women, Letters and the Novel* (New York, 1980).

——and BROWNLEY, MARTIN WATSON (eds.), *Mothering the Mind: Twelve Studies of Writers and their Silent Partners* (New York, 1984).

Poovey, Mary, *Uneven Developments: The Ideological Work of Gender in Mid-Victorian England* (Chicago, 1988).

Prior, Mary (ed.), *Women in English Society: 1500–1800* (London, 1985).

Pykett, Lyn, *The 'Improper' Feminine: The Women's Sensation Novel and the New Woman Writing* (London, 1992).

Radford, Jean (ed.), *The Progress of Romance: The Politics of Popular Fiction* (London, 1986).

Radstone, Susannah (ed.), *Sweet Dreams: Sexuality, Gender and Popular Fiction* (London, 1988).

Radway, Janice, *Reading the Romance: Women, Patriarchy, and Popular Literature* (Chapel Hill, NC, 1984).

Reilly, Catherine (ed.), *Scars upon my Heart: Women's Poetry and Verse of the First World War* (London, 1981).

Robinson, Jane, *Wayward Women: A Guide to Women Travellers* (Oxford, 1990).

Roe, Sue (ed.), *Women Reading Women's Writing* (Brighton, 1987).

Rogers, Katherine M., *Feminism in Eighteenth Century England* (Urbana, Ill., 1982).

Rose, Mary Beth (ed.), *Women in the Middle Ages and the Renaissance: Literary and Historical Perspectives* (Syracuse, NY, 1986).

Sage, Lorna, *Women in the House of Fiction: Post-War Women Novelists* (Basingstoke, 1992).

Sanders, Valerie, *The Private Lives of Victorian Women: Autobiography in Nineteenth-Century England* (Brighton, 1989).

Schofield, Mary Anne, *Masking and Unmasking the Female Mind: Disguising Romances in Feminine Fictions* (Newark, Del., 1990).

——and Macheski, Cecilia (eds.), *Fetter'd or Free? British Women Novelists 1670–1815* (Athens, Oh., 1986).

————*Curtain Calls: British and American Women and the Theater 1660–1820* (Athens, Oh., 1991).

Scott, Bonnie Kime (ed.), *The Gender of Modernism: A Critical Anthology* (Bloomington, Ind., 1990).

Sellers, Susan, *Feminist Criticism: Theory and Practice* (Hemel Hempstead, 1991).

Showalter, Elaine, *A Literature of their Own: British Women Novelists from Brontë to Lessing* (Princeton, NJ, 1977; rev. 1982).

——(ed.), *Speaking of Gender* (London, 1989).

Simons, Judy, *Diaries and Journals of Literary Women: From Fanny Burney to Virginia Woolf* (London, 1990).

Sizemore, Christine Wick, *A Female Vision of the City: London in the Novels of Five British Women* (Knoxville, Tenn., 1989).

Smith, Hilda, *Reason's Disciples: Seventeenth Century English Feminists* (Urbana, Ill., 1982).

Spacks, Patricia Meyer, *The Female Imagination* (London, 1976).

Spencer, Jane, *The Rise of the Woman Novelist: From Aphra Behn to Jane Austen* (Oxford, 1986).

SPENDER, DALE, *Mothers of the Novel: 100 Good Women Writers before Jane Austen* (London, 1986).

——(ed.), *Living by the Pen: Early British Women Writers* (London, 1992).

SQUIER, SUSAN MERRILL (ed.), *Women Writers and the City: Essays in Feminist Literary Criticism* (Knoxville, Tenn., 1984).

STALEY, THOMAS (ed.), *Twentieth-Century Women Novelists* (London, 1982).

STEBBINS, LUCY POATE, *A Victorian Album: Some Lady Novelists of the Period* (London, 1946).

——*London Ladies: True Tales of the Eighteenth Century* (New York, 1952).

STOWELL, SHEILA, *A Stage of their Own: Feminist Playwrights of the Suffrage Era* (Manchester, 1992).

STUBBS, PATRICIA, *Women and Fiction: Feminism and the Novel 1880–1920* (London, 1979).

SUTHERLAND, JOHN, *The Longman Companion to Victorian Fiction* (London, 1988).

SWINDELLS, JULIA, *Victorian Writing and Working Women: The Other Side of Silence* (Cambridge, 1985).

TODD, JANET, *Women's Friendship in Literature* (London, 1980).

——*The Sign of Angellica: Women, Writing and Fiction, 1660–1800* (London, 1989).

——(ed.), *Women Writers Talking* (New York, 1983).

——(ed.), *A Dictionary of British and American Women Writers 1660–1800* (London, 1984).

TOMPKINS, J. M. S., *The Popular Novel in England, 1770–1800* (London, 1932; repr. 1969).

TRAVITSKY, BETTY (ed.), *The Paradise of Women: Writings by Englishwomen of the Renaissance* (London, 1981).

TURNER, CHERYL, *Living by the Pen: Women Writers in the Eighteenth Century* (London, 1992).

TYLEE, CLAIRE M., *The Great War and Women's Consciousness: Images of Militarism and Womanhood in Women's Writings 1914–16* (Basingstoke, 1990).

WALBANK, F. ALAN, *Queens of the Circulating Libraries* (London, 1950).

WALLAS, A., *Before the Bluestockings* (London, 1929).

WARNICKE, R. M., *Women of the English Renaissance and Reformation* (London, 1983).

WAUGH, PATRICIA, *Feminine Fictions: Revisiting the Modern* (London, 1989).

WEEKES, ANN OWENS, *Irish Women Writers: An Uncharted Tradition* (Lexington, Ky., 1990).

WILLIAMS, MERRYN, *Six Women Novelists* (London, 1987).

WILLIAMSON, MARILYN L., *Raising their Voices: British Women Writers, 1650–1750* (Detroit, 1990).

WILSON, KATHARINA M., *Medieval Women Writers* (Athens, Ga., 1984).

——(ed.), *Women Writers of the Renaissance and Reformation* (Athens, Ga., 1987).

——and WARNKE, FRANK J. (ed.), *Women Writers of the Seventeenth Century* (Athens: Ga., 1989).

WILSON, MONA, *These were the Muses: Essays on Women Writers* (London, 1924).

WOLFF, ROBERT LEE, *Nineteenth-Century Fiction: A Bibliographical Catalogue*, 5 vols. (New York, 1981–6).

WOODBRIDGE, LINDA, *Women and the English Renaissance: Literature and the Nature of Womankind 1540–1620* (Brighton, 1984).